Rick Steves®

ISTANBUL
WITH EPHESUS & CAPPADOCIA

By Lale Surmen Aran & Tankut Aran

CONTENTS

Post-Pandemic Travels: Expect a Warm Welcome...and a Few Changes

Research for this guidebook was limited by the COVID-19 outbreak, and the long-term impact of the crisis on our recommended destinations is unclear. Some details in this book will change for post-pandemic travelers. Now more than ever, it's smart to reconfirm specifics as you plan and travel. As always, you can find major updates at RickSteves.com/update.

Welcome to Rick Steves' Europe

Travel is intensified living—maximum thrills per minute and one of the last great sources of legal adventure. Travel is freedom. It's recess, and we need it.

In my 20s, I finished several European trips in a row with a visit to Istanbul. I didn't plan to...it was the subconscious cherry on top of every adventure. I've been sharing my love of travel ever since—through my bus tours, public television and radio shows, and travel guidebooks. And I remain passionate about how Istanbul offers an accessible, enriching experience in the Muslim world.

Istanbul is a complex destination, and you deserve the expertise of locals to guide you. To co-author this book, I partnered with talented tour guides (and Istanbul residents) Lale Surmen Aran and Tankut Aran. Lale and Tankut wrote the first edition, my team of guidebook researchers and editors (including Cameron Hewitt and Gene Openshaw) shaped it, and I personally traveled with their work, adding my own perspective.

This book offers you a balanced mix of Istanbul's top sights and lesser-known gems. And its self-guided museum tours and neighborhood walks provide insight into Istanbul's vibrant history and today's living, breathing culture.

Lale, Tankut, and I advocate traveling simply and smartly. Take advantage of our money- and time-saving tips. Try local, characteristic alternatives to expensive hotels and restaurants. In many ways, spending more money only builds a higher wall between you and what you traveled so far to see.

We visit Istanbul to experience it—to become temporary locals. Thoughtful travel engages us with the world, as we learn to appreciate other cultures and new ways to measure quality of life.

Güle güle! Happy travels! *Rick Steves*

ISTANBUL

Istanbul is one of the world's great cities, period. For millennia, it's been at the crossroads of civilizations, where Europe meets Asia. Few places on earth have seen more history than this sprawling metropolis on the Bosphorus.

As you wander this colorful, dynamic city—where fishermen sell sandwiches from bobbing boats, shops offer saffron-hued mounds of spices, and sturdy trams and ferries carry thousands of people daily—it can be easy to forget that you're walking in the footsteps of Roman emperors and Ottoman sultans.

Over the centuries, Istanbul served as the capital of two grand empires: first as Constantinople, the capital of the Byzantine Empire (AD 313-1453), and then as Istanbul, the renamed capital of the conquering Ottoman Empire (until Ankara was made the capital of modern Turkey in 1923).

In the lively Old Town, monuments to those empires still stand and impress. Hagia Sophia, the greatest Byzantine church, became the Ottomans' most important mosque. The multidomed Blue Mosque, with its soaring interior, is among the world's most beautiful. The colorfully tiled Topkapı Palace was home to the ruling sultans and their harems.

Turkey today is a proud republic. While it's no longer the capital, Istanbul is still the country's historical, cultural, and financial center. You'll see the nation's red flags flying everywhere.

A focus of "East meets West" trade since ancient times, Istanbul is famous for its bustling markets. The biggest is the

A vendor displays a scarf at the Grand Bazaar; a man washes before prayers at a mosque.

world's oldest mall, the Grand Bazaar, a sprawling warren of shops with eager merchants selling jewelry, housewares, sandals, clothing, and Turkish carpets. Bargaining and banter go hand in hand, and English is the common language.

Istanbul literally links Europe and Asia, with several bridges and tunnels crossing the Bosphorus Strait. To sail between two continents, take a relaxing Bosphorus cruise toward the Black Sea (on your right—Asia). As you return to Istanbul, you'll glide into the shimmering inlet of the Golden Horn as the sunset glows on the city's spine-tingling skyline, bristling with minarets.

As the showpiece city of a moderate Muslim nation, Istanbul offers curious travelers from other backgrounds the opportunity to witness the Islamic faith in action. Five times a day, the call to prayer echoes across the rooftops. People stop to pray...or not. Close up, it's easier to see similarities between faiths than differences.

Day or night, Istanbul is a hive of human activity. Sample sweets at the busy Spice Market. Stroll the two-level Galata Bridge, where vendors sell sesame-seed bread rings *(simit)* from steamed-up carts and fishermen cast lines into the water below. Inhale apple-flavored smoke from a water pipe in a trendy *nargile* café. Marvel at the mesmerizing spinning of whirling dervishes as they meditate on universal harmony. At

Istanbul Slice-of-Life Stroll

Just walking through the streets of Istanbul can give you a look at the cuisine, culture, and character of this captivating city.

You'll see vendors' carts and hole-in-the-wall restaurants selling *döner kebab* (roasted meat wrapped in pita bread) and *gözleme* (flatbread folded over cheese and spinach). Turkish cuisine is Mediterranean-healthy, making tasty use of olive oil, stuffed veggies, lentils, seafood, and grilled meats. A local favorite to try—or avoid—is *kokoreç* (sheep intestines, grilled and served with tomatoes and green peppers; it's better than it sounds).

Shop windows display towers of Turkish delight (soft, chewy sweets) and honey-soaked baklava. Ice cream shops sell thick, stretchy Turkish ice cream; get a cone for your walk.

People fill the streets. Most Turks wear Western dress, though more conservative Muslim women wear headscarves over their hair.

In the back streets you're likely to see specialty clothing shops. The brightly colored silky capes hanging in windows are for boys to wear at their circumcision party. It's a big celebration. Turks call it "a wedding without the in-laws," where a good time is had by...well, nearly everyone.

You'll spot "evil eye" amulets tacked in doorways and dangling from souvenir stands. These popular blue-and-white glass good-luck charms, with big googly eyes, are thought to ward off evil.

Exotic yet down to earth, Istanbul inspires thoughtful travelers to want to know more about the country's intriguing culture and gregarious people. Make the most of Turkish hospitality to connect, ask questions, and learn. ▇

Tasty snacks on wheels; sweet Turkish delight; boys dressed up for a traditional circumcision party

Whirling dervish performance; family-friendly Sultanahmet Park in the Old Town

a Turkish bath, get cleaner than you've ever been. Linger over a seafood feast overlooking the Sea of Marmara, and sway to live Turkish music in a New District nightclub. Join the happy crowd in Sultanahmet Park, between Hagia Sophia and the Blue Mosque. It's breathtaking at night, when hard-pumping seagulls dart between floodlit minarets against the black sky.

With more time, consider a short-flight side trip to the ancient Roman city of Ephesus, on Turkey's Aegean coast, or the geologic wonderland of Cappadocia, with "fairy chimneys" and early Christian settlements, located deep in the country's heartland.

The mix of Muslim faith, Western outlook, and warm hospitality make Turkey a rewarding stop for travelers. The country's best sights are its people—they're among the friendliest on the planet. It's easy to strike up conversations, whether you're asking a fisherman about his catch, haggling over a Turkish carpet in the Grand Bazaar, or playing backgammon with a grizzled elder. Many conversations lead to an invitation to drink tea *(çay)* together. If you accept, little tulip-shaped glasses of steaming liquid appear within minutes, and soon the language barrier dissolves faster than a sugar cube in hot tea.

Istanbul's incomparable sights will wow you, while its open-hearted welcome makes you feel you're among friends. It's a crossroads not only of commerce but humanity. And according to the Turkish proverb, every guest is a gift from God.

Istanbul by Neighborhood

Sprawling Istanbul (with a population of over 15 million) straddles two continents: Europe and Asia. Tourists focus on Istanbul's European side, which consists of the Old Town and "New District," split by the Golden Horn inlet. Across the Bosphorus Strait is the mostly residential Asian side of Istanbul.

TOP NEIGHBORHOODS

Old Town

The Old Town is corralled on a peninsula bordered by the Sea of Marmara, Bosphorus Strait, and Golden Horn.

The city's blockbuster sights—Hagia Sophia, Blue Mosque, and Topkapı Palace—are clustered in the central, welcoming neighborhood called Sultanahmet, which also has the highest concentration of hotels and restaurants. Also here are the Istanbul Archaeological Museums and the Turkish and Islamic Arts Museum.

To the west of Sultanahmet, on a long hill spilling down to the Golden Horn, are the Grand Bazaar (the world's oldest market), the Mosque of Süleyman the Magnificent, and the bustling Spice Market.

Farther west, just inside the old city walls, is the Chora Church, with beautiful Byzantine mosaics.

Golden Horn

The Golden Horn, a tapering inlet of the Bosphorus, runs roughly northwest to southeast, separating the Old Town from the New District. Humming with ferries, the Golden Horn is spanned by the people-friendly Galata Bridge, itself abuzz with pedestrians, fishermen, food carts, and eateries.

At the south end of the Galata Bridge is the lively Eminönü district (near the Spice Market), with ferry docks offering day-long Bosphorus cruises and trips across the strait to the Asian side.

New District

North of the Old Town, the triangle of land flanked by the Golden Horn and the Bosphorus is what I call the "New

Opposite: Mosque of Süleyman the Magnificent. *Clockwise from top:* Spice Market; Chora Church mosaics; Galata Bridge action; İstiklal Street tram

Clockwise from top: *Kadıköy market; New District skyline with Galata Tower; ballooning in Cappadocia; friendly shopper*

District." This urban, European-feeling area is full of life day and night. The delightful pedestrian street called İstiklal teems with window-shoppers, stores, and eateries, and connects huge Taksim Square to the Tünel funicular, which conquers the steep hill down to the Galata Bridge in seconds.

The New District's major sights are the Pera Museum (Orientalist art), the Galata Dervish Monastery (Sunday performances), and the 14th-century Galata Tower (for great views).

The New District also hosts hotels, restaurants, and lots of nightlife. Farther north, the trendy Ortaköy neighborhood draws crowds for its fun nightlife scene on the Bosphorus.

Across the Bosphorus

The eastern half of Istanbul, across the Bosphorus Strait, hosts two contrasting and easy-to-visit neighborhoods. Üsküdar, the traditional starting point for trips to Mecca, has a religious vibe, numerous mosques, and a view of Istanbul's stunning skyline. Modern, energetic Kadıköy offers a cacophony of colorful market activity, shop-lined streets, and busy eateries.

The Bosphorus, crowded with ships, tankers, fishing boats, and ferries, is a sight in itself. Its shores are lined with historic fortresses, Ottoman palaces, luxury hotels, and parks and gardens—best viewed from a public ferry that sails nearly to the Black Sea.

Beyond Istanbul

Turkey's most rewarding sights outside of Istanbul are Ephesus and Cappadocia, each a short flight away.

The ancient city of **Ephesus,** one of the grandest in the Roman Empire, is impressive even in ruins, with marble-paved boulevards, the Library of Celsus, and a huge theater where the Apostle Paul once spoke. Ephesus, on Turkey's western Aegean coast, is a popular excursion for cruise ships docking at the shopping mecca of Kuşadası.

The **Cappadocia** region in central Turkey is a sprawling landscape of fantastical geological spires, cave dwellings, early Christian sites (even underground cities), open-air museums, and down-to-earth villages. Hot-air balloon rides offer thrilling overviews.

Planning and Budgeting

The best trips start with good planning. Here are ideas to help you decide when to go, design a smart itinerary, set a travel budget, and prepare for your trip. For our best general advice on sightseeing, accommodations, restaurants, and more, see the Practicalities chapter.

PLANNING YOUR TIME

As you read this book and learn about your options...

Decide when to go.

Istanbul has a moderate climate year-round. It is generally hot and humid from mid-July to mid-August, and it can snow during January and February. The peak-season months (with the best weather) are from April to late June and September through November. In the off-season, you can generally find better deals and smaller crowds; the weather is usually good, and all the sights are open. Weather conditions can change throughout the day—especially in spring and fall—but extremes are rare. Summer temperatures generally range from 65 to 85 degrees Fahrenheit (42-60 degrees in winter). Temperatures below freezing and above 90 make headlines. For more information, check the climate chart in the appendix (and www.mgm.gov.tr for a daily forecast).

Keep in mind that Istanbul is more crowded and has higher hotel prices during Christian holidays such as Easter, Christmas, and New Year's.

Work out a day-by-day itinerary.

The following day plans offer suggestions for how to maximize your sightseeing, depending on how many days you have. You can adapt these itineraries to fit your own interests. To find out when sights are open, check the "Daily Reminder" in the Orientation chapter. Consider whether you'll want to buy a Museum Pass or tickets for major sights in advance.

Istanbul deserves a minimum of two full days, but you'll need four days to do it justice. And if you have up to a week, the city will keep you busy and entertained.

To include both Ephesus and Cappadocia, add another three to five days.

Day One

In the morning, focus on the Sultanahmet district in the Old Town. Take the self-guided Historic Core Walk in this book to get your bearings, visiting Hagia Sophia, the Basilica Cistern, and the Blue Mosque. Then follow the self-guided tour of the Turkish and Islamic Arts Museum (across from the Blue Mosque).

Evening Options: On any evening, consider dinner in a sea-view restaurant, a whirling dervish performance, or live music and clubbing in the New District. Enjoy a Turkish bath, or catch the sunset from a city viewpoint like the Galata Tower. Stroll the Galata Bridge, the Old Town's Sultanahmet Park, or İstiklal Street in the New District.

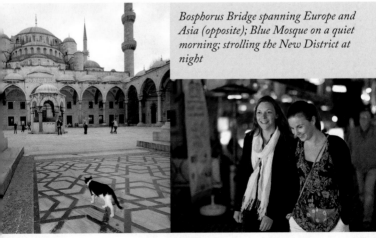

Bosphorus Bridge spanning Europe and Asia (opposite); Blue Mosque on a quiet morning; strolling the New District at night

Clockwise from top: Gates of Topkapı Palace; bread rings for sale; viewing art in the Pera Museum; a relaxing Bosphorus cruise

Day Two

Follow this book's self-guided tours of the sprawling Topkapı Palace and nearby Istanbul Archaeological Museums. For a break, Gülhane Park is next door.

Then take a taxi to the Chora Church for a self-guided tour of its Byzantine mosaics. From here, you could follow this book's self-guided City Walls and Neighborhoods Walk, which starts near the church.

With only two days for Istanbul, skip the church and instead take a self-guided New District Walk.

Day Three

Spend today on this book's self-guided Old Town Back Streets Walk—stopping along the way to tour the Grand Bazaar and the Mosque of Süleyman the Magnificent—then visit the Rüstem Paşa Mosque and the Spice Market. You'll finish near the Galata Bridge, where you could end your day with a self-guided Golden Horn Walk.

Day Four

Devote today to the New District, following this book's self-guided walk along the street called İstiklal, including visits to the Pera Museum and Galata Tower.

To fit in more New District sights, choose from the Military Museum (near Taksim Square) or the Quincentennial Museum of Turkish Jews (near Galata Tower). Or take a funicular from Taksim Square down to the Bosphorus and Dolmabahçe Palace (sultans' 19th-century digs; book a tour in advance). Catch a taxi to the Chora Church in the Old Town (if you didn't go on Day Two).

Day Five

Go to Asia. Set sail on the Bosphorus Strait, following this book's self-guided Bosphorus Cruise by public ferry. You'll spend a full day cruising up toward the Black Sea, stopping at the Asian village of Anadolu Kavağı before returning to Istanbul.

17

Or, for a quicker visit to Asia, catch a ferry across the Bosphorus to Üsküdar or Kadıköy, and follow this book's self-guided walks through those local neighborhoods.

With More Time

With extra time in Istanbul, choose among many smaller museums, mosques, outlying sights, and experiences such as a Turkish bath, a *nargile* (water pipe) café, a cooking class, or shopping.

Or catch a flight to Ephesus or Cappadocia, or visit both. Ephesus merits a day, while the Cappadocia region warrants two to four days. Flights connect Cappadocia and Ephesus.

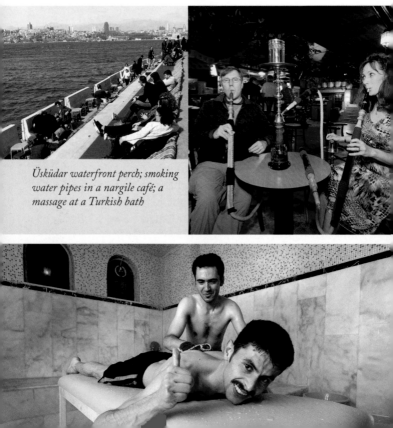

Üsküdar waterfront perch; smoking water pipes in a nargile café; a massage at a Turkish bath

PLANNING YOUR BUDGET

Run a reality check on your dream trip. You'll have major transportation costs in addition to daily expenses.

Flight: A round-trip flight from the US to Istanbul costs about $600-1,500, depending on where you fly from and when.

Public Transportation: For a one-week visit, allow about $15-20 per person for public transportation (each individual trip costs about a dollar). It's cheap to treat yourself to a cab—$10-20 will cover the cost of connecting virtually any two sights listed in this book. Add $35-50 if you plan to take a taxi between the airport and your hotel in the Old Town or New District.

AVERAGE DAILY EXPENSES PER PERSON

$215
Applies to cities, figure on less for towns

Lodging
Based on two people splitting the cost of a $190 double room
$95

Meals
$15 for lunch, $25 for dinner, and $2 for coffee or ice cream
$42

City Transit
Trams, light rail, funicular, Metro, ferries, and buses
$3

Sights and Entertainment
This daily average works for most people.
$75

To add on Ephesus or Cappadocia, figure about $150 for a round-trip flight to either destination.

Budget Tips: To cut your daily expenses, take advantage of the deals you'll find throughout Istanbul and mentioned in this book.

A Museum Pass saves avid sightseers time and money (see the Sights chapter for details). Or, visit only the sights you most want to see, and seek out free sights and experiences (people-watching counts).

Some businesses—especially hotels—offer discounts to my readers (look for the RS% symbol in the listings in this book).

Reserve your rooms directly with the hotel and book good-value rooms early. Some hotels offer a discount if you pay in cash and/or stay three or more nights (check online or ask). Rooms can cost less outside the peak spring and fall seasons. And even seniors can sleep cheaply in hostels (most have private rooms) for about $30 per person. Or check Airbnb-type sites for deals.

It's no hardship to eat inexpensively in Istanbul. You can get tasty, affordable meals at self-service cafeterias and from street vendors (*döner kebabs*, bagel-like *simit*). Cultivate the art of picnicking in atmospheric settings.

When you splurge, choose an experience you'll always remember, such as a cooking class, a Turkish bath, or a hot-air balloon ride over Cappadocia. Minimize souvenir shopping; focus instead on collecting wonderful memories.

A budget-friendly, tasty, and satisfying cafeteria meal; a welcoming hotel room with all the comforts

BEFORE YOU GO

You'll have a smoother trip if you tackle a few things ahead of time. For more information on these topics, see the Practicalities chapter and Ricksteves.com, which has helpful travel tips and talks.

Make sure your travel documents are valid. You need a passport and a visa, but no shots, to travel in Turkey. If your passport is due to expire within six months of your ticketed date of return, you need to renew it. Allow up to six weeks to renew or get a passport (www.travel.state.gov). You must buy your visa before you enter Turkey (at www.evisa.gov.tr/en or at an embassy or consulate).

Arrange your transportation. Book your international flights. Overall, Kayak.com is the best place to start searching for flights. If you'll be traveling in Turkey beyond Istanbul (to Ephesus or Cappadocia), book a flight on a Turkish airline, and consider reserving a rental car for Cappadocia.

Book rooms well in advance, especially if your trip falls during peak season or any major holidays or festivals.

Buy a pass or advance tickets for major sights, and reserve splurge experiences. To avoid ticket lines at Istanbul's sights, purchase a Museum Pass or buy advance tickets for just the biggies, such as Topkapı Palace (www.muze.gov.tr is a one-stop shop). If you're adding Cappadocia and want to splurge on a hot-air balloon ride or a folk show, reserve far ahead.

Hire guides in advance. If you want to hire a guide, reserve ahead by email. Popular guides can get booked up.

Consider travel insurance. Compare the cost of insurance to the cost of your potential loss. Check whether your existing insurance (health, homeowners, or renters) covers you and your possessions overseas.

Call your bank. Alert your bank that you'll be using your debit and credit cards in Europe. Ask about transaction fees, and get the PIN number for your credit card. You don't need to bring Turkish lira for your trip; you can withdraw lira from cash machines in Turkey.

Use your smartphone smartly. Sign up for an international service plan to reduce costs, or rely on Wi-Fi in Europe instead. Download any apps you'll want on the road, such as maps, translators, transit schedules, and **Rick Steves Audio Europe** (see sidebar).

Pack light. You'll walk with your luggage more than you think. I travel for weeks with a single carry-on bag and a day pack. Use the packing checklist in the appendix as a guide.

Rick's Free Video Clips and Audio Tours

Travel smarter with these free, fun resources:

Rick Steves Classroom Europe, a powerful tool for teachers, is also useful for travelers. This video library contains over 400 short clips excerpted from my public television series. Enjoy these videos as you sort through options for your trip and to better understand what you'll see in Europe. Check it out at Classroom.RickSteves.com (just enter a topic to find everything I've filmed on a subject).

Rick Steves Audio Europe, a free app, makes it easy to download my audio tours and listen to them offline as you travel. For this book, I've recorded an audio tour of ancient Ephesus (look for the 🎧). The app also offers interviews from my public radio show with experts from Europe and around the globe. Find it in your app store or at RickSteves.com/AudioEurope.

Travel Smart

If you have a positive attitude, equip yourself with good information (this book), and expect to travel smart, you will.

Read—and reread—this book. To have an "A" trip, be an "A" student. Note opening hours of sights, closed days, crowd-beating tips, and whether reservations are required or advisable. Check the latest at RickSteves.com/update.

Be your own tour guide. As you travel, get up-to-date info on sights, reserve tickets and tours, reconfirm your hotel and travel arrangements, and check transit connections.

Carry identification. You're required to have proof of identity and your tourist visa with you at all times in Turkey. You may be asked to show your passport when entering sights or using a credit card.

Outsmart thieves. Pickpockets abound in crowded places where tourists congregate. Treat commotions as smokescreens for theft. Keep your cash, credit cards, and passport secure in a money belt tucked under your clothes; carry only a day's spending money in your front pocket or wallet. Don't set valuable items down on counters or café tabletops, where they can be quickly stolen or easily forgotten.

Minimize potential loss. Keep expensive gear to a minimum. Bring photocopies or take photos of important documents (passport and cards) to aid in replacement if they're lost or stolen. Back up photos and files frequently.

Beat the summer heat. If you wilt easily, choose a hotel with air-conditioning, start your day early, take a midday siesta at your hotel, and resume your sightseeing later. Take frequent breaks for cold drinks and snacks at teahouses or coffee shops.

Guard your time and energy. Taking a taxi can be a good value if it saves you an exhausting walk across town or a long wait for a cheap bus. To avoid long lines, follow the crowd-beating tips in this book, such as getting a Museum Pass, buying tickets in advance, or sightseeing early or late.

Be flexible. Even if you have a well-planned itinerary, expect changes, closures, sore feet, bad weather, and so on. Your Plan B could turn out to be even better.

Attempt the language. Many Turks—especially in the tourist trade and in cities—speak English, but if you learn some Turkish, even just a few pleasantries, you'll get more smiles and make more friends. Practice the survival phrases near the end of this book, and even better, bring a phrase book.

Connect with the culture. Interacting with locals carbonates your experience. Enjoy the friendliness of the Turkish people. Ask questions; most locals are happy to point you in their idea of the right direction. Set up your own quest for the best viewpoint, most unusual sight, or most interesting conversation with a local. When an opportunity pops up, make it a habit to say "yes."

Istanbul...here you come!

ORIENTATION TO ISTANBUL

Istanbul is sprawling, confusing...and magnificent. Take a deep breath, then use this orientation to traverse the city with ease.

With just over 15 million people, Istanbul sprawls over an enormous area on both banks of the Bosphorus Strait (Boğaziçi). The western half lies in Europe, and the east in Asia, thus making the city a "crossroads of continents." Asian Istanbul is mostly residential, while European Istanbul is densely urban and contains the city's main attractions. The two sides are connected by three suspension bridges, a rail tunnel, a car tunnel, and commuter-friendly ferries.

Navigating such a huge city can be intimidating. There's no central square (in fact, the Turkish word for "square"—*meydanı*—actually means "area"). Instead, Istanbul is a collection of landmarks and neighborhoods interconnected by twisty alleys. But though big, the tourist's Istanbul is surprisingly compact and walkable, especially when augmented by its impressive public-transportation network.

This chapter offers crucial advice on basic survival—things like staying healthy (don't drink the water) and avoiding theft (pickpockets abound)—as well as helpful hints and details on Istanbul's tourist services, a rundown of options for getting around, and recommendations for organized tours. (For an overview of the city's neighborhoods and detailed day plans, see the previous chapter.)

Perhaps most important, Istanbul requires cultural orienta-

Istanbul Place Names

English	Turkish
Basilica Cistern	Yerebatan Sarayı (yeh-reh-bah-tahn sah-rah-yuh)
Blue Mosque	Sultanahmet Camii (sool-tah-nah-meht jah-mee)
Bosphorus Strait	Boğaziçi (boh-ahz-ee-chee)
Burned Column (and major tram stop)	Çemberlitaş (chehm-behr-lee-tahsh)
Chora Church	Kariye Müzesi (kah-ree-yeh mew-zeh-see)
Divan Yolu (main street in Old Town)	Divan Yolu (dee-vahn yoh-loo)
Galata Bridge	Galata Köprüsü (gah-lah-tah kohp-rew-sew)
Galata Dervish Monastery	Galata Mevlevihanesi (gah-lah-tah mehv-leh-vee-hah-neh-see)
Galata Tower	Galata Kulesi (gah-lah-tah koo-leh-see)
Golden Horn	Haliç (hah-leech)
Grand Bazaar	Kapalı Çarşı (kah-pah-luh chahr-shuh)
Gülhane Park	Gülhane Parkı (gewl-hah-neh pahr-kuh)
Hagia Sophia	Aya Sofya (eye-ah soh-fee-yah)

tion. In this chapter you'll find tips on everything from mosque etiquette (wear scarves and long pants) to dealing with aggressive salesmen.

Now, relax. With the proper approach and a measure of patience, you'll fall head over heels for Istanbul—Europe's most exotic destination.

Overview

TOURIST INFORMATION

Istanbul's state-run tourist offices, abbreviated as **TI** in this book (and marked with an *i* sign in Istanbul), suffer from long lines and scant information. The only reason to visit one is to pick up the good, free city map. The TI staff, many of whom are not fluent in English, will try to help you with your requests, but likely with mixed results.

If you must visit a tourist office, here are some handy locations (all have sporadic hours; generally daily 9:00-17:00): in the **Sultanahmet** neighborhood, in the center of the Old Town (until 22:00 in summer, Divan Yolu Caddesi 3, at the bottom of the Hippodrome, next to the tram tracks, +90 212 518 8754); at the **Sirkeci** train station, near the Golden Horn in the Old Town's Eminönü

English	Turkish
Hippodrome	Hipodrom *(hee-poh-drohm)*
Sultanahmet (Old Town historic core)	Sultanahmet *(sool-tah-nah-meht)*
İstiklal Street	İstiklal Caddesi *(ees-teek-lahl jahd-deh-see)*
Mosque of Süleyman the Magnificent	Süleymaniye Camii *(sew-lay-mah-nee-yeh jah-mee)*
New District	Pera, Beyoğlu *peh-rah, bay-yoh-loo*
Rüstem Paşa Mosque	Rüstem Paşa Camii *(rew-stehm pah-shah jah-mee)*
Sirkeci Train Station	Sirkeci Tren Garı *(seer-keh-jee trehn gah-ruh)*
Spice Market	Mısır Çarşışı *(muh-suhr chahr-shuh-shuh)*
Süleymaniye (district)	Süleymaniye *(sew-lay-mah-nee-yeh)*
Taksim Square	Taksim Meydanı *(tahk-seem may-dah-nuh)*
Topkapı Palace	Topkapı Sarayı *(tohp-kah-puh sah-rah-yuh)*
Tünel (funicular)	Tünel *(tew-nehl)*

district (until 20:00, +90 212 511 5888); and near **Taksim Square** in the New District (at Mete Caddesi 6).

There are also TIs at **Istanbul Airport,** the city's main airport (open until 23:00, +90 212 813 3839) and at **Sabiha Gökçen Airport**, the city's alternate airport on the Asian side (+90 216 588 8794).

For current information on cultural activities, entertainment, shopping, and restaurants, pick up *The Guide,* a magazine published every two months and written by Turks and expats (10 TL, at bigger newspaper stands and major bookstores on İstiklal Street in the New District; also available online at www.theguideistanbul.com).

The monthly *Time Out Istanbul* magazine lists sights, hotels, restaurants, nightclubs, and more (6 TL, sold at most Istanbul newsstands, www.timeout.com/istanbul).

ARRIVAL IN ISTANBUL

For a rundown of Istanbul's train stations and airports, see the Istanbul Connections chapter.

HELPFUL HINTS

Don't Drink the Water: Drinking Istanbul's tap water can make you sick. Brush your teeth with bottled water, and avoid get-

ORIENTATION

ting tap water in your mouth while showering, shaving, and so on. Any bottled or canned beverages are fine. Most restaurants sell safe water in cheap little plastic cups with peel-off tops. Tea and coffee are usually made with bottled or filtered water. Better restaurants wash produce with filtered water. At cheaper restaurants, choose cooked food instead of raw.

Dealing with Diarrhea: No matter how careful you are, you might get a touch of "Istanbul intestines." Don't panic, revise your diet, and take it easy for 24 hours. For a day or so, eat very bland food (bread, rice, applesauce, boiled potatoes, clear soup, toast, weak tea). Keep telling yourself that tomorrow you'll feel much better, because you probably will. If loose stools persist, drink lots of water to replenish lost liquids.

Pharmacies: Pharmacies (*eczane;* edge-zah-neh) are generally open Monday through Saturday (9:00-19:00) and closed Sunday. In every neighborhood, one pharmacy stays open late and on holidays for emergencies. These *nöbetçi eczane* (noh-bet-chee edge-zah-neh; "pharmacy on duty") are generally within walking distance or a short cab ride from wherever you are. Just ask your hotelier for help. Or, if you're on your own, the location of the nearest *nöbetçi eczane* is posted by the entrance to any pharmacy. When interpreting signs, note these translations: *bu gece* (tonight), *Pazar* (Sunday), and *gün/günü* (day).

Medical Problems: In an emergency, dialing 112 will get you an ambulance to a public hospital (you may need to ask a local to help with translation—but Turks are eager to help). Istanbul's public hospitals *(hastane)* usually have 24-hour emergency care centers (*acil servis;* "emergency service") but are short on English-speaking personnel. Unless you need to be rushed to the nearest hospital, go to a private facility with English-speaking staff. For recommendations, see the Practicalities chapter.

Theft Alert: In Turkey, travelers are rarely mugged, but often pickpocketed. Thieves thrive on fresh-off-the-plane tourists. You'll be better off without your best clothes, expensive-looking gear, and fancy jewelry. Be alert on all public transportation and in crowds. Watch for distraction tactics such as dropped coins, "accidental" spills, and locals who ask you for directions.

If you're out late, avoid dark back streets or any place with dim lighting and minimal pedestrian activity. Ignore anyone who asks if you need help or a cab ride. Wear a money belt, be smart with your bags, sling your daypack across your front, and keep change in buttoned or front pockets.

Daily Reminder

Open Every Day: Hagia Sophia, Basilica Cistern, Bosphorus cruise boats, Galata Tower, Chora Church, Miniatürk, and most Turkish baths welcome tourists daily. Mosques are open daily, but close to tourists five times each day, when worshippers come to pray. Specific prayer times change daily but can be found online (search "prayer times Istanbul"). For tips on the etiquette of visiting a mosque, see page 71.

Sunday: The Grand Bazaar is closed.

Monday: Most of Istanbul's museums are closed today, including those operated by the Ministry of Culture—such as the Istanbul Archaeological Museums, and the Turkish and Islamic Arts Museum. The Dolmabahçe Palace, Galata Dervish Monastery, Military Museum, Istanbul Modern, Pera Museum, Sakıp Sabancı Museum, and Rahmi Koç Industrial Museum are also closed. Topkapı Palace is open.

Tuesday: Topkapı Palace, Hagia Irene, and the Military Museum are closed.

Wednesday: Closed sights include the Rumeli Fortress and Sadberk Hanım Museum. Because Topkapı Palace is closed on Tuesday, it may be especially crowded first thing this morning.

Thursday: All sights are open. Istanbul Modern is open until 20:00.

Friday: The Blue Mosque is closed until after the Friday noon service. All other mosques are closed during this important service, and very crowded before and after. The Quincentennial Museum of Turkish Jews closes at 13:00.

Saturday: Everything is open except the Quincentennial Museum of Turkish Jews.

Ramadan: During the Muslim holy month, a big, convivial, multigenerational festival breaks out each evening at sunset. For most visitors, the Hippodrome square is the most convenient place to join in. For more information, see page 72.

Religious Holidays: The Grand Bazaar and the Spice Market are closed during religious festivals. Museum hours are also adjusted for the first day of religious holidays, with closures either in the morning or for the entire day.

Advice for Women: Modesty is valued in Turkish culture; it's best to cover your shoulders and knees, and avoid form-fitting clothes. Carry a scarf to cover your hair while inside mosques as a sign of respect.

Buses and trams are very crowded, and some physical contact with other people is unavoidable. But if someone tries to touch you in a deliberate way, be clear about your disapproval. Push the offender away and say in a loud voice, "*Çek elini*" (check eh-lee-nee; Get your hands off me).

Advice for Men: Men should consider wearing lightweight pants instead of shorts, as Turkish men generally don't sport shorts beyond the beach. When visiting mosques, it is respectful to wear clothing that covers your knees and shoulders.

Street Safety: Be extremely cautious when crossing streets that lack traffic lights or crosswalks. Look both ways, since many streets are one-way, and be wary of seemingly vacant bus, tram, or taxi lanes. Don't assume you have the right-of-way, even in a crosswalk. When crossing a street, keep your pace constant and don't stop suddenly. Drivers calculate your speed and won't hit you—provided you don't alter your route and pace. (Don't expect them to stop for you; they probably won't.)

Finding Addresses: An Istanbul address can have several elements. Sometimes it's as straightforward as a street name (*Caddesi*—"street," or *Sokak*—"alley"), followed by a number, such as Akbıyık Caddesi 21. The address is sometimes preceded by the name of a larger street that's nearby (such as İstiklal Caddesi, Meşelik Sokak 10) to help you or your cabbie find the general location (İstiklal Caddesi) before searching for a tiny alley (Meşelik Sokak 10). And sometimes the address is followed by the name of the neighborhood it's in; for example: Şifahane Sokak 6, Süleymaniye.

Aggressive Sales Pitches: As you walk through the Old Town, you'll constantly be approached by people who greet you enthusiastically, offer help, ask where you're from, and tell you about a cousin who just happens to live in your hometown. Before long, what began as a friendly conversation devolves into an aggressive sales pitch. These salesmen—who prey on Americans' gregariousness and desire to respond politely to a friendly greeting—are irritating and can waste your valuable sightseeing time. While not dangerous, the salesmen can be particularly intimidating to single women. Just smile and say, "No, thank you!" without breaking stride...then ignore the escalating attempts to grab your attention (or elbow) as you walk past.

Public WCs: You'll generally pay 1-2 TL to use a public WC. The İstanbulKart (see page 35) is valid in some public WCs. Carry toilet paper or tissues with you, since some WCs are poorly supplied. Use the WCs in museums (likely free and better than public WCs), or walk into any sidewalk café or American fast-food joint as if you own the place and find the WC in the back (if you encounter a lock, ask permission or make a small purchase).

In the heart of the Old Town, plumbing isn't always up to modern standards. Rather than flush soiled toilet paper, locals dispose of it in a designated trash can next to the toilet. It's culturally sensitive—and sometimes essential plumbing-wise—for visitors to do the same (especially if there's a sign requesting this).

Western-style toilets are the norm, but you may run across a "squat" toilet. This squat-and-aim system is basically a porcelain hole in the ground flanked by platforms for your feet. If this seems outrageous to you, spend your squatting time pondering the fact that those of us who need a throne to sit on are in the minority; most humans sit on their haunches and nothing more.

Baggage Storage: Easy-to-use lockers are available at Istanbul Airport (fees vary with item size). Some hoteliers will store bags if you're leaving Istanbul and returning later.

English-Language Church: Christian services are held in English every Sunday at the **Dutch Chapel** (Union Church of Istanbul, just off İstiklal Street by the Dutch Consulate at #393, contemporary service at 9:30, traditional worship at 11:00, +90 212 244 5212, http://ucistanbul.org).

GETTING AROUND ISTANBUL

Even though Istanbul is a huge city, most of its tourist areas are easily walkable. You'll likely need public transportation only to connect sightseeing zones (for example, going from the Old Town to the New District across the Golden Horn). Istanbul has a slick, modern, and user-friendly network of trams, funiculars, and Metro lines. Once you learn the system, it seems custom-made for tourists, with stops within a short walk of most major attractions. Round out your transportation options with taxis (abundant and affordable) and ferries (handy in this water-laced city).

On religious festival days—when public transit may be free or discounted—buses and trams can be loaded with locals visiting their families and heading to parks, fairs, and theaters. Expect crowds on transit and in the streets.

ORIENTATION

Turkish Do's and Don'ts

Turkey gives Western visitors a refreshing dose of culture shock. Here are a few finer points to consider when interacting with your Turkish hosts:

Don't signal to someone with your hands or your fingers, except when hailing a cab or trying to get your waiter's attention. In any other situation, it's considered rude.

Don't get too close to people as you talk. Allow for plenty of personal space (an arm's length is fine). Especially when talking to someone of the opposite sex, keep your distance and don't touch them as you talk.

Be careful with gestures: A "thumbs up" is—and means—OK. But putting your thumb between your index and middle finger and making a fist is equivalent to showing your middle finger in the US. (And you always thought Grandma was "stealing your nose.") Making a circle with your thumb and index finger while twisting your hand is a homophobic insult.

Be aware of Turkish body language for "yes" and "no." A Turk nods her head down to say yes. She shakes it back and forth to say no, like Westerners do. But she might also say no by tilting her head back. Learn the Turkish words for "yes" (*evet*; eh-veht) and "no" (*hayır*; hah-yur) to confirm.

If you're offered food or a gift, either keep it for yourself or politely decline. Turkish people love to share what they have, but what they offer to you is for you alone. If you don't want the food or gift, don't wave it away. Do as the Turks do: Either put your right hand on your heart and say, "Thank you" (*teşekkür ederim*; teh-shehk-koor eh-deh-reem), or if it's food, pat your abdomen to indicate that you're full.

Don't blow your nose at the dining table—either leave the table, or turn to face the other way. And afterward, don't shake hands right away. (Come to think of it, that's a rule everyone could use.)

By Taxi

Taxis are generally an efficient, affordable way to get around town (5-TL drop fee, then roughly 3.10 TL/kilometer; no nighttime tariff). Figure about 25-40 TL for a longer trip within the Old Town or New District.

Taxi Tips: Use only official taxis: These are painted yellow, with their license plate number, name, and home-office phone number displayed on the front doors.

If a taxi's top light is on, it's available—just wave it down. Drivers usually flash their lights to indicate that they'll pick you up. Taxis can take up to four passengers. If you have difficulty hailing a cab off the street, ask where you can find a taxi stand. You can also call a taxi company, usually for no extra charge. Hotels, restaurants, museums, and even shopkeepers almost always have the phone number of a nearby taxi company—just ask.

Or try the **İtaksi** app (meaning "Istanbul taxi"). It's a good way to make sure you'll get an official taxi and be charged the right fare (in English; see details at www.itaksi.com).

All cabs have electronic meters and cabbies should use them. To ask for the meter to be turned on, use the phrase "*taksi metre lütfen*" (tahk-see meh-treh lewt-fehn; meter, please).

The cabbie may claim you have to pay bogus extra charges; for example, if he claims that you owe him a 5-TL "luggage charge" for a 15-TL ride, politely refuse and pay what's on the meter. If your cabbie incurs toll charges, though, you should expect to pay them.

Some cab drivers use a sleight-of-hand trick with bill denominations. For example, they'll take your 50-TL bill, then insist you gave them only a 5-TL bill (while showing you a 5-TL bill they have ready and handy for this scam). If you must pay your fare with a big bill, announce the bill's denomination as you give it to the cabbie.

Tipping: Although some cabbies are con artists, many are honest and deserve a tip. To tip, simply round up the bill (generally 2-4 TL; for exceptional service, you could add a few liras more). If you need a receipt, ask: "*Fiş, lütfen*" (fish lewt-fehn; receipt, please).

By Public Transportation

Istanbul's transit is convenient and inexpensive. Tram, funicular, and Metro lines intersect at central locations, and use the same cards and passes. A transit system map is included at the back of this book, and you can find timetables and maps at www.metro.istanbul.

Trams

The seemingly made-for-tourists ***tramvay*** (trahm-vay) cuts a boomerang-shaped swath through the core of Istanbul's Old Town, then crosses the Golden Horn to the New District, where it continues along the Bosphorus. Destinations are

Paying for Public Transportation

Istanbul's public transportation is fairly easy to use, with one caveat: The city is constantly tinkering with the ticketing system. For the latest, check the Istanbul public transportation website (www.metro.istanbul).

To buy one token, insert money into the machine and press the green button on the right. To buy several tokens, insert money, hit the dark blue button to select the number you want, and press the green button to confirm. Collect your tokens and change from the slot at the bottom.

Single or Multiple-Ride Cards: These nonrechargeable electronic cards should cover all forms of public transit. A single-ride card costs 5 TL; multiple-ride cards offer lower fares (2-ride card-8 TL, 3 rides-11 TL, 5 rides-17 TL, 10 rides-32 TL). Buy these cards from ticket booths at major bus, tram, light rail, Metro, and ferry stops (not available through vending machines).

posted on the outside of the tram—just hop on the one heading in the direction you want to go. Key tram stops include (from south to north):

Beyazıt and **Çemberlitaş:** Flanking the Grand Bazaar in the Old Town.

Sultanahmet: Dead-center in the Old Town, near Hagia Sophia, the Blue Mosque, the Hippodrome, and most recommended hotels and restaurants.

Gülhane: At the side entrance to the Topkapı Palace grounds, near the Istanbul Archaeological Museums.

Sirkeci: Sirkeci train station, near the Golden Horn and several Bosphorus ferry terminals.

Eminönü: On the Golden Horn in the Old Town, near the

IstanbulKart Pass: If you're staying more than a few days and plan to use public transit frequently, consider the reloadable IstanbulKart transit card to cut your per-ride costs. There's a non-refundable 6-TL charge to buy the card, then each ride costs 2.60 TL (a deal compared to a 5-TL single-ride card). Transfers within a two-hour window are even cheaper, at about 1.85 TL per ride (up to five transfers; you must wait at least 15 minutes between the start of your first ride and your transfer; no time limit between additional transfers). The pass works on all forms of transit, including double-decker buses that cross the Bosphorus (3 TL with pass) and ferries to the islands (4 TL with pass).

IstanbulKart passes are sold at ticket booths and newsstands; to reload the card, use a vending machine or visit a tobacco shop near central stops. If reloading at a vending machine, do not use large bills, as machines do not give change and will load the entire amount onto the card.

To use the IstanbulKart, hold it over the card reader as you go through the turnstile. The screen will show your remaining balance. For more information about the İstanbulKart, call +90 212 444 1871, visit www.istanbulkart.istanbul, or download the app.

Spice Market, Galata Bridge, and additional Bosphorus ferry terminals.

Karaköy: In the New District (directly across Galata Bridge from the Old Town), near the Galata Tower and Tünel train up to İstiklal Street.

Tophane: Near the Kiliç Ali Paşa mosque.

Kabataş: End of the line in the New District, next to the funicular up to Taksim Square (described later) and a few blocks from Dolmabahçe Palace.

There's also the **Nostalgic Tram** that runs up and down İstiklal Street, through the middle of the New District. For details, see the New District Walk chapter.

Funiculars

The easy one-stop, two-minute underground *füniküler* connects Taksim Square (and the top of İstiklal Street) in the New District with the Kabataş tram stop along the Bosphorus below. At

Kabataş, the tram and funicular stations are side by side; to find the funicular station from Taksim Square, look for the combined funicular/Metro entrance at the center of the square, across from the Marmara Hotel, and follow *Kabataş-Füniküler* signs.

A second underground funicular, called **Tünel,** climbs the steep hill from the Galata Bridge on the Golden Horn to Tünel Square, at the bottom end of İstiklal Street. This late-19th-century funicular is as historic as it is convenient (for details, see page 276).

Metro

The underground Metro line 2—generally not useful for tourists—begins at Yenikapı, stops at Taksim Square, and then heads north into the business and residential Levent district. To find a Metro entrance, look for big *M* signs.

Marmaray Rail

Marmaray (mahr-mah-rahy), the underground (and underwater) commuter rail system, provides by far the fastest connection between the two banks of the Bosphorus. Trains run between Kazlıçeşme (just outside the Old Town) and Ayrılık Çeşmesi (close to Kadıköy in Asia; switch to the Metro here to get to Kadıköy). For visitors, the most convenient stop to begin the journey to Asian Istanbul is from Sirkeci Station in the Old Town. See the Asian Istanbul Walks chapter for details.

Light Rail

Istanbul's light rail is of little use to most travelers, unless you arrive in Istanbul by bus (see the Connections chapter).

Buses

Although the bus system was designed for commuters, it can work as a last resort for tourists (but avoid buses during the busy morning and evening rush hours). Bus numbers on a particular route are clearly marked on signs at stops (bus info at www.iett.gov.tr/en). Buses are mostly useful for sights along the Bosphorus, including the Rumeli Fortress, Sakıp Sabancı Museum, and Sadberk Hanım Museum.

To ride a bus, you'll need either a transit card or İstanbulKart, as bus drivers do not take cash or tokens.

By Ferry

In this city where millions of people sail across the Bosphorus to work each day, the ferry system had better work well...and it does. In fact, locals much prefer ferries to avoid heavy car traffic crossing the Bosphorus, especially during rush hour. Ferries are convenient and inexpensive—many cost as little as 5 TL one-way (2.60 TL with İstanbulKart).

In European Istanbul, the main ferry docks are in the Old

Town's **Eminönü district**, near the mouth of the Golden Horn (by the Spice Market and Galata Bridge). This area is a major transit hub, where tram, bus, and ferry systems link up. Here you'll find terminals for ferries heading to **Asian Istanbul** (Üsküdar—2-4/hour in peak times, 20 minutes; Kadıköy—2/hour, 25 minutes) as well as Bosphorus cruise boats (both public ferries and private tour boats; for details, see the Bosphorus Cruise chapter). There are also piers at **Eyüp** (near the Eyüp Sultan Mosque, outside the old city walls), **Ayansaray** (near the walls' endpoint on the Golden Horn), **Karaköy** (across the Golden Horn from Eminönü, in the New District) and **Beşiktaş** (on the Bosphorus).

At every ferry dock, terminals are named for the ferry's destination. So, if you're at Eminönü and headed to Kadıköy, simply head to the Kadıköy terminal. Destinations are clearly marked on the terminals and above passenger entrances. For more on commuter ferries, see the Golden Horn Walk chapter.

You may see "sea buses" *(deniz otobüsü)* on the water, but these are geared for commuters, not tourists.

Tours in Istanbul

Note that tour companies and local guides often list prices in dollars or euros (not Turkish lira) and prefer to be paid in those currencies. This is partly for convenience, but also to protect vendors against currency fluctuations.

Hop-on, Hop-off Bus Tours

Narrated **Bigbus** double-decker tours should enable you to hop off, tour a sight, then catch a later bus to your next destination—but it isn't very practical. The tour amounts to a pricey two-hour ride in heavy traffic with recorded, multilingual commentary. The bus does offer views from the top deck, making it a convenient and scenic place to munch a kebab or picnic (and thanks to a convertible roof, this option still works in rainy or cold weather). But strictly for transportation, the Old Town's single tram line will take you to the major sights without the hassle and for a lot less money. The bus loop starts across from Hagia Sophia at Sultanahmet, but you can hop on at nearly any of the major sights along the route. Buses run year-round (€45, valid 24 hours, departures every 30 minutes, +90 212 283 1396, www.bigbustours.com).

Basic Boat Tours

Turyol offers 1.5-hour cruises on the Bosphorus. You won't see all of the Bosphorus, and there's no narration, but you can follow the route using the first part of this book's Bosphorus Cruise chapter. You don't need a reservation. Boats leave from the Golden Horn, right behind the Eminönü bus stop, across from the Spice Market

The Bosphorus Tunnel

Istanbul's Asian districts are mostly residential. That means millions of people commute to work across the strait using the bridges and ferries (which don't run in bad weather—making the commute a nightmare over the jammed-up bridges). Seeking to solve crowded Istanbul's never-ending traffic mess, a third bridge (Yavuz Sultan Selim) was constructed and opened in 2016.

A new option for transiting between continents is the rail tunnel beneath the Bosphorus—constructed as part of the ongoing, $2.5 billion Marmaray (a.k.a. Marmara Rail) project. The Marmaray incorporates a new commuter light-rail system into existing public transit, extending the system roughly 50 miles across both continents and carrying about 150,000 passengers per hour. The mile-long, rail-only Bosphorus Tunnel connects the Old Town to the busy Üsküdar district across the Bosphorus. And now a second tunnel (the twin-deck Eurasia Tunnel) has been opened for motor vehicles.

(25 TL, about hourly on weekdays and Sun, every half-hour on Sat; see the Bosphorus Cruise chapter for specifics, www.turyol.com).

Bosphorus and Black Sea Cruises

Guided cruises up the Bosphorus to the Black Sea are rare and can take most of the day. However, if you have the time and interest, İBO sails all the way to the Black Sea. If it's warm, you can even swim in the Bosphorus. Cruises depart from Kabataş and stop at Ortaköy, Küçüksu Pavilion, and Rumeli Fortress. An included lunch is served on board, and the swimming break (weather permitting) is at Poyrazköy Bay (north on the Bosphorus). Prices include admission to all sights (cruises operate April-Sept, €79, cheaper for kids, half-day cruises available, +90 212 528 0475 or +90 212 528 0476, www.ibocruise.com, owner İbrahim Şancı). For a self-guided cruise on a public ferry, see the Bosphorus Cruise chapter.

Local Guides

There are plenty of very good private guides in Istanbul. In Turkey, tour guides must be certified, and only travel agencies are authorized to make travel arrangements such as reserving minibuses or plane tickets. I've indicated which of the listed guides also run travel agencies so you'll know what they're allowed to arrange for you. All guides listed here are certified with the appropriate authorities. It's best to use an official guide or travel agency—otherwise you might be left in the lurch without the tour or services you paid for... and no legal recourse for a refund.

Lale and **Tan**, co-authors of this book and the owners of **SRM Travel,** run city tours, food walks, and cooking classes; develop custom itineraries for Istanbul, Cappadocia, Ephesus, and the rest of Turkey; and can book a private guide for you (including some who lead or help with Rick Steves' Europe tours). Lale and Tan can also refer travelers to gay-friendly guides and services in Istanbul. Mention this book to receive free travel consulting when you buy any travel service (private guiding from $235/half-day, from $265/full day, +90 216 266 5839, www.srmtravel.com).

Other recommended travel agent/guides include **Kağan** and **Lale Koşağan** of KSG Tours (€250/half-day, +90 216 343 4215, mobile +90 532 234 2042, www.ksgtours.com). **Attila Kılınç** can book you with a guide and provide private travel services (from $150/half-day, $200/full day, mobile +90 532 294 7667, www.marmaratours.com).

The following certified tour guides have also served my readers well: **Hakan Başar** ($200-220/half-day, $220-250/full day, mobile +90 532 417 1744, hakanbashar@gmail.com), **Nilüfer İris** ($225/half-day, $300/full day, especially good with senior travelers, +90 212 273 1142, mobile +90 532 244 1395, niluferiris@hotmail.com), and **Pınar Çağlayan** ($250-325/full day, offers food tours and classes too, mobile +90 538 315 5888, guidepinar@hotmail.com).

ORIENTATION

SIGHTS IN ISTANBUL

The sights in this chapter are arranged by neighborhood for handy sightseeing. Some of the city's most important sights have the shortest listings (and are marked with a 📖). That's because they are covered in much more detail in one of the self-guided walks or tours included elsewhere in this book.

The Old Town's major sights have long been discovered, which is why this area gets approximately three million visitors every year. Yet Istanbul is so wonderfully rich that hidden gems known only to locals wait to be explored outside the main tourist zones.

SIGHTSEEING STRATEGIES

Renovations: Istanbul is one of the fastest-changing cities in Europe. Add to this the fluctuating agenda of the government and the wait-until-the-last-minute attitude of its officials, and even locals have a hard time keeping up. Renovation projects are announced late, and the information is often inaccurate. Expect changes during your visit—ask your hotelier or the TI for the latest news about the sights you're planning to visit.

Opening Hours: If a sight is a must-see for you, check its hours in advance (by calling or asking at a TI—websites often are not accurate), and visit well before the closing times listed here.

Museum Pass: The five-day Museum Pass Istanbul (currently 325 TL) covers many of the city's top sights, including the Topkapı Palace (but not its Harem), Galata Tower, Istanbul Archaeological Museums, Istanbul Mosaic Museum, Turkish and Islamic Arts Museum, Chora Church, and others. The pass can save you money and lets you bypass ticket lines at the most popular attractions. Validate the pass only when you're ready to tackle covered sights on consecutive days. The pass is sold online (www.muze.gov.tr) and at ticket offices and vending machines at participating sights (buy it at a less-crowded sight—not Topkapı Palace).

Advance Tickets: If you don't need a pass, you can avoid lines by buying advance tickets at www.muze.gov.tr for museums including Topkapı Palace, Istanbul Archaeological Museums, Turkish and Islamic Arts Museum, and Chora Church.

Going with a Guide: You can skip the line without buying tickets ahead of time if accompanied by an official tour guide. Make sure your guide is registered with the appropriate authorities (for recommended guides, see page 38).

SIGHTS

In the Old Town

Istanbul's highest concentration of sights (and hotels) is in its Old Town, mostly in the Sultanahmet neighborhood.

IN THE SULTANAHMET AREA

📖 The Historic Core Walk chapter links Hagia Sophia, the Blue Mosque, the Basilica Cistern, and the Hippodrome.

▲▲▲Hagia Sophia (Aya Sofya)

It's been called the greatest house of worship in the Christian and Muslim worlds: Hagia Sophia (eye-ah soh-fee-yah), the Great Church of Constantinople. Built on the grandest scale possible by the Byzantine emperor Justinian in AD 537, it was for a thousand years the cathedral of Constantinople. Later, conquering Ottomans converted Hagia Sophia into a mosque, which it remained for almost five centuries until its conversion to a museum in 1934 by the secular Turkish Republic. Controversially, in 2020 the building was returned to its status as

a mosque. But whether church, mosque, or museum, Hagia Sophia remains the high point of Byzantine architecture. Enjoy the Christian and Islamic elements that meld peacefully under its soaring arches.

Cost and Hours: Free, generally open daily around the clock but closed to visitors five times a day for prayer; details for tourist visits to Hagia Sophia in flux at time of publication—best to confirm locally; in the heart of the Old Town at Sultanahmet Meydanı, +90 212 522 1750, www.muze.gen.tr.

📖 See the Hagia Sophia Tour chapter.

Istanbul at a Glance

In the Old Town

▲▲▲**Hagia Sophia** Constantinople's great church, later converted to an Ottoman mosque, then a museum, and recently reestablished as a mosque. **Hours:** Generally open daily around the clock but closed to visitors five times a day for prayer. See page 41.

▲▲▲**Blue Mosque** Ahmet I's response to Hagia Sophia, named for its brightly colored tiles. **Hours:** Generally open daily one hour after sunrise until one hour before sunset, closed to visitors five times a day for prayer and Friday mornings. See page 44.

▲▲▲**Topkapı Palace** Storied residence of the sultans, with endless museum exhibits, astonishing artifacts, and the famous Harem. **Hours:** Wed-Mon 9:00-19:00, until 17:00 off-season, closed Tue. See page 49.

▲▲▲**Grand Bazaar** World's oldest shopping mall, with more than 4,000 playfully pushy merchants. **Hours:** Mon-Sat 9:00-19:00, closed Sun and during religious holidays. See page 53.

▲▲▲**Mosque of Süleyman the Magnificent** The architect Sinan's 16th-century masterpiece, known for its serene interior and the tombs of Süleyman and his wife, Roxelana. **Hours:** Mosque—generally open daily from one hour after sunrise until one hour before sunset, closed to visitors five times a day for prayer. Mausoleums—daily 9:00-17:00, until 18:00 in summer. See page 53.

▲▲**Basilica Cistern** Vast sixth-century subterranean water reservoir built with recycled Roman columns. **Hours:** Daily 9:00-17:30. See page 45.

▲▲**Turkish and Islamic Arts Museum** Carpets, calligraphy, ceramics, and other traditional arts on display at the former İbrahim Paşa Palace. **Hours:** Tue-Sun 9:00-20:00, until 18:00 off-season, closed Mon. See page 45.

▲▲**Istanbul Archaeological Museums** Complex covering Istanbul's ancient civilizations, including sumptuous tiles and highly decorated sarcophagi. **Hours:** Tue-Sun 9:00-20:00, until 18:00 off-season, closed Mon. See page 51.

▲▲**Spice Market** Fragrant and colorful spices, dried fruit, and roasted nuts inside a 350-year-old market hall. **Hours:** Mon-Sat 8:00-19:30, until 19:00 off-season, Sun 9:30-18:00 year-round, closed during religious holidays. See page 54.

▲▲**Chora Church** Modest church outside the Old Town with

some of the best Byzantine mosaics in captivity. **Hours:** Daily 9:00-19:00, until 17:00 off-season. See page 54.

▲**Hippodrome** Roman chariot racetrack-turned-square, linking Hagia Sophia and the Blue Mosque. See page 45.

▲**Rüstem Paşa Mosque** Small 16th-century mosque of Süleyman's Grand Vizier with extravagant tile decor. **Hours:** Generally open daily one hour after sunrise until one hour before sunset, closed to visitors five times a day for prayer. See page 54.

On the Golden Horn
▲▲**Galata Bridge** Restaurant-lined bridge spanning the Golden Horn, bristling with fishermen's poles and offering sweeping views of the Old Town and New District. See page 56.

In the New District
▲▲▲**İstiklal Street** Cosmopolitan pedestrian-only street in the New District, teeming with shops, eateries, and people. See page 61.

▲▲**Galata Tower** 14th-century stone tower with the city's best views. **Hours:** Daily 10:00-21:00, Fri-Sat until 23:30. See page 65.

▲**Taksim Square** Gateway to the pedestrianized Istiklal Street, and heart of Istanbul's New District. See page 60.

▲**Pera Museum** Compact New District collection of world-class Orientalist paintings, Anatolian weights and measures, and Kütahya tiles. **Hours:** Tue-Sat 11:00-18:00, Sun 12:00-18:00, closed Mon. See page 61.

▲**Galata Dervish Monastery** Meeting place for dervishes, who whirl here once a week. **Hours:** Tue-Sun 9:00-19:00, until 17:00 in winter, closed Mon; dervish services generally Sun at 17:00. See page 64.

Along the Bosphorus
▲▲▲**Bosphorus Cruise** Public ferry ride on the Bosphorus Strait, offering a glimpse of untouristy Istanbul (and an Asian adventure). **Hours:** Daily April-Oct at 10:35 and 13:35, additional departures possible in summer; Nov-March at 10:35 only. See page 66.

▲**Dolmabahçe Palace** Opulent 19th-century European-style home of the sultans, accessible only by guided tour. **Hours:** Tours run Tue-Sun 9:00-16:00, closed Mon. See page 67.

SIGHTS

Sultans' *Türbes*

A *türbe* (tewr-beh) is a mausoleum—a monumental tomb for high-ranking religious and political leaders. Several imperial Ottoman *türbes* are in Hagia Sophia's garden (separate entrance). This is where sultans Selim II, Murat III, Mehmet III, and Mustafa I (rulers in the 16th and 17th centuries) are buried, side-by-side with their heirs and other relatives. To go inside a *türbe,* you'll need to remove your shoes on its entrance porch.

Cost and Hours: Free, daily 9:00-19:00, along the south side of Hagia Sophia—entrance on Bab-ı Hümayün Caddesi.

Visiting the *Türbes:* Walk past the first four elaborately decorated *türbes* to reach the simplest mausoleum, that of **Sultan Mustafa I.** This was built over the Hagia Sophia baptistery. Through the glass (on the right as you enter), you can see the baptistery's former courtyard and the massive baptismal pool.

The twin-domed *türbe* of **Sultan Murat III** is particularly striking. Its interior is decorated in coral-red İznik tiles bordered with excerpts from the Quran and inlaid wood. The *türbe* of **Sultan Selim II,** designed by the great Ottoman architect Sinan, is one of the most elaborate in the city, with an exterior paved with marble and İznik tile. Notice the tile panels on either side of the entry: The one on the right is the 16th-century original, while the one on the left is a replica. In 1895, a French art collector took the original panel to France, ostensibly for restoration. It ended up in the Louvre.

▲▲▲Blue Mosque (Sultanahmet Camii)

Officially named for Sultan Ahmet I, its patron, this mosque is nicknamed for the cool hues of the tiles that decorate its interior.

The Blue Mosque was Ahmet I's 17th-century answer to Hagia Sophia. Its six minarets rival those of the Great Mosque in Mecca, and beautiful İznik tiles with exquisite floral motifs fill the interior. The tombs of Ahmet I and his wife Kösem Sultan are just outside the mosque precinct. The building is undergoing an extensive renovation, and parts of it may be behind scaffolding when you visit.

Cost and Hours: Free, generally open daily one hour after sunrise until one hour before sunset, closed to visitors five times a day for prayer and Friday mornings, Sultanahmet Meydanı.

📖 For a visit inside the Blue Mosque, see the Historic Core Walk.

▲▲Basilica Cistern (Yerebatan Sarayı)

Stroll through an underground rain forest of pillars in this vast, subterranean water reservoir. Built in the sixth century AD to store water for a thirsty and fast-growing capital city, the cistern, with a capacity of more than 20 million gallons, covers an area about the size of two football fields. Your visit to the dimly lit, cavernous chamber includes two stone Medusa heads recycled from earlier Roman structures. The cistern also hosts occasional concerts and art exhibitions.

Cost and Hours: 20 TL, daily 9:00-17:30, Yerebatan Caddesi 1/3, Sultanahmet, +90 212 512 1570, www.yerebatan. com.

📖 For a visit inside the Basilica Cistern, see the Historic Core Walk.

▲Hippodrome (Sultanahmet Meydanı)

This long, narrow, park-like square in the center of Istanbul's Old Town was once a Roman chariot racetrack. Today it's the front yard for many of Istanbul's most famous sights, including the Hagia Sophia, Blue Mosque, and İbrahim Paşa Palace (home to the Turkish and Islamic Arts Museum). Strolling the Hippodrome's length, you'll admire the Egyptian Obelisk, Column of Constantine, and German Fountain—monuments that span the ages.

📖 For more on the Hippodrome, see the Historic Core Walk.

▲▲Turkish and Islamic Arts Museum (Türk-İslam Eserleri Müzesi)

Housed in the former İbrahim Paşa Palace across from the Hippodrome, this museum's 40,000-piece collection covers the breadth of Islamic art over the centuries. The compact exhibit displays carefully selected, easy-to-appreciate works from the Selçuks to the Ottomans, including carpets, calligraphy, ceramics, glass, and art represented in wood, stone, and metal.

Cost and Hours: 20 TL, Tue-Sun 9:00-19:00, until 17:00 off-season, closed Mon, last entry one hour before closing, Sultanahmet Meydanı—across from the Hippodrome's Egyptian Obelisk, +90 212 518 1805, www.muze.gov.tr.

📖 See the Turkish and Islamic Arts Museum Tour chapter.

SIGHTS

SIGHTS

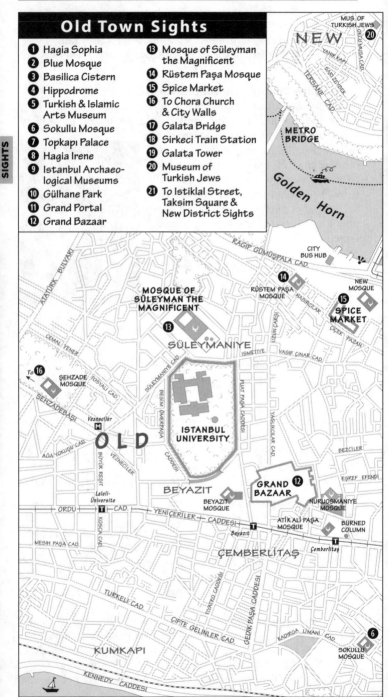

Old Town Sights

1. Hagia Sophia
2. Blue Mosque
3. Basilica Cistern
4. Hippodrome
5. Turkish & Islamic Arts Museum
6. Sokullu Mosque
7. Topkapı Palace
8. Hagia Irene
9. Istanbul Archaeological Museums
10. Gülhane Park
11. Grand Portal
12. Grand Bazaar
13. Mosque of Süleyman the Magnificent
14. Rüstem Paşa Mosque
15. Spice Market
16. To Chora Church & City Walls
17. Galata Bridge
18. Sirkeci Train Station
19. Galata Tower
20. Museum of Turkish Jews
21. To Istiklal Street, Taksim Square & New District Sights

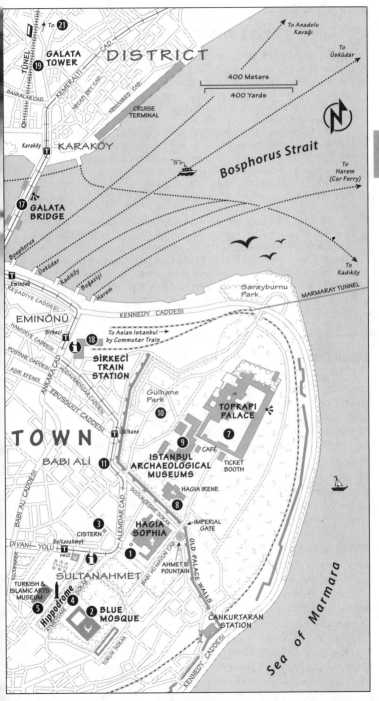

The Tulip Era (1718-1730)

During the early 18th century, the Ottoman Empire enjoyed an unprecedented era of peace and prosperity. For a half-century, there were no wars, no border disputes, and no uprisings. The Ottomans signed treaties with long-standing rivals such as Russia, Austria, and Venice...and then found themselves out of enemies. Thus began the so-called Tulip Era.

Sultan Ahmet III (r. 1703-1730) reigned over this era. But historians give more credit to his grand vizier, İbrahim Paşa—called the Damat (the "Groom") because he married the sultan's daughter. Famed as an able statesman, Damat İbrahim Paşa was also an intellectual, with interests in science, history, art, and literature. He set the tone for the cultured upper-class lifestyle of the Tulip Era.

This time of political, social, and cultural advancement was something of an Ottoman Renaissance. Free from political and economic worries, people could explore and celebrate the finer things in life. The city's first printshop was established (more than 200 years after the printing press became commonplace in Europe). Literature, especially poetry, came into fashion—even the sultan was a poet. There was a newfound appreciation for fine arts, particularly tile production. Turkish tiles from this period

Sokullu Mosque (Kardirga Sokullu Camii)

This 16th-century mosque, a few hundred yards from the Hippodrome, is more down to earth than the big showpiece mosques around Sultanahmet but contains some notable decorations. The famous imperial architect Sinan built the Sokullu Mosque in 1571-72 for Grand Vizier Sokullu (for more on Sinan, see the sidebar on page 209). A fine example of Sinan's mature work, the mosque is decorated with İznik tiles even older than those used in the Blue Mosque. But what makes the Sokullu Mosque unique are several gold-framed fragments of the Black Stone of Kaaba—priceless relics for Muslims, who believe that this stone descended from the heavens to show the Prophet Abraham where to build a temple. One piece is displayed above the mosque's main door, another is directly above the mihrab (prayer niche), and a third is on the entrance to the *minbar* (pulpit).

Cost and Hours: Free, generally open daily one hour after sunrise until one hour before sunset, closed to visitors five times a day for prayer; imam may lock the door if there are no visitors, but he's usually nearby, so try waiting a few minutes; located at Şehit Mehmet Paşa Yokuşu 20-24, Sultanahmet.

Getting There: Leave the Hippodrome at its south end (past the Column of Constantine) and take the street called Şehit Mehmet Paşa Yokuşu to the right of the big building at the bottom

SIGHTS

decorate monuments and museums all over the world. Gardening caught on among the wealthy, as "Tulipmania" swept the country. A single sought-after bulb could sell for more than 30 ounces of gold. Hedonism took hold, as lavish waterfront parties sprawled along the Golden Horn at night—lit by candles placed on the backs of hundreds of roaming tortoises.

But as with any time of prosperity and decadence, the Tulip Era couldn't last. The sultan's peacetime frivolity was funded by outrageous tax increases on the common people. Before long, revolution was in the air, led by Patrona Halil, a bath attendant. Halil gathered a mob, recruited the royal guards, stormed Topkapı Palace, and beheaded Damat İbrahim Paşa. The rioters also executed several scholars, poets, and philosophers, and burned down tulip gardens all over the city. Ahmet III left the throne to ease the anger of the rebels. When the dust cleared, Halil and several others were executed as Sultan Mahmut I took the throne. Since Halil was Albanian, one of Mahmut I's first acts was to ban Albanian attendants in the city's baths.

of the square. Follow this road downhill, and after it makes a sharp right turn, continue for another block. You'll see the mosque on the left, at the corner of the intersecting Su Terazisi Sokak. Walk a little farther and take the steps to the north to enter the courtyard.

TOPKAPI PALACE AND NEARBY

This walled zone, at the tip of the Old Town peninsula, is a five-minute walk from the heart of the Sultanahmet district. On the sprawling grounds of the Topkapı Palace complex you'll find the former residence of the sultans, one of Istanbul's top museums, and all the historical trappings of a once-thriving empire.

▲▲▲Topkapı Palace (Topkapı Sarayı)

For centuries, this was the palace where the great sultans hung their turbans. Built on the remains of ancient Byzantium, Mehmet II (the Conqueror) established this palace as an administrative headquarters and royal residence, but it was Süleyman the

Ottoman Fountains

Throughout old neighborhoods in Istanbul, you'll find elegant fountains, souvenirs of a genteel age. The most famous is the Ahmet III Fountain, just outside the Imperial Gate of Topkapı Palace.

In the 17th century, there were more than 10,000 fountains scattered throughout the city—at intersections, mosques, parks, and gardens. Because most private homes did not have plumbing, people used public fountains as their water source. Most of the fountains relied on a water system constructed by the imperial architect Sinan in the mid-1500s. To begin with, the fountains were generally simple structures, built to be functional. The tap was mounted on a marble panel and a basin was placed underneath.

Some fountains were built by the royal family and/or local administrators, but most were donated by the wealthy. It was considered prestigious to build a handsome fountain, and those commissioned by the rich were quite fancy and decorative. These charming fountains (whose water effects are often drowned out by the noise of 21st-century traffic) come with decor typical of the Muslim Ottomans: a flamboyant Arabic script rendering a Quranic verse, perhaps a poem or proverb, the name of the benefactor, and a line acknowledging the donation.

Although no longer as common, the custom of building fountains continues today. People in the countryside sometimes build roadside fountains for travelers.

Magnificent who turned Topkapı Palace into a home. During your wander through the many pavilions and courtyards you'll see a 16th-century kitchen, 10,000 pieces of fine Chinese porcelain, traditional weapons, royal robes, ceremonial thrones, and Sultan Ahmet III's tulip garden. The Imperial Treasury is home to the famous emerald-encrusted Topkapı Dagger and the stunning 86-carat Spoonmaker's Diamond. The Holy Relics exhibit contains sacred Islamic objects, including some associated with the Prophet Muhammad. A separate ticket covers the cloistered rooms of the famous Harem, where the sultan's wives and concubines lived. Note that parts of the Treasury and the Harem may be under renovation during your visit.

Cost and Hours: Palace-100 TL (line-skipping Fast-Track ticket-135 TL); Harem-70 TL; Wed-Mon 9:00-19:00 (until 17:00 off-season), closed Tue, last entry two hours before closing (one hour in off-season), exhibits may begin closing one hour earlier; audioguide-45 TL; between the Golden Horn and Sea of Marmara in the Sultanahmet district, +90 212 512 0480, www.millisaraylar. gov.tr.

📖 See the Topkapı Palace Tour chapter.

Hagia Irene (Aya Irini)

This important early Christian church hides inside the outer Topkapı Palace wall. Often mistakenly interpreted as "St. Irene," the church's name actually means the "Divine Peace," an attribute of Christ. The original Hagia Irene church that stood on this site is thought to have been built by Constantine. The present structure dates back to the reign of Emperor Justinian in the sixth century, when this church and Hagia Sophia were rebuilt after a catastrophic fire.

Soon after Constantine split the Roman Empire between West and East—with the Eastern capital here, in Byzantium (renamed Constantinople)—Hagia Irene hosted the Second Ecumenical Council to set the course for the new church (in AD 381). Decisions made in this building shaped Christian traditions for centuries to come. In the short term, the council—which discussed theological questions such as whether Jesus was human, divine, or both—sparked social struggles and riots in the early history of the capital.

Hagia Irene served as the patriarchal (main) church of Constantinople until Hagia Sophia was built. Under Ottoman rule, Hagia Irene was used as an arsenal by the imperial guards and later to store artifacts from the Istanbul Archaeological Museums.

Cost and Hours: 60 TL, Wed-Mon 9:00-16:45, closed Tue; between the Golden Horn and Sea of Marmara in the Sultanahmet district.

▲▲Istanbul Archaeological Museums (Istanbul Arkeoloji Müzesi)

In a city as richly layered with the remains of fallen civilizations as Istanbul, this complex of three museums (all covered by the same ticket) is an essential stop. The variety and quality of the collections rival any in Europe. The Museum of Archaeology houses a vast exhibit on the Greeks, Romans, and other early civilizations of the Near East. The star attraction here is the world-class collection of ancient sarcophagi, including the elaborately decorated and remarkably well-preserved Alexander Sarcophagus. (Parts of

the Museum of Archaeology are undergoing renovation; in the interim, collection highlights are being displayed in temporary galleries.) The Tiled Kiosk Museum sparkles with a staggering array of sumptuous ceramics and tiles. And the Museum of the Ancient Orient shows off striking fragments from the even more ancient civilizations of Mesopotamia and Anatolia, such as the 13th-century BC Kadesh Treaty—the first written peace agreement in world history.

Cost and Hours: 50 TL includes all three museums; Tue-Sun 9:00-20:00, until 18:00 off-season, closed Mon, last entry one hour before closing; audioguide-25 TL, Osman Hamdi Bey Yokuşu, Gülhane, Eminönü, +90 212 520 7740, www.muze.gov.tr.

📖 See the Istanbul Archaeological Museums Tour chapter.

▲Gülhane Park

Originally Topkapı Palace's imperial garden, this welcoming swath of open green space is Istanbul's oldest park. Located on the hillside below the palace, with terraces stretching to the shore below, Gülhane is a favorite weekend spot for locals. Come here to commune with Turks as they picnic with their families and enjoy a meander along the park's shady paths. On some summer weekends, the park hosts free concerts.

Grand Portal (Bab-ı Ali, a.k.a. Sublime Porte)

In the 19th century, this grand gate near Topkapı Palace, with its wavy roof and twin fountains, was the entrance to the office of the grand vizier (the sultan's first minister), where the business of the Ottomans was conducted. The word *bab* (door) refers to the authority of the state; historically, official pronouncements and decisions were announced at a palace gate. Each Wednesday and Friday, commoners could enter here and tell their problems to public officials. It was here that all domestic and foreign affairs were discussed and presented to the sultan for a final decision. The surrounding neighborhood (also known as Bab-ı Ali) was the center of the Turkish news media for about 50 years (until the 1990s). Now it's a dull administrative district. But you can still find the historic gate just outside the old palace walls, near the Gülhane tram stop (see the "Old Town Sights" map, earlier in this chapter).

FROM THE GRAND BAZAAR TO THE GOLDEN HORN

The area north and west of Sultanahmet is more residential and less touristy; here you can delve into the "real" Istanbul at some of the city's best mosques and markets. While some attractions here—such as the Grand Bazaar—are tourist magnets, the lanes connecting them are filled mostly with local residents.

📖 The Old Town Back Streets Walk links many of the following sights and describes the Rüstem Paşa Mosque and Spice Market in greater detail.

▲▲▲Grand Bazaar (Kapalı Çarşı)

Shop till you drop at the world's oldest market venue. Although many of its traditional stalls have been overtaken by souvenir shops,

in many ways Istanbul's unique Grand Bazaar remains much as it was centuries ago: enchanting and perplexing visitors with its mazelike network of more than 4,000 colorful shops, fragrant eateries, and insistent shopkeepers. Despite the tourists and the knickknacks, the heart of the Grand Bazaar still beats, giving the observant visitor a glimpse of the living Istanbul.

Cost and Hours: Free, Mon-Sat 9:00-19:00, closed Sun and during religious holidays, https://www.kapalicarsi.com.tr. It's across the parking lot from the Çemberlitaş tram stop, behind the Nuruosmaniye Mosque.

📖 See the Grand Bazaar Tour chapter.

▲▲▲Mosque of Süleyman the Magnificent (Süleymaniye Camii)

This soothing, restrained, but suitably magnificent house of worship was built by the great 16th-century architect Sinan for his

sultan, Süleyman. Although less colorful than the Blue Mosque, this mosque rivals it in size, scope, and beauty. Enjoy the numerous courtyards and tranquil interior, decorated in pastel hues and stained glass. Out back are the elaborate tombs of Süleyman the Magnificent and his wife, Roxelana.

Cost and Hours: Mosque—free, generally open daily from one hour after sunrise until one hour before sunset, closed to visitors five times a day for prayer; mausoleums—free, daily 9:00-17:00, until 18:00 in summer. It's on Sıddık Sami Onar Caddesi, in the Süleymaniye district.

☐ See the Mosque of Süleyman the Magnificent Tour chapter.

▲Rüstem Paşa Mosque (Rüstem Paşa Camii)

This small 16th-century mosque, designed by the prolific and talented architect Sinan, was built to honor Süleyman the Magnificent's grand vizier, Rüstem Paşa. It's elevated above street level in a bustling market zone, its facade studded with impressive İznik tiles. But the wall-to-wall decorations inside are even more breathtaking. Note that ongoing restoration may obscure your view of the tiles; check locally.

Cost and Hours: Free, generally open daily from one hour after sunrise until one hour before sunset, closed to visitors five times a day for prayer, on Hasırcılar Caddesi, Eminönü.

▲▲Spice Market (Mısır Çarşışı)

This market was built about 350 years ago to promote the spice trade in Istanbul...and, aside from a few souvenir stands that have wriggled their way in, it still serves essentially the same purpose. Today the halls of the Spice Market are filled with equal numbers of locals and tourists. In addition to mounds of colorful spices (such as green henna and deep-red saffron), you can also get dried fruits (including apricots and figs), fresh roasted nuts, Turkish delight, supposed aphrodisiacs, imported caviar, and lots more.

Cost and Hours: Free to enter; Mon-Sat 8:00-19:30, until 19:00 off-season, Sun 9:30-18:00 year-round, closed during religious holidays. It's right on Cami Meydanı Sokak along the Golden Horn, at the Old Town end of the Galata Bridge, near the Eminönü tram stop.

NEAR THE OLD CITY WALLS

▲▲Chora Church (Kariye Müzesi)

This small but remarkable ancient church is packed full of some of the most impressive Byzantine mosaics anywhere (parts may be under renovation during your visit). It's tucked just inside the old city walls, removed from the rest of Istanbul's Old Town sights, but art lovers and history buffs find Chora Church to be worth the trip. Tilt back your head and squint at the thousands of tiny tiles artfully plastered on the ceilings and domes. Mosaics depict the birth, life, and death of Christ, as well as the Holy Family, saints, and other Christian figures. Note that the Turkish government has

Istanbul's Best Views

Galata Tower: This medieval, distinctively Italian tower offers visitors perhaps the best view of Istanbul, from the Golden Horn to the Bosphorus, over the rooftops of the European side and across to Asian Istanbul (see page 65).

Ferry to Kadıköy: A ferry ride from the Galata Bridge to the Asian side of town reveals the Old Town from a different perspective, as well as the contemporary New District skyline and the bustling Asian side; views extend out to the Sea of Marmara (one-way ride-5 TL, ferries available from Eminönü and Karaköy piers, at either end of Galata Bridge).

Galata Bridge: The sidewalks of this bridge are a great perch for photographers. From the west side, enjoy an unobstructed view of the Mosque of Süleyman the Magnificent; from the east side, take in the Bosphorus and Topkapı Palace. A viewing platform on the bridge's lower, restaurant level offers a panorama of Europe, the Bosphorus, and Asia—all in one frame (from midspan, to reach the lower level, descend the stairs on the east side).

Mosque of Süleyman the Magnificent: The mosque's huge courtyard offers an outstanding view, over centuries-old domes and chimneys, all the way to the mouth of the Golden Horn, across to the New District, and up the Bosphorus Strait.

Adamar Hotel: This recommended hotel's terrace, above the restaurant floor, has a spectacular view of Hagia Sophia and the Blue Mosque rising above the Old Town. The blue waters of the Bosphorus serve as a backdrop (Yerebatan Caddesi 37, Sultanahmet, www.adamarhotel.com).

Restaurants: Some eateries have superb views, including the recommended Cankurtaran Sosyal Tesisleri, Mimar Sinan Café, Hamdi Restaurant, 360 Restaurant, and Bilsak 5.Kat (see the Eating in Istanbul chapter).

announced the impending conversion of the building to a mosque. Confirm hours and admission details locally before visiting.

Cost and Hours: 65 TL, daily 9:00-19:00, until 17:00 off-season, audioguide-25 TL, +90 212 631 9241, www.muze.gov.tr.

Getting There: The church is in the Edirnekapı district, west of downtown, a 40-50 TL taxi ride each way from Sultanahmet.

📖 See the Chora Church Tour chapter.

Walls of Constantinople and Theodosius II

When Constantine laid out his new capital city in the early fourth century, he erected defensive walls that arced from the Golden Horn to the Sea of Marmara. Theodosius II reinforced and expanded the boundary of that wall system in the fifth century, making it one of the most extensive fortifications in history. The land walls were complemented by sea walls encircling the rest of the peninsula. Together the walls protected the city from invaders for more than 1,000 years. Many sections still survive.

Cost and Hours: Best viewed by day; located about four miles northwest of the historic core. The best way to see the land walls is to walk there after touring Chora Church (see listing, earlier).

◫ See the City Walls and Neighborhoods Walk chapter (including details for the Tekfur Palace Museum, where it's possible to climb a portion of the walls).

SIGHTS

On the Golden Horn

The following sights are located along the Golden Horn waterway. The first two—Galata Bridge and Sirkeci Train Station—are at the mouth of the inlet, near the Spice Market, in the Old Town district called Eminönü (a major transit hub for trams, buses, and ferries). The remaining sights are farther up the inlet, but can be easily reached by taxi or bus (for locations, see the "Istanbul Transit" map at the back of this book).

▲▲Galata Bridge (Galata Köprüsü)

In 1994, this modern bridge replaced what had been the first and, for many years, only bridge spanning the Golden Horn. Now, lined with hundreds of fishermen dipping their hooks into the water below, the Galata Bridge is an Istanbul fixture. A stroll over the bridge offers panoramic views of the Old Town and across the Bosphorus to Asian Istanbul. Consider stopping for a drink or a meal at one of the many restaurants on the bridge's lower level, where there's also a viewing platform (access lower level from either end of bridge or at midspan; tram stops: Eminönü on the Old Town end of the bridge, and Karaköy on the New District end).

◫ The area around the Old Town side of the Galata Bridge is covered by the Golden Horn Walk chapter.

Sirkeci Train Station (Sirkeci Tren Garı)

This 19th-century example of European Orientalism architecture was the terminus of the Orient Express. The famous train, which traveled from Paris through "exotic" eastern Europe to Istanbul, was immortalized by Agatha Christie in her classic crime novel *Murder on the Orient Express*. Today the station is used mostly by local commuters; it's also an alternative entry for the Marmaray Metro station. The modest Railway Museum inside the station is worth a look.

Cost and Hours: Railway Museum—free, Tue-Sat 9:00-12:30 & 13:00-17:00, closed Sun-Mon; near the Eminönü ferry docks, tram stop: Sirkeci, +90 212 527 1201.

Istanbul with Kids

Among the many sights described in this chapter, some are definite kid pleasers:

- Spooky Basilica Cistern
- Attraction-filled Miniatürk Park
- Breezy Bosphorus Cruise
- Bustling Grand Bazaar
- Fragrant Spice Market
- Gadget-filled Rahmi Koç Industrial Museum, with a Golden Horn cruise
- Nostalgic Tram down İstiklal Street.

A few other sights are worth considering:

Santral Istanbul is an industrial museum (formerly a power plant) that's popular with school kids. In the Museum of Energy, they can explore the original turbine rooms, have fun in the Energy Play Zone, try interactive science experiences, generate energy, morph into batteries, and make magnetic sculptures (free, daily 10:00-18:00, closed on the first day of religious holidays; Eski Silahtarağa Elektrik Santrali, Kazım Karabekir Caddesi 2, Eyüp, +90 212 311 7878, www.santralistanbul.org). A free shuttle runs between the museum and Atatürk Cultural Center at Taksim Square (see museum website for details). You can also take the Golden Horn ferry from Karaköy and get off at the Eyüp stop; from there, it's a short walk to the museum (see the Golden Horn Walk chapter for ferry details).

The **Istanbul Aquarium** (Istanbul Akvaryum), set in a 20-acre rainforest, has more than 1,500 species and 15,000 animals in exhibits organized geographically from the Black Sea to the Pacific Ocean. Try to schedule your visit to overlap with the daily feeding at 15:00 (109 TL, 79 TL for students—ID required, young kids are free, family discounts; daily 10:00-20:00, west of the Old Town at Şenlikköy Mahallesi Yeşilköy Halkalı Caddesi 93, Florya, +90 212 444 9744, www.istanbulakvaryum.com. A free shuttle connects the aquarium with the Old Town (from a stop near the ATMs in Sultanahmet Meydanı) and Taksim Square (stops at Atatürk Cultural Center; both routes 4/day, every 2 hours starting at 10:15 or 10:30, see aquarium website for details).

Eyüp Sultan Mosque (Eyüp Sultan Camii)

This mosque attracts a conservative pilgrim crowd, making it one of the most interesting people-watching experiences in the city. You'll be surrounded by Turks who are humble in mood and attire, each looking for spiritual fulfillment.

Ayyub El Ansari, called Eyüp Sultan by the Turks, was the Prophet Muhammad's standard-bearer and companion. He died outside the city walls during the siege of Constantinople by Muslim Arabs and was buried where he fell. Centuries later, Sultan Mehmet II built a mosque and mausoleum at the location of Eyüp's grave. Over the years, the mosque became an important religious center and destination for Muslim pilgrims. This where new Ottoman sultans received their sword of sovereignty as they took the throne. The complex you see today dates from the 1800s.

The Eyüp Sultan Mosque is thronged with locals at all times of day. Crowds increase at prayer times—particularly on Fridays for the midday service—and for religious festivals. Year-round, especially from late spring to early fall, you'll see boys in fancy circumcision outfits and newlyweds in their gowns and tuxedoes, here for a prayer. In the mausoleum, people pray in front of the tomb of Eyüp Sultan, as well as at the glass screen covering a supposed footprint of the Prophet Muhammad. There are no prayers to the dead in Islam, but it is a tradition to invoke the names of the deceased (such as Eyüp Sultan or Muhammad) to give prayers more weight with Allah.

Because this is a religious shrine, dress modestly, even if you're not going into the mosque—women should cover their hair with a scarf; everyone should cover their shoulders and knees.

Cost and Hours: Free, generally open daily from one hour after sunrise until one hour before sunset, closed to visitors five times a day for prayer.

Getting There: The address is Camii Kebir Caddesi, Eyüp. From Eminönü in the Old Town, take bus #99 (Eminönü-Akşemseddin Mahiye) to the Eyüp Sultan stop. The bus may use an alternative stop, so ask the driver or another passenger where to get off. Other buses that will get you there include #36CE, #399B, and #399C. By taxi it's a quick 20-TL ride (consider a detour to see some of the old city walls along the way; ◫ see the City Walls and Neighborhoods Walk chapter).

For a fun and scenic alternative, take the 35-minute ferry ride to the mosque from the Karaköy ferry pier in the New District (it's just east of the Galata Bridge) to the Eyüp pier near the mosque. See the Golden Horn Walk chapter for more on this option.

Rahmi Koç Industrial Museum (Rahmi Koç Müzesi)

This museum is located in a historic shipyard that once produced anchors and parts for Ottoman navy vessels. Inspired by the Henry Ford Museum in Michigan, Turkey's industrial giant, Rahmi Koç, started this museum in 1994 with his private collection of artifacts dedicated to the history of industry, transport, and communication. Today the collection has been expanded to include a vast number of metalworking tools, engines of all sizes and applications, scientific instruments, machinery, and vehicles including motorcycles, bicycles, a submarine, and a small train.

Off the beaten path, the Rahmi Koç stands out for its optional but highly recommended 45-minute Golden Horn cruise (offered only in summer) aboard a fully restored, 65-foot, 1936 steam-powered tugboat. Most travelers to Istanbul don't get to see this part of the Golden Horn, let alone in an antique boat. The Rahmi Koç isn't essential if your time in Istanbul is limited, but it's worth considering on a longer visit.

Cost and Hours: Museum-21 TL, Golden Horn cruise-10 TL, submarine-10 TL; museum open Tue-Sun 9:30-19:00 (until 17:00 off-season), closed Mon; cruises run June-Aug Sat-Sun at 13:00, 14:30, 16:00, and 17:30, check for weekday departure times, may also run in May and Sept—call to confirm; Hasköy Caddesi 5, +90 212 369 6600, www.rmk-museum.org.tr. The museum's Halat Restaurant serves great food.

Getting There: It's on the Golden Horn in the Hasköy neighborhood. The easiest way to get there is on the Haliç Hattı ferry (5 TL one way, usually hourly, departs from the Karaköy pier on the Golden Horn—east of the Galata Bridge on the New District side. Disembark at Hasköy, walk straight to the main road, turn left, and walk along the wall of the museum for about 50 yards to reach the entrance on the left. You can also go by taxi; the ride from Eminönü should cost around 20 TL.

Miniatürk Park

This huge park, with more than 100 scale models of Turkish monuments, is a wonderful, fun family scene, especially on sunny weekends. The displays—divided into monuments of Istanbul, the rest of Turkey, and elsewhere in the former Ottoman Empire—give you a glimpse of the parts of Turkey you're not visiting.

A janissary band—an Ottoman military band *(mehter bandosu)*—occasionally performs on Sundays at 16:00, playing music that once inspired Mozart; their costumes are colorful, their mustaches are big, and their drums are huge. Other kid-friendly highlights include a small pond with remote-control boats, a go-cart track, a mini train that tours the grounds, a maze, and a trampoline.

Within Miniatürk are two other, smaller museums: The Victory Museum tells the story of the War of Independence (after World War I, 1919-1922), while the tacky Crystal Museum displays laser carvings of monuments in crystal.

Cost and Hours: 15 TL; daily 9:00-18:00, last entry one hour before closing; children's playground, İmrahor Caddesi, Borsa Durağı Mevkii, Halıcıoğlu, Sütlüce, +90 212 222 2882, www.miniaturk.com.tr.

Getting There: The park is located near the west end of the Golden Horn. It's a 20-minute taxi ride from Taksim Square or

Eminönü. By public transport, you can take bus #36T from Taksim or #47 or #47E from Eminönü.

In the New District

The New District, across the Golden Horn from the Old Town, offers a modern, urban, and very European-flavored contrast to the historic creaks and quirks of the Old Town.

📖 The New District Walk chapter covers the best of these sights, which are listed here roughly in the order you'll reach them going from Taksim Square toward the Golden Horn.

ON OR NEAR TAKSIM SQUARE
▲Taksim Square (Taksim Meydanı)

At the center of the New District is busy, vibrant Taksim Square. Taksim is the gateway to Istanbul's main pedestrian thoroughfare, İstiklal Street, with its historic buildings and colorful shops. This enormous square is the New District's version of Grand Central Station, connecting to the rest of the city by bus, Metro, funicular, and Nostalgic Tram (for more on this tram, which runs from one end of İstiklal to the other, see the New District Walk chapter).

Military Museum (Askeri Müze)

Organized with military precision, this museum focuses on the progress of Turkish military might over the centuries. The collection itself—including imperial tents of Ottoman sultans and the sword of Süleyman the Magnificent—thrills military historians, but bores everyone else.

The trip can be worth it, though, to hear the janissary band, rated ▲, which puts on a one-hour performance at 15:00 each day the museum is open. Such Ottoman-era groups were the first military marching bands *(mehter bandosu)* of their kind, eventually prompting other European monarchs to create similar ensembles of their own. The band's primary role was to lead the army into war, but in peacetime it also entertained the public with Turkish folk tunes. Today's costumed concerts evoke the golden age of the Ottoman Empire, with all the regal pomp of ages past.

Cost and Hours: 6 TL includes janissary band performance; museum open Wed-Sun 9:00-16:30, closed Mon-Tue, last entry one hour before closing; band performances Wed-Sun at 15:00 at the Atatürk auditorium; one-hour demonstration of traditional archery with visitor participation Wed and Sat at 14:00; Harbiye district, +90 212 233 2720.

Getting There: The Military Museum is a huge, walled complex at the end of Cumhuriyet Caddesi, the main avenue leading north from Taksim Square into trendy residential and business districts. You can walk there from Taksim Square in about 15 minutes (you'll see the museum on the right just before the avenue forks, past the multistory military club). Or take the Metro from Taksim one stop to Osmanbey, then backtrack a few blocks on Halaskargazi Caddesi to the museum (on your left, just as Halaskargazi runs into Cumhuriyet).

ON OR NEAR İSTIKLAL STREET
▲▲▲İstiklal Street (İstiklal Caddesi)
Linking Taksim Square with the Tünel district (and, below that, the Galata district), İstiklal Street is urban Istanbul's main pedestrian drag, passing through the most sophisticated part of town. The vibrant thoroughfare, whose name translates as "Independence Street," is lined with a lively mix of restaurants, cafés, shops, theaters, and art galleries. The street's beautiful Art Nouveau facades intrigue visitors, as does the multicultural mix of tourists, businesspeople, and locals thronging the sidewalks.

📖 For more on İstiklal Street, see the New District Walk chapter.

▲Pera Museum (Pera Müzesi)
This museum beautifully displays its modest but interesting collection of historic weights and measures, Kütahya tiles, and Orientalist paintings and portraits. It's housed in a renovated late-19th-century building typical of the once high-end Pera neighborhood.

Cost and Hours: 25 TL, free Wed all day and Fri 18:00-22:00; open Tue-Sat 11:00-18:00, Sun 12:00-18:00, closed Mon; worthwhile 35-TL audioguide covers only the paintings; Meşrutiyet Caddesi 65, Tepebaşı, Beyoğlu, +90 212 334 9900, www.peramuseum.org.

Visiting the Museum: Floor 1 displays centuries of **weights and measures** from the Anatolian peninsula. Circling clockwise, you'll watch the weights evolve more or less chronologically—from prehistoric times to the modern Republic—to suit an ever-more-sophisticated economy. Look for the weights shaped like fine statues.

Also on Floor 1 is a collection of **Kütahya tiles,** named for the city southeast of Istanbul where their production flourished. During the 18th and 19th centuries—the scope of this collection—İznik tiles were used by the Ottoman court, Çanakkale tiles were for the common folk, and Kütahya tiles were for both. This exhibit shows off pieces that Turks of that time bought to decorate their homes.

On Floor 2, you'll find the museum's most striking exhibit:

SIGHTS

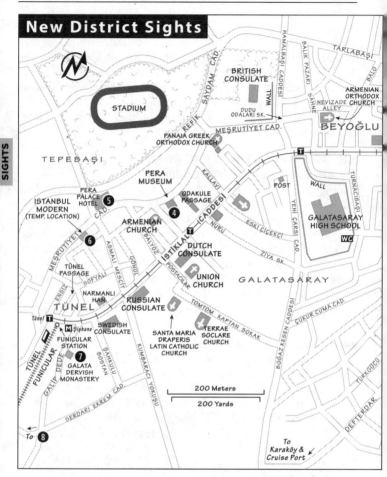

New District Sights

one of the world's best collections of **Orientalist paintings.** More than 300 canvases capture both royal pomp and everyday life during Ottoman times. Dating from the 17th to the 19th century, most of these works were painted by visiting Europeans, who were mesmerized by the "mysteries of the Orient" they found here. Imagine a painter from buttoned-down Victorian England or Habsburg Austria traveling to this faraway land, with its pointy minarets, exotically scented spices, and off-limits harems. Indeed, one of the themes of the exhibit is Ottoman women and harems, and the way their reputation became distorted through a European lens. The paintings are works of fancy, as the painters never set foot in a harem. (For the real story on harems, see the sidebar on page 138.)

You'll also see works by Osman Hamdi (1842-1910), the leading late Ottoman painter who worked in an Orientalist style but from a more accurate point of view than his Western colleagues.

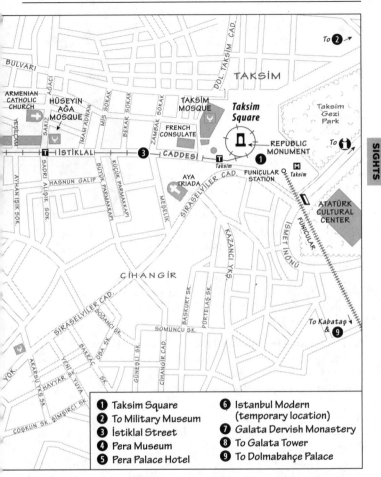

1. Taksim Square
2. To Military Museum
3. İstiklal Street
4. Pera Museum
5. Pera Palace Hotel
6. Istanbul Modern (temporary location)
7. Galata Dervish Monastery
8. To Galata Tower
9. To Dolmabahçe Palace

Find Hamdi's masterpiece, *The Tortoise Trainer*. The patience required to train slow-motion tortoises is a metaphor for the patience required to live life.

Rounding out the collection is a who's who of royal portraits, depicting both Ottoman bigwigs (find the sultans you've been learning about) and foreign ambassadors wearing Ottoman clothing (to curry favor with the sultan).

Pera Palace Hotel

Agatha Christie fans will want to visit this hotel down the street from the Pera Museum (just past the multistory Hotel Pera Marmara), especially since this historic landmark has been extensively renovated.

By the late 19th century, the Orient Express train service to Istanbul from Western Europe had become all the rage (for more about the Orient Express, see page 253). But Istanbul lacked a European-style hotel elegant enough to impress the posh passengers arriving on those trains, so in 1892 this top-of-the-top hotel was built. It was the first modern hotel in Istanbul to have electricity.

Allied forces used the hotel as a base during the occupation of Istanbul at the end of World War I. In World War II, it was a hotbed of spies and counterspies. The hotel's guest book reads like a history lesson: Atatürk, Mata Hari, the Duke of Windsor, Yugoslav president Josip Broz Tito, Jackie Kennedy, and Agatha Christie (who stayed here several times in the 1920s and 1930s while writing *Murder on the Orient Express*).

Some of Atatürk's personal belongings and medals are displayed in Room 101 (free, but attendants expect a tip; open to visitors daily 10:00-11:00 & 15:00-16:00; hotel located at Meşrutiyet Caddesi 52, +90 212 377 4000, www.perapalace.com).

Istanbul Modern (İstanbul Modern Sanat Müzesi)

The main museum in Istanbul dedicated to the works of contemporary Turkish artists, Istanbul Modern offers a look at the city's current art scene—and the well-heeled crowd it attracts. Originally located in a huge warehouse in the port area, the museum is temporarily housed in a bright and user-friendly space near the Pera Palace Hotel until its new building on the Bosphorus is completed (2022 or later).

Cost and Hours: 72 TL, open Tue-Sat 10:00-18:00, Thu until 20:00, Sun 11:00–18:00, closed Mon, closed on the first day of religious holidays, near the Pera Palace Hotel at Asmalı Mescit Mahallesi, Meşrutiyet Caddesi 99, Metro stop: Şişhane, +90 212 334 7300, www.istanbulmodern.org.

▲Galata Dervish Monastery (Galata Mevlevihanesi)

This *mevlevihane* serves as one of the few meeting places left for dervishes in Istanbul. Poke into the modest courtyard and the surrounding religious buildings. The museum is dull, but the monastery is worth visiting on Sundays for the once-a-week dervish services conducted here.

Cost and Hours: Museum—18 TL, Tue-Sun 9:00-19:00, until 17:00 in winter, closed Mon; dervish services—120 TL, Sun at 17:00, extra services may be held on Sat; see page 370 for details and ticket information, Galip Dede Caddesi 15, +90 212 245 4141.

IN THE GALATA DISTRICT

The Galata neighborhood, until recently more seedy than chic, climbs up a hill from the Golden Horn into the İstiklal Street area. An old-fashioned subterranean funicular called Tünel runs beneath the hill (the entrance at the top is at the north end of İstiklal Street; down below, it's near the Karaköy tram stop and Galata Bridge). You can visit these sights after finishing the New District Walk; they're listed in order from the top of the hill down to the waterfront.

▲▲Galata Tower (Galata Kulesi)

The most prominent feature of the New District skyline, the 205-foot-tall stone Galata Tower (sometimes called the Genoese

Tower) has been used over the centuries as a fortification, a fire tower, a barracks, a dungeon, and even as a launch pad to test the possibility of human-powered flight.

In the Middle Ages, when Byzantines controlled the historic core of the city, they granted land concessions to their Italian trading partners to use for docks and warehouses. The Galata area was the territory of Genoa. The Genoese rebuilt this tower (once a lighthouse) in the mid-14th century as part of the fortifications of their colony. With a key location facing the Byzantine capital across the Golden Horn, the dramatic tower's purpose was likely as much to show off as to defend.

Today, the tower offers visitors perhaps the best view of Istanbul. An elevator takes you as far as the sixth floor; from there, you'll spiral up about 70 steps to the observation terrace on the eighth floor. An interactive model of the city (on the seventh floor) makes it easy to identify Istanbul's highlights.

As you enjoy the view, ponder the legend of a 17th-century aviation pioneer, Hezarfen Ahmet Çelebi. He was so inspired by the drawings and models of Leonardo da Vinci that he built his own set of artificial wings, with which he launched himself from the top of this tower, across the Bosphorus, to Asian Istanbul.

Cost and Hours: 30 TL, daily 10:00-21:30, Fri-Sat until 23:30, Büyük Hendek Sokak, +90 212 293 8180, www.galatakulesi. com.tr.

Quincentennial Museum of Turkish Jews (500 Yıl Vakfı Türk Musevileri Müzesi)

In 1492, King Ferdinand and Queen Isabel of Spain ordered their Sephardic Jewish population to accept the Christian faith—leave and "dare not return." The Ottoman sultan Beyazıt P the only monarch of the time who extended an invitation to take in these refugees. Jewish people—many of whom can still trace their roots back to Spain—remain a vibrant part of Turkey's cultural mosaic. This museum, founded 500 years after the Spanish expulsion and housed in the Neve Shalom Synagogue, commemorates those first Sephardic Jews who found a new home here. The building was an early-19th-century synagogue built on the remains of a much older synagogue; now it displays items donated by the local Jewish community. Particularly interesting are the ethnographic section, showing scenes from daily life, and a chair used in the Jewish circumcision rite.

Cost and Hours: Free, Mon-Thu and Sun 10:00-17:00, Fri until 13:00, closed Sat and during Jewish holidays, Bereketzade Mahallesi, Büyük Hendek Caddesi 39, Beyoğlu, +90 212 292 6333, www.muze500.com.

Getting There: The museum is near the Şişhane Metro stop. From the Metro stop, walk downhill on Yolcuzade İskender Caddesi and take the first left onto Büyük Hendek Caddesi. The entrance is on the small side street directly after the synagogue.

Along the Bosphorus

Many of these sights along the Bosphorus Strait can be reached by ferries that depart from piers in the Eminönü district (under the Galata Bridge, near the Spice Market). To combine a Bosphorus cruise with visits to the Rumeli Fortress, Sakıp Sabancı Museum, and/or Sadberk Hanım Museum, see the sidebar on page 292.

▲▲▲Bosphorus Cruise

For a relaxing day-long cruise on the Bosphorus Strait, catch a ride on a public ferry. The round-trip ferry cruise goes by mansions, fortresses, and two intercontinental bridges before stopping at an Asian fishing village, a good spot for lunch. Alternatively, take the ferry as far as Sarıyer, then hop on a bus to access sights north of Istanbul.

Cost and Hours: 40 TL round-trip, daily April-Oct at 10:35 and 13:35, additional departures possible in peak season; Nov-March at 10:35 only. The public ferry leaves from the first terminal east of the Galata Bridge on the Old Town side of the Golden Horn. Private cruises are also available nearby.

☐ See the Bosphorus Cruise chapter.

A Quick Trip to Asian Istanbul

...rything described in this book is in European Istanbul. ...ck and easy taste of Asia—where millions of Istanbul- ...p a ferry or a train to the other side of the Bosphorus. ...self-guided walks covering two neighborhoods on the Asian side: traditional **Üsküdar**, with grand views back on the Old Town and Golden Horn, and access to the iconic, castaway Maiden's Tower; and modern, vibrant, progressive **Kadıköy**, a bit deeper in Asia, offering a vivid slice of workaday life, including a visit to a thriving market area. Both neighborhoods are easy to reach, either by a scenic commuter ferry ride across the Bosphorus or a much faster trip under the strait on the Marmaray train line. To really dive in, you can connect the two areas with a fun and very local ride on a *dolmuş* (shared minibus)—an Istanbul experience in its own right.

🔲 See the Asian Istanbul Walks chapter.

SIGHTS

▲Dolmabahçe Palace (Dolmabahçe Sarayı)

This palace was the last hurrah of the Ottoman Empire. By the late 19th century, the empire was called the "Sick Man of Europe," and

other European emperors and kings derided its ineffective and backward-seeming sultan. In a last-ditch attempt to rejuvenate the declining image of his empire, Sultan Abdül-mecit I in 1844 built the ostentatious Dolmabahçe (dohl-mah-bah-cheh) Palace as his official residence. With all the trappings of a European monarch's showpiece abode, it took the place of the unmistakably Eastern-feeling Topkapı Palace. It didn't work—instead, Dolmabahçe was the final residence of the long line of Ottoman sultans, falling empty when the royal family was exiled in 1922.

Two parts of the palace—the administrative wing *(selamlık)* and the residential wing *(harem)*—can be visited, but only with a tour (each about an hour long). Visit the *harem* only if you have time to spare; it's nothing compared to the administrative side. But leave time for the beautiful palace grounds, which are large, beautiful, and right on the Bosphorus.

Cost and Hours: The palace is accessible only with a guided tour, available in English, which should be booked in advance; *selamlık*-90 TL, *harem*-60 TL, combo-ticket for both—120 TL; tours run Tue-Sun 9:00-16:00, closed Mon; reserve ahead by calling +90 212 327 2626, ask to be connected to an English-speaking agent. If you hear a recording in Turkish, just wait to be connected; reservation office hours Mon-Sat 9:00-17:45, closed Sun; Dolmabahçe Caddesi, Beşiktaş, +90 212 236 9000, www.millisaraylar. gov.tr.

Services: Just as you pass the ticket-taker, WCs are behind the wall to your right, and the baggage check is to your left. A café and a bookstore are on the way to the exit, on the left.

Getting There: It's a few blocks from the Kabataş tram/funicular stop. From Taksim Square, take the funicular to Kabataş; from the Old Town, take the tram to Kabataş. Once at Kabataş, walk along the water with the Bosphorus on your right. You'll pass a mosque (with slender, balconied minarets), then a parking lot and a clock tower. The ticket office is to the left just before the palace's huge gates (wave at the statuesque honor guard—he's real).

Visiting the Palace: Dolmabahçe (meaning, roughly, "filled-in garden") sits on what was once a bay, on land long ago reclaimed from the Bosphorus. Built over a decade by an Ottoman-Armenian father-and-son team of architects and completed in 1853, the palace is a fusion of styles—from Turkish-Ottoman elements to the frilly Rococo that was all the rage in Europe at the time. Its construction drained the already dwindling treasury, and the empire had to take a foreign loan to complete the project. Today the building belongs to the Turkish Parliament, which uses it only for important occasions.

After buying your ticket, you'll walk through the palace's well-manicured garden, past a small pool flanked by lion statues, and up the steps to the entrance. Before you line up inside for the tour, take a look at the magnificent ceremonial gate in the palace wall to your left. When the palace was the sultan's home and seat of government, this was the door through which royal processions entered the palace grounds.

The decorations in the *selamlık* section are alternately breathtaking and chintzy. Standouts include huge, hand-woven Turkish carpets; the sultan's alabaster bathroom; crystal (much of it Bohemian), including a Baccarat crystal staircase; and the Imperial Hall, built to accommodate up to 2,500 people. This room's dome is 118 feet high—you can't see it from outside—and the world's largest crystal chandelier hangs down from its center, weighing in at some four tons.

The *selamlık* tour ends outside the throne room. Those continuing on to the *harem* can stick with the guide; otherwise, take your time to enjoy the gardens and the view of the Bosphorus.

📖 For more about Dolmabahçe Palace, see page 285 of the Bosphorus Cruise chapter.

Rumeli Fortress (Rumeli Hısarı)

Ottoman Sultan Mehmet II built this mighty fortress in 1452, a year before his conquest of Constantinople. The honorific "Conqueror" (Fatih, fah-tee) was given to him after he succeeded in capturing the city.

Completed in a record 80 days, Rumeli stands at a strategic

location up the Bosphorus from the Old Town, across from an earlier, smaller fortress (the Anatolian fortress of Sultan Beyazıt I). With strategic views of both banks of the Bosphorus, Rumeli was perfectly situated for controlling the strait and preventing aid from reaching Constantinople while the city was under siege. It was renovated and turned into an open-air museum in the 1950s. Although the mosque that once stood at the castle's center is no longer there, you can see a section of its brick minaret.

The fortress alone isn't worth the trip. But if you're returning from a Bosphorus cruise, consider hopping off the boat at Sarıyer to see the fortress on your way back to town (this option is explained in the sidebar on page 292). The fortress can also be combined with a visit to the Sakıp Sabancı Museum and/or Sadberk Hanım Museum (both described next).

Cost and Hours: 18 TL, Thu-Tue 9:00-17:00, closed Wed; near the second bridge (FSM Bridge) up the Bosphorus, on the European shore at Yahya Kemal Caddesi 42; +90 212 263 5305.

Getting There: From the Old Town, take the tram to Kabataş, then take northbound bus #25E (Kabataş-Sarıyer). From Taksim Square in the New District, take the funicular to Kabataş, and then bus #25E; from Sarıyer (where you can disembark from the Bosphorus cruise), take southbound bus #25E (Sarıyer-Kabataş). Buses stop at Rumelihisarı, near the fortress.

Sakıp Sabancı Museum (Sakıp Sabancı Müzesi)

This attractive private museum has two main collections: paintings and Ottoman calligraphy. The calligraphy collection is outstanding—one of the best and most extensive in the world. Temporary exhibits are usually well done and worthwhile.

The museum is located on the grounds of a waterfront mansion called Atlı Köşk ("Horse Mansion"). This glamorous property, with a wonderful view of the Bosphorus, was the residence of a giant of Turkish industry, Sakıp Sabancı. A philanthropist and an art admirer, he developed a significant collection of traditional artworks, which he donated to Sabancı University, along with this mansion, just before his death. The museum has a trendy restaurant, MSA (Tue-Sat 12:00-23:00, Sun from 8:00, closed Mon), and a gift shop offering a fine selection of art and history books.

Cost and Hours: 40 TL, Tue-Sun 10:00-18:00, closed Mon and on the first day of religious holidays, Sakıp Sabancı Caddesi 42, Emirgan, +90 212 277 2200, www.sakipsabancimuzesi.org.

Getting There: Follow the Rumeli Fortress directions (in the previous listing), but get off the bus at the Çınaraltı stop.

Sadberk Hanım Museum (Sadberk Hanım Müzesi)

Two 19th-century mansions overlooking the Bosphorus display separate exhibits dedicated to archaeology and art history. Their collections rival, and sometimes surpass, that of the Turkish and Islamic Arts Museum.

Opened in the 1980s, this was one of the first private museums in the country. (It's named for Sadberk Hanım, wife of a prominent businessman.) While not worth a dedicated trip, it works well when combined with the Sakıp Sabancı Museum and/or Rumeli Fortress.

Cost and Hours: 15 TL, Thu-Tue 10:00-17:00, closed Wed, Piyasa Caddesi 27-29, Büyükdere, +90 212 242 3813 or +90 212 242 3814, www.sadberkhanimmuzesi.org.tr.

Getting There: Follow the directions in the Rumeli Fortress listing, get off the bus at the stop called Sefaret (seh-fah-reht), and walk south a few blocks along the coastal road.

EXPERIENCES IN ISTANBUL

Istanbul's best attractions aren't in its museums, but in its streets, mosques, and neighborhood cafés, baths, and barber shops. Watch a gathering of Muslims as they wash their hands and feet at a fountain before entering a mosque, or celebrate along during Ramadan as they break their fast at sundown. Visit a café or teahouse, where you can sip high-octane Turkish coffee, take a slow drag of sweet apple-flavored smoke from a traditional water pipe, or challenge a local to a game of backgammon. Enter a Turkish bath and let an attendant wash and scrub you—or a barber shop to get a very close shave (using thread or fire). These Istanbul experiences will fill your trip with colorful memories.

Visiting a Mosque

Touring a few of Istanbul's many mosques offers Westerners a ▲▲▲ opportunity to better understand the Muslim faith. (For a primer, see the Understanding Islam chapter.) Just as touring a Christian church comes with a certain protocol, the following guidelines should be observed when visiting a mosque (*camii* in Turkish; pronounced jah-mee).

WHEN TO GO

Most mosques are open to worshippers from the first service in the morning (at sunrise) until the last service in the evening (at sunset). Tourists are generally allowed to enter, except during the five daily services.

EXPERIENCES

Ramadan

Every year, devout Muslims keep the month-long observance of Ramadan—or *Ramazan* in Turkish. Ramadan dates are based on the lunar calendar and shift each year (see "Holidays and Festivals" in the appendix for current dates).

During Ramadan, Muslim people refrain from eating during daylight hours. This fasting is intended to turn the heart away from the world and toward God. By allowing people of all classes to feel hunger pangs, it also encourages generosity toward the less fortunate: For many Muslim families, Ramadan concludes with acts of charity and gift-giving.

Ramadan turns Istanbul's Old Town into a particularly colorful place—especially in the evenings, when locals pack the Hippodrome area. The happy, multigenerational partying that follows the breaking of the fast at sunset every night is a memorable travel experience, and not to be missed if you're in town during this time.  After hours of fasting, people are ready for the first meal of the day as the sun goes down. Many rush home, while others stop for a quick bite at one of many temporary food stands. Restaurants that have been empty all day now have long lines stretching up the street.

There's hardly a tourist in sight as the fun builds, the sun sets, the call to prayer rings out, people eat, and the party starts. On and near the Hippodrome, the city presents shadow puppet theaters, public concerts, and traditional folk dances. The Blue Mosque's interior courtyard turns into a huge market with religious books and other items for sale.

After going to bed late, be ready for traditional drummers to wake you up early. These drummers go from street to street in the Old Town a couple of hours before dawn, reminding people to get up and have a small bite to eat—or at least a glass of tea—before fasting resumes at sunrise. The drummers start practicing long before Ramadan, and some even sing a bit as they bang out their wake-up call.

During Ramadan, the minarets of many mosques are decorated with strings of lights and banners with Muslim sayings. After Ramadan concludes, Turks celebrate the three-day religious festival of Eid al-Fitr, when they spend time with their families and visit the graves of deceased family members. (The Grand Bazaar and Spice Market are closed during Eid al-Fitr.) On these days, Istanbul has a festive atmosphere—its streets are packed with people, and its public transit (often free at this time) is jammed with locals enjoying their time off.

Specific opening times can vary, but figure that most mosques are open to visitors from one hour after sunrise until about an hour before sunset.

Because mosques are active places of worship, visitors are not allowed inside from about 30 minutes before each service until the end of the service. (The five daily services each last about 15-30 minutes.) If you are already inside, you may be asked to leave so as not to disturb the congregation. Prayer times are dictated by the position of the sun and shift daily.

To plan ahead, ask your hotelier about service times, or check online (search "prayer times Istanbul"). If you're visiting a mosque on Friday, avoid going around the midday service, which is more heavily attended than others, and longer, because it includes a sermon.

AT THE MOSQUE

Both men and women should cover their knees and shoulders. Some major mosques (such as the Blue Mosque) loan cover-ups for this purpose.

As a sign of respect, women should also cover their hair with a scarf. It's best to carry one around with you at all times (they're easy to buy at a market), though if you don't have one, most mosques have loaners available.

Everyone must remove their shoes before entering. If you'll enter and exit the mosque through different doors, borrow a plastic bag at the entrance to carry your shoes with you. Otherwise, leave them on the wooden rack by the entry door. You'll also see Muslims performing ablutions before they enter—washing their bodies at water taps as part of a purification ritual.

Inside the mosque, a large area close to the mihrab (prayer niche) is often cordoned off and reserved for worshippers. Stay behind this line. Areas in the back of the mosque behind screens, or the upper-level galleries, are reserved for female worshippers.

It's OK to take photos and videos inside a mosque, but be subtle, and ask for permission before taking pictures of worshippers.

Turkish Coffee

Though the texture and taste of Turkish coffee can be difficult to appreciate, visiting a café and sampling one is an interesting ▲▲ activity while you're in Istanbul.

In a cup of Turkish coffee, the grounds float freely in the brew, leaving behind a layer of "mud" at the bottom. To make it, coffee (*kahve;* kah-veh) is added to cold water in a copper pot. (Some use hot or lukewarm water to speed up the process, but you can taste the difference—Turks call this hasty version "dishwater.") The coffee-and-water mixture is stirred and slowly heated over medium heat. Just before the water boils, the pot is set aside to allow its contents to settle. Then the pot is put back on to boil. This time, half is poured into a cup, while the rest is reheated and used to top off the drink. Turks joke that the last step is to put a horseshoe in it— if the horseshoe floats, you know it's good coffee.

Locals prefer Turkish coffee without sugar, but first-timers —even coffee-loving ones—often prefer to add sugar to make its powerful flavor a bit more palatable. Sugar is added while the coffee is being heated, so you'll need to ask for it when you place your order: *az şekerli* (ahz sheh-kehr-lee) is a little sugar; *orta şekerli* (ohr-tah sheh-kehr-lee) is a medium scoop; for a generous amount of sugar, just say *şekerli* (sheh-kehr-lee).

Because it's unfiltered, the coffee never completely dissolves. When drinking Turkish coffee, the trick is to keep swirling your cup to remix the grounds with the water. Otherwise you'll be sipping weak coffee and wind up with a thick layer of grounds at the bottom when you're done.

THE BEST COFFEE IN TOWN

Turkish coffees at these places cost about 5-15 TL.

Şark Kahvesi is an Istanbul institution and a good place to sample Turkish coffee for the first time (Mon-Sat 9:00-18:30, closed Sun, in the Grand Bazaar at Yağlıkçılar Caddesi 134, +90 212 512 1144; for location, see the map on page 197).

Fes Café serves Turkish coffee with different aromas, such as coffee with mastic (the resinous Greek version) or with cardamom (the Arabic version), at two locations at the Grand Bazaar—one inside the bazaar (Mon-Sat 9:00-18:30, closed Sun, Halıcılar Caddesi 32) and the other outside the bazaar (Mon-Sat 9:00-19:00, closed Sun, Ali Baba Türbe Sokak 25/27, Nuruosmaniye, +90 212 526 3070).

Kahve Dünyası, a national coffee chain, has premium-quality Turkish coffee (with or without mastic), as well as international coffees at reasonable prices. Branches are spread around Istanbul, including a convenient location near the Grand Bazaar (Mon-Sat 7:30-20:30, Sun 9:00-19:00, Nuru Osmaniye Caddesi 79, +90 212 527 3282).

Café Grand Boulevard is actually a Turkish-style coffee shop, though the name sounds French. There's nothing grand about this place, except for the experience and location, in a spacious atrium of a century-old historical passage on İstiklal Street. As you sip your coffee, observe the bustle of an old-fashioned lingerie shop, a handmade-hat store, and an old book shop. You can try a variety of coffees and natural herbal infusions (a.k.a. teas), such as sage, linden, and rosehip (daily 10:00-22:00, Hazzopulo Passage, Hangeçidi Sokak 116/3A, İstiklal Caddesi).

Reis Café has fine coffee and an authentically shabby atmosphere, with tiny stools and tables in the shade of a historic inn (Mon-Sat 6:00-20:00, closed Sun, Vezirhan Caddesi, Alibaba Türbe Sokak 13, Çemberlitaş).

Mandabatmaz is a tiny coffee shop in a characteristic narrow alley off busy İstiklal Street. The name translated literally means "water buffalo won't sink in," suggesting the rich thickness of the shop's coffee. The marble counter dominates the snug interior, leaving room for a few low coffee tables and stools; the outdoor seating is popular with locals (daily 9:00–22:00, İstiklal Caddesi, Olivia Geçidi 1/A).

In Asian Istanbul: Open since 1923, **Fazıl Bey'in Türk Kahvesi** (Mr. Fazıl's Turkish Coffee) is a tiny coffee shop in Kadıköy's market area with a local clientele that keeps it busy every hour of the day. Its meticulous coffee preparation makes it one of the best in the business (daily 8:30-23:00, Serasker Caddesi 3, Kadıköy Çarşısı, +90 216 450 2870; for location, see the map on page 310).

Water Pipes

Sucking on a *nargile* (nahr-ghee-leh)—also known as a "water pipe," "hookah," "hubbly-bubbly," "shisha," or "really big bong"—

is a relaxing social ritual. And it's fun to lounge while you play with the pleasant-smelling smoke. Even nonsmokers enjoy this ▲▲ experience.

While similar instruments are happily—and usually illegally—used by marijuana enthusiasts back home, the water pipes you'll see in Istanbul are filled not with pot, but with low-nicotine tobacco leaves mixed with molasses and dried fruit or herbs (apple is the most common, but you'll also see cappuccino, strawberry, and other flavors). Because the fruit-infused tobacco contains zero to very little nicotine, it's not addictive and provides no buzz, but it's still fun to let the taste and rich aroma linger in your mouth. Even without much tobacco, you're still inhaling smoke, but it's filtered and cooled by the water before you inhale, allowing you to breathe it deeply.

One of Turkey's oldest traditions, the water pipe originated in India before migrating to Anatolia (the Asian part of Turkey, east of the Bosphorus Strait). A *nargile* has a glass water jar at the bottom, called a *şişe* (shee-sheh). Attached to the top of the *şişe* is a long metal body with a little metal plate on top that holds a container (the *lüle*; lew-leh). The tobacco goes in the *lüle*, with a piece of glowing coal (*mangir*; mahn-gheer) on top. A long, flexible hose (*marpuç*; mahr-pooch) with a wooden mouthpiece at the end (*ağızlık*; ah-uhz-luhk) is connected to the body. When you inhale, smoke fills the *lüle*, moves down into the bottle, and makes the water bubble. Impurities are filtered out, and the smoke (as clean and cool as smoke can be) heads up the tube to your mouthpiece.

You can order a water pipe in various coffee shops and trendy *nargile* cafés in the Old Town and New District (figure on paying roughly 10-15 TL per group). A *nargile* is shareable, and everyone gets their own plastic mouthpiece to insert into the bigger wooden mouthpiece (sometimes for a fee). After you take a drag, remove your mouthpiece and pass the hose to the next person. When you're done, keep your mouthpiece as a souvenir...or use it next time.

Backgammon

From the ancient Greeks to the Romans, to the teahouses of today, backgammon has been around for thousands of years. Walking the marble-paved streets of ancient sites in Turkey, such as Ephesus and Aphrodisias, you'll see backgammon boards carved on stones.

Even today, most people in Turkey know how to play backgammon. You'll often see locals playing the game in Istanbul's coffee shops. Watching one of these games is an interesting experience; but challenging someone to a game can be even more engaging (and worth ▲▲).

While a man can challenge anyone to a game, there are certain conventions for women. It's fine for a woman to challenge a man if she's traveling with a group that includes men, or in a coffee shop in one of the more modern districts (such as the side alleys of İstiklal Street, the Ortaköy district, and the Kadıköy area on the Asian side). However, it's considered inappropriate for a woman on her own to challenge a man in a traditional coffee shop, where most of the clientele is male.

Backgammon is a game of luck and skill, but it's not as drawn out or cerebral as chess. Turks tend to play very quickly, making moves instinctively rather than following a carefully plotted strategy. Onlookers often gather and give players tips on how to win. Money is almost never involved. Instead, locals typically play for baklava, or the loser might pay the bill (usually a few glasses of tea).

Because backgammon is of Persian origin, Turks still call it by its Persian name *(tavla)* and tend to use the Persian words for numbers. They'll be tickled and impressed if you do the same:

English	Persian
one	*yek* (yehk)
two	*dü* (dew)
three	*se* (seh)
four	*cahar* (jah-hahr, jahr)
five	*beş* (behsh)
six	*şeş* (shehsh)

HOW TO PLAY

Whether you're observing or joining in, here's a primer on Turkish backgammon.

There are two players, each with 15 checkers. The board is divided into four quadrants, each containing six triangle-shaped spaces, called "doors" (*kapı;* kah-puh), for a total of 24 doors. Each player has a "home board" (the quadrant closest to you on your right, numbered starting with 1) and an "outer board" (on your left). Each player starts with 2 checkers on the 24 door, 3 on the 8 door, and 5 each on the  6 and 13 doors. The goal is to be the first to bring all your checkers "home" and remove them from the board.

Roll to determine who goes first. Dice are called *zar* (zahr) in Turkish, but their nickname is *kemik* (keh-meek), which means bone (dice were originally made from bone). Take turns rolling and moving your checkers counterclockwise, toward your home board. A checker can only be moved to an "open" door (one that is occupied by no more than one opposing checker). For luck, kiss the dice in your fist, and as you roll, say, *"Hadi kemik!"* (hah-dee keh-meek)—"Come on, dice!"

Each die indicates the number of doors that can be moved. For example, if you roll a 3 and a 6, you may move one checker three doors and a different checker six doors; or move a single checker three doors, then six more doors (but only if the third or sixth door is open). If you roll a double, you can use each number twice—so if you roll double 3s, you can move three doors four times. (Got that?) If you have to choose between two moves, you must make the larger one. If no move is possible (because of closed doors), your checkers stay put.

If you land on an open door that contains one of your opponent's checkers, you can "hit" it and remove it from play. Your opponent must put the checker back into play on the opposing home board by rolling a number that corresponds with an open door. Your opponent can't move any of their existing checkers until they bring back the one that was hit.

Once you've moved all 15 checkers to your home board, you'll roll to remove checkers. If the roll is higher than any of your checkers' doors (for example, you roll a 6 but have no checkers on the six door), you can remove the highest checker on your board. If one of your checkers is hit and removed from the board, you must return it to your home board before you can continue collecting your checkers.

If you win the game, you get a point. If you collect all your checkers before your opponent gets all their checkers to their home board, you get two points (called *mars* in Turkish). Typically you play until one player reaches five points. Good luck!

Turkish Baths

A visit to a *türk hamamı* (tewrk hah-mah-muh; Turkish bath) is perhaps the best way to rejuvenate your tired body while soaking in Turkish culture. It's a ▲▲ experience, but it's not for everyone: Baths are hot and humid, bathers are at least partially naked, and attendants touch your bare skin. Still, for most of those who've tried it, one visit isn't enough.

BATH PROCEDURE

The whole experience generally takes an hour and a half to two hours. Avoid eating a huge meal or drinking alcohol before going to a Turkish bath. It's useful to bring along a hairbrush, shampoo, clean underwear, flip-flops (though most baths supply plastic slippers), and a bottle of water. It's also smart to bring a *kese* (keh-seh; a raw-silk mitten used to exfoliate dead skin). If you don't, bath attendants will scrub you with a used one. *Keses* cost around 5 TL and make nice souvenirs.

While nudity is the norm at Turkish baths, it's not required. If you're uncomfortable, you can wear a bathing suit or underwear. Most Turks prefer to keep a *peştemal* (pehsh-teh-mahl; a large cot-

The Turkish Bath

Going to a Turkish *hamam* (bath) on a regular basis is one of the region's oldest traditions. Baths are still popular in today's Turkey, especially in the countryside. Ritual cleansing is an essential part of the Muslim religion and an important element of Turkish culture.

Turks brought the steam bath from Central Asia, blended it with the Roman bath culture they found here, and created

the synthesis we call the Turkish bath. There are no pools for soaking; instead, Turkish-style baths use heat, steam, and humidity to stimulate perspiration, followed by a dousing with cool water and a vigorous massage.

The Turkish bath was introduced to Europe by the ever-encroaching Ottoman Empire. Europeans loved this exotic experience, especially painters of *turqueries* (fantastical representations of imagined Turkish culture), who used the baths as an excuse to paint frolicking naked girls.

Over time, baths became an integral part of everyday Turkish life. The *hamam* of the past was both health club and beauty parlor—like many spas in the US today. Rubdowns with a raw-silk mitten, herbal therapy, and oil massage became popular treatments.

Baths were also a place for social interaction. Two centuries ago, a woman could ask for a divorce if her husband failed to finance her twice-weekly bath visits. The baths were a place where Muslim women could socialize outside of their homes. Here they could look for a suitable bride for their sons or celebrate the birth of a new child. Meanwhile, men met at the baths to mark circumcisions, religious festivals...and for bachelor parties.

Turkish baths remain a part of the culture, especially in rural areas and in folk songs and proverbs. A common Turkish maxim about facing the consequences of one's actions goes, "He who enters a bath, sweats."

ton towel provided at the bath) wrapped around their bodies. Since most Turks find mixed-sex bathing unacceptable, it's common to find single-sex baths, as well as baths with different entry times or segregated areas for men and women. At these baths, you'll be attended by staff of the same sex. (In co-ed baths, most attendants are male, serving both men and women.)

As you enter the bath, you'll find yourself in a waiting chamber with sofas and maybe a decorative fountain. You'll be directed to a changing room or cabin and given a *peştemal*. Lock your clothes and valuables in the changing room or locker (at most places you'll wear the key on your wrist). Leave glasses in the locker, as the steam will fog them up. All of the sweating will dehydrate you, so drink lots of water.

The central section of the bath is the hot, wet caldarium, or *sıcaklık* (suh-jahk-luhk). Marble basins are spaced out along the walls. Sit next to a basin, adjust the water temperature (it should be as hot as you can stand), dip the provided metal bowl into the basin, and pour water on yourself. This will soften your skin and prepare it for exfoliation. Spend the next 20-25 minutes lazily pouring hot water over yourself to achieve maximum sweating and relaxation.

At the center of the chamber is a large marble slab. When it's your turn, an attendant will ask you to lie down on this slab. Men keep their *peştemal* on the entire time. Women generally remove their *peştemal* to lie on the slab (except in co-ed baths).

If you brought your own *kese*, hand it over to the attendant for your scrub-down. Attendants often have a sense of humor, and they may toss you around on the slippery marble. Submit and go along for the ride. You may be amazed by what comes off as the attendant scrubs your skin. If you want the attendant to be gentle, say *"yavaş"* (yah-vahsh; "slow"), use hand gestures, or simply say "Ouch."

After the scrub, the attendant takes a piece of sponge or knitted wool, dips it into soapy water, bathes you with bubbles, and gives you a short, relaxing massage. (If you're a glutton for punishment, you can get what locals call the "bone-crunching massage.") After your massage, go back to the basin to wash your hair.

By the time you're finished, you're cleaner than you've ever been, and your skin is softer than a baby's. Take a towel from an attendant when you're ready to return to the waiting chamber. As you cool off for 10-15 minutes in the waiting chamber, you'll usually be offered tea. When you're relaxed and ready to go, it's time to get dressed.

CHOOSING A BATH

Baths in the Old Town and New District have become quite touristy. On the upside, this means attendants are usually accustomed to the needs and expectations of international visitors. Don't worry—you're still getting a fairly authentic Turkish bath experience.

When choosing a bath, check their policy on mixed-gender bathing. It's also smart to confirm the price and find out what's included. In touristy baths, expect to pay 400-500 TL for the experience, plus a tip of about 10-15 percent for the otherwise poorly compensated attendants. (In some baths, tips motivate the over-worked attendants—if the attendants just hang around without showing any interest in you, check with the supervisor and consider tipping before you start.)

Baths in the Old Town

Çemberlitaş Hamamı, designed by the famous architect Mimar Sinan in the late 16th century for the sultan's mother, is known for its fine architecture (segregated, daily 7:30-24:00, credit cards accepted, next to Çemberlitaş tram stop, across from Burned Column, Vezirhan Caddesi 8, +90 212 522 7974, www.cemberlitashamami.com).

Another of Sinan's creations, the **Süleymaniye Hamamı** baths were built to be part of the larger mosque complex (co-ed—only couples and families with children ages 4 and up are admitted, daily 10:00-21:00, right next to Mosque of Süleyman the Magnificent, Mimar Sinan Caddesi 20, +90 212 519 5569 or +90 212 520 3410, www.suleymaniyehamami.com.tr).

Cağaloğlu Hamamı is one of the more attractive historic baths in Istanbul, and recently restored (segregated, reservations required, daily 8:00-22:00, halfway between Underground Cistern and Grand Bazaar, Prof. Kazım İsmail Gürkan Caddesi 24, +90 212 522 2424, www.cagaloghamami.com.tr).

The historic **Ayasofya (Hürrem Sultan)** bath—commissioned by Süleyman the Magnificent's wife Roxelana and built by Sinan—has been restored to its original purpose. At the heart of the Old Town, between Hagia Sophia and the Blue Mosque, everything is fit for royalty, spotlessly clean, and well-kept. All of the attendants have been formally trained and are paid accordingly, and the management knows and appreciates Rick Steves readers. The luxury is reflected in the prices (segregated, reservations required; packages from €55 to €185; €135 Zevk-i Sefa package covers the expected services, requires a tip, and takes about 80 minutes—but you can stay afterward to enjoy the facility as long as you want; RS%—show this book to receive a free organic *peştemal;* open daily 8:00-23:00, last entry at 21:30; Aya Sofya Meydanı 2, Sultanahmet, +90 212 517 3535, www.ayasofyahamami.com).

Baths in the New District

Only recently discovered by travelers, **Büyük Hamam** is the most "local" bath of the bunch. Though the staff is not yet accustomed to serving tourists, they're helpful and make an effort. Enjoy the beautiful surroundings—built by Sinan—for a far more reasonable price than the other baths listed here. Women should bring their own bath accessories, as this place only provides men the necessary supplies, like a towel and a *peştemal*—though upon request, they'll borrow these from the men's section (segregated, men's section daily 5:30-22:30, women's section daily 8:30-19:00, Büyük Cami yanı, Potinciler Sokak 22, men's section +90 212 253 4229, women's section +90 212 256 9835). It's located in the Kasımpaşa (kah-suhm-pah-shah) neighborhood, near the Kasımpaşa Mosque, at the edge of the New District (best to take a cab).

The nicely restored **Galatasaray Hamamı** baths have a local clientele (segregated, men's section daily 7:00-22:00, women's section daily 8:00-20:00; 25 percent discount with Museum Pass; a block off İstiklal Street at Turnacibasi Sokak 24, general info and men's section +90 212 252 4242, women's section +90 212 249 4342, www.galatasarayhamami.com).

Kılıç Ali Paşa Hamamı is on the Golden Horn and close to historic shipyards—it was built to serve the Ottoman navy in the 16th century. The bath's creator and namesake, Kılıç Ali Paşa, was grand admiral of the Ottoman fleet (he appears in Cervantes' *Don Quixote* as the character Uchali). Well-trained staff welcome you with a cup of traditional chilled fruit juice *(şerbet)*, then provide bathing, scrubbing, and foam massage for around an hour—but you can stay as long as you want (women's hours daily 8:00-16:00, men's hours daily 16:30–23:30, reservation required, Kemankeş Mahallesi, Hamam Sokak 1, Tophane, +90 212 393 8010, http://kilicalipasahamami.com).

Turkish Shaves

For male travelers, a memorable ▲▲ experience is to get a shave at a neighborhood barber shop (ask your hotelier to recommend a place). Barbers start with a razor, then follow up with silk thread or fire to get rid of the fine hairs. Because a good shave can last several days, many Turkish men prefer to have it done by a barber instead of doing it at home.

Besides the shave, you can also get a haircut. It can be as little as 50 TL for both. For a shave, say *"Sakal"* (sah-kahl); for a haircut, it's *"Saç"* (suhch); for both, say, *"Saç sakal."* If doing both, the barber will likely start with the haircut, as it's faster. The whole experience can take up to an hour. If you're in a hurry, tell them how much time you have before the barber starts.

For the shave, the barber will go around your face with a shaving brush to spread the lather, then drives a straight edge razor across your face and neck several times. Notice that the barber transfers what he shaves off to the other hand and gets rid of it all at the end, rather than disposing of it after each stroke.

Following the razor shave, the barber will use a silk thread, fire, or both to pick up the fine hairs the razor could not collect, including those up your nostrils and around your ears. For the fire

EXPERIENCES

treatment, the barber will wrap a small piece of cloth or gauze around the end of a stick, light it, and dart the flame back and forth around your ears and nose until the excess hair is gone. To clean up the fine hair at your cheekbones, he may run a silk thread over the area (which may sting a bit).

At the end of the shave, the barber will wash your face in the sink, then bathe his hands in scented *kolonya* and give you a quick face, neck, and shoulder massage. Tipping is expected, and 20-30 percent is an ideal tip.

HISTORIC CORE WALK

Sultanahmet, Blue Mosque, and Hippodrome

Just like Rome, Istanbul's Old Town was built on seven hills. On top of the first hill sits the historic core of the city, where emperors built their palaces and sultans built their mosques.

On this walk, we'll see monuments from every layer of the city's long history: Roman, Byzantine, Ottoman, and modern. We'll see ancient Greek columns, a Roman horse-race track, the greatest church in Byzantine Christendom, and the greatest mosque in Ottoman Islam. We'll go inside two of the city's best sights: the famed Blue Mosque (for an introduction to everyday Islam) and the mysterious Basilica Cistern. Use this walk to get oriented, both geographically and historically, and see sights you may want to visit in depth later, especially Hagia Sophia. The walk is a lively one, as all of this history sits smack-dab in the middle of a vibrant, people-friendly zone in today's Istanbul—a city still turning heads after all these years.

Orientation

Length of This Walk: Allow about three hours, including sightseeing, for this short walk.

Getting There: If coming by tram, get off at the Sultanahmet stop, then walk to the park between the Blue Mosque and the Hagia Sophia.

Renovations: Both Hagia Sophia and the Blue Mosque are undergoing renovations. Expect scaffolding in some places.

Hagia Sophia: Free, generally open daily around the clock but closed to visitors five times a day for prayer, Sultanahmet Meydanı.

Basilica Cistern: 20 TL, daily 9:00-17:30, Yerebatan Caddesi 1/3.

Blue Mosque: Free, generally open daily one hour after sunrise until one hour before sunset, closed to visitors five times a day for prayer and Friday mornings, Sultanahmet Meydanı.

Mosque Etiquette: To enter a mosque, knees and shoulders must be covered, shoes must be removed, and women should cover their hair with a scarf. (For more mosque-visiting etiquette, see page 71.)

The Walk Begins

• *Start in Sultanahmet Park, the vast space in between Hagia Sophia and the Blue Mosque. The round pond with the fountain in the middle of the park is a great place to get oriented.*

❶ Sultanahmet Park

Start by just checking out the scene around you: men in business suits, women in veils, street vendors selling chestnuts and bagel-like *simit*, kids playing amid palm trees and ever-greens, tourists snapping selfies . . . in short, there are people from all over the globe. Istanbul—the city that straddles the continents of Europe and Asia—certainly lives up to its name as a "crossroads of the world."

Spin 360 degrees clockwise to take in the major sights: At one end of the square is (orange-hued) Hagia Sophia, once the greatest Christian church in the world. Behind Hagia Sophia (though not visible from here) sits the Topkapı Palace, the fabled home of the Ottoman sultans. Spinning to the right, the row of domes bordering the park mark another great Ottoman-era addition, the Haseki Baths. At the far end of the park is the fabulous Blue Mosque, one of Islam's greatest structures. To the right of the Blue Mosque (not visible from here) is the Hippodrome, the huge ancient horse-race track dotted with renowned monuments. The tiny green dome peeking through the trees is the German Fountain and marks the Hippodrome's near end. Continuing your clockwise spin, the park-like area (through the trees) is the jumping-off point for modern Istanbul—its trams, main roads, and modern businesses.

With Hagia Sophia bookending one end of the square and the Blue Mosque the other, you're standing in the middle of the 2,000-year-old story of Istanbul.

• *Of all of Istanbul's sights, perhaps the most influential is...*

Historic Core Walk

1. Sultanahmet Park
2. Hagia Sophia
3. Milion Stone Column
4. Basilica Cistern
5. Haseki Baths
6. View of Blue Mosque
7. Outer Courtyard
8. Inner Courtyard
9. Blue Mosque Interior
10. Hippodrome
11. Egyptian Obelisk
12. Serpent Column
13. Walled Obelisk
14. German Fountain
15. View of Istanbul

HISTORIC CORE

❷ Hagia Sophia

Still regal after all these years, this church-turned-mosque encapsulates much of the story of Istanbul. As you survey the majestic

outlines of this structure, consider its place in world culture. Built by the last great Roman emperor, Justinian I (around the year 530), Hagia Sophia reigned as the supreme church for Orthodox Christians for the next 900 years. When the Ottomans conquered the city (1453), Hagia Sophia carried on (now with minarets) as one of Islam's

greatest mosques. Hagia Sophia's distinct architecture—a central dome surrounded by smaller domes—inspired countless dome-topped buildings and mosques, including its mirror image the

Just Enough History for This Walk

For more than two millennia, Istanbul/Constantinople has been one of the world's greatest cities. On this walk, you'll see monuments from each of these eras of Istanbul's long history:

- The Greek city founded for its strategic location atop a hill surrounded on three sides by water (700 BC-AD 300)
- The grand eastern capital of the Roman Empire (AD 333-476)
- Its thousand years as the greatest city in Byzantine Christendom (476-1453)
- Its four hundred years as a Muslim capital of the vast Ottoman Empire (1453-1920)
- The modern metropolis of today, encompassing Muslim, Christian, and secular residents (1920-today)

Blue Mosque. After the fall of the Ottoman Empire at the end of World War I, Hagia Sophia was again transformed, this time into a secular museum befitting the modern Republic of Turkey. Only recently was it once again converted into a mosque.

Picture Hagia Sophia at its peak around the year 1000, when it was the heart of Constantinople, population 500,000—the greatest city in the world. Hagia Sophia was the spiritual polestar for millions of the world's Christians—the "eastern Vatican." The Byzantine world stretched from here to Italy, from the Danube to North Africa, and eastward to Asia. While Western Europe was stumbling through the "Dark" Ages, Constantinople was a beacon of light. And this vast empire was ruled by emperors who lived in the enormous Great Palace, which once stood right where you're standing now: today's Sultanahmet Park.

• *If you'd like to go inside Hagia Sophia now,* 📖 *see the next chapter for a detailed tour. Otherwise, let's check out a few more sights from the glory days of Constantinople.*

Walk toward Hagia Sophia, turn left, and head toward a stubby stone tower. As you cross the tram tracks, glance to the right as the road curves downhill. That way lies the Istanbul Archaeological Museums, home to many of the statues and relics that once adorned old Constantinople (see page 146).

Approach the stone tower. This water tower was just one small part of the ingenious system of aqueducts that once brought fresh water to the city. (We'll learn more about that in a minute.) For now, turn your attention to a much smaller gray column to the left of the tower. This marble stub is all that's left of the...

❸ Milion Stone Column

This bit of ruined marble was once a column that supported a big

triumphal arch—50 feet wide and six stories tall, topped with a dome and statues
of the Roman emperor Constantine and
his beloved mom, Helena. The arch was
built in the fourth century when Constantine enlarged the city to make it the new
capital of the Roman Empire. (Constantine officially renamed it "New Rome,"
but everyone else just ended up calling it
Constantinopolis—"Constantine's City.")
The Milion was the ceremonial starting
point of the city's main street (the Mese),
which headed west from here (following
the same course as today's tram-lined

Divan Yolu street) on its way to the city of Rome. The Milion
(shorthand Latin for "milestone") was "point zero" of the entire
empire—the spot from which all distances were measured.

• *Next we visit part of the water-supply system that fed the great city of
Constantinople. The entrance to the Basilica Cistern is beyond the Milion, up cobbled Yerebatan street. Buy your ticket, enter, and descend the
stairs into a dark and mesmerizing realm.*

❹ Basilica Cistern

This vast underground reservoir—lined with columns and mysteriously lit—looks like a subterranean cathedral with plumbing issues.
Because it stands atop an earlier basilica, it
was called the "Basilica Cistern," though
Turks today call it "the sunken palace."

It's huge: 150 yards long and 70 yards
wide. A forest of 336 columns supports
the cross-vaulted brick ceiling. The walls
are four feet thick. In its day, the cistern
was completely filled with fresh water.
It could hold more than 20 million gallons—enough to fill 30 Olympic-sized
swimming pools or serve the daily needs
of 100,000 Byzantines. (These days, to
accommodate tourists, the water level is
kept low, and they've added a walkway
and schools of plump carp.)

The cistern was built 1,500 years ago by Emperor Justinian—
the same man who built Hagia Sophia. Over 7,000 slaves labored
on the project. This was the city's largest cistern, and it served the
emperor's Great Palace. It was just one cistern of hundreds in the
city's vast water-supply system. Fresh water from 10 miles away
was channeled here through underground pipes and across raised

aqueducts. (A half-mile long section of the Valens Aqueduct still stands a mile west, near Atatürk Boulevard.)

Stroll up the walkway toward the far end. Check out the columns up close. They're all a uniform 30 feet tall, but each has a different capital at the top—from simple Doric to scroll-shaped Ionic to leafy Corinthian—because the columns were recycled from earlier ruins. Imagine touring the basilica by rowboat—as tourists once could (like in the James Bond film *From Russia with Love*).

A few odd columns stand out. One column's shaft is carved with rounded shapes that some call "tears" and others call "pea-cocks' eyes." (Stick your thumb in the hole and spin it for luck.) Signs lead you to the two "Medusa" columns. These stand atop big pedestals carved with faces of the Medusa— that mythological snake-headed gorgon whose gaze turned people to stone. Why Medusa? Maybe  because pagans believed the gorgon would scare off plunderers or evil spirits. Or maybe Christians buried these pagan monstrosities where they'd never see the light of day again. Here's a more practical theory: Notice that one Medusa head is upside down (making it taller), while the other is turned sideways (making it shorter). The architect may have simply needed to shim up the mismatched columns to the correct height...and Medusa did the trick.

As you return to the exit, you'll see huge, blocky concrete columns built recently to support the structure. Also, notice the performance stage in the water. The cistern hosts occasional arts exhibitions and concerts, mainly for traditional Turkish music. (Check the events schedule at the ticket office.)

The cistern served Constantinople for nearly a thousand years. But by the year 1453, it had become much like the Byzantine Empire itself—crumbling, weak, and dysfunctional. That's when everything changed.

• *Let's turn to the next chapter in the city's history. Exit the Basilica Cistern. (The exit spills you out a block away from where you entered.) Turn right and return to where this tour began—Sultanahmet Park.*

Once there, peruse that building we saw earlier—the one with the row of domes bordering the park, the...

❺ Haseki Baths

This bath house embodies the city's dramatic makeover from Christian Constantinople to Muslim.

In 1453, the city was conquered by Sultan Mehmet II (known as the Conqueror). Almost overnight, the Byzantine Empire was now the Ottoman Empire. Hagia Sophia was converted into a mosque, the Great Palace was abandoned for the sultans' Topkapı Palace, the Basilica Cistern was renovated to serve the Topkapı, and the Haseki Baths were built. The Ottomans loved their *hamams* just as Turks do today. In fact, this is still a working spa—now the restored **Ayasofya (Hürrem Sultan)** baths (see page 81).

The original baths had hot rooms, massage rooms, and cold plunges, each section topped with a dome. Domes became all the rage in Constantinople, thanks to the man who designed these baths—Mimar Sinan. After studying Hagia Sophia's geometrically complex dome, Sinan went on to create a hundred other (mostly domed) buildings and mosques in the city, including the Mosque of Süleyman the Magnificent. Sinan's signature style later got the supersized treatment when his trusty apprentice, Mehmet Aga, built the massive (and domed) Blue Mosque.

The Haseki Baths were financed by Roxelana, the red-headed concubine-turned-wife of Süleyman the Magnificent. As an advisor to her husband, she set the tone for a century of mighty female sultans called the "reign of the ladies." (For more on this power couple, see the sidebar on page 206).

• *Roxelana also gave birth to a line of highly artistic sultans, who continued to beautify the city. Her grandson was none other than Sultan Ahmet I, who commissioned the "Sultan Ahmet Mosque," better known as the Blue Mosque. Turn your back to Hagia Sophia and cross the park to see it.*

❻ View of Blue Mosque and Its Six Minarets

This gorgeous mosque, nicknamed for the rich blue decor inside, is one of the world's finest. It was built in just seven years (1609-1616) by the architect Mehmet Aga, Sinan's student. (Mehmet Aga also famously renovated the Kaaba, the holiest shrine of Islam—that giant black cube at the center of the mosque in the holy city of Mecca.) The enormous Blue Mosque was built atop ruins of the Byzantines'

Great Palace, hammering home the point that the Ottomans were now in charge.

Survey the mosque from one of the benches in front. To your right (with all those minidomes and chimneys) is the madrassa, a school of theology. Also, beneath one of those domes lies the tomb *(turbe)* of Sultan Ahmet I. Now, face the mosque again.

The Blue Mosque is unique because it has six minarets—when only one should be enough. A mosque's minaret is a tower the imam (prayer leader) or the muezzin (a man chosen for his vocal talents) climbs five times a day to call the faithful to prayer. On hearing this warbling chant, Muslims are to come to the mosque to worship. Today, an imam or muezzin still performs the call to prayer from the Blue Mosque, but now it's amplified by loudspeakers.

So why does the Blue Mosque have six minarets? A story popular with tour guides is that Sultan Ahmet I asked the architect for a gold *(altın)* minaret—but the man thought he said "six" *(altı)*. More likely, Ahmet probably requested six to flaunt his wealth. At the time, the central mosque in Mecca also had six. The people of Mecca feared that Ahmet's new mosque would upstage theirs—so the sultan graciously built a seventh minaret at Mecca.

• *Ready to go inside?*

Blue Mosque Visit

If this is your first mosque experience, don't stress. The Blue Mosque is extremely welcoming. Because the mosque is visited by many tourists, it goes out of its way to accommodate non-Muslims (but does enforce a dress code: knees and shoulders must be covered, and women should cover their hair with a scarf).

Note that the mosque is undergoing an extensive renovation and that many of the beautiful blue tiles of the interior may be obscured by scaffolding.

○ Self-Guided Tour: The walkway leads through a gate in the wall into the park-like setting of the mosque's...

❼ Outer Courtyard: You're facing the Mosque's main facade, but the entrances are around the right side. Continue straight ahead, where you reach a small staircase. Before going in, notice the line of water taps to the right—for the ritual cleansing of the body Muslims perform before worshipping, as directed by Islamic law.

• *Now take the stairs up into the...*

❽ Inner Courtyard: The spacious courtyard is surrounded by columns and arches providing a

shaded arcade. Stroll around, snap photos, and take in the scene. In the center of the courtyard is a six-sided domed fountain, once used for ablutions but now just decoration. The courtyard serves as overflow if the mosque gets too crowded, but these days such jam-packed services are rare. Muslims are no longer required to go to the mosque five times a day; they can pray anywhere. The exception is the midday service on Friday—the "Muslim sabbath"—when the Quran says all worshippers must worship together.

• *Let's go inside the mosque. You'll see an entrance here in the courtyard—but that's only for Muslims saying prayers. Instead, follow signs to the visitors entrance to the right, around the corner. (If there's a line, you could use the time to read the Understanding Islam chapter.) As you enter, take a plastic bag from the container and use it to carry your shoes, which you'll remove before stepping onto the carpet.*

❾ **Interior:** Stepping through the heavy leather drape into the interior, you'll understand why this is called the Blue Mosque.

The walls are covered with blue (and some red) tiles. Add in the blue-tinted windows and blue paint, and the whole atmosphere takes on an azure glow. It's a vast, sparsely decorated worship space with intensely decorated walls.

Approach the railing for a closer look. The area beyond is reserved for worshippers, who pray while going through a series of ritual gestures—bowing, kneeling, standing back up, and so on. They face toward the touchstone of their faith—the holy city of Mecca, birthplace of Muhammad, 1,500 miles away in Saudi Arabia. As in all mosques, that direction is marked by the **mihrab.** The Blue Mosque's mihrab, pointing southeast toward Mecca, is on the far wall—look for the tall gray-stone niche, surrounded with gilded ornamentation.

To the right of the mihrab is a steep, narrow staircase leading up to a platform with a cone on top. This is the *minbar*, or pulpit. The imam mounts this staircase to deliver a sermon on Fridays and on religiously important days. As a sign of respect for Muhammad, the imam stands only halfway up the staircase. The *minbar* is symbolic of the growth of Islam—Muhammad had to stand ever higher and higher to talk to his growing following.

Sultan Ahmet I and Kösem

Ahmet the First (1590-1617), who commissioned the Blue Mosque, epitomizes the many complex aspects of being a "sultan." Like many other sultans, he ascended the throne at a young age—only 14. He survived the palace intrigue so typical of the times, where princes were often murdered by their rivals. When Ahmet took power, he was expected to kill his own brother (to eliminate any threats), but Ahmet, known for his compassion, spared his brother's life.

As sultan, Ahmet was both the all-powerful ruler of the empire and a divinely appointed religious figure. Ahmet came to represent all that was good about the sultanate. Unlike earlier warrior-sultans, Ahmet was a true Renaissance Man—educated, artistic, a horseman, a scholar who spoke several languages, a man of faith, and an able statesman.

Ahmet's greatest achievement was the Blue Mosque, which in many ways represents the peak of Ottoman power

and majesty. Unfortunately, Ahmet died (of typhoid) only a year after its completion, at the tender age of 28. And after that, the sultanate began its slow centuries-long decline into debauchery and irrelevance.

Ahmet was succeeded by his young son, but the real power behind the throne was Ahmet's ambitious wife, Kösem (1590-1651). Like so many other sultan's wives, Kösem proved to be a major force in Ottoman history. She'd begun as a concubine of Ahmet's when she was only 15. She rose to be his wife, then mother of the crown prince. When their son Murat became sultan at age 11, Kösem essentially ran the empire through him. Her control continued through the reign of her second son, İbrahim I (a.k.a. İbrahim the Mad), who suffered with mental illness. Kösem's reign was finally cut short—in typical Ottoman style—when her rivals murdered İbrahim and sent eunuchs to strangle her in her sleep.

Today, Ahmet and Kösem lie together for eternity in a tomb alongside their magnum opus—the Blue Mosque.

Farther to the right is a fancy marble platform elevated on columns. This is where the choir sings hymns—generally *a cappella*, as Islam rarely uses instruments.

Mosque services are segregated: Men use the main hall, while women use the colonnaded area along the back wall or the upper galleries. Although some visitors see this division as demeaning to women, most Muslims feel it's a respectful way for both genders to concentrate on God.

The huge **dome**—140 feet high and 110 feet across—is modeled after the one in Hagia Sophia. That was the first building in the world to successfully place a round dome atop a rectangular building. You can see how the dome's weight is ingeniously distributed downward onto four spindly "legs" that rest atop four massive "elephant-foot" columns. The dome is further buttressed by the half-domes around it that push back in. These supports allow the walls to be opened up to glorious stained glass (260 panes, much of it original), giving the mosque an airy and spacious feeling. Thanks to the Blue Mosque's success, these architectural elements spread to mosques all over the Islamic world.

Overhead are ornate chandeliers. Though fitted with light bulbs now, these were once oil lamps with floating wicks, supported by a system of wires that allowed the chandeliers to be raised and lowered to tend to the lamps. Under your feet are rich padded carpets—essential for a worship space without pews. The carpets have lines to organize the worshippers into efficient rows.

Notice that, in this whole mosque, there's not one statue, painting, or mosaic of a saint. Islamic tradition forbids the portrayal of living beings in places of worship, which could distract people from worshipping Allah as the one God. As a result, the Muslim world excelled at nonfigurative art, like the glorious geometric designs here.

More than 20,000 ceramic **tiles** decorate the mosque. The lower walls have the famed İznik tiles, a world-class porcelain factory 50 miles south of here. If you could get a close-up look, you'd see that each tile is hand painted, and features one of 50 different designs based around Turkey's favorite flower—the tulip. İznik tiles are used all over Istanbul, especially the Topkapı Palace, as well as in museums around the world.

The mosque also has artful Arabic **calligraphy**, which quotes the Quran or the sayings of Muhammad. The two medallions high above the mihrab read *Muhammad* (left) and *Allah* (right, with its distinctive "cursive w" shape).

Soak it all in. The Blue Mosque represents the pinnacle of Ottoman architecture.

It also marks the beginning of the empire's decline. Thanks to the enormous cost of its construction, the treasury was exhausted, the Ottoman Empire became stagnant, and never again would they build a mosque of such splendor.

Despite the Ottoman decline, Constantinople continued to be a great city—the caretaker of an imperial legacy stretching back thousands of years.

• *Exit into daylight and make your way back to that inner courtyard we were in earlier (with the tiny domed fountain in the center).*

Before you exit the complex completely, just soak up the scene. The crowd is a fun mix of Turkish tourists, wide-eyed cruise groups, and devout pilgrims. Try out a little Turkish: *"Merhaba"* means "Hello." Every Turkish school kid knows how to say in English, "What is your name?" and "How old are you?"

• *Now, with your back to the mosque, head through the exit gate in the courtyard's back wall. (As you pass through, turn around for a great photo-op of the mosque's graceful cascading-domes design, framed by the portal.) Continue down the stairs, where you enter a looooong, skinny square with an Egyptian obelisk. This is the site of the...*

⑩ Hippodrome

This oblong square—five football fields long—was once a chariot-race course. Picture the scene here circa AD 500: Grandstands

surround the stadium, filled with 100,000 roaring fans. The chariots line up at the far right end (near the small green dome)...and they're off! They'd race past the obelisk, make the dangerous hairpin turn at the far-left end, and race back. Two teams, the Blues and the Greens, vied for fans' loyalty. Rivalries grew so fierce that, in 532, the Nika riots broke out, with rebels attacking Emperor Justinian and burning down his home church. Justinian responded by quelling the revolt, launching construction of a new Hagia Sophia, and executing 30,000 rebels here in the Hippodrome.

The race course dates from the city's earliest years, back when it was a Greek city called Byzantion. As the city grew into a Roman capital, the race course was augmented to accommodate grand spectacles and rallies. Each successive ruler added monuments proclaiming the city's greatness.

• The greatest of the Hippodrome's monuments was the...

⓫ Egyptian Obelisk

This served as the race track's center point, anchoring the raised platform (the *spina*) that the chariots raced around.

Approach the obelisk for a closer look. Sixty feet tall and made of red granite, the obelisk is very old—dating from 1,500 years before the birth of Christ. Its hieroglyph inscription trumpets the triumphs of Pharaoh Thutmose III. In Roman times, the obelisk was taken down by Emperor Theodosius the Great (390) and shipped across the Mediterranean to Constantinople.

The obelisk's base is carved with fourth century reliefs that tell the story. Start with the north panel (the side that faces Hagia Sophia). It shows the citizens of Constantinople, ruled over by Emperor Theodosius (seated at top-center). At the bottom of the relief, we see the obelisk on its side, being transported. Then workmen struggle to turn pulleys as they raise the obelisk up in its new location—the Hippodrome.

Circle counterclockwise to the west panel. It shows awe-struck citizens kneeling at Theodosius's feet, thanking him for the obelisk.

At the bottom, an inscription in Greek proclaims that "only the Emperor Theodosius dared lift this column up, executed in 32 days."

The south panel depicts the chariot races in action. The fans are seated in the bleachers, with Theodosius at top-center in his private box on the 50-yard line (on the Blue Mosque side). At the bottom, we see chariots racing along, pulled by four muscular horses.

In the east panel, the race is over, and Theodosius stands to give the laurel-wreath prize to the winner. The inscription below (in Latin), heaps more praise on "Theodosius and his everlasting descendants," and claims he raised the obelisk, not in 32 days, but a mere 30. "All things must yield to Theodosius!"

As it turned out, Theodosius would be the last Roman emperor to rule a united Roman Empire. A century later, the western half was in ruins, while Justinian struggled to hold it all together.

Regardless, Constantinople kept chugging on as the enlightened capital of the Byzantine half, and the Hippodrome continued hosting races and spectacles.

• *Let's turn our attention to a few...*

Other Hippodrome Monuments

The next treasure adorning the *spina* was the ⓬ **Serpent Column.** This 25-foot-tall, bronze-green, corkscrew-shaped column

originally depicted a coiled snake with three (now-missing) heads. The column was built to commemorate ancient Greece's victory over Persia (479 BC) that ushered in the Golden Age. The column was famous in ancient times, as it stood for 800 years at the sacred site of the Delphic Oracle. When Constantine made Constantinople his capital, he erected the column in the Hippodrome, instantly giving the city a distinguished heritage.

HISTORIC CORE

Next comes the so-called ⓭ **Walled Obelisk.** This 100-foot-tall stone pillar, once covered in gilded

bronze, was built way back in...well, nobody actually knows how old it is. We know it was renovated in the 10th century by the Byzantines to celebrate their victories over enemies and seemingly never-ending dominance as Europe's greatest power.

• *But all empires end, and the Hippodrome also testifies to that. Stroll around while you ponder the...*

Decline of the Hippodrome and Byzantine Empire

Constantinople continued through medieval times as Europe's supreme city. Then in the year 1204, everything changed.

The city was surrounded by an army of fellow Christians—Crusaders led by Venice. (The situation was complicated, but basically the Crusaders were hoping to collect unpaid debts, avenge a massacre of western Christians, assert the power of the pope over the Orthodox world...and feast on the vast wealth of Europe's richest city.) The Crusaders breached the mighty walls and began sacking and looting. The Walled Obelisk was stripped of its precious metals. Statues and columns were melted down or vandalized. Four bronze horses that once adorned the Hippodrome's starting line were carried off as booty to decorate Venice's St. Mark's Basilica.

The city was traumatized, and never really recovered, while the Hippodrome fell into ruin.

When the Ottomans arrived in 1453, they used the Hippodrome as little more than a meadow for their horses. They recycled the grandstands' stones to build the Blue Mosque. They dumped the construction dirt in the Hippodrome, which is why it's now six feet higher than the (sunken) monuments. The Ottomans built their own impressive buildings, like the stone **İbrahim Paşa Palace** (now the Turkish and Islamic Arts Museum), which borders the Hippodrome's long side, near the Egyptian Obelisk. (The museum is a good place to get a glimpse of Ottoman greatness—see the Turkish and Islamic Arts Museum Tour chapter.)

For the next 400 years, the sultans ruled Constantinople. But as we saw, their empire eventually declined until it was known as the "Sick Man of Europe." Meanwhile, modern Europe was on the rise.

• *Let's see a monument from that transition period. Head for the other end of the Hippodrome (closest to Hagia Sophia), to the small green dome, known as the...*

⓮ German Fountain

This octagonal structure—with a Byzantine-style dome atop eight porphyry columns—is a public water fountain. You can see the (still-working) bronze water taps. Like thousands of other fountains erected in Ottoman times, it gave ordinary citizens access to fresh water. Sultans and the rich donated these and vied with each other to make them the fanciest. (For more on the city's fountains, see the sidebar on page 50.)

This particular fountain, however, was not the gift of an Ottoman sultan but a German Kaiser. Wilhelm II had visited Constantinople to schmooze with the sultan. He was seeking lucrative trade deals and an alliance with the sultan in case of war.

Wilhelm sent this fountain in 1900 to woo the sultan. Its style is a mix of Byzantine (mosaics under a dome) and Islamic (like the Blue Mosque's courtyard fountain), plus European technology: It was constructed in pieces in Germany, then shipped to Istanbul and reassembled on this location.

The Kaiser and the sultan (see their imperial medallions in the dome's mosaic) struck a deal, so when Germany started World

War I, the Ottomans were drawn into the bloody conflict and
ended up on the losing side. In 1918 the war ended, the last sultan
died, and the Ottoman Empire was carved up by Europe's victors.

Out of the ashes rose a whole new era—the Turkish Republic. The visionary new leader, Mustafa Kemal Atatürk, westernized
and secularized the nation, and Constantinople got a new name:
Istanbul.

• *We'll finish our walk by surveying the modern city of Constantino—
excuse me, I mean "Istanbul."*

*From the German Fountain, turn left and head through the trees
into a small park. Continue about 200 yards, making your way uphill,
up a set of steps, past bubbling fountains, to a small brick-paved terrace.
Turn around, and survey the wonderful...*

⓯ View of Istanbul

From here, you get a sense of today's city—a mix of old and new.
In the distance are the minarets of the Blue Mosque. Closer to you
is the minaret of Firuz Ağa Camii, one of the 2,000 mosques that
dot this city. At your feet is a modern amphitheater. It sits beside
piles of ruined columns from the Byzantine era. Turks relax in the
park or hurry about on business. From ancient Constantinople to
modern Istanbul, we've come full circle—the city is yours.

• *If you're up for more sightseeing, remember that **Hagia Sophia** is just
downhill from here, with the **Topkapı Palace** beyond that.*

*To your left is the Sultanahmet tram stop, where my **Old Town
Back Streets Walk** to the Grand Bazaar and Spice Market starts. The
Sultanahmet **tram** line can take you to many of Istanbul's best sights:
the Istanbul Archaeological Museums, the Golden Horn/Spice Market/
Galata Bridge, and the New District.*

HAGIA SOPHIA TOUR

Aya Sofya

Simply put, Hagia Sophia is one of the most magnificent, influential, historic, and revered buildings on earth.

For a thousand years, it served as the greatest church in Christendom. It was home to the Byzantine Emperor and Orthodox Patriarch (the "eastern pope"), and a beacon of civilization during Western Europe's dark ages.

When Muslims conquered Constantinople, this great church suddenly became one of the world's greatest mosques. And when it was secularized in the 20th century, Hagia Sophia remained world-class, as a stunning museum of priceless artifacts. In mid-2020, to the surprise of many (and delight of Istanbul's conservatives), the building reverted to its status as a mosque.

On this visit, we'll see elements from Hagia Sophia's entire 1,500-year history— as church, mosque, and museum. We'll marvel at its sheer size—the vast nave, soaring dome, and cutting-edge design. We'll contemplate glimmering mosaics of saints and emperors, some of the world's finest. We'll see the big, ornate marble monuments added in the Muslim years, fit for a sultan. And along the way, we'll stumble across a few oddities found nowhere else—from a 50-foot-tall angel, a marble belly button, and Viking graffiti to a famously sweaty column.

In a sense, Hagia Sophia is Istanbul in a nutshell: ancient, grandiose, a bit sprawling and unruly, and a fascinating blend of east and west.

Orientation

Hagia Sophia in Flux: In mid-2020, the Turkish government changed the status of Hagia Sophia from a museum to a mosque. At the time of publication of this book, details regulating visits to the monument were in flux, including opening hours, access to the upper galleries, and the availability of tours. Assume that you'll follow the protocols for a visit to any mosque (see page 72), but check locally for the latest information.

Cost and Hours: Free, generally open daily around the clock but closed to visitors five times a day for prayer.

Information: +90 212 522 1750, www.muze.gen.tr

Dress Code: Modest dress (covered knees and shoulders) is expected for men and women, and women should have a headscarf (available at door). You'll need to remove your shoes.

Getting There: Hagia Sophia is in the heart of the Old Town, facing the Blue Mosque. The main entrance is at the southwest corner of the giant building, across the busy street with the tram tracks (Divan Yolu). Arriving by tram, get off at the Sultanahmet stop and walk a couple of hundred yards downhill along Divan Yolu. Cross the wide street at the traffic light.

Tours: You may find local guides outside Hagia Sophia offering to take you around for a fee (generally 70 TL). But, with this self-guided tour, you won't need their help.

Length of This Tour: Allow at least one hour for the main floor and 30 minutes or more for the upper galleries.

Services: There is no bag check. WCs are near the main entrance.

Nearby: The imperial mausoleums of several Ottoman sultans, known as the Sultans' *Türbes*, are in the garden along the south side of Hagia Sophia. Free to visit, they are worth a look (daily 9:00-19:00). For details, see page 41.

Starring: The finest house of worship in the Christian and Muslim worlds.

The Tour Begins

• *Start in Sultanahmet Park, the vast landscaped square between Hagia Sophia and the Blue Mosque.*

❶ Hagia Sophia's Exterior

Take in the majestic outlines of Hagia Sophia (hah-gee-yah soh-FEE-yah; or in Turkish *Aya Sofya*). It's a massive square building topped with a dome and surrounded by a waterfall of smaller domes

cascading down. When Muslims arrived and added the pointy minarets, the iconic "look" the world has come to know was complete. Compare Hagia Sophia with its neighbor, the Blue Mosque. It's clear that the venerable Christian church set the template for countless mosques around the world.

The church was built between AD 532 and 537, in the waning days of the Roman Empire by Justinian I, the last great Roman emperor. By now, Constantinople was the empire's capital, as the city of Rome had fallen to barbarians. By building Hagia Sophia, Justinian was sending a message to the world that the grandeur of Rome would continue for centuries to come.

Justinian (reign 527-565) envisioned a church of mind-boggling proportions. He spared no expense. Some 10,000 architects, stonemasons, bricklayers, plasterers, sculptors, painters, and mosaic artists worked around the clock. Unbelievably, they completed it in just five years.

Hagia Sophia became an instant legend. For a while, it was the biggest building in the world, period. It would remain the biggest cathedral for nearly a thousand years. Its gleaming dome was the first thing visitors would see arriving on ships and caravans. Word spread across the globe of its size and its perfect—almost mystical—proportions.

On Christmas Day of the year 537, Hagia Sophia hosted its first service, overseen by Justinian and the Patriarch of Constantinople. The church was dedicated with a Greek name, capturing its seemingly heaven-sent presence. They called it Hagia Sophia—"Holy Wisdom."

• *Enter the complex and follow the walkway straight ahead to the main entrance. Before going inside Hagia Sophia, survey it from outside.*

❷ Main Entrance

As you get close, the building seems to rise up like a massive mountain of stone. Take in the **four large buttresses** framing the entrance. The church was built mostly of bricks held together with mortar, with larger blocks for the buttresses. Frankly, from the outside, Hagia Sophia can look a bit clunky, but these buttresses were essential. They pushed inward to hold the structure together. By putting structural elements like these on the exterior, the architects opened up the interior (as we'll soon see) into a magnificent worship place on a scale never seen before.

The area outside is littered with broken columns and sunken foundations. These are not from Hagia Sophia but **remnants of the two earlier churches** that previously stood on this spot. These structures were so grand they were called "Megalo Ekklesia"—the "Great Church." But when that "great" church was utterly destroyed by frenzied revolutionaries (in the Nika riots, AD 532), Emperor Justinian I decided to punctuate his victory over the rebels with something that would make earlier churches look puny.

His huge church would accommodate large-scale religious spectacles in what became the Orthodox Christian tradition. As emperor, he would enter the church through the grand entrance—coincidentally, the same entrance used by tourists today. Imagine the scene: the emperor in his jeweled robe accompanied by his entourage—the empress, patriarch, priests, scholars, and eunuchs.

• *Enter Hagia Sophia like an emperor, through the grand main entrance. You first pass through the **outer narthex**, a long, narrow, bare-brick (and no longer impressive) hallway. In the Orthodox tradition, this is where the entourage would pause, light candles, revere icons of saints, and get into the proper frame of mind before they entered the sacred space. Continue into another similar (but more impressive) anteroom, called the...*

❸ Inner Narthex

With its golden mosaic ceiling, walls of green and red marble, and huge bronze doors, this hallway gives a tiny glimpse of Justinian's original vision. As emperor of Rome, he decorated this entryway with two Roman specialties: mosaics and marble.

The **mosaics** here are the oldest in the church, from Justinian's day. The ceiling is an elaborate pattern of squares, circles, and arches. Looking closer, you see that those elements are themselves composed of leaves, flowers, crosses, and eight-pointed stars. Mosaics like these were made of small cubes of colored glass interspersed with semi-precious stones. When lit by candles (the original light source for this space), the golden background and intricate patterns flickered to life.

Notice that these mosaics mostly depict geometric designs. In Justinian's day, mosaics depicting people were not popular. As we'll see, Orthodox Christians were often skeptical of realistic mosaics of human figures. The simple geometric designs spared these mosa-

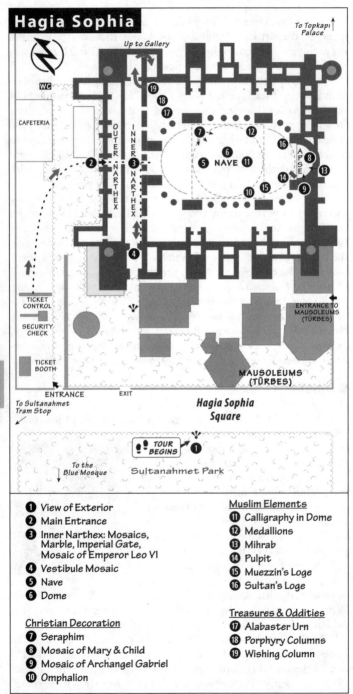

Hagia Sophia

To Topkapı Palace

Up to Gallery

WC

CAFETERIA

OUTER NARTHEX

INNER NARTHEX

NAVE

APSE

TICKET CONTROL

SECURITY CHECK

TICKET BOOTH

ENTRANCE TO MAUSOLEUMS (TÜRBES)

MAUSOLEUMS (TÜRBES)

ENTRANCE   EXIT

To Sultanahmet Tram Stop

Hagia Sophia Square

TOUR BEGINS ➊

To the Blue Mosque

Sultanahmet Park

HAGIA SOPHIA

➊ View of Exterior
➋ Main Entrance
➌ Inner Narthex: Mosaics, Marble, Imperial Gate, Mosaic of Emperor Leo VI
➍ Vestibule Mosaic
➎ Nave
➏ Dome

Christian Decoration
➐ Seraphim
➑ Mosaic of Mary & Child
➒ Mosaic of Archangel Gabriel
➓ Omphalion

Muslim Elements
⓫ Calligraphy in Dome
⓬ Medallions
⓭ Mihrab
⓮ Pulpit
⓯ Muezzin's Loge
⓰ Sultan's Loge

Treasures & Oddities
⓱ Alabaster Urn
⓲ Porphyry Columns
⓳ Wishing Column

ics when so-called "Iconoclasts" vandalized human-centric mosaics they considered sacrilegious (see the "Iconoclast Era" sidebar, later in this chapter).

The **marble** on the walls and floors is also from Justinian's time. To create these mirror-image Rorschach blots, workers laboriously sawed through the thin marble blocks, then folded them out like a book. The inch-thick panels were then glued to the wall with stucco and pinned with iron rods. Even after 15 centuries, the panels hang on.

The big central doorway is called the **Imperial Gate** and was opened only for the emperor. The 23-foot doors are made of bronze plating covering an oak core that supposedly came from Noah's Ark. The doors were already 700 years old when Justinian brought them here from a famed Greek temple—giving Hagia Sophia instant historical status.

Above the door is a **mosaic of Emperor Leo VI,** which, though not one of Justinian's originals, is still very old (c. AD 900). Obviously, it was made during a generation when depictions of human figures were back in vogue. The mosaic features Christ Pantocrator, or "Ruler of All," a pose familiar to Orthodox Christians to this day. Seated on his heavenly throne, he raises his right hand in a blessing, and holds a Bible in the other. Christ is flanked by Mary and the Archangel Gabriel. At Christ's feet, Emperor Leo prostrates himself—possibly (as legend says) to

atone for his scandalous sex life. As we'll see, mosaics depicting these types of figures—Christ, Mary, angels, and emperors— were once everywhere in Hagia Sophia.

• *Before entering the nave, let's see one of the building's finest mosaics. It gives us a glimpse of the man who built the church— Emperor Justinian I. Facing the Imperial Gate, turn right, and head out the far end of the narthex. As you step through the door, turn around and look back up to find the...*

❹ Vestibule Mosaic of Mary, Justinian, and Constantine

This mosaic, from around AD 1000, represents Byzantium's peak of power and height of mosaic-making skill.

Mary is seated on a throne, with baby Jesus posed on her lap like a pint-sized Pantocrator, flashing the three-fingered sign of the Trinity. Mary is depicted in her role as "Mother of God" (as the abbreviation "MP OV" says). Such mother-and-child mosaics were especially popular in this particular church, because, by giving birth to Jesus, it was Mary who brought God's "Holy Wisdom" (or Hagia Sophia) into the physical world.

Flanking Mary are the mighty emperors who made this church possible. On the right, holding a model of Constantinople, is Constantine the Great, who founded the city and whose son built the first Christian church on this site. On the left is Justinian, with a model of the even-greater church he added—Hagia Sophia. Unlike today's structure, the church back then was painted blue, with a cross on top and no minarets.

Note that both emperors wear imperial garb—blue silk robes with gold-brocaded shawls—symbolizing the continuity of rule from ancient to Byzantine times. Justinian's Greek inscription calls him the "Emperor of Illustrious Memory." His glorious reign called up the long tradition of emperors that stretched from Caesar Augustus to Constantine the Great to the man who dared to build a Christian church on a Roman-size scale—Emperor Justinian.

• Now let's enter the heart of Justinian's Hagia Sophia. Backtrack to the Imperial Gate and step through it into the vast nave. It's said that when Justinian first set foot inside his church, he compared it with the Holy Temple of Israel and exclaimed, "Solomon, I have surpassed you!"

❺ Nave: The Grandeur of Justinian's Church

Stroll around this spacious setting and try—just try—to take it all in. It's huge—the massive pillars, the high ceiling, the soaring dome...even the scaffolding (for ongoing renovation) is on a supersized scale. The building has a long oblong nave flanked by two side aisles. All in all, the interior is 250 feet long, 240 feet wide, and 180 feet high (at the dome). With a footprint of over

60,000 square feet, it could host nearly 20,000 worshippers. (Or stage a dozen basketball games at once.) Justinian's church surpassed even the pope's church, St. Peter's in Rome. Paris' Notre-Dame could do the limbo beneath Hagia Sophia's great dome.

Close this book for a second and just absorb the experience: You are in Hagia Sophia, the crowning achievement of the Byzantine Empire.

(And, we're back.) After ogling the church's sheer size, turn to its decoration. The upper half is covered with golden mosaics, part of nearly four acres of mosaics. The lower walls are faced with panels of multi-colored marble: green, red, and yellow. Even the floor has expensive slabs of marble making a wavy pattern, symbolizing the cosmic ocean.

On either side of the nave are enormous 45-foot-tall **columns** of speckled-green marble topped with lacy white capitals. These big columns are matched by smaller ones midway up in the gallery (which we'll visit later). Think of the engineering challenge: Each column was quarried in Greece, dragged to a port, shipped across the Aegean, transported to this site, and erected in place, using ropes and pulleys and lots of sweaty workers. And that was just one column of more than a hundred, just one small part of this huge undertaking.

Despite its size, the overall effect of Hagia Sophia is not of heavy solidity but of airy space and light. The acoustics here are perfect. A diffuse light filters through the windows—some made of glass, some of translucent sheets of alabaster. The light reflects off the mosaics to create a thick golden atmosphere—like the Orthodox vision of heaven.

• *Approach the center of the church and gape upward into the...*

❻ Dome

What blew everyone away was Hagia Sophia's most unique feature—the dome. It's 105 feet across and hovers 185 feet off the ground. It seems to rest on nothing at all—seemingly float-

ing atop a ring of light, formed by the 40 windows at its base. It was meant to convey the feeling of being "suspended from heaven" on a chain of gold.

The dome was the central element in the church's groundbreaking design. Placing a round dome atop a square building seems simple, but at the time, it was revolutionary. In fact, having a square church at all was unheard of in the Christian world, where basilicas were always long, narrow, and low-ceilinged.

To appreciate Hagia Sophia's complex design, look at its **footprint** on the map on page 104. The building has a circular dome in the center, enclosed by a square. From here, four arms radiate out to form a Greek Cross (or a plus sign). This cross is itself enclosed in a larger square. This design was so bold that only a few churches in the west (such as Venice's St. Mark's) dared to follow. But in the east, it set the pattern for thousands of Orthodox houses of worship.

Take a moment to appreciate Hagia Sophia as an engineering marvel. Justinian hired two scholarly geometricians, Anthemius of Tralles and Isidore of Miletus, to figure out how to fit the round peg of a dome into the square hole of the church. When Anthemius tried to explain how difficult that was to Justinian, the emperor simply told him: "Have faith in God."

The architects' solution was a complex interplay of forces: First off, their dome would be partly supported by the church's thick walls, heavy pillars, and stout columns. But more importantly, it would rest on the four big **arches** directly beneath it. It's the arch (not the barely solid wall beneath it, perforated with windows) that bears most of the weight. The arch passes the dome's weight outward to the massive piers at the corners.

That's where the **half-domes** flanking the central dome come in. They distribute some of the weight outward to the exterior buttresses (which we saw) that push back in to hold everything in place.

Thanks to this intricate scheme, the heavy dome essentially rests on four spindly legs—the triangular-shaped **"pendentives"** beneath the dome decorated with the four winged angels. These pendentives support the dome while delicately balancing their dainty ballerina toes atop the walls.

Anthemius and Isadore had accomplished their mission: "to apply geometry to solid matter." As you look around, you'll see the basic principle found in all Byzantine architecture: symmetry.

Hagia Sophia as a Church

For nearly a millennium, the church of Hagia Sophia was the heart of this large, Christian, Greek-speaking civilization. But, like all empires, Byzantium slowly declined. And the church itself underwent many changes. Iconoclasts destroyed old artwork, while icon-lovers added new ones. The church (which rests on a major fault line) suffered through numerous earthquakes and rebuilds. (Even the central dome collapsed once—a mere 20 years after completion—only to be rebuilt by none other than the nephew of Isidore of Miletus, one of the original geometricians.)

After its peak in the year 1000, Byzantium suffered a series of body-blows. In 1054, the pope's ambassador was excommunicated in Hagia Sophia, prompting the Great Schism between Orthodox and Catholic Christians. In 1204, Constantinople was sacked by Venetian crusaders, who looted Hagia Sophia and (temporarily) used it as a Catholic church. The Byzantine empire shrank, and its once-vigorous trade routes faded as other European sea-powers took over. By the year 1400, the once-great "empire" was little more than Constantinople itself—a crumbling city with a big old church.

Such mathematical perfection reflected the order God had placed in the world. The structure sent a message to every awe-struck visitor: Justinian's church was a physical incarnation of God's "Holy Wisdom."

• *Now let's focus on some of the church's...*

Christian Decoration

Start with Hagia Sophia's biggest images—the four 50-foot-tall angels in the pendentives beneath the dome. These are the ❼ **sera-phim**—the fiery six-winged body-guards of God's heavenly throne. Each of them is unique, with their wings in a different pose. According to the Bible (Isaiah 6:2), these angels covered their bodies with their wings. Find the one angel whose original face still peeks out from the flurry of wings.

Now turn your attention to the apse, with its colorful ❽ **mosaic of Mary and the Christ Child.** Mary is huge—16 feet tall. Lit by the four windows beneath her, she floats in a gold-mosaic heaven. On her lap, Christ is dressed in gold and wearing a cross-shaped halo. He's a little kid with curly blonde hair, rosy cheeks, and a welcoming smile. Mary rests one slender hand on Jesus's shoulder and the other on his knee. They're both sitting on a jeweled throne (with no back), resting on pillows.

This is the oldest surviving mosaic in the nave (ninth century). It's a perfect example of a Byzantine "icon," or image of a holy person. It reflects the long-standing controversy over icons. Early Christians had strong feelings about whether icons were a good or a bad thing (see the "Iconoclastic Era" sidebar). Consequently, Hagia Sophia's mosaics were periodically vandalized, then replaced again, depending on the mood of the times. This Mary-and-Child was the first major mosaic done after the greatest wave of Iconoclasm.

It seemed to strike an acceptable compromise. On one hand, Mary is an ethereal presence in a faraway heaven (pleasing the Iconoclasts). On the other, she's plunked down on an earthly bench with three-dimensional solidity. Similarly, Christ poses like a symbolic Pantocrator, but he's also cute as a button. In the endless debate over whether Christ was a flesh-and-blood mortal or an all-powerful god, this pleasant mosaic captured a nice balance.

To the right of Mary (at the base of an arch), find the 30-foot-tall ❾ **mosaic of Archangel Gabriel.** Though it's badly damaged, you can still make out Gabe's youthful (almost feminine) face, blonde hair, and voluminous feathery wings. In one hand he holds a staff while the other cradles a crystal ball. This angel (along with Archangel Michael who was once on the other end of the arch) served as guardians of Mary and Jesus in the apse, the same way soldiers attended the Byzantine emperor.

Speaking of the emperor, find the ❿ **omphalion,** the emperor's personal place in this imperial church. The omphalion is

a big gray-green marble circle in the pavement of the church floor, beneath (but not directly beneath) the dome. The big circle is surrounded by smaller circles of various colors, all enclosed in a 19-foot square.

This was the coronation spot for Byzantine emperors. A golden throne would be set in the circle, and the patriarch would crown him emperor. Long

Iconoclast Era (730-840) and the Banning of Icons

The religious use of icons—depictions of human figures in mosaics, frescoes, and statues—was controversial throughout Christian Byzantine history. The Bible specifically forbids making "graven images." Iconoclasts ("image breakers") argued that icons were like idols, worshipped like a false god. On the other hand, the masses tended to like icons, as a way to make a personal connection with faraway saints.

Over the centuries, the pendulum swung back and forth  between icon-lovers and Iconoclasts. It caused huge divisions in the church. Even images of Christ could spark controversy. If Christ was divine, how could his nature be depicted by only showing his mortal form?

In AD 730, the controversy came to a violent head. Emperor Leo III banned all icons, and zealous Iconoclasts destroyed statues, paintings, and mosaics throughout the city. Many of Hagia Sophia's treasured mosaics were vandalized and lost forever.

A century later, public opinion swung the other way. Artists were once again free to portray saints and emperors (who loved to be seen as semidivine).

The Iconoclastic debate was never fully resolved. Over time, Byzantines seemed to settle onto a kind of compromise. Today, their icons tend to be just realistic enough to depict flesh-and-blood human beings, but abstract enough to suggest the unknowable divine.

after the Roman empire fell in the west, Byzantine emperors still liked to think of themselves as heirs to the "Roman" Empire that stretched back to Caesar Augustus.

Imagine this spot during a coronation. Byzantine rituals were a spectacle. The emperor and patriarch processed into the church in a cloud of incense. An army of priests also paraded in, swinging silver incense burners, carrying golden crosses, and waving colorful banners of saints. From the gallery, a large choir sang Gregorian-chant-like hymns. The dignitaries paraded to the altar through an enormous chancel screen made of 40,000 pounds of silver. Then the emperor took his seat on the throne in the marble circle. The patriarch placed the crown on his head and—dut dutta dah!—he was now emperor. The whole event was watched over by a large image that once graced the dome overhead—Christ Pantocrator ("Ruler of All"), blessing the scene.

The word "omphalion" is Greek for "navel," and this spot was considered the symbolic center of the entire empire. By the year 1000, the Byzantine world stretched from Syria to Naples, from the Danube to Athens. Its traders plied the Mediterranean and rode camels to China. While Western Europe was mired in poverty and war, the Byzantines reigned supreme as Europe's most enlightened power. And it was all ruled from this spot, the center of civilization itself—the Byzantine belly-button.

• *Then came the Muslims, and Hagia Sophia turned the page to a new chapter in its illustrious history. Let's focus now on Hagia Sophia's...*

Muslim Elements

On May 29, 1453, Constantinople was conquered by the Ottomans. The Christian city was now Muslim, the Byzantine empire was the Ottoman Empire, and—on the very day the city fell—Hagia Sophia was transformed from one of the world's greatest churches to one of its greatest mosques.

The sultans embraced Hagia Sophia, lavishly restoring and beautifying the aging structure. They furnished it with the things you'd find in mosques anywhere, but on a grandiose scale. Minarets were placed at the corners. In the nave, new chandeliers (originally holding glass oil lamps with floating wicks) improved the lighting. Christian-themed mosaics (especially those depicting human figures) were plastered over and replaced with geometric designs.

In the central dome, the figure of Christ Pantocrator was replaced with elaborate ❶ **calligraphy.** The Arabic letters proclaim a well-known verse from the Quran (24:35): "Allah is the light of the world." The seraphim were allowed to stay, but were given a new job—guarding the Islamic (not Christian) heaven. To discourage anyone from worshipping these supernatural creatures as gods (which Muslims abhorred as much as Christians did), the angels' faces were covered over with 3-foot-wide gold-leaf hubcaps in the shape of stars. (The one face that does show through was uncovered in the 21st century.)

The nave was decorated with eight 25-foot ❷ **medallions with calligraphy.** The Arabic script was done by the same well-known calligrapher who did the dome. They're made of wood wrapped with leather, inscribed with huge letters. Each medallion honors a famous figure in Islamic history. The four under the dome name the first four caliphs—those immediate successors of

Muhammed that every Muslim schoolkid knows. The two most important medallions flank the apse: The one to the left (with its unique squiggle) reads "Muhammed." The medallion to the right (with what looks like a cursive "w" and "l") says "Allah."

• *In and around the apse you'll find the most important trappings—the ones used in...*

Muslim Worship

Inside the apse, the gilded-marble rectangle against the wall is the **⓭ mihrab.** This is the ceremonial niche found in every mosque that shows the precise direction to face during prayers—namely, toward Mecca. Note that this particular mihrab is slightly off-center, because Hagia Sophia was built (following the Christian tradition) facing roughly east, while Mecca is actually southeast. The mihrab is flanked by two thick candleholders brought here as booty by the Ottomans' great Renaissance sultan, Süleyman the Magnificent.

On the right side of the apse is a steep, narrow staircase topped with a pointy turret—the **⓮ pulpit** *(minbar)*, which also points to-

ward Mecca. Here the imam (the congregation's pastor) delivered his Friday sermon from a point halfway up the stairs, reserving the uppermost step for the Prophet Muhammad as a sign of respect. Although every mosque has something similar, few can match Hagia Sophia's ornately-carved marble beauty.

Farther to the right (near the omphalion) is the **⓯ muezzin's loge**—a rectangular, honey-hued marble structure supported by pointed arches. During a service, the muezzin would go inside here and mount a staircase to the roof to lead prayers during the service. Because Hagia Sophia is so big, they needed five such platforms—this one is the oldest and nicest.

To the left of the apse is a six-sided pavilion atop columns—the **⓰ sultan's loge.** This was the sultan's private viewing area during services, shielded by an elaborate gilded screen.

Looking at all these great Muslim additions, you can't help but feel that each Ottoman sultan used Hagia Sophia as a showcase for their power, wealth, and devotion to the faith.

HAGIA SOPHIA

• *Through its entire existence, Hagia Sophia has been a kind of museum or treasury of cultural artifacts from the world's great civilizations—Christian, Muslim, and even pagan. Let's see some of these pieces. Start heading back through the nave (toward where we came in), pausing along the way to see some...*

Cultural Treasures and Oddities

Veer to your right to find a five-foot-tall, egg-shaped ❼ **alabaster urn.** (There's a matching one on the opposite side of the nave.) These

urns are more than 2,000 years old. Each one can hold 333 gallons. They were brought here from the sophisticated Hellenist-Greek city of Pergamon (on Turkey's Aegean coast). A sultan graciously donated them to the congregation of Hagia Sophia. Note the tap mounted in the side. These one-of-a-kind ancient treasures were used for a traditional Muslim purpose—to provide drinking water for worshippers.

Behind each urn stand two ❽ **purple porphyry columns.** These are among the dozens of columns in Hagia Sophia—of different colors, shapes, and heights—brought here from distant lands and historic temples and incorporated into the church. Symbolically, this was a way of appropriating and building on previous empires. These particular columns were chosen by Justinian to recall the royal-purple color favored by ancient Roman emperors. They're made of a rare stone found only in one particular quarry in Egypt. (Their iron girdles were placed around them long ago to prevent these precious objects from cracking.)

The columns' white capitals give them a distinctive "Byzantine" look. They're inverted trapezoids with intricate filigree acanthus-leaf intertwining and Ionic scrolls. They support tall Byzantine horseshoe-shaped arches. If you look closely at the capitals, you can find circular medallions with the initials (in Greek) of Justinian and his wife Theodora.

About 10 yards farther, beyond the columns, is a square pillar partly covered with metal plating—the quirky, "perspiring," and purportedly miraculous ❾ **Wishing Column.** According to legend, ever since St. Gregory the Miracle Worker miraculously appeared here, the column has "wept" holy water reported to cure ailments from cataracts to infertility.

How does it work? Put your thumb in the hole, make a complete 360-degree circle (clockwise), and if it comes out feeling damp, your prayer will be answered. Millions of true believers have polished the column over the years.

Want another legend? When the Ottomans conquered Constantinople, Sultan Mehmet II knelt here and wished that his newly christened mosque actually faced Mecca. An angel appeared, stuck his thumb in the column, and started to tu-u-u-urn the entire building. Unfortunately, he was spotted by a mortal and disappeared—leaving the mihrab slightly off-center as it remains today.

Before moving on, look midway up the nave and find our next destination—the **upper galleries.** This balcony overlooks the interior of the church, and from there we'll see some of the church's (and the world's) finest mosaics. They're so well preserved thanks in part to two Swiss architects hired by a 19th-century sultan to do a major renovation of Hagia Sophia. The Fossati brothers rediscovered many of the original Christian mosaics the Muslims had plastered over. They cleaned, repaired, and catalogued them, then carefully covered them up again, preserving them until they were fully revealed in the 20th century.

• *To get to the upper galleries, return to the inner narthex. (There's a convenient door next to the Wishing Column.) Once in the narthex, turn right. At the end of the narthex, climb the long, stone-paved ramp to the upper galleries. Why a ramp? Because those of exalted rank were either carried up by their servants, or rode up on horseback. As you step off the ramp, you enter the upper gallery. Keeping to the right, start in the...*

⑳ West Gallery

Take in the great view of the vast nave, with the apse at the far end. In Byzantine days, women attended church services in this hallway, while men worshipped below.

The prime viewing spot was reserved for the empress. You'll find it midway along the hall next to the railing, marked by a green marble circle in the pavement—the **empress' loge.** Here between the green columns the empress would sit on her throne to watch services, attended by her entourage.

Before moving on, check out a few other West Gallery sights. From here you get a close-up view of the massive medallions with Arabic script, made of linden wood and hung with sturdy chains. Find some graffiti carved onto the balcony railing. And admire the standing chandeliers lining the hall, with their green marble columns, nice capitals, and ironwork lamps.

• *Continue through the West Gallery, turning left into the...*

Hagia Sophia Upper Gallery

⓴ West Gallery & View of Nave
⓱ Gate of Heaven & Hell
⓲ Deesis Mosaic
⓳ Tomb of Doge Enrico Dandolo
⓴ Viking Graffito
㉕ Emperor John II Komnenos Mosaic
㉖ Empress Zoe Mosaic

HAGIA SOPHIA

South Gallery

You'll reach a marble partition, known as the ⓱ **Gate of Heaven and Hell**. Made in Justinian's day, it's cleverly carved to look like the kind of paneling you'd find on an expensive set of wooden doors, right down to the ring-shaped "door handle." This partition marked off a sacred room reserved for the emperor, patriarch, and other high-ups, who met here for the most important council meetings. In 1166, a famous synod of dignitaries from across the Christian world met here to try to settle one of Christianity's most nettlesome questions: whether Jesus Christ was a man, a God, or some combination of both. (They failed, and the debate still goes on.) By the way, the frescoes on the ceiling that look ancient? They're actually copies of ancient designs—another work by those clever Swiss Fossati brothers.

Pass through the marble door and immediately look right, near the first window, to find the ⓲ **Deesis Mosaic.** The mosaic (from the late-1200s) is quite damaged, but still has its most important feature: the expressive faces. This mosaic has

been called (with a bit of hype) the most important work of art of the entire Middle Ages. Its trailblazing realism inspired Renaissance painting.

The theme of the mosaic was a common one in Orthodox churches, but the artist charged it with tender human emotion rarely seen before. It shows Christ Pantocrator, with Mary and John the Baptist pleading with him to go easy on sinful humanity. Mary's and John's heads tilt slightly toward Christ, breaking the stiff iconic mold of earlier works. Their eyes are sad as they reflect on Man's pitiful state. Christ is a dispassionate judge, seeing all. (Including you. His eyes follow you as you move.)

Get up close. See how minuscule and finely cut the glass and stone pieces are. Christ's face alone is composed of literally thousands of tiny bits. If the surface looks rough, it was done intentionally, so the jagged pieces would reflect the light. As you walk around, Christ's golden robe sparkles and the faces come alive.

The mosaic has elements of proto-Renaissance realism. Christ, Mary, and John are larger than life but fully human. Unlike traditional icons who stand stiffly staring straight ahead, Mary and John are depicted at the harder-to-draw three-quarter profile. Less-accomplished mosaics have heavy coloring-book outlines filled in with single blocks of color. This mosaic uses subtle gradations of color. Christ's pink cheeks blend seamlessly into light flesh-tones. His nose is a patchwork of light and dark, capturing the shadows cast by a three-dimensional object. Two centuries before the Renaissance, this innovative artist was building figures with tiny mosaic pieces the way a painter creates with dabs of paint.

The soft faces of Mary, John, and Jesus say it all. They communicate a message of divine compassion—not through abstract symbolism but by touching the viewer's heart.

Nearby, find a couple of reminders of the many cultural strands that went into Byzantium's diverse history. On the floor, a panel marks the ㉓ Tomb of Doge Enrico Dandolo, the Venetian crusader who sacked Constantinople in 1204 and turned Hagia Sophia into a Catholic church. (Coincidentally, the Deesis Mosaic was created to celebrate the church's rededication to Orthodox.) Atop the balcony railing, find a bit of ㉔ Viking graffito, probably carved by a bored Norse mercenary working as a bodyguard for the Byzantine emperor. It reads: "Halvdan was here."

• *To complete this tour, continue to the far end of the South Gallery, where you run into two mosaics side by side depicting saints and emperors.*

East Gallery

The mosaic on the right (12th century) depicts ㉕ **Emperor John II Komnenos** and his wife Irene flanking a Madonna-and-Child. Christ extends one hand in blessing while holding a scroll in his other. The purpose of this mosaic was to announce that this church

HAGIA SOPHIA

was brought to you by generous donors like these. The emperor offers Christ a bag of money and the empress a scroll.

Enjoy the mosaic's shimmering details. Emperor John wears the traditional jeweled robe and the inlaid crown with pearl tassels dangling down. Nicknamed "The Moor," John has a dark beard, while his Hungarian wife Irene has long red braids.

Finish with the mosaic (11th century) on the left—the ㉖ **Empress Zoe Mosaic.** Zoe stands with her husband Emperor Constantine IX, as they present their donations to Christ Pantocrator on his cushioned throne. The couple's robes and crowns are even more stunning than in the previous mosaic.

Note the inscription above the emperor's head: "Sovereign of Romans, Constantine Monomachus." And the empress is identified as "Zoe, the most pious Augusta."

In fact, Zoe was famously glamorous, ambitious, and ruthless. She married for power, exiled her own sister, and climbed the ranks as her exes died under mysterious circumstances. Constantine was husband number three. Look closely at his inscription. You can see that parts were erased, then clumsily restored in a different font. It's clear that, by the time husband #3 came along, it was easier to change his inscription than his face. And Zoe made sure that, despite being almost 70 years old, her face depicted all her youthful beauty, preserved here for eternity.

Hagia Sophia's Legacy

This is a good place to end our tour—with (literally) iconic and timeless images. Here in Hagia Sophia, Byzantium seems to live on forever. Take a final look over the structure below and reflect on its long history: built by Roman Emperor Justinian I, embellished by his Byzantine successors, given a makeover by Islamic sultans, and renovated in modern times—first as a museum and more recently as a mosque. Hagia Sophia's legacy is long: its groundbreaking architecture of domes and half-domes inspired countless buildings, from Orthodox churches to Muslim mosques.

It's clear that this great building does not belong to any single faith or culture, but to the whole world. It stands as a symbol of how many cultural strands can weave together into something beautiful. Here in Hagia Sophia, the golden glory of 2,000 years still shines like a kind of..."Holy Wisdom."

• *To return to the ground floor and the exit, retrace your steps around the gallery to where you entered, and follow* exit *signs. The route takes you back downstairs to the inner narthex. Following* exit *signs, you'll emerge into the light of day past a nice 18th-century Ottoman fountain.*

HAGIA SOPHIA

TOPKAPI PALACE TOUR

Topkapı Sarayi

This sprawling palace was the lavish home and center of power for the Ottoman sultans for 400 years. It was the de facto capital of Islam and the heart of an empire that spanned three continents—from Persia to Africa, and from Mecca to Vienna.

Today, the Topkapı (tohp-kah-puh)—expanded over the centuries in the architectural style du jour—is a vast complex of buildings in a walled, parklike setting. You'll wander through colorfully tiled rooms and opulent pleasure pavilions amid gardens and reflecting pools. Though bare of furnishings, the buildings still echo with splendor. A highlight is the sultan's private residence—the Harem—with some of the most magnificent rooms.

In addition, the Topkapı has several mini museums of the sultans' personal collections: stunning jewels, holy Islamic relics, ceremonial swords, and priceless dinnerware.

Now, let's explore the Topkapı's eclectic sights. We'll see where sultans were crowned and harem concubines lounged. We'll see a jewel-encrusted dagger and strands of Muhammad's beard. Along the way, we'll learn about the Ottoman world and the lifestyle of its rulers, even delving into their most intimate secrets. (Yes, I mean s-e-x.)

Orientation

Cost: Palace-100 TL, 135 TL for Fast-Track ticket; Harem-70 TL.

Hours: Wed-Mon 9:00-19:00, until 17:00 off-season, closed Tue, last entry two hours before closing (one hour in off-season), exhibits may begin closing one hour earlier.

Information: +90 212 512 0480, www.millisaraylar.gov.tr.

Renovation: Parts of the Harem and Imperial Treasury may be undergoing renovation, and other sections may close without notice.

Crowd-Beating Tips: A Museum Pass (see page 40) allows you to skip the ticket line and head directly to the security check. Or get a Fast-Track ticket, which comes with shorter security lines (sold from booth near regular ticket windows). You can also save time by buying regular tickets from machines in the kiosk next to the ticket booth (credit cards only).

If you arrive at or before the 9:00 opening time, you'll have to wait outside the Imperial Gate; to avoid the early crowd, arrive at 10:00. Since the museum is closed on Tuesdays, Mondays and Wednesdays tend to be more crowded.

Dress Code: Women may need to cover their heads, knees, and shoulders to enter the Treasury's room of Holy Relics.

Getting There: Topkapı Palace is in the Old Town's Sultanahmet district. To trace these directions, see the "Old Town Sights" map on page 46.

From the **Sultanahmet tram stop,** cross the street and face Hagia Sophia, with the Blue Mosque at your back. Walk around the right (eastern) side of Hagia Sophia, following brown signs for *Topkapı Sarayı* to reach the Imperial Gate and the start of this tour.

From the **Gülhane tram stop,** go in the gate on the side wall of the Topkapı complex, and bear right up the hill. You'll pass the Istanbul Archaeological Museums on your left, then emerge into the First Courtyard (with the Gate of Salutation and inner Topkapı complex to your left), joining this tour at our second stop.

Getting In: The outer Topkapı complex is free to enter; tickets are required to access the inner part (the palace museum and Harem). Palace tickets are sold at windows to the right as you face the Gate of Salutation (note some windows are reserved for guides/groups); the Harem requires a separate ticket (sold at a booth in the courtyard outside the Harem entrance).

Tours: A 45-TL audioguide covers both the palace and the Harem. While the information is skimpy, the narration makes it easy to meaningfully navigate the sight. The rental booth is in the second courtyard, just past the ticket turnstile.

Length of This Tour: Two hours for the palace, plus another hour if you visit the Harem.

Services: A good gift shop is near the ticket booth, just outside the Gate of Salutation. The bookstore is just inside past the security checkpoint, to your left before the exit. There is no cloakroom.

Eating: At the far end of the palace (in the Mecidiye Pavilion in the Fourth Courtyard), the **$$$ Konyalı** restaurant serves

Turkish fare in two sections: sit-down (slow service) or self-service (can be crowded). It's expensive but convenient, with sweeping views across the Bosphorus. Drinks and snacks are sold next to the Harem entrance, and at a little café in the Palace Kitchens' inner courtyard.

Starring: The jewel-encrusted Topkapı Dagger, an 86-carat diamond, some remarkable Muslim relics from Mecca, the famous Harem of the sultan (minus the dancing girls), and several centuries of Ottoman history.

The Tour Begins

• *We'll start at the impressive Imperial Gate in the palace's outer wall (opposite Hagia Sophia's northeast corner). To locate the gate, see the "Old Town Sights" map on page 46.*

❶ Imperial Gate

This massive gate was the palace's main entrance. After Sultan Mehmet II took Constantinople in 1453, he solidified his conquest

by building the Topkapı Palace (c. 1460-78). The palace was protected by this imposing wall with guard towers and a crenellated sentry walk. Mehmet inherited the wall from the Byzantines. For a thousand years, it had famously rebuffed all invaders...until the arrival of Mehmet II, known as "the Conqueror."

At first, Mehmet II's new palace was more of a fortress—"Topkapı" means "cannon gate." It sat at a strategic location, overlooking the Sea of Marmara, the Bosphorus, and the Golden Horn. This imposing wall is just the first of several layers of defense we'll pass through as we make our way into the sultan's intimate realm.

Above the gate's door is a medallion with Mehmet II's imperial signature, or *tuğra*. Just above that, an Arabic inscription proclaims: "By the grace of Allah, the foundations of this great castle were laid by Sultan Mehmet, conqueror of Constantinople. May Allah exalt his residence above the brightest stars of the heavens."

Before going in, survey the impressive structures nearby. Check out Hagia Sophia's towering minarets and bunker-like buttresses, and the 18th-century **Ahmet III fountain**—one of the best examples of the city's many public fountains. It has water taps on each side, flanked with mihrab-like niches, and is decorated with colorful tiles, gilded designs, and calligraphy—including the

phrase, "Turn the tap with the name of Allah, the Protector, and the Merciful. Drink the water, and say a prayer for Sultan Ahmet."

• *Pass through the gate into the palace's outer grounds, as we make our way—layer by layer—into the sultan's private world.*

❷ First Courtyard

Stroll through this vast park-like area, known as the First Courtyard. In Ottoman days, the First Courtyard was the buffer zone between the city and the inner palace. Various buildings (mostly gone now) housed the royal mint, government offices, and soldiers' barracks. The courtyard was generally open to the public (if they passed security at the Imperial Gate) from sunrise to sunset.

On the left is the domed church of **Hagia Irene.** This venerable Christian church—dating back to the very foundations of Constantinople—was used by the sultans as a storeroom and arsenal. (It's still a fascinating sight worth a visit; for details see page 51.)

• *Along the right side of the courtyard is the ticket office for the Topkapı Palace. Once you have your ticket, continue toward the far end and face the intimidating gate with twin pointed towers, the...*

Gate of Salutation: Reminiscent of a European castle, this gate—the entrance to the inner palace—was an effective defensive structure. If the palace were under attack, soldiers could man the crenellations and shoot arrows through the slits in the walls. Above the doorway you'll see a sultan's signature and the phrase, "There is no other God but Allah, and Muhammad is his prophet."

This gate also served as the palace's execution site. After slicing off a criminal's head, the executioner would wash his hands and blade at the **Executioner's Fountain**—the white marble niche embedded in the wall to the right.

• *With that cheerful thought, let's enter. In Ottoman days, everyone except the sultan had to leave their horse here and walk in. So tie up your horse, get ready to present your Topkapı ticket or Museum Pass, and enter through the gate's iron doors.*

TOPKAPI PALACE

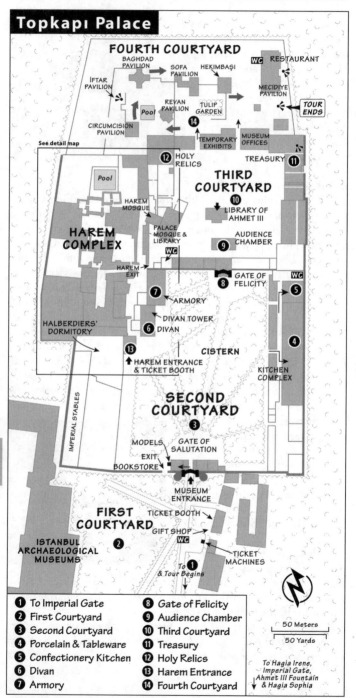

Topkapı Palace

FOURTH COURTYARD

BAGHDAD PAVILION
SOFA PAVILION
HEKİMBAŞI
IFTAR PAVILION
REVAN PAVILION
TULIP GARDEN
CIRCUMCISION PAVILION
Pool
14
RESTAURANT
WC
MECIDIYE PAVILION
TOUR ENDS
TEMPORARY EXHIBITS
MUSEUM OFFICES

See detail map

12 HOLY RELICS
Pool
HAREM MOSQUE
PALACE MOSQUE & LIBRARY
HAREM COMPLEX
HAREM EXIT
HAREM ENTRANCE & TICKET BOOTH
13
HALBERDIERS' DORMITORY
ARMORY **7**
DIVAN TOWER
DIVAN **6**
TREASURY **11**
THIRD COURTYARD
10 LIBRARY OF AHMET III
AUDIENCE CHAMBER **9**
WC
8 GATE OF FELICITY
WC
5
4
KITCHEN COMPLEX
CISTERN

IMPERIAL STABLES

SECOND COURTYARD
3
MODELS
EXIT BOOKSTORE
GATE OF SALUTATION
MUSEUM ENTRANCE

FIRST COURTYARD
TICKET BOOTH
GIFT SHOP
WC
TICKET MACHINES
ISTANBUL ARCHAEOLOGICAL MUSEUMS
2
1 To Imperial Gate & Tour Begins

To Hagia Irene, Imperial Gate, Ahmet III Fountain & Hagia Sophia

1. To Imperial Gate
2. First Courtyard
3. Second Courtyard
4. Porcelain & Tableware
5. Confectionery Kitchen
6. Divan
7. Armory
8. Gate of Felicity
9. Audience Chamber
10. Third Courtyard
11. Treasury
12. Holy Relics
13. Harem Entrance
14. Fourth Courtyard

50 Meters
50 Yards

TOPKAPI PALACE

Pass through security and scan your ticket at the turnstile. You're now in the palace's...

❸ Second Courtyard

This courtyard was the palace's workaday center.

Get oriented. Start with the two **models** to the left of the entrance. One shows the entire rectangular palace complex, atop a bluff, surrounded by stone walls and its "walls" of water—the Sea of Marmara and Golden Horn. (A pennant in the model marks where you are—at the two-steepled gate.) The place is huge! It originally covered some 173 acres (or 75 million square feet, the size of two Disneylands) and consisted of hundreds of buildings, courtyards, gardens, and fields. You can clearly see the various layers of defense: a series of walls enclosing four courtyards, each one more secure and private.

The second model is a close-up of the central core of the palace, which we're about to tour. (Find that two-steepled gate to get oriented.) On the wall nearby, **maps** show the Ottoman world—a vast empire spanning Europe, Asia, and Africa—all ruled from this spot.

Now take a few steps in and survey the expansive **Second Courtyard**—150 yards long and 120 yards wide, enclosed by marble columns. Unlike towering palaces elsewhere in the world, the Topkapı Palace is a low-rise structure of one- or two-story buildings. It grew over the centuries, as each sultan added on, in a funhouse of architectural styles. This particular courtyard took shape under Süleyman the Magnificent (c. 1520-60), who helped turn Mehmet II's stark fortress into a luxurious home.

On the left side of the courtyard rises the **Divan Tower.** Its main purpose was symbolic. The tower was tall enough to be visible all over the city, even to ships at sea, proclaiming to all that their sultan was here, bringing justice to the world. At the tower's base are some sights we'll see shortly: the Divan, Armory, and Harem. On the right side of the courtyard, looking like an ocean liner with smokestacks, is the palace kitchen.

The Second Courtyard was the beating heart of the palace. Typical of all Islamic residences, everyday life revolved around this cool, tree-lined space. The Topkapı Palace was a self-contained city with a population of 5,000. It had its own water supply (a cistern beneath your feet), apartments, mosques, schools, a hospital, a small army of soldiers, and an army of workers.

Mentally replace tourists with turbaned Ottomans and imagine this courtyard buzzing with activity. Bakers carry sacks of flour to the kitchen. Eunuchs guard the Harem entrance. The sultan's viziers (advisers) scurry to the Divan for an important meeting of the imperial council. Long-haired porters carry feed to the nearby stables. Red-jacketed janissaries (the sultan's elite bodyguards) patrol the grounds. And wandering about everywhere are tame peacocks.

To feed them all, the palace had the enormous, chimney-topped royal kitchen (on your right).

Kitchen Complex

The 190-yard-long royal kitchen complex covers the entire length of the courtyard. Foundations of the complex date back to the late 1400s, the reign of Mehmet II. It was later redesigned by the great royal architect Mimar Sinan (see page 209), who turned to his signature architectural element: the dome. Sinan built a row of 10 separate chambers, each with an elevated dome and a tall chimney for ventilation. Some chambers fed workers, some the harem. Others turned out specialty foods, from pastries to drinks to desserts. Most important of all, they created the delicacies enjoyed by the sultan and his family.

• *Step through the vaulted entryway at the right of the courtyard into a long, narrow courtyard. A few steps to the right and through the first door on the left, enter the kitchen to find an impressive collection of kitchenware, glass, and porcelain.*

❹ Porcelain and Tableware

Imagine dozens of chefs, cooks, and assistants working around the clock to feed thousands every day. Kitchens were simple, designed to be extremely functional and to operate with precision. Gaze up at Sinan's innovative dome and chimney.

This part of the complex was recently renovated to reflect the royal kitchen's former glory. Many of the original architectural elements are missing, but enough remain to give you an idea of the layout.

Work your way counterclockwise around

the collection, with copper objects from a 2,000-piece collection, and 800 years of Chinese porcelain (covering four dynasties: Sung, Yuan, Ming, and Ching). We'll focus on the Chinese porcelain, which had a huge impact on the Topkapı Palace's interior decor.

Why is there so much Chinese porcelain in Turkey? The sultans insisted on eating from the finest dinnerware in the world—and that meant Chinese. Ottoman merchants trekked the Silk Road to China, returning with camels bearing precious porcelain. More than 10,000 pieces survive (about half of the sultan's original stash), and a few dozen are on display here.

From the Sung and Yuan periods come green-hued plates, pitchers, and cups fired with the glaze called celadon. Suspicious sultans especially loved celadon because the dishes supposedly changed color if the food had been poisoned. Dragon and fish designs were popular, as well as plant and geometric patterns. The 700-year-old Yuan dynasty pieces are especially cherished, valued today in the millions.

The highlights of the collection are the exquisite blue-and-white pieces from the Ming Dynasty (1368-1644). Note that, besides the traditional Chinese designs, many were made-to-order for the Ottoman sultan, with Arabic script, fit-for-Islam abstract patterns, and excerpts from the Quran. Ming-era porcelain was enormously influential in the 1500s, when global trade was first coming into its own. In Europe, Chinese technology inspired blue-and-white Delftware, manufactured in Holland. In Turkey, porcelain factories in İznik and Kütahya began cranking out knock-off Chinese vases and wall tiles. Throughout the palace, you'll see splendid Chinese-inspired tilework.

• *Return to the courtyard, turn right and enter the last door on the right to the...*

❺ Confectionery Kitchen

The Confectionery Kitchen displays earthenware containers, massive cauldrons, stone mortars, purpose-built counters, and part of an original drain.

The round stone block in the connecting chamber was used for grinding herbs. This chamber was where they made desserts, such as halva, a soft candy made with sesame oil and tahini. It's also where the royal doctor concocted the "sultan's paste," an herbal mix famed for its strength-boosting (and aphrodisiac) qualities.

• *More rooms hold fine glasswork, utensils, and dinnerware (including silver items and European-style porcelain, which became trendy in the late empire), and an entire section dedicated to the coffee culture through centuries...but let's move on.*

Exit back into the Second Courtyard. Straight across the courtyard is our next stop—the Divan.

What's for Dinner?

The palace's kitchens didn't feed just the sultan. They routinely dished up chow for thousands of people—up to 10,000 for religious festivals and when the hungry janissaries (soldiers) had their payday. In the 18th century, the royal kitchens employed up to 20 chefs, 200 cooks and their assistants, 100 specialized cooks, another 100 dessert experts...and more than 300 busboys to clean up the mess. And this doesn't even count the bakers. As the head of such an immense staff, the master of the kitchens was as important as a vizier.

Sultans spent fortunes on buffet-style receptions for foreign envoys, weddings, circumcisions, and open-invitation

public feasts on important religious days (such as the end of Ramadan). The circumcision gathering for one crown prince lasted several days. Each evening, the menu included rice pilaf for a thousand people and 20 whole roasted cows.

The catering complex had separate kitchens, each run by a specialized chef. For example, the Has (royal) Kitchen cooked only for viziers, Harem residents, and staff. There were two meals a day: midmorning and before sunset. Food was distributed by boys carrying large trays. The most used ingredients in the kitchens were butter, saffron, and sugar.

The sultan's food was prepared in a special kitchen. His personal master chef and 12 cooks were carefully chosen from among the best. The master chef was also the caretaker of the fine porcelain used by the sultan and viziers of the Divan, and for the banquets for visiting envoys and ambassadors. When the sultan went on a military campaign, his cooks went with him—occasionally, they'd grab a sword and join the battle.

Mealtime etiquette changed through time, but until the 19th century, there were still no dining tables at the palace. The sultan sat cross-legged in front of a large tray and usually ate alone. Food and beverages were served in celadon-colored porcelain ware and metal cups. A typical sultan's dinner menu include mutton (steamed or kebab), a variety of grilled meats (mutton, quail, etc.), and baklava or rice pudding. The sultan didn't drink water during the meal, but instead sipped from a large bowl of chilled, stewed fruit juice (şerbet), as well as Turkish coffee. To set the proper mood, the room was filled with aloe-wood incense, and the sultan was entertained by mute dwarfs.

❻ Divan

Pass through the Divan's golden-grilled entrance and make your way to the far-left room. Until the 1700s, the entire Ottoman Empire was ruled from these three adjoining rooms. The first room was

the most important. The sultan and his viziers met here four times a week to dictate the laws that governed the lives of 30 million people. Laws were debated in this first room, written down in the next, and archived in the last.

Another space designed by the great imperial architect Sinan, a century later this room was slathered with the frilly Rococo style we see today. Picture the scene: Viziers from across the empire gather, dressed in long robes and tall conehead hats. They take their seats on the cushions that ring the room—that is, the "divan" (which gave us our English word for a long, low, backless couch against the wall). They're surrounded by blue-and-white tiles from İznik, beneath a dome of the heavens and a dangling golden ball symbolizing the earth the sultan ruled.

The imperial congress begins when the grand vizier—the empire's prime minister—arrives. He takes his place on the central cushion, directly opposite the entrance.

Where is the sultan? He stands out of sight behind the golden-grilled window above the grand vizier—called "the Eye." Though the empire was an absolute monarchy, sultans wanted to project an image of being above earthly squabbles. So from here, he can simultaneously maintain an imperial distance, while listening in, whispering instructions, and literally looking over his vizier's shoulder.

• *The Harem entrance is just around the corner—consider visiting it now if there's no line. Otherwise, let's look at how the sultan's transcontinental empire was kept in order—by force. Head a few doors down, to the...*

❼ Armory

The sultans saw themselves as heirs to a centuries-old line of warriors. This collection of their personal weaponry includes medieval swords, pikes, and chain mail, plus early rifles and pistols. Touring the room counterclockwise, keep an eye out for these exhibits:

The huge swords were captured during the Ottoman invasion of Hungary that brought the Islamic world right to the gates of Vienna. Early rifles were state-of-the-art weaponry. Find the famed sword of Mehmet II, with its inscription along the blade in golden Arabic letters: "Praise be to Allah who blesses the faithful with bright, shining words and sharp, shining swords." The wavy sword belonged to Mehmet's son and successor, Bayazit II, who solidified his father's conquest and helped build the city we see today. Find several yatağans—the lightweight, curved swords

carried by the janissaries (see sidebar). The ornate black-and-gold chain-mail suit belonged to Mustafa III, the 18th-century sultan who was more poet than warrior, epitomizing the once-fierce empire's slow decline.

• *Head back out into the Second Courtyard and stand before the porch-covered gate at the far end.*

❽ Gate of Felicity

Located roughly in the middle of the Topkapı complex, this gate was its symbolic center, dividing the palace's public area from the

sultan's private realm. This is where the reclusive ruler met his adoring fans, in elaborately choreographed ceremonies.

The striking gate, with a wide roof supported by four delicate columns, is topped with a dome and ornamented with golden frills and landscape paintings. It made a dramatic

backdrop for the empire's most important events, including sultans' funerals, Ramadan festivities, proclamations of war, and visits by foreign ambassadors.

The most important ceremony of all was the coronation of a new sultan. The throne was set in front of the gate, atop a large carpet, framed by the porch. Palace inhabitants gathered in the courtyard. Hundreds of red-jacketed janissaries lined the walls, standing like statues. Rows of dark-skinned eunuchs in golden silks and viziers in turbans bowed as one toward their sultan-to-be. Ambassadors and imams (prayer leaders) waited patiently for their turn to kiss the hem of his caftan. Then the sultan-to-be would take his seat on the throne and be inaugurated, not with a crown, but with something more befitting of a warrior—a sword.

The Janissaries

The sultans' highly trained personal army of troops and body-guards were known as janissaries.

As the Ottoman empire grew, they needed a standing army. Beginning in the 14th century, the empire instituted a kind of "draft" to recruit soldiers (financed through taxes on large landowners). By the time Mehmet II (the Conqueror) vanquished Constantinople, his hodgepodge army was not enough to control the vast empire. So, he incorporated defeated armies—mostly Christians—into his own elite corps. From then on, Christian boys were taken from their families, converted to Islam, and raised to be soldiers. The best and brightest were trained at schools in the Topkapı Palace.

Though it sounds cruel, being a janissary had its advantages. Janissaries were not slaves but professional soldiers—paid a salary even in peacetime. A janissary's parents became exempt from taxes. Graduates of the Topkapı's janissary school often went on to greater things—as generals, keepers of the treasury, or even becoming viziers.

The janissaries became the backbone of Ottoman military might. In later years, they were often more powerful than the sultan himself. If angered, they were known to launch coups and dethrone or literally strangle a sultan. And because they tended to prefer the status quo, they often stood in the way of much-needed reforms. In fact, many historians claim that one cause of the empire's decline was the very thing that had made it great—the janissaries.

• *Let's continue into the next layer of the palace—the private realm of the sultan. Approach the Gate of Felicity, and pause under the porch, at the hole in the pavement. Whenever the empire went to war, the centuries-old Battle Flag of Muhammad—black with a white crescent—was unfurled here.*

Continue through the gate. The building straight ahead is called the...

❾ Audience Chamber

To project an aura of divine majesty, sultans rarely spoke or appeared in public. Instead, the sultan received visitors in this room, designed to impress.

Imagine being a foreign ambassador. You walk over carpets that lead the way through the Gate of Felicity and on to the Audience Chamber, passing the speckled-marble columns that support the striped arches below

TOPKAPI PALACE

the colorful roof. You notice the sultans' golden signatures flanking the door, and Quran verses above. (To the right, a helpful illustration of a sultan receiving a foreign envoy helps today's visitors envision the scene.)

Now you step inside to greet the sultan. His "throne" is a plush couch under a canopy. There he sits, cross-legged, warming himself by the cone-chimney furnace, under an ornate Rococo ceiling. Elaborately brocaded and jeweled 16th-century silk rugs serve as "throne covers," cushioning his royal tush.

As a visitor, you're required to stand and wait in silence. Highly educated deaf-mute eunuchs, adept at communicating nonverbally, stand in attendance. Finally, when it pleases the sultan, you're signaled to approach the throne. You kneel and bow, touching your head to the floor. Then you rise, present your gifts, and heap praise on the mighty sultan.

• *Exit out the far end of the Audience Chamber, where you find yourself in the...*

⓾ Third Courtyard

This was the private domain of the sultan, his family, and his closest courtiers. It's a kind of Islamic oasis but on a sultan-size scale, with exotic trees and landscaping, surrounded by a marble colonnade. The big white-domed building in the middle is the Library of Ahmet III, which held the sultan's extensive book collection. Enter on the far side to see its fancy doors inlaid with mother-of-pearl.

• *Now let's see some of the sultans' most cherished possessions. Start in the Third Courtyard's far-right corner, to enter the...*

⓫ Treasury

Browsing these four rooms (just follow the signs on a one-way route), you'll enjoy countless extravagant objects—the "crown jewels" of the Ottoman Empire. Besides ceremonial regalia, the collection holds many gifts from foreign rulers to the sultans, from gem-studded rifles to gold-filigree ice-cream bowls.

First Room: Start with the imperial thrones. Each sultan chose his own design: The throne of Ahmet I is essentially an elaborate wooden chair with a built-in canopy. Another throne is covered with gold leaf, with huge dangling emeralds. The ebony-and-ivory throne belonged to Süleyman the Magnificent. Another throne—a gift from Persia's Nādir Shāh—is essentially a backless couch with an accompanying footrest, or "ottoman."

• *Backtrack and follow signs to the second room, with jade and jewels. Then continue to the...*

Third Room: By the fireplace, find a gold-ruby-and-turquoise helmet (right), and (to the left) two 100-pound solid-gold candle-sticks—brought here from Muham- mad's tomb in Medina by Ottomans retreating during World War I.

• *Your route continues across a balcony with sweeping views of the Bosphorus Strait, Bosphorus Bridge, Asian Istanbul, and the Sea of Marmara.*

Fourth Room: In the far-right corner (past a bowl of emeralds and quartz) is the famous **Topkapı Dagger.** Its hilt is studded with three golf-ball-size emeralds surrounded by diamonds and gold. Another octagonal emerald at the top flips up to reveal a small clock, decorated with more diamonds. This magnificent dagger was cre- ated here in the palace workshop in 1747 for Sultan Mahmut I. Its beauty inspired a 1964 Hollywood heist movie *(Topkapi)* about the attempted theft of this treasure.

Nearby is the 86-carat pear-shaped **Spoonmaker's Dia- mond**—one of the biggest diamonds in the world. It's nestled in- side a double row of 49 more tiny diamonds. According to legend, a poor man found this diamond in the dirt and traded it to a spoon- maker for a few paltry spoons, who in turn sold it to a jeweler for only a few coins.

Finally, as you leave, find the gilded wood cradle that once rocked a newborn crown prince when he was presented to his proud daddy.

• *As stunning as these imperial treasures are, there's one more collection that the sultans considered infinitely more precious—the Holy Relics. To get there, continue circling the courtyard counterclockwise.*

Before entering the Relics rooms, look to the left to find the sultan's **Funeral Platform.** *When a sultan died, his body was washed, wrapped in a white shroud, and laid on this marble slab for viewing at his fu- neral. There are platforms like this in virtually every mosque, but only the sultan was laid next to the most treasured objects in Islam, the...*

⓬ Holy Relics

These are some of the most holy treasures of the Muslim faith. The collection began with Egyptian booty brought here by Sultan Selim I in 1517; his successors added more relics over the years.

This room of sacred objects has become a kind of pilgrimage spot for devout Muslims from all over the world. You'll see many people praying with their hands open. Read the rules on the sign next to the entrance, and be respectful.

• *Now, enter through the impressive door whose inscription proclaims: "There is no other God but Allah, and Muhammad is his Prophet."*

The central room is dedicated to relics of the Kaaba—the big black cube-shaped building in Mecca that Muslims make a once-in-a-lifetime pilgrimage to visit. You may see objects like the building's keys, locks, door, and fancy rain gutter. The most precious relic is a golden case made to hold the famed **Black Stone**—the rock that descended from heaven and that Muhammad himself placed on the corner of the Kaaba. (The stone itself is still in Mecca, where pilgrims reverently kiss it.)

The room to the left displays **relics of the prophets**. The Muslim faith honors holy people of several religions—Judaic, Christian, and Muslim—all considered messengers of God. You may see Moses' staff, which he used to part the Red Sea. The granite cooking pot belonged to Abraham, the founding father of both the Israeli people and Muhammad's forebears. There's the turban of Joseph, the sword of giant-slayer David, and bone fragments of Jesus' cousin John the Baptist. (You may be skeptical about these strangely well-preserved objects, but step back a second and observe the "Wow-there-it-is" reactions of some of your fellow visitors.)

Finally, the room on the opposite side is dedicated to God's next great messenger, "the last prophet," **Muhammad.** In the year 610, this humble Arabian businessman was visited by the angel Gabriel, who dictated the Quran to him and inspired him to dedicate his life to the one God, Allah. Objects on display here help make this larger-than-life figure seem more human. You might see Muhammad's footprint (pressed into clay), his sandals, some hair from his beard (encased in crystal), and even a piece of his tooth. His sword and bow are from the years when he had to go to war against opponents of his new faith. In an adjoining room, you can glimpse a gold chest containing his mantle. There are also relics from Muhammad's well-known successors, like swords of the caliphs (similar to the early Christian apostles who carried on after Jesus) and the cape of Muhammad's beloved daughter Fatima.

As you survey these relics, you can hear a man chanting over a microphone. The Quran is read 24/7, 365 days a year—just as imams have done here nonstop for more than 400 years.

• *Now that you have a sense of the complex personality of the sultans, it's time to see where they actually lived—the* **Harem.** *Take note of where you are right now—the Third Courtyard.*

This is where you'll end up again after your Harem visit.

Start by backtracking to the Harem entrance: Remember, it's in the Second Courtyard, near the Divan, at the base of the Divan Tower. You'll need to buy a separate Harem ticket at the entrance.

If you have extra time, consider a quick detour through the **Dormitory of the Halberdiers with Tresses** *(guards and servants), to the left of the Harem entrance, covered by the same ticket.*

Now enter the...

⓭ Harem

This part of the palace is where the sultan actually lived. He shared these 400 rooms with his wives, children, concubines, mom, and extended family—plus the hundreds of workers who waited on them. The Harem was a world unto itself, with bedrooms, dining rooms, bathrooms, schools for the kids, doctors' offices, and mosques. On our route, we'll see about 20 grand rooms, with exquisite decoration—soaring domes, bubbling fountains, and colorful tiled walls.

• *Go through the turnstile, and walk straight ahead along the inlaid-pebble path, until you emerge in the long, narrow...*

Ⓐ Courtyard of the Eunuchs

"Harem" literally means forbidden place. The Harem's entrance came with a strict security check: All visitors' credentials were checked closely. The women could come and go—to shop, picnic, or socialize—but only in draped carriages and under close supervision.

The only men allowed here were the palace guards—a crack squad of 100 men dubbed the Black Eunuchs. Their ranks were filled with African slaves who'd been castrated to discourage dalliances with the sultan's women. They were educated in Turkish, converted to Islam, and taught the finer elements of court life. Their chief was one of the most powerful men in the palace. (There were also White Eunuchs who guarded the

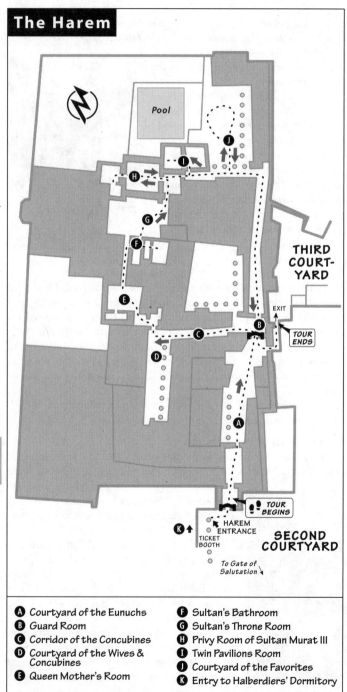

The Harem

TOPKAPI PALACE

A Courtyard of the Eunuchs
B Guard Room
C Corridor of the Concubines
D Courtyard of the Wives & Concubines
E Queen Mother's Room
F Sultan's Bathroom
G Sultan's Throne Room
H Privy Room of Sultan Murat III
I Twin Pavilions Room
J Courtyard of the Favorites
K Entry to Halberdiers' Dormitory

palace school and taught classes for future viziers and up-and-coming janissaries.)

The Black Eunuchs lived in the rooms along the left side of this courtyard. The farthest room (look through the windows to see some mannequins) was the posh private apartment of the chief eunuch.

At the far end of the courtyard, enter the small ❽ **Guard Room.** From this security checkpoint, doors led to the various parts of the palace. Using mirrors much like today's security guards use video monitors, the Black Eunuchs could easily survey multiple directions.

• *Let's enter the women's part of the Harem. Turn left and go down the* ❻ *Corridor of the Concubines. At the end of the hall, turn left into the...*

❼ Courtyard of the Wives and Concubines

This was where the sultan's women lived—in rooms surrounding this central gathering space. The three apartments along the right

side of the courtyard housed the sultan's wives—one each for wives #2, #3, and #4, plus their children and servants. (The sultan's favorite wife got special accommodations elsewhere in the palace.) The left side of the courtyard was the women's bathhouse, laundry, and kitchen—note the water taps.

At the far end of the courtyard were the concubines' quarters. Though the word "concubine" is often used interchangeably with "mistress" or even "sex slave," it's not that simple. Concubines were simply female servants.

They began as young slave girls trained to serve the senior women. Becoming a concubine could be a major opportunity: Many were granted their freedom after serving in the Harem. Only a few were chosen to have sex with the sultan and be granted "favorite" status, which came with wealth and influence.

The relationship between the women who lived around this courtyard was, well, complicated. The sultan's wives vied with each other to promote the interests of their own sons, hoping they'd rise to power or even sultanhood. The wives constantly competed for the sultan's favor, and for the gifts he lavished on them (which they squirreled away for financial security). The wives knew their status was fragile, and their most feared enemy was often the wife next door. Even a concubine might catch the sultan's eye, and bear his son, thus posing a threat.

TOPKAPI PALACE

Harem 101

Contrary to Western fantasies about nubile sex slaves satisfying a sultan's every desire, the harem was actually a family-oriented place where the sultan and his women lived. (Oh, but there was still plenty of sex, so don't stop reading.) Let's pull back the veil on this mysterious and titillating phenomenon.

The word "harem" refers to both the women (wives, favorites, mothers, and concubines) and the part of the palace where they lived. Turks today use the word for the most private part of a Turkish house, reserved for family members, specifically the women. To Turks, "harem" connotes family closeness—not sexual fantasy.

The Topkapı's harem was run according to strict social rules that helped ensure the longevity of the Ottoman Empire. Its primary role was to provide future heirs to the Ottoman throne, an essential responsibility that was too important to be left to impulsive urges.

Here's how it worked: The sultan was the head of the household. But he couldn't have sex with just anyone. His sex partners were generally chosen by either his wives or his own mom—the "mother sultan," or

queen mother. The sultan could have up to four wives, with one considered the senior, most influential wife. Any sons they bore him were in line to be the next sultan.

On the other hand, the wives chose which concubines a sultan could sleep with. (In other words, the man's wives chose his girl-friends.) But of all the women in the Harem, one was the most powerful of all—the elderly lady down the hall: the mother sultan.

• *Keep going through a few small rooms until you emerge in a large, ornate, yellow-and-green room, the...*

❺ Queen Mother's Room

This apartment's fanciful decor was tailored for the sultan's revered mother. Picture the queen mum reclining on her sofa in a cozy alcove—eating, taking tea, pampered by concubines, chatting with the wives, or laughing with her chief Black Eunuch—all while being entertained by singers and dancers.

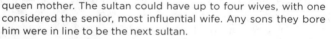

Here's where it gets interesting. Also living in the harem were hundreds of "concubines"—that is, female housekeepers. From among the concubines, the sultan—or, more often, his mother or wife—might select up to four "favorites" with whom he could

become more, ahem, familiar. A favorite who bore a child of the sultan was often treated as a wife. Again, the sultan could only have sex with chosen women, not with anyone he wanted. Every night he spent with a woman had to be documented in writing.

Sultans often preferred "favorites" to the entanglement of marriage. They were wary of weakening the dynasty line through marriage or losing a wife to a rival—like the wife of Sultan Beyazıt who ended up a prisoner of the conqueror Timur, sweeping his palace floors.

When a sultan died, all his women—wives, mothers, and favorites—had to leave the harem, though they were given new housing and a healthy pension.

Thanks largely to the harem and its strict protocols, the Ottoman Empire avoided many of the battles for succession that dogged other great empires. As a result, the line of Ottoman emperors was unbroken for nearly 600 years.

Despite the İznik tilework, this is the most European room in the palace. The upper walls are painted with Western-style scenes from nature. It's a realistic and lush leafy landscape with a river running through it, with grape vines in the dome. The room's doors are of carved wood with incredible mother-of-pearl inlay. The Rococo curlicues, trompe l'oeil classical columns, and crystal chandelier are more typical of another well-known palace of the day: Versailles.

This room was strategically located between the wives-and-concubines' apartments and the sultan's. The queen mother ruled the Harem. She set the rules and was the social gatekeeper, deciding whom her son could sleep with, and fixing him up with only the best women.

Besides ruling the Harem, the queen mother also helped rule the empire. "Mother sultan" was an official title, granting her broad political powers. Queen mums made their mark on Istanbul—building schools, mosques, and public fountains. For a century (c. 1533-1656, a period called the "Women's Sultanate"), a series of

TOPKAPI PALACE

Polygamy in Turkey

Contrary to popular belief, most Turks have always been monogamous. Even though the Quran permits a man to marry up to four times, this is generally reserved for extraordinary situations. When the rule was instituted, wars had decimated the male population, leaving more women than men. With no modern social-welfare network to care for war widows, men began to take additional wives. The Quran sets strict criteria for polygamy: The man must have the financial means to support all his wives, and he must treat each one equally. Under Ottoman rule, polygamy was practiced mainly among minorities, traditional Arab communities...and, of course, the ruling class who could afford it.

Polygamy is illegal in today's Turkey (although it continues in some mostly Arab communities of eastern Turkey). In most of the country, today's progressive Turkish women would never accept their husbands' taking second wives. Legally, Turkish women have had equal rights with men since the Turkish Republic was established, including the right to vote and run for office.

queen mothers and ambitious wives ruled the Ottoman Empire as "sultans," while their sons or husbands were either too young or incompetent. It's little wonder that when the ambassador of Venice visited here, he reported back: "All goodness and all evil comes from the mother sultan."

• *Continue down a corridor, into the rooms where the sultan himself lived. Don't overlook the ❽ **sultan's bathroom**, all in marble, with a bathtub, dressing room, heated floors, and golden privacy screen. Nearby, find the sultan's porcelain-footprint-hole-in-the-ground "Oriental toilet." Next you enter a very large room, with a dome and a couch-like throne, the...*

❾ Sultan's Throne Room (a.k.a. the Imperial Hall)

You're in the heart of the Harem, the private realm of the sultan. The centerpiece of this room is a canopy arching over a "throne" that looks more like a couch from La-Z-Boy. (As we've seen, we get many of our English words for furniture pieces from the Turks: ottomans, divans, and sofas.) Despite the room's pompous name, this was not used for stuffy political ceremonies—it was really the family's private party room. Here were held weddings and receptions,

coronation after-parties, and impromptu gatherings. Imagine the scene: The sultan presides from his sofa-style throne, while his favorite wives, concubines, and mom look on from the balcony. The metal brazier in the center of the room keeps everyone warm.

Because the Ottoman world encompassed so many cultures, the decor has a variety of styles. The dome is typically Islamic (with its Arabic calligraphy), but it's also painted with European-style vases. The room has Baroque balustrades, blue-and-white Delftware tiles (from Holland), ceramic vases (from China), and Venetian mirrors. The Ottomans were trying to keep up with the other great palace in the world—Versailles—so you'll see Rococo elements like pastel tones, a teardrop chandelier, and gold-leaf trim.

• *The following rooms were the sultan's private (or "privy") rooms—his palatial man cave. Two of them deserve special attention. Exiting the sultan's throne room, bear left when you can to reach a large domed room with a trickling fountain.*

⓫ Privy Room of Sultan Murat III

As the Harem's best-preserved room, this space retains the vision of its creator, the famed architect Sinan. Like many of his other

works in Istanbul, it features a soaring central dome atop a square base (a design he learned from Hagia Sophia). Sinan's distinct style used broad arches, lots of light, playful water, and colorful decorative elements like red-blue-green İznik tile and ornamental calligraphy. The blue frieze running around the room quotes the Quran's best-known verse: "Allah!" (spelled with the distinctive "w-" and "l"-shaped letters)..."There is no God but Him, the living and eternal...His throne encompasses the heavens and the earth..." (Surah 2:255).

The room's fountain still works, trickling down stairsteps. Water—so rare and precious in the Islamic world—was the purest symbol of life. The Topkapı was decorated with water, water everywhere: standing still in courtyard pools, bubbling up from fountains, masking secret conversations, and drip-dropping playfully.

The two golden canopies were added later, beneath which sultans relaxed (by day) and slept (at night) on their sofas.

• *At the room's far end, you could check out the more intimate and tranquil Library of Ahmet I, and the wood-paneled and flowery Fruit Room. When you're ready, backtrack, continue straight, and take your first left into a suite of two rooms connected by a doorway.*

❶ Twin Pavilions Room
(a.k.a. the Apartments of the Crown Prince)

These twin rooms are furnished to create a sense of intimate luxury. The stained-glass glows, and the tilework features slender cypress trees, flowers, and vases, as if the princes were lounging in a cool leafy garden, beneath a golden-sun dome. The ceiling rises like a garden tent, or "pavilion."

These rooms were where the sultan's #1 son—the crown prince—grew up. All the sultan's sons were educated here in the Harem.

The rooms were nicknamed "the Cage," as the prince was kept in seclusion—for his own protection. Ambitious rivals to the throne sometimes killed their brothers. But isolation had its downside. Having spent his entire life under lock and key, the prince never learned how to run an empire. Ideally, princes grew up here, then served an apprenticeship as a regional governor to learn the ropes of rulership. Nevertheless, many historians blame the Topkapı's life of gilded-cage isolation as one reason why so many sultans were incompetent, hastening the empire's decline.

• *Our final stop in the Harem is just a few steps down the corridor. You'll reach an open-air courtyard with buildings on the right and a view on the left.*

❶ Courtyard of the Favorites

This place is aptly named, as it was here that the sultan's favorites concubines lived—in the white two-story building with wooden shutters. As they threw open those shutters in the morning, think of the stunning views they'd have, overlooking a big pool (remnants are still visible) and a lush garden.

Remember that most concubines were simply female slaves. But occasionally one would catch his eye. Or she'd be presented to him by his mother or one of his wives. This might open the doors to a great future.

One who epitomized the concubine success story—and even changed the course of history—was named Roxelana. Kidnapped as a young girl in Poland, Roxelana was sold into the slave trade and eventually ended up as a concubine at Topkapı Palace, hauling water and sweeping floors. She showed promise, was taught to read, and learned the arts and court etiquette.

One day, this red-haired beauty was noticed by none other than Sultan Süleyman the Magnificent, who took her to bed. Roxelana soon became one of his "favorite" mistresses. Next, she became his official wife, then his favorite wife, then mother to his son Selim, who became the crown prince and eventually succeeded him. (Roxelana never achieved the rank of mother sultan only because she died before her son took the throne.) Roxelana's political savvy made her one of Süleyman's wisest and most trusted advisors. Eventually, she ruled alongside him as a virtual co-sultan. From her humble origins as a concubine, Roxelana kickstarted the "reign of the ladies" that carried the Ottoman Empire through a century of greatness.

• *Our Harem tour is done. Now let's see the final part of the Topkapı Palace: the Fourth Courtyard.*

To get there, follow signs to the Harem exit. You'll spill out in familiar territory—the Third Courtyard. As you exit, notice that the stone-and-mortar mosque here is aligned at an off-kilter angle—so its prayer niche faces Mecca.

Make your way to the far end of the courtyard. Then go down a set of stairs between buildings and enter the complex's inner sanctum, the...

⑩ Fourth Courtyard

This was the most private realm of the sultan, his personal pleasure garden. It's dotted with a half-dozen small buildings. The idea was to create a kind of nature preserve where the sultan could go camping (or "glamping") in these tent-like buildings. Free-standing, open-sided pavilions like these are called kiosks (which gives us our English word for small booths doling out smoothies or tourist info).

• *As you enter the Fourth Courtyard, turn left, and tour the area clockwise. You'll wind your way from kiosk to kiosk, through landscaped gardens, pools, trickling fountains, and flower beds, up and down staircases, and along a terraced hillside with great views. The first building up is the octagonal...*

Revan Pavilion: Built by Sultan Murat IV in the mid-17th century, this has many of the typical features of other pavilions we'll see, with grilled windows and a jutting roofline creating a shaded walkway around the building. Inside, it's decorated with typical blue-and-white İznik tiles and topped with a central dome. The window shutters and cupboard doors are inlaid with mother-of-pearl and tortoiseshell. It's easy to imagine the sultan kicking back here on a couch, looking out at views of the gardens, warmed by the fireplace, and luxuriating in the diffuse light from the skylights and stained glass windows.

• *Next, you'll come to the...*

Circumcision Pavilion: On the outside, it has elaborate blue-and-white İznik tiles—some of the Topkapı's finest, inspired by Ming Dynasty porcelain. The pavilion was built by Murat's younger brother İbrahim, as the place where princes were ritually circumcised. (No wonder they called him İbrahim the Mad.)

• *Next up is a wide balcony with stunning views, the...*

İftar Pavilion: The sultan and his family would gather here at sunset daily during Ramadan to celebrate with a fast-breaking *(iftar)* evening meal. Take in the views across the Golden Horn to the New District. Find the conical Galata Tower, and the tall skyscraper topped with a black box that marks Taksim Square.

• *Now enter the blue-tiled...*

Baghdad Pavilion: This pavilion is noted for its splendid dome and silver brazier—a gift from France's Louis XIV. (Because

these kiosks have a certain similarity, it's easy to get kind of ho-hum about it. But really—it's pretty spectacular, isn't it?) This pavilion was a built by Sultan Murat IV to celebrate his conquest of Baghdad. Murat was the poster child of the all-powerful Ottoman sultanate, feared by everyone. He carried an iron mace to intimidate troublemaking janissaries. He banned alcohol, not because he was against it, but so he could execute violators. But after a long day of decapitating drunks, Murat retreated here to his Baghdad Pavilion to find peace. Surrounded by nature, he read lyrical poetry and listened to soothing music.

• *Head down the stairs and continue toward the white wooden building just ahead, the...*

Sofa Pavilion: This is the airiest and brightest kiosk of all. Its walls are almost nothing but windows. It's decorated with lush drapes, a carved wood ceiling, and ringed with the eponymous sofa. Some sultans used it as a guest house. For others, it was their box seat for gymnastics tournaments in the gardens.

• *The Sofa Pavilion is set in the palace's famed...*

Tulip Garden: It was the Ottomans who introduced tulips to Western Europe. Turks brought them along from central Asia, cultivated the species, and shipped bulbs to Holland and the rest of Europe. Tulip designs became a popular motif on Turkish tiles and textiles. In this garden, Sultan Ahmet III grew rare bulbs. He presided over an period of peace and prosperity known as "The Tulip Era" (see sidebar on page 48).

• Take the stairs by the pavilion down to one last platform that marks the limits of the museum grounds. Walk straight to the edge to see the marble **Column of the Goths,** *standing in the park beyond. It's topped with a Corinthian capital, and the Latin inscription at its base commemorates a Roman victory over the invading Goths.*

Now make your way (to the right as you face the column) toward the European-style...

Mecidiye Pavilion: As you walk toward the pavilion, look to your left to see a ramp leading down to a guarded gate on the wall. The sultan used this gate whenever he wanted to leave the palace grounds in secret.

This pavilion, from the mid-1800s, was the last great building constructed at Topkapı Palace. It looks more European than Oriental. By now, Europe was on the rise, and this was the sultan's attempt to keep up. By this time, Topkapı Palace was old-fashioned—unfit for a modern ruler. No sooner was the pavilion built than the sultans abandoned the Topkapı altogether. After 400 years, they packed up their hookahs and harem pants and moved the seat of the empire across town to more modern digs—Dolmabahçe Palace.

• To finish your Topkapı tour, make your way to the **terrace** *with a stunning view. Gaze across the Sea of Marmara to the continent of Asia— where Ottoman culture was born. Look down to see the old walls of the Byzantines—the culture the Ottomans assimilated into their growing empire. To your left, take in the Bosphorus—where the sultans built a new palace to live out their final days.*

Now, head down the steps to the restaurant, where you can enjoy a well-deserved rest after your palace tour...and dine like a sultan.

ISTANBUL ARCHAEOLOGICAL MUSEUMS TOUR

Istanbul Arkeoloji Müzesi

The three Istanbul Archaeological Museums offer a collection that rivals any on earth, with intricately carved sarcophagi, an army of Greek and Roman sculptures, gorgeous İznik tiles, ancient Babylonian friezes, the world's oldest peace treaty, and an actual chunk of the chain that the Byzantines stretched across the Golden Horn.

The main Museum of Archaeology features the world-renowned Alexander Sarcophagus, a selective and engaging collection of ancient sculpture, and archaeological finds from the Trojans and the Byzantines (predominantly from the sixth century BC on). The 15th-century Tiled Kiosk Museum, one of the oldest examples of Ottoman civic architecture, contains an outstanding collection of centuries-old Turkish tiles. And the Museum of the Ancient Orient displays artifacts from early Mesopotamian and Anatolian cultures, mostly dating from before the sixth century BC (with some going all the way back to 2700 BC).

There's a lot of ground to cover here. If your time is limited, spend most of it at the Museum of Archaeology. The Tiled Kiosk Museum and the Museum of the Ancient Orient are small enough to merit at least a quick walk-through.

Orientation

Cost: 50 TL includes entry to all three museums.

Hours: Tue-Sun 9:00-20:00, until 18:00 off-season, closed Mon, last entry one hour before closing.

Information: +90 212 520 7740, www.muze.gov.tr.

Advance Tickets: Buying a ticket in advance online or using a Museum Pass allows you to skip the ticket line and head directly to the security check.

Getting There: The museum complex is inside the outer wall of the Topkapı Palace complex, at Osman Hamdi Bey Yokuşu. It's easiest to reach by tram; get off at the Gülhane stop. From the stop, walk two blocks away from the Golden Horn along the old palace wall, go through the entryway with three arches into Gülhane Park, and bear right up the cobbled lane. The complex is near the top of this lane, on the left.

You can also access the museums from the First Courtyard of the Topkapı Palace (see the Topkapı Palace Tour chapter). After entering the First Courtyard through the Imperial Gate, go diagonally to the left (with the Hagia Irene church on your left), pass through the arched entryway, and follow the alley down the hill to the museums (on your right).

Getting In: Pass through the complex's big entrance gate and find the ticket seller to the left. After the security check, go through the turnstile: The Museum of the Ancient Orient is directly to your left; the Tiled Kiosk Museum is ahead on the left; and the main Museum of Archaeology (where this tour begins) is ahead on the right.

Expect Changes: The Museum of Archaeology may still be undergoing renovation when you visit; parts of the collection may be moved to temporary galleries. The Tiled Kiosk Museum and Museum of the Ancient Orient remain open. Look for signs at the entry gate that list temporary displays and closures.

Tours: Audioguides cost 25 TL.

Length of This Tour: Allow at least two hours to tour all three museums. If you're in a hurry, spend an hour at the Museum of Archaeology, sprint through the Tiled Kiosk Museum, and skip the Ancient Orient.

Eating: An outdoor café hides among trees and columns on a pleasant terrace overlooking Gülhane Park (between the Museum of the Ancient Orient and the Tiled Kiosk Museum, limited menu, may close in winter). The Museum of Archaeology has a small coffee shop serving sandwiches and cookies.

Starring: A slew of sarcophagi (including the remarkable Alexander Sarcophagus), sumptuous İznik tiles, the ancient Kadesh Treaty, and several millennia of Turkey's past.

ARCHAEOLOGICAL MUSEUMS

The Tour Begins

• *We'll begin at the museum's highlight: the Museum of Archaeology. Ongoing renovations may affect the location of some collections described below. In that case, consider this tour as an overview, then just enjoy what's currently on display.*

Use the first of the museum's two entrances, directly opposite from the café.

MUSEUM OF ARCHAEOLOGY

This ornamental building has two entrances, framed by pediments supported by four tall columns—resembling the designs on some of the museum's sarcophagi. Inside you'll find those sarcophagi, as well as piles of artifacts from the Greeks, Romans, Byzantines, Trojans, and more.

• *As you go through the door, you'll enter a lobby dominated by a colossal statue of...*

❶ Bes

This statue dates back to the first century AD. Often confused with Hercules, Bes was a demigod of ancient Egypt and a popular figure in the Cypriot pantheon of gods at the time. Here we see Bes holding a lion by its legs. Scholars' best guess is that the statue served as a fountain.

• *Facing Bes, head left. You'll pass the cloakroom and the gift shop (WCs are nearby). Connecting halls ahead of you display the museum's...*

Sarcophagi Collection

These sarcophagi were brought here in the 1880s from the royal necropolis of Sidon (in present-day Lebanon, but part of the Ottoman Empire back then). Discovered accidentally by a villager digging a well, they are among the most important classical works ever unearthed.

• *Go through the doorway, and look for...*

❷ Tabnit's Sarcophagus

Just as you enter is an Egyptian sarcophagus carved from dark diorite (similar in texture to granite). Dating from the sixth century BC, this is the oldest sarcophagus found in the Sidon excavations. Hieroglyphs on the lid describe the first owner, an Egyptian commander named Penephtah. He was later moved from his tomb to

make room for the local king, Tabnit of Sidon (whose mummified corpse lies next to the sarcophagus). The inscription at the foot is Tabnit's epitaph.

Across the hall, two light-colored, Egyptian-style sarcophagi lie side by side. Beginning in the fifth century BC, Greek sculptors carved Egyptian-looking sarcophagi for their wealthy clients. Although the basic style was Egyptian, the Greeks felt free to play around with the design. The result: archaic Greek figures trapped in an Egyptian sarcophagus. The extensions at the shoulders were used to lift or carry the sarcophagus, then chopped off once it reached its final destination.

• *In the middle of the hall, you'll see the...*

❸ Lycian Sarcophagus

Dating from the late fifth century BC, this sarcophagus is named for Lycia—a small area in Mediterranean Turkey—because its shape

resembles the distinctive, monumental tombs built into the side of a cliff there. But that's where the connection ends: The three-quarter poses of this sarcophagus' figures and their Thracian attire—popular in Athens at the time—instead link it to the Greek mainland, as does the layered portrayal of horses and hunters on the casket's long sides. This experimentation with 3-D perspective winds up as a clutter of horse heads and hooves—like equine Rockettes.

The two long sides feature detailed, lifelike hunting scenes: a lion on one side, a wild boar on the other. The horses show their Arabic and European ancestry, with large foreheads, deep chests, and lean bellies—similar to the horses in friezes at the Parthenon in Athens.

On one end, two centaurs fight over a deer. One is naked, while the other—wearing a panther skin—is about to spear his opponent in the eye. On the other end, centaurs beat a man to death. This half-buried man is Kaineus, the mythological centaur slayer. The centaur on his left is about to hit him with an amphora jug. The

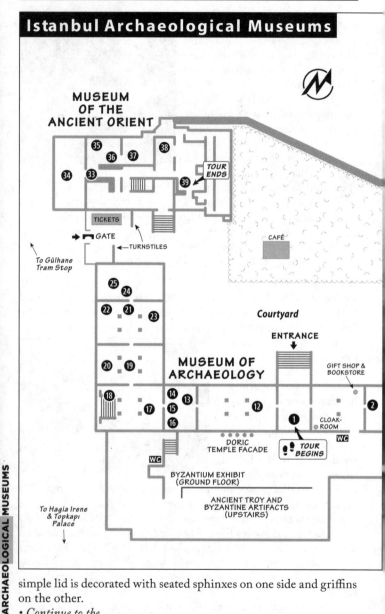

Istanbul Archaeological Museums

simple lid is decorated with seated sphinxes on one side and griffins on the other.

• Continue to the...

❹ Satrap Sarcophagus

A "satrap" was a Persian governor, akin to a viceroy ruling in a king's name. This sarcophagus dates from the fifth century BC. Its specific occupant is unknown, but the scenes on the sides of the

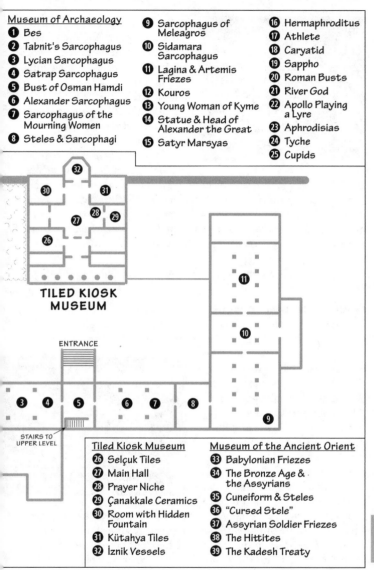

casket trace the life of a powerful satrap. The once-bright colors of the palm- and lotus-flower borders faded long ago. On one long side, the satrap and his men prepare his chariot for a ride. As you walk around the sarcophagus to the right, the short end shows the satrap reclining on a bench in his private chamber, accompanied by his wife (resting her back on the border). A servant pours wine, while a second servant stands by with a cloth in one hand and an unseen fan in the other. In the next scene, on the opposite long

side, the satrap uses a spear to hunt a panther. The final short end shows the satrap's grooms with their spears, helping him out of a potentially embarrassing situation.

• *Exit the hall. You are now in a lobby dedicated to Osman Hamdi Bey, the museum's founder (find his ❺ bust near the staircase to the right). Backlit panels and the central showcase give details about his life and paintings.* Famous in his own time as a painter, Osman Hamdi (1842-1910) is today regarded as the father of Turkish museums. Hamdi directed the excavations in Sidon and discovered the next two sarcophagi completely intact in separate burial chambers, where they had been insulated from humidity and water damage.

• *Continue into the connecting hall to see the two marble sarcophagi, starting with the outstanding...*

❻ Alexander Sarcophagus

The museum's star exhibit is inside a large, red-framed glass case. Other than a few dents in the marble caused by careless movers, this fourth-century BC sarcophagus is in excellent condition. Although it's known as the Alexander Sarcophagus—that's Alexander the Great portrayed in the scenes of battle and hunting on the sides—it was actually carved to hold King Abdalonymos of Sidon.

While faded after two thousand years, some of the sarcophagus' colors remain, and the bas-reliefs that decorate the casket and its lid are impressive. Some figures are almost freestanding, giving the impression that their next step will take them right out of the scene and into the room with you. Nearby, look for a color model of the "Alexander on his horse" scene, offering a better idea of how the relief may have looked in full sarcophi-color.

One side of the casket shows Alexander's army battling the Persians in the Battle of Issus in 333 BC. Alexander's victory here paved the way for him to conquer the Middle East. The battle also changed the life of Abdalonymos, the sarcophagus' likely "owner": Distantly related to Sidon's royal family, he was appointed as the new king when the Macedonians marched into Sidon. It's easy to tell

ARCHAEOLOGICAL MUSEUMS

who's who: Persian troops wear long pants, several layers of loose shirts, and turbans. The Macedonians are either naked or half-naked, in short tunics. On the far left, Alexander wears a lion pelt as he attacks a Persian soldier from horseback. His arm

is raised as he prepares to hurl a (missing) spear.

Move counterclockwise around the sarcophagus. The battle scene continues on the short end of the casket to the right. The relief on the lid, in the triangular pediment, is another battle scene—

likely the battle of Gazze (312 BC), in which King Abdalonymos was killed. The dominant red color is best preserved on this side.

The next, long side of the sarcophagus depicts two separate hunting scenes. This relief, less crowded than the battle scene, is dominated by the lion hunt at its center. The lion's body is pierced at several points, and blood flows from his wounds. Still, he manages to bite and claw at the horse's shoulder. The rider of the horse is King Abdalonymos, dressed in a traditional Persian outfit. Pay attention to the different garb of the soldiers—here, they're all hunting together. This was a scene Alexander fought for: to create a united empire. The Macedonian on the horse behind the lion is Alexander's general, Hephaestion, who appointed Abdalonymos as king. Alexander is on horseback to the left of Abdalonymos.

On the final short end is a panther hunt, but this time all the hunters are dressed in the same Persian style. There's more fighting in the pediment, but the figures here are not as refined as the rest. Apparently the first sculptor ran out of time to complete his work, so another took up the hammer.

• *Near the Alexander Sarcophagus is another perfectly preserved sarcophagus, the...*

❼ Sarcophagus of the Mourning Women

The museum building you are in was modeled after this mid-fourth-century BC sarcophagus, arguably the best example of its kind. Although Greek in style, it has Eastern influences that are apparent in the mourning figures' wailing gestures and long robes (called chitons).

The sarcophagus belonged to King Straton of Sidon. Professional mourners—women hired to cry and wail at funerals—were common when he died around 360 BC, but the women portrayed on this sarcophagus were members of Straton's harem and seem genuinely affected by his death. Notice that their gestures are very natural, almost lifelike. Scholars believe the sculptor may have used models to create such realistic emotion. The designs along the lid's long sides show the funerary procession. From right to left, find the young man leading the cortege, two horses to be sacrificed at the service, a Persian quadriga (chariot with four horses), and a funeral cart pulled by four horses, followed by the attendants.

Optional Detour

If you're not yet sick of sarcophagi, you could continue through the doorway at this end of the hall to take a quick look at several fairly well-preserved ❽ **steles and sarcophagi** from Sidon and other places in the Middle East. Continue into the next rooms to see two standouts: the second-century ❾ **Sarcophagus of Meleagros,** decorated with mythological figures and motifs, and the third-century ❿ **Sidamara Sarcophagus,** known for its sheer size and detailed sculptures. And at the far end of the exhibit are some remarkable ⓫ **friezes** from two ancient temples in southwestern Turkey: the temple of Artemis at Magnesia ad Maeandrum and the temple of Hecate at the Carian city of Lagina.

• *From here, retrace your steps to the Bes statue (where we entered) and continue through the doorway on the other side to find...*

Greek and Roman Sculpture
• *You're greeted by the head of a...*

⓬ Kouros

This kouros (a Greek statue of a boy), dating from 600 BC, was brought from the Greek island of Sámos. His face is round, with a blunt profile, almond eyes, and raised eyebrows. His lips are closed and straight, but grooves at the corners give the impression that he's smiling. In south Aegean art, kouros statues represented the idealized Greek youth. Similar heads and statues have been found in excavations on Sámos, Rhodes, Kos, and other Greek islands. Two other kouros statues stand stiffly at either side.

The rest of the hall is dedicated to a time period when Anatolia was under Persian rule (from the mid-sixth century BC to the Hellenistic age).

• *Continue about 30 yards into the next hall, dedicated to...*

Hellenistic Sculpture (330 BC-First Century BC)

This hall contains a beautiful example of the Hellenistic period: a fine statue of a ⓭ **young woman** from ancient Kyme. Rather than noble, idealized gods, the Hellenistic artists gave us real people with real emotions.

But the highlight of this exhibit is a pair of Alexander the Great artifacts. Both were discovered at Pergamon, the world-famous acropolis in Aegean Turkey.

Swooping down from ancient Macedonia (located in present-day Macedonia and the far north of Greece) in the fourth century BC, Alexander the Great's father conquered the Greeks and embraced their culture—one of Alexander's tutors was Aristotle. When Alexander took the throne after his father's assassination, he spread Greek customs and philosophy as he marched across the Middle East. By the time he died, in 323 BC, his empire—and Greek culture—stretched all the way to India. Every city's main square had a Greek temple, and Greek was the language of his vast domain.

From an artistic perspective, Alexander's conquests marked the end of the Greek Golden Age, when balance was celebrated above all. The Hellenistic period that followed was characterized not by idealized and composed beauty but by rippling energy and jump-off-the-stage exuberance.

Carved from fine white marble, the powerful ⓮ **statue of Alexander the Great** dates from the second century BC. It's likely he once held a bronze spear in his right hand, although his right arm and hand are missing. The hilt of the sword he held in his left hand remains. The statue bears a rare inscription naming its sculptor: "Menas of Pergamon, son of Aias."

The very natural-looking **head of Alexander the Great** also dates from the second century BC. Some believe it was carved to decorate the renowned "Altar of Zeus" at Pergamon (the altar is now in Berlin). This head is a copy of the fourth-century BC original, by the renowned sculptor Lysippus. Alexander has a slightly tilted head, round eyes with heavy eyelids, and an open mouth that doesn't show his teeth. Gentle lines, deep furrows on the forehead, and the overall natural rendering of the face are characteristic of Hellenistic Pergamon sculpture.

Look for the third-century BC statue of the ⓯ **satyr Marsyas.** Marsyas isn't stretching—he's tied to a tree by his arms, his face contorted in terrible pain. According to myth, Marsyas, provoked by peasants, invented a flute and challenged Apollo to a musical contest. Marsyas lost the contest, and Apollo hung him from a branch and skinned him alive. Though Marsyas is usually portrayed alone, this statue was found in a group, next to Apollo...with a slave by his side, ominously sharpening his knife.

Also found in Pergamon was a six-foot-tall statue of the Greek god ⓰ **Hermaphroditus,** with both male and female attributes.

• *The next hall is dedicated to statues from two other ancient Aegean cities.*

Magnesia and Tralles

These statues were found in the late 19th century in Magnesia and Tralles. As you enter this larger hall, you'll see a statue of a cloaked ⓱ **athlete** (some say he was a wrestler), which probably decorated the gymnasium at ancient Tralles in the first century AD. The muscular young man with the playful smile relaxes against a column, having just finished his exercise.

Find the beautifully shaped ⓲ **caryatid**—a support column carved as a woman. Dressed in a traditional gown, she looks well suited for her architectural role.

• *Enter the doorway on the right to a hall with bays on either side, separated by columns.*

At the center of this hall is the head of the poet ⓳ **Sappho,** born 2,700 years ago on the island of Lesbos. Her romantic poems to other women, including Aphrodite, gave us the words "lesbian" and "Sapphic." The left bay is dedicated to ⓴ **Roman portrait busts.** The statue and bust (second century AD) of Emperor Marcus Aurelius, and the bust of Empress Faustina, are particularly interesting and realistic.

• *The next hall displays findings from...*

Ancient Cities in Turkey

This hall is marked by a reclining ❷ **river god** (second century AD). Brought to the museum from Ephesus, this is Oceanus, a personification of the river thought by ancients to encircle the world. He's shown here as an old man, but his arms still ripple with muscle.

In the left bay are statues from Miletus and Ephesus. Find the statue of ❷ **Apollo playing a lyre.** In this second-century Roman copy of the Hellenistic original, Apollo is portrayed as more graceful than divine. His missing fingers were on the strings, and his right hand holds the plectrum (used to pluck the strings)—ready to play. Here and there are traces of the reddish brown and blue paint that once decorated the statue.

The right bay is dedicated to the ancient city of ❷ **Aphrodisias,** which had its own school of fine arts and a distinct artistic style. The room is named for Kenan Erim, the professor who spent a lifetime excavating at Aphrodisias. (Asked why he never married, Erim said he already was married—to Aphrodite.) Erim was buried at the site, next to the monumental entry to the Temple of Aphrodite.

• *Past the river god, enter the last exhibition hall, with statues from the...*

Roman Imperial Period

Although of lesser importance, a few of these statues stand out for their intricate work—like ❷ **Tyche,** the city goddess. Also check out the two ❷ **cupids**—betting on a rooster fight (in a glass case).

• *You've now seen the best of the Museum of Archaeology. If you're getting museumed out, head for the exit and make your way to the Tiled Kiosk Museum.*

Or, if you can't get enough of ancient Turkey, consider an optional detour upstairs to see artifacts from...

Ancient Troy and Byzantium

• *To go upstairs, backtrack to the lobby dedicated to Osman Hamdi Bey, just before the Alexander Sarcophagus. Head up the stairs and pass through the hall with a bronze statue of Emperor Hadrian to find the annex.*

Start by touring the humble exhibit of artifacts from the ancient city of **Troy.** At the end of this long hall, dip into the section to the left, which displays findings from a **tumulus** (ancient burial mound). Then backtrack to the end of the Troy exhibit, and take the stairs (across from the tumulus exhibit) down to the mezzanine level. Halfway down the stairs is an exhibit of **Byzantine artifacts.** Follow the zigzag tour route past a few interesting items, including part of the impressive chain the Byzantines pulled across the mouth of

the Golden Horn to block enemy fleets (to your immediate left as you enter); fine Byzantine church frescoes; and massive Byzantine water pipes carved out of marble and caked with lime deposits. You'll also have views down into the atrium, where you can see a replica of the facade from the Doric Temple of Athena at Assos (580 BC).

At the bottom of the far staircase is the entrance (and exit) for the **Byzantium** exhibit (on the ground level, WC nearby), which may be worth a few minutes if you have the interest for even more late Roman and Byzantine artifacts. You'll emerge near the gift shop.

• *As you leave the Museum of Archaeology, the small, older building directly ahead of you—fronted by a gorgeous two-story colonnade, and to the right of the little park and café—is the...*

TILED KIOSK MUSEUM

The word "kiosk" comes from the Turkish word *köşk,* meaning "mansion" or "pavilion." This kiosk contains some of the finest

examples ever assembled of Selçuk, Ottoman, and regional tiles. As you tour the sumptuous collection, keep in mind that in Turkey, "tile" (*çini;* chee-nee) refers to a high-quartz-content material that can be used to decorate architectural surfaces (with flat tiles) or to create functional vessels (such as bowls, vases, and cups). While much of what you'll see inside might be called "ceramics" or "pottery" in English, Turks consider them all "tiles."

The collection is displayed on one easy floor, so you can treat it like eye candy, lingering only at your favorite pieces to read the fine English descriptions.

The steps leading up to the entrance are in the center of the lower gallery, hiding behind the stone wall with the barred window. The Arabic **inscription** above the doorway explains that the building was constructed in AD 1472, during the reign of Mehmet II (the Conqueror)—roughly 20 years after the Ottomans had taken Constantinople from the Byzantines. The building represents the earliest stages of Ottoman civic architecture and is the only one of its kind in Istanbul dating from this period.

As you step into the lobby (its floor is covered in glass to protect the original pavement), head for the large **map** on the opposite wall, which shows the historically important tile-manufacturing regions in Turkey and throughout the Middle East and Asia.

• *The lobby is flanked by two small rooms. Enter the room on the left, which contains some of the oldest objects in the exhibition.*

㉖ Selçuk Tiles

This room is dedicated to the early tiles of Selçuk (the Turkish em-

pire before the Ottomans) and Middle Eastern origin. As you enter the room, the case in front of you displays Syrian and Iranian pieces; the one behind it has some fine examples of Selçuk pottery.

At the end of the room, on the right wall, are decorative tile pieces with colored glaze from a 13th-century mosque. This turquoise-colored glaze is still in use, although only a few master potters remain who can apply it correctly. On the opposite wall are **star-shaped wall tiles** with animal and floral designs. Dating from the 13th century, these are from the sum-

mer palace of the Selçuk sultans in Konya (central Turkey).

• *Return to the lobby, and take the door to your left into the ㉗ main hall, where you'll see...*

More Tiles and Ceramics

The hall is filled with Selçuk, Anatolian, and Ottoman treasures. The objects that look like vases (in the larger case in the center) are actually **ceramic lamps.** These 16th-century oil-burning lamps, from the tile-making center of İznik, were hung from the ceilings of mosques by those little handles. They were probably the best available lamps in the market at the time.

ARCHAEOLOGICAL MUSEUMS

The colorful circa-1430 **❷⓼ prayer niche** was brought from a mosque in Konya in central Turkey. Its pieces are fired with colored glaze.

An annex off the main hall displays curiously designed 18th- and 19th-century **❷⓽ ceramics** from Çanakkale (a city on the Dardanelles).

• *Now walk to the end of the room, across from the entrance.*

Find the two **glazed plates,** displayed in the side walls, across from each other. Dating from ad 1500, these are two of the fin-

est surviving pieces of İznik tile—frequently showing up in reference books as textbook examples of Turkish tiles.

• *Walk past the plates, and go through the doorway on your left, which opens into a highly decorated room.*

The walls contain color-glazed tiles and intricate gold designs known as "gold embroidery." It may be a little over-the-top to today's eyes, but it was the height of style in its day. At the end of the room, on the left corner, is a beautiful **❸⓿ hidden fountain.**

The room to your right displays **❸⓵ Kütahya tiles.** The town of Kütahya (south of the Sea of Marmara) began making tiles during the 18th century, using techniques similar to those of the master potters at İznik but never quite matching their quality.

For the real deal, head into the final room, with masterpiece blue-and-white **❸⓶ İznik vessels** from the early 15th century.

• *When you're done in the Tiled Kiosk Museum, exit back into the courtyard and turn right. Head toward the entrance gate. Just inside the gate, on the right-hand side, are stairs leading up to the...*

MUSEUM OF THE ANCIENT ORIENT

This small collection offers an exquisite peek at the ancient cultures of the Near and Middle East. Most of what you'll see here comes from Mesopotamia, between the Tigris and Euphrates rivers (parts of present-day Iraq and Syria). On this one-way loop you'll meet Sumerians, Akkadians, Babylonians, and Assyrians (all of whom were sovereign in the Middle East), as well as the Hittites (who ruled today's Turkey)—peoples who paved the road to modern civilization.

• *The entry area offers some maps and other posted information worth skimming for a background understanding of the "Ancient Orient."*

Walk through the first room of the museum—stopping to see the Babylonian sundial (on the left)—and head for the doorway on the right (next to the adorable little sphinx). Turn left into a corridor, and take a moment to enjoy the tile friezes lining the walls.

❸❸ Babylonian Friezes

These tile friezes once decorated the gate of the ancient city of Babylon (located in today's Iraq). The colorful designs of lions,

bulls (which, thanks to stylized perspective, look more like unicorns), and dragons (up top, looking like snakes with lions' paws in front and eagles' feet in back) represented Babylon's mighty gods.

• *Beyond the friezes, at the end of the corridor, you'll emerge into a room with artifacts from...*

❸❹ The Bronze Age and the Assyrians

The marble head of Lamassu—a half-human, half-bull Assyrian creature—guards the doorway. Turn left and tour the collection clockwise. First you'll see early Bronze Age objects from the Sumerian and Akkadian civilizations. If you know your prehistory, you'll notice that Anatolia and Mesopotamia were technologically advanced, progressing through the metal ages (such as the Bronze Age) thousands of years ahead of continental Europe. So while a Mesopotamian sword was made around 3000 BC, its European counterpart wouldn't have been created until 1000 BC.

Continuing around the room, you reach a small showcase with **weight and measurement units** used in Mesopotamia, including the talent, mina, and shekel. Using these units, along with accurate scales, the Mesopotamians developed the first formal monetary system, based on the weights of gold and silver.

Keep going, into the collection of **Assyrian objects.** The two tall, freestanding statues of kings (ninth century BC) were carved from basalt; although the shorter statue is unfinished, the big one shows fine detail, with cuneiform script pressed into his uniform.

• *For more cuneiform, head back toward the corridor, then take the first left into the collection of...*

❸❺ Cuneiform and Steles

On the back wall is a group of five steles—small pillars used to commemorate major events. The cases on either side of the steles display **cuneiform tablets.** The wedge-shaped script is the world's first writing system, invented 5,000 years ago by the Sumerians (of southern Iraq) and developed into a syllabic alphabet by their descendants, the Assyrians.

The case on the left traces the progress of cuneiform script. At the bottom left is one of the oldest tablets in the museum (2700 BC). The nail-shaped object nearby is actually an inscribed piece. To its right, the item shaped like a roll of paper towels chronicles the acts of the Babylonian king Nebuchadnezzar, describing the temples he built and the reconstruction of Babylon's city walls.

The case to the right of the steles holds interesting tablets, such as the **Ur-Nammu law,** a legal code of ancient Mesopotamia dat-

ing from 2050 BC. Another tablet records the Assyrian kings' genealogy, while others list sacred marriage rites, poison remedies, and the court verdict for a man who put off an engagement. There's also a resume and job application, a book of proverbs, and a steamy love poem that conveys the timelessness of passion ("My groom, lover of my heart / Your beauty is unquestionable, sweeter than honey. Lion, my heart's treasure... / Let us take joy in your beauty").

Notice the ❸❻ **"cursed stele"** on the wall (to the left of the doorway to the next room). This eighth-century BC stele records the will of an Assyrian palace administrator, Bel-Harran. He tells about a city that he founded and a temple he constructed and dedicated to the gods. He declares that his citizens will be protected and exempt from tax. And at the end, he tacks on a curse to scare away vandals: "I pray that the great gods of Assyria destroy the future of whoever might destroy my words and my name, and the gods shall have no mercy on them." Maybe that explains how this stele has survived intact for 2,700 years.

• *Continue into the next room. On the right, notice the long army of knee-high Munchkins marching along the wall.*

❸❼ Assyrian Soldier Friezes

The first few of these Assyrian troops carry taxpayers' money on the trays balanced on their heads. At the front of the line (at the opening in the wall) is a highly decorated basalt altar

Who's Who in the Ancient Orient

Who were the peoples of the Ancient Orient, and how did they relate to one another—and to today's Middle East? Here's an oversimplified family tree to help you get your bearings.

One of the clearest ways to track an ethnic group's lineage is to examine its language. Today's Arabs and Jews share a common Semitic language, meaning that they probably also share common ancestors. Today's Turks, Persians (most Iranians), and Kurds speak non-Semitic languages, which indicates that they aren't related to the Arabs.

The earliest of the peoples you'll meet in this museum are the **Sumerians** (c. 3000-2000 BC). While their origins are unclear, they weren't Semitic. The Sumerians invented a writing system called cuneiform, which marks the beginning of humankind's recorded history.

The **Akkadians** (c. 2300-2100 BC) and the **Babylonians** (c. 1900-1600 BC) were of Semitic origin—the ancestors of today's Arabs. Because the city of Babylon is located in today's Iraq, you could say the Babylonians were "ancient Iraqis."

The **Assyrians** (c. 1900-600 BC) were descendants of the Akkadians, and also Semitic (Arab). They created a very efficient trade system throughout the lands they conquered. To secure their borders and prevent uprisings, the Assyrians forced the people they conquered to migrate to other areas of the empire, contributing to the Middle East's ethnic complexity. Today's Assyrian descendants speak Syriac, a form of Aramaic.

The **Hittites** (c. 1700-1200 BC) spoke an Indo-European language—meaning their language, and probably their ethnicity, were closer to Europe than to Asia. The Hittites came from the north and ruled today's Turkey and the Middle East for centuries.

from Cappadocia, in central Turkey. The altar dates from the fifth century BC. Both the reliefs and the altar have Aramaic text—a "newer" style of writing that replaced cuneiform. Aramaic was also the language spoken by Jesus Christ and most other New Testament figures.

• *After a quick look around in this room, backtrack through the previous room (with the cuneiform tablets and steles). From there, turn left into the main corridor and follow it to its end, into a room with artifacts from...*

㉛ The Hittites

The Hittites once controlled a big chunk of Anatolia, reaching their peak in the 13th century BC. The huge relief on the wall depicts a king praying to Tarhunza, the Hittite storm god. Although the king stands on a tall mountain, he still can't reach the height of

the gigantic god. Tarhunza was also the god of plants—he carries grapes in one hand and wheat in the other. His curly beard and hair, as well as the flares on his skirt, reflect Assyrian influence, while the helmet is Hittite-style. The horns on the helmet are a barometer of his divine importance: The more horns, the more important the god.

• *Go through the doorway on the right, and look to your right. A small case displays the exhibit's highlight.*

❸❾ The Kadesh Treaty

These few clay fragments are a record in cuneiform script of the world's oldest surviving peace accord: the Kadesh Treaty. This document, created in 1283 BC, ended the decades-long war between the Hittites and the Egyptians. Even the United Nations recognizes the importance of this early peace agreement: A large copy of the treaty is displayed at the UN headquarters in New York City.

The text was initially engraved on silver tablets that have been lost to time. Three ancient copies exist. The version you see here was found in the archives of the Hittites' capital, Hattusha (100 miles north of present-day Ankara). It's written in Akkadian cuneiform, the language of diplomacy at the time.

Egyptian King Ramses II and Hittite King Hattusili III each had their own copy of the treaty—and each version claims victory for that copy's owner. But otherwise, the copies are similar, and they include many elements still common in modern-day peace agreements, such as provisions for the return of prisoners and refugees, and a mutual-aid clause. The treaty ends with a curse: "To whoever acts against these words, may the thousand gods of the Land of Hatti and the thousand gods of Egypt destroy his home, his land, and his servants." These final words dictate that the treaty's conditions would be honored by the kings' successors forever. After the Kadesh Treaty, the Middle East enjoyed uninterrupted peace for seven years—which, back then, was a pretty impressive run.

• *Our tour is finished. Avoid the curse—leave in peace.*

ARCHAEOLOGICAL MUSEUMS

TURKISH AND ISLAMIC ARTS MUSEUM TOUR

Türk-Islam Eserleri Müzesi

With a thoughtful and manageable collection of artifacts spanning the course of Turkish and Islamic civilizations, this museum is a convenient place to glimpse the rich cultural fabric of Turkey and the Middle East. You'll see carpets, calligraphy, ceramics, metalwork, woodwork, and lots more. Almost as interesting as the collection is its setting: the İbrahim Paşa Palace, one of Istanbul's great surviving Ottoman palaces.

Orientation

Cost: 50 TL.

Hours: Tue-Sun 9:00-20:00, until 18:00 off-season, closed Mon, last entry one hour before closing.

Information: +90 212 518 1805, www.muze.gov.tr.

Getting There: It's in the Old Town's Sultanahmet area, across from the Hippodrome's Egyptian Obelisk and the Blue Mosque. From the Sultanahmet tram stop, cross the park toward the Blue Mosque, then jog to the right when you hit the Hippodrome.

Length of This Tour: Allow one hour.

Services: WCs are located under the staircase that leads up to the central courtyard.

Cuisine Art: A cafeteria is to the right as you enter the central courtyard.

Starring: Carpets, ceramic tiles and containers, rare calligraphy, and other artifacts of the Islamic world's religious and cultural heritage.

OVERVIEW

The original İbrahim Paşa Palace was much bigger, rivaling that of the sultan. But today, its smaller size makes the museum's U-shaped layout easy to figure out.

The palace's original reception hall is today's south wing, with a small wooden balcony facing the Hippodrome. Its north and west wings were once palatial guest rooms. Today the museum's upstairs north, west, and south wings focus on historical artifacts, while the downstairs (garden level) south wing focuses on lifestyles. Temporary exhibits are located on the entrance level. In the chamber behind the ticket/information desk, you'll find remains of the Hippodrome's Byzantine infrastructure. On this tour, we'll start in the north wing, dip into several rooms along the west wing, then enter the large south wing.

I've given dates for artifacts according to the Western calendar, though a few items in the museum are dated only by the Islamic calendar.

The Tour Begins

• *After you enter the large central courtyard, turn 180 degrees, and then go through the first door (to the right of the cafeteria) to enter the north wing.*

NORTH WING

• *At the top of the entry staircase, turn around. On the back wall of the corridor (on the elevated section behind the staircase) are the...*

❶ Samarra Palace Artifacts

The Abbasid dynasty ruled the Muslim world for more than five centuries, from AD 700 to 1250. Abbasid caliphs (political and religious leaders) employed non-Muslim slave-soldiers, mainly Turkic people from the north who had been abducted by slave traders or sold into slavery by impoverished parents. In time, these soldiers became a powerful military caste, establishing their sovereignty in North Africa and the Middle East.

The presence of these troops caused friction with the public in Baghdad, capital city of the Abbasid dynasty. In 836, largely pressured by local leaders in Baghdad, the caliph decided to move the center of the caliphate from Baghdad to the new city of Samarra, which was then a simple military garrison. Thousands of masons were brought in from all over the Middle East to build immense structures. Even the homes of officials and administrators were huge palaces. The masons created some of the finest examples of early Islamic civil architecture, with summer and winter sections that incorporated baths, canals, and pools.

The display case holds composite column capitals, wall frescoes, tiles, and other decorative pieces unearthed during early 20th-century excavations.

• *Before you continue, notice the beautiful ceramic vase with a dark blue glaze (13th century, Raqqah, Syria) in the wall display to your left. This gives you an idea of what is through the doorway, in the chamber dedicated to...*

❷ Raqqah Ceramics

Through the Middle Ages, Raqqah (in northern Syria) produced both polychrome and monochrome ceramics. The monochrome Raqqah ware, in a dominant turquoise color and transparent glaze, was the most popular. The collection displayed here comes from archaeological digs done in 1905.

• *Leave the room, start down the main corridor, and go through the first door on the right (behind the staircase) to three connecting rooms showcasing...*

❸ Objects from Early Caliphs and Islamic Dynasties

These three rooms are dedicated to Islamic art dating back to the early caliphates. Following the first four caliphs of the newborn religion, the two caliphate dynasties—the Umayyad (660-750) and the Abbasid (700-1250)—carried the influence of Islam beyond the Arabian Peninsula. During their reign, territories of the Islamic Empire extended from central Asia to Spain (see sidebar).

The first room displays objects from the Umayyad period. In

Turkish & Islamic Arts Museum

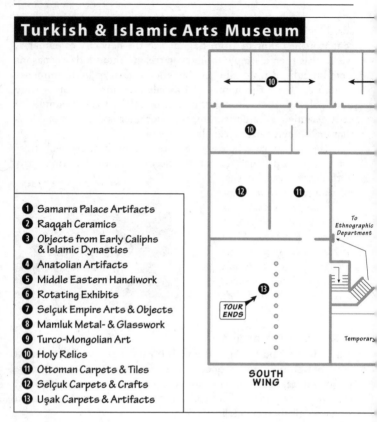

1. Samarra Palace Artifacts
2. Raqqah Ceramics
3. Objects from Early Caliphs & Islamic Dynasties
4. Anatolian Artifacts
5. Middle Eastern Handiwork
6. Rotating Exhibits
7. Selçuk Empire Arts & Objects
8. Mamluk Metal- & Glasswork
9. Turco-Mongolian Art
10. Holy Relics
11. Ottoman Carpets & Tiles
12. Selçuk Carpets & Crafts
13. Uşak Carpets & Artifacts

the display case, the eighth-century Quran chapter *(Juz)* deserves particular attention.

The stones you see here on the wall, dating from the seventh and eighth centuries, are some of the oldest pieces in the museum's collection. The slab on the left is a milestone, with an inscription in Arabic that states that you are only at the beginning of your journey.

The next room boasts fine decorative pieces of ninth-century Abbasid palace art. Cases in the room display wall frescoes from the palace harem (the larger fresco of the two dancers is particularly appealing), wooden fragments used for wall decoration, an intricate marble bowl, and ceramics.

The last room is dedicated to a vast collection of Islamic calligraphy called the "Damascus documents" (they were kept in the Damascus Umayyad Mosque for centuries). Among these are the earliest copies of the Quran, including parchment sheets on which the Quran was initially written.

• *Head back to the corridor and enter the next room on the right.*

TURKISH & ISLAMIC ARTS

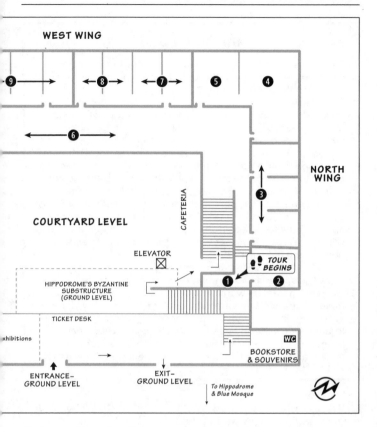

❹ Anatolian Artifacts (10th-15th Century)

In the last quarter of the 11th century, the Selçuks (the first of the powerful Muslim Turkish states) invaded Anatolia, aiding an ex-

tensive migration of Turkic tribes into the region also known as Asia Minor (the Asian part of present-day Turkey). The Artuqid state (1100-1400) is one of the many states that were founded during this transition period.

As insignificant as the Artuqid state was, it produced some remarkable metalwork. Some of the most attractive pieces in the museum are in this section—such as the two intricate bronze drums. However, the main attraction here, in the large corner room, is the monumental door

TURKISH & ISLAMIC ARTS

İbrahim Paşa

The Turkish and Islamic Arts Museum is housed in the former palace of Ibrahim Paşa, the grand vizier (prime minister) of Süleyman the Magnificent.

Enslaved as a child, Ibrahim was appointed to serve young Prince Süleyman, and advanced quickly when Süleyman succeeded to the throne. Ibrahim married the sultan's sister, Hatice, and was named grand vizier in 1523.

Ibrahim's wealth and influence grew as the Ottomans expanded their empire. After the conquest of Budapest, he placed looted bronze statues of Apollo, Artemis, and Hercules in front of his palace. The pagan symbols offended the public, leading a popular poet of the time to write, "Two Ibrahims came to this world. One (Prophet Abraham) destroyed idols—and the other re-erected them." Ibrahim could not stand the criticism, forcing the poet to crawl the streets of Istanbul and then having him hanged.

The grand vizier's arrogance and increasing power produced strong enemies, among them Süleyman's wife, Roxelana. Fearing Ibrahim would interfere with her sons' succession, Roxelana turned Süleyman against him. The grand vizier was invited to Topkapı Palace for dinner...and the next morning, Ibrahim's lifeless body was found outside the palace walls. Süleyman had his former slave turned trusted advisor buried in an unmarked grave, and confiscated his enormous wealth.

of the mid-12th-century Grand Mosque of Cizre (today a small town in eastern Turkey west of the Tigris River).

This magnificent door is made of wood, sheeted with copper, held together with iron nails, and reinforced with brass rods. Patches were made from recycled metal items and used to replace missing sheets on the door's panels. Look at the dragon-shaped handles. The one on the left was stolen in 1969 and somehow showed up in a Copenhagen museum. The lion-shaped middle piece is still on the door wing. Lions and dragons, considered talismans, were common designs in Anatolia in the Middle Ages.

• *As you face this door, the doorway on the left leads into a display of...*

❺ Middle Eastern Handiwork (12th-15th Century)

Founded by Selahaddin Eyyubi, the Eyyubid state (1170 to mid-15th century) ruled Egypt and the entire Middle East at its height. Eyyubi, known in the West as Saladin, led the Muslim opposition

The Great Caliphates

After the death of the Prophet Muhammad in AD 632, Islamic leaders created the position of caliph to serve as both the religious and social leader of the Muslim community. But as the first four caliphs (who served consecutively) died, people wondered how to choose their replacements: Some Muslims thought caliphs should be elected, while others felt the position should be hereditary and pass only to direct descendants of Muhammad.

At first the title of "caliph" was handed down through family dynasties, taking on more of a political significance. The **Umayyads** (661-750) became the first significant caliphate dynasty and ruled from Damascus, in present-day Syria.

Then the **Abbasids**—the descendants of Muttalib, the uncle of Muhammad—used the lineage argument to seize the caliphate, moving its base from Damascus to Baghdad and eventually to Samarra. Beginning in the early eighth century, the Abbasids ruled the Middle East and the Islamic world. Although their power waned over time, they kept the caliphate title until the early 1500s, when the Ottomans took over.

Because the **Ottomans** were Turks rather than Arabs, their claim to the caliphate was less convincing to the Arab communities within their empire. But once the Ottoman sultan's name was officially recorded as the caliph, his authority was accepted.

In the early 20th century, as Turkey was poised to become a modern republic, the caliphate came into question again. Because Atatürk's vision for the new republic included a separation of mosque and state, Turkey's parliament abolished the caliphate in 1924, once and for all.

against Christian Crusaders. On display here are two 13th-century intricate wood columns, turquoise Raqqah ceramic ware, and vessels for daily use.

• *Step through the doorway, back to the corridor.*

WEST WING

• *Beyond this point, the corridor through the west wing is used for* ❻ *rotating exhibits from the museum's collection, occasionally with audiovisual displays. Go through the next door to find...*

❼ Selçuk Empire Arts and Objects

The Selçuk Turks governed from 1000 to the early 1300s, maintaining power over the Near East (mainly present-day Iran), the Middle East, and Anatolia. While Islam was the dominant culture where the Selçuks ruled, you will find extensive traces of their Turkish roots and local cultures in their art. The decline of the

Selçuks in the early 14th century cleared the way for the autonomy of future Turkish dynasties. Just over a century later, the Ottomans would unify the Turks once again.

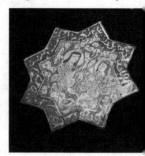

The first room boasts some very fine examples of 12th-to-13th-century Selçuk metalwork, pottery, and tiles. On the back wall, look for a star-shaped 12th-century tile piece that depicts a courting couple (a reminder of the many behind-closed-doors affairs that took place in the Selçuk palace).

Decorative star-shaped tiles in blue, turquoise, and purple, usually painted both under and over the glaze, have their roots in central Asia. With high quartz content, these tiles were made to

last for centuries (we'll learn more in the "Selçuk Carpets and Crafts" section, later). Even at the time they were made, they were considered unique and precious items. The painted figures have classic Turkic features: round faces, almond eyes, and small noses and mouths. A halo indicates aristocratic status, and armbands on caftans and jackets indicate social rank.

The adjacent room is reserved for everyday items, from earthenware objects to metalwork, that were both decorative and functional.

❽ Mamluk Metal and Glasswork

The next two rooms display artifacts of Mamluk origin. The Mamluks (1250-1500) were slave-soldiers of non-Muslim origin under the Abbasid caliphs. This powerful military caste ruled over Egypt and the Middle East until the Ottoman occupation in the early 1500s.

The giant 15th-century brass lantern (third room, wall display) shows off skilled craftsmanship. Beaten metal parts were painstakingly decorated by carving and punching.

Labeled *badiye*, the 15th-century brass bowl in the wall display (fourth room, next to the door) is a true work of art. Further decorated with silver and

gold, the inscriptions praise the Mamluk sultan for a victory in battle.

Also note the intricate glass lan-
terns in the large case across the room,
with colorful enamel designs.

• *Step through the doorway, back to the
corridor. If you have time for a detour,
turn right into a section dedicated to...*

❾ Turco-Mongolian Art (13th-20th Century)

The works in these rooms is from the
two Turco-Mongolian dynasties—the
Ilkhanids (1255-1350) and Timurids
(1370-1500)—along with the Safavids (1500-1720, founded by the
Safavviya Sufi order) and the Turkmen Qajars (1795-1925, who
ruled Persia—today's Iran).

You'll see some fine examples of religious calligraphy and
decoration, as well as diverse
items, such as the 642-page,
14th-century album of Persian
poetry that also includes attractive landscape paintings (*Mec-
mua*, Timurid, second room).
Notice the highly decorated,
boat-shaped brass bowl from
the 17th century, used by dervishes to collect alms and offerings
(marked as *Keşkül*, Safavid, third room in the wall display).

• *Continue to the end of the corridor. The last section in this wing contains...*

❿ Holy Relics

The long, single case on
the corridor wall displays
a 19th-century Kaaba belt.
It was a tradition for the
house of the ruling caliph
to annually present em-
broidered fabric covers and
belts to decorate the stone
walls of the Kaaba, the holiest Muslim shrine, locat-

ed in Mecca (in today's Saudi Arabia). Ottomans used thick woven
textiles such as silk, velvet, or wool, embroidered with threads of

real silver and gold, for the decorative belts and door covers. The texts are excerpts from the Quran.

Along the left wall, the 18th-century *kıblenüma* (compass pointing in the direction of the Kaaba, toward which Muslims pray) and the 13th-century scroll *(Hac Vekaletnamesi)* deserve particular attention. Devout Muslims are expected to make the pilgrimage, or hajj (pron. "hahdge"), to the Kaaba at least once in their lifetimes. In the Middle Ages, this was a long, arduous journey. Believers who were unable to do it would sponsor someone else to

make the pilgrimage on their behalf, as inscribed in this scroll.

Items in the connecting rooms include hair from the Prophet Muhammad's beard, his footprint, and two highly decorated verbal descriptions of his qualities—all the more important in Islam in the absence of physical portraits. Called a *hilye* (heel-yeh), or *Hilye-i Şerif*, the poetic text describes the Prophet's attributes, such as generosity, honesty, and gentleness. It combines two traditional arts—*hat* (calligraphy) and *tezhip* (decoration)—into one artwork.

Traditionally, a *hilye* was given to a young man about to get married, with the hope that he would read it and be inspired to model himself after the Prophet. Similarly, a bride's dowry chest contained a Quran, so that she could pattern herself after the woman to whom an entire chapter in the holy book is dedicated—Mary, the mother of Jesus.

• *Now continue into the...*

SOUTH WING

• *As you enter the south wing, the left wall of the entrance hall is covered with fine examples of...*

⓫ Ottoman Carpets and Tiles

The European love affair with Turkish, or "Oriental," carpets began in the 13th century. For centuries, upper-class Europeans considered a Turkish rug the ultimate status symbol. If you couldn't afford to buy an actual rug, you'd pay an artist to paint one to hang on the wall—or to paint a rug hanging in the background of a portrait.

A few of the carpets here are named for the German painter Hans Holbein the Younger (1497-1543). Holbein, considered a master portrait artist, served as a court painter to Henry VIII and illustrated the first German translation of the Bible. He and other artists of his time liked to paint Oriental carpets (and other handicrafts) in the backgrounds of paintings and court frescoes. Europeans who had seen these designs in the paintings wanted to own a similar carpet in real life...and Turkish weavers happily obliged. A particularly famous Holbein portrait, *The Ambassadors*, featured an Anatolian carpet—hence the term "Holbein carpet."

Holbein carpets often have large eight-pointed stars, a motif more common in earlier Selçuk carpets (shown in the next section).

The carpets you see here are mainly based on designs from the Turkish towns of Uşak (oo-shahk) and Bergama (known in ancient times as Pergamon). Today, a limited number of carpets are still being woven in Bergama. (We'll see more examples of Uşak carpets later.) Crafted in a predominantly red color, these carpets have a traditional design and are extremely fine, especially considering the density of their wool.

The prayer rugs on display here—or what's left of them after centuries of constant use—have bare spots worn by the foreheads, knees, and toes of worshippers. They have repeating prayer-niche designs that reflect their purpose.

In the large central case, you will find a few examples of early Ottoman tiles and ceramics, including decorative fragments of a 15th-century inscription. Pieces called Miletus ware were thought to resemble the ceramics of Miletus, an ancient city along the Aegean Sea, near Ephesus. But they're actually late 14th- and 15th-century ceramics manufactured in İznik (ancient Nicaea),

a town to the east of the Sea of Marmara. Miletus ware, which was produced for just a short time and represents a transition from traditional Selçuk to fine Ottoman tiles, usually features purple and cobalt-blue colors on a white undercoat, with basic geometric shapes and plant and animal motifs.

• *Walk through the doorway by the fireplace into the next section, which is reserved for...*

⑫ Selçuk Carpets and Crafts

Only a handful of 13th-century **Selçuk carpets** have survived, and more than half of those are displayed in this room. They were gathered from mosques and shrines in central Turkey, especially in Konya, the capital city of the Selçuk Empire. Each carpet here is unique in color and design, with floral and animal motifs adapted into geometric forms and stylized almost to the point of abstraction. Designs feature eagles, arrowheads, crescents, and eight-pointed stars, as well as Kufic letters (which are also commonly used to decorate borders), often in repeating patterns. The carpets, made of pure wool, use a double-knot technique known as the "Turkish knot."

On the opposite wall, you will find rare and highly intricate examples of traditional wood carving. The larger, 13th-century

walnut window shutters, brought from a tomb in the early 1900s, represent painstaking craftsmanship. Arabic script on the upper panels reads, "There is no greater virtue than to avoid ambition and earthly desires." The detailed ceremonial wood sarcophagus dates back to 1250. The smaller walnut doors are more recent, and not Selçuk.

On the north wall hangs a 13th-century tiled-brick panel made in a traditional fashion. The Selçuk Turks used tiles to decorate both the interiors and the exteriors of their monuments. The secret to their artistry was the fine clay they used, which contained a large amount of quartz. The quartz made the tiles durable enough to survive even the harsh weather of the steppes of central Asia. To create the tiles, Selçuk artisans spread a layer of clay several inches thick on a tray and cut it into smaller shapes such as triangles, rectangles, and stars. Then they painted the pieces with colored glazes and fired the tiles. Unlike thin-surface tiles used elsewhere, the Selçuks' thick, glazed tiles were integrated into the walls, ceilings, and minarets.

To the right of the panel, find the rare pieces of Selçuk stone carving, including a relief with two Selçuk warriors and two others with griffin motifs. In the Selçuk tradition, stylized reliefs display birds, beasts of prey, and griffin and dragon motifs embedded in intricate floral designs. The Selçuk Turks used these motifs extensively in wood and stone to deco-

rate facades and entrances on civil as well as religious architecture.
• *Pass through the doorway next to the stones and into the last and largest hall of the museum to see...*

⓮ Uşak Carpets and Artifacts

You've arrived at the pinnacle of traditional all-wool carpet weaving in Turkey. An average Uşak carpet has about 103,000 knots in ten square feet. (Wool carpets don't come any denser.) The most common design features medallions; the second-most common uses repetitive star patterns. The museum has a large inventory of these Uşak "palace carpets"; others are displayed at the Carpet Museum (at the northeast corner of the Hagia Sophia, by the Imperial Gate of Topkapı Palace).

The first case beyond the carpet display has some attractive items from the Ottoman era. Standouts are two 17th-century gilded copper candlesticks adorned with floral motifs and semiprecious stones, a highly decorated 15th-century copper lantern, and a 17th-century incense burner-candlestick featuring curved arms that end in tulips.

Continuing around the room counterclockwise, in the next case you'll find a scroll with the imperial signature (known as the *tuğra*) of Sultan Süleyman the Magnificent himself. This particular type of scroll is called a *ferman*, meaning "the word of the monarch." Though the scroll is incomplete, the part we can see has, unsurprisingly, words of praise for the sultan. The scroll (with its signature) is a great example of traditional *hat* art, which combines Arabic writing with artistic calligraphy. The calligrapher *(hattat)* plays with the shape of letters, creating beautiful forms that remain grammatically correct but can be hard to read. (For more on this art, including information about how to see it being made, see page 363.)

The next display case boasts ornate woodwork and outstanding decorations. This late 16th-century Quran holder (the taller of the two displayed) was brought here from the library of Hagia Sophia. The wood is studded with ebony, ivory, turtle shell, and mother-of-pearl, and the interior of the domed cover has exquisite paintwork.

Also on display are two 17th-century *rahles*, or Quran stands.

A *rahle* supported the fragile binding of the Quran (or another book) while it was read.

The last case displays a masterpiece of Ottoman calligraphy and traditional book decoration. Renowned calligrapher Seyyid Lokman created the book, *Religions, Islam, and Ottoman History*, at the end of the 16th century on the order of the sultan. The book's miniatures and decorations were painted by skilled artisans in watercolor and glaze. The 55 miniatures depict personalities of religious significance, as well as Ottoman sultans.

• *Exit down the staircase to return to the central courtyard. Next to the base of the stairs is the entrance to the...*

ETHNOGRAPHIC DEPARTMENT

This section of the museum is dedicated to traditional Turkish lifestyles and art. If it's open when you visit, it may be worth a quick look.

You'll see why **textiles,** especially those that can be used as furniture in a Turkish home, are the flagship of Turkish arts and crafts. Once produced for basic needs, textiles eventually turned into a pleasing art form, especially as the Turks prospered under Ottoman rule.

You'll find more examples from the museum's immense **carpet collection**, including a custom-designed silk carpet depicting 19th-century Istanbul. Turkish carpets are usually known by the name of the region where they are made, and traditional wool-on-wool carpets from the same region almost always have similar designs and colors. This is not only because traditional designs are passed down through the generations but also because the

plants used to dye the wool are grown only in certain areas.

A number of cases display women's clothing and jewelry. Notice the **white bridal gown** embellished with gold threads—the traditional Turkish bridal dress was either completely red or dominated by red, but as Western influence grew, more brides began wearing white.

Theater is represented here as well, in the form of the **shadow**

play, long popular among Turkic people in central Asia.

For centuries, the shadow play was enjoyed as local entertainment. But under the Ottomans, it became a major influence as the cast of stock characters expanded to include ethnicities found across the empire. (Audiences could always find someone onstage to identify with.) Simple animated stories turned into plays examining complex social relations, but two main characters were always present— Karagöz, a rather unruly peasant who tended to get himself in trouble, and Hacivat, his educated (and pompous) foil. Hence the Turkish name for the traditional shadow play: Karagöz-Hacivat.

• *Our tour is over. As you walk back across the garden, notice the* **terrace** *overlooking the Hippodrome, with sweeping views of the Hippodrome monuments and the Blue Mosque.*

OLD TOWN BACK STREETS WALK

From Sultanahmet to the Spice Market

This walk leads you through the back streets of Istanbul's Old Town, giving you a taste of the authentic city (rather than its tourist-filled historic core). You'll share sidewalks with residents going about their daily routines, and walk streets that haven't changed in centuries, lined with shops that cater to locals.

The major sights of this walk are markets and mosques. The Old Town has been a bustling commercial center for centuries, and you'll enjoy two of its most famous and bustling marketplaces: The Grand Bazaar's aggressive salesmen and tempting souvenirs will threaten to empty your wallet, while the Spice Market's intoxicating aromas and offers of "Turkish Viagra" will titillate your senses. We'll drop into two of the city's most interesting and important mosques: one grand (the Mosque of Süleyman the Magnificent, the finest of all Ottoman mosques in Istanbul), and one cozy (the gorgeously tiled Rüstem Paşa Mosque). In between these main attractions, we'll see a side of Istanbul few tourists experience.

Orientation

Length of This Walk: Allow at least four hours, not counting the Grand Bazaar; if you linger in the shops at the Grand Bazaar and Spice Market, it could fill an entire day.

Getting There: We'll start at the Sultanahmet tram stop in the heart of the Old Town.

Grand Bazaar: Mon-Sat 9:00-19:00, shops begin to close at 18:30, closed Sun and during religious holidays, across the parking lot from the Çemberlitaş tram stop, behind the Nuruosmaniye Mosque.

Mosque of Süleyman the Magnificent: Mosque—Free, generally open daily from one hour after sunrise until one hour before sunset, closed to visitors five times a day for prayer. Mausole-ums—Free, daily 9:00-17:00, until 18:00 in summer. Located on Sıddık Sami Onar Caddesi, in the Süleymaniye district.

Rüstem Paşa Mosque: Free, generally open daily from one hour after sunrise until one hour before sunset, closed to visitors five times a day for prayer, on Hasırcılar Caddesi, Eminönü.

Spice Market: Free to enter, Mon-Sat 8:00-19:30 (until 19:00 off-season), Sun 9:30-18:00, closed during religious holidays, at the Old Town end of the Galata Bridge, near the Eminönü tram stop.

Mosque Etiquette: To enter a mosque, knees and shoulders must be covered, shoes must be removed, and women should wear a headscarf (see page 71 for details).

Starring: Some of Istanbul's best markets and mosques...and its people.

The Walk Begins

• *Begin at the Sultanahmet tram stop (200 yards uphill from the Hagia Sophia and the Basilica Cistern; to locate it, see the "Historic Core Walk" map on page 86). From here, we'll walk five blocks uphill along the tram tracks to an ancient column from Byzantine Constantinople (at the Çemberlitaş tram stop).*

Divan Yolu

The bustling street called Divan Yolu—lined with shops and restaurants and with traffic mostly limited to buses and **trams**—has been the city's main thoroughfare since Byzantine times. Istanbul's first horse-drawn *tramvay* opened in 1872 and by the 1950s electric trams reached all corners of the city. Trams were phased out to make way for cars in the 1960s. A few decades later people realized trams were cleaner—and faster—than cars stuck in traffic. Now trams are back as a small but integral part of Istanbul's public transit system.

The small **mosque** near the Sultanahmet tram stop is the Firuz Ağa Camii, one of the few mosques in Istanbul from before 1500. If you haven't already visited the **park** beyond the mosque, now's a good time to do so, to take in the grand views of the Blue Mosque. The bust you pass as you leave the park depicts the poet Mehmet Akif, who wrote Turkey's national anthem.

After enjoying the view, continue up Divan Yolu (with the Hagia Sophia behind you). Walk another block up the street, and cross the tracks at the traffic lights (by the Yapı Kredi Bank). Ahead, an old **cemetery** filled with Ottoman bigwigs is behind the wall on your right. For a detour to see the tombs, enter near the corner, walk in 15 paces, and look to your right. Amid the tradi-

Old Town Back Streets Walk

1 Çemberlitaş
2 Nuruosmaniye Mosque
3 Grand Bazaar
4 Beyazıt District
5 Istanbul University
6 Mosque of Süleyman the Magnificent
7 Uzun Çarşı Caddesi
8 Rüstem Paşa Mosque
9 Hasırcılar Caddesi
10 Food Vendors
11 Eminönü Square
12 New Mosque of Mother Sultan
13 Spice Market

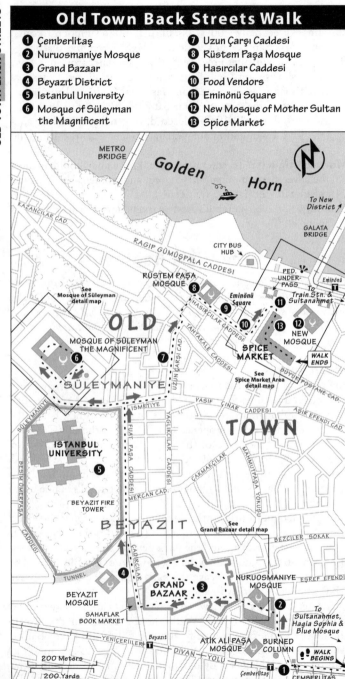

tional pillar- and turban-shaped tombstones, find the unique stone resembling a ship's sail (it marks the grave of a high-ranking naval officer).

The big **mausoleum** at the far end of the cemetery honors Sultan Mahmut II (1785-1839), who ruled in the first half of the 19th century, overseeing a time of reforms, modernization, and increasing interaction with Western Europe. His mausoleum (free, donation requested, remove shoes before entering) represents the eclectic taste of the time and includes a beautiful crystal chandelier hanging down from the center of the dome. Two other sultans and a handful of relatives share this grand space with Mahmut. As was traditional, the "caskets" you see are actually empty—the bodies are buried underground. Caskets with hats were for men; flowers were for women. You may see a visitor saying a prayer for the soul of the deceased.

• *Back on Divan Yolu, continue along the tram tracks. After one block, you'll see a towering Byzantine column called...*

❶ Çemberlitaş (Burned Column)

Also known as the Column of Constantine, Çemberlitaş means "stone with hoops"—referring to the nearly 115-foot-tall col-

umn's six-drum construction. Dating from the fourth century a.d., Çemberlitaş once held aloft a larger-than-life statue of Constantine depicted as the god Apollo. In Constantine's day, this column marked the center of the Forum, the city's main square, ringed with public buildings and churches. When the statue was lost (well before the Ottomans took over the city), it was replaced with a golden cross—which is also now missing. Now the column stands empty, forlorn behind the tram stop. Adding insult to injury, frequent fires in this district left the column permanently scorched.

After all those years of abuse, it's finally being restored—so it may be covered with scaffolding when you visit.

• *At the column, turn right (passing a recommended Turkish bath, Çemberlitaş Hamamı, on your right—see the Experiences chapter) and head down the hill toward the big, ornate...*

❷ Nuruosmaniye Mosque

Continue straight past the line of tour buses and walk along the outer wall of this late Ottoman-era mosque (opened in 1755). The tourist shops on the left were built as part of the complex, to provide funds to maintain the mosque. Find the entrance into the court-

yard (on your left, across from a pedestrian street), a shady, picturesque oasis. You can step into the mosque if you like—but be careful not to tire yourself out too early in the walk.

• *Continue through the mosque courtyard (WCs at the far end of courtyard, on the left) to enter the Grand Bazaar through its Nuruosmaniye Gate (look for the sign above the gate—Nuruosmaniye Kapısı). As you enter the crowded market, it's smart to tuck away your valuables and be alert for pickpockets.*

❸ The Grand Bazaar

This remarkable roofed warren of shops—with Byzantine foundations and an Ottoman floor plan, bustling with merchants and

shoppers—is one of Istanbul's top attractions. Of course, this is a colorful and convenient, if predictable, place to do your souvenir shopping. But it also hides authentic shops and craftspeople that offer rich, vivid insights into the Turkish culture of yesterday and today.

• *To carry on with this walk, simply walk straight through the bazaar on its main street, Kalpakçılar Caddesi, to the far end. Or, to explore the bazaar with a self-guided tour, ☐ see the Grand Bazaar Tour chapter (and allow 1-3 hours). Either way, you'll exit the bazaar at the same place, through the Beyazıt gate (Beyazıt Kapısı).*

❹ Beyazıt District

This next stretch—through the Beyazıt district from the Grand Bazaar and the Mosque of Süleyman the Magnificent—involves about a half-mile walk, and gives you a glimpse at a pocket of everyday life in a neighborhood surrounded by tourism.

Across and to the right from where you exited the bazaar is the entrance to **Sahaflar Çarşısı,** Istanbul's oldest secondhand book market. Precious old books, modern textbooks, traditional calligraphies, and miniature paintings rub elbows in a shady courtyard. For two centuries, this has been a magnet for bibliophiles seeking rare collector's items with fancy illustrations. At the center of the courtyard you'll find a statue of Ibrahim Müteferrika, an 18th century publisher and printer, presiding over it all.

Walk along Çadırcılar Caddesi through vendors selling clothing and textiles. At the end of the busy **textile market,** you emerge facing the wall of Istanbul University's main campus (across the street). This area, between the market and the university, is crowded with a mix of shoppers, tourists, and students. On Fridays, when the mosques are packed, you might see people roll out their prayer mats in the street to join in the midday prayer.

Notice that many stores along here sell **kitchen utensils.** This district was once Istanbul's coppersmith center. Even up until the early 1980s, many people still used copper utensils. But modern materials and methods have taken over, coppersmiths are mainly a thing of the past, and most of the utensils along here are now made of steel, aluminum, or pressed copper or brass.

• *Keeping the university wall to your left, continue straight down the right side of the busy street (Fuat Paşa Caddesi). After a block or so, cross the street to the left side. We'll continue about a quarter-mile straight downhill along this road.*

At the fenced gate in the wall, the landmark 280-foot-tall Beyazıt **fire-watch tower** *marks the grounds of...*

❺ Istanbul University

This state-subsidized school (closed to tourists) is the city's biggest university, drawing over 60,000 students from all over Turkey. The larger of Istanbul University's two main campuses, the sprawling grounds were originally a Roman forum, then an Ottoman palace.

The fire-watch tower itself is also an important piece of city history: Istanbul's homes used to be built mainly of wood, and a single spark could set the whole city ablaze. This stone watchtower dates to 1826; it replaced an earlier wooden version that was destroyed in a fire.

• *After the shops end, the wall continues. Keep going until the end of the wall. Now's the time to decide if you'll visit the massive Mosque of Süleyman the Magnificent (allow about an hour and follow the wall 300 yards uphill to your left) or turn right, steeply downhill toward the Rüstem Paşa Mosque.*

❻ Mosque of Süleyman the Magnificent

Perched high on a hill overlooking Istanbul, this stately mosque befits the most "Magnificent" sultan of the Ottoman Empire. Designed by the empire's greatest architect (Sinan) and dedicated to one of its greatest sultans, the

Mosque of Süleyman the Magnificent gives the Blue Mosque a run for its money. Its pastel interior is a serene counterpoint to the Blue Mosque's vivid colors. The mosque complex holds the mausoleums of Süleyman and his wife, Roxelana, and its "backyard" offers sweeping views of the city below. The surrounding Süleymaniye neighborhood includes a former madrassa (school) that now hosts restaurants and tea gardens.

• *For a self-guided **tour** of the mosque, 📖 see the Mosque of Süleyman the Magnificent Tour chapter. If you follow the tour, come back to this intersection afterward.*

From here, follow İsmetiye Caddesi heading downhill about 100 yards to the second street on your left (Uzun Çarşı Caddesi—look for a sycamore tree on the corner and Vakıf Bank across the street). Turning downhill and left onto this street, you'll see the brick minaret of a 15th-century mosque straight ahead and, behind it, the minaret of Rüstem Paşa Mosque.

❼ Uzun Çarşı Caddesi

As you walk straight ahead along this street—which soon becomes a narrow alley, near the brick minaret—you'll be jostled by shoppers and nudged by delivery trucks trying to sneak their way into the commercial sprawl. Shops on either side cater to locals: hardware stores, stationery shops, toy stores, quilt-makers, sportswear vendors, shoe stores, and so on. If you're looking for a traditional backgammon board—without that shiny, fake mother-of-pearl and wood inlay that strain your eyes as you play—you'll find it here, and pay a lot less.

• *The alley runs directly into a two-story stone building with an arched entryway. Go through the humble doorway and take the stairs up into the courtyard of the...*

❽ Rüstem Paşa Mosque

Built by Sinan in the 16th century, this mosque stands on an elevated platform, supported by vaults that house shops which once provided income for the mosque's upkeep. The mosque's namesake, Rüstem Paşa (ruhs-tehm pah-shah), was a Grand Vizier of Süleyman the Magnificent (after the mysterious death of İbrahim Paşa—see page 170). He found great success in this role, not just because he was Süleyman's son-in-law (he married Süleyman and Roxelana's daughter Mihrimah, whose tomb is next to Süleyman's), but also because he was clever and efficient. Like King Midas, Rüstem

Paşa could turn anything into revenue, and he filled the sultan's treasury. But the public hated him because he taxed everything in sight, and he was frequently accused of embezzling funds.

Admire the giant portico that covers most of the courtyard, and notice that the Rüstem Paşa mosque seems to be missing one feature found at almost every mosque: a fountain for ablution. Because of the limited space in this courtyard, Sinan placed the fountain at street level (down the stairs across the courtyard from where you entered).

The mosque's facade is slathered in gorgeous 16th-century İznik tiles, but the interior is even more impressive. To enter, go around the left side to find the visitors' entrance. Inside, virtually every surface is covered with floral-designed tile panels. (Locals say that if the Blue Mosque is Istanbul's Notre-Dame, this tiny gem is its Sainte-Chapelle.) Scaffolding for ongoing restoration work may obscure your view of the tiles; check locally.

• *Because the next alley we'll be using is always packed with people—especially on Saturdays—consider reading the following section before you start walking. Leave the mosque complex through the door you entered, passing some enticing tile souvenirs. Turn left and walk down...*

❾ Hasırcılar Caddesi

Hasırcılar Caddesi ("Mat-Weavers' Alley") is a real-life market street—part of the commercial sprawl surrounding our next sight, the Spice Market.

As you walk, notice the porters and the carts squeezing their heavy, wide loads through the alley. You'll pass old *bedestens* (traditional commercial buildings) and stores, many of them family-owned for generations. If you had strolled this street a century ago, only the shoppers' clothes would have been different.

At the first corner on your left, notice the store selling hunting knives and rifles. Turkey has strong gun-control laws, but they don't extend to hunting rifles—you just need a hunting license to own one of these weapons.

One block before the Spice Market entrance, you'll smell the aroma of fresh-roasted coffee and spices. If you're in the market for spices, dried fruits, sweets, and nuts, start checking the prices along here—they're cheaper than in the high-rent Spice Market. Ask for a sample, and don't feel obligated to buy. While bargaining has become common in the Grand Bazaar, around here you'll generally pay what's on the price tag for food and spices—though you can haggle for souvenirs and exotic items (such as saffron and imported caviar).

• *Half a block before the arched entry to the Spice Market (the big brick-and-stone building at the end of the alley), you'll be immersed in a lively bazaar of...*

❿ Food Vendors

On your left, look for a thriving deli, **Namlı Şarküteri** (a.k.a. NamPort), with large containers of olives, pickled peppers, and hanging pastramis out front (get a sample inside). It's been here for over a century, selling a wide range of traditional cold *mezes* (appetizers): dry salted fish, spicy tomato and pepper pastes, pickles, *sucuk* (soo-jook; spicy veal sausage), Turkish pastrami, and a variety of white cheeses made from sheep's and cow's milk. They also make a high-cholesterol sandwich called *kumru* (koom-roo; meaning "dove"), stuffed with spicy sausages, salami, and smoked cow's tongue. Wander through to get a feeling for what locals buy at the grocery store, and say hello to Zeki, the guy who runs the place. Upstairs is an oasis of a cafeteria (air-con, bright, cheery, and fast).

A little farther ahead on the right, just before the Spice Market entrance, is one of the best coffee vendors in town: the venerable **Kurukahveci Mehmet Efendi Mahdumları** (say it three times fast). This is the locals' favorite place to get ground coffee. Remember that only sealed packets can be taken through US Customs, and pick up the leaflet with preparation instructions when you check out. There's often a long line of loyal customers waiting at the cashier. If you can't find it on the map, just follow your nose.

• *Just after the coffee shop is the Spice Market's Hasırcılar Gate. But rather than entering the market here, let's walk around the side of the L-shaped building to its main entrance, facing the Golden Horn.*

Turn left and continue along the street (following the Spice Market wall). Along this alley you'll spot several more shops displaying spices, dried fruits, and sweets, alongside butcher, fishmonger, and dairy shops. The Turks have a word for this vibrant scene: pazar *(pah-zahr), which gave us the English word "bazaar."*

The alley opens to your left into the large...

⓫ Eminönü Square (Eminönü Meydanı)

This square, with the Golden Horn (not quite visible from here) on the other side of the busy street, was once a huge outdoor bazaar. You may still see a few makeshift stands with **vendors** hawking anything from clothes to fake jewelry to giant posters of pop stars. The vendors, who "forget" to pay taxes, are routinely rounded up by local police—so don't be surprised if you see a string of people running up the street with merchandise in their hands, chased by city inspectors.

Also notice the **pigeons:** Many Turks believe that getting pooped on by a bird is good luck—and reason enough to buy a lottery ticket. Unless you're interested in putting this to the test, don't get too close to the buildings (where the birds are likely to be perched overhead, just waiting to bestow luck).

Our next stop is the Spice Market. Before we dive in, consider your **options:** You could take a break, sitting with locals on the platforms by the side of the square, watching the people pass by. (If you've bought some munchies, here's a good place to picnic. You can get a beverage from a nearby store, or from the newsstand straight ahead.)

If you'd like a cup of coffee or tea, walk to your immediate left down the alley bordering the square to find **Café Society,** usually crowded with locals. It has tables and chairs out front where you can sit down and relax. Or if you're hungry for a

meal, go next door to the recommended **Hamdi Restaurant,** which specializes in meaty kebabs.

• *Continue around the corner of the Spice Market to the right. The square in front of the Spice Market is dominated by the ⓬ New Mosque of Mother Sultan, a good example of a classical, traditional-style Ottoman mosque (opened in 1665).*

With the mosque on your left, you're facing the front of the Spice Market. Notice the outdoor plant and pet market to the left. A WC is in the inner corner of the "L" formed by the Spice Market. Now enter the...

⓭ Spice Market

Built at the same time as the not-so New Mosque, this 17th-century market hall was gradually taken over by merchants dealing in spices, herbs, medicinal plants, and pharmaceuticals. While it's quite a touristy scene today, most stalls still sell these traditional products, and the air is heavy with the aroma of exotic spices. Locals call it the Mısır Çarşışı (Egyptian Bazaar) because it was once funded by taxes collected from Egypt.

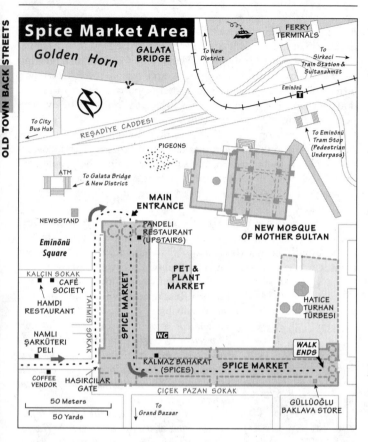

Spice Market Area

Golden Horn

GALATA BRIDGE

FERRY TERMINALS

To New District

To Sirkeci Train Station & Sultanahmet

Eminönü

To City Bus Hub

REŞADIYE CADDESI

PIGEONS

To Eminönü Tram Stop (Pedestrian Underpass)

ATM

To Galata Bridge & New District

MAIN ENTRANCE

NEWSSTAND

PANDELI RESTAURANT (UPSTAIRS)

NEW MOSQUE OF MOTHER SULTAN

Eminönü Square

KALÇIN SOKAK

CAFÉ SOCIETY

HAMDI RESTAURANT

SPICE MARKET

TAHMIS SOKAK

PET & PLANT MARKET

HATICE TURHAN TÜRBESI

WC

NAMLI ŞARKÜTERI DELI

WALK ENDS

KALMAZ BAHARAT (SPICES)

SPICE MARKET

COFFEE VENDOR

HASIRCILAR GATE

ÇIÇEK PAZAN SOKAK

50 Meters

50 Yards

To Grand Bazaar

GÜLLÜOĞLU BAKLAVA STORE

(To the left as you enter, a staircase leads up to the recommended and historic **Pandeli Restaurant**.)

First Wing: While smaller and less imposing than the Grand Bazaar, the Spice Market is more colorful and more traditional. On either side of the long, vaulted central hall are a wide range of **merchant stalls,** most of them with sacks and barrels out front showing off their wares. While merchants once sat quietly, cross-legged, next to their shops, today they engage in a never-ending game of one-upmanship, competing for the attention of passersby. If you're offered a sample, feel free to accept—but be warned that it can be difficult to pry yourself away from the sales pitch that's sure to ensue.

Aside from the **spices,**

you'll also see natural sponges, lentils and beans, pistachios and hazelnuts, and several kinds of sweets—including, of course, **Turkish delight.** While most Westerners think of Turkish delight as being colored and fruit-flavored, locals prefer more adventurous varieties: with double-roasted pistachios, or the kind with walnuts in grape or mulberry molasses called *sucuk* (also the name of the spicy veal sausage).

Look for the granddaddy of spices, **saffron.** Locals still use saffron (mostly in rice pilaf and dessert), though not as much as they used to. The best saffron is Spanish; the local kind—cheaper and not as dark-red—usually comes mixed with other herbs. The caviar you see isn't local; it's mostly from Iran or Russia. More authentic are the Turkish dried fruit, especially **apricots** and **figs.** Dried vegetables, eggplant, and green peppers hang from the walls. Cooks use these to make dolma (dohl-mah; "to stuff"), stuffing them with rice and raisins, or rice and meat. You'll also see lots of sacks full of green powder. This is **henna,** traditionally used as a hair dye and for skin care. In the countryside, young women stain the palms of their hands with henna the night before they get married. For tips on what to buy in the Spice Market, see the Shopping chapter. Lately these old-fashioned shops are being joined by souvenir shops and jewelry stores, making this a mini Grand Bazaar of sorts.

• *Walk to the far end of the hall. Straight ahead is a gate leading to an always-busy street that heads five blocks up to the Grand Bazaar; to the right is the Hasırcılar Gate and the alley that leads to the Rüstem Paşa Mosque. And to your left is the Spice Market's side wing. Turn left.*

Side Wing: The Spice Market's side wing is less crowded and less colorful than the main concourse. After a few steps, look for a tiny shop on the left (second from the corner) called **Kalmaz Baharat.** *Baharat* (bah-hah-raht) means "spice," and this is one of the few shops that still sells the most exotic spices of the past. Adnan, the owner, has herbal teas, thick aromatic oils, natural-fiber bath gloves, and olive-oil soap (white is better than green). He also sells the aphrodisiac called "sultan's paste" (more recently dubbed "Turkish Viagra"). This mix of several kinds of herbs and spices supposedly gave the sultan the oomph to enjoy his harem, and is still used as an all-purpose energy booster today.

TURKISH VIAGRA
IF YOU TAKE
YOU CAN MAKE
LOVE 5 TIMES
IN THE NIGHT

Browse your way to the end of this wing (notice the great **Güllüoğlu Baklava** store on the right, the third shop before the exit). You probably deserve a treat about now!

• *Our tour is complete. For more suggestions in the Spice Market, see the Shopping chapter.*

*When you're ready to leave, retrace your steps to the main entrance. You'll be facing the **Galata Bridge** over the Golden Horn, with the New District beyond. To reach the bridge, use the pedestrian underpass (ahead and to the left, with an ATM nearby). Notice the many restaurants on the lower level of the bridge (this area is described in the Golden Horn Walk chapter).*

*To reach the **Eminönü tram stop**, walk to the right between the New Mosque and busy Reşadiye street. Where the mosque ends, you'll see the entrance to another pedestrian underpass. Halfway through the underpass, steps lead up to separate tram platforms: The first is for the Old Town; the second is for the New District.*

*You can generally wave down a **cab** along the main street right in front of the Spice Market.*

GRAND BAZAAR TOUR

Kapali Çarsi

The world's oldest shopping mall is a labyrinthine warren of shops and pushy merchants—a unique Istanbul experience that shouldn't be missed, even if you're not a shopper. While parts of the bazaar are overrun with international visitors, it also has many virtually tourist-free nooks and crannies that offer an insightful glimpse into the "real" Istanbul.

Sprawling over a huge area in the historic city center, Kapalı Çarşı (kah-pah-luh chahr-shuh; "Covered Market") was a bustling market during Byzantine times, and grew even larger when the Ottomans arrived. Anchored by traditional *bedestens* (commercial complexes of related shops and workshops), over time the diverse merchant shops were connected and roofed into a single market hall. At its prime, the Grand Bazaar was the center for trade for the entire Ottoman Empire, guarded by a hundred soldiers like a fortified castle.

By the 1950s, the Grand Bazaar had 4,000 shops, bursting with everything from jewelry to silk, and from traditional copperware to exotic imports. But then came the tourists, and many local merchants were displaced by glitzy jewelry, souvenir, and carpet shops.

Even though the bazaar has lost some of its traditional ambience, a visit here is still an irreplaceable part of any trip to Istanbul. Because navigating the bazaar can be confusing, I've designed a short, (fairly) easy-to-follow tour to get you started. We'll go through the schlocky tourist zones but also sample a bit of the outer fringe, still frequented more by Turks than tourists.

Orientation

Cost and Hours: Free to enter and browse, open Mon-Sat 9:00-19:00, closed Sun and during religious holidays.

Information: A useful map is online at www.kapalicarsi.com.tr.

Getting There: It's behind the Nuruosmaniye Mosque, across the parking lot from the Çemberlitaş tram stop. From Sultanahmet, follow the tram tracks uphill on Divan Yolu Caddesi for about five blocks. Turn right at the Çemberlitaş column, and you should see the Nuruosmaniye Mosque towering beyond the parking lot. Walk through the mosque courtyard to find the starting point of this tour. (For a narrated walk from Sultanahmet to the Grand Bazaar, see the beginning of the Old Town Back Streets Walk chapter.)

Navigating the Bazaar: The Grand Bazaar is a giant, maze-like commercial complex with named "streets" *(caddesi)* and "alleys" *(sokak)*. But few of these streets and alleys are well marked, and the few signs are often obscured by merchandise, so relying on these names isn't always successful. Navigate using the map in this chapter and by asking people you encounter for help. (But be aware that asking a merchant for directions may suck you into a lengthy conversation about the wonders of his wares.) Most of the specific shops described in this tour are well-established landmarks.

Length of This Tour: Allow between one and three hours, depending on how much shopping you plan to do.

Pickpocket Alert: The Grand Bazaar probably contains the highest concentration of pickpockets in Istanbul. Watch your valuables.

Shopping Tips: This tour goes hand-in-hand with the Shopping chapter. Consider reading that chapter beforehand, perhaps while nursing a cup of Turkish coffee in the bazaar (focus on the bargaining tips if you plan to buy anything). For advice on dealing with overly zealous shopkeepers here (and elsewhere), see the "Dealing with Aggressive Merchants" sidebar.

Eating: For recommended eateries within and near the Grand Bazaar, see the Eating in Istanbul chapter.

Rainy Day: This tour is a good bad-weather activity, since almost the entire bazaar is covered.

The Tour Begins

• *Enter the Grand Bazaar through the* **Nuruosmaniye Gate** *(beneath its Ottoman coat of arms), and pause a moment to take it all in.*

Dealing with Aggressive Merchants

Throughout the Grand Bazaar—and just about everywhere in the Old Town—you'll constantly be barraged by people selling everything you can imagine. This can be intimidating—or fun if you loosen up and approach it with a sense of humor. The main rule of thumb: Don't feel compelled to look at or buy anything. Vendors prey on Americans' gregariousness and tendency to respond politely to anyone who offers a friendly greeting. They often use surprising or attention-grabbing openers:

"Hello, Americans! Where are you from? Chicago?! I have a cousin there!"

"Are you lost? Can I help you find something?"

"Nice shoes! Are those Turkish shoes?"

"Would you like a cup of tea?"

The list is endless—collect your favorites.

If you're not interested, simply say a firm, "No, thanks!" and brush past them, ignoring any additional comments. This may seem cold, but it's the only way to get through the market without constantly getting tied up in unwanted conversations.

If, on the other hand, you're looking to chat, merchants are often very talkative—but be warned that a lengthy conversation may give them false hopes that you're looking to buy, and could make it even more difficult to extract yourself gracefully from the interaction.

❶ Entrance

You're immediately thrust into a sensory overload of bustling shoppers and aggressive merchants, lit by thousands of electric bulbs. Welcome to the Grand Bizarre . . . er, Bazaar.

This part of the market is typical of the ever-changing Grand Bazaar: Once the humble Kalpakçılar, or the "Hatmakers' Street," it's now dominated by glitzy jewelry. As we'll see, Turks love

GRAND BAZAAR TOUR

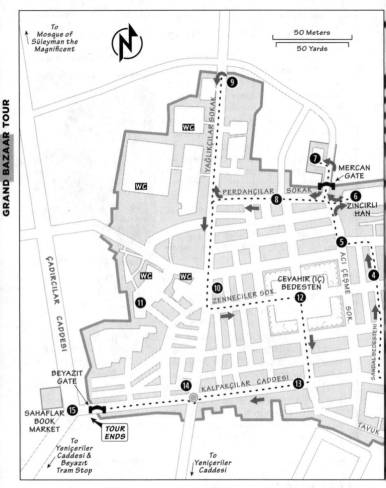

gold, not because they're vain or greedy, but because they're practical: Since local currency can be unstable, people buy gold bracelets or necklaces as a tangible way to hang onto their savings.

• *Take a few steps along Kalpakçılar. Detour for a quick look through the first entryway on your right, which leads into the...*

❷ Sandal Bedesteni

Traditionally, each section of the bazaar had its own unique product. The specialty here was once *sandal* (not shoes but instead a luxury textile made of a blend of silk and cotton, woven with threads the color of sandalwood), though now you'll see a wide array of tourist items. But the *bedestin* still has the same 15th-century layout—a central courtyard surrounded by product-selling shops and product-making workshops.

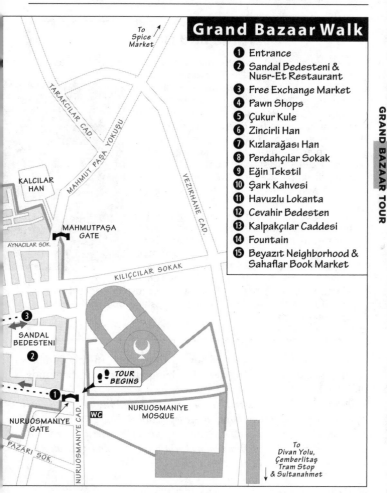

Grand Bazaar Walk

1. Entrance
2. Sandal Bedesteni & Nusr-Et Restaurant
3. Free Exchange Market
4. Pawn Shops
5. Çukur Kule
6. Zincirli Han
7. Kızlarağası Han
8. Perdahçılar Sokak
9. Eğin Tekstil
10. Şark Kahvesi
11. Havuzlu Lokanta
12. Cevahir Bedesten
13. Kalpakçılar Caddesi
14. Fountain
15. Beyazıt Neighborhood & Sahaflar Book Market

Today the courtyard is entirely occupied by the upscale Nusr-Et Restaurant, a chain steakhouse owned by Turkish chef and social media phenom Nusret Gökçe (nicknamed the "Salt Bae" for his unique meat-seasoning technique—Google it).

• *Continue on Kalpakçılar and turn right at the first intersection, going downhill on Sandal Bedesteni Sokak ("Sandal Street"). After about 50 yards, turn right at the next alley to the...*

❸ Free Exchange Market

You'll hear it before you see it. From about 10:00 until 17:00, this area is full of hundreds of boisterous men shouting into their phones and waving their arms. These are currency brokers, trading Turkish lira into other currencies and back again—a kind of poor man's Wall Street. Because the Turkish lira's value fluctuates, many

Turks and Gold

Traditionally, Turks celebrating special occasions—such as a wedding or a boy's circumcision—receive gold as a gift. In fact, in the most traditional corners of Turkey, the groom's family still must present the bride's family with gold bracelets before the couple can marry.

Because gold is used primarily as an investment, and only secondarily as an accessory, it's most commonly sold in the form of simple 22-carat bracelets (24-carat is too soft to wear). If you see a woman whose arm is lined with five or six gold bracelets, she's not making a fashion statement—she's wearing her family's savings on her sleeve, literally. Recently, jewelers have started selling more elaborately decorated designer pieces. These are more expensive and less appealing to thrifty locals (since you're paying for the workmanship, not just the gold itself). Instead, locals who want jewelry for fashion buy cheaper 14- or 18-carat bracelets.

Turks play the money market hoping to win big. In this humble setting, people are cutting deals involving hundreds of thousands of dollars.

• *Backtrack to "Sandal Street," turn right, and continue on. You'll pass by a number of* ❹ *pawn shops, where locals can exchange their "investment jewelry" for hard cash. Continue to where the street dead-ends at a T-intersection. Turn left to find a charming brown-and-gold wooden structure clogging the intersection ahead.*

❺ Çukur Kule

This adorable structure, built as a teahouse in the 17th century and known as the "Oriental Kiosk," sells jewelry today. The fountain next to the kiosk is called the "Bitter Fountain." Avoid the water here...just in case. And watch for falling motorcycles—in the James Bond movie *Skyfall*, a motorcycle crashes through the roof and onto the (now rebuilt) kiosk.

• *From here, let's see some less-touristy shops and a few actual workshops (called "hans") where goods are made. Turn right at the kiosk (onto Acı Çeşme) and walk toward the end of the alley. On your right, just before the bazaar exit, marked by an arrow hanging from the vaulted ceiling, is the entrance to...*

❻ Zincirli Han

Rough steps take you into this quiet little courtyard surrounded by (mostly jewelry) shops and workshops. Zincirli Han (zeen-jeer-lee hahn; "Chain Han") is less fancy, but also less aggressive, than the more touristy zones.

Check out a few shops. At the far end of the courtyard, **Merim Kuyumculuk** makes its own jewelery. The owner, Ferdi, may let you see his tiny workshop upstairs.

Osman's Carpet Shop—run by a hard-to-miss "professor of carpets" nicknamed Şişko (sheesh-koh; "Fatty")—is a good place for high-quality (read: expensive) carpets and expert advice. The staff here is low-pressure and informative. This fifth-generation shop is hardly a secret—notice the celebrity photos and press clippings on the wall.

• *Let's go even more local. Backtrack to where you entered the* han, *turn right (on Acı Çeşme), and exit the Grand Bazaar through the Mercan Gate into the light of day (past traditional gold-bracelet shops). Then turn left (at #94), into the...*

❼ Kızlarağası Han

This humble courtyard hosts humble workers who recycle secondhand gold and silver into something usable. The low-profile teahouse serves simple glasses of tea to an almost exclusively local crowd. Buy a glass, join the gang playing backgammon, and chat with the kids (who generally know a few words of English). Get your shoes shined by friendly Cafer (jah-fehr, 2-4 TL), and leave with slick shoes and a shiny memory.

Find the shop (across from the teahouse) of **Ayhan Usta** (eye-hahn oos-tah; "Ayhan the Master"), one of the goldsmiths. Ayhan

speaks only Turkish, but if you peek into his shop, he may wave you in. Cautious at first, Ayhan enjoys showing travelers how he melts cast-off gold shavings down for reuse. You need not pay or tip him in return—he simply likes to share his craft with curi-

What Is a *Han*?

An important element of commerce in Ottoman times, a *han* (hahn) was an inn located in an urban business district to accommodate tradesmen, diplomats, students, and travelers. The concept brings to mind the caravanserais (secure lodging for caravans) popular along eastern trade routes. *Hans* eventually developed into commercial centers, with production facilities and markets for various handicrafts. Later, *hans* specialized in the trade and production of a particular item. Most were (and still are) owned by state trusts, although some were privately owned.

Traditional *hans* usually had a rectangular floor plan, with rooms and passages around a central courtyard. The main gate into the complex was designed to be large enough to accommodate animals loaded with goods. While some of Istanbul's *hans* have three floors, most have two: The first (ground) floor contained a storage area, stables for animals, and repair shops. Dormitory-style guest rooms were located on the second floor. Guests spread sleeping mats on the floor at night and tucked them away in wall niches during the day.

A typical *han* had a *mescit* (mehs-jeet; small mosque) in the courtyard. In *hans* frequented by Jews or Christians, synagogues or chapels were common.

ous travelers. Stay safely away from the fire (burning at 2,200°F)—especially when he tosses in some white powder to increase the temperature as he melts the gold.

Ayhan belongs to a dying breed of craftsmen. Today most gold-working is done in large factories outside the city. But locals believe the Grand Bazaar needs both shops and workshops to be successful. If a product isn't perfect, the shopkeeper can send it to his workshop for an adjustment. And if workshops like Ayhan's are forced out by high rents and replaced with more "Made in Taiwan" gift shops, the soul of the Grand Bazaar will be lost.

• *Return to the Grand Bazaar. As you enter, take the first right, down a big lane called* ❽ *Perdahçılar Sokak, lined with a colorful mish-mash of shops. Follow this lane 100 yards, to a T-junction, then turn right onto Yağlıkçılar Sokak and walk toward the bazaar exit. To the right, just inside the exit door, find the textile store called...*

GRAND BAZAAR TOUR

❾ Eğin Tekstil

This textile shop is steeped in history: The storage annex in the back wall was constructed in Byzantine times. They have been in business for more than 150 years, and owner Süleyman—who continues the family tradition even though he's a doctor by trade—still has the Ottoman deed to the store.

Go inside and say hello to Süleyman or one of his assistants, who'd be happy to tell you about their shop's history...and, of course, what they are selling. Their specialty is *peştemal* (pash-tah-mahl), the traditional cotton towel for visits to a hamam. Prices are marked, fixed, and fair. (They value Rick Steves readers—show this book for attentive service and a possible RS% discount or token of appreciation.)

• *Exit, turn left to dive back into the maze, and backtrack on Yağlıkçılar Sokak. Continuing past the intersection with Perdahçılar Sokak, watch on the left for the* ❿ *Şark Kahvesi (shark kah-veh-see) coffee shop. This Istanbul institution is a good place to sample Turkish coffee (see page 74). Just past Şark Kahvesi, a lane on the right leads to the recommended* ⓫ *Havuzlu Lokanta restaurant.*

But we're turning left, going downhill on the alley called Zenneciler Sokak. Soon the lane opens up into a somewhat spacious courtyard.

⓬ Cevahir Bedesten

You've reached the center of the Grand Bazaar labyrinth. Cevahir Bedesten was originally a 15th-century freestanding warehouse for merchants—with domed bays supported by eight massive pillars. It's taller than the rest of the bazaar, classier, and a bit quieter. You'll find icons, jewelry, miniatures, coins, cameras, worry beads, and (always a good gift idea) daggers.

• *From the center of Cevahir Bedesten, turn 90 degrees to the right and leave through the door into the bustling alleys of the bazaar. Continue up this zone packed with souvenir and carpet shops. After 50 yards, you'll reach the intersection with the bazaar's main street,* ⓭ *Kalpakçılar Caddesi.*

To leave the market the way we came in (at the start of our tour), you could turn left (downhill), going 100 yards to reach the Nuruosmaniye Gate (and the Çemberlitaş tram stop beyond).

But we'll turn right on Kalpakçılar Caddesi. About 100 yards along, you'll pass a ⓮ *fountain (with nice leather and textile shops to the right). Keep going another 100 yards, where you'll exit the Grand Bazaar through the Beyazıt Gate.*

⓯ Beyazıt Neighborhood

You've entered the Beyazıt (beh-yah-zuht) district, where market crowds and students from the nearby Istanbul University mix. To your right is a crowded clothing and textiles market, popular with bargain-hunters; nearby is Istanbul's old **book market,** the Sahaflar Çarşısı (described in the Old Town Back Streets Walk chapter).

• *This is a pleasant place to end our Grand Bazaar shopping experience. If you want more of the Grand Bazaar, you've now got a good orientation to explore more of its 4,000 shops. The Beyazit tram stop is just 100 yards away. Or, from here you can pick up my* 📖 *Old Town Back Streets Walk.*

MOSQUE OF SÜLEYMAN THE MAGNIFICENT TOUR

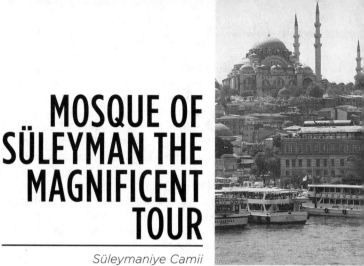

Süleymaniye Camii

Built for the sultan by his prolific architect, Sinan, and completed in 1557, the Mosque of Süleyman the Magnificent almost outdoes the Blue Mosque in its sheer size, architecture, and design. Its subtly understated interior is decorated in pastel tones.

The term "Süleymaniye" applies not just to the mosque, but to the huge network of related buildings that nestle around it on a hilltop overlooking the city. Within this complex are the ornate mausoleums of Süleyman and his wife, Roxelana, as well as a former madrassa (theological school).

Imagine the pomp and circumstance on the summer day in 1550 when construction began: Sultan Süleyman the Magnificent arrives on his horse, along with the clergy. He orders his guards to give alms to the poor and to sacrifice rams for a fortunate start. As the crowd recites verses from the Quran, the head of the clergy sets the first stone of the foundation. Within six years, the dome would be complete; the following year, the mosque would open for worship. The whole shebang took only a decade to finish.

The mosque has been renovated in recent years, and today is almost as clean and shiny as it was the day it opened.

Orientation

Cost and Hours: Mosque—Free, generally open daily from one hour after sunrise until one hour before sunset, closed to visitors five times a day for prayer. Mausoleums—Free, daily 9:00-17:00, until 18:00 in summer.

Dress Code: You'll need to remove your shoes. Modest dress (covered knees and shoulders) is expected for men and women, and women should wear a headscarf. For more tips, read "Visiting a Mosque" in the Experiences chapter.

Getting There: The mosque is on a hill near Istanbul University, on Sıddık Sami Onar Caddesi in the Süleymaniye neighborhood. It's a short walk from most places in the Old Town (and an easy stop on my Old Town Back Streets Walk). Coming from Taksim or further north, take the Metro to Vezneciler Station.

Length of This Tour: Allow one hour.

Services: WCs are located just outside either end of the mosque wall, and at the opposite corner of the mosque's outer courtyard. Restaurants and a coffee shop are located within the former madrassa alongside the mosque.

Starring: One of Sinan's great mosques; the mausoleums of Süleyman and his wife, Roxelana; and the Süleymaniye neighborhood.

The Tour Begins

• *Enter the mosque complex at its southern corner, by the large street* ❶ *fountain.*

Standing in the square with the mosque to your right, to your left is the ❷ **madrassa.** Originally, this school of theology was divided into three sections: The first two were devoted to interpreting the Quran, while the third (at the far end, with the flagpole at its entrance) was a medical school—now it's a hospital.

This peaceful space, stretching along the mosque's outer courtyard wall, today is lined with decent restaurants.

• *Now use the gate near the big fountain to enter the mosque's...*

❸ Outer Courtyard

As you enter this courtyard, walk straight ahead to the gate leading into the ❹ **cemetery.** Just before you enter the cemetery, look to your left to see two elevated stone slabs—these are used to support the coffin during a funeral service. According to Muslim tradition, the body of the deceased is washed and wrapped in a white shroud, then placed in a wood coffin and brought to stone slabs such as these. Relatives and friends gather nearby, and the imam (cleric) leads them in one last prayer for the soul of the deceased. The body is then taken into the cemetery and buried, still in the shroud but without the coffin. Just as a Muslim faces Mecca to pray, the body of a Muslim is buried so that it points eternally toward Mecca.

• *Go through the gate into the cemetery with the...*

SÜLEYMAN MOSQUE

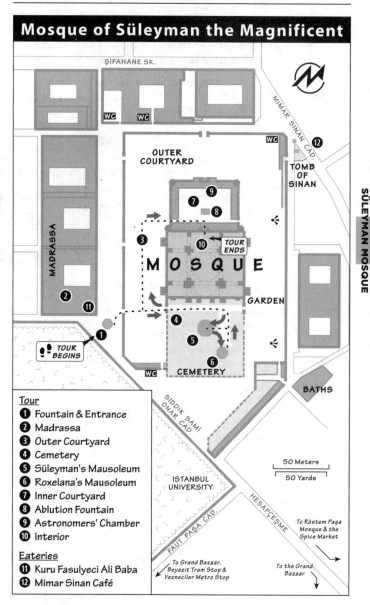

Mosque of Süleyman the Magnificent

Tour
1. Fountain & Entrance
2. Madrassa
3. Outer Courtyard
4. Cemetery
5. Süleyman's Mausoleum
6. Roxelana's Mausoleum
7. Inner Courtyard
8. Ablution Fountain
9. Astronomers' Chamber
10. Interior

Eateries
11. Kuru Fasulyeci Ali Baba
12. Mimar Sinan Café

SÜLEYMAN MOSQUE

Mausoleums of Süleyman the Magnificent and Roxelana

As you walk through the headstones (some dating back to the early 17th century), notice that each tomb has two stones. The larger stone was inscribed with the epitaph, while the smaller one was for decoration.

Süleyman the Magnificent (1494-1566) and Roxelana (c. 1498-1558)

Süleyman the Magnificent, the 10th sultan of the Ottoman Empire, ruled for nearly a half-century (1520-1566). His reign was the Golden Age of Ottoman history, when the Ottoman Empire was the world's greatest power. The treasury was bursting, and the empire's borders stretched from North Africa to Central Europe to the Near East. One-third of the population in Western Asia and around the Mediterranean lived under the Ottoman flag.

Süleyman ruled during the age of powerful leaders. His contemporaries were Holy Roman Emperor Charles V, King François I of France, and King Henry VIII of England. A peace treaty ending a dispute with Austria refers to Süleyman as the "Emperor of the East and the West"—the first time someone had laid claim to that title since the Byzantine Emperor Justinian, a thousand years prior. In signing the treaty, Charles V accepted Süleyman's superiority despite his own title of "Holy Roman Emperor."

While Westerners know him as Süleyman the Magnificent, the Turkish people call him "Süleyman the Legislator" or "Süleyman the Law Giver." His greatest contribution was to codify Ottoman law. As the ruler of a multinational empire, Süleyman realized that different regions and different peoples needed different laws.

Süleyman's first son (and presumptive heir), Crown Prince Mustafa, was born to his chief consort, Gülbahar. But Süleyman later fell deeply in love with one of his concubines, Roxelana. Kidnapped by traders from her native Poland and sold into the slave market at Constantinople, Roxelana was sent to the palace harem. She was ambitious and managed to get herself presented to the sultan, drawing his attention by daring to laugh in his pres-

• *Follow the stone path to the first and bigger* ❺ *mausoleum (on your right).*

In 1566, the aging Süleyman the Magnificent went on one last military campaign, where he died silently in his tent during his army's siege of Szigetvár, a fortress in southern Hungary. His clever Grand Vizier knew that the army would disband if they found out the sultan was dead, so he hid the sultan's death and covertly had Süleyman's body mummified. (Meanwhile, the Grand Vizier sent a note to Süleyman's son, Selim, telling him to grab the throne before another one of his relatives did.) The magnificent sultan's death

ence. Süleyman named her "Hürrem"—his "Cheerful One."

Underestimating this humble girl, the jealous Gülbahar snubbed Roxelana, addressed her as "slave," and even physically attacked her. Süleyman had Gülbahar banished, and Roxelana became his chief consort. She persuaded Süleyman to legally marry her—a first for a slave concubine—and bore the sultan five children (four sons and a daughter).

Gülbahar's son, Crown Prince Mustafa, remained an obstacle for Roxelana, who hoped one of her sons would become sultan after Süleyman. She convinced Süleyman that Mustafa was plotting against him, and Süleyman had him strangled.

Of Roxelana's four sons, two died of natural causes, and a third was strangled on Süleyman's orders. The remaining son survived to eventually take the throne as Selim II.

Roxelana's influence grew as Süleyman turned to her for advice in all his decisions. She was the first of several powerful women who ruled the Ottoman Empire from behind the scenes over the next 150 years. Relentless in her ambition, Roxelana is said to have orchestrated dozens of murders to secure her surviving son's crown. In what may have been a sort of public apology, Roxelana later spent her personal fortune creating charitable institutions.

When Roxelana died in 1558, Süleyman had a separate mausoleum built for her. After Süleyman's death eight years later, he was buried in a mausoleum of his own—forever separated from the strong-willed woman who'd changed his life.

was kept secret until after the army returned in victory to Istanbul, when his body was interred next to the mosque that bears his name.

• *At the entrance porch, remove your shoes and stow them on the wooden shelves, then step inside.*

A year after Süleyman's death, the best stonemasons and marble-workers in the empire came here to build a *türbe* (tuhr-beh), or mausoleum, that would mirror Süleyman's fame. They were led by Sinan, the master architect who'd also built the mosque. The mausoleum was considered complete when it was decorated with precious tiles from İznik (bordered with Arabic inscriptions—excerpts from the Quran). Candles and oil lamps were lit, Süleyman's robe was laid over the green cover of the ceremonial coffin, and imams began reading aloud from the Quran...and didn't stop for years.

On either side of the entrance are some of the most beautiful tile frames anywhere. Above the door are inscribed the words, "There is no other God but Allah, and Muhammad is his Prophet." The larger tomb (cenotaph) at the center of the mausoleum is Süleyman's. On either side are Süleyman's two heirs, their relatives, and Süleyman and Roxelana's daughter (to his right). Notice the room's gorgeous details: floral-designed İznik tiles, marble paintwork, beautiful woodwork on the window and door shutters, and decorative ostrich eggs and colored replicas in the frame hanging from the ceiling.

As you exit, the entrance to ❻ **Roxelana's mausoleum** is to your right. While not as impressive as her husband's, it's worth a look. Enjoy the attractive tiles, and notice the "stalactites" decorating the niches between the windows. Roxelana's cenotaph is the first one, surrounded by an elegant inlaid wood panel. Take a close look at the workmanship—thousands of tiny wood pieces fitted together.

• *Exit the cemetery back into the outer courtyard, turn right, and walk along the mosque. You'll see stairs leading up to a gate reserved for worshippers (usually no visitors are allowed). Continue beyond this gate to the far end of the mosque, and climb a few stairs into the...*

❼ Inner Courtyard

Like the rest of the Süleymaniye complex, this courtyard was designed by the architect Sinan. He was a master of creating spaces that were at once plain and tranquil. Looking around the courtyard, appreciate Sinan's command of architectural grace: It's not ostentatious, but the surrounding porticos and soaring minarets make it feel appropriately majestic. Take a moment to consider the architectural beauty of what is not only the finest mosque in Istanbul, but also one of the finest in all of Islam.

If you've already been to the Blue Mosque, you'll notice some similar features here: The domed porticos around the perimeter look decorative, but they're also functional, providing shade in

Turkey's Greatest Architect: Mimar Sinan (1489-1588)

Mimar Sinan was one of the greatest architects the world has ever seen. Born to a Christian family in a small village in Kayseri (ancient Caesarea, in central Turkey), he spent his childhood as an apprentice to his father, a mason and carpenter. When he was about 23 years old, Sinan was conscripted into the sultan's service, where he converted to Islam and was assigned to the elite janissaries. (For more on the system of janissaries, see the sidebar on page 131.)

Sinan received the customary janissary education, living with a Turkish family to learn the Turkish language and culture. He built tile kilns in İznik, developing an appreciation for tiles (and later using them to adorn his most important works). He also worked in the construction of government and military buildings, polishing his skills and learning techniques that would serve him well as an architect.

Sinan traveled extensively with the army, from Vienna to Baghdad. He was a student of architecture everywhere he

went, examining what made structures strong or weak, beautiful or ugly. During military campaigns, Sinan built bridges, forts, siege towers, and canals. His abilities, which literally paved the way for the army, impressed the sultan. Sinan became the royal architect in 1539, serving Süleyman the Magnificent and two of his successors. Sinan worked until the day he died, at age 99. During his prolific career, he built over 450 monuments, including 20 royal mosques in Istanbul alone. Most of his buildings are still standing—including his masterpiece, the Mosque of Süleyman the Magnificent.

Less visually striking, but arguably more important, were Sinan's improvements to Istanbul's water-distribution infrastructure. Süleyman was so happy with the results that he allowed Sinan to pipe running water into the architect's own home, a privilege previously enjoyed only by the sultan.

Sinan was an intellectual, a researcher, and an avid reader who spent extravagant sums on books. One of his greatest joys upon becoming the royal architect was gaining access to the royal library. Though he achieved personal glory and success, Sinan always remained a loyal servant to the Ottoman dynasty, praising those who encouraged him to follow his passion. While largely unfamiliar to Westerners, this contemporary of Leonardo da Vinci and Michelangelo certainly ranks among those greats.

summer and shelter in winter. The shutters are opened for ventilation in the summer. The portico that runs along the front of the mosque is elevated, giving it a grand appearance; this area is used for overflow worshipers when services fill up. The old marble ❽ **fountain** in the middle of the courtyard was used for ablution—ritual cleansing before worship.

The main gate of the courtyard is across from the entrance to the mosque. (This door is usually kept closed, but we'll see it from the other side later on this tour.) Notice the first shutters on either side of this door and the windows above them. These appear identical to the other shutters around the courtyard, but they ac-

tually hide the entrance to a special ❾ **chamber** used by astronomers—who had the important responsibility of calculating the exact time for worship, five times each day, based on the position of the sun.

This mosque has four minarets. Mosques financed by sultans often had more than one minaret, to show off the sultan's wealth. Here, the extra minarets symbolize the initial four caliphs (religious and social leaders who succeeded the Prophet Muhammad). Notice that there are a total of 10 balconies on the minarets. This is also symbolic: Süleyman was the 10th sultan of the Ottoman dynasty.

• *Enter the mosque, removing your shoes and placing them on the wooden shelves. Notice the beautiful stalactite designs on the niche over the door, and the woodwork on the door wings. There's no fee to enter the mosque, but you can leave a donation as you exit. Now go through the leather curtain and into the mosque's...*

❿ Interior

Tranquility. Especially compared to the riot of color and design in the Blue Mosque, the sedate interior of Süleyman's mosque puts the worshipper at ease. Appreciate the genius of the architect Sinan: Somehow the seemingly plain pastel decoration and tasteful stained-glass windows merge in a harmonious whole.

The architect behind this building—whom Turks call "Sinan

the Great"—struggled his whole life to engineer a single dome that could span an entire building, without bulky support arches and pillars. He considered this mosque an important milestone in his quest. (He later succeeded with the Selimiye Mosque in Edirne, near the Turkish-Bulgarian border.)

For this mosque, Sinan used four irregularly shaped "elephant's feet" **pillars** to support the arches and the dome. His simple and elegant design masks the pillars with an arcaded gallery. The bulky buttresses blend in with their surroundings, giving the impression of an uncluttered space. You have to look hard to see the pillars (unlike the Blue Mosque, where the pillars immediately pop into view).

The impressive **dome** (flanked by two semi-domes, as at Hagia Sophia) has a diameter of 90 feet. While Renaissance architects in Europe were struggling to sort out the basic technical difficulties of building domes, Sinan succeeded in creating an elegant, masterful dome that included such details as open earthenware jars embedded between the brick layers to enhance acoustics.

Look around to find the typical features of a mosque. The wooden barrier marks an area reserved for worshippers. At the end of the apse, a marble niche, the **mihrab,** shows the direction of the holy city Mecca (toward which Muslims face to pray). To the right is the decorated *minbar,* the staircase where the imam stands to deliver his sermon. In front of that is an elevated marble platform for the choir. And in the left corner, behind the giant support leg, is the sultan's **lodge** (on pillars). The decor is nonfigurative: floral designs, stained-glass windows, tiles, and calligraphy.

• *Our tour is over. For a sultan's view of the Bosphorus, Europe, and Asia, visit the **garden** on the far side of the mosque (see map in this chapter).*

For a bite to eat, the recommended **Kuru Fasulyeci Ali Baba** restaurant or the **Mimar Sinan Café** are nearby (see listings on page 343). Also, consider a visit to the recommended **Süleymaniye Hamamı** Turkish bath, just outside the complex walls (see the Experiences chapter).

To join (or rejoin) **the Old Town Back Streets Walk,** retrace your steps to the entrance of the mosque complex.

CHORA CHURCH TOUR

Kariye Müzesi

Certain art forms are indelibly associated with a specific place, time, or civilization. The trademark art form of the Byzantines is the wall mosaic, and this tiny, underrated museum—hiding out on the edge of town—is home to some of the best examples of late-period Byzantine mosaics anywhere. Mosaic art existed in this region a thousand years before Christ but originally was found only in floors. It was the Byzantines who refined the technique, used lighter material with better plaster, and mastered the application of mosaics to walls and ceilings. The mosaics in the Chora Church are among the most beautiful surviving examples of this classic Byzantine art form. The formal name of the church is St. Savior in Chora, but most locals know it by its Turkish names, Kariye Müzesi or Kariye Camii.

Note to Readers: As this book was going to press, the Turkish government announced plans to convert the Chora Church to a practicing mosque. Ticketing information and hours listed in this chapter are subject to change—check locally before visiting.

Orientation

Cost: 65 TL.

Hours: Daily 9:00-19:00, until 17:00 off-season.

Information: +90 212 631 9241, www.muze.gov.tr.

Renovation: Partial restoration of the church is ongoing. Some areas may be unavailable for viewing as the work progresses.

Getting There: The church is just inside Istanbul's old city walls, about four miles northwest of the historic core, in the Edirnekapı (eh-deer-neh-kah-puh) district. The church is on a little square, facing a big café with outdoor tables and lots of

Chora vs. Ravenna

Visitors to Istanbul who have traveled in Italy tend to compare the mosaics at the Chora Church with the mosaics in the Basilica of San Vitale in Ravenna, near Venice. But they were completed in very different historical periods.

Ravenna's sixth-century mosaics were commissioned by Emperor Justinian (who ruled the Byzantine Empire from Constantinople and constructed the Hagia Sophia). The basilica in Ravenna was an imperial project intended to show off the emperor's power and wealth. It was a gigantic self-made shrine, and Justinian spent a great deal of money from the royal treasury to bring it to completion.

The Chora's mosaics came much later, in the 14th century, and were commissioned by the wealthy Byzantine bureaucrat

Theodore Metochites. Instead of showing emperors and empresses standing proudly next to holy figures, as at Ravenna's basilica, the Chora's mosaics generally portray the donors as humble and vulnerable. The style, use of light, and perspective are also different. Compared with the classical Byzantine mosaics at Ravenna, the newer Chora mosaics show a better sense of 3-D perspective, with more realism, action, and emotion.

While Justinian's reign marked the heyday of the Byzantine Empire, by the time Metochites was decorating the Chora Church, the empire was approaching its final days. The Black Death had killed hundreds of thousands. To the west, the Serbs were a serious threat, while to the east the Turks were at Constantinople's gates. Amid this chaos, the Chora's artists managed to produce works that are glorious in every respect, with mosaics that shine brighter than the troubled era of their creation.

CHORA CHURCH

souvenir stands. It's easiest to get there by **taxi** (about 40-50 TL from the Sultanahmet area).

It's also possible to take **public transit.** From the Old Town, take the tram to the Eminönü stop, near the Galata Bridge (from the New District, take the funicular and tram). Then catch bus #32 (Eminönü-Cevatpaşa) or #910 (Eminönü-Otogar) beneath the yellow signs directly across from the Spice Market. Buses #37E and #38 also work.

Get off at the Edirnekapı stop (it's just after the huge, sunken stadium and right before the big fragment of the city wall; for location, see the "City Walls & Neighborhoods Walk" map on page 233). At Edirnekapı, face the city wall: The church is down the hill to your right (follow signs for *Kariye Oteli*, a hotel right next to the church, and look for the old dome with the simple minaret).

Tours: Audioguides cost 25 TL.

Length of This Tour: Allow one hour.

Services: Free WCs are located on the north side of the church.

Eating: Basic tourist restaurants, cafés, and souvenir stands line the leafy square in front of the church. For better cuisine, consider the **Asitane** restaurant, in the Kariye Hotel next door.

Nearby: Consider combining your visit to the Chora Church with a walk along the nearby city walls. A visit to the Tekfur Palace museum allows you to climb the walls for a rewarding view. See the next chapter for details.

Starring: Thousands upon thousands of glittering little tiles, plus several walls and ceilings slathered with vivid frescoes, all from about 1300.

BACKGROUND

The Chora Church can be crowded inside, and you'll be craning your neck to see all of its little details. Read the information in this chapter before you arrive, or at the small café across the square from the church.

Locals call this church Kariye (kah-ree-yeh)—the Arabic interpretation of the Greek word *chora*, which means "territory" or "land." When a church was first built here in the fourth century, it was outside Constantine the Great's city wall. A century later, the walls were enlarged, and the church was folded within the city limits. But the name "Chora" stuck, likely because the word had other meanings. In Byzantine religious literature, Mary herself is often referred to as "Chora," in the same sense as an uncultivated field—in other words, a virgin. When she became pregnant with Jesus, Mary (or the "Chora") became "a container for the uncontainable." Greek inscriptions in the church refer to *He chora ton zon ton* ("the house of the living") and *He chora tou achoretou* ("the house of the uncontainable"—the One that cannot be kept within boundaries, a.k.a. Jesus Christ).

The current church—built after an earthquake damaged the original—dates back to about 1100. The church was damaged by Crusaders in the 1200s. Then, in the early 1300s, the Byzantine prime minister Theodore Metochites was selected as the Chora's patron, and oversaw the church's reconstruction. It was the first time someone other than a royal was honored with the title of patron for an imperial monastery. Powerful and rich, Metochites invested generously in the project, commissioning the sumptuous mosaics that attract tourists today.

In the early 16th century, 60 years after the Ottomans took Constantinople, the church was converted into a mosque. A mihrab (prayer niche) was built off-center in the main apse (to face Mecca), and the bell tower was replaced with the minaret you see today. The Byzantine-era frescoes and mosaics were whitewashed over and remained hidden from daylight until the late 1940s, when they were rediscovered and restored.

Artistically, the Chora Church's decorations were influential models for depictions of Christian figures and events. After the Church split between east and west (Eastern Orthodox and Roman Catholic) in the 11th century, western churches became provincial, focused on their own local customs and saints—with church art that splintered into many different, idiosyncratic visions. Meanwhile, the Eastern Orthodox Church remained consolidated under the stable and wealthy Byzantine Empire. Church power was centralized, so artistic decisions made in Constantinople filtered down to churches throughout the Byzantine world, bringing consistency to medieval church decorations. For example, an artist's depiction of Mary, Joseph, and Baby Jesus here became the norm for Eastern Orthodox church art. Lacking a similarly coherent western Christian artistic tradition, artists across the generations embraced these Eastern Orthodox archetypes. The artistic vision realized here in the Chora eventually trickled down to decorations in today's Christian churches in Italy, Indonesia, and Iowa.

OVERVIEW

Theodore Metochites said of the Chora Church, "The mosaics and frescoes in the church show how God became a mortal on behalf of human beings." On this tour, we'll concentrate on important events in the lives of Jesus and Mary, to whom the church and its monastery, respectively, were dedicated.

The decoration in the church is meant to transform Eastern Orthodox liturgy into reality. Standing before these images of Christ, the Virgin, and the saints, the believer feels present with them at that very moment and place. A pilgrimage to the Holy Land has never been a priority for Orthodox Christians, because the neighborhood church brings the Holy Land to them.

The church contains some images of holy figures and biblical stories that may seem less familiar to Western eyes. They are drawn from apocryphal writings—versions of scripture that are not part of the Bible.

Theodore Metochites

You're here today because of Theodore Metochites, the man who commissioned these mosaics. Metochites was born in Constantinople in 1270, a few years after the city was taken back from the Crusaders. His father supported the unification of the Eastern Orthodox and Roman Catholic churches—a view that earned the family exile in Nicaea (the present-day Turkish city of İznik, south of Constantinople). Metochites' parents tried to steer him away from politics, encouraging their son to devote his life to science. But politics was in his blood. By the time he reached his 20s, Metochites was writing essays and critiques.

His work came to the attention of Emperor Andronicus II, who invited Metochites to serve in the palace in Constantinople. He got his start arranging political marriages for royal family members—including a wedding between the emperor's five-year-old daughter and a middle-aged Serbian king. In the early 1300s, Metochites became treasurer, and then prime minister. Anyone who wanted access to the emperor had to see Metochites first. He acquired land and wealth but wasn't the most effective bureaucrat. Decorating the Chora Church distracted him from the Italian merchants who were becoming superior in naval trade.

As the Ottoman Turks became a clear threat to the empire, panic and chaos led to civil war between Andronicus II and his grandson Andronicus III. The grandson won, and in 1328 Metochites lost his protector. A mob burned his palace, his wealth was confiscated, and Metochites was exiled. Metochites was eventually allowed to return to Constantinople, where he entered the Chora's monastery, took the name Theoleptos, and died in 1332.

The layout of the church is fairly straightforward. The main part is a single nave, facing east (like all European Christian churches of the time). Behind the nave are two narthexes: inner and outer. These narthexes hold most of the mosaics. Running next to the nave is a long corridor called a *parekklesion*, or side chapel. This section is decorated with frescoes, not mosaics.

Give your neck a good stretch before you begin—most of what there is to see is a few feet above eye level. You'll be whirling like a dervish trying to see all the details. To make things easier, we'll focus on the most interesting or important scenes—explaining some Bible stories out of order and skipping lesser figures and events.

The Tour Begins

Facing the church, the ticket booth is to the left of the original front door. This main entrance will likely be the one open to visitors during the restoration. Through the front door, you go straight into the outer narthex.

However, depending on restoration work, you may instead be directed to an alternate access point to the left of the church. From here, you'll circle behind and around the church to reach the alternate entry on the far side. If you happen to go this way, notice the giant buttress at the back of the church. This originally held up the church...but now the church supports the buttress.

Orientation Walk

The interior visit has four parts—outer narthex, inner narthex, central nave, and *parekklesion*. The art tells a story that unfolds as the worshipper enters the building, so we'll view it as a Christian would have during Byzantine times, beginning in the outer narthex (see map).

Before studying the mosaics, it's helpful to take a quick walk around to understand the general structure of the church: The **outer narthex** tells the story of Jesus—from his conception and childhood through his baptism as an adult.

Walking into the next chamber, the **inner narthex,** you encounter art that teaches the delicate balance between Jesus (on the right, curing the sick and working miracles) and Mary (on the left, with scenes from her life).

Stepping into the **central nave,** you enter a place of worship that functioned as a mosque for 500 years. The centuries-old Christian altar was replaced by the Islamic prayer niche, or mihrab. Notice that the mihrab is made with marble that matches the exquisite original walls of the much-older interior—it was cut from the same quarry. Rather than destroy the Christian frescoes and mosaics, the Muslim Ottomans covered them over with whitewash.

The last part of your visit is the *parekklesion* (to the right of the nave), a chapel for important tombs that's decorated with frescoes.

Now let's return to the outer narthex and study some of the Bible scenes depicted in the fine mosaic art. (Use the map with keyed numbers to locate each scene.)

Outer Narthex

❶ **Incarnation of Jesus Christ:** Here the Virgin Mary holds the divine Baby Jesus in her womb. She is the Chora, the dwelling place of the uncontainable. The placement of this scene—just above the church's front door—is interesting. It's likely that when the panel was made, you could see the walls of Constantinople through this

CHORA CHURCH

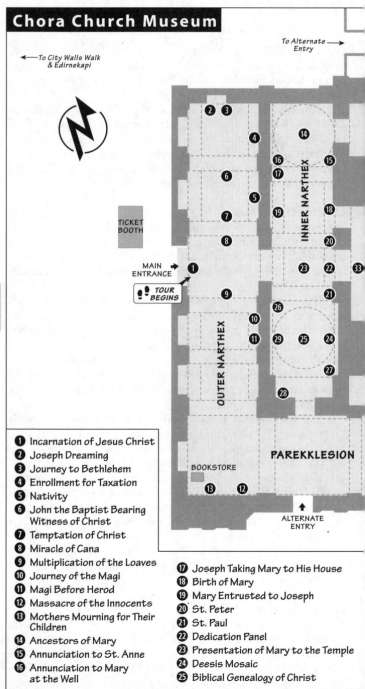

Chora Church Museum

To Alternate Entry →

← To City Walls Walk & Edirnekapi

TICKET BOOTH

INNER NARTHEX

MAIN ENTRANCE →

👣 TOUR BEGINS

OUTER NARTHEX

PAREKKLESION

BOOKSTORE

↑ ALTERNATE ENTRY

1 Incarnation of Jesus Christ
2 Joseph Dreaming
3 Journey to Bethlehem
4 Enrollment for Taxation
5 Nativity
6 John the Baptist Bearing Witness of Christ
7 Temptation of Christ
8 Miracle of Cana
9 Multiplication of the Loaves
10 Journey of the Magi
11 Magi Before Herod
12 Massacre of the Innocents
13 Mothers Mourning for Their Children
14 Ancestors of Mary
15 Annunciation to St. Anne
16 Annunciation to Mary at the Well
17 Joseph Taking Mary to His House
18 Birth of Mary
19 Mary Entrusted to Joseph
20 St. Peter
21 St. Paul
22 Dedication Panel
23 Presentation of Mary to the Temple
24 Deesis Mosaic
25 Biblical Genealogy of Christ

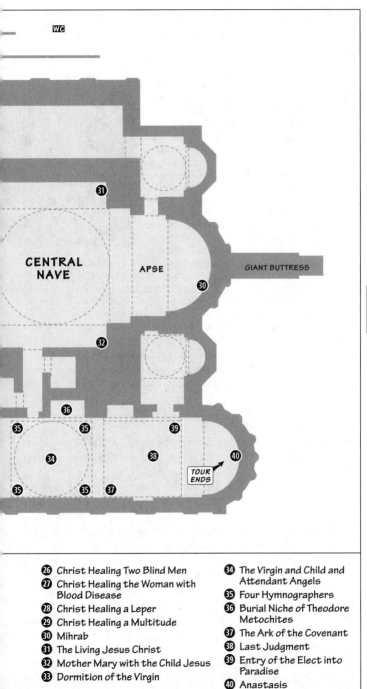

CHORA CHURCH

26 Christ Healing Two Blind Men
27 Christ Healing the Woman with Blood Disease
28 Christ Healing a Leper
29 Christ Healing a Multitude
30 Mihrab
31 The Living Jesus Christ
32 Mother Mary with the Child Jesus
33 Dormition of the Virgin
34 The Virgin and Child and Attendant Angels
35 Four Hymnographers
36 Burial Niche of Theodore Metochites
37 The Ark of the Covenant
38 Last Judgment
39 Entry of the Elect into Paradise
40 Anastasis

Mosaics 101

Expensive and time-consuming to create, Byzantine mosaic art is generally seen only in royal residences or in houses of worship supported by wealthy patrons. Mosaicists usually worked in groups, like a small union or guild. The most experienced—the master—was usually the leader. A city like Constantinople supported several competing mosaicist groups.

Mosaics are made of tiny pieces (tesserae) of glass or other materials stuck to moist plaster to create a larger image. It took about three years to complete the mosaics in the Chora Church. The Chora's art was ahead of its time, and in a way anticipated the Renaissance: art for the sake of religion, but without neglecting aesthetics. You'll notice an attempt to create emotive faces, moving bodies, and realistic perspective. The Chora Church was often used after sunset, lit by candles and oil lamps. Imagine the flickering light sweeping across the walls, each tile glittering in turn.

Feeling inspired? Here's a recipe for your own Byzantine mosaic:

1. Prepare a **blueprint**. Mosaics require detailed planning.
2. Gather the **mosaic pieces**. Common materials include glass, stone, marble, and brick. Gold and silver tesserae are not

door. When the city was in danger, the people would bring icons of Mary to the walls to protect the city. Perhaps this panel was part of that tradition.

❷ Joseph Dreaming: In Joseph's dream, the angel explains Mary's pregnancy to him. Behind him are the Virgin and a companion.

❸ Journey to Bethlehem: Mary is seated on a donkey; in front of her is Joseph's son (not Jesus—explained later). Joseph walks at the back, trying to catch up. The city behind the hill is Nazareth.

❹ Enrollment for Taxation: The governor of Syria is seated on a throne, wearing the outfit and hat of Byzantine's high government officials. He likely represents Theodore Metochites, who served as a tax collector on his way to becoming prime minister. At the center, another official holds an unrolled scroll. On the right is pregnant Mary, her tunic stretching to contain her belly. Joseph is behind her.

❺ Nativity: This representation of the birth of Jesus Christ is typically Byzantine, with all the events related to Jesus' birth shown

solid metal but a thin layer of metal sandwiched between two glass pieces. Very thin, pink marble can represent some human skin tones.

3. **Stud the walls** at random with nails, leaving about one inch of the nail exposed. This helps the plaster adhere to the wall. (But don't use iron nails—in the past, rusting iron nails ruined many mosaics when they expanded and forced chunks of plaster to crack and fall.)

4. Apply three layers of **plaster,** up to two inches thick. The first layer—made of crushed lime and straw—should cover the entire work surface. When the first layer is completely dry, score it and apply a second layer of more finely crushed lime and straw pieces. While the second layer is still damp, apply the third and finest layer of plaster, of crushed lime and marble dust.

5. Transfer your blueprint to the plaster in the form of a **rough painting**. This will serve as your guide. (Often, the underlying blueprint can be seen in older mosaics where pieces have fallen out.)

6. Begin by applying **smaller pieces** to define the contours of your mosaic design, then fill in the rest with **bigger pieces**. The frame, hands, feet, face, and hair require the most skill and are traditionally completed first by the master mosaicist. Then the other mosaicists fill in the rest. Place your pieces at different angles to capture the light.

7. Stand back and enjoy.

CHORA CHURCH

next to one another. Notice the stable, animals, Joseph in deep thought, Mary resting, and maids bathing the newborn Christ.

❻ **John the Baptist Bearing Witness of Christ:** John talks with a group of priests and Levites and gestures toward Christ. The fiery-eyed Baptist is dressed in his usual animal-skin outfit and sports the long beard of a hermit.

❼ **Temptation of Christ:** The story of the temptation of Christ is told in four scenes arranged in a semicircle in the vault, with Satan represented as a dark, ugly winged creature. In the first section, Satan appears above a box full of stones, asking Jesus to turn them into bread. Next, Satan offers Jesus the world's many kingdoms (the tiny kings with crowns ruling over Legoland). In the third scene, we see Jesus on a hill, overlooking the kingdoms. In the last scene, Jesus stands on a tower, as Satan asks him to prove his divinity by jumping down without hurting himself.

❽ **Miracle of Cana:** Here we see Jesus turning water into wine at a wedding party. Jesus is holding a small scroll with the Virgin

Mary behind him. A servant is pouring water into one of five huge jars. Notice that the jar mosaics are made of terracotta—the same material the actual jars would have been made of.

❾ Multiplication of the Loaves: By blessing five loaves of bread, Christ feeds a multitude. Jesus is seen behind three big baskets of bread, giving pieces of bread to his disciples, who pass them to the crowd. If you follow the vault to the right, you'll see the happy conclusion: After everyone was fed, the remaining bread filled 12 large baskets.

❿ Journey of the Magi: Three wise men on horseback—Melchior, Balthasar, and Caspar—follow the star to find the newborn Christ Child.

⓫ Magi Before Herod: The wise men offer their gifts to Herod, who sits on a throne.

⓬ Massacre of the Innocents: Herod orders the murder of all young male children, in an effort to find and kill the Baby Jesus. The flying cloaks imply motion and action.

⓭ Mothers Mourning for Their Children: Grief-stricken mothers cradle the bodies of their brutally slain children. Above the next window to the right you see Elizabeth and her baby, John the Baptist, hiding safely in a cave.

Inner Narthex

⓮ Ancestors of Mary: At the center of the dome, in the medallion, is Mary with the Baby Jesus. Notice the two figures between the ribs in each section. The upper figures are the genealogical ancestors of Mary and Jesus, starting with King David; the lower figures are ancestors outside the official lineage.

⓯ Annunciation to St. Anne: St. Anne, the mother of Mary, wears a long, red scarf over a blue garment and a red shawl that falls down to her knees. Above the fancy fountain before her is a flying angel giving the good news that she will bear a daughter.

⓰ Annunciation to Mary at the Well: Now it's Mary's turn. Mary is dressed in a blue tunic and holds a golden pitcher. She's surprised by the approach of the angel, who tells her she will give birth to the Christ Child.

⓱ Joseph Taking Mary to His House: A young and helpless-looking Mary follows her new husband. In front of them is Joseph's son. While this figure may be surprising to some Christians, this version of Mary's life comes from the apocryphal Gospel of St. James, which holds that Joseph was a widower with several children when he wed Mary. Joseph seems a little confused, too—which way is he walking?

⓲ Birth of Mary: The newborn, naked baby Mary is held by a midwife as a maid prepares a bath. Another maid fans St. Anne while attending women present gifts.

❶⓳ **Mary Entrusted to Joseph:** On the left side, the local priest Zechariah is behind young Mary, his hand protectively on her head as he presents her to Joseph. Other suitors stand to the side.

⓴ **St. Peter** and ㉑ **St. Paul:** St. Peter is on the left side of the door, holding the keys to heaven. On the right side is bald

and wrinkled St. Paul, holding the codex of Epistles in his left hand (the wrinkles on Paul's broad brow are said to represent his intellect). The Byzantines often decorated either side of a church's nave door with the twin figures of St. Peter and St. Paul—fathers of the early Christian Church.

㉒ **Dedication Panel:** The enthroned Jesus Christ is at the center, holding the Bible and making the sign of the Trinity. On his right side, squeezed in the corner, is church patron Theodore Metochites, offering Jesus a model of the church (a common Byzantine way to represent a donation). Metochites wears a fancy garment and a big hat reminiscent of a Turkish turban—both are symbolic of his status.

㉓ **Presentation of Mary to the Temple:** Mary's parents enthusiastically urge their daughter to go to the priest—Zechariah, father of John the Baptist—who welcomes the Virgin. Behind them, in a separate scene, we see Mary receiving holy bread from an angel.

㉔ *Deesis* **Mosaic:** In Greek Orthodox churches, a *deesis* mosaic such as this one would traditionally show Christ flanked by both Mary and John the Baptist, interceding on behalf of sinners. But John must have been late for his Chora Church sitting, because he's not depicted here. Instead, behind Jesus and Mary are two small figures representing church donors. Mary is asking Jesus to forgive their sins. The woman kneeling before Christ is Melanie, the illegitimate daughter of a Byzantine emperor (depicted below Mary) who married a Mongolian king. After the king died, she came back to Constantinople and lived as a nun.

㉕ **Biblical Genealogy of Christ:** In the center, Jesus Christ—in the usual pose—holds the Bible in one hand and makes the sign of the Trinity with the other. In the flutes of the dome are Christ's

CHORA CHURCH

Mary Rules the Orthodox World

Christianity has always proved remarkably adaptable to local traditions. From the Christmas tree to the Easter egg, many "Christian" traditions have pagan roots. It was no different in Anatolia (Turkey), where the long tradition of a female "mother-goddess" figure provided a convenient foundation for Mary.

The idea of a mother-goddess originated in Anatolia (likely in the early sixth millennium BC), and her popularity spread to encompass virtually all of Mediterranean Europe, western Asia, and North Africa. No matter what she was called or how she looked, the mother-goddess always displayed the maternal qualities of fertility and nurture. She also possessed miraculous gifts. For example, the Phrygian goddess Cybele was a figure of power and protection. Often, a mother-goddess figure would give birth to a deity. Leto was impregnated by the Greek god Zeus and gave birth to the twins Apollo and Artemis—both highly revered as gods. The mother-goddess Aphrodite (Venus) was born pregnant with her child, Eros, the god of love.

When Christianity arrived, Mary easily took her place among these powerful mother-goddess figures. Like those before her, Mary is looked to for comfort and healing in times of trial. As the "container of the uncontainable," she gave birth to the son of God, Jesus Christ. And according to Christian tradition, when she completed her earthly life, she was transported ("assumed") body and soul directly to heaven, as no other mere mortal has been.

Old Testament ancestors. Though most of us can't read the Greek names, many of the figures come with attributes that help to identify them. The cycle starts in the upper level with Adam, standing on a snake (he's the one with a long white beard under Jesus' left hand).

If your neck isn't killing you, spend some time here and try to identify other familiar figures—such as Noah carrying an ark. Hmm...a vessel for holding precious life...yet another metaphor for the Virgin. Nearby, many of Christ's miracles are depicted: ㉖ **Christ Healing Two Blind Men;** ㉗ **Christ Healing the Woman with Blood Disease;** ㉘ **Christ Healing a Leper;** and ㉙ **Christ Healing a Multitude.**

Nave

This square, domed room is the oldest section of the building, probably dating from around 1100. Straight ahead is the main apse—the holiest section of the church, where the altar once stood.

• *The marble niche a little to the right of center is the...*

❸⓿ Mihrab: This was added by the Muslim Ottomans when this church became a mosque. Representing a symbolic doorway leading to the holy city of Mecca, the mihrab shows Muslims the correct direction in which to pray.

• *Two mosaics in the central nave use the word "Chora" to describe Jesus and Mary. On the left side of the wall, before the apse, is a framed mosaic depiction of...*

❸❶ The Living Jesus Christ: The inscription originally read "Dwelling-Place (Chora) of the Living."

• *On the right wall before the apse is...*

❸❷ Mother Mary with the Child Jesus: The inscription originally read "Dwelling-Place (Chora) of the Uncontainable." (The mosaic lettering HXOPA spells "Chora.")

• *Turn around and look above the door where you entered. This is one of the church's most impressive panels, the...*

❸❸ Dormition of the Virgin: Byzantine Christians struggled with the theological issue of Mary's identity. In the early fifth century, the Church declared her the "Mother of God." This was actually good marketing, as Anatolians were already comfortable with goddesses.

Whether Mary died at the end of her life or fell asleep (which "dormition" seems to imply) is debated among theologians. But either way, she passed from this life (or was "assumed") into heaven. August 15 is celebrated as the feast of the Assumption of Mary by both the Eastern Orthodox and Roman Catholic worlds.

Mary is shown here on her last earthly bed. The scene is made of very small mosaic pieces, allowing the artists to show palpable emotion in the faces of the apostles and other mourners around her deathbed. Behind her, in a large heavenly halo, is Jesus Christ. He holds the innocent soul of Mary, in the form of a baby. Angels appear in the outer ring of the halo. To the left of the bed, St. Peter swings an incense burner, while on the right, St. Paul bends toward the bed in sorrow.

A gray bubble is taking her soul to heaven. Follow this: In heaven Mary has morphed into a baby (as a child of God). Since God and Jesus are one, baby Mary is the mother of Jesus...or God. It's beyond us. But the point is that she made it to heaven, where she's a busy part of God's administration in both the Eastern Orthodox and Roman Catholic churches to this day.

Take a few moments in the nave to study the marble, and notice the slender recycled pieces in the panels placed higher on the walls—these were columns before being cut into panels.

Parekklesion

This side chapel, which functioned as a mortuary chamber for Theodore Metochites and his family, is decorated entirely with frescoes. In a fresco, paint is applied to wet plaster, which absorbs and preserves the pigment—making frescoes more durable than regular wall paintings.

Most of the frescoes on the *parekklesion* walls deal with the afterlife and salvation—appropriate themes for a burial chamber. Unlike many other Byzantine churches, here the dead were not interred in the ground but instead laid to rest in the now-empty niches in the chapel walls.

• *Again referring to the map, you'll see the following scenes:*

❸❹ The Virgin and Child and Attendant Angels: Mary is depicted here as the Queen of Heaven, dressed in her usual blue tunic, now decorated with gold. This is another ribbed dome, made more impressive by the light from windows at its base. Within the dome's sections are winged angels worshipping Mary and Christ. The angels wear clothing typical of Byzantine officials.

❸❺ Four Hymnographers: These four serious-looking Byzantines are poets who were renowned for their verses in Mary's honor: John of Damascus, in the northeast corner wearing a turban; Kosmas the Poet, in the southeast corner with a blank book in his lap; Joseph the Poet, in the southwest corner holding a scroll; and Theophanes Graptos, in the northwest corner, where he's writing verses.

❸❻ Burial Niche of Theodore Metochites: The largest of all the chapel's burial niches probably belonged to Theodore Metochites. Most of its decorations were lost over the ages, although the

The Marble of Marmara

Most of the marble used in the Chora Church came from Marmara Island, which is in Turkey's Sea of Marmara. (In fact, *marmara* means "marble" in Greek.) But

some of the marble was recycled from buildings in Italy, Greece, and North Africa. These pieces were cut again before being reused.

Most of the marble panels in the building are slices of stone, cut in half and placed next to one another. The workmanship involved in cutting marble was as painstaking as the workmanship of the mosaics. Only a couple of inches of marble could be cut each day, using a smooth piece of metal that—combined with sand—was used as a saw.

Notice the marble slabs of the nave's upper level. These tall, slender, recycled pieces were formed from columns cut into slices.

The marble lintels above the church's doors and door frames, and most of the column capitals, were recycled as well. The marble arches decorating the *parekklesion* are the best examples of stone carving from the late Byzantine period.

Whether recycled or newly quarried, Chora's marble decorations fit harmoniously with the rest of the structure. Originally, many of the marble works were painted or glazed with gold. The small holes and niches in the marble (which you'll see throughout the church) once held icons, crosses, lamps, and holy relics.

inscriptions and decorations in some of Chora's other burial niches are among the best sources of information about the lives of 14th-century Byzantine aristocrats.

㊲ The Ark of the Covenant: Men are carrying something that looks like a coffin. This is the Ark of the Covenant being taken to Solomon's Temple. This ark, like Noah's ark, is a metaphor for the Virgin Mary: All three contain the treasures of God.

• *Look above the vault to see the most impressive fresco in the church, the...*

㊳ Last Judgment: This colorful fresco depicts scenes from the Book of Revelation: Christ's victory over death and the salvation of the righteous. Jesus sits on a glorious throne in the center, flanked by the Virgin Mary and John the Baptist. The 12 apostles, holding books, are seated at either side. Behind them are groups of angels.

The white shell-like object held aloft by an angel represents the sky at the end of time. All around the vault are choirs of the chosen, floating in clouds.

Below this triumphant scene is the dramatic Weighing of the Souls—the ultimate "thumbs-up" or "thumbs-down." Christ's right palm is turned up, showing the lucky bunch who will go to heaven. His left hand is turned down and points toward the condemned, as does the river of fire flowing from his left foot.

Notice the stigmata (marks of the Crucifixion) on Jesus' hands. Try to imagine his gold-colored robe and the halo behind his head as they once appeared, covered in sheets of gold (some of the gold still remains in his halo).

Beneath Jesus are the figures of Adam and Eve on their knees. Farther down, you can see a scale. Naked bodies on the right are the souls awaiting judgment. At the center, another naked soul trembles while he is judged. Barely visible is a little demon, craftily trying to pull down the scale. Look closely at the river of fire to see ugly little demons giving the condemned a helpful push.

㊴ Entry of the Elect into Paradise: A cherub with closed wings protects the entrance into heaven. On the left, St. Peter unlocks the door. The Good Thief—carrying a cross—greets the chosen and points toward the Virgin Mary on her throne.

㊵ Anastasis: This fresco depicts the standard Byzantine representation of the Resurrection, when Christ descends into hell to save the righteous people of the Old Testament. You can see Jesus (like a biblical Rambo) pulling Adam and Eve by their arms out of their coffins. Under Jesus' feet are the broken gates of hell, scattered keys, and Satan, bound and powerless.

• *With that promising image, this tour is over. Congratulations. Give yourself a well-deserved rest and neck rub. From here you might explore the **city walls** and the colorful Lonca, Balat, and Fener neighborhoods (see the next chapter), or catch a **taxi** to the most conservative religious scene in town at the Eyüp Sultan Mosque (see page 57). You can also return to the Old Town or other points by taxi or public transit.*

Note: Taxis picking up right at the church tend to overcharge. It's best to have the nearby Kariye Hotel call you a cab, or walk up the hill on Kariye Camii Sokak to Hoca Çakır Caddesi and stop a cab there (either direction is OK).

CITY WALLS & NEIGHBORHOODS WALK

From Chora Church to Eğrikapı Gate & Greek Orthodox Patriarchate

The Walls of Constantinople rank among the most impressive city walls in the world. Istanbul was born on this peninsula, flanked by the waters of the Golden Horn and the Bosphorus, in part because it was so easy to fortify: Simply build a wall across the narrow thumb of land. The first wall was built by Greek settlers. When Constantine the Great made Constantinople his capital, he enclosed the city with new defensive walls (early fourth century). By the time Theodosius II (r. AD 408-450) was in command, however, the city had grown well beyond Constantine's walls. Theodosius erected new fortifications to encompass an even greater area. In total, Constantinople's land and sea walls stretched 13 miles around the city and remained virtually impenetrable for more than 1,000 years. These massive walls were breached only twice—by the Fourth Crusade in 1204 and by the Ottoman invasion in 1453.

The walls that stretch across the Old Town peninsula lie about four miles northwest of the historic core. The first part of this walk focuses on the walls and nearby sights (between the Chora Church and the Eğrikapı Gate). Then we'll cut through residential neighborhoods as we head back toward downtown, learning more about the ethnic diversity that shaped Istanbul. As this is a conservative neighborhood, you'll see more traditional dress here.

Orientation

Length of This Walk: Allow 2.5 hours for the entire 1.5-mile walk: one hour for the first part, from the Chora Church to the Eğrikapı Gate (with an optional detour to a viewpoint outside the walls), and another 1.5 hours from the gate to the Greek Orthodox Patriarchate, passing through untouristed residential neighborhoods and a colorful market district. For many, the first part of the walk is enough, but the full walk is worthwhile for those with time and interest.

When to Go: The walls are best viewed by day. After dark, the streets are sparsely populated, and some travelers may not feel comfortable.

Getting There: We'll start at the Chora Church. To get there, it's easiest to take a **taxi**, but a **tram-bus** combination to the Edirnekapı (eh-deer-neh-kah-puh) neighborhood will also bring you within short walking distance. For details, see "Getting There" at the beginning of the previous chapter.

If you've taken a taxi to visit the Eyüp Sultan Mosque (a recommended sight outside the city walls—see page 57), it's easy to have your cabbie drop you off at the Chora Church on your way back.

Starring: The Walls of Theodosius, Tekfur Palace (with a great wall-top viewpoint), the Dungeons of Anemas, and various religious sights (churches and synagogues and mosques, oh my).

The Walk Begins

CHORA CHURCH TO EĞRIKAPI GATE

• *Begin at the* ❶ *Chora Church. With the church behind you (and the street fountain to your right), walk uphill for about 50 yards and take the first right on Kuyulu Bahçe Sokak (labeled* Şeyh Eyüp *on the left). Follow Kuyulu Bahçe as it bends left and then right. At the outer wall of Çakır Ağa Mosque, turn left down a narrow alley. You'll emerge on Hoca Çakır Caddesi (Hoca Çakır Street), facing the...*

❷ Walls of Theodosius

Constantinople surrounded itself with land walls and sea walls. Because the sea itself provided natural fortification (like a giant moat), the land walls were stouter and more impressive. These early fifth-century walls stretch for 3.5 miles north to south, from the shores of the Golden Horn up the hill to the Edirnekapı district, and then downhill to the shoreline of the Sea of Marmara.

Fortified with 185 towers, each about 65 feet high, the Walls of Theodosius were actually two separate walls—an outer wall and a stronger inner ring, separated by a defensible no-man's land about 55 feet wide. And just outside the outer wall, a huge moat further protected the fortification.

After the Ottoman conquest, the walls

fell into disrepair, as they were no longer needed for protection. While most of the inner walls are long gone, the outer walls still stand.

• *Turn right and head down Hoca Çakır Street along the wall. Less than 100 yards beyond the Çakır Ağa Mosque, watch for a wide opening in the wall to your left. On weekends a* **bird market** *springs up here, where pigeon fanciers buy and sell "Turkish tumblers"— domesticated pigeons prized for their acrobatic backflipping skills. The hobby has many avid fans; some birds can sell for thousands.*

Where the wall sharply bends to the left, you'll see a more recent structure—with fancy, arched windows and a balcony out front—built into the top of the wall. This is the...

❸ Tekfur Palace (Tekfur Sarayı)

Sandwiched in a bend between the inner and outer Theodosian walls, Tekfur Palace was constructed during the late 13th or early 14th century at the southern end of the larger Blachernae Palace complex (which we'll visit later on this walk). Tefkur's red-brick and marble facade and three-story outer wall are all that remain of Istanbul's only surviving Byzantine palace. A recent renovation enclosed part of the structure and reopened the palace as a museum (20 TL, daily 9:00-18:00, www.tekfursarayi.istanbul). It's worth going in. Three levels of audiovisual displays and artifacts detail the restoration, and you can climb to the top of the wall for an excellent view.

The vaulted entryway leads into a central **courtyard.** Before going into the exhibit (to your left, in the palace building), cross the open-air courtyard to check out the interior of the wall—or what little survives of it after centuries of disrepair.

Next, make your way through the **exhibits,** which explain the palace's colorful history: royal Byzantine residence damaged in the Ottoman conquest, 16th-century imperial menagerie (it housed elephants and giraffes), 17th-century tile workshop, 18th-century Jewish poorhouse, and finally, 20th-century bottle factory.

You can access the **top of the wall** from the second level of the

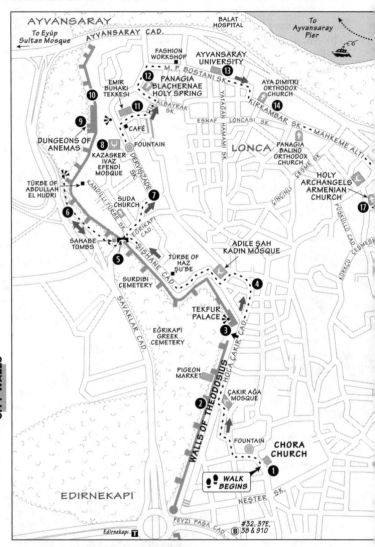

palace building. With the Old Town at your back, look out beyond the wall. The patches of green on either side of the busy road are centuries-old **cemeteries,** both Muslim and Eastern Orthodox. This location outside the city boundaries was a hygienic, logical place to bury the dead. In the distance (to your right) are the Golden Horn and the Haliç bridge with its eight busy lanes of traffic.

Looking to your left, find the massive tower built to guard **Edirnekapı,** the grand gate of ancient Constantinople (with the same name as this modern-day district of Istanbul). The physical gate is long gone, and Fevzi Paşa Street passes unchallenged

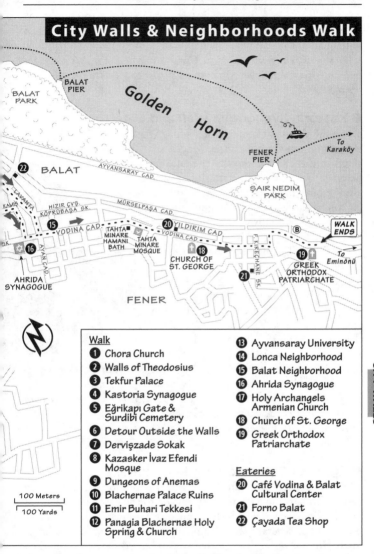

City Walls & Neighborhoods Walk

Walk
1. Chora Church
2. Walls of Theodosius
3. Tekfur Palace
4. Kastoria Synagogue
5. Eğrikapı Gate & Surdibi Cemetery
6. Detour Outside the Walls
7. Derviszade Sokak
8. Kazasker İvaz Efendi Mosque
9. Dungeons of Anemas
10. Blachernae Palace Ruins
11. Emir Buhari Tekkesi
12. Panagia Blachernae Holy Spring & Church
13. Ayvansaray University
14. Lonca Neighborhood
15. Balat Neighborhood
16. Ahrida Synagogue
17. Holy Archangels Armenian Church
18. Church of St. George
19. Greek Orthodox Patriarchate

Eateries
20. Café Vodina & Balat Cultural Center
21. Forno Balat
22. Çayada Tea Shop

100 Meters
100 Yards

CITY WALLS

through a large opening in the wall. But the two huge towers that once protected and flanked the gate still stand like sentinels.

Sultan Mehmet II, the Conqueror, rode triumphantly through this gate into Constantinople in 1453, ending the Byzantine era and ushering in the Ottoman age. In Ottoman times, Edirnekapı continued as the official gate into the city—and it was a busy one. Sultans left the city through this gate when visiting the Eyüp Sultan Mosque for Friday prayers. Common folk, caravans of merchants, and soldiers on the way to their posts also passed through

Edirnekapı. Guarded by a squad of janissaries, the gate was locked at the end of the day.

• *When you exit, return to Hoca Çakır Street and continue down the hill. In less than 100 yards, the street curves to the left. To your right are the...*

❹ Kastoria Synagogue Wall and Gate

These are the scant remains of a synagogue built in 1453 by Jewish immigrants from Kastoria, Macedonia. The building was renovated in the 1800s, but over the ensuing decades, many Jewish families moved away from this neighborhood. Without its congregation, the synagogue fell into disrepair. Eventually it was torn down and turned into a parking lot, earning the ruins the nickname "the drive-in synagogue."

On the still-standing main gate, among other Hebrew writings, you'll see the year "5653"—which, in the Hebrew calendar, equals 1893, most likely the year the synagogue was last renovated.

• *Continue down the hill. Take the first left (Sulu Sokak), then turn right at the Adile Şah Kadın Mosque onto Şişhane Caddesi; follow it as it twists through a residential neighborhood. Just ahead, the street makes a left turn. A block later, stick with the street as it bends sharply to the right. Continue down the hill to the intersection with Eğrikapı Street. Turn left onto Eğrikapı and walk a few steps to the...*

❺ Eğrikapı Gate and Surdibi Cemetery

Eğrikapı (eh-ree-kah-puh; "bent gate") is one of the minor city gates. Through the gate and just outside the city walls is the small Surdibi Cemetery. This Muslim cemetery is known as the legendary burial site of several *sahabe* (companions of the Prophet Muhammad). The *sahabe* are said to have been buried here in unmarked graves, having fought and died as members of the Arab army that attacked Constantinople in the seventh century.

When Sultan Mahmut II started a major westernization project in the early 19th century, his opponents tried to discredit him by portraying him as an infidel who had turned away from Islam. To prove his faith, the sultan initiated a search to pinpoint and mark *sahabe* burial sites. The historical legitimacy of these gravesites is—for Muslims—authenticated by faith. Look for the gravestones marked *Sahabe'den*.

• *We've reached the mid-point of this walk. From here, those willing to*

The Jews in Turkey

The Byzantines were not very tolerant of Jews. Jewish people couldn't ride on horseback within Istanbul's city limits; they weren't allowed to build houses taller than those of their Christian neighbors; and their synagogues couldn't have domed roofs. Emperor Justinian was particularly harsh. He outlawed the reading of the Torah in Hebrew and ordered that it must be recited in Greek. The emperors who followed imposed heavy taxes on the Jewish minority. In the sixth century, the Jews were expelled from the city and required to live outside the walls in Haskoy and Galata (today's New District). These Greek-speaking "Romaniots" made up the small Jewish minority in Constantinople when the Ottomans took over the city.

The Jews fared better under the Ottomans, who encouraged more Jewish immigration to populate the city and boost the economy. The first to come were Jews from the Balkans (Ashkenazi Jews). Then, in the late 15th century, 200,000 Sephardic Jews were expelled from Spain. Ottoman Sultan Beyazıt II welcomed them to Turkey, saying, "Ferdinand of Spain is a wise king; however, he is making his land poor and ours rich."

Later, under the Turkish Republic, the Jews were unfairly targeted by a WWII "wealth tax." Despite being neutral during the war, Turkey increased its military spending and levied taxes on wealthy citizens to pay for arms and soldiers. The tax was applied more heavily to non-Muslims, and although it was later lifted, it caused many Jews to leave the country.

At the same time, Turkey offered refuge to many prominent German Jews escaping the Holocaust. Later, Jewish professors played an important role in the development of the Turkish education system.

Today, Turkey's Jewish community is estimated at 25,000 people, about 95 percent of whom are Sephardic Jews—descendants of those Spanish exiles. The majority of Turkey's Jews live in Istanbul, but about 2,500 live in İzmir, on the Aegean. Turkish Jews are legally represented by a chief rabbi, a post currently held by Istanbul native Izak Haleva.

brave the traffic can detour for an impressive view of the walls (see next). Then the second part of this walk awaits: See "Eğrikapı Gate to Greek Orthodox Patriarchate," later.

If you're walled out, from Eğrikapı Gate you can catch a taxi to the Old Town/Eminönü neighborhood (east); walk to the Ayvansaray dock to catch a boat to Karaköy (just across the Galata Bridge from Eminönü); or retrace your steps to the Chora Church, then return by taxi or public transit to central Istanbul. (Or, for more sightseeing, you can continue west to the Eyüp Sultan Mosque by taxi—see page 57.)

❻ Detour Outside the Walls

To get a great view of the walls, you'll need to walk on a sidewalk alongside a busy highway. Don't go beyond the viaduct, or you'll end up in the middle of the highway.

Take the walkway on the right (through the cemetery), and keep walking along the wall. Farther down the road, the wall bends again and gradually splits off from the road. Here you'll see the final section of the wall leading all the way to the Golden Horn. Look down about midway along the last stretch of wall, where two towers stand next to each other, sharing a common base. The first tower (on the right) is the Bastion of Isaac II Angelus. The tower on the left marks the Dungeons of Anemas, built as a prison in the early seventh century as part of Blachernae Palace (described later). Just behind the towers is the 16th-century Kazasker İvaz Efendi Mosque (we'll see the bastion, dungeons, and mosque again later, from inside the wall).

Beyond the Dungeons of Anemas, the rest of the wall forms a fortress with huge hexagonal towers. This is where the land walls connected to the sea walls on the Golden Horn. The sea walls, which ran a little less than four miles, were shorter and largely unfortified, making them the weak link in Constantinople's defenses. As additional security, the Byzantines sealed off the Golden Horn to enemy vessels by stretching a thick chain across its entrance. But a clever attack rendered the entire network of walls irrelevant. In 1453, in a remarkable feat of military ingenuity and engineering prowess, Mehmet II, the Conqueror, dragged his warships on rollers through today's New District under cover of darkness, launched them into the Golden Horn, and executed a successful surprise attack on Constantinople—ending Byzantine rule and opening a new chapter in the city's history.

EĞRİKAPI GATE TO GREEK ORTHODOX PATRIARCHATE

The next part of this walk explores the residential areas of Lonca, Balat, and Fener, inside the walls. The people you're meeting along the way don't see many tourists. Greet them with a friendly *"Merhaba"* as you pass.

• *From Eğrikapı Gate, head east on Eğrikapı Street toward the Old Town. Next to a little grocery store and a manly tea house, take the third alley to the left (Dervişzade Sokak).*

❼ Dervişzade Sokak

As you walk along, imagine how the city walls lost their protective function as the centuries went by. No longer needed for fortification, they became a handy quarry for locals needing stone for home additions or to build walls of their own. Many homes were constructed right up against the wall (to save on building materials), so in a way the Walls of Constantinople remain integral to the foundation of this grand city.

An ongoing urban rehabilitation project (supported by UNESCO and the European Union) seeks to preserve the authenticity of the Lonca, Balat, and Fener neighborhoods while being mindful of the inhabitants and their needs. A few years ago, tourists walking these alleys would have faced a tough local attitude. Residents feared that the renewal project would force them from their homes. Tour guides were hired to take locals on cultural tours of their own neighborhoods to learn what the project is all about.

• *Follow Dervişzade Sokak as it curves to the right and then left (and gets wider). Straight ahead, you'll see an old fountain in the middle of the alley. To the left of the fountain is the entrance to the...*

❽ Kazasker İvaz Efendi Mosque

This mosque, built in 1585 by the architect Mimar Sinan or one of his students, honors Kazasker İvaz Efendi, one of the highest-ranking military judges in the Ottoman Empire, who conferred directly with the grand vizier. Located on what was one of the terraces of the sprawling Blachernae Palace, this mosque is unusual for its entry, which has double doors (women right, men left) at either side instead of the traditional central entrance. You're welcome to enter the courtyard and mosque. Peer over the balustrade into the cemetery with its Arabic calligraphy and turbans carved in stone. If the imam is around, ask him to open the mosque so you can see

its delightful original interior. Wander upstairs behind the jalousies.

• *Return to the alley and follow the mosque's courtyard wall to a view—*

*point next to Anemas Café. From here you can look out over the ruins of
the Dungeons of Anemas and Blachernae Palace. (Ongoing renovation
may cause some areas to be cordoned off or blocked from view.)*

❾ Dungeons of Anemas

The two towers are known as the Dungeons of Anemas—named
for their first prisoner, a Byzantine soldier of Arab origin named
Michael Anemas. He was imprisoned here after a failed attempt to
murder the Byzantine emperor in 1107. Legend says the emperor's
daughter later helped Anemas escape, while historians believe he
served jail time but was spared being blinded, thanks to the daughter's fervent pleading.

This prison was also where overthrown emperors were locked
up and tortured. Emperor Isaac II Angelus was blinded and held in
the dungeons (next to his bastion) for years when his elder brother
usurped the throne.

All three floors inside the towers have collapsed, so what you'll
see is an empty shell. The basement (not visible from the platform)
contains remnants of the walls that once separated the cells. Imagine the sunlight beaming through narrow openings.

❿ Blachernae Palace Ruins

The remains of the foundations, vaulted galleries, and underground
tunnels of the once-great Blachernae Palace, administrative center
of the Byzantine Empire, lie before you, all along the wall.

Blachernae (vah-lah-hehr-nah) Palace dates back to the sixth
century. Over time, it grew more extensive, incorporating part of
the city wall. In the 12th century, Emperor Alexios I Komnenos
abandoned Constantine's run-down royal palace in the city center
(where the Blue Mosque stands today), and the royal family made
Blachernae their primary residence. The emperor brought royal traditions with him to the "New Palace," including having a priest
lock the palace doors each afternoon and open them again at sunrise the next day.

Alexios I and his grandson Manuel I expanded and improved
the palace. Everything at Blachernae was designed to impress. Visitors and envoys were admitted with much pomp and circumstance
to the highly decorated throne room, where the emperor and his
officials awaited in fine robes and jewel-encrusted crowns.

The showiness backfired. Latin envoys, as impressed as they
were envious, brought home stories of the wealth on show here,
and in 1204, Crusader armies plundered Constantinople and the
riches of Blachernae. The palace was still standing when the Crusaders left, but likely never regained its former glory, even after
the Byzantine emperor retook the throne. By the 14th century, the

treasury was empty, the palace was in disrepair, and the emperor was drinking his wine from an earthenware cup.

Excavation and restoration work has been going on for some time now, closing this site to visitors. If by chance you are permitted to enter, watch out for unstable, loose ground.

• *Next, take the narrow alley (Ahmet Rufai Sokağı) across from Anemas Café. To your left as you walk is the...*

⓫ Emir Buhari Tekkesi (Emir Buhari Lodge)

The popular dervish spiritual leader Emir Buhari lived in the late 15th and early 16th centuries. As his name suggests, he came from the city of Bukhara (Buhara in Turkish), in today's Uzbekistan. Buhari introduced a dervish sect with roots in the spiritual side of Islam. This lodge (not open to the public) was built by the sultan to serve as a gathering place for Buhari's followers. To the left of the lodge are the burial places of sect leaders who followed Emir Buhari.

Religious orders, dervish lodges, and sheiks like Buhari played an important role in Istanbul's social, religious, and political life in the past—and to some extent, they remain influential even now. When the Turkish Republic was established in 1923, religious organizations like this were banned, and *tekkes* (lodges) were closed down. But the sects lived on, practicing dervish traditions in secret, under different names. These sects still exist—unofficially.

• *Continue until the alley ends (keep left) at a staircase. Looking straight down from the top, you'll see the Panagia Blachernae Church, our next stop. At the bottom of the staircase, turn left and keep the wall to your right as you go around the block to the church entrance.*

⓬ Panagia Blachernae Holy Spring and Church (Vlaherna Meryem Ana Church)

A holy spring (one of the Orthodox faith's three most sacred springs in Istanbul) was once part of the Blachernae Palace complex, with a small church at the site. The church housed a sacred relic—a scarf purported to have been Mary's—that was believed to protect the city from disasters. When the church and scarf were destroyed in a fire, churchgoers believed that the city would fall to invaders. Two decades later, the Ottomans conquered Constantinople.

The word *panagia* refers to the Mother Mary and means the "all holy." Many churches in Istanbul dedicated to Mother Mary are named *panagia*—this one is Panagia Blachernae, or the All Holy of Blachernae.

If it's open, step inside the church for a quick look at the holy spring (inside the church building by the end of the courtyard—look for the basket of small plastic bottles). The water is believed

The Fighting Roma of Lonca

The Roma of Lonca are famous for their "street fights." Don't worry; these aren't violent conflicts. When a family has a problem to resolve with another family, they invite that family to a "fight." A date and time are set, and a location selected (it could be outside on a common street, or inside a coffee shop). Neighbors are invited to attend as witnesses, and both families prepare food to serve the audience. At the appointed date and time, musicians and dancers from both families take turns trying to outdo one another's performances. The family that receives the most applause from the audience wins the "fight"— and prevails in whatever issue it was that needed to be settled.

to have healing properties. Many visitors come here from Greece, filling their bottles at the spring to take home.

You may see Muslims—mostly women—visiting this church to ask the priest for help. Superstitious Turks believe in charms and spells, and that a certain type of spell can only be undone by a faithful Orthodox priest.

Back outside the church, look across the street to the shop with many colorful and extravagant cabaret costumes hanging outside. This is the workshop of **Kobra Murat,** a Roma fashion designer known as the Versace of Istanbul. Many Roma performers and those attending special events come here when they need fancy garb.

• *With the church entrance behind you, turn right and walk along Mustafa Paşa Bostanı Sokak (called Bostan Sokak by locals).*

⓭ Ayvansaray University

You'll pass (on the right) a recently restored building that's now part of Ayvansaray University (the main campus is across the street). A new trend among Turkish universities is to locate campuses within the heart of the historical city (rather than a more spacious suburban campus), to connect students to real life. And that explains several little cafés in the neighborhood, catering to students.

• *Continue on to the end of Bostan Sokak, where it sharply bends to the right and connects to Kırkambar Sokak. You are now in the...*

⓮ Lonca Neighborhood

Long ago, Istanbul's Roma (Gypsy) families wearied of traveling and settled in the neighborhoods of Lonca and Balat. Laundry hanging from lines stretched across the street; young children running around, hollering for attention; and elderly women sitting out on doorsteps, chatting and sipping tea—these are common scenes in the alleyways of Lonca and Balat. You won't see many older kids around during the day—if they're not at school, they're usually on a mission to help the family economically. As the Roma say, "The wealth of a Roma family is determined by the number of their children."

Lonca's residents are known for being talented musicians, fortune-tellers, and street florists. The musicians you come across in *meyhanes* (taverns) across Istanbul are usually from this neighborhood. As you wander Lonca's alleys, you may hear music coming from "musicians' coffee shops," which function as a sort of informal musicians guild.

• *On Tuesdays, the **Aya Dimitri Orthodox Church** on your left marks the start of a lively street market. If you're here then, the crush of people is a good reminder that pickpockets like a crowd (secure your wallet).*

*Continue straight ahead another 100 yards onto Mahkeme Altı Caddesi, passing (to your right) the **Panagia Balino Greek Orthodox Church**. Continue until you reach a fork, then keep to the left, following Lavanta Sokak as it turns into Ayan Caddesi (the hard-to-notice doorway of the historic **Yanbol Synagogue** is to your right). Ahead of you is the...*

⓯ Balat Neighborhood

Until the 1950s, Balat was a bustling Jewish neighborhood with a lively market (Balat Çarşısı). But in the decades since Turkey

became a republic, many Jewish people who could afford it have moved to more desirable neighborhoods elsewhere in Istanbul. Today's Balat is missing the taverns, jewelers, fabric merchants, and bankers of the past—they've been replaced by hardware stores, metal repair shops, butchers, wholesalers, and green grocers. And yet this little downtown somehow retains a hint of its traditional charm.

Thanks to a European Union project, Balat has had a facelift in recent years. With many of its once-dilapidated buildings restored, the neighborhood is evolving into a trendy design district, with a smattering of artists' studios and craft workshops. Nowadays, it's cool to hang out here.

• *At the intersection, turn right onto Kürkçü Çeşmesi Sokak. To your left is the...*

⓰ Ahrida Synagogue

This synagogue is the only one in the city that can be dated with certainty to the Byzantine period. It was built in the early 15th century by Jewish settlers from the Macedonian city of Ohrid and has

---

Catching Your Breath in Balat

A handful of newly opened, rustic, and cozy cafés and restaurants in Balat are ideal for a break or simple lunch. For locations, see the map earlier in this chapter.

Look for homey **$ Café Vodina** in the Balat Cultural Center (Balat Kültür Evi), the meeting place of the Turkish Soroptimist Federation, an organization of professional women. The café and cultural center are focused on empowering the women of Balat—who staff and run the facility (daily 10:00-18:00, Vodina Caddesi 39, +90 212 531 0057, www.balatkulturevi.com).

$ Forno Balat is a small and friendly *pide* shop that feels more like a large kitchen than a restaurant. The chef works at a long marble counter running along one wall, while regulars socialize at the large central table (Tue-Sun 10:00-20:00, closed Mon, off Vodina Caddesi at Fener Kireçhane Sokak 13, +90 212 521 2900).

With coffee shops trimming every corner of the city, **$ Çayada** ("Tea Island") is a haven for tea enthusiasts. The simple interior is colorful and cheerful with wall paintings, flower pots, and a kaleidoscope of glass chandeliers; a pleasant outdoor terrace has views of the Golden Horn. They serve cold sandwiches as well as cookies and tea (daily 9:30-24:00, Mürselpaşa Caddesi 201, +90 212 531 3148).

---

been welcoming worshippers ever since. The last renovation was in 1992, marking the 500th anniversary of the arrival of Sephardic Jews in Istanbul.

The synagogue is open to the public only during the first week of September (Jewish Week in Europe). The rest of the year you'll need advance permission from the Chief Rabbinate (www.turkyahudileri.com, click on "Admissions"). If you get a chance to peek inside, look for the bema, the elevated platform from which the Torah is read to the congregation. Built from varnished wood in the shape of a ship's prow (said to be Noah's Ark), it's the most interesting part of this synagogue. Ottoman-style floral designs decorate the wooden ceiling.

• *From here, if you're interested, it's a short detour to the Holy Archangels Armenian Church. With your back to the synagogue, take the alley (Düriye Sokak) directly across from you, and turn left onto Kamış Sokak by the church wall.*

⓱ Holy Archangels Armenian Church (Surp Hıreşdagabet)

Dating from the 19th century, this church replaced an earlier Greek Orthodox structure. In the 1600s, the sultan gave it to the Armenian congregation to return a favor. The holy spring in the

The First Patriarch After the Ottoman Conquest

When Mehmet II conquered Constantinople in 1453, the patriarchal throne had been empty for a few years. Even before the conquest, ongoing discussions about the reconciliation of the Catholic and Orthodox churches were creating friction. Realizing that a unified Church would be a threat to his throne, Mehmet sought to derail the negotiations. He picked the theologian Gennadius Scholarius—a strong opponent of unification—as patriarch of the Orthodox Church. Unfortunately Gennadius wasn't around: He'd been taken captive during the conquest of Constantinople and was being held in a slave market in a neighboring city. Mehmet's soldiers found Gennadius and brought him back to Constantinople, where he became not only the patriarch of Constantinople but also the ethnarch—the political representative of the entire Orthodox population living under Ottoman rule.

Gennadius was an important scholar and theologian even before his ascension to the patriarchal throne. He's best known for writing the *Confession*, a book about Christianity that was presented to Mehmet. Today, a mosaic panel depicting Sultan Mehmet II and Gennadius decorates the entrance hall of the Patriarchate administrative building.

basement—a typical feature of a Greek Orthodox church—is dedicated to St. Andonios (church open to the public Thu 8:30-10:30 & 12:00-14:00, Sun 9:30-14:00, closed Mon-Wed and Fri-Sat).

• *Back at the synagogue, return to the junction of Kürkçü Çeşmesi and Ayan Caddesi. Walk straight across onto Vodina Caddesi. Continue past the* **Tahta Minare Hamamı** *(bath) and stay on Vodina as the street bends to the right. After 200 yards, on the right at #45, behind the massive stone wall, is the...*

⓲ Church of St. George (Aya Yorgi)

This Orthodox church has had a long connection with the Patriarchate of Jerusalem. Every year, on April 23, the patriarch of Jerusalem and the Ecumenical Greek Orthodox patriarch hold a special joint service here, conducted in three languages: Arabic, Greek, and Turkish.

If you're here outside the visiting hours, the caretaker may unlock the main gate into the large garden, with ancient earthenware jars lined up along the side (open to visitors Sat-Sun 14:00-17:00, donation expected).

• *Walk roughly three blocks to the end of Vodina, and turn left and then right onto Yıldırım Caddesi. Walk another block to reach the...*

⓳ Greek Orthodox Patriarchate

This unassuming complex holds the modern offices of the head of the Greek Orthodox Church and its roughly 300 million followers worldwide. The Patriarchate in Istanbul is as important to followers of the Orthodox faith as the Vatican in Rome is to Catholics. The current patriarch, who has the status of "first among equals" among the various branches of the Orthodox Church, is Bartholomew I (270th archbishop of the historic throne of Constantinople), a Turkish-born Greek. Because of his work on behalf of environmental causes, he is known as the "Green Patriarch."

Hagia Sophia was the seat of the patriarch until the Ottoman conquest in 1453. After that, the Patriarchate moved to several different locations before finally finding a permanent home here in the Fener neighborhood in the early 1600s, making this the center of Greek Orthodox life in the city. The name "Fener" is often used as a nickname for the Patriarchate, just as the name "Vatican" is used as shorthand for the leaders of the Catholic Church. Though only a couple of thousand Greek Orthodox Christians reside in Istanbul today, the Greek Orthodox Church remains very influential here.

You'll see three gates at the entrance to the complex. The main gate (at the center) was welded shut in honor of Patriarch Gregory V, who in 1821 was hung here by Sultan Mahmut II for supporting the Greek uprising against Ottoman rule in the Peloponnese. The three crosses on the gate symbolize the patriarch and the two *metropolitans* (similar to archbishops) who were killed with him. The gate on the right opens to the administrative side of the complex.

That leaves the gate on the left—you can use it to enter the courtyard. Straight ahead is another **Church of St. George**, where services are held and holy relics are kept (including those of St. Euphemia). On the facade, above the church's main door, you can spot a double-headed eagle relief, the symbol of the Byzantine Empire. The buildings on the right are the administrative offices and patriarchal residence. To your left, the single-story narrow building is where myrrh, the holy ointment for baptism, is prepared for the Greek Orthodox world.

The Patriarchate and the Church of St. George are open to visitors daily from 8:30 to 16:30. You're welcome to attend services at 16:30 (print out a church tour at www.patriarchate.org).

• *Our walk is finished. From here, you can take a taxi or a bus to Taksim (#55T) or Eminönü (several lines) from the nearby Fener bus stop.*

GOLDEN HORN WALK

From the Galata Bridge to Sirkeci Train Station

The famous Golden Horn—a strategic inlet branching off the Bosphorus Strait—defines Istanbul's Old Town peninsula. The city's fate has always been tied to this stretch of sea: The Golden Horn is Istanbul's highway, food source, and historic harbor all rolled into one. While much of the Old Town area feels dedicated to tourists these days, a visit to the Golden Horn has you rubbing elbows with fishermen and commuters.

This walk offers a handy orientation to the city and affords a sweeping panorama of the Old Town peninsula. Because it's near the terminals for the various Bosphorus ferries, this walk also works well either before or after a cruise of the strait (see the Bosphorus Cruise chapter). The walk is short (about a third of a mile) but allow around 45 minutes if you like to linger.

GETTING TO THE GALATA BRIDGE
The walk begins on the New District (north) end of the Galata Bridge, across from the Eminönü district in the Old Town.

From the Old Town: Take the tram (direction: Kabataş) to Karaköy, the first stop after you cross the Galata Bridge.

From Taksim Square, in the New District: You have two options: Take the funicular down to Kabataş, then ride the southbound tram to the Karaköy stop. Or follow the self-guided New District Walk down İstiklal Street to Tünel (see the next chapter; with less time, link Taksim to Tünel on the Nostalgic Tram). From Tünel you can either take the old funicular down to the bottom of the hill or walk down on Bankalar Caddesi.

The Walk Begins

• *Start on the embankment, on the east side of the Galata Bridge (see map—if you wind up on the wrong side of the bridge, take the pedestrian underpass connecting the two sides). Position yourself on the waterfront, noticing the tulip shapes decorating the railing. With the water at your back, you're facing the neighborhood called...*

Karaköy

The New District covers the area from Karaköy to Taksim Square, a few blocks up the hill. In Byzantine times, this area was inhabited by commercial colonies of Gen-oese and Venetian settlers. In the late Ottoman era, it became a residential area for non-Mus-lims, including Jews, Catholics, and Eastern Orthodox Chris-tians. Today, this part of the city is dominated by the famous Galata Tower (you can just see its cone-shaped top up the hill).

Karaköy is also one of Istanbul's main passenger-ferry ports. As you turn and face the Old Town across the Golden Horn, you'll see public ferry and sea bus docks along the embankment to your left. The area has been the scene of an extensive rebuilding project, as rundown buildings make way for art galleries, deluxe hotels, and convention centers. Locals grumble about political connections that made the project possible, but it's too late to go back now.

If you have the time and interest, you can take a short cruise from the Karaköy ferry pier to see more of the Golden Horn (fer-ries run Mon-Sat at :10 past the hour from 8:10-16:10 and :20 past the hour from 17:20-20:20, Sun at :10 past the hour from 11:10-16:10 and :20 past the hour from 17:20-21:20; 35 minutes; one-way 5-TL trip). Passengers are mostly devout Muslims heading to the Eyüp Sultan Mosque (the last stop; for its religious significance—see page 57) or intrepid travelers looking for "Back Door" scenes.

• *The bridge has two levels. We'll start by walking across the top level, then duck down to the lower level. Climb the stairs and wander across the bridge—dodging fishing poles as you walk.*

Fishermen

Enjoy the chorus line of fishing rods, dancing their little jig. While some of these intrepid folks are fishing for fun, others are trying to land a little extra income. They catch mostly mackerel or ancho-vies—better than nothing, especially during the commercial fish-ing ban (no nets or sonar) that's in effect from June to September.

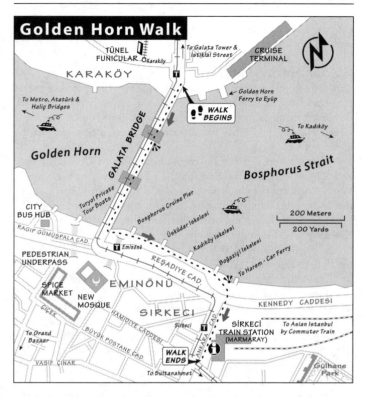

Golden Horn Walk

TÜNEL FUNICULAR · Karaköy
To Galata Tower & İstiklal Street
CRUISE TERMINAL
KARAKÖY
To Metro, Atatürk & Haliç Bridges
Golden Horn Ferry to Eyüp
WALK BEGINS
Golden Horn
GALATA BRIDGE
To Kadıköy
Bosphorus Strait
CITY BUS HUB
Turyol Private Tour Boats
Bosphorus Cruise Pier
200 Meters
200 Yards
RAGIP GÜMÜŞPALA CAD.
Üsküdar İskelesi
Kadıköy İskelesi
PEDESTRIAN UNDERPASS
Eminönü
REŞADIYE CAD.
Boğaziçi İskelesi
To Harem · Car Ferry
SPICE MARKET
NEW MOSQUE
EMINÖNÜ
KENNEDY CADDESİ
ÇİÇEK
SİRKECİ
HAMIDIYE CADDESİ
Sirkeci
SİRKECİ TRAIN STATION (MARMARAY)
To Asian İstanbul by Commuter Train
To Grand Bazaar
BÜYÜK POSTANE CAD.
ANKARA CAD.
WALK ENDS
VASIF ÇINAR
To Sultanahmet
Gülhane Park

During the ban, most of what you find in the market is the expensive daily catch, imported frozen fish, or farm-raised fish.

Approach a fisherman and wish him well, saying *"Rastgele"* (rustgeh-leh; "May you catch some"). Ask to see his catch of the day: *"Bakabilir miyim?"* (bah-kah-bee-leer mee-yeem; "May I see?"). Each one has a bucket or Styrofoam cooler full of  wriggling fish he'd love to show off. If you're having fun with the language, try this: Point to someone's bucket of tiny fish and ask playfully, *"Yem mi, yemek mi?"* (yehm mee yeh-mehk mee; "Is that bait or dinner?").

Watch out for flying hooks as you walk among the fishermen—occasionally they get careless as they swing back for a cast.
• *The part of the bridge between its two low-profile towers can be raised*

GOLDEN HORN

to let big ships pass. This is a good place to find a spot out of harm's way and ponder the famous...

Golden Horn (Haliç)

This four-mile-long horn-shaped inlet glitters like precious metal at sunset. But its strategic value is also worth its weight in gold. Protected from the prevailing north winds, the Golden Horn has served as a natural harbor for centuries: It is an integral part of the history of Istanbul.

This was once the main commercial port of Constantinople and a base for the Byzantine fleet. To block enemy fleets sailing into the heart of the city, and to more effectively levy taxes on ships, the Byzantines hung a massive chain across the entrance of the Horn (you can see some of the historic links in the Istanbul Archaeological Museums). The chain was breached only a couple of times, by the Vikings (10th century) and by the Crusaders during the Fourth Crusade (1204).

In 1453, when the young Ottoman Sultan Mehmet II set out to capture Constantinople, he knew it was crucial to gain control of the Horn. Rather than breaking the chain, he decided to bypass it altogether. His troops pulled their fleet of ships out of the waters of the Bosphorus, slid them on greased logs over the hills through what later became the New District, and launched them back into the Horn—all in just one night.

During Europe's Industrial Revolution, the Ottoman Empire was slow to adapt to the fast-changing new world. It began the industrial race well after the West, then rushed to catch up, often without careful planning. The Horn became more and more polluted as industrial plants and shipyards were built along its banks.

In the 1980s, a clever Istanbul mayor with light blue eyes used a great gimmick to clean things up: He got people on board by saying his project would make the Horn as blue as his eyes. Factories were closed and moved outside the city. Rotting buildings along the water with no historic significance were torn down, and empty space was converted into public parks. The area's entire infrastructure was renewed—a process that's ongoing.

• *Now look inland over the tram tracks and up the Golden Horn (with your back to the Bosphorus), to see the...*

Bridges over the Horn

Four bridges over the Golden Horn connect the Old Town to the New District. The first one you see is the Metro Bridge, completed in 2013 as part of the project to extend the underground Metro line to the Old Town.

Right behind the Metro Bridge is the low-lying Atatürk Bridge, on floating platforms, and beyond that is the taller main highway bridge, called Haliç (hah-leech)—also the local name for the Golden Horn.

The original Galata Bridge was the first and, for decades, the only bridge spanning the Horn. It's the one you see in historic postcards from Istanbul. But the huge platforms it was built on blocked water circulation, worsening the Horn's pollution woes. So, in 1994, this historic bridge was replaced with the new Galata Bridge—the one you're standing on. A public outcry of nostalgia eventually compelled city leaders to reassemble the original bridge farther down the Horn, but it also blocked the current, and today only a small chunk remains (not visible from here).

• *Now take in the...*

Old Town Panorama

Use this sweeping vista of the Old Town to get your bearings. Straight ahead from the end of the bridge, you can see the main entrance to the famous **Spice Market** (it's the stone-and-brick building with three small domes), which sells souvenirs, caviar, dried fruits, Turkish delight, "Turkish Viagra"...and, oh yeah, spices.

The handsome mosque just to the left of the Spice Market (partly obscured by the bridge tower) is the New Mosque of Mother Sultan, or simply the **New Mosque.** Dating from the 17th century, it's one of the last examples of classical-style Ottoman mosques. After that time, mosques were built in an eclectic style, heavily influenced by Western architecture.

Behind the Spice Market, twisty streets lined with market stalls wind their way up the hill toward the famous **Grand Bazaar.** While the Spice Market and Grand Bazaar are deluged with tourists, this in-between zone sells more housewares and everyday textiles than souvenirs—meaning that it's packed tight with locals looking for a bargain, particularly on Saturdays. Thanks to these crowds—and a steady stream of delivery trucks and carts blocking the streets—it can take a half-hour to walk just the four blocks between the markets. This is the "real" Istanbul—gritty and authentic.

Farther to the right, past the open space and near the Golden Horn, you see the **Rüstem Paşa Mosque.** This tiny mosque, with its single dome and lone minaret, is dwarfed by the larger mosques around it. But a visit there offers a peek at fine 16th-century Ottoman tiles in a cozy setting.

On the hillside just above the Rüstem Paşa Mosque is the

16th-century **Mosque of Süleyman the Magnificent,** with its handsome dome and four tall minarets. Elaborate and impressive, yet tastefully restrained, this mosque offers an insightful contrast to the over-the-top and more famous Blue Mosque.

To the left of Süleyman's mosque is the single, tall **Beyazıt Tower.** Sometimes referred to as the "fire tower," it marks the location of bustling Beyazıt Square and Istanbul University's main campus (next door to the Grand Bazaar).

Now look to your left. At the end of the Historical Peninsula, you can see the lush gardens marking the grounds of **Topkapı Palace.** Most of what you see from here are the palace's lower gardens, called Gülhane, now a public park. You can also see the tower marking the entrance to the Harem complex.

To the right of the palace (up the hill, above the modern buildings), notice the gorgeous dome and minarets of **Hagia Sophia**— once the greatest church in Byzantium, then a mosque, then one of Istanbul's best museums, and today again a mosque. The famous Blue Mosque, which faces Hagia Sophia from across Sultanahmet Park, is not quite visible from here.

If you look far to the left, beyond the Topkapı Palace gardens, you can see the Bosphorus Strait and **Asian Istanbul** (the hilltop that bristles with TV towers, like a sea of giant minarets). The Bosphorus Bridge, an impressive suspension bridge, is visible from here (unless it's really hazy).

• *Continue along the bridge to the second tower. Go inside the tower and take the stairs down...*

Under the Bridge

As you descend the stairs, look up for a fun view of dozens of fishing rods twitching along the railing of the bridge. As you walk down here, watch your head—sometimes an amateur fisherman carelessly lets his weight swing under. And keep an eye out for the flicker of a little silvery fish, thrashing through the air as he's reeled in by a happy predator.

Walk along the bridge (toward the Old Town), enjoying this "restaurant row." Passages lead to the other side of the bridge, which is lined with still more restaurants. As you walk, aggressive waiters will try to lure you into their restaurants. Don't be shy—look around, get into a conversation, and compare prices. You may end up here tonight for a fish dinner or, better yet, on the other side of the bridge, where you can watch the sun set

over the Golden Horn. Even if you don't want a full meal, consider picking up a sandwich or having a drink at a café. The last restaurant, with dozens of simple brown tables, sells barbecued fish sandwiches to go—handy to eat as you walk (you'll smell the outdoor barbecue before you see it). If you cross under, you'll find a line of trendy teahouses and bars facing up the Golden Horn—great for backgammon, drinks, and sunsets. At the end of the bridge on the Old Town side, venerable "fish and bread" boats sell cheap fish sandwiches literally off the boat.

• *At the end of the bridge, turn left and continue along the...*

Commuter Ferry Terminals

This embankment bustles with thousands of commuters heading to and from work (during morning and evening rush hours) and shopping chores (especial-ly Saturdays). Peek into the pedestrian underpass beneath the bridge for a taste of the shoulder-to-shoulder commute that many locals endure.

This area is also a hub for intercontinental traffic. Public ferries carry mil-lions of commuters every year between the European and Asian districts of Istanbul. Until the first bridge over the Bosphorus was built in the early 1970s, boats were the only way to cross from Europe to Asia. Locals still prefer the ferries, which are a convenient and cheap way to avoid the gridlock on the bridges.

From this vantage point, you can assess how crowded with tourists Istanbul is at the moment. When cruise ships dock (at piers on the edge of the New District), the big boats routinely unload several thousand tourists apiece, inundating the city's top three sights: the Blue Mosque, Hagia Sophia, and Topkapı Palace.

Here on the Old Town side, the first terminal, the **Bosphorus Cruise Pier,** is where you can catch a public ferry for a cruise up the Bosphorus (allow 5.5-7 hours with stop at fishing village; seasonal schedule and route described in the Bosphorus Cruise chapter). Just beyond are **private tour boats** (look for the *Bosphorus Tours* sign). For about 25 TL (hawkers ask more), these boats take you as far as the second bridge on the Bosphorus and back again in 1.5 hours. Ignore the posted schedule: Boats leave when they fill up, so just hop on board whenever you're ready. While it's easy to take a public ferry for a Bosphorus curise, these tour boats—which don't go as far up the strait, and don't make any stops—are faster and worth

GOLDEN HORN

considering if you're pressed for time and just want a taste of the strait.

The next terminal is **Üsküdar İskelesi,** with boats heading to the Üsküdar district on the Asian side. It's followed by **Kadıköy İskelesi,** with boats heading to Asian Istanbul's Kadıköy district (for more on Üsküdar and Kadıköy, and getting there by ferry, see the Asian Istanbul Walks chapter). Next is **Boğaziçi İskelesi,** another commuter port.

The last terminal is for the car ferry to **Harem**—not a place with sultans' wives, but the major commercial harbor in Asian Istanbul (near Üsküdar). Harem is a handy shortcut to the Asian side, and it's definitely the cheapest intercontinental crossing for cars (every 30 minutes, 25 minutes). One-way passenger trips on the Üsküdar, Kadıköy, and Harem ferries are covered by single-ride public transit tickets/passes—see page 34.

• *When you spot the Harem ferry, it's time to head inland. For a nice panorama over the Galata Bridge and the New District, you could climb the pedestrian overpass. But for where we're going next, it's better to cross the street at the stoplight in order to stay on the proper side of the tram tracks.*

After you cross the street, you're in the Sirkeci neighborhood, and a few steps from the historic train station of the same name.

Sirkeci Train Station

This is a surprisingly low-key train station for having once been the terminal of the much-vaunted Orient Express. An old locomotive decorates the corner of the station, honoring this footnote in history. Pass the locomotive and turn left, finding your way to the station's main entrance (along the modern wall with the white doors, under the sign for *İstanbul Gar*). Inside, a TI and ticket windows are to your left—and a statue of Atatürk is staring down at you from the head of the tracks.

Wander deeper into the station, past the ticket windows, and go left to find evidence of a more genteel, earlier age. Consider popping into the humble little **Railway Museum,** with its old photos and equipment (free, Tue-Sat 9:00-12:30 & 13:00-17:00, closed

Sun-Mon). To the right of the museum is the old passenger waiting room, with wooden benches and stained-glass windows that recall the station's former glory.

The **Orient Express** train line began in the 1880s. You could board a train in Paris and step off into this very station three days later (after passing through Munich, Vienna, Budapest, and Bucharest). Traversing the mysterious East, and headed for the even more mysterious "Orient," passengers were advised to carry a gun. The Orient Express was rerouted to avoid Germany during the Nazi years, and was temporarily disrupted during both world wars, but otherwise ran uninterrupted until May 1977. While this is the most famous route, almost any eastbound train from Western Europe could be called an "Orient Express." The train line was immortalized in literature and film—most famously by Agatha Christie, whose *Murder on the Orient Express* takes place on the Simplon Orient Express (Paris' Gare de Lyon station to Milan, Belgrade, Sofia, and Istanbul).

Sirkeci no longer serves international trains, but the station is still a busy stop on the Marmaray commuter rail line that runs under the Bosphorus Strait to the Üsküdar district in Asia.

• *Your walk is finished. To head back to Sultanahmet, you can take the tram (which departs from directly in front of the station) two stops uphill to the Sultanahmet stop, or simply follow the tram tracks on foot (10–15 minutes).*

NEW DISTRICT WALK

From Taksim Square & Istiklal Street to Tünel Funicular

To fully appreciate the urban Istanbul of today, leave the Old Town and plunge into the lively, sophisticated, and very European New District. Start at the vast Taksim Square and stroll the length of teeming İstiklal Street (İstiklal Caddesi)—the city's jam-packed main pedestrian drag. Lined with Art Nouveau facades, cafés, restaurants, pubs, bookstores, music stores, art galleries, cinemas, theaters, and a rainbow of other shops, İstiklal Street is probably the most cosmopolitan part of European Istanbul. Pastry shops and restaurants that once served only the upper crust now open their doors to commoners like you and me.

Orientation

Length of This Walk: Allow one hour for the walk...but you'll need much longer if you succumb to the many temptations along the way.

Getting There: From the Old Town, ride the northbound tram to the Kabataş stop (the end of the line) and follow the crowds directly into the funicular station.  Take the handy little one-stop funicular up to Taksim Square (transfer-2.5 TL, runs every 8 minutes, daily 6:00-24:00) and exit following signs for *İstiklal Caddesi*.

Nostalgic Tram: This tram runs quietly up and down İstiklal Street between Taksim Square and the Tünel funicular station. It's a handy way to quickly skip ahead or backtrack during this walk (single ride-3.5 TL, runs every 5-10 minutes, daily 7:30-22:45).

Tünel Funicular: This underground funicular, inaugurated in 1875, connects the bottom end of İstiklal Street with the Galata Bridge, Karaköy, and the tram line back to the Old Town (single ride-4 TL, covered by transit passes, runs every 4-7 minutes, daily 7:00-22:45; see the end of this chapter for more on the Tünel).

The Walk Begins

• *Start at Taksim Square, next to the Republic Monument.*

❶ Taksim Square and Republic Monument

Taksim Square (Taksim Meydanı) is the New District's transportation hub, connected to other parts of Istanbul by bus, Metro, fu-

nicular, and the Nostalgic Tram. Long an emblem of modern Turkish life, Taksim Square also marks the beginning of Istanbul's trendiest business and residential neighborhoods, which stretch beyond the square in the direction of the adjoining Taksim Gezi Park.

At the east end of Taksim Square, the redesigned **Atatürk Cultural Center** is gradually rising as a new setting for opera and classical music (may be open in 2021). Across from it stands the brand-new and imposing **Taksim Mosque,** a controversial project championed by conservatives.

The mosque squares off (physically and symbolically) against the patriotic **Republic Monument** (Cumhuriyet Anıtı, in the middle of the square), unveiled in 1928 to commemorate the fifth

anniversary of the founding of the secular Turkish Republic. When the government ran out of money to fund the monument, the people of Turkey dug into their own pockets to finish it.

Designed by Italian sculptor Pietro Canonica, the monument shows two aspects of Atatürk, the father of modern Turkey. On the north side, he's wearing his military uniform, as the hero of the Turkish War of Independence. On the

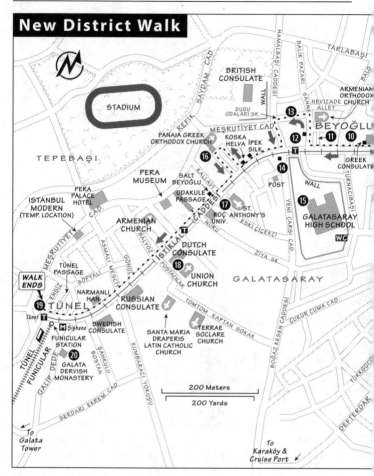

New District Walk

STADIUM

TEPEBAŞI

BRITISH
CONSULATE

ARMENIAN
ORTHODOX
CHURCH

NEVIZADE
ALLEY

BEYOĞLU

TARLABAŞI

HAMALBAŞI CADDESI

BALIK PAZARI

SAHNE

MEŞRUTIYET CAD.

DUDU
ODALARI SK.

PANAIA GREEK
ORTHODOX CHURCH

KOSKA
HELVA IPEK SILK

13
12
11
10

16

PERA
MUSEUM

SALT
BEYOĞLU

KALLAVI

ODAKULE
PASSAGE

17

KOÇ
UNIV.

ST.
ANTHONY'S

14

POST

GREEK
CONSULATE

WALL

TURNACIBAŞI

15

GALATASARAY
HIGH SCHOOL

WC

YENI ÇARŞI

ESKI ÇIÇEKÇI

ISTANBUL
MODERN
(TEMP. LOCATION)

PERA
PALACE
HOTEL

MEŞRUTIYE CAD.

ARMENIAN
CHURCH

BALYOZ

İSTIKLAL CADDESI

NURU

ZIYA SK.

DUTCH
CONSULATE

18

UNION
CHURCH

GALATASARAY

TÜNEL
PASSAGE

WALK
ENDS

19

TÜNEL

NARMANLI
HAN

RUSSIAN
CONSULATE

SOFYALI

ENSIZ

GÖNÜL

ASMALI MESÇIT

TOSTACILAR

TOMTOM KAPTAN SOKAK

BOGAZ KESEN CADDESI

ÇUKUR CUMA CAD.

Tünel

Şişhane

FUNICULAR
STATION

20

GALATA
DERVISH
MONASTERY

GALIP DEDE

TÜNEL
FUNICULAR

SWEDISH
CONSULATE

ŞAHKULU
BOSTANI

SANTA MARIA
DRAPERIS
LATIN CATHOLIC
CHURCH

TERRAE
SOCLARE
CHURCH

KUMBARACI YOKUŞU

SERDARI EKREM CAD.

200 Meters

200 Yards

To
Galata
Tower

To
Karaköy &
Cruise Port

REFIK SAYDAM CAD.

flip side, civilian Atatürk is shown as modern Turkey's first president, surrounded by figures representing the proclamation of the republic.

Two medallions near the top of the monument represent women before (veiled) and after the founding of the republic. Scholars say that one of the women depicted is actually Sabiha Bengütaş—the republic's first female sculptor, the first female student admitted to the sculpture department at the Turkish Academy of Fine Arts (today's Mimar Sinan University of Fine Arts), and the first Turkish woman to win the Prix de Rome scholarship (to attend the French Academy in Rome). Later, Bengütaş worked with Canonica and assisted him with this monument.

• *From Taksim Square, the Nostalgic Tram loops around the monument and runs to the end of İstiklal Street (and the top of the Tünel funicular,*

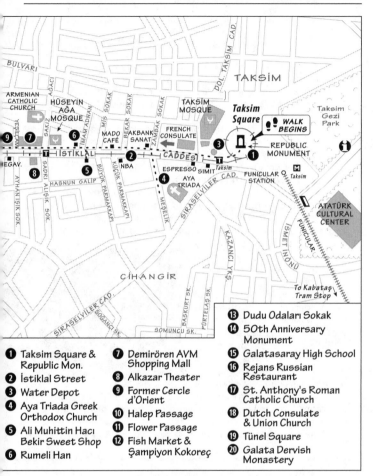

① Taksim Square &
   Republic Mon.
② İstiklal Street
③ Water Depot
④ Aya Triada Greek
   Orthodox Church
⑤ Ali Muhittin Hacı
   Bekir Sweet Shop
⑥ Rumeli Han
⑦ Demirören AVM
   Shopping Mall
⑧ Alkazar Theater
⑨ Former Cercle
   d'Orient
⑩ Halep Passage
⑪ Flower Passage
⑫ Fish Market &
   Şampiyon Kokoreç
⑬ Dudu Odaları Sokak
⑭ 50th Anniversary
   Monument
⑮ Galatasaray High School
⑯ Rejans Russian
   Restaurant
⑰ St. Anthony's Roman
   Catholic Church
⑱ Dutch Consulate
   & Union Church
⑲ Tünel Square
⑳ Galata Dervish
   Monastery

which leads down to the Galata Bridge). That's precisely the course we'll
walk. Before you leave the square, take a minute to read about...

❷ İstiklal Street

İstiklal Caddesi (ees-teek-lahl jahd-deh-see; "Independence
Street") was born after a devastating 1870 fire. The Ottoman gov-
ernment took the opportunity to rebuild the area as a showpiece of
Art Nouveau style.

While immersed in the crowds that enliven this boulevard,
stand still for a moment just to watch the river of people. İstiklal
Street is today's Turkey. Where is everyone going? Just "out." Are
they Turkish? Yes. Nine out of every ten people you see on this
promenade are Turks—modern Turkey is a melting pot of some
20 different ethnic groups. Observe the haircuts and fashions as

NEW DISTRICT

"I Was in Taksim"

Taksim Square and İstiklal Street have always been a gathering point for crowds—the place to go if you want to draw attention to your cause. Any event organized here makes the news.

For decades, labor-union members celebrated Labor Day (May 1) in Taksim Square, and for years the rallies ended peacefully. May 1, 1977, was different. Half a million workers crowded the square that day, and tempers flared. Suddenly, gunshots were heard, and in the ensuing panic and chaos, 37 people died (the shooter was never identified). Many locals consider this a particularly dark day in the city's history. The following year, union members again assembled at the square, this time to protest against the government they held responsible for the previous year's melee. In response, the government banned May 1 gatherings on the square for three decades. In 2009, the unions finally got permission for a Labor Day

rally, and in 2010, more than 100,000 workers demonstrated peaceably.

But Taksim Square had never seen anything quite like the massive demonstrations that took place here in May 2013. Sparked by police action against a peaceful group of young environmentalists, the demonstration became a prolonged rally, with protesters decrying increasing government intrusions into citizens' private lives and erosion of Turkey's secularism.

The driving force behind the huge May 2013 demonstrations

---

everyone from teenagers to businesspeople makes the scene. Stop and talk with someone in this living celebration of diversity.

From here, this walk slopes gradually downhill. Along the way, cafés and eateries offer second-floor refuges from the crowds and fine vantage points from which to view the scene below. To make the route super-simple, follow the tram tracks and match the handy red-metal numbered plates on the buildings with the addresses included in this walk—odd numbers on the left, even on the right (ignore the old blue plaques).

Thronged with people, İstiklal Street is no fun for claustrophobes. (The crowds can be so thick that occasionally the tram simply cannot run.) When the street is jammed, it's easier to go with the flow by sticking to the right, as local strollers do.

• Let's start down İstiklal Street. Follow the tram tracks to the octagonal building known as the...

came from an unexpected (to the government) source: Turkey's younger generation, not the older, pro-secular members of society. These persistent, computer-savvy kids used methods that were hard for the government to deal with—social media and humor—and attracted large numbers of supporters.

Successive waves of protests rippled across the nation, even reaching remote, traditionally pro-government towns in the east. Officials say three million citizens took to the streets, but the number was undoubtedly higher. Local authorities called it the largest anti-government uprising in the history of the Republic. Authorities also said that it was the first time then three-term prime minister Recep Erdoğan and his party suffered a defeat.

Erdoğan's government responded with a violent crackdown, using tear gas to disperse the protestors. Eleven people died, thousands were injured, and over 3,000 were arrested. The government reaction left deep scars in the Turkish psyche. To some, Taksim Square is considered Turkey's version of Tiananmen Square.

What happened at Taksim is an outgrowth of a major shift away from the liberal ideals that originally brought Erdoğan and his AKP party to power in 2003. Civil unrest and a faltering economy have led the AKP to adopt ever more conservative policies to retain power—and conservative votes. Erdoğan's election as president in 2014 (and survival of a military-backed coup in 2016) cemented AKP as the dominant force in Turkish politics.

For many, the restrictions on personal freedoms, censorship and arrests of journalists, and suppression of social media and public gatherings are unacceptable. Depending on what happens next, to say, "I was in Taksim," may take on an even greater meaning.

❸ Water Depot (Taksim Maksemi)

This historic building is a reminder that *"taksim"* means "distribution," and that this square was once part of the town's water system. The ground floor is faced in marble, and above the rounded entrance door, a three-line inscription gives the date, 1732. Look up to see two intricate birdhouses on the facade, just below the roofline—a charming feature often seen in Ottoman-era architecture. On the side of the building facing the square is a marble fountain. Also on the square (just behind the fountain) is the free **Republic Art Gallery** (Cumhuriyet Sanat Galerisi), which showcases exhibits of contemporary art.

• *Opposite the water depot, check out the...*

Food Corner at the Top of İstiklal Street

This first corner has long been a fast-food stop. Fresh-squeezed orange juice and just-sliced *döner kebab* are traditional favorites, but American fast-food joints are also popular.

• *A few steps in, take a closer look at a truly local fast-food place...*

Simit Sarayı (#3)

A *simit* (see-meet) is like a bagel: bread dough dipped in grape molasses *(pekmez)*, rolled in sesame seeds, and then baked. You'll see street vendors with old-fashioned carts selling these bread rings all over town (a filling snack starting from 2 TL). The popular Simit Sarayı chain has all of Istanbul munching on its *simit* sandwiches of cheese, sausages, and olives.

• *A little farther down the street, on the left, you'll see the...*

Espresso Lab (#15)

Since Turks love coffee (heck, they claim to have invented it), Turkey is an appealing market for international chains. Australia's Gloria Jean's was the first modern coffee shop to hit Istanbul, with Seattle's green mermaid and the UK's Caffè Nero close behind. The local Kahve Dünyası (Coffee World) challenges the big boys by selling coffee at a fraction of the others' prices, and now Espresso Lab is a bold new contender in this expanding coffee war.

Across the street (at #4) is the **French Consulate.** During Ottoman times this was the most European-friendly district of Istanbul, and many European consulates (Russian, Dutch, Greek, to name a few) and churches are located here.

• *Continue down İstiklal Street. After half a block, turn left at the alley (Meşelik Sokak). On your left is the...*

❻ Aya Triada Greek Orthodox Church

Aya Triada—or, as the locals call it, the Grand Church—is the largest active Orthodox church in town. While it's often closed, the guard will usually let you in (for a donation to the church offering box). Built in the Neo-Gothic style in 1880, the church has some interesting flourishes, such as the delicate paintings that line the sanctuary walls. Also enjoy the colorful frescoes and Baroque-style decorations on the ceiling and dome. This is the first of many Christian churches we'll see along this walk—reminders that, historically, this was one of the most diverse, cosmopolitan areas of Istanbul.

• *Head back out to İstiklal Street to continue our walk. Notice the six-story building on the opposite corner, a part of Istanbul's...*

Art Gallery Scene

Several art galleries are located on İstiklal Street and nearby. This building is **Akbank Sanat** (#8), a contemporary art gallery and arts center, with studio space for artists and dancers. We'll go by other galleries (such as **Salt Beyoğlu** at #136) which display permanent and temporary exhibitions of both well-established artists and rising stars in the art world. This is a good opportunity to check out Turkey's often-overlooked contemporary art scene (most galleries are free to enter).

• *Across the street, on the left, notice the...*

NBA Store (part of Adidas, #59)

American professional basketball is hugely popular in Istanbul. This is the first NBA store to open anywhere outside the US. In 2000, Hidayet "Hido" Türkoğlu became the first Turkish-born player in NBA history. Following Türkoğlu's footsteps, Mehmet Okur played for the 2004 NBA champion Detroit Pistons and became the first Turk to play in an All-Star game (other Turkish NBA stars include Ersan İlyasova and Cenk Akyol). In 2006, the NBA began actively promoting the sport in Europe, including Italy, Spain, Britain...and Turkey. Turks hold out hope that the NBA could expand to Europe someday.

• *Ahead on the right is...*

MADO (#38)

This chain is a local favorite for its Turkish-style ice cream. Made with goat's milk and powdered wild orchid bulbs, it has a thick, stretchy texture. The café also serves good *börek* (savory pastries) and traditional Turkish desserts such as baklava. Two scoops of their ice cream over a serving of baklava is a real treat.

• *If you didn't buy ice cream, you may want to cross the street to be tempted by the offerings at...*

Mustafa Kemal Atatürk (1881-1938)

Atatürk, the George Washington of the Turks, almost single-handedly created modern-day Turkey. As the map of Europe was being redrawn at the end of World War I, this confident war hero put forth a clear and complete vision that persuaded the Turks, on the brink of crisis, to forge a modern nation.

By the early 20th century, the Turkish people were in dire straits. After centuries of decline, the Ottoman Empire allied itself with Germany and was pulled into World War I. But even as the Ottoman Empire floundered, a wily officer named Mustafa Kemal proved his military mettle, successfully defending Gallipoli against a huge armada with a handful of poorly equipped soldiers.

As the war came to an end, victorious European armies occupied Istanbul and made plans to dole out pieces of the former Ottoman Empire to their allies. In 1919, the Greeks took the city of İzmir (on the south coast of Turkey) and began pushing toward Istanbul. With lightning speed, the war hero Kemal gathered an army to defend Turkish territory. Over the three-year Turkish War of Independence, he chased out French and Italian troops and repelled the Greek invasion. With the Treaty of Lausanne in 1923, the Ottoman Empire was history, the Turkish Republic was born, and Mustafa Kemal became the most beloved Turkish leader in centuries. The National Assembly elected Mustafa Kemal as the first president

❺ Ali Muhittin Hacı Bekir (#83)

Turkish kids cheer when their parents bring home a box of *lokum*—Turkish delight—and Hacı Bekir's is considered the best. *Lokum* (loh-koom) is a sweet, flavorful cube of gooey gelatin dusted with powdered sugar and sometimes embedded with nuts. Browse the selection; *lokum* comes in boxes of all shapes and sizes, packed with many different flavors and add-ins (pistachios are favorites). Their almond paste, hard candies, and *helva* (a sesame oil and tahini treat) are also good. Prices are by the kilogram—buy a small amount to taste. About 2 TL will get you 50 grams, about five pieces of Turkish delight. For an assortment, ask for *karışık* (kah-ruh-shuhk) *lokum*. Or pay 3 TL to get the same amount of double-roasted pistachio *lokum* (the real stuff).

• *Ahead on the right, admire the façade of...*

NEW DISTRICT

of the Republic, and dubbed him Atatürk—literally, "father of the Turks"; in this context, it also means "great leader" or "grand Turk."

Rescuing his nation from the chopping block would have been enough to get his name in the history books, but Atatürk was not finished. He envisioned a modern, progressive Turkey that would leave behind the outmoded values of the Ottoman Empire in favor of European-style secular democracy. Rarely in history has anyone exerted such power with such effect in so short a time. In less than 10 years, Atatürk did the following:

- aligned Turkey with the West
- separated religion and state (removed Islam as the state religion and upheld civil law over Islamic law)
- adopted the Western calendar
- decreed that Turks should have surnames, similar to Western custom
- changed the alphabet from Arabic script to Roman letters
- abolished the sultanate and caliphate, and outlawed the fez and veil
- abolished polygamy
- adopted women's suffrage

Atatürk died at 9:05 on November 10, 1938—and every year, all of Turkey still observes a minute of silence at 9:05 on that day to honor the man they regard as the greatest Turk. For a generation, many young Turkish women worried that they'd never be able to really love a man because of their love for the father of their country. Because of Atatürk, millions of Turks today have a flag—and reason to wave it.

❻ Rumeli Han (#48)

Notice the eclectic decorations on the entrance to this old residen-

tial and shopping building—Greek Ionic columns, lions' heads, Arabic script, and more. It was built as a mansion in the 1870s for the grand vizier Ragip Pasha (who served Mustafa III) by the same architects who designed the seaside Dolmabahçe Palace. Later it became a commercial complex with shops, cafés, art studios, and office space on the upper floors. It's hard to tell from here, but this huge complex was constructed in the style of a traditional Ottoman *han* (a combo

In Istanbul, North Is "West"

The area I call the "New District" was once known as Pera ("The Side Across"). Many locals still use this term, which dates from the Middle Ages. When Constantinople's Orthodox Christians clashed with its minority Roman Catholics, the Catholics moved outside the city walls—to "The Side Across," north of the Golden  Horn. Ever since, the northern part of Istanbul (the New District) has looked west to Europe, while the southern part (the Old Town) identifies more with the East.

During the Fourth Crusade, in 1204, the gap between Constantinople's Orthodox and Catholic populations widened. The crusaders stayed here for half a century, establishing relations with Venetian and Genoese merchants, who dominated world trade. For political and economic reasons, the emperors reluctantly gave up their claim to Pera, offering it to the Genoese as a self-governing commercial base.

When the Ottomans conquered Constantinople in the 15th century, the Genoese immediately recognized the rule of the young Ottoman sultan. In return, they were granted privileges and commercial rights that would last for centuries.

As the Ottoman Empire became a more powerful player on Europe's political stage, Pera became a home base for visiting envoys and ambassadors. Genoa, France, Spain, England, Holland, and many of Europe's other great powers built embassies here.

marketplace and inn for merchants), set around a central courtyard. It takes up about a third of the block.

• Walk on down İstiklal Street. To your right, just past the 16th-century Hüseyin Ağa Mosque (the only mosque on the street) and covering an entire city block is the...

❼ Demirören AVM Shopping Mall

Construction of this controversial mall—which has four subterranean and five aboveground floors—was opposed by many neighborhood shop owners and residents. But none were as powerful as the company building the mall—the Demirören group, one of Turkey's leading development companies. The mall's grand-opening ceremony was hosted by the head of the Demirören group (he's also the ex-president of one of Turkey's top soccer teams, Beşiktaş) with a special guest appearance by the popular Brazilian soccer player Ronaldo. Nearby shop owners had to close up early or risk being

Beginning in the 16th century, these embassies became deeply involved in business interests. Foreign merchants wanted to live near their embassies, turning Pera into a particularly desirable and genteel corner of the city. Schools, churches, and communal buildings were built to meet the needs of the ever-growing expatriate population. Soon İstiklal Street became known as the Grand Rue de Pera, and the district became a "little Europe" within the boundaries of greater Istanbul. This cosmopolitan area also began to draw the city's other non-Muslim minorities, such as Greeks, Armenians, and Jews.

The mid-19th century was a time of great change. A new bridge over the Golden Horn connected the still very Eastern-feeling Old

Town to newer, European-style neighborhoods in the north. Tired of being viewed as backward by his European contemporaries, the sultan moved out of the historic Topkapı Palace and into the new Western-style Dolmabahçe Palace in the New District.

The ties between "The Side Across" and Europe are still palpable today. Strolling down the very European-feeling İstiklal Street, tourists sometimes forget they're just a short boat or train trip from Asia. Like the Genoese merchants, ambassadors, and clever sultans before them, today's visitors are figuring out that here in Istanbul, you go north to find the West.

overrun by the chaotic crowd of soccer fans. Turkey's first Virgin Megastore was located in this mall.

• *Across from the mall is the...*

❽ Alkazar Theater (Alkazar Sineması, #111)

This narrow storefront—with a fancy pseudo-arch supported by pedestaled statues—used to hide one of the first movie theaters in Istanbul, dating from just after World War I. In those first years of the early republic, this was a gathering place for the aristocracy, but by the 1970s and 1980s, the only way it could pay the bills was to show erotic films. Nonetheless, with the Turkish film industry on the upswing—thanks

The Brave Grocer Against the Supermarket

For several seasons in the 1980s, the satirical play *The Brave Grocer Against the Supermarket* (Kahraman Bakkal Süpermarkete Karşı) drew full houses in Istanbul.

Istanbul's first modern shopping mall opened in 1988 to newspaper headlines and public acclaim. It was large, there was plenty of parking, fine brands filled the many shops, you could eat on-site, there was even an ice-skating rink...and it was expensive. Luxury wasn't cheap, and Turkish shoppers were willing to pay for the convenience.

Contractors noticed the trend, and soon malls were going up throughout the city, and across Turkey. Supermarket chains followed the trend, supersizing themselves and securing locations in or next to the malls.

As a result, Turkish shopping trends changed radically. Locals who had been accustomed to shopping in neighborhood markets abandoned their familiar haunts and rushed to these giant shopping utopias. Small businesses, groceries, neighborhood eateries, and bakeries tried very hard to survive, but some were forced out of business.

Today, many shoppers have realized that while the big malls offer one-stop convenience, they lack the personal touch. Many consumers are again seeking out their neighborhood shops, and starting the day with a chat with the corner baker. While malls are still everywhere, now they are the ones trying to survive.

to bigger-budget attractions, foreign films, and the buzz created by Istanbul's International Film Festival—this theater managed to survive for another two decades.

Ultimately, though, the theater's prime location doomed it—a victim of developers hungry for commercial real estate. Construction work here will continue into 2021 (but the original facade will be saved).

• *A short distance down the street, peek down the lane on the right called Yeşilçam.*

Yeşilçam Alley (across from #115)

This alley was once the heart of the film industry—the "Turkish Hollywood." While actors, directors, and producers have moved on to other parts of town, "Yeşilçam" is still the nickname for the local film industry.

In Turkey, filmmaking is all about making a good movie on a small budget. Turkish soap operas give Bollywood and Brazilian productions a run for their money—both in Turkey and abroad—

with ratings that surpass even those of Hollywood productions. They pull the best ratings in the Middle East, the Balkans, and Greece, where the Bishop of Thessaloniki warned citizens against watching *Magnificent Century* (about Süleyman the Magnificent, who conquered Rhodes), saying that Greeks surrender to Turks simply by watching the show. In Iran, authorities blame Turkish soaps for pushing a liberal lifestyle.

• *On the corner with Yeşilçam (look for the Madame Tussauds) is...*

❾ Former Cercle d'Orient (#56-58)

This building (its wide facade stretches all the way from Yeşilçam to the Greek Consulate, halfway down the block) was designed in the 1880s by architect Alexander Vallaury as a residence for Abraham Paşa, a wealthy Armenian Catholic. Paşa rented the top two floors to the Cercle d'Orient, a gentlemen's club (more like a political and financial-interest group). Early club members included top-ranking Ottoman officials and officers as well as foreign diplomats.

Even with his huge fortune, Paşa fell into debt and lost the building to his bank, and the Cercle d'Orient, which still exists under the name Büyük Kulüp, eventually moved elsewhere. Today the entire complex has been redeveloped into the Grand Pera shopping mall, despite valiant efforts to save this cultural landmark.

• *Across the street look for...*

Megavizyon (#125)

As pop music grows ever more popular among young Turks, new stars seem to crop up every day. You'll see their posters decorating music-store showcases and billboards. As in many countries, music and book piracy are problems in Turkey. There used to be several flagship stores like this Megavizyon on İstiklal Street, but few are left now that streaming services and online shopping are so common.

On the retail front, Turkey's electronics giant Teknosa (the Turkish Best Buy) and international superstores (such as Media-Markt) have taken over where small businesses once thrived. As in other parts of the world, big chains are increasing in Turkey, no matter how popular or successful a local business is.

• *Just down the street on the right, past the Greek Consulate, is the entrance to a passageway signed...*

❿ Halep Passage (Halep Pasajı, #62)

Thousands walk past this building complex every day without realizing that it houses one of the few independent theaters in the country. The passageway connects to a second building, at the back, built as a theater in the 1880s. For decades it has been run by a dedicated theater company, led by actor Ferhan Şensoy. His long-running (three decades) one-man play, a political satire based on news-making head-lines in the country, is not so popular among conservative crowds. Look for a poster just above the entrance. The company is devoted to incorporating traditional Turkish theater with contemporary and classic works (imagine Anton Chekhov's *Cherry Orchard* with American humor).

• *Continuing on to the next block you'll find...*

Traditional Food at Otantik Anadolu Yemekleri (#80A)

In the window of this recommended restaurant, a woman prepares and bakes *gözleme* (gohz-leh-meh) in the traditional way: She rolls out the thin flat bread with a rolling pin, piles on savory fillings like cheese, potatoes, and spinach, folds over the dough, and then puts it in the oven. It's simple, delicious...and a good quick snack midway along this walk. Pick the ingredients (10 TL, depending on fillings). To get it wrapped to go, say, "*Paket, lütfen*" (pah-keht lewt-fehn).

• *Next door is the . . .*

⓫ Flower Passage (Çiçek Pasajı, #80)

The original Flower Passage was built in the Neo-Baroque style in the 1870s, with apartments above and shops in the passageway.

Until the 1940s, it was filled only with flower shops. Over time, lively pubs and taverns began to sprout up. The Flower Passage became a gathering place for writers, newspaper correspondents, students, and intellectuals sitting around beer-barrel tables.

But in 1978, a century after it was built, the Flower Passage collapsed due to lack of maintenance. It remained in ruins for a decade until the city decided to rebuild it. What you're looking at is a nostalgic reproduction of a place that's long gone. While some people enjoy the new version (and travel writers seem to love it), most locals are skeptical. Part of the original Flower Passage's original charm was its casual, spontaneous atmosphere—nothing like the white-tablecloth uniformity of today's incarnation.

The Turkish Flag

While the modern Turkish Republic was founded only in 1923, its heritage is much older. Today's flag is very similar to the design used by the Ottomans for centuries, often with a red or green background. All were decorated with a crescent moon (and sometimes a verse from the Quran) as a symbol of Islam. Under Ottoman Sultan Selim III (1789-1807), an eight-point star was added to the flag; today's five-point version replaced it some 150 years later. The design and exact proportions of the Turkish flag were standardized by law in 1937.

The red of the flag is said to represent the blood shed to create the Turkish nation. The crescent and star are the subject of a curious legend. Following the Ottoman victory at the Battle of Kosovo, Sultan Murat I was killed by a Serbian captive. The crescent moon and a star are said to have been seen reflected in a pool of Turkish blood at the scene—inspiring the design for the flag. Interestingly, the date of the battle (July 28, 1389) actually was a night when Jupiter and the moon were side by side in the night sky over this part of the world. So, it is possible that someone could have seen a reflection that matches the moon and the star on the Turkish flag.

• At the next corner, notice the wrought-iron arch over the alley to the right. This is the entrance to the. . .

⑫ Fish Market (Balık Pazarı)

True to its name, the Balık Pazarı (bah-luhk pah-zah-ruh) is *the* place in the New District to shop for fresh fish. But you'll find other uniquely Turkish taste treats here, too.

A few steps into the alley, notice **Şampiyon Kokoreç** on the left. *Kokoreç* (koh-koh-retch; sounds like—but doesn't taste like—"cockroach") is chopped-up sheep intestines, grilled and served with tomatoes, green peppers, and fresh seasonings and herbs. Order *kokoreç* by itself on a plate (*porsiyon;* pohr-see-yohn) or as a half-sandwich (*yarım;* yah-

NEW DISTRICT

ruhm) or quarter-sandwich (*çeyrek;* chey-rehk). To enhance the flavor, doll up your sandwich with the hot peppers in the jars.

As you munch, ponder how seriously Turks take their *kokoreç*. A few years ago, a rumor flew through the streets that stringent new EU regulations would outlaw the beloved *kokoreç*. Before the story was proved untrue, many Turks did some soul-searching and decided that if they had to choose, they'd gladly pass up EU membership for *kokoreç*.

As you wander along the fish stalls and tiny shops selling herbs, dried fruits, and nuts, you're seeing the reality of workaday Istanbul. About halfway down the alley on the right, a narrow door leads into the courtyard of the Holy Trinity Armenian Orthodox Church (also known as the Armenian Church of the Three Altars, or Surp Yerrortutyan). Just beyond this doorway is Nevizade Sokak, an alley lined with lively, down-to-earth restaurants and *meyhanes* (traditional Turkish taverns). The ambience here is local, and the service is usually attentive. It's busiest near sunset, when district residents stop by after work to chat with friends and have a drink or an extended dinner.

• *Backtrack in the direction of the Armenian church and turn into the alley (on the right) named...*

⓭ Dudu Odaları Sokak

Packed with shops that sell a variety of foods, this narrow alley is a great place for one-stop picnic shopping. It's a bit like the Fish Market, but with specialties of its own.

Bakeries start things off early, around 7:00, and gradually are joined by more shops and eateries. Some don't open until noon, since they don't close until 21:00 or even later.

The prices you see are per kilogram, but you can buy items in any amount you want (half a kilo is roughly a pound). With simple gestures, you can signal that you'd just like a small sample, or a handful.

Midyeci Memet (#22), a dedicated supplier of stuffed mussels, has been on this street for five decades. Memet and his hardworking wife Edibe cook up a fresh pot every two hours, nearly around the clock (from 8:00 to 6:00 the next morning). Aside from their regular customers, many restaurants also buy their mussels. Try their mainstay—mussels stuffed with rice, onions, and herbs—or their mussels stuffed with shrimp or calamari (1.5-3 TL/serving).

Cumhuriyet İşkembecisi (#15B) is known for its tripe soup (yes, as in cow stomach, but remember, sausages are made using animal guts, too). In Turkey, if you're hungry—or drunk—late at night, you go out for tripe soup (this shop stays open until 5:30 in the morning). Try a bowl; it's a great Turkish experience. Locals dress it with vinegar, garlic, and red-hot chili peppers. The shop also serves head of sheep—the brain, tongue, and eyes (you can opt out on the eyeballs). The specialty salad is brain salad. Soups are around 11 TL a bowl, a portion of sheep head is 13 TL, and brain salad is 12 TL.

Üç Yıldız Şekerleme (#7) is one of the oldest confectionery shops in the city, famous for its Turkish delight (2.50-4 TL/100 grams—about 8-10 pieces), including varieties flavored with resinous *mastic* and jelly candies. The shop carries a variety of hard candies as well. It's owned and managed by a father-son duo who speak excellent French; the son also speaks English. If you understand some French, it's a delight to hear Feridun, the father, recount stories of good old Istanbul.

Sakarya Tatlıcısı (#3) makes more traditional Turkish desserts, including varieties of baklava (about 35-45 TL/kg). A serving of their specialty, quince dessert, with *kaymak* (kai-mahk; clotted cream made from water-buffalo milk) is 8 TL.

Petek Turşuları (#1D) is a gourmet sour-pickle shop. Turks love sour pickles (*turşu;* toor-shoo) and pickle juice (*turşu suyu;* toorshoo soo-yoo). Even if pickles aren't your thing, they're displayed so well that this shop makes a great photo op. The shop's specialties are plum-and-okra pickles (15-18 TL/kg), beet juice (6 TL/liter), and marinated grape leaves for dolma (10 TL/kg). The store carries some of the finest olives and virgin olive oil from Ayvalık, a town on Turkey's Aegean coast.

• *At the end of Dudu Odaları Sokak, head left and back to İstiklal Street. In a small square across the street, you can see an abstract* ⓮ *monument (resembling a cluster of tubes) that commemorates the 50th anniversary of the Turkish Republic (1923-1973). The square is often the scene of colorful demonstrations as well as performances by talented—and sometimes not so talented—street musicians and jugglers. Behind the tall, fancy gate beyond the monument is...*

⓯ Galatasaray High School

Set in the middle of a huge garden surrounded by a wall marked with a gigantic ornamental gate, this "Royal School" (Mekteb-i Sultani), founded in 1870, was designed to properly raise and educate a new generation of public servants and officials. Its founders hoped to boost the Westernization of the struggling Ottoman Empire. Classes were taught in Turkish and French (the lingua franca of Europe at the time). The school's first principal was a visionary Frenchman who pursued a secular curriculum years before this was common in Europe. The secular teaching outraged the Catholic pope, the Greek Orthodox patriarch, and leading Muslim clerics alike.

As the Ottoman Empire declined, so did the quality of Turkish education. Many of this school's teachers were sent to fight in World War I and never returned. In 1917, only five students graduated. After the Turkish Republic was founded, Galatasaray High School's fortunes improved. Today it's one of the best schools in the country, with a primary school, a high school, and a university.

Across from the high school gate, at #90, is a fine example of Art Nouveau architecture: Built in 1875 for the Sivajian family, this building was later converted into a post office and is now a center for culture and the arts.

• *You've reached the midpoint of İstiklal Street. If you need a pick-me-up, about halfway down the block is...*

Hazzopulo Passage (Hazzopulo Pasajı, #116)

Need a short break or a Turkish coffee? Pop through this narrow, unremarkable entryway into the spacious atrium of this century-old historic passage. Here you'll find the Café Grand Boulevard, a traditional-style coffee shop (see page 74) that's frequented by locals. Sip your coffee or tea while seated at one of the short legged-tables scattered around the courtyard, and watch the commotion of people going about their daily routines.

• *Back on İstiklal Street, look for the...*

State Lottery Administration (Milli Piyango, #120A)

Turkish authorities outlawed private casinos and gambling several years ago after discovering money laundering schemes. (When the tax office would ask someone shady about a sudden, huge influx of cash, the predictable answer was, "I won it gambling.") So the nationwide lottery is hugely popular, with prizes in the millions of dollars. The government runs the lottery and all other legal betting opportunities in Turkey (except horse races; your bet on a winning horse is handled by a private broker). Also popular are the *kazi kazan* (scratch-to-win) cards and *İddia* (eed-dee-ah; literally "to bet"), a lottery game in which players bet on Turkish and European soccer scores. Conservative Muslims debate the morality of state-organized betting games, and yet lottery agents are everywhere, even in the remote ghettos of the city.

• *Just a few steps farther is the…*

İpek Silk Shop (#120)

This fine shop features fixed prices, reliable quality, and a friendly and knowledgeable staff. Isaac and his employees speak English and are happy to demonstrate the latest in scarf fashion. Ask to see the various ways to wear a scarf, depending on your religious leanings. (Rick Steves readers are valued here—show this book for attentive and informative service).

Koska Helva Shop (#122)

It's time to taste another delicacy: *helva* (hell-vah). The word is Arabic and means "sweet." Today, several countries claim the original recipe. Turkish *helva* is made of crushed sesame seeds, wheat flour, and sugar. Pistachios, vanilla, or cacao is added to create different flavors. *Helva* is also associated with social rituals. For example, when someone dies, loved ones will prepare a certain type of wheat *helva* (without the sesame seeds) and serve it to visitors offering condolences. *Helva* is prepared in large blocks (10-20 TL/kg). If you go inside and ask for 2 TL of *karışık* (kah-ruh-shuhk; assorted) *helva,* you'll end up with a mixed bag of about 100 grams (roughly a quarter-pound).

• *Just around the corner from Koska Helva, make a one-block detour down the alley called Emir Nevruz Sokak and take the first left to the site of the historic…*

⓰ Rejans Russian Restaurant

After the 1917 Russian Revolution, many of the deposed czar's officers fled to Turkey. For the next 30 years, this area was an enclave of Russian culture, with Russian restaurants, pubs, music, shows, and dances. Though they had lost the war for their homeland, these Russian transplants spent the rest of their lives pretending they were still living high on the hog in Mother Russia. The locals continued to call them by their former titles: Baron Colonel, Count General, Grand Duke, and so on.

Founded by Russian aristocrats, Rejans (reh-zhahn)—named for Le Régence Restaurant in Paris—retained the caviar-and-vodka trappings of that era for decades to come. Proud of the restaurant's heritage, the owners eagerly shared stories of their famous patrons, including Atatürk, Greta Garbo, and Agatha Christie. During World War II, neutral Turkey was a hotbed of diplomatic negotiation and espionage—much of it conducted by German and

NEW DISTRICT

British ambassadors and foreign service officers who rubbed shoulders in Rejans' wood-paneled dining room.

• *From here, follow the alley back to İstiklal Street, passing people sucking big water pipes (nargile) at the Sefa Nargile Café (at #1B, daily 10:00-24:00; for details on trying a water pipe, see the Experiences chapter). At #1A, Mandabatmaz Coffee serves some of the best (they take it quite seriously) Turkish coffee in the city. Once back on İstiklal Street, look for the arches across the street that open up to...*

⓱ St. Anthony's Roman Catholic Church (between #167 and #173)

Remember that even back in Byzantine times, this neighborhood was where Western-oriented minorities settled. Franciscan priests built a church here in the 13th century. That church became known as the Hagia Sophia of the Roman Catholic minority in Constantinople (which was then mostly Eastern Orthodox). After that church burned down in the late 17th century, the Franciscans chose to rebuild on this site. The current Neo-Gothic building, with a particularly impressive facade, dates from 1912. St. Anthony's still serves an active Roman Catholic congregation with weekly Mass, and the Christmas service here has become a major social event in Istanbul, attended by Turkey's jet set (even many Muslims). This part of the city is home to several active churches of different denominations, and church hopping on Christmas Eve has become a popular way to observe how each community celebrates this joyful event. If the church is open, feel free to take a quick trip west by popping inside.

• *About four storefronts down from the church, you'll see...*

Koç University (#181)

Private universities are fairly new in Turkey, arriving on the scene just over 20 years ago. Koç University, founded by the industrial giant Koç family, seeks to establish an academic culture in the tradition of Ivy League universities. This building houses the university's bookstore, alumni club, and Anatolian Civilizations Research Center.

Pera Detour

If you're interested in the worthwhile **Pera Museum,** now's a good time to detour to see its displays of Kütahya tiles, Orientalist paintings, and ancient weights and measures (described on page 61). To reach the museum, take the pedestrian lane under the brown Oda-kule office building (a half-block ahead, on the right). The museum is on the left corner at the end of the passage. Down the street from the Pera Museum, fans of opulent hotels may want to visit the historic **Pera Palace Hotel** (see page 63); fans of contemporary art museums might drop by the temporary home of **Istanbul Modern** (see page 64).

When you're done with the museums and hotel, you can back-track to İstiklal Street to continue our walk.

⓲ Dutch Consulate (at #197) and Union Church of Istanbul

Continuing down İstiklal, on the left you'll see the Dutch Consul-ate. Behind the consulate is the Union Church of Istanbul, which holds English services each Sunday (to reach it, walk to the end of the block and turn left on narrow Postacılar Sokak and go halfway down—the entry is on the left). The church was founded by Ameri-can Congregational Church missionaries in the 1830s. Soon after, the Dutch ambassador invited them to build a permanent home on the embassy grounds. Unfortunately, the chapel's interior is generally closed except for Sunday services: at 9:30 (contemporary worship in English), at 11:00 (traditional worship in English), and at 13:30 (in both English and Turkish; +90 212 244 5212, www. ucistanbul.org).

• *Continue down İstiklal Street, passing the Russian Consulate (on the left). When you come to the Swedish Consulate (on the left), stop to ad-mire the recently renovated...*

Narmanlı Han (at #180)

Built in the 1830s, this striking, peach-colored, columned build-ing is a longtime landmark of European Istanbul. It served as the home of the Russian Con-sulate for 50 years and later hosted local painters, writers, and publishers. After its recent renova-tion, international chain stores replaced the shabby coffee shops once crowded with young people. And the cats that were regulars

in the courtyard garden are now nowhere to be seen.

• *Follow the tram tracks as they curve toward the right and arrive at their terminus, bringing us to the end of this walk and the funicular called...*

⓳ Tünel

To Istanbul natives, "Tünel" (tew-nehl) refers both to this neighborhood (at the bottom of İstiklal Street) and to the underground funicular that goes from here to the bank of the Golden Horn, below. Look for the entrance to the Tünel funicular at the end of the Nostalgic Tram line.

In the 19th century, as the Golden Horn became Istanbul's bustling commercial hub, it became clear that the narrow alley connecting İstiklal Street to the waterway below was not sufficient to transport the increasing volume of goods and people. When French engineer Henri Gavand visited and saw 50,000 people walking or riding their horses up and down this hill each day, he decided there must be a better way. Funded by the British government, and approved by the sultan, Gavand spent four years building a tunnel for an underground funicular.

When it opened in 1875, Tünel became the second subterranean people-mover in the world (after London's Tube). The roofless cars were lit by gas lamps and had no seats, so passengers had to stand. At first the public was uncomfortable traveling underground, so most of the cars carried goods and livestock. But ultimately the efficiency and ease of the Tünel trip won out. Locals still use this old-fashioned underground funicular to get between İstiklal Street and Karaköy, a few blocks down the hill, near the Galata Bridge on the Golden Horn.

Opposite the Tünel entrance, the Tünel Passage (Tünel Pasajı) is a fun place to celebrate the end of your walk with a drink. Enjoy the festive, cozy atmosphere.

• *From here, you have several options. You can ride the Tünel funicular down to the Galata Bridge and Karaköy, where you can catch the main tram line to the* **Old Town** *(Sultanahmet stop) and beyond.*

Or skip the funicular, and stroll the colorful streets leading downhill to the Galata Bridge—the left fork (Galip Dede Sokak) goes down to the ⓴ **Galata Dervish Monastery** *(see page 370) and the* **Galata Tower** *(see page 65), then steeply downhill to the Galata Bridge.*

Or catch a taxi to your next destination (a taxi stand is just beyond the Nostalgic Tram terminus).

Or you can ride the romantic Nostalgic Tram back to Taksim Square, along the same street you just explored.

BOSPHORUS CRUISE

From Eminönü to Anadolu Kavagi

In addition to separating two continents, the Bosphorus Strait serves as Istanbul's main highway. A never-ending stream of vessels—from little fishing dinghies to gigantic rusted oil tankers to luxury cruise ships—sails up and down this strategic corridor, day in and day out. The Bosphorus is one of the busiest waterways in the world; churning ship engines and clanging horns are Istanbul's constant soundtrack. This carnival of commerce is the only outlet to the Mediterranean for Russia, and the only route to any sea for the other countries on the Black Sea: Romania, Bulgaria, Ukraine, and Georgia.

In Turkish, the Bosphorus is Boğaziçi (boh-ahz-ee-chee), which means "pass" or "strait." This 19-mile-long waterway curves like a snake as it connects the Black Sea in the north with the Sea of Marmara and—eventually—the Mediterranean in the south. Istanbul's various districts line up along the bays, and the coastline is peppered with cute neighborhoods. Many of these areas, once separate communities, have been incorporated into Istanbul as the town has sprawled from north to south over the past several decades. Today Istanbul extends pretty much all the way up to the Black Sea. But a few neighborhoods in the north retain a village-like quality, where men still fish for a living.

Cruising the Bosphorus—a ▲▲▲ experience—is the best way to appreciate the massive size and scale of 15-million-strong Istanbul, and a convenient way to see many of its outlying landmarks, with a visit to the fishing village of Anadolu Kavağı, on the Asian side.

The Turks view the Bosphorus as much more than just a body of water—to them, it's a sacred inheritance. Locals take joy in it, and can sit for hours on a bench by the Bosphorus just watching the beautiful scenery as a United Nations of boats drifts past.

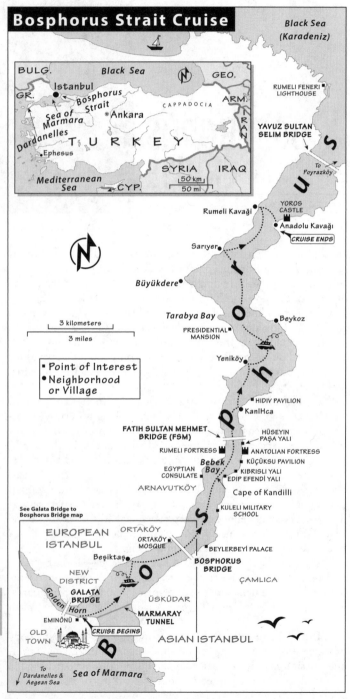

Bosphorus Strait Cruise

Black Sea (Karadeniz)

BULG.   Black Sea   GEO.
Istanbul
GR.   Bosphorus   ARM.
Strait   CAPPADOCIA
Sea of   •Ankara
Marmara   T U R K E Y   IRAN
Dardanelles
Ephesus   SYRIA   IRAQ
Mediterranean
Sea   CYP.
50 km
50 mi

RUMELI FENERI LIGHTHOUSE

YAVUZ SULTAN SELIM BRIDGE

To Poyrazköy

YOROS CASTLE

Rumeli Kavağı•   •Anadolu Kavağı
CRUISE ENDS

Sarıyer•

Büyükdere•

Tarabya Bay   •Beykoz

PRESIDENTIAL MANSION

3 kilometers

3 miles

Yeniköy•

■ Point of Interest
• Neighborhood
  or Village

HIDIV PAVILION
KanlIca

FATIH SULTAN MEHMET BRIDGE (FSM)
HÜSEYIN PAŞA YALI
RUMELI FORTRESS ■   ■ ANATOLIAN FORTRESS
Bebek   KÜÇÜKSU PAVILION
EGYPTIAN   Bay
CONSULATE ■   ■ KIBRISLI YALI
    ■ EDIP EFENDI YALI
ARNAVUTKÖY   Cape of Kandilli

■ KULELI MILITARY SCHOOL

See Galata Bridge to
Bosphorus Bridge map

EUROPEAN   ORTAKÖY
ISTANBUL   ORTAKÖY
    MOSQUE
NEW   Beşiktaş•   ■ BEYLERBEYI PALACE
DISTRICT
GALATA   BOSPHORUS   ÇAMLICA
BRIDGE   BRIDGE
Golden   ÜSKÜDAR
Horn
EMINÖNÜ ■   MARMARAY
CRUISE BEGINS   TUNNEL

OLD
TOWN   ASIAN ISTANBUL

To
Dardanelles &   Sea of Marmara
Aegean Sea

Orientation

Public Ferry: It's easy to take a day-long cruise on the public ferry, which leaves from the first terminal east of the Galata Bridge on the Old Town side of the Golden Horn. For a shorter cruise, consider a private tour operator (described later, under "Private Tours").

Ferry Cost: 40 TL round-trip to Anadolu Kavağı, less for children. You can return directly to Eminönü, or hop off early to see outlying sights on your way back to town.

Ferry Schedule: The ferry to Anadolu Kavağı leaves April-Oct at 10:35 and 13:35 (additional departures possible in peak season); Nov-March departs at 10:35 only. Confirm these times before you set out (ask your hotelier, drop by the dock, or check online at www.sehirhatlari.istanbul/en—under "Timetables" select "Bosphorus Tours," then "Full Bosphorus Cruise").

When to Go: The 10:35 departure puts you in Anadolu Kavağı just in time for lunch and gets you back to Istanbul early enough for a little evening sightseeing. If you're in Istanbul for several days, check the forecast and plan your cruise during good weather.

Crowd-Beating Tips: Weekdays are best—the ferry can be miserably crowded on weekends, especially from late spring through early fall. Arrive at least 30 minutes before your scheduled departure time, as the best seats fill fast (on a sunny weekend, show up even earlier). As you board, you can find a seat, but to keep it you'll need to stay in one place the entire trip (and won't be able to see the other side of the Bosphorus very well). Or you can stand, giving you maximum flexibility for moving around and taking photos, but leaving you without a guaranteed seat (although seats may free up as people move around or disembark at later stops on the route).

Getting There: The public ferry leaves from the Bosphorus Cruise Pier ferry terminal in the Old Town's Eminönü district (near the mouth of the Golden Horn, along the embankment next to the Galata Bridge; see the "Golden Horn Walk" map on page 247).

To reach the ferry landing from the Old Town, take the tram (direction: Kabataş) and get off at the Eminönü stop.

When you emerge from the pedestrian underpass, look for the ferry-terminal building marked *Bosphorus Cruise Pier.*

To reach the ferry from Taksim Square in the New District, you can either walk or take the Nostalgic Tram down İstiklal Street to Tünel, then take the Tünel funicular down to Karaköy at the Galata Bridge. Walk across the bridge and turn left along the embankment to find the terminal labeled *Bosphorus Cruise Pier.* Alternatively, you can ride the funicular down the hill from Taksim Square to Kabataş, and take the southbound tram (direction: Bağcılar) from there to Eminönü.

Ferry Route: The ferry goes from Eminönü in downtown Istanbul to the Black Sea end of the Bosphorus, where it takes a break in the Asian fishing village of Anadolu Kavağı before returning to Eminönü. It makes several other stops along the way, but only docks long enough to pick up or drop off passengers.

Length of Ferry Cruise: A round-trip Bosphorus cruise by ferry takes about 5.5-7 hours, depending on wind, weather, and traffic conditions on the Bosphorus, as well as how long your boat lingers in Anadolu Kavağı (expect about 3 hours of actual sailing time, plus a 2- to 3-hour break in Anadolu Kavağı).

Heading north from Eminönü, the boat stops at Beşiktaş, Kanlıca, Yeniköy, Sarıyer, Rumeli Kavağı, and Anadolu Kavağı. On the way back to Eminönü, you can expect the same stops in reverse order.

Sarıyer Shortcut: If you'd rather not go all the way to the end, consider getting off about 1.25 hours into the trip at the Sarıyer stop and taking the bus back (see sidebar on page 292). This gives you the option of visiting the Rumeli Fortress, Sakıp Sabancı Museum, Sadberk Hanım Museum, and Dolmabahçe Palace, all described in the Sights chapter. Or, get off at Sarıyer on the return trip to see some of these sights on your way back.

Services: WCs and snack bar are on board.

Private Tours: For a shorter Bosphorus cruise, consider a private excursion. Various companies sell 25-TL cruise tickets on either side of the Old Town end of the Galata Bridge (behind the bus stops on the west side of the bridge, and next to the Bosphorus ferry cruise pier on the east side of the bridge—look for *Bosphorus Tours* sign). These boats will take you as far as the Fatih Sultan Mehmet Bridge) and back in 1.5 hours, with no stops. There's no set schedule (at least, not one that's strictly adhered to). Boats depart as soon as they have enough people. Just buy your ticket and hop on. These cruises are a good option if you're short on time, but you'll see less of the Bosphorus and won't get a glimpse of the Black Sea. In general, the cruises stick closer to the European side on the way north and the Asian side on the way back south.

One of many options is the **Turyol** company, with departures about hourly on weekdays (10:00-21:00) and Sun (11:00-18:45), and every half-hour on Saturday (12:00-19:00) from the west side of the Galata Bridge, next to the fish-sandwich boats and behind the bus stops (+90 212 527 9952, www. turyol.com).

A different cruise (private, day-long) goes all the way to the Black Sea (see page 38).

Starring: Bridges between the continents, imperial Ottoman palaces, fancy waterfront mansions, fortresses, castles, and the fishing village of Anadolu Kavağı.

GETTING STARTED

Buy your ticket at the windows facing the busy street, then go through the turnstile to reach the ferry. Hang on to your ticket— the ticket-taker will check it again on your return journey.

If you arrive at least 30 minutes early, there will usually be some seats left (but show up even earlier if you want to snag a seat on a sunny weekend). On the way up the Bosphorus, most of the attractions are on the left (European) side of the boat, so pick your spot accordingly. Ideally you'd like a clear look at both sides, though because of the width of the boat and the crowds on board, this often isn't possible. The lower deck has unobstructed view seats along the water. If you don't mind seeing only one side, grab one of these seats on the left. The open upper decks in the front and back of the boat are ideal for avid photographers. If all the good seats are taken, consider staking out a standing spot on the left near the back of the boat. Realize that people will constantly be jostling for position for the prettiest photos—so no matter where you sit or stand, you may not have the place to yourself.

Coming back, the sunlight is better for taking photos of the Asian side (during the afternoon, the sun is in your eyes looking at the European side). So a smart plan is to always sit on the left side (views of the European side on the way there and the Asian side on the way back).

On the upper deck is a snack bar where you can get a *simit*, candy bar, sandwich, or beverage. Attendants also walk around the ferry selling tea, coffee, fresh-squeezed orange juice, and water. The WCs are on the lower deck, on the sides, toward the front (past the stairs to the second deck).

For the first half-hour or so, the boat moves fast and there's a lot to see. Consider reading ahead so you're ready for the attractions as you pass them.

BOSPHORUS CRUISE

The Bosphorus Strait: A Critical Location

The Bosphorus Strait—17 nautical miles long—connects the Black Sea with the Sea of Marmara (which, at its western end, flows

through the Dardanelles to the Aegean Sea, and then out to the Mediterranean Sea). The great commercial and strategic importance of the Bosphorus was a factor in the establishment of the city of Constantinople here in AD 330. Today, private boats and passenger ferries make more than 2,000 runs on the strait each day, carrying 2.5 million people between the two continents. Add in the hundreds of commercial vessels—you'll see many at anchor just offshore in the Sea of Marmara—plus fishing boats out for the daily catch, and you've got a lot of traffic.

Navigation through the strait can be extremely difficult due to its narrow width (just a half-mile across at its narrowest, between the Anatolian and Rumeli fortresses), sharp turns (there are 12 course-changing bends), tricky currents, and the immense size of the tankers and cruise ships that ply its waters. Powerful currents funnel through this narrow north-south strait. Less salty water flowing south from the Black Sea creates a strong surface current, which is generally strengthened by prevailing northerly winds. Note the fishing boats off the Old Town peninsula, straining to stay in place with their bows pointed toward the Bosphorus.

Making things even more complicated, another, saltier current flows beneath the surface in the opposite direction, toward

The Tour Begins

• *Anchors aweigh!*

Eminönü to Beşiktaş

• *The first few sights are on the right side of the boat.*

As the boat pulls away, you're treated to a fine panorama of the Old Town peninsula—made even more dramatic by the boats scurrying around the harbor and the embankments and streets teeming with people. You see **Hagia Sophia** first, with its dome and minarets. Sirkeci train station is right behind the car ferry dock. As you move along the peninsula, the gardens of **Topkapı Palace** come into view—including Divan Tower, with the buildings of the Harem complex to its left.

On the waterfront, past the car ferry port, is the **Sepetçiler**

the Black Sea. Clever ancient mariners figured this out; they lowered weighted baskets on lines down into the water to catch the lower current to pull their boats northward.

In 1936, Turkey signed the Montreux Convention, which regulates boat traffic through the Bosphorus and the Dardanelles. In

those days, ships were smaller and weren't required to use a local pilot to negotiate the dangerous Bosphorus; an oversight that proved disastrous. The location of the Bosphorus, flanking populous Istanbul, magnified the consequences of shipboard accidents as the number and size of boats traveling the strait steadily increased. Boats collided in fiery explo-

sions, tankers leaked thousands of gallons of crude oil into the fragile waters, and more than one disabled ship ran aground—smacking right into waterfront houses. An Istanbul resident reported: "I heard an unusual sound getting louder and louder, and all of a sudden, I saw the bow of the ship going right into the room!"

Now local pilots are required and boat traffic is more strictly controlled, managed by radar towers along the Bosphorus. In addition, oil pipelines from the eastern Black Sea, the Caucasus region, and the Caspian Sea are providing an alternative way of transporting oil, which is helping to alleviate the bottleneck of tanker traffic through the strait.

Pavilion (seh-peht-chee-lehr; "basket weavers"), today a fine restaurant used mostly for banquets.

Within a few minutes, you reach Seraglio Point, the tip of the Old Town peninsula. This is where the Golden Horn ends and the

Bosphorus begins. As you get farther from the Old Town, behind Hagia Sophia you'll notice the minarets, and later the dome, of the **Blue Mosque.** Soon the skyline of old Istanbul will be dominated by domes, minarets, and

towers. Add a layer of haze, and you have a magical, mystical-looking silhouette.

Galata Bridge to Bosphorus Bridge

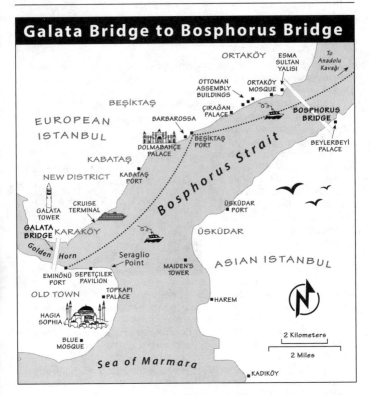

Just off Seraglio Point, you can see the end of the Bosphorus—where it joins the **Sea of Marmara.** Around the base of the Old Town peninsula are intact portions of the Byzantine wall that fortified the city until the Ottomans conquered it in the 15th century. As the boat turns left, you'll begin to get some good views on the right side of Asian Istanbul, across the Bosphorus. The cranes mark the main commercial port of the city. From this angle, the Princes' Islands appear to the south in the Sea of Marmara, usually as a silhouette a few miles off Asian Istanbul. On a clear day, you can even see the southern shores of Marmara.

• *Look toward Asia.*

Offshore from Asian Istanbul is one of the city's symbols, the old Byzantine tower often called the **Maiden's Tower** (just left of the harbor, but before the radar tower). Today this landmark is used as a lighthouse and a restaurant.

• *That's all for Asia for a while. The boat picks up speed—yes, it'll go this fast the whole time—and*

moves closer to Europe. Get settled and start reading ahead. Now focus your attention on the left, on the Karaköy district of European Istanbul.

You'll see the massive construction site of Istanbul's new **cruise port,** a $2 billion project to build new terminals and service areas to accommodate large cruise ships and their passengers. The old and inefficient terminals, piers, and warehouses at Karaköy are being phased out of use.

Soon you go by the Kabataş district and its sea-bus and ferry ports. Beyond that is the **Dolmabahçe Palace** complex, the 19th-century palace of the Ottoman sul-

tan. The first building of the complex is the Dolmabahçe Mosque, built exclusively for the sultans and sharing the same eclectic style as the palace itself. Next door is the clock tower, built as an extravagant accessory. Right behind the tower is a soccer stadium that seats 30,000 people—but since it's ingeniously designed to fit into its surroundings, you barely notice it. Unfortunately, the same cannot be said of the tall glass building above, the Ritz-Carlton. The other eyesore is the Swissotel, right above the palace.

Centuries-old trees partially block your view of the monumental gate, to the right of the clock tower, leading to the palace. This also marks the start of a waterfront fence, guarded by soldiers. At the back side of the garden, just before the palace starts, you can see a second massive entryway, built for the sole use of the sultan and his guests.

The first wing of the building, including the tall middle part, was the palace's public, administrative section *(selamlık).*

The side gate was for officials and envoys, whom the sultan received in the front-corner rooms, each with sweeping Bosphorus views. The next wing was the residential section *(harem),* which extends behind the visible section. The building to the right, set apart from the palace, was for guests and palace employees.

Impressive as Dolmabahçe is from here, a century and a half of humidity and saltwater has taken its toll on the palace's facade. Though the palace walls facing the Bosphorus are ornate, the back is plain and dull—left undecorated when the sultan ran out of money.

The palace fence ends at an abandoned ferry port, named for **Barbarossa,** the famous pirate-turned-Ottoman admiral. When Barbarossa sailed the seas, the Ottoman armada controlled the entire Mediterranean. The park just beyond the dock, and the mosque behind the park, are also named for the beloved Barbarossa. There's a larger-than-life Barbarossa statue in the park, and his tomb is in the mosque complex. The fenced park belongs to the Naval Museum.

While you were ogling the palace, you may have noticed the ferry starting to slow down for its first stop, at **Beşiktaş** (beh-sheek-tahsh). Enjoy your last views back toward the Old Town, which is now little more than an outline. While the boat docks, look down into the water, swirling with garbage and jellyfish—two good reasons why you'll rarely see swimmers in this part of the Bosphorus.

Beşiktaş to Kanlıca

• *Keep watching the left (European) side.*

As you leave Beşiktaş, the next building is one of Istanbul's private universities. In front of the building, you'll see people fishing—either for sport or to catch dinner. Many local fisherfolk have favorite spots along the Bosphorus. These embankments are even more crowded on weekends, with people walking, fishing, enjoying the day with their families. Keep an eye out for barbecue grills, used to cook up the fish as they're pulled from the water.

Past the university, the palatial building—formerly a state guesthouse—is a Four Seasons hotel. Next to it is the **Çırağan Palace** (chuh-rah-ahn), another late-Ottoman residence. Built two decades after Dolmabahçe Palace, in the same eclectic style by the same architect, it mysteriously burned to the ground in 1910—some say because of faulty wiring, others say arson. Only a chunk of the facade remained standing, and a local soccer team used the empty space for practice. More recently, an international hotel chain restored the palace in exchange for the right to build a hotel complex next door, the Çırağan Palace Kempinski Hotel (with the big swimming pool in front). Presidents Clinton and Bush (the Elder) have both stayed here (though not at the same time). It has theme restaurants and a ballroom, as well as a popular—and expensive—jazz bar.

The next building is a maritime high school (easy to recognize, thanks to the ship's mast in front). The three long buildings standing side by side, painted various shades of yellow, were the 19th-century **Ottoman Assembly.** In the late days of the Ottoman Empire, when it was becoming the "Sick Man of Europe," pressure from elsewhere in Europe—and from forces within the empire, especially the military—compelled the sultan to agree to the creation of an advisory committee. The parliament lasted only a few decades, and vanished with World War I.

Past the assembly buildings, we enter the lively **Ortaköy** (or-tah-koy) district (with the towers of Istanbul's business zone in the background). Just before the Bosphorus Bridge is the striking 19th-century **Ortaköy Mosque**—with a Western style similar to the Dolmabahçe Mosque we passed earlier. Right next to the mosque is a 19th-century mansion,

Esma Sultan Yalısı, which once belonged to a sultan's daughter. After the birth of the Republic, the building endured years of ne-glect, a fire, and use as a tobacco and coal depot. More recent own-ers, a hotel group, have redecorated the structure with stylish glass and metal elements, converting the mansion into a banquet hall for dinners, cultural activities, and concerts. For more on the happen-ing Ortaköy scene, see the Entertainment chapter.

Now you are crossing beneath the first bridge to connect two continents—the **Bosphorus Bridge.** It is the first of three suspen-sion bridges over the Bosphorus. A Turk-ish-British corporation completed the span in 1973, on the 50th anniversary of the Turkish Republic. Almost two-thirds of a mile long, it carries six lanes of traffic between the continents.

• *Now look to the right (Asian) side.*

Just to the left of the bridge is **Bey-lerbeyi,** the late-19th-century summer palace of the sultan. The hill rising behind the palace is Çamlıca (chahm-luh-jah). Half of the city's TV and radio transmit-ters are on that hill: At roughly 1,200 feet, it's the highest point in greater Istanbul.

• *Look back to the left (European) side.*

Just past the bridge is a string of nightclubs—some of the most popular places in the city for the jet set. There's even a small island that belongs to a private sports club.

We've been cruising along the European coastline since leav-ing Beşiktaş. Now the boat will adjust its course and head for the other side of the strait. (To follow our route from here, turn back to the overview map on page 278.) As the boat passes the center of the strait, see if you can spot any dolphins heading north on their way to the Black Sea.

To the Black Sea by Land

Cruising the Bosphorus is an adventure in itself, but if you simply want to experience a beach day near the Black Sea, you can save considerable time and money by hiring a local taxi for a do-it-yourself excursion (negotiate with the driver in advance; figure 400 TL for 4 hours). Avoid this trip during rush hour to save yourself from sitting in traffic.

Head straight for the charming village of Poyrazköy, 40 minutes outside Istanbul on the Asian side of the strait. The arcing, mostly sand beach is a fine place to settle in: Each stretch has changing rooms, chairs and umbrellas to rent (50 TL for two chairs and umbrella), and a corresponding café. If you're ambitious, hike above the harbor to a ruined fortress for a sweeping view of the new Yavuz Sultan Selim "Third" Bridge and the entrance to the Black Sea.

• *As the boat heads for Asia, so should your gaze. Look right.*

Coming up on the Asian side is a very wide two-story white building. Named **Kuleli** ("with towers") for the towers on either end, it was built in the early 1800s as an army barracks. Today it's being converted into a museum.

Beyond Kuleli, the population starts to thin out. Small villages once dotted the shoreline, but today luxury yachts have replaced simple fishing boats. Especially along the Asian side, from Kuleli all the way to the second bridge, you'll see lots of impressive private waterfront **mansions** (*yalı*; yah-luh) belonging to wealthy families. Pay attention to those made of wood—quite a few are more than a century old, although many have been renovated. Laws once prohibited the use of non-original materials in restoring historic buildings. But many historic wooden *yalı* mysteriously burned down, only to be quickly replaced with new, modern constructions. This led to a compromise: The core of the structure can be rebuilt according to modern specifications, but a replica of the original wooden facade must adorn the front. Regardless of their historical value, these multimillion-dollar homes on the Bosphorus are among the most expensive in the city.

Next you'll pass the **Cape of Kandilli** (kahn-dee-lee; "with candles"), named for the lamps lit to warn ships of the strong current here. The cape is marked by a hill topped with a huge electric pole, transferring high-voltage wires across to Europe. At the tip of the cape is another radar tower. Next to it is the two-story white-and-gray wooden *yalı* of **Edip Efendi**, an Ottoman minister of finance in the 19th century.

• *Now look back to the left (European side).*

Across from the cape is the trendy Arnavutköy district (named after early Albanian settlers) and, following that, **Bebek Bay** (beh-behk; "baby"). This town on the bay is known for its almond paste, sometimes flavored with pistachios. The apartments and condos here cost a small fortune to buy or rent. Notice the many private boats anchored in the bay. To the left of the bay, the unusual-looking gray building with a French-style roof and large flag is the **Egyptian consulate.**

• *Look back to Asia (right).*

Beyond the cape, the Bosphorus makes a sharp turn into a bay. Watch for more impressive homes, especially the terracotta-colored one with three antique columns in its garden (it belongs to one of the wealthiest families in Turkey) and the expansive 18th-century **Kıbrıslı** *yalı*, with a fancy second-floor balcony.

Deeper into the bay, you'll notice the Western-looking 19th-century hunting pavilion of the sultans, named for a nearby freshwater creek, **Küçüksu**. It was a remote getaway for the royals, who were hunting peace and quiet more than anything.

Less than half a mile from the pavilion, past the pink building (a teachers' social club), notice the round and square towers of an old fortress rising among the houses. This is the **Anatolian fortress** (Anadolu Hisarı), built by the Ottoman sultan Beyazıt I at the end of the 14th century. Known as "Thunderbolt" for his speed on the battlefield, Beyazıt built this fortress at one of the narrowest points of the Bosphorus

to cut off aid to Constantinople during a siege. Fifty years later, Beyazıt's grandson, Mehmet II, conquered Constantinople by following his grandpa's example across the strait....

• *Now look across to the European side (left).*

Here you see the much bigger **Rumeli Fortress** (Rumeli Hisarı), built by Sultan Mehmet II a year before the conquest of Constantinople in 1453. Con-

struction was completed in just 80 days. Once the Ottomans had fortresses on both banks of the Bosphorus, it was virtually impossible for a ship to pass without permission. This one-

two punch of mighty fortresses was a key component of Mehmet II's ultimately successful siege of Constantinople. (Read more about the Rumeli Fortress on page 68.)

• *Look back to Asia (right).*

As you near the second bridge, look for the oldest surviving *yalı* on the banks of the Bosphorus: the mansion of **Hüseyin Paşa.** Run-down but currently under renovation, this terracotta-painted *yalı* was built by the Ottoman Grand Vizier around 1700. It's taller than you'd expect for a single-story building, because it rises up on wood supports above a stone retaining wall.

Next up is the **Fatih Sultan Mehmet Bridge** (locals call it FSM for short). Newer than the Bosphorus Bridge, it was built in 1988 by a Turkish-Japanese corporation and is longer (almost a mile) and wider than the Bosphorus Bridge.

As we approach **Kanlıca,** enjoy the view of impressive *yalıs,* many with drive-in "garages" for private boats. Kanlıca is a popular weekend spot, with many cafeterias and eateries along the water for locals to enjoy a cup of tea while soaking up the beautiful scenery. Kanlıca is also famous for its yogurt, served in small plastic containers and sprinkled with powdered sugar. As you leave the port, servers will scamper around the boat selling fresh yogurt just picked up here.

Kanlıca to Yeniköy

• *Keep watching Asia.*

After cruising less than a mile, look up the hill and into the woods at the fancy tower of the renowned **Hidiv Pavilion.** It was built in the Art Nouveau style at the end of the 19th century for the

hidiv—the Ottoman governor of Egypt. You'll get a better view of the building as the boat slides away from the Asian shore.

• *The next stop is on the European side (left).*

Now the boat heads back across the Bosphorus to dock at **Yeniköy** (yeh-nee-koy; "new village"). This trendy, high-end district has some of the most elaborate houses on the Bosphorus. Some are traditional wood constructions, but quite a few newer ones have a distinctly modern style. American travelers often compare these with the mansions along the Mississippi River.

Yeniköy to Sarıyer

• *Keep watching the European side (left).*

About five minutes after you leave Yeniköy, you'll see the **Presidential Mansion.** Built in the 19th century, this has been the summer mansion for the president of Turkey since 1985. The mansion's two three-story pavilions rise behind a long, tall stone wall running along the coastal road. The closest pavilion has a steep tile roof and a decoration that looks like a little onion dome at the front-left corner.

The small **Tarabya Bay** is marked by the multistory hotel complex at its right end. Here is where you'll start to feel a cool breeze from the north. It's the prevailing wind all year long, cooling Bosphorus temperatures quite a bit in the summer.

• *Turn back to Asia (right).*

Half a mile past Tarabya Bay, from the right side of the boat, you'll get your first glimpse of the **Black Sea.**

• *And then turn back to Europe again (left).*

Our next stop, **Sarıyer** (sah-ruh-yehr), is at the far end of the large bay. Transit-pass holders can consider getting off at Sarıyer—either now, or on the way home—to return to downtown Istanbul overland by bus, stopping to see some sights en route (see sidebar).

Sarıyer to Rumeli Kavağı

• *Watch the European side (left).*

As you leave Sarıyer, you'll cruise very close to the bank for one more stop on the European side before the boat heads to its last stop on the Asian side. Beyond this point, the wind gets stronger. Locals call this wind Poyraz (poy-rahz), after Boreas, the Greek god of wind.

Cruising along fishing communities and narrow marinas where fishing boats are tied up, you'll soon come to the village of **Rumeli Kavağı** (roo-meh-lee kah-vah-uh). Then the ferry heads for its last stop: the fishing village of Anadolu Kavağı on the Asian side, right across from Rumeli Kavağı.

Rumeli Kavağı to Anadolu Kavağı

• *Keep watching the European side (left).*

As the boat turns toward Asia, from the left side you can enjoy a great view of the Bosphorus opening into the **Black Sea.** You should also be able to see the third Bosphorus bridge, the Yavuz Sultan Selim Bridge (abbreviated as YSS), one of the world's widest suspension bridges. The first two Bosphorus bridges are used

Returning Overland from Sarıyer

To cut your Bosphorus cruise short, you can get off the ferry at Sarıyer and use the bus to visit some interesting sights on the way home. A ride on southbound bus (#25E to Kabataş or #25T to Taksim) back to central Istanbul can take from 45 to 60 minutes, depending on the time of day and traffic. The bus stop, signed with bus numbers, is one block from the Sarıyer port: With the port behind you, walk right along the park and look for the bus stop across the street, where the street makes a sharp curve. Once on board, tell your driver (or fellow passengers) where you'd like to get off so they can help you find the right stop.

Bus #25E: For a pleasant ride back to the city, take southbound bus #25E (Sarıyer-Kabataş). This bus follows a scenic route along the Bosphorus and connects easily with the Old Town tram and the Kabataş-Taksim funicular. Bus #25E also provides a convenient connection to the Sadberk Hanım Museum, Sakıp Sabancı Museum, and Rumeli Fortress, as well as the popular Ortaköy district by the Bosphorus Bridge.

To reach the **Sadberk Hanım Museum,** walk (south) from the Sarıyer ferry stop for about 10 easy minutes. Or take southbound bus #25E and get off at the Sefaret (seh-fah-reht) stop, then walk a few blocks south along the coastal road (with the Bosphorus on your left). After you visit the museum, catch the same bus to Kabataş. Or, if you enjoy strolling near the water, keep heading south until you get tired, then catch a bus.

mostly for local city traffic, but the YSS sees more intercity and international travel (for example, trucks are required to use the YSS).

Even the casual tourist senses the dark, foreboding aura of this zone, where wind and rainstorms can gather within minutes, even in the middle of summer.

Up the shore on the European side are some extremely dangerous hidden rocks that have long plagued navigators. If you know the tale of Jason and the Argonauts, you may remember the **Clashing Rocks** (or Symplegades) the crew encountered as they sailed into the Black Sea. These rocks of legend are believed by some to be based on this stretch of the Bosphorus. In Jason's time, the rocks would dangerously lunge toward one another, demolishing any boats that tried to pass. To make it through, the Argo-  nauts let loose a dove, which was guided by the goddess Athena and led them to safety. After this, the rocks stopped clashing, but remained a potentially destructive obstacle. Byzantine emperors erected a huge column here to warn passing ships. It worked...ex-

For the **Sakıp Sabancı Museum,** take bus #25E to the Çınaraltı stop.

For the **Rumeli Fortress,** take bus #25E to the Rumeli Hisarı (roo-meh-lee hee-sah-ruh) stop. Catch your return bus where you got off, or walk to the next stop, Aşiyan, on the hillside just past the cemetery (next to the fortress).

For the **Ortaköy district,** take bus #25E to the Ortaköy (ohr-tah-koy) stop and enjoy one of Istanbul's most picturesque pedestrian areas. Popular among the younger generation, Ortaköy is crowded on weekends, sunny days, and all summer long. It's also full of eateries: seafood restaurants, fast-food joints, cafés, and tea shops. Students and artists display their handicrafts for sale—usually souvenirs and simple jewelry.

Bus #25T: This is the quickest way to get from Sarıyer to **Taksim Square** in the New District, but what you make up in time you lose in scenery, since it takes the inland freeway. Bus #25T runs every 15-60 minutes. Take this only if you want to make a beeline back to Taksim Square.

At Sarıyer: If you have time to spare before catching a bus, detour to the Sarıyer fish market. With the port behind you, follow the road to the right, and take the first right, soon after the street curves left. The fish market is a couple of blocks down on the right, behind the little square. Try the specialty: deep-fried mussels.

cept when thick fog made this part of the Bosphorus nearly impossible to navigate. It's still difficult today, even with state-of-the-art electronic equipment.

• *Turn toward Asia (right) as we near our final stop...*

Anadolu Kavağı

Welcome to Asia: the small fishing village of Anadolu Kavağı (ah-nah-doh-loo kah-vah-uh). *Anadolu* comes from the Greek word *anatoli*, meaning "the land to the East," while *kavak* means "controlled pass." From Byzantine times to the present, this has been a strategic checkpoint for vessels going through the Bosphorus. As you approach the Asian side, watch for the Byzantine **Yoros Castle** that dominates the hilltop above the village. Below that, notice the modern military instal-

lations: The area between here and the Black Sea is a restricted-access zone.

The ferry takes a break here in Anadolu Kavağı, usually for two to three hours. Look for the scheduled departure time posted near the dock or ask the attendant what time to be back. Be sure to arrive back at the boat at least 10 minutes before the departure time—or earlier, if you want to secure a prime seat for the return trip.

Planning Your Time: Anadolu Kavağı has two main activities—eating lunch or hiking up to Yoros Castle (parts of the castle may be closed for renovation). If you're speedy or have a longer break, you'll probably be able to squeeze in both; if you'd like a more leisurely experience, choose one.

Overland Return to Istanbul: Don't miss the boat. But if you do, it's simple to return to Istanbul by taxi (figure 90 TL), or bus. You can catch the bus at the town center, a block straight ahead from the ferry port. Begin by taking bus #15A (Anadolu Kavağı-Kavacık) to the Körfez (Beykoz) stop. From there you can take bus #15P and #15T to Üsküdar or #15F to Kadıköy (both on the Asian side), where you can catch a ferry back to Eminönü in the Old Town.

Eating in Anadolu Kavağı

Anadolu Kavağı is made-to-order for enjoying a leisurely lunch. The town is packed with down-to-earth restaurants that cater to Bosphorus cruise passengers—both international tourists and Istanbul residents who come here for a nice meal on the weekends. As you step off the boat, the streets just ahead of you and for two blocks to the left are filled with nothing but restaurants. (The path leading up to the castle is also lined with eateries, but their quality isn't as reliable.)

The specialty is seafood, of course. You can find a wide range of fish straight out of the strait. Most eateries advertise *midye tava* (meed-yeh tah-vah)—deep-fried mussels. Popular all over Istanbul, these are mussels dipped in batter, deep-fried, and served with *tarator* (tah-rah-tohr) sauce—made from bread, crushed fresh garlic, lemon juice, yogurt, olive oil, salt, and vinegar. Upscale restaurants sometimes add crushed walnuts to the mix. Fried calamari is also common, but beware: It's not native to Istanbul and is usually frozen, not fresh.

Before settling in, ignore the hawkers and stroll around to find the place that looks best. Most of the cheaper eateries sell a fixed-price meal for 30-35 TL that includes grilled fish, fried mussels, French fries, salad, bread, and a drink. Fancier restaurants have a wider (and more expensive) menu. If you opt to go à la carte, one portion of *midye tava* can be a light meal. For about 45 TL, two people can get two portions of *midye tava,* two drinks, and split a fresh fish fillet.

Other options include sandwiches, salads, *pide* (pee-deh; Turkish flatbread topped with vegetables and cheese), kebabs, and even waffles, although your options may be limited in the off-season. For dessert, try the *lokma* (lohk-mah) advertised by stalls and restaurants. This is a crispier version of a doughnut hole, made by dipping wheat dumplings into hot syrup. Locals love it and have been known to travel to Anadolu Kavağı just for fresh-cooked *lokma.* **Yosun Restaurant,** to your immediate left as you stand with the ferry dock at your back, has a *lokma* stand at the corner.

The grocery store and the bakery are good places to pick up supplies for a people-watching picnic on a bench in the square, or to munch up at the castle. To find them, follow the narrow street straight ahead from the port. The bakery is on the other side of the intersecting street, just before the parking lot, and the grocery store is past the parking lot. The bakery's specialty is anchovy bread (*hamsili ekmek;* hahm-see-lee ehk-mehk)—a Black Sea delicacy made with corn flour, leeks, tomatoes, fresh peppers, and fresh anchovies.

Yoros Castle (Yoros Kalesi)

Aside from having a meal and wandering the town, the only other activity in Anadolu Kavağı is to hike up to Yoros Castle, on the hilltop above town. Parts of the castle may be undergoing renovation when you visit. Check its status with the ferry staff or with locals when you arrive at Anadolu Kavağı.

While this run-down castle ruin hardly reflects the glory of its past, it does afford fine views over the Bosphorus and to the Black Sea. You can combine a castle hike with a picnic purchased at the grocery store in town. Public WCs are en route. You'll notice lots of litter, as well as friendly but hungry stray dogs eyeing you, hoping for your leftovers.

The moderately strenuous hike takes about 20 minutes each way. Most of the way up, you'll be passing through a military-controlled zone, so put your camera away. Once at the castle, feel free to take photos. Our hike goes up the south side of the hill where there are fewer breezes, so it may feel a little warmer than you'd expect.

Castle Hike: Standing with your back to the ferry port, walk

The Fish of the Bosphorus Strait and the Sea of Marmara

Fish are an essential part of Istanbul's cuisine, offering a flavorful alternative to kebabs. Many locals can tell at a glance just how many hours a fish has been out of the water. But with Istanbul's population now exceeding 15 million, the Bosphorus' once-abundant native fish are becoming scarcer. Fishing stocks have been depleted by the use of large fishing boats, which consequently are now banned from June to September. However, fishing for sport is still allowed, and many people fish along the Bosphorus. Fishermen yell at passing boats that get too close and scare away their potential catch.

While perusing Istanbul's menus, keep an eye out for the following fish. In some cases, we've listed the months when they're most abundant, but you may also find them at other times.

Barbun (bahr-boon): This little red mullet, which lives along the muddy seabed, can be caught year-round. A local delicacy, it's delicious when deep-fried and is often served as a side dish or hot appetizer. No need to remove the bones—just crunch them down.

Çinekop (chee-neh-kohp): This bluefish is popular when grilled and is available from early October through late November.

---

straight ahead toward the large, square street fountain (with the gold Arabic script). After the fountain, take the street to your left, and walk about 100 yards (bearing left at the fork) until you reach the corner of the yellow, 16th-century Ali Reis Mosque (you'll see a sign to *Yoros Kalesi*—that's Yoros Castle—across the street). Turn right and walk with the mosque on your right-hand side. Soon you'll see the Navy station fence on your left. After about 100 yards, you'll come to a fork—keep to the left.

The road gets steeper and bears right as you continue up and up. After passing a stand of cypress trees, the road makes a sharp curve to the left, offering glances of the Bosphorus beyond the parking lot. Up ahead, you also see part of the lower wall of Yoros Castle. Keep walking.

Past the wall fragments, there's another fork—keep right (the left fork goes to a military checkpoint). Less than 100 yards later, after the road curves left, you'll see a large aerial photo of the castle on the wall to your left (with a sign reading *To Castle/Ceneviz*

Hamsi (hahm-see): A delicacy from the Black Sea, this anchovy is in season from November to March. Natives cook this small fish in dozens of ways—including fried, steamed, and grilled, as well as mixed in casseroles and even added to cornbread. Hamsi are especially good when steamed in large trays with onions, tomatoes, green peppers, and lemons—creating a traditional dish called *hamsi buğulama* (hahm-see boo-oo-lah-mah).

Istavrit (ees-tahv-reet): This mackerel, generally served fried, is available throughout the year.

Kalkan (kahl-kahn): Best when pan-fried, this delicious turbot lives in the Sea of Marmara and is usually in the markets from December to April. As it's becoming rarer, you may find it only in upscale restaurants. It has round bones that locals call "buttons"; the female fish have fewer bones than the males.

Levrek (lehv-rehk): While its tastier wild cousins are expensive, farm-raised sea bass is cheap and available year-round. Although it's not wild, it's still worth a try—especially grilled.

Lüfer (lew-fehr): Its lack of a "fishy" taste makes this type of bluefish extremely popular in Istanbul. It's becoming rare—and expensive—and is usually available from late September to January.

Mezgit (mehz-geet): Fish-sellers hawk this whiting throughout the year. It's best either pan-fried or steamed with vegetables, though natives of Istanbul have never developed a real taste for its chicken-like flavor.

Kalesi). Follow the steps next to the sign, up past the café tables. Keep to the right as the path, punctuated with simple steps, leads you through more humble eateries on its way to the castle entrance. You'll soon see the castle wall to your left, as well as public WCs, picnic tables, and hammocks.

Reaching the end of the path, take the stairs to your left, through Yoros Café (ignore the plaster lion statues and menus—the steps are public, not part of the restaurant). These steps lead all the way up, straight to the gate of Yoros Castle. After passing through the gate (free, always open), you're in an open courtyard with several rough paths and the graffiti-marred remains of the former military fortress. Head up to the top of the courtyard for your reward: spectacular views of the Bosphorus and the Black Sea—and the cool northerly breeze. Yoros Castle is quite popular on weekends in good weather, when it's packed with locals.

• *Enjoy the view and the town below, then head back to the ferry for the cruise back to Europe, and Istanbul.*

BOSPHORUS CRUISE

ASIAN ISTANBUL WALKS

Across the Bosphorus to Üsküdar and Kadıköy

While most of Istanbul's top sights are on the European side of the Bosphorus, the city itself spills over the strait into Asia. More than a third of Istanbul's 15 million residents (including this book's co-authors) live in Asian Istanbul, or Anadolu Yakası (ah-nah-doh-loo yah-kah-suh, "the Anatolian side").

This chapter offers two neighborhood walks that introduce you to this sprawling, vibrant area. Getting there is half the fun: You'll take an intercontinental metro ride under the Bosphorus, or cross that historic waterway on a scenic passenger ferry.

The **Üsküdar View Walk** features the Bosphorus waterfront, with views back on historic European Istanbul and its iconic skyline, bristling with turrets, spires, and domes. The **Kadıköy Neighborhood Walk** dives deeper into modern Asia, focusing on a thriving fish market where you can shop and eat like a local. You can choose just one walk or do both, connecting them with a memorable shared-minibus *(dolmuş)* ride through residential streets.

Orientation

Length of These Walks: Allow at least four hours to do both walks (including transport back and forth from the European side); with more time, you can linger or have a meal here in Asia. To visit just one part—either Üsküdar or Kadıköy—allow a couple of hours round-trip.

When to Go: These walks—especially in Üsküdar—work well in the morning, when the light is best looking toward European Istanbul. You can finish your excursion with a leisurely lunch in Kadıköy before heading back to Europe. It's best to avoid rush hour (8:00-9:30 and 16:00-19:30), when commuters flock

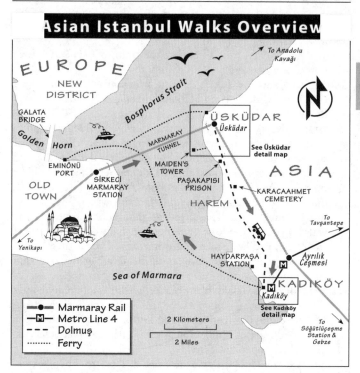

between the Asian and European parts of the city, and transport and public spaces are very congested.

Getting to Üsküdar: The fast option is to take the **Marmaray commuter rail line** under the Bosphorus—catch it at Sirkeci train station in the Old Town. Hop on a train going toward Gebze and get off just three minutes later at the first stop, Üsküdar (3.50 TL with İstanbulKart). Follow exit signs to *Hakimiyeti Milliye Caddesi*, and you'll emerge at the heart of Üsküdar, the square called Üsküdar Meydanı (ews-kewh-dahr may-duh-nuh).

For a slower but very scenic alternative, catch the **ferry** at the commuter pier at Eminönü (near the Eminönü tram stop). It's on the Old Town side of the Golden Horn, near the Galata Bridge. Look for the *Üsküdar* terminal (just next to the *Kadıköy* terminal; 2-4/hour in peak times, 20 minutes, runs 7:30-22:00; 7 TL one-way with token, 3.65 TL with İstanbulKart; signs show the ferry destination above the terminal and passenger entrance).

The boat ride is enjoyable—the views alone justify the trip. Upon arriving in Asia, simply walk away from the Bosphorus to the walk's starting point. To return to Eminönü, head back to the port where you arrived, and look for the *Eminönü* terminal.

For variety, mix it up: take the train to Asia and a ferry home, or vice-versa.

Getting to Kadıköy: Take the same **Marmaray commuter rail line** from Sirkeci train station (direction: Gebze), but stay on until Ayrılık Çeşmesi (second stop in Asia, 3.50 TL with İstanbulKart), then switch to the Metro and ride one stop to Kadıköy (discounted transfer with İstanbulKart). To get there by **ferry**, catch the boat from the Eminönü dock in the Old Town. The terminal (next to the Üsküdar terminal) should be marked *Kadıköy* (2/hour, 25 minutes, runs 7:00-21:00; 7 TL one-way with token, 4 TL with İstanbulKart).

Mosque Etiquette: You'll pass a few neighborhood mosques as you walk. If you choose to enter, remember that women must cover their hair, and both men and women must cover their shoulders and knees and remove shoes. Bring a bag to carry your shoes during your mosque visits.

Market Hours: In Üsküdar, the market we'll explore on our walk (Üsküdar Çarşısı) is open daily 8:00-20:00. The lively Kadıköy Market closes between 18:30 and 19:00, but eateries stay open until 21:00. After 21:00, crowds vanish (though places serving alcohol stay open until late).

Süreyya Opera House Performances: It's worth buying tickets in advance to see a performance at the Süreyya Opera House in Kadıköy. Tickets are cheap, but they can sell out a month in advance (buy online at www.operabale.gov.tr; see more tips in the Entertainment in Istanbul chapter). Consider timing a visit to the opera with the end of the Kadıköy walk.

Starring: The classic view of old Istanbul's skyline from Üsküdar, plus Kadıköy's bustling food market district.

BACKGROUND

The Asian side of the Bosphorus has long been home to small towns and villages, but today Asian Istanbul consists mostly of modern sprawl. Development boomed here after the first bridge over the Bosphorus opened in 1973 (though regular ferry service started in the 1850s). While European Istanbul is known for its historic quarters and time-honored ways of life, Asian Istanbul boasts modern infrastructure, bigger homes, and the efficiencies of contemporary life. Each day, millions of people commute across the Bosphorus from their homes in Asia to their jobs in Europe.

This chapter explores two parts of Asian Istanbul—each with its own character. Üsküdar—historically the launchpad for trips to Mecca—has a more traditional, religious feel. Meanwhile, the residents of Kadıköy tend to be more progressive and secular than

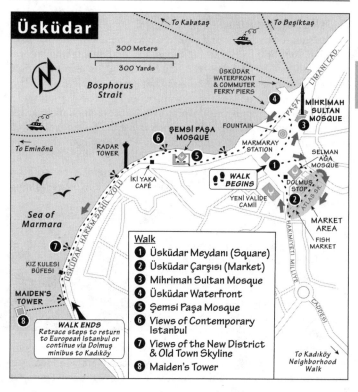

Üsküdar

300 Meters
300 Yards

Bosphorus Strait

To Kabataş *To Beşiktaş*

ÜSKÜDAR WATERFRONT & COMMUTER FERRY PIERS **4**

MİHRİMAH SULTAN MOSQUE **3**

To Eminönü

RADAR TOWER

ŞEMSİ PAŞA MOSQUE **6** **5**

FOUNTAIN

MARMARAY STATION **1**

SELMAN AĞA MOSQUE

İKİ YAKA CAFÉ

WALK BEGINS

YENİ VALİDE CAMİİ

DOLMUŞ STOP **2**

Sea of Marmara

7

KIZ KULESİ BÜFESİ

MARKET AREA

FISH MARKET

MAIDEN'S TOWER

8

WALK ENDS
Retrace steps to return to European Istanbul or continue via Dolmuş minibus to Kadıköy

ÜSKÜDAR HAREM SAHİL YOLU

HAKİMİYETİ MİLLİYE

To Kadıköy Neighborhood Walk

Walk
1 Üsküdar Meydanı (Square)
2 Üsküdar Çarşısı (Market)
3 Mihrimah Sultan Mosque
4 Üsküdar Waterfront
5 Şemsi Paşa Mosque
6 Views of Contemporary Istanbul
7 Views of the New District & Old Town Skyline
8 Maiden's Tower

their counterparts across the strait. (For example, you'll see fewer women wearing headscarves, and the area is a voting stronghold for the modern Social Democrat party.) Attentive travelers tune into these subtle differences as they explore this Asian side of the city.

Üsküdar View Walk

In the Ottoman era, Üsküdar was the gathering and departure place for pilgrims and caravans heading to Mecca, giving it a spiritual ambience that is still apparent today. Countless mosques and Sufi lodges (Muslim counterparts of Christian or Buddhist monasteries) were built here, attracting religious communities. Even today, strolling the streets of Üsküdar, you may notice locals' more conservative lifestyle. Observe how people here dress and socialize—then compare with what you'll experience in Kadıköy later on—a striking contrast.

• *Exiting the Marmaray Üsküdar station, you emerge into the central square called...*

❶ Üsküdar Meydanı

As the square bustles around you, consider the history of this part of Asian Istanbul. In Byzantine times, this settlement was known unofficially as Chrysopolis—the "City of Gold." Its prime location on the ancient maritime route was the source of its wealth. The town administration collected transit fees and port taxes from trade vessels sailing through the Bosphorus and those anchoring at its harbor for supplies. Later, this area was a base for squadrons of shield-carrying soldiers, called Scutarii—the origin of the name Üsküdar.

With the Marmaray entrance behind you, the early-18th-century **Yeni Valide Camii** (New Mosque of the Mother Sultan) stands just ahead of you, with its spindly gray minarets. Just before the mosque, notice a cluster of **yellow *dolmuş* vans**. Remember this location—if continuing to Kadıköy, you'll catch your ride here.

To your left and across the street is the **Selman Ağa Mosque,** with its stouter brick minaret. Although it's one of the oldest monuments in Üsküdar (from the early 1500s), until recently it was completely hidden by a cluster of commercial buildings. Now it sets apart, uncovered and restored to its former charm.

• *Head toward the Selman Ağa Mosque: Cross the street (called Hakimiyeti Milliye Caddesi) at the traffic light (some walkways may be blocked due to construction). With the mosque to your right, continue straight down the street called Selmani Pak Caddesi. (For a caffeine boost, stop in the **Eminönü Kahvecisi** coffee shop on your right, just behind the mosque.) Back on Selmani Pak Caddesi, turn right down the first alley (Atlas Sokak), to enter the...*

❷ Üsküdar Çarşısı (Üsküdar Market)

This market (*çarşısı*, chahr-shuh-suh) area takes up an entire city block. Its narrow back streets are lined with retail shops, old-fashioned cafés and restaurants, butchers and offal shops, green grocers, and a local fish market displaying today's catch. The fish market is particularly lively in the morning.

This is the most congested part of Üsküdar. Atlas Sokak extends roughly 100 yards, all the way through a smelly fish market slinging the fresh catch of the day. Other vendors along this strip sell brightly colored produce, sweets, nuts, meat, and baked goods. Revel in the sights and smells as you wander through this bustling street until you reach the main drag, Hakimiyeti Milliye Caddesi.

Who Gets to Be Called Sultan?

The title of sultan indicates rule and authority (like the terms king, duke, queen, or duchess). You may at first be surprised to see Turkish women with the title "sultan," but the word is versatile—used for both men and women. For men, the title precedes the name, but for women, it follows the name. So Sultan Ahmet is a man, Mihrimah Sultan is a woman. Even when used for women, the term is still sultan—not sultana (she's a royal, not a raisin).

Under Ottoman rule, the sovereign was the sultan, and his mother, siblings, and children were given similar titles. The mother of an heir to the throne was known as the "master woman." If that heir ascended to the throne, the mother adopted the title of sultan (the equivalent of "Queen Mother" in Britain).

• *Turn right on Hakimiyeti Milliye Caddesi, heading back towards the Marmaray station (you've just made a big loop). Continue along this street for a block, heading toward the water. As the walkway gets wider and you pass through the square where we began, look to your right for another dominating landmark, the...*

❸ Mihrimah Sultan Mosque

This mosque was commissioned by Mihrimah Sultan and built by the great architect Sinan in 1548—predating his masterpiece, the Mosque of Süleyman the Magnificent (for more on Sinan, see page 209). The mosque was just one part of a sprawling complex that at one time included a primary school, madrassa, bath, mausoleum, inn, hospital, bazaar, and a public fountain—all fronting the Bosphorus.

Mihrimah was the daughter of Sultan Süleyman and Roxelana. A sultan's daughter was expected to marry a man of the highest rank and with the brightest future. Per the tradition, Mihrimah married statesman Rüstem Paşa, who eventually became the grand vizier, the sultan's powerful chief minister (for more on Rüstem Paşa, see page 186).

The great architect Sinan is rumored to have been deeply in love with Mihrimah Sultan. Because he could not profess his affection to her directly, he immortalized it in the two mosques he built for her—one in European Istanbul (by the Walls of Theodosius, close to Chora Church), and the other here in Asia. The placement of each mosque is highly symbolic: In Persian, *"mihr"* means "the sun," and *"mah"* means "the moon." On March 21, the birthday of Mihrimah, the sun rises by her mosque in Üsküdar and sets behind the one in Europe—giving way for the moon to rise in the same direction.

Go up the steps of the mosque to the colonnaded portico for a good view of the square and European Istanbul across the Bosphorus. Then step inside to appreciate the early architectural flourishes that paved the way for Sinan's later works. The building behind the mosque (accessible through the courtyard) was the madrassa of the complex. Built in a traditional fashion, with rooms surrounding a central atrium, it now serves as a medical facility.

Üsküdar's mosques are popular among the pious. If you're in Üsküdar on a Friday morning, you'll likely see women in headscarves and elderly men on their way to a mosque. You may also see a few devout women in the black, robelike attire called a *çarşaf* (similar to a burka). For more on the tradition of Muslim headscarves, see page 447.

• *Just outside the mosque, by the pedestrian crossing, is the handsome 18th-century* **Fountain of Sultan Ahmet III**. *The marble fountain was originally built right on the shore. It was moved to its current location during renovation of the square.*

At the traffic light by the fountain, cross the street (Paşa Limanı Caddesi) to the....

❹ Üsküdar Waterfront

To your right are the commuter ferry piers. For decades, commuter ferries were practically the only means of transportation for millions of workers commuting across the city. The 2013 opening of the Marmaray tunnel—and the connecting rail system—eased this traffic greatly. But for many commuters and tourists, ferries are still an efficient and scenic way to travel. And for some, nothing can replace *simit*-and-tea breakfast on a ferry (the local

equivalent of a coffee and doughnut on the subway). From here, ferries run regularly to Beşiktaş (right across the Bosphorus) and to Eminönü in the Old Town (consider taking the ferry back to Europe after your Asian Istanbul walks). Although not as frequent, there are also scheduled services to remote piers along the Golden Horn.

Facing the water, turn left and head south along the wide promenade dotted with benches and coin-operated telescopes. You'll see Roma women selling flower bouquets and romantic couples enjoying the view.

• *Continue a few hundred yards to the small, waterfront...*

❺ Şemsi Paşa Mosque

This little mosque, though not as striking as some of Sinan's earlier works, was built by Sinan in 1580, during the last decade of his long life. The mosque was built for Şemsi Paşa, a vizier to Sultan Süleyman the Magnificent.

Around Istanbul, you'll notice that pigeons flock around the domes of many mosques. But Şemsi Paşa mosque is an exception, with few birds circling above. Locals like to say that because Şemsi Paşa had a reputation for bribery and corruption, his memory is so tarnished that not even a bird would land on his mosque. The real reason is that Sinan intentionally located the mosque at the intersection of strong winds to protect the structure from corrosive bird droppings.

The mosque is surrounded by an L-shaped madrassa, with 12 domes and chambers. Through the garden, you can enter the school to see its modest interior—today a library busy with students.

At the far end of the garden, a marble doorway makes a picturesque frame around the view of the strait and European Istanbul. Walk through the doorway to emerge onto a waterfront strip, then turn left to continue along the water. Just beyond the mosque, you'll reach the **İki Yaka Café** (on the left), selling ice cream and thin, crunchy wafers called *kağıt helva*—a favorite of local kids. This sweet treat comes with nougat or caramelized sugar inside and can be eaten as is, or used to create an ice-cream sandwich.

• *Grab a* kağıt helva, *find a spot along the water, and enjoy the...*

❻ Views of Contemporary Istanbul

Looking across the Bosphorous, you can easily spot the western-style **Dolmabahçe Palace** on the waterfront (almost straight ahead from where you stand). Despite its impressive appearance, this mid-19th-century Ottoman palace stands as a reminder of a declining empire—and the sultan's last-ditch attempt to revive it. Until the early republic, Dolmabahçe Palace marked the northern boundary of European Istanbul (other than a few fishing communities farther north). Just above the palace, the modern **Swissotel Bosphorus** (built in the 1980s) was a controversial addition to the cityscape, as locals feared its imposing location would overshadow the palace.

To left of the palace, notice the fancy little mosque of the Dolmabahçe complex. Farther to the left is the new and extended **Kabataş pier** that will serve thousands of commuters a day (it's scheduled to be completed in 2021). Kabataş is also the terminus of two public transit lines: the central tram line through the Old Town and New District, and the funicular from Taksim Square.

Behind the pier and all the way up the hill, the green high-rise building (Marmara Taksim Hotel) marks the location of **Taksim Square,** the bustling center of the New District. And north and northeast of Taksim Square, you'll notice the many high-rise buildings that comprise the business and financial districts of today's cosmopolitan Istanbul.

Looking north of the Dolmabahçe complex (to the right), you'll see middle and upper-middle class residential neighborhoods that sprawl all the way to the Bosphorus Bridge and beyond, cluttered only by few buildings of historic significance—including the waterfront **Çırağan Palace.** Built in the same eclectic fashion as Dolmabahçe (but two decades later), Çırağan Palace was the last of several Ottoman palaces built there. The original palace was dedicated to opulent Tulip Era parties. Named after the Persian word for light, *çerağ,* it became known as the Çırağan Palace—meaning "Luxurious Palace." Today, Çırağan is part of an international hotel chain. Behind Çırağan, **Yıldız Parkı**—once an imperial garden, but now a public park—is one of the largest in Istanbul.

Back on this side, just beyond the İki Yaka Café, look up at the distinctive **radar tower** before you. This is part of an extensive radar control system built to coordinate the heavy maritime traffic through the Bosphorus. You're now at the waterfront strip called Salacak Sahili (Salacak Waterfront), a popular spot for amateur fishermen. On weekends, this area is crowded with locals out walking, jogging, and enjoying the fresh air.

• *Continue along the waterfront, taking in the great views of the New District and Old Town skyline. Soon the promenade begins to cascade toward the water in cement tiers, with carpeted seating, large pillows, and tiny tables where cafés serve coffee and tea. Stop at **Kız Kulesi Büfesi** to sip coffee while you take in the...*

❼ Views of the New District and Old Town Skyline

You are now standing right across from the mouth of the Golden Horn, the waterway that separates the two halves of Istanbul's core, the New District and the Old Town. This was the area that comprised the city until the 1950s. The Galata Bridge crosses the opening of the Golden Horn.

North of the Golden Horn, the lone medieval tower you see is the 14th-century **Galata Tower** (or the Genoese Tower), dominating the New District skyline. The Genoese were among the first to settle on the north banks of the Horn, negotiating and acquiring trade privileges from the Byzantine emperor. The tower and surrounding land were considered Genoese territory. (Though the Ottomans sought to promote commerce with such trade deals, by the 19th century, the empire's economy could no longer compete with the industrialized west, contributing to the decline of the Ottoman Empire.)

Beyond the tower are a series of neighborhoods I've dubbed the **New District.** In the 1800s, the New District became densely populated with foreign diplomatic and religious missions and entrepreneurs. The district grew into a European-looking city, gradually evolving into a modern and lively neighborhood. Before this time, the Old Town was where everyone (Muslim and non-Muslim) wanted to live and work. But by the early 1900s, the New District became the trend.

Shift your gaze south of the Golden Horn. Nothing seems to match the majestic skyline of Istanbul's **Old Town**. Occupied without interruption since King Byzas (founder of Byzantium), the Old Town served as the proud capital of some of history's greatest empires—and it shows.

The view is impressive whether seen in the sun or under a blanket of snow: the choppy waters of the Bosphorus, the intact Byzantine **sea walls** running all along the coastline, countless domes and cupolas of the **Topkapı Palace** on the hillside, and massive domes and minarets of **Hagia Sophia** and the **Blue Mosque** in the backdrop. But the skyline really becomes magical—almost mystical—in the haze.

• *Farther along the Asian coastline—and just off the embankment where you stand—you've probably already noticed another Bosphorus landmark.*

❽ Maiden's Tower

This tower sits on a natural rock outcropping just off the coastline. While the current structure dates only from the 19th century,

this has been an important spot since the fifth century BC. Scholars believe that on this rock the Romans built a fort, which later became a prison, a customs office, and even a quarantine ward during the cholera pandemic of the 1830s. Finally, it was rebuilt as a lighthouse.

While the tower comes with many silly legends, my favorite is the love story of Hero and Leander. Hero, a priestess of Aphrodite, lived an isolated life and refrained from worldly pleasures. But upon meeting the handsome Leander, her passion overcame her dedication to the goddess. To hide their affair, Hero and Leander would meet in secret on this rocky islet. Hero would light a torch every night, and Leander would swim towards the light to meet her. One night, heavy winds carried the torch away, and Leander lost his sense of direction and drowned. Devastated by her lover's death, Hero jumped into the sea and also drowned. (The tower's nickname is "Leander's Tower.")

Romantics with plenty of time can go out to visit the Maiden's Tower. Continue along the waterfront about 150 yards to reach a tiny pier from where boats shuttle visitors over (30 TL one-way, frequent departures daily 9:00-19:00, more in April-Oct). At the lighthouse, you'll have 360-degree views of both banks of the Bosphorus. There's also a tacky museum dedicated to tower myths (www.kizkulesi.com.tr).

• *Our walk is over. If you've had enough sightseeing for now, you can head back to the* **Old Town:** *Retrace your steps back along the waterfront to the ferry pier, then catch a boat to Eminönü, or head to the Marmaray station for the commuter train back to Sirkeci.*

Or you can carry on to another Asian Istanbul experience, the **Kadıköy Neighborhood Walk.** *For that, retrace your steps to Üsküdar Square, where we began, and take a* dolmuş *van to Kadıköy (see next).*

Dolmuş Ride From Üsküdar to Kadıköy

To connect Üsküdar and Kadıköy, you'll ride about two miles in a *dolmuş* (shared minibus). This can take anywhere from 20 to 40 minutes, depending on traffic. If you have yet to ride a *dolmuş* in Istanbul, this is a great opportunity for a distinctly Turkish experience.

Yellow *dolmuş* vans are parked in front of the Üsküdar Marmaray station (facing the Yeni Valide Camii mosque). Each minibus has its destination clearly marked (look for *Kadıköy*). Vans depart as they fill up. Pay the 3.25-TL fare directly to the driver (or hand your fare up, if you are seated at the back, exact change preferred). Tell the driver you want to get off at **Haldun Taner Sahnesi** (hahl-doon tah-nehr sah-neh-see) **Theater**— it's right before the minibus' last stop. (There are no "official" stops—vans make arbitrary stops to drop and pick up passengers.)

Here's what you'll see along the way as your *dolmuş* zips through the streets of Asian Istanbul. Note: During rush hour (roughly 8:00-9:30 and 16:00-19:30), the driver may choose a faster route to avoid traffic, and you may not see everything described here.

Leaving Üsküdar Square, the first half of the ride is uphill, through residential neighborhoods. Rows of condos are interrupted by a public park at the end of the steep Doğancılar Caddesi (on the left). About a block up on the right from the park is a 200-year-old penitentiary, **Paşakapısı Cezaevi**. It's behind an imposing, hard-to-miss wall with barbed wire. The complex, built in 1800 by Sultan Selim, was a hunting palace before it became a prison. Today its occupants are convicted civil servants.

At the edge of Üsküdar, you'll drive along the massive **Kara-caahmet Cemetery**. The cemetery, which predates the Ottoman conquest of Istanbul, is the final resting place of an estimated five million people. (Adherents of different sects of Islam are buried in different areas within the cemetery.) The cemetery is also an unofficial nature preserve—a welcome green space in this very densely built city. Centuries-old plane trees, laurels, hackberries, cypress trees, and wild berries create a habitat for local and migratory birds (such as woodpeckers, kestrels, storks, starlings, falcons, and owls). You may even spot a few exotic escaped parrots. Through the summer, locals come here to pick fruit and berries.

You'll cross a railroad bridge over the D-100 intercity highway, crossing into **Kadıköy**. Once over the bridge, you'll notice some of Istanbul's specialized hospitals *(hastane)* on either side of you. Then, look to your right to spot the historic **Haydarpaşa Train Station.** Built in 1908 (partially on reclaimed land), the structure stands on a platform supported by over 1,000 pillars. This railway station was commissioned to connect Istanbul to Baghdad and Mecca, an ambitious but never completed project. Bypassed when Istanbul built its Marmaray commuter rail line, the landmark station has been closed for years but may see service again as a terminus for intercity rail.

You're entering the bustling (or, during rush hour, downright chaotic) center of Kadıköy. The driver should drop you off by the **Haldun Taner Sahnesi Theater** or the *konservatuar* (kohn-sehr-vah-too-ahr)—a conservatory and theater we'll cover on our walk. Head behind the theater to the Eminönü and Karaköy pier, where we'll start our Kadıköy neighborhood walk. (If you miss the stop, don't worry: The *dolmuş* route ends about 200 yards away, and you can easily walk back.)

Kadıköy Neighborhood Walk

Historic Kadıköy predates even the Byzantine Empire. Settled in ancient times by Greek colonists, this area was known as Chalcedon. Dorian Greeks from Megara (near Athens) came here around the seventh century BC to access its vast, cultivable lands. And through the Byzantine and Ottoman periods, Chalcedon was the "bread basket" of the capital. Far

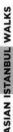

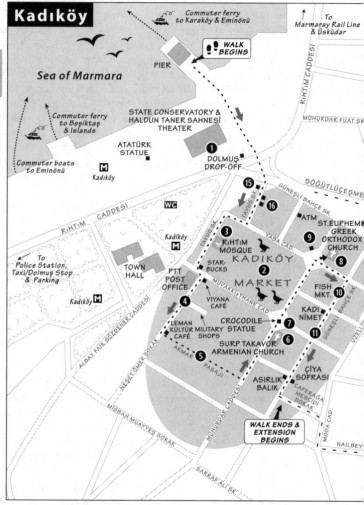

from the city center, it also provided seclusion for Christian monasteries. Later it became known as Kadıköy—"village of the judge"—for the righteous judge, Hızır Bey, who once lived here.

Today's Kadıköy, with over a million people, is a modern commercial and residential district that has grown up around its ferry hub. Upon arrival in Kadıköy, you'll see that it's well designed to deal with hordes of commuters. Trains and buses fan out from the ferry dock. Shops and restaurants fill the grid-planned commercial zone that stretches inland. Notice the shopping-mall ambience, youthful energy of the crowds, and modern efficiency of the commerce. Progressive and western-looking, Kadıköy is for many a stronghold of the secular state.

Walk

1 State Conservatory & Haldun Taner Sahnesi Theater

2 Kadıköy Market

3 Rıhtım Mosque

4 Neşet Ömer Sokak

5 Akmar Pasajı & Bookstores

6 Surp Takavor Armenian Church

7 Bronze Crocodile

8 Saint Euphemia Greek Orthodox Church

9 Şekerci Cafer Erol Candy Shop

10 Fish Market

11 Güneşli Bahçe Sokak Eateries

Walk Extension

12 Bahariye Caddesi

13 Süreyya Opera House

14 Bull Statue

More Eateries

15 HD İskender

16 MADO & Fazıl Bey

• *Our walk starts at the Eminönü and Karaköy pier. If you came by ferry or by* dolmuş, *you're already there. If you came on the Metro, walk 100 yards (past the Atatürk statue at the center of the square) to the pier.*

With the pier behind you, the large, terracotta-painted building in the middle of the square is the...

❶ State Conservatory and Haldun Taner Sahnesi Theater

Surrounded by Roma flower stands, this building is a typical example of Early Republic architecture (from 1927). It served as a main produce market until the early 1980s, when it was converted into Istanbul University's State Conservatory.

This is one of Turkey's most prestigious schools for music and the performing arts. (Listen for classical music echoing from its windows.) Art, culture, education, and health services are largely state-subsidized in Turkey. The municipality sponsors all productions staged in the Haldun Taner Sahnesi Theater. That means tickets are affordable (just a few dollars, much less for children)—so people of all economic classes can enjoy some culture here.

• *With the conservatory building to your right, walk to the busy street (Rıhtım Caddesi). At the traffic light, cross the street to the middle section, head right to the next set of lights, then cross the intersecting road and tram tracks and approach the massive...*

❷ Kadıköy Market (Kadıköy Çarşısı)

This sprawling market area is the historic core of Kadıköy—and it doesn't get more authentic than the surrounding neighborhood.

Here in the market area, you'll find everything from grocers and fishmongers to popular delis and specialty olive oil shops. (Watch for a live goose, the shopkeepers' mascot, waddling around on the loose.) The surrounding streets are lined with boutiques, bookstores, fast-food kiosks, cafés, bars, and restaurants (which come alive in the late afternoon, but get sleepy after 21:00). As busy as it is around here during the day, it gets even more crowded at rush hour. Commuters make a stop here to shop and enjoy a drink or meal with friends.

After crossing the street and tram tracks, you're at the start of a street called Tavus Sokak. On the right is the chain restaurant **HD İskender**, serving up only one main dish: *İskender kebap*. Named after its inventor, the dish consists of thin slices of *döner kebab* over fresh *pide* bread, topped with tomato sauce and sizzling hot butter, and served with thick yogurt on the side. Across from HD İskender, look for **MADO** and **Fazıl Bey's** Turkish coffee shops, side-by-side. If you're here around lunch time, consider making this little spin tour into a meal: enjoy a filling *İskender kebap*, dig into a baklava topped with ice cream at MADO, and finish with a Turkish coffee at Fazıl Bey's.

• *At the end of this alley, turn right. Then follow Tavus Sokak as the street bends left. Midway along the next block, look to your left for the narrow entry to a humble mosque that stands behind the row of buildings.*

❸ Rıhtım Mosque, a.k.a. Mosque of Sultan Mustafa III

During his reign, the 18th-century Ottoman Sultan Mustafa III built three mosques: one in Üsküdar, another on the outskirts of the Old Town, and this one in Kadıköy. Much to his frustration, none of the mosques were named after him. Instead, they're named after nearby locations (*rıhtım* refers to the nearby boat dock).

• *Continue along Tavus Sokak, and at the end of the block (by the Starbucks), cross diagonally through the little square (don't turn left), passing between the Viyana Café and the post office (PTT) onto the street called…*

❹ Neşet Ömer Sokak

Also known as the "alley of pubs," this strip (and the surrounding blocks) buzzes with performance centers and lively pubs and bars. During the day, you'll spot seniors nursing a cup of tea or a beer, but by sunset, this becomes a clubbing zone.

A few steps down this street, look left down **Kadıköy Çarşısı**—a passage (with the same name as the greater market area) with shops selling military supplies, uniforms, accessories, boots, and more. In Turkey, military service is compulsory for all male citizens and is seen as a milestone event. The more educated a man is, the less time he is required to serve. Shops like these (and their patrons) offer a look into this formative part of a Turkish man's life.

Continue down Neşet Ömer Sokak. On your left, it's easy to spot the bright yellow exterior of the **Leman Kültür Café**. Inside, its walls and tables are decorated with pages of comic strips. The café is run by the owners of a highly controversial cult comic magazine. The café was initially a grubby hangout for cartoonists and stand-up comedians. Eventually it morphed into the slick, commercial café it is today—which, critics say, is the opposite of the irreverent spirit that *Leman* magazine stood for.

Just beyond Leman Kültür Café is ❺ **Akmar Pasajı**, a small passageway that runs straight through the block to Mühürdar Caddesi (the street parallel to Neşet Ömer Sokak). A bibliophile's heaven, this passage has several bookstores with dusty shelves crammed with a hodgepodge of books. Purists say that you can find any book you need here—and for much less than at a modern bookstore. As you browse, look for books labeled *KPSS, ALES, LGS,* and *YKS*. These are prep books for various types of public education and public service standardized tests. More than four out of five Turkish students attend public schools, and spaces at prestigious institutions are highly competitive—so test prep is big business here.

• *Walk all the way through the passage. Emerge and turn left onto Mühürdar Caddesi, following it toward the intersection with Muvakkıthane*

Caddesi. At the corner, behind the wall on your right is the wooden bell tower of the...

❻ Surp Takavor Armenian Church

This church, originally built in the early 1700s (the current build-ing is from 1936), is one of 36 active Apostolic Armenian Churches in the city. Turkey is home to about 60,000 Armenians (a rec-ognized minority), and most live in Istanbul. If it's Sunday, you can visit the church discreetly during the holy liturgy.

• *In the small square formed by the streets meeting in front of the church, look for a marble block topped with a small...*

❼ Bronze Crocodile

On the marble base of this popular landmark, an inscription by the first-century Greek historian Strabo reads: "By the entrance of Pontus [the Black Sea], there is the village of Chrysopolis [today's Üsküdar] and Khalkedon [today's Kadıköy] established by Mega-rons, and the Temple of Khalkedon. There is a small spring where crocodiles feed themselves." Despite the objections of scholars—who doubted that crocodiles ever lived here—this bronze crocodile was commissioned in honor of this quote. Later they realized the quote was mistranslated. In reality, it was lizards that lived here—not crocodiles.

• *Continue straight through the square along Mühürdar Caddesi for an-other two short blocks until you reach the intersection with Yasa Caddesi.*

*In the middle of this small square, notice the **stone-and-metal blocks** that feature symbols of the produce sold in the market. On the ground, a Turkish phrase is spelled out in marble. It's a translation of the Latin term* Ex oriente lux *("Light comes from the east")—Con-stantine's rationale for choosing Byzantium as the new capital for the Roman Empire.*

Ahead of you on the right, behind the pale yellow wall topped with a white cross, is...

❽ Saint Euphemia Greek Orthodox Church

This church, dating from 1694, honors the saint considered to be the protector of the Orthodox faith. Euphemia was the daughter of a Roman senator in Chalcedon (ancient Kadıköy). Chalcedon governor Priscus demanded that all inhabitants offer a sacrifice to Ares, the god of war. Because of her Christian faith, Euphe-

mia refused. As punishment, she was brought before Priscus, tortured, and killed by a bear in an arena. Greeks believe that the relics of St. Euphemia are in a silver coffin in the Church of St. George at the Greek Orthodox Patriarchate in Istanbul's Fener neighborhood. However, the small Croatian town of Rovinj also claims to own the relics (which mysteriously washed up there in a huge stone sarcophagus in the year 800). Just to be certain, check out both and decide for yourself.

• *Facing the church, head to the left across the square to the navy awning of the...*

❾ Şekerci Cafer Erol Candy Shop

This local confectionary shop has been in business for five generations—since the early 1800s. Inside the colorful shop you

can browse shelves loaded with candies, Turkish delights, marzipan, macarons, baklava, and other sweets. Keep an eye out for these favorites: *fıstık ezmesi* (pistachio paste similar to marzipan); *acıbadem kurabiyesi* (Turkish macarons made with almond); and *akide şekeri* (hard candy—the cinnamon and clove flavors are popular). Upstairs, **Cafer Erol Café** is a good place to catch your breath...and sample some candies.

• *Exiting the shop, cross the square with St. Euphemia Church on your left, and head a short block uphill on Yasa Caddesi. Where the street intersects with Güneşli Bahçe Sokak, you're standing at the heart of Kadıköy's traditional...*

❿ Fish Market

Güneşli Bahçe and the intersecting narrow alleys are lined with specialty local food stores selling everything from sweets to fresh and dried vegetables to dairy prod-

ucts. The classic Kadıköy ambience has remained the same here for decades. Linger in this colorful part of the market and enjoy perusing the produce and joining the commotion. This market is crowded with locals any time of day, but it gets far busier during the evening rush hour.

• *When you're ready to move on, head right down Güneşli Bahçe to experience the...*

⓫ Güneşli Bahçe Sokak Eateries

If you didn't go for the *İskender kebap* at the beginning of this walk, consider eating along this street. Some fish vendors here double as eateries: Just choose a fish from the display, and they'll cook it up and serve it to you on the spot. About a block up on the right, **Kadı Nimet** was one of the first restaurants on this stretch to start cooking up their fish for hungry customers. (More food is coming up soon.)

About 100 yards down the street on the left is the down-to-earth **Çiya Sofrası** restaurant. Chef Musa Dağdeviren is dedicated to reviving traditional recipes of Asia Minor and Mesopotamia. Today's specialties are displayed at the entrance, and the staff is happy to explain each dish (vegetarian options available). If you eat here, be aware that the self-service salad and *meze* bar is priced by weight.

Across from Çiya Sofrası, **Asırlık Balık** seafood restaurant is a reasonably priced gem that's often crowded with locals (but undiscovered by tourists).

• *If you're ready to finish your walk here, backtrack to the intersection of Güneşli Bahçe and Yasa Caddesi. Turn left on Yasa Caddesi and walk straight downhill to Tavus Sokak, then retrace your steps all the way back down to the Kadıköy pier. But to explore a bit more, stick with me for this optional extension.*

More Sights in Kadıköy

The rest of this walk leads through older, middle-class neighborhoods of downtown Kadıköy.

• *Just past the Çiya Sofrası restaurant, turn left into narrow Caferağa Mescidi Sokak. At the end of the alley, bear right on Moda Caddesi, then take the first left onto Nailbey Sokak. Walk about 400 yards until you reach the pleasant and pedestrianized...*

⓬ Bahariye Caddesi

Officially named for General Asım Gündüz, locals still call this street by its traditional name, Bahariye. Once a trendy designer street with upscale shops, today it's less posh but very popular with Kadıköy's casual, middle-class residents and students. This was one of the earliest pedestrian zones in the city (the tram came later). Though locals were skeptical at first, they quickly found that the lack of cars here made life easier—especially for students running late for classes.

• *Turn right onto Bahariye Caddesi. Within the block, and to your left, you'll see the...*

⓭ Süreyya Opera House

While the city's main fine arts venue—the Atatürk Cultural Center (AKM, near Taksim Square)—is under construction, this is Istanbul's main space for opera and ballet. Built in 1923, it was commissioned by Süreyya Paşa, a foreign affairs minister in the waning days of the Ottoman Empire. The architect, Master Kavafyan, modeled the building after its European counterparts (on a smaller scale). The ceiling of the auditorium is decorated with reliefs of cherubs. If the lobby is open, see if you can peek inside. Even those casually interested in opera should consider attending a performance here—for details see the Entertainment in Istanbul chapter.

If your plans change and you can't make the show, do as the locals do and offer your ticket up to someone in Kadıköy—ask *"Bilet isteyen?"* (bee-leht ehs-tay-ahn, "Anyone looking for a ticket?"). Students are particularly appreciative of a free ticket.

• *From the opera house, turn around and walk back down Bahariye Caddesi (back in the direction from where you came). About a block down, on the right, watch for the small passageway called* **Opera Onur Çarşısı**. *For locals attending a wedding, a ball, or a special event, this alley is a one-stop shop for evening gowns and cocktail dresses. Most of the ensembles you see here are modeled after the red-carpet dresses of Turkish and international celebrities.*

Continue downhill for about 300 yards, where the street ends. You'll end up by a...

⓮ Bull Statue

This iconic statue was made in Paris by the French sculptor Isidore Bonheur in 1864. It represents the anger of the French regarding the Alsace-Lorraine border dispute with Germany. On a trip to Paris, the sultan of the time, Abdülaziz, spotted a similar statue and commissioned two more from the sculptor for his private residences. However, the bull's anatomical accuracy offended fundamentalists in his court, so the statue was moved to various low-profile locations around town...before ending up here, in Kadıköy.

• *Our walk is finished. The bull is headed down Söğütlüçeşme Caddesi. Follow his lead and walk down the hill all the way to the pier. From here, you can catch a ferry back to the Old Town. Or, walk left along the water, past the State Conservatory and Haldun Taner Sahnesi Theater to reach the Metro. Ride one stop to Ayrılık Çeşmesi, then connect to the Marmaray commuter rail line back to the Old Town's Sirkeci train station.*

SLEEPING IN ISTANBUL

Istanbul has an abundance of comfortable, well-located hotels. I've focused my recommendations on two safe, handy, and colorful neighborhoods: the historic Old Town (the Sultanahmet and Sirkeci districts); and the New District (near İstiklal Street). For each neighborhood, I also offer tourist and transit tips. For recommended restaurants in these neighborhoods, see the Eating in Istanbul chapter.

I've also listed a few hotels in prime waterfront locations along the Bosphorus. Many visitors to Istanbul look forward to staying on the banks of the Bosphorus for views not only of the sea, but also of another continent across the water. These views often come with hefty price tags; I've purposefully selected seaview hotels that won't break the bank. In general, be aware that Istanbul hotel websites sometimes overstate their views, which may only be visible if you crane your neck or stand on the hotel's rooftop terrace.

When comparing hotels, don't be surprised to see prices quoted in euros instead of Turkish lira. Many travel companies, including hotels, publish their prices in euros as a hedge against Turkey's currency fluctuations.

A designation called "Special Class" (indicated in the listings below as **SC**) indicates the hotel is either itself a historic building or a former residential building converted to lodging—in other words, it has a unique character. Some are upscale; others are run-down. While the rooms can be quite comfortable, most don't have amenities such as saunas, pools, multiple restaurants, or parking. Many of the Old Town's Special Class hotels are equivalent to two- or three-star hotels.

I rank accommodations from $ budget to $$$$ splurge. For information and tips on pricing, getting deals, types of rooms, making reservations, renting an apartment, and more, see the "Sleeping" section of the Practicalities chapter.

In the Old Town

The Old Town, Istanbul's 3,000-year-old Byzantine core, is a welcoming, visitor-friendly area where hotels surround the city's most famous sights. Proximity to the sights is a mixed blessing: Many traditional old Ottoman houses in this area have been converted into hotels and pensions, and few locals can afford to live here anymore. So although the buildings are authentic, the demographic is touristy. Many of the Turks you encounter here are trying to sell you something—an inaccurate and unfortunate first impression of a kind and generous people.

Most of the accommodations recommended here are in a compact central district called Sultanahmet, but a few lovely gems are a bit farther north in the bustling Sirkeci neighborhood.

The **Sultanahmet** district is named for the Blue Mosque (officially called the Sultan Ahmet Mosque, after its namesake). The neighborhood is also home to some of Istanbul's other big sights—Hagia Sophia and the Grand Bazaar. My recommended hotels are located within a 10-minute walk of these historic buildings. Daylight hours here are lively—the neighborhood is full of cafés and shops tucked into narrow streets originally built for horse-drawn carriages. In the evenings, many locals who work nearby go home, leaving the restaurants and cafés to tourists.

Busy **Sirkeci** is just a bit north of Sultanahmet, down the hill towards the Golden Horn. You'll find a potpourri of tech stores, market shops, historic bazaars, restaurants, and fine, small hotels. This neighborhood is also the home of Sirkeci train station, the last stop of the famous Orient Express (and today a hub for the Marmaray commuter rail line to Asian Istanbul). Staying here also gives you easy access to Eminönü, ferry ports on the Golden Horn, and trams to the New District.

Tourist Information: The Sultanahmet TI is at the bottom of the Hippodrome, across from Hagia Sophia (generally daily 9:00-17:00, until 22:00 in summer). The Sirkeci TI is in the Sirkeci train station (generally daily 9:00-20:00).

Transit Connections: The very convenient Sultanahmet tram stop on the main tram line is on Divan Yolu, about 200 yards up from Hagia Sophia. The Sirkeci and Gülhane tram stops are convenient to Sirkeci hotels. The tram connects you to Eminönü (a hub for public buses and ferries) and can also take you north of the Golden Horn to the New District. For more on getting around Istanbul, see the Orientation chapter.

SULTANAHMET

$$$$ Hagia Sophia Mansions is a row of restored historic Ottoman homes on a peaceful cobblestoned street between Hagia Sophia and the Topkapı Palace. The property, run by Hilton, offers outdoor gardens, terraces, and other common areas—a rare feature in the densely built Old Town. Other than two rooms facing the wall of Topkapı Palace, all have street views (RS%—email manager directly, air-con, Soğukçeşme Sokak, Sultanahmet, +90 212 912 4212, https://curiocollection3.hilton.com, info@hagiasofiamansions.com, manager Melis Okay). Be sure to check out the on-site Sarnıç Restaurant, situated in a glowing Byzantine cistern.

$$$$ Vogue Hotel Supreme, on the same street as the Basilica Cistern, is in the heart of the Old Town. It offers 103 large, modern, and crisp rooms, and the café in front is a nice place to relax (air-con, elevator, Yerebatan Caddesi 13, +90 212 513 1616, www.voguehotelsupreme.com/vogue-istanbul, istanbul@voguehotelsupreme.com).

$$$$ Hotel Sultanhan SC is an elegant hotel just off Divan Yolu, close to the Grand Bazaar and within walking distance of the Blue Mosque and Hagia Sophia. Its 40 rooms—larger than the norm for most Old Town hotels—have been carefully restored, and the staff is especially attentive (RS%, air-con, elevator, Piyer Loti Caddesi 7, +90 212 516 3232, www.hotelsultanhan.com, info@hotelsultanhan.com, manager Enis Akça).

$$$ Blue House SC has 26 smartly decorated rooms with bold color schemes. Some rooms have views of the nearby Blue Mosque. The terrace restaurant is wonderfully peaceful and offers great views of the Blue Mosque, the Sea of Marmara, and a bit of Hagia Sophia (RS%, air-con, elevator, Dalbastı Sokak 14, +90 212 638 9010, www.bluehouse.com.tr, info@bluehouse.com.tr).

$$$ Deluxe Hotel Golden Horn Sultanahmet, behind the Turkish and Islamic Arts Museum, is very close to Divan Yolu and the Sultanahmet tram stop. Recently renovated, its 75 rooms—some with views of the sea and the Blue Mosque—boast stylish furniture and decor (RS%, air-con, Binbirdirek 1, +90 212 518 1717, www.deluxegoldenhornhotel.com, info@deluxegoldenhornhotel.com).

$$$ Azade Hotel SC, about three blocks downhill from the Blue Mosque, was converted from an old Ottoman house. Its 33 rooms manage an old-fashioned charm, and the breakfast terrace has sweeping views of the Bosphorus, Sea of Marmara, and the Blue Mosque (RS%, family rooms, some seaview rooms, air-con,

SLEEPING

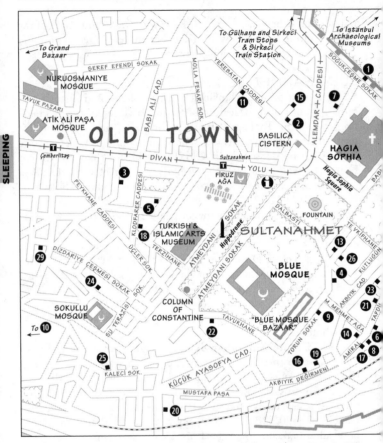

elevator plus some stairs, Mimar Mehmet Ağa 17, +90 212 517 7173, www.azadehotel.com, info@azadehotel.com, helpful staff includes manager Ömer Sümengen, receptionist Sinan, and reservations supervisor İbrahim). Its sister hotel, **Azade Premier,** shares the same courtyard and offers slightly more expensive rooms ("Oriental" rooms are larger, RS%, +90 212 458 1230, www. azadepremier.com, info@azadepremier.com).

$$$ Ottoman Hotel Imperial SC is a freshly renovated former Ottoman school and hospital right across the street from Hagia Sophia. Its 27 rooms—plus 25 more in an annex building— are comfortable and plush. Managers Serdar Balta and Kenan Özkan cherish Rick Steves readers (RS%—use discount code "RCKSTV15" when you book, "premium" rooms have Hagia Sophia views and elevator service, air-con, laundry service, Caferiye Sokak 6/1, +90 212 513 6151, www.ottomanhotelimperial.com, info@ottomanhotelimperial.com).

$$$ Sümengen Hotel is one of the older small hotels in

Old Town Hotels

1. Hagia Sophia Mansions
2. Vogue Hotel Supreme
3. Hotel Sultanhan
4. Blue House
5. Deluxe Hotel Golden Horn Sultanahmet
6. Azade Hotel & Azade Premier
7. Ottoman Hotel Imperial
8. Sümengen Hotel
9. Sultan Ahmet Palace
10. To Ottoman Hotel Park
11. Adamar Hotel
12. Hotel Valide Sultan
13. Uyan Hotel
14. Hippodrome Hotel
15. And Hotel
16. Sphendon Hotel
17. Romantic Hotel
18. Lausos Hotel
19. Erten Konak Hotel
20. Harmony Hotel
21. Agora Guesthouse
22. Hotel Sultan Hill
23. Zeugma Hotel
24. Stone Hotel
25. Basileus Hotel
26. Avrasya Hostel
27. Orient Hostel
28. Sultan Hostel
29. Aslan Apartments

this area, with a cozy feel and reliable staff. Its rooms are larger than average in the Old Town, and some have large Jacuzzis with views of the Sea of Marmara and islands. The top-floor breakfast room also has great views (RS%, elevator, Mimar Mehmet Ağa Caddesi 7, +90 212 517 6869, www.sumengenhotel.com, info@sumengenhotel.com).

$$$ Sultan Ahmet Palace SC, with 45 classy rooms across the street below the Blue Mosque, will have you feeling like a guest of the sultan. From the quiet street, you'll pass through a lush garden, then an elegant lobby, to reach the reception desk. In your bathroom, you'll find faux-Turkish bath fixtures. This place is likely to have space when others are full (air-con, no elevator, Torun Sokak 19, +90 212 458 0460, www.sultanahmetpalace.com, saray@sultanahmetpalace.com).

$$$ Ottoman Hotel Park SC, about a 10-minute walk from the heart of the Old Town, is finely decorated in a modernized Ottoman style. The three types of rooms differ only in size—all have

Old Town Versus New District: Where to Sleep?

The character of your stay in Istanbul can be determined to a great extent by where your hotel is located.

To experience romantic and classic old Istanbul—calls to prayer, graceful minarets outside your hotel, rough cobbled lanes, and must-see sights (mosques, bazaars, and palaces) within an easy walk—go for the Old Town's Sultanahmet or Sirkeci districts. The surroundings are traditional and the neighborhoods are tourist-friendly.

To experience the tempo of today's Istanbul—stylish shoppers and office workers strolling down big noisy streets, energizing the main pedestrian boulevard until late—make the New District your home base. Hotels here serve more businesspeople than tourists, and the neighborhood offers a diverse selection of restaurants and nightlife. Karaköy, the New District's historic banking center, is newly trendy, with small boutique hotels, fine restaurants, and inviting shops. Its proximity to the Old Town and easy access to both parts of the city make Karaköy an especially handy place to stay.

---

the same amenities. Managers Serdar Balta and Kenan Özkan are eager to please (RS%—use discount code "RCKSTV15" when you reserve, air-con, elevator, +90 212 516 0211, Kumkapı, Kadırga Limanı Caddesi 85, www.ottomanhotelpark.com, info@ottomanhotelpark.com).

$$ Adamar Hotel SC has an uninspired lobby, but its terrace has a panoramic view of the Old Town and the New District, and some of its 25 minimalist rooms also have exceptional views. It's on the same street as the Basilica Cistern (family rooms, air-con, elevator, laundry service, Yerebatan Caddesi 37, +90 212 511 1936, www.adamarhotel.com, info@adamarhotel.com, manager Serkan Doğan).

$$ Hotel Valide Sultan SC ("Sultan's Mother") is 100 yards down the busy street from the Topkapı Palace's Imperial Gate. This 19th-century Ottoman mansion has 17 tidy rooms, friendly staff, and an imperial lobby with elegant furnishings, though it's a bit past its prime (RS%, some rooms have sea views, air-con, elevator, İshak Paşa Caddesi, Kutlugün Sokak 1, +90 212 517 6558, www.hotelvalidesultan.com, vsultan@hotelvalidesultan.com).

$$ Uyan Hotel SC is family-run and convenient. It's a very short walk to the Blue Mosque, Hagia Sophia, and Topkapı Palace, and offers great views from its terrace. The 29 tidy rooms are as advertised: Single rooms are true singles, and "small doubles" are compact with no views. The basement family suite is a good value if you're traveling with two or three kids (air-con, elevator, Utangaç

Sokak 25, +90 212 516 4892 or +90 212 518 9255, www.uyanhotel. com, info@uyanhotel.com).

$$ Hippodrome Hotel SC, owned by the nearby Azade Hotel (listed earlier), rents small but comfortable rooms (RS%, family rooms, breakfast at Azade Hotel, air-con, elevator in main building only, Mimar Mehmet Ağa 22, +90 212 517 6889, www. hippodromehotel.com, hippodrome@hippodromehotel.com). In the building across the street, they also rent two three-bedroom apartments with room for six, and a two-bedroom apartment with room for four—ideal for families.

$ And Hotel is ideally located on the same street as the Basilica Cistern and a very short walk from the Old Town's major sights. The 44 rooms are small and basic, but the breakfast room terrace offers an amazing view (air-con, elevator, Yerebatan Caddesi 18, +90 212 512 0207, www.andhotel.com, andhotel@andhotel.com).

$ Sphendon Hotel SC is a cute place with a tiny seaview terrace and a delightful patio out back where breakfast is served in the summer. Its 12 rooms are within walking distance of the heart of the Old Town (air-con, Akbıyık Değirmeni Sokak 50, +90 212 518 5820, www.hotelsphendon.com, info@hotelsphendon.com, owner Erdal Demirli).

$ Romantic Hotel SC's nine smallish rooms are warm and woodsy, tucked inside a converted old mansion only three blocks down from the Blue Mosque. Some rooms have great views and balconies, and breakfast is served on a teeny terrace with a magnificent view of the Sea of Marmara (air-con, Amiral Tafdil Sokak 17, +90 212 638 9635, www.romantichotelistanbul.com, info@ romantichotelistanbul.com, friendly Atilla and Erdal).

$ Lausos Hotel SC, with 30 rooms, is a couple of blocks from the Hippodrome. Some rooms have views of the Blue Mosque and/or the Sea of Marmara and Princes' Islands (air-con, elevator, Klodfarer Caddesi 33, +90 212 638 0707, www.hotellausos.com, info@hotellausos.com, manager Mustafa Özduman).

$ Erten Konak Hotel SC is set in two renovated Ottoman houses on a quiet street, a few blocks down from the Blue Mosque (reception is in the smaller house). The decor is lively, with antique paintings on glass and swirling, gold designs on white walls. Breakfast is served in a greenhouse-like space in the pleasant garden (air-con, no elevator, Akbıyık Değirmeni Sokak 8-10, at intersection with Akbıyık Caddesi, Sultanahmet, +90 212 458 5000, www. ertenkonak.com, info@ertenkonak.com, owner Atahan Erten).

$ Harmony Hotel is a budget hotel with 22 small rooms and a family room for four. Like most other hotels in this part of the city, the terrace has a nice view of the Sea of Marmara. Breakfast is served in the well-lit basement (Küçük Ayasofya Mahallesi, Aksakal Caddesi 26, +90 212 518 8700, www.istanbulharmony.com, info@istanbulharmony.com).

$ Agora Guesthouse offers basic doubles, triples, and dorm rooms (air-con, Akbıyık Caddesi, Amiral Tafdil Sokak 6, +90 212 458 5547, www.agoraguesthouse.net, info@agoraguesthouse.com).

$ Hotel Sultan Hill SC, immediately behind the Blue Mosque and a few steps off the Hippodrome, has 17 clean, comfortable rooms on three floors of an old Ottoman house. Straightforward managers Nilgün and Sedat enjoy helping American travelers (RS%, family room, air-con, Tavukhane Sokak 15, +90 212 518 3293, www.hotelsultanhill.com, info@hotelsultanhill.com).

$ Zeugma Hotel, located amid hostels on backpacker-friendly Akbıyık Caddesi, offers simple, well-kept, budget rooms (air-con, Akbıyık Caddesi 35, +90 212 517 4040, www.zeugmahotel.com. tr, info@zeugmahotel.com). A plethora of cafés and restaurants are just out the front door.

$ Stone Hotel SC, two long blocks from the Hippodrome (across from the Sokullu Mosque) in a quiet, mostly residential neighborhood, has a relaxing stone garden out back (RS%, air-con, elevator, Binbirdirek Mahallesi, Şehit Mehmet Paşa Yokuşu 34, +90 212 638 1554, www.stonehotelistanbul.com, info@ stonehotelistanbul.com).

$ Basileus Hotel is a small, well-maintained budget hotel on a relatively quiet street southwest of the Blue Mosque and a short walk from the Hippodrome and Akbıyık Caddesi. Its 20 rooms come with basic furnishings, but some have French doors and small balconies—the natural light makes them seem grander. You'll be welcomed by a friendly staff with warm hospitality (RS%, family room, air-con, Küçük Ayasofya Mahallesi Şehit Mehmet Paşa Sokak 1, +90 212 517 7878, www.basileushotel.com, info@ basileushotel.com).

SIRKECI

$$$$ Sirkeci Mansion, tucked on a silent street between the outer wall of Topkapı Palace and Sirkeci train station, is famous for its exceptional hospitality. It's a "large" small hotel with 52 rooms, a complimentary sauna, spa, and a small indoor pool. The bright, spacious deluxe rooms on the top floor—with private terraces overlooking historic Gülhane Park—are ideal for families and longer stays (elevator, complimentary refreshments in lobby, Taya Hatun Caddesi 5, +90 212 528 4344, www.sirkecimansion.com, info@ sirkecimansion.com).

$$$ Lalahan Hotel is a crisp and tiny place on the busy main street midway between the Sirkeci and Gülhane tram stations. The third bed in the triple rooms is not a fold-out or a bunk bed, but an orthopedic bed disguised as a couch (elevator, Hüdavendigar

Sirkeci Hotels & Restaurants

Golden Horn

CITY BUS HUB

RAGIP GÜMÜŞPALA

GALATA BRIDGE

Turyol Private Tour Boats

Bosphorue Cruise Pier

Üsküdar Iskelesi

Kadıköy Iskelesi

Boğaziçi Iskelesi

To Harem - Car Ferry

Eminönü

NEW MOSQUE

KEŞADİYE

SPICE MARKET

BÜYÜK

HAMİDİYE CAD

POSTANE CAD

VASIF ÇINAR

AŞIR EFENDİ

KENNEDY CADDESİ

Commuter Rail to Asian Istanbul

Sirkeci

SİRKECİ TRAIN STATION

ANKARA

HÜDAVENDİGAR

EBUSSUUT

Gülhane

To Hagia Sophia & Blue Mosque

Gülhane Park

TOPKAPI PALACE

ISTANBUL ARCHAEOLOGICAL MUSEUMS

200 Meters
200 Yards

❶ Sirkeci Mansion
❷ Lalahan Hotel
❸ Legacy Ottoman Hotel
❹ Elanaz Hotel
❺ Can Oba Restaurant & Şehzade Erzurum Çağ Kebabı
❻ Hocapaşa Pidecisi

SLEEPING

Caddesi 26, +90 212 512 1301, www.lalahanhotel.com, info@lalahanhotel.com, geniune Zerrin and Meriç).

$$$ Legacy Ottoman Hotel is an architect's dream. Dating from the early 20th century, it was built by prominent architect Mimar Kemaleddin Bey. The domes at either side of the building feature the same design as the Dome of the Rock mosque in Jerusalem, which was restored by Kemaleddin Bey. Though the decor feels a little tired, this is an elegant place. Some rooms on higher floors (and the hotel restaurant) have beautiful views of the Bosphorus, while rooms overlooking the atrium can feel a little gloomy (air-con, elevator, Hoybar Caddesi 16, +90 212 527 6767, www.legacyottomanhotel.com, reservation@legacyottomanhotel.com).

$$ Elanaz Hotel, a short walk to the Sirkeci train and tram stations—and surrounded by restaurants and cafés—is family-owned with decent-size, modern rooms (some view rooms, elevator, Orhaniye Caddesi 34, +90 212 528 2426, www.elanaz.com, info@elanaz.com).

HOSTELS

These three hostels are located on or near the bustling-with-backpackers Akbıyık Caddesi ("White Moustache Street"), a couple of blocks below the Blue Mosque (toward the Sea of Marmara). For locations, see the "Old Town Hotels" map, earlier in this chapter. Each offers dorm beds and some double rooms, plus a simple

Turkish breakfast. If you're trying to avoid American backpackers and other international travelers, this is not the street for you. The Agora Guesthouse (listed earlier) also offers hostel-type accommodations.

¢ **Avrasya Hostel,** just up the street from the Four Seasons, is nicely located and well-run. Its 70 beds are filled with travelers who enjoy hanging out in the basement bar or rooftop terrace (Kutlu Gün Sokak 35, +90 212 516 9380, www.hostelworld.com).

¢ **Orient Hostel** is an official HI hostel and a backpacker mecca. The 152 beds in more than 35 rooms are a bit institutional, but a steady stream of Australian and Kiwi backpackers keeps the place lively (RS%, Akbıyık Caddesi 9, +90 212 518 0789, www.orienthostel.com, info@orienthostel.com).

¢ **Sultan Hostel** is another HI hostel, but feels less institutional than the Orient Hostel (Akbıyık Caddesi 21, +90 212 516 9260, www.sultanhostel.com, sultan@sultanhostel.com).

APARTMENTS

$ **Aslan Apartments** offers four 1- to 3-bedroom contemporary units with well-equipped kitchens in a residential neighborhood within walking distance of the Old Town sights. Most have views, and all have balconies or patios (RS% when you pay in cash, seaview apartments for 4-5 people, duplex garden apartments for 8-10 people, 2-night minimum, air-con, laundry facilities, courtyard garden; near the Çemberlitaş tram stop, Piyer Loti Caddesi Satır Sokak 5, Emin Sinan Mahallesi, Sultanahmet; for location see the "Old Town Hotels" map, earlier; +90 212 251 8530, mobile +90 553 221 4224 or +90 533 273 3042, www.aslanapartments.com, info@aslanapartments.com).

In the New District

Staying near İstiklal Street (İstiklal Caddesi) in the area I call the "New District" puts you right at the center of the living city. This hip part of town never sleeps. From restaurants, cafés, theaters, and art galleries to bookstores, boutiques, bars, and jazz clubs, there's something here for everyone. In the New District, you can rub elbows with locals and become part of this energetic scene.

Recently, the municipal government has undertaken projects to upgrade Taksim's infrastructure and preserve its Art Nouveau buildings. Due to the New District's popularity, prices here are higher than in the Old Town. Renting an apartment may be a good budget alternative.

Tourist Information: The TI is a short walk from Taksim Square (generally daily 9:00-17:00, Mete Caddesi 6).

Transit Connections: The New District is well-connected

to the Old Town (and other parts of the city). Two options are the most convenient for reaching the Old Town sights. From Taksim Square (near the first group of hotels listed next), take the funicular down to Kabataş, then can catch the tram to zip into the historic core (get off at Sultanahmet for Hagia Sophia, the Blue Mosque, and other Old Town attractions). Or, from the opposite end of İstiklal Street (near the Şişhane Metro station), take the old-fashioned funicular from Tünel down to Karaköy, where you can catch the same tram mentioned above. Within the New District, the convenient Nostalgic Tram runs down the center of İstiklal Street, between Taksim Square and Tünel.

NEAR TAKSIM SQUARE

$$ Germir Palas Hotel SC, on a busy street near Taksim Square, comes with an old-fashioned but tastefully stylish lobby and 49 heavily perfumed rooms. Comfortable and classy, in a sophisticated Art Nouveau shell and with a smartly uniformed staff, this place is a winner (air-con, elevator, Cumhuriyet Caddesi 7, +90 212 361 1110, www.germirpalas.com, hotel@germirpalas.com). From Taksim Square, with İstiklal Street behind you, walk up the busy street (Cumhuriyet) that runs alongside a big park; the hotel is on the left after two blocks, across from the park.

$$ Triada Residence SC is just below Taksim Square, facing Aya Triada Church a half-block off İstiklal Street. This small, friendly place offers 10 good-size, no-nonsense, updated apartments. Its reasonable rates and excellent location make it popular—book far in advance (RS%, air-con, elevator, İstiklal Caddesi, Meşelik Sokak 4, +90 212 251 0101, www.triada.com.tr, info@triada.com.tr).

$$ Inntel Hotel, a short walk from Taksim Square, is simple and focused on client satisfaction. It's in the pedestrian-friendly area popular with international business travelers and convention-goers due to its proximity to the Lütfi Kırdar Congress Center (RS%, air-con, elevator, Kocatepe Mahallesi, Dolapdere Caddesi 49, Taksim, +90 212 361 9292, www.inntelhotelistanbul.com).

ON OR NEAR İSTIKLAL STREET

$$$$ Tomtom Suites SC has 20 plush suites in a Galatasaray neighborhood building that was once a Franciscan convent. Guests have access to a small library (with comfy sofas and books on Istanbul) and a nice terrace with views of the Old Town (laundry service, Boğazkesen Caddesi, Tomtom Kaptan Sokak 18, Beyoğlu, +90 212 292 4949, www.tomtomsuites.com, info@tomtomsuites.com).

$$$ Mr. Cas Hotels is in the center of the İstiklal Street action, right across from the Flower Passage. Housed in a late-19th-

SLEEPING

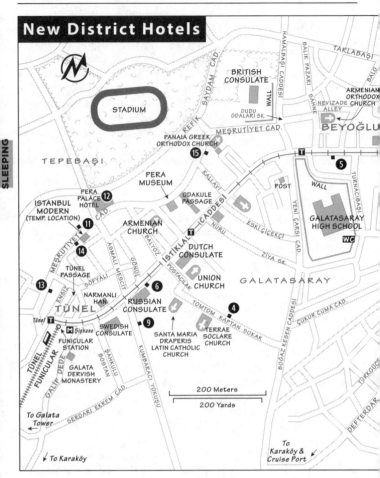

New District Hotels

century building, Mr. Cas rents 35 smartly-appointed rooms with high ceilings—though some street-facing rooms can be noisy until late. The colorful rooftop bar, restaurant, and view terrace provide a nice place to wind down (air-con, elevator, reception is one flight up the stairs as you enter, İstiklal Caddesi 153-1, Beyoğlu, +90 212 293 0007, www.mrcashotels.com, info@mrcashotels.com). The hotel also hosts a small museum dedicated to fashion designer Yıldırım Mayruk, a star of Turkish haute-couture.

$$ Richmond Hotel has 103 small, business-class rooms without any personality—it's all about the location, just a few blocks up İstiklal Street from the Tünel funicular station (air-con, elevator, İstiklal Caddesi 227, +90 212 252 5460, www.richmondint. com.tr, info.istanbul@richmondint.com.tr).

$ Stories Hotels is a small local chain of four boutique hotels near İstiklal Street. Each one is charming—set in beautiful, neat-

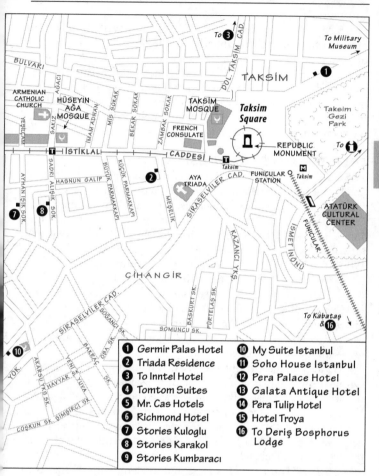

1. Germir Palas Hotel
2. Triada Residence
3. To Inntel Hotel
4. Tomtom Suites
5. Mr. Cas Hotels
6. Richmond Hotel
7. Stories Kuloglu
8. Stories Karakol
9. Stories Kumbaracı
10. My Suite Istanbul
11. Soho House Istanbul
12. Pera Palace Hotel
13. Galata Antique Hotel
14. Pera Tulip Hotel
15. Hotel Troya
16. To Deriş Bosphorus Lodge

ly furnished historic buildings with high ceilings. Most of their rooms have kitchenettes (breakfast not included, +90 212 292 2980, www.storieshotel.com.tr, reservation@storieshotel.com.tr). **Stories Kuloglu** and **Karakol**, on the same block, each offer well-equipped rooms and a 24-hour front desk (elevator, Kuloglu: Ayhan Işık Sokak 30, Karakol: Sadri Alışık Sokak 26). **Stories Kumbaracı** is larger and closer to Tünel, with 24 rooms and a pleasant lobby. The popular restaurant next door, Yeni Lokanta, offers a special €10 breakfast deal for hotel guests. Some rooms have Bosphorus views (elevator, Kumbaracı Yokuşu 66). **Stories Galata,** also called the **Rezidans,** is an apartment-hotel on the edge of the Karaköy neighborhood, with units available for longer-term rental. Reception is staffed during the day and there's a common lounge and kitchen in the well-lit basement (apartments, breakfast-€10, Kumbaracı Yokuşu 37—for location, see "Karaköy Hotel & Restaurants" map).

$ My Suite Istanbul is just a few minutes' walk from İstiklal Street in the Cihangir neighborhood, the SoHo of Istanbul—full of very local little shops, restaurants, and cafés. They offer two inviting hotel rooms and fifteen apartments, all decorated with warm and cheerful colors. Their central office is open 8:00-20:00; management is available by mobile phone 24/7 (Firuzağa Mahallesi, Türkgücü Caddesi 74/A, Cihangir, mobile +90 530 384 0111, www.mysuiteistanbul.com, info@mysuiteistanbul.com).

ON MEŞRUTIYET CADDESI

$$$$ Soho House Istanbul is part of a chain of pricey and elegant hotels. The hotel's public spaces are housed in a 19th century palace that was once the home of a Genoese merchant (the building later housed the American consulate). The large rooms, located in the annex, are tastefully opulent, with a decor that recalls the building's history (air-con, elevator, Meşrutiyet Caddesi 56, Beyoğlu, +90 212 377 7100, www.sohohouseistanbul.com).

$$$$ Pera Palace Hotel is the famous and historic hotel in which Agatha Christie supposedly penned her *Murder on the Orient Express*. The stately hotel has had a facelift but it still offers historic charm—and an Agatha Christie room (air-con, elevator, Meşrutiyet Caddesi 52, +90 212 377 4000, www.perapalace.com, reservations@perapalace.com).

$$$$ Galata Antique Hotel SC is housed in a 122-year-old Ottoman-French mansion designed by the same architect who did the original Pera Palace. This family-owned boutique hotel, located close to Tünel, has lots of personality, with 22 rooms differing in size and decor (RS%, air-con, "historic" elevator, Meşrutiyet Caddesi 119, Tünel, +90 212 245 5944, www.galataantiquehotel.com, info@galataantiquehotel.com).

$$ Pera Tulip Hotel is large and modern, with 85 spacious rooms on seven floors. Top-floor "executive balcony" rooms have Golden Horn views, while other rooms have windows opening to a ventilator shaft. Renowned Turkish jazz musicians sometimes perform in their lounge (air-con, elevator, Meşrutiyet Caddesi 103, Tepebaşı, +90 212 243 8500, www.peratulip.com, sales@peratulip.com).

$ Hotel Troya SC is a newly renovated hotel just a short walk from İstiklal Street. Ask for a room with a real window—some of its 77 rooms face a ventilation shaft (air-con, elevator, Meşrutiyet Caddesi 45, +90 212 251 8206, www.hoteltroya.com, troya@hoteltroya.com).

NEAR THE GALATA TOWER

$$ Anemon Galata SC is next door to the Galata Tower on the edge of the Karaköy neighborhood. This historic building has been converted into a classy boutique hotel with 28 small, Old World-plush rooms and six suites, some with impressive Bosphorus or Golden Horn views (air-con, elevator, breakfast terrace with spectacular view, Bereketzade Mahallesi, Büyükhendek Caddesi 5—for location see the "Karaköy Hotels & Restaurants" map, +90 212 293 2343, www.anemonhotels.com, galata@anemonhotels.com).

KARAKÖY

$$$ 10 Karaköy, located in the former banking and financial district of the Ottomans, is a short walk from the Golden Horn and Galata Bridge. Its 70 rooms are well appointed, fresh, and modern (RS%—includes upgrade based on availability, air-con, elevator, Kemeraltı Caddesi 10, Karaköy, Beyoğlu, +90 212 703 3333, www.morganshotelgroup.com, 10karakoy.info@mhgc.com).

$$$ Karaköy Rooms, in an elaborate early 20th-century building, offers nine simple, designer-decorated rooms with hardwood floors, plain white walls, and exposed copper pipes. Some rooms have Bosphorus views (breakfast-€10, Necatibey Caddesi, Galata Şarap İskelesi Sokak 10, Karaköy, +90 212 252 5422, www.karakoyrooms.com, info@karakoyrooms.com).

$$ The Haze Karaköy—very close to the Karaköy pier—rents rooms in two connected buildings. A simple breakfast is served on the terrace, with partial views of the Bosphorus. Helpful manager Rafi is eager to host Rick Steves readers (RS%, air-con, elevator, Necatibey Caddesi 36, Karaköy, +90 212 293 9955, www.thehazeistanbul.com, info@thehazeistanbul.com).

$$ Momento Hotel Golden Horn is right next to the Tünel funicular. Rooms here are standard and modern—and those on the fifth floor and up offer excellent 180-degree views of the Old Town and the Golden Horn. The top-floor Tersane restaurant, owned and operated by a renowned chef, offers similar views (air-con, elevator, Tersane Caddesi 24, Karaköy, +90 212 653 5050, www.momentohotelsistanbul.com, sales@hotelmomento.com).

$$ SuB Karaköy is small and charming, with modern, minimalist rooms and breakfast served in its popular café. It's located on the main artery of the Karaköy district (Necatibey Caddesi 91, Karaköy, +90 212 243 0005, http://subkarakoy.com, stay@subkarakoy.com).

$ Karaköy Port Hotel is a little tacky, with inexpensive, gold-gilded furniture, but the gasp-inducing terrace view—including the Bosphorus, Old Town, and Golden Horn—makes up for it. Its location, with many nearby eateries, comes with noise (some rooms with Bosphorus views, Tophane İskele Caddesi 10, Beyoğlu, +90 212 243 9868, www.karakoyporthotel.com, info@karakoyporthotel.com).

$ Manesol Galata Hotel is on a small street next to the

SLEEPING

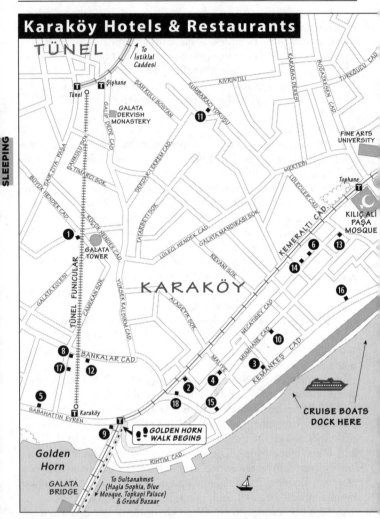

Karaköy Hotels & Restaurants

Tünel funicular. Its neat, cookie-cutter rooms are larger than average for this part of the city. Economy rooms have no windows—request a front-facing room with window when you book (air-con, elevator, Arap Cami Mahallesi, Billur Sokak 1/A, Karaköy, +90 212 245 0000, www.manesolgalata.com, info@manesolgalata.com).

$ **Nordstern Galata** is a small, 20-room hotel in a 130-year-old neo-Gothic building right next to the Galata Bridge. The rooms have high ceilings, and some have stately chandeliers and wonderful views. Rooms only have queen or king sized beds—no twins (air-con, elevator, Tersane Caddesi 5, Kara-

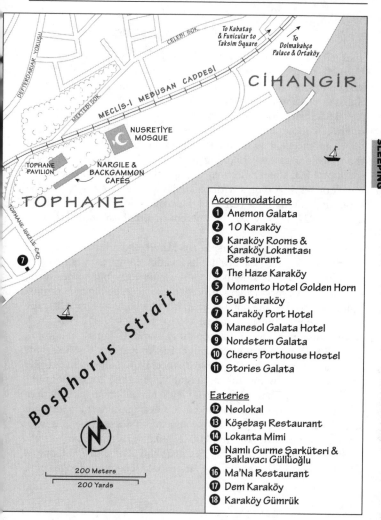

Accommodations
1. Anemon Galata
2. 10 Karaköy
3. Karaköy Rooms & Karaköy Lokantası Restaurant
4. The Haze Karaköy
5. Momento Hotel Golden Horn
6. SuB Karaköy
7. Karaköy Port Hotel
8. Manesol Galata Hotel
9. Nordstern Galata
10. Cheers Porthouse Hostel
11. Stories Galata

Eateries
12. Neolokal
13. Köşebaşı Restaurant
14. Lokanta Mimi
15. Namlı Gurme Şarküteri & Baklavacı Güllüoğlu
16. Ma'Na Restaurant
17. Dem Karaköy
18. Karaköy Gümrük

köy, +90 212 358 2222, www.nordsternhotelgalata.com, info@ nordsternhotelgalata.com).

HOSTEL

¢ **Cheers Porthouse Hostel,** a 10-room place with cheerful colors and simple decor, is one short block from the Bosphorus, and close to several fine eateries and public transportation. Family rooms and connecting rooms are available (Kemankeş Mahallesi, Mumhane Caddesi 31, Karaköy, +90 212 292 3850, www.cheersporthouse. com, info@cheersporthouse.com).

On the Bosphorus

These first two places are scenically located to the north of the New District, right on the water in the trendy Ortaköy neighborhood, known for its busy party scene. The third is on the waterfront in Kabataş, close to Dolmabahçe Palace.

$$$$ The Stay Bosphorus belongs to a hip local chain. The small, 26-room hotel is cheerful and tastefully decorated and offers an excellent value for this location. Breakfast is served in the first-floor café overlooking the strait. Though the rooms are soundproofed, street noise may be a problem for light sleepers. The top-floor seaview rooms with balconies and terraces match super-expensive competitors (Ortaköy Salhanesi Sokak 1/A, Ortaköy, +90 212 327 7787, www.thestay.com.tr, info.bosphorus@thestay.com.tr).

$$$ Radisson Blu Bosphorus Hotel, though part of a characterless chain, is a great deal for its location compared to surrounding competitors. Its smallish rooms are uniform but comfortable, and some have spectacular views of the water. A generous breakfast buffet is served in the hotel restaurant, which has a terrace literally on the water (Çırağan Caddesi 46, Ortaköy, +90 212 310 1500, www.radissonblu.com, info.bosphorus.istanbul@radissonblu.com).

$$$ Deriş Bosphorus Lodge, in the Kabataş district, rents seven apartments close to Dolmabahçe Palace. It's conveniently located near tram and funicular stations and the commuter ferry port. Some units have Bosphorus views, and all come with modern furniture, kitchens, and washing machines, making them ideal for families and long stays (panorama apartment sleeps 5, 5-night minimum, reception desk daily 8:00-23:00, overnight security staff, İnebolu Sokak 5/A, Kabataş Setüstü, +90 212 252 7913, www.derisbosphoruslodge.com, reservation@derisbosphoruslodge.com).

EATING IN ISTANBUL

Turkey's cuisine, with its roots in the Imperial Ottoman kitchen, reflects the rich cultural interaction of its ethnic ancestry: Turkish, Arab, Persian, and Greek. Indeed, what qualifies as Turkish food—and what doesn't—can be a bit ambiguous. You'll find many similar foods in the countries that neighbor Turkey. Given the immense and diverse territories that once made up the Ottoman Empire, it's no surprise that modern Turkish cuisine is multiethnic. The cuisine is further enriched by Turkey's fertile land—the varied geography and climates produce a great array of crops, vegetables, and fruits.

Turkish diners usually sit down to eat between 20:00 and 21:00, but most restaurants are ready to serve dinner much earlier. Be aware that during the religious festival of Ramadan restaurants are likely to be empty or even closed in daylight hours but busy after sunset.

I rank eateries from $ budget to $$$$ splurge. A 10 percent tip in cash is customary at sit-down cafés and restaurants; you can leave it on the table or hand it to your server when you sign the credit-card slip. While a tip isn't expected at self-service, cafeteria-style places, bussers appreciate an extra lira or two. For more details on tipping, as well as other aspects of dining in Istanbul—including types of restaurants, advice on eating during Ramadan and navigating self-service eateries, and a rundown of Turkish cuisine—see the "Eating" section in the Practicalities chapter.

In addition to my recommended restaurants, consider Turkish street food, which is cheap, filling, and easy to find, especially in high-traffic areas such as Istiklal Street. Avoid drinking tap water in Istanbul: Restaurants often serve water in plastic cups with peel-off tops, and bottled water is easy to find.

In the Old Town

SULTANAHMET AREA

These restaurants—along with many recommended hotels and much of Istanbul's best sightseeing—are concentrated in the Sultanahmet area.

$$$ Matbah Restaurant—where the manager and chef share their nearly two decades of research into imperial Ottoman cuisine—has a seasonal menu using fresh ingredients. Try the lamb neck with apricots and plums served alongside saffron rice with grape molasses; lamb shanks served with smoked eggplant puree; or *nergis kalyesi,* a vegetarian stew with mixed vegetables, walnuts, dill, and sour grapes (daily 11:30-23:30, next to Hagia Sophia in the Ottoman Imperial Hotel, Caferiye Sokak 6/1, Sultanahmet, +90 212 514 6151, www.matbahrestaurant.com).

$$$ Blue House Restaurant, located in the Blue House Hotel near the city's most important sights, boasts an outdoor terrace with amazing views of the Blue Mosque and Sea of Marmara. The atmosphere is peaceful and relaxed, and there is something for every taste on the simple menu. The staff is attentive and friendly (Dalbastı Sokak 14, Sultanahmet, daily 12:00-23:00, +90 212 638 9010).

$$$ Deraliye Ottoman Palace Cuisine is a successful example of a restaurant re-creating the sultan's food—the date of the original recipe is on the menu. Though it feels upscale with its decor and attentive staff, most diners are everyday visitors looking for unrushed, well-prepared Ottoman cuisine (Ticarethane Sokak 10, Sultanahmet, +90 212 520 7778, www.deraliyerestaurant.com).

$$$ Albura Kathisma, on eatery-lined Akbıyık Street, is a versatile restaurant where caring staff busily serve from 10:00 until midnight. It's built over the remnants of a great Byzantine palace—don't leave without peeking into the "cistern" in the basement. You have three seating options: outdoors on the front patio, in the casual and cozy interior, and on the elegant covered terrace. If you have a seating preference, consider making a reservation (Akbıyık Caddesi 36, Sultanahmet, +90 212 517 9031, www.alburakathisma.com).

$$ Cankurtaran Sosyal Tesisleri is a spacious, family-friendly restaurant located within the Byzantine city walls south of Cankurtaran Meydanı. You can eat inside or out, and the outdoor tables have a great view of the Bosphorus, Sea of Marmara, and Asian side of Istanbul (the downside is the noise from the four-lane road on the other side of the wall). The food is remarkably good and inexpensive. Their specialty, Topkapı Kebab, is a mix of chicken, veal, mushrooms, and tomatoes topped with cheese. They also serve delicious *künefe*—a sweet cheese pastry (daily 8:30-22:00, no alcohol, Ahırkapı İskele Sokak 1, Cankurtaran, +90 212 458 5414). Their simple cafeteria in the garden serves only beverages.

$-$$ *On the Backpackers' Strip:* **Akbıyık Caddesi** ("White Moustache Street") is lined with casual restaurants serving simple food and beer to a United Nations of gregarious young travelers. Eateries usually open early in the morning to offer breakfast to youth hostelers. Several small grocery stores selling basic food items and fruit are on the same street (one block below the Blue Mosque, toward the Sea of Marmara).

Budget Eateries on Divan Yolu, in the Heart of Sultanahmet

The first two famous—and very convenient—restaurants stand side-by-side on busy Divan Yolu, across the tram tracks from Hagia Sophia and the Hippodrome (just downhill from the Sultanahmet tram stop).

$$ Sultanahmet Köftecisi ("Sultanahmet Meatballs") is so famous for its meatballs that it has inspired an epidemic of copycat joints, rolling out knockoff *köfte* throughout Turkey. The very limited menu includes just two main courses (*köfte* and *şiş kebab*), four sides (including a tomato-and-onion salad and the local favorite, *piyaz*—a white-bean salad in olive oil), and two desserts. You can't come to Istanbul without sampling these *köfte* (daily 11:00-23:30, Divan Yolu 12, +90 212 520 0566, www.sultanahmetkoftesi.com).

$$ Lale Restaurant is the **"Pudding Shop,"** where a generation of vagabond hippies started their long journey east on the "Freak Road" to Kathmandu in the 1960s. (Enjoy the hippie history shared on its wall full of clippings.) Today, this much tamer but still tourist-friendly self-service cafeteria cranks out a selection of freshly cooked, seasonal Turkish food and chicken and beef kebabs. It's a well-oiled machine, but don't expect personal attention when it's crowded (daily 7:00-22:30, RS%—show this book to the cashier before you pay, Divan Yolu 6, +90 212 522 2970, www.puddingshop.com).

$$ Caferağa Medresesi, in an old madrassa (Muslim school) next to Hagia Sophia, serves basic food (mostly grilled meat and chicken) to students, amateur artists, and a handful of in-the-know locals. Drop in for a cup of traditional Turkish coffee or a meal. The setting is casual and friendly, with tables in the atrium, which is filled with hundreds of tulips in the spring (lunch served 11:00-16:00, drinks until 19:00, Sogukkuyu Çıkmazı 5, entrance on dead end off Caferiye Sokak—the alley that runs along Hagia Sophia's outer wall, +90 212 513 3601). The madrassa trains students in tra-

EATING

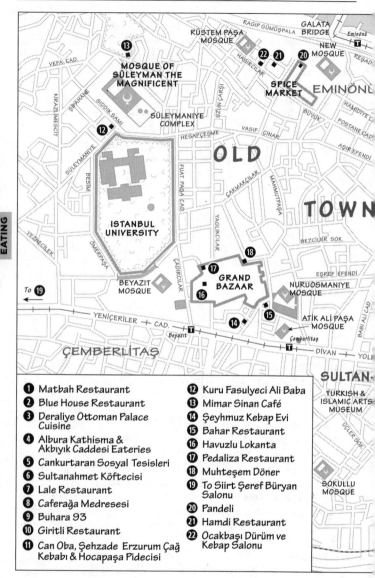

Map legend:

1. Matbah Restaurant
2. Blue House Restaurant
3. Deraliye Ottoman Palace Cuisine
4. Albura Kathisma & Akbıyık Caddesi Eateries
5. Cankurtaran Sosyal Tesisleri
6. Sultanahmet Köftecisi
7. Lale Restaurant
8. Caferağa Medresesi
9. Buhara 93
10. Giritli Restaurant
11. Can Oba, Şehzade Erzurum Çağ Kebabı & Hocapaşa Pidecisi

12. Kuru Fasulyeci Ali Baba
13. Mimar Sinan Café
14. Şeyhmuz Kebap Evi
15. Bahar Restaurant
16. Havuzlu Lokanta
17. Pedaliza Restaurant
18. Muhteşem Döner
19. To Siirt Şeref Büryan Salonu
20. Pandeli
21. Hamdi Restaurant
22. Ocakbaşı Dürüm ve Kebap Salonu

ditional Turkish arts and crafts, including tile painting, calligraphy, gold gilding, miniature painting, and the reed flute. Email in advance to join one of their workshops (caferagamedrese@tkhv.org).

Budget Eatery Behind the Blue Mosque, near the Top of the Hippodrome

To reach this popular budget option from the Hippodrome, face the

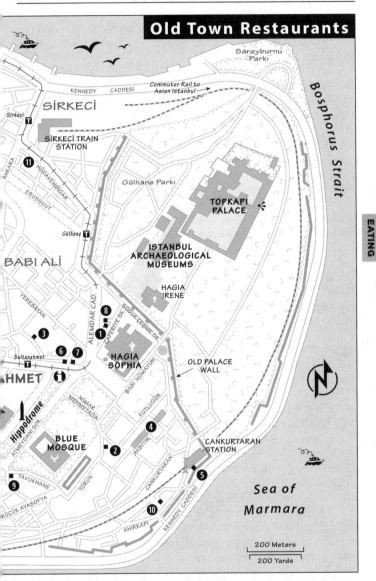

Old Town Restaurants

EATING

Column of Constantine with the Blue Mosque on your left, then leave the Hippodrome on the street to the left, and hook downhill to the right...following the sound of happy al fresco diners.

$$ Buhara 93 serves up affordable, down-to-earth food that tastes like your Turkish grandma just cooked it: simple and tasty. Their *lavaş* (flat bread) is baked after you order and served right out of the wood-fired oven. This is also a good place to sample *pide*—pitas with toppings (daily 8:00-22:30, can be crowded at lunch and early dinner but no reservations needed, no alcohol, Nakilbend Caddesi 15, +90 212 518 1511, mobile +90 544 433 9202, www. buhararestaurant.com).

Seafood Splurge near the Sea of Marmara

$$$$ Giritli Restaurant, a short hike from the Blue Mosque action, is a splurge, serving a single multicourse feast with booze. On cold evenings you'll dine in a two-story 19th-century mansion with a dressy white-tablecloth ambience. When it's hot, food is served across the lane in a walled, poolside garden with a Greek-island feel (its owners emigrated from Crete; *giritli* means "Cretan"). The mother-daughter team of İpek and Ayşe will treat you like a personal guest. The menu ranges from Aegean- and Mediterranean-style seafood to Cretan-style *mezes* and raw fish. The fixed-price meal includes rice, salad, your choice of 16 varieties of cold *mezes* and three kinds of hot *mezes* (octopus, calamari, or *pide*), a fish main course, and a bottomless local beverage—including *rakı*, beer, and wine. While expensive, it's a fine value if you enjoy seafood and wine (daily 12:00-24:00, RS%—show this book before you pay, reservations smart, several blocks south of the Blue Mosque at Keresteci Hakkı Sokak 8, +90 212 458 2270, www.giritlirestoran.com).

ELSEWHERE IN THE OLD TOWN

Arranged by neighborhood, these eateries are handy to the Old Town's various sights.

Near Sirkeci Train Station

$$$ Can Oba looks and feels like any other restaurant in the Old Town, but its owner, Chef Can Oba, was trained by a Michelin-star chef in Germany. The regular menu is similar to other area restaurants, so ask for the special seasonal menu, revised weekly (daily 12:00-22:30, a few blocks south of the train station at Hobyar Mahallesi, Mimar Vedat Sokak 5, +90 212 522 1215).

$$ Şehzade Erzurum Çağ Kebabı, a carnivore's fantasy, specializes in *yatık döner*—meat rotated over an Eastern-style horizontal coal or wood-fire grill until tender but crisp, then finely cut and served on skewers with *lavaş* bread (Mon-Sat 11:30-21:30, closed Sun, Hocapaşa Sokak 4/6, +90 212 520 3361).

$$ Hocapaşa Pidecisi is an unpretentious little eatery, with communal tables filled with locals, plus a few tourists who appear to have dropped in accidentally. Third-generation owner Yusuf Bey seems to do all the work, including preparing and baking the pita-like *pide*. Try the excellent *kavurmalı pide,* topped with dried meat—an uncommon menu item (daily 12:00-19:00—or until food is gone, no alcohol, Hocapaşa Sokak 19, +90 212 512 0990).

Near the Mosque of Süleyman the Magnificent

$ Kuru Fasulyeci Ali Baba, in the mosque's former madrassa (Muslim school), has been Istanbul's favorite bean restaurant since 1939. *Kuru fasulye* (koo-roo fah-sool-yeh) is a staple that's eaten at home at least once a week by every Turkish family. The bean soup is made with dried white beans and chunks of beef or pastrami and served with a side of rice pilaf. After the meal, try the pumpkin dessert (daily 10:00-21:00, Prof. Sıddık Sami Onar Caddesi 1/3, next to fountain and just across from entrance to mosque's outer courtyard, +90 212 520 7655). Other bean joints—not as famous or established, but fine in a pinch—populate the rest of the madrassa.

$ Mimar Sinan Café, a simple coffee shop on the large terrace of the historic Mimar Sinan Inn, offers great views of the Old Town. While the food (cheese rolls and meatballs) is basic, the hospitality and view more than make up for it (daily 8:00-22:30, Demirtaş Mahallesi, Fetva Yokuşu, Süleymaniye, Mimar Sinan Hanı 34, next to Istanbul Müftülüğü—the Directorate of Religious Affairs of Istanbul, +90 212 514 4414).

In or near the Grand Bazaar

$$ Eating at Şeyhmuz Kebap Evi is like taking a trip to the Syrian border. Its owners cook traditional kebabs just the way they do it in their hometown of Mardin, in southeast Turkey. You can hear the knives chopping meat in the open kitchen from the street. Try the *lahmacun* (*pide* topped with meat, onions, and parsley). Their specialty, *Şeyhmuz kebap,* is also good: a mix of lamb and veal served with vegetables, cheese, or pistachios (Mon-Sat 11:30-18:30, closed Sun, Atik Ali Paşa Sokak 2, Çemberlitaş, +90 212 526 1613 or +90 212 512 4102). Walk downhill from the Çemberlitaş tram stop toward the Nuruosmaniye Mosque, turn left just past the parking lot, walk a block, and take the first left.

$$ Bahar Restaurant, in Yağcı Han just outside the Grand Bazaar, is another well-known workers' restaurant. They're famous for their *abant kebab,* a mix of beef and chicken with onions, tomatoes, and green peppers, as well as their *begendili kebab*, made with lamb and eggplant (Mon-Sat 12:00-16:00, closed Sun, no alcohol, Nuruosmaniye, Yağcı Han 13, +90 212 512 7439). As you face the Grand Bazaar's Nuruosmaniye Gate, walk to your left, and then take the first right to Yağcı Han.

$$ Havuzlu Lokanta, inside the Grand Bazaar, serves a sped-up version of traditional Ottoman cuisine, with a continually changing menu. Look for the *beykoz kebab,* prepared with eggplant, veal, mushrooms, and sweet peas. The vast interior can accommodate an army of tourists (it's in all the guidebooks), but the quaint fountainside seating out front keeps you in the midst of the Grand Bazaar action (Mon-Sat 12:00-16:00, closed Sun, look for sign near Şark Kahvesi café, Gani Çelebi Sokak 3, +90 212 527 3346, www.havuzlurestaurant.com).

$$ Pedaliza Restaurant, with typical local cuisine, decent service, and high turnover, is popular among business owners in the Grand Bazaar. It's a little more upscale than other workers' restaurants, with tablecloths and pleasant outdoor seating, and it's open only until the food's gone—get there early (Mon-Sat roughly 11:00-16:00, closed Sun, Yağlıkçılar Caddesi, Cebeci Han 55, +90 212 522 5903).

$ Muhteşem Döner is a small traders' restaurant offering *döner kebab,* lamb and chicken stews, and wraps. They serve basic and hearty food, offering quick service and no frills. It's located just outside the Grand Bazaar a short walk from the Mercan Gate (Mon-Saturday, 12:00-16:00, Mercan Çıkmazı Kırıcılar Sokak 1, +90 212 519 3006).

Near the Aqueduct (Bozdoğan Kemeri)

$$ Siirt Şeref Büryan Salonu is a local favorite for its signature dish of succulent, juicy *büryan kebab*—marinated whole lamb cooked in a pit for more than two hours—served with *pide* and *perde pilavı,* a thin pastry shell filled with rice pilaf, almonds, pistachios, black pepper, and currants. The yogurt drink called *ayran* is served in large copper cups. Located in a big historic house in a conservative neighborhood, it's an easy 10-minute walk from the Mosque of Süleyman the Magnificent (daily 11:00-22:00, until later in summer, Zeyrek Mahallesi, İtfaiye Caddesi 4, Fatih Kadınlar Pazarı, +90 212 635 8085, mobile +90 535 345 3603, www.serefburyan.org).

In or near the Spice Market

$$$ Pandeli, on the Spice Market's second floor, is open for lunch only. Started by Chef Pandeli in the 1930s, it still serves a mouth-watering traditional Turkish-Ottoman menu, including an especially good eggplant *börek.* Although the restaurant always appears crowded with businesspeople, they eat quickly, so you won't wait long for a table (daily 11:30-19:00, go up tiled staircase just inside Spice Market's main entrance at Eminönü Mısır Çarşısı 1, +90 212 527 3909, www.pandeli.com.tr).

$$ Hamdi Restaurant is a smart-casual, white-tablecloth place with vested waiters, a bright glassed-in roof terrace, and great views of the city and over the water—ask for third-floor seating. They serve a variety of traditional kebabs from southeast Turkey (upper Mesopotamia), such as pistachio lamb, grilled eggplant, plum lamb, and grilled garlic lamb. The delicious *beyti* (behy-tee) *kebab*—a mix of barbecued beef and lamb wrapped in thin phyllo bread—takes longer to make. The wheat pilaf, called *firik* (fee-reek), is also good. For dessert, try the pistachio *katmer* or the baklava (daily 11:30-23:30, next to Spice Market, Kalçın Sokak 11, +90 212 528 0390, www.hamdi.com.tr). Take the elevator to the crowded third-floor terrace—the views are best from the narrow balcony (if there's an empty table here, grab it).

$$ Ocakbaşı Dürüm ve Kebap Salonu is exactly what its name suggests: *Ocakbaşı* means "by the grill." Grab a chair by the grill or join a communal table indoors or out. Specialties include the Adana kebab (spicy-hot ground beef on skewer), Urfa kebab (similar to Adana but less spicy), and chicken *şiş*—all are succulent (Mon-Sat 11:00-18:30, closed Sun, Hasırcılar Caddesi 61, +90 212 526 3229).

In the New District

ON AND NEAR İSTIKLAL STREET

These eateries are on or within a short stroll of İstiklal Street.

Near Taksim Square

$ Taksim Sütiş, while technically a "pudding shop," is a time-warp cafeteria serving everything from puddings to omelets to *döner kebabs*. Among its famous puddings, *tavuk göğüsü* (tah-vook gooh-sew) stands out. It's made with finely shredded chicken breast, but doesn't taste like chicken at all. Locals love the rice pilaf with chicken and the baklava. Consider the *su böreği* (soo boh-reh-ee), a layered pastry. On a cold day, try the *sahlep* (sah-lehp), a warm, creamy sweet drink made with the powdered roots of wild Taurus mountain orchids and served with cinnamon. The photo menu is convenient, but you can also step up to the display case and point to what you want (daily 6:00-24:00, İstiklal Caddesi 7, +90 212 251 3270).

$ Beyoğlu Halk Döner is a budget, cafeteria-style eatery right on İstiklal Street. It's bright, modern, fast, clean, and a fine value. Choose your meal from the fresh food displayed on the buffet at the entrance, and take advantage of the spacious seating areas on three floors (daily 10:30-24:00, İstiklal Caddesi 10, Beyoğlu, +90 212 243 6759).

$$ Zencefil Café is a vegetarian restaurant with a relaxing interior and a lovely garden a block away from the crowded main drag. It's also frequented by carnivores for its appetizing and healthy food and great prices. The menu of freshly grown products changes with the season. It also offers pomegranate, blueberry, and cherry fruit wines (Mon-Sat 10:00-22:30, closed Sun, at #8A on Kurabiye Sokak—a lane that runs parallel to İstiklal Street, +90 212 243 8234).

$$ Nizam Pide, part of a chain, makes great *pide*. It's like a typical traders restaurant, dishing up hearty portions, and is

EATING

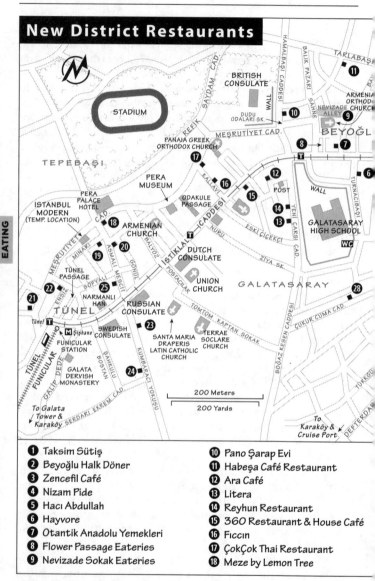

New District Restaurants

1. Taksim Sütiş
2. Beyoğlu Halk Döner
3. Zencefil Café
4. Nizam Pide
5. Hacı Abdullah
6. Hayvore
7. Otantik Anadolu Yemekleri
8. Flower Passage Eateries
9. Nevizade Sokak Eateries
10. Pano Şarap Evi
11. Habeşa Café Restaurant
12. Ara Café
13. Litera
14. Reyhun Restaurant
15. 360 Restaurant & House Café
16. Ficcin
17. ÇokÇok Thai Restaurant
18. Meze by Lemon Tree

frequented by clubbers during the wee hours for their delicious soups (daily 8:00-very late, İstiklal Caddesi, Büyükparmakkapı 18, Beyoğlu, +90 212 249 7918, www.nizampide.com).

Along Central İstiklal Street

$$$$ **Hacı Abdullah,** near the Hüseyin Ağa Mosque, is popular by locals and can be very busy. The specialty is Özel Hacı Abdullah Tabağı ("Abdullah's Special Hacı Platter"), loaded with eggplant

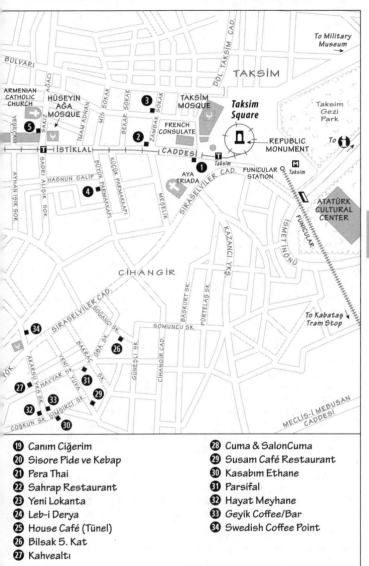

19 Canım Ciğerim
20 Sisore Pide ve Kebap
21 Pera Thai
22 Sahrap Restaurant
23 Yeni Lokanta
24 Leb-i Derya
25 House Café (Tünel)
26 Bilsak 5. Kat
27 Kahvaltı

28 Cuma & SalonCuma
29 Susam Café Restaurant
30 Kasabım Ethane
31 Parsifal
32 Hayat Meyhane
33 Geyik Coffee/Bar
34 Swedish Coffee Point

kebab, lamb shanks, and two other kebabs—enough for two. Also good are the quince desserts with honey and bananas topped with water buffalo cream, and the fresh pomegranate juice from eastern Turkey (soups and salads, several fixed-price meals, daily 11:00-22:30, closed until sundown during Ramadan, no alcohol, extra charge for water and bread, 10 percent service charge for groups of 4 or more, Atıf Yılmaz Caddesi 9/A, +90 212 293 8561, www.haciabdullah.com.tr).

EATING

The New Istanbul Style

Istanbul's new wave of restaurants and chefs are adapting to the tastes of its elite, educated young people, who want traditional but innovative food and classy but unpretentious decor. These places, clustered in the New District, tend to be well-lit, with a refined, elevated ambience where chefs interact with diners. Many offer tasting menus for a set price.

$$$ Yeni Lokanta has a somewhat experimental menu based on traditional Turkish food. Owner Civan Er, a famous chef and columnist who enjoys talking to guests, creates delicious dishes with unusual combinations, such as ravioli stuffed with dried eggplant. The place has a smart bistro feel with geometric floor tiles, traditional İznik tiles on the bar, and bread served in copper pots. Reservations are a good idea for weekend dinners (tasting menu for two, prices a bit higher for dinner, Mon-Sat 12:00-16:00 & 18:00-22:30, closed Sun, just off İstiklal Street at Kumbaracı Yokuşu 66, Beyoğlu, +90 212 292 2550, www.yenilokanta.com).

$$$ Meze by Lemon Tree, fronted by wall-to-wall windows, is small, simple, and friendly. It's the kind of place where locals casually chat between tables and owner/chef Gencay explains the food. His culinary creations evolve with the seasons, featuring whatever's freshest at the market (tasting menu for two, near historic Pera Palace Hotel at Meşrutiyet Caddesi 83/B, Beyoğlu, +90 212 252 8302, www.mezze.com.tr).

$$$$ Neolokal, the trendy restaurant of renowned Chef Maksut Aşkur, boasts a well-educated team of cooks who prepare delicious, innovative international and local dishes, always with the best ingredients. It is located on the top floor of SALT Galata, a cultural center and modern art gallery. The structure is a historical landmark built by a famous 19th-century architect, Alexandre Vallaury. The dining area is elegant, and the floor-to-ceiling window offers amazing views of the domes and minarets of the Old Town. Their set-price tasting menu for two offers a sampling of some of their best items (daily 18:00-24:00 or later, Salt Galata, Bankalar Caddesi 11, Karaköy, +90 212 244 0016, www.neolokal.com, see map on page 334).

$-$$ Hayvore, tucked into a long and narrow space near Galatasaray High School, is the place for Black Sea cuisine. Specialties include red mullet and anchovy dishes, fish and kale soups, bean stews, and a Black Sea fondue with cheese, corn flour, and butter called *muhlama* (daily 08:00-22:30, no alcohol, Turnacıbaşı Caddesi Sokak 4, Beyoğlu, +90 212 245 7501).

$$ Otantik Anadolu Yemekleri is so successful that it quickly became a chain. Next to the entrance to the Flower Passage, it serves traditional Anatolian food, representing different ethnic groups living within Turkey. It's a great opportunity to sample affordable cuisine from around the country. Watch as the costumed cooks prepare the *gözleme* bread. The restaurant has the ambience of a practical diner, with a handy photo menu that makes ordering easy, and four floors of seating that ensure that there's plenty of space (daily 9:00-24:00, İstiklal Caddesi 80/A, +90 212 293 8451).

$$$ In the Flower Passage (Çiçek Pasajı): The Flower Passage is not one restaurant, but a row of seafood places with six-seat tables (you'll share) in a historic, beautifully restored passage on İstiklal Street. The 10 restaurants are mostly interchangeable, with similar value, quality, and a genteel late-19th-century atmosphere. In the evening, some have live music, usually traditional Istanbul songs. But the area is grotesquely touristy and overpriced, and because many menus include unlimited alcohol, drunkenness crescendos as the night wears on (daily 12:00-24:00, İstiklal Caddesi). For more on the history of the passage, see page 268.

$$$ On Nevizade Sokak: This lane, just a block off İstiklal Street, past the fish market, is home to several reliably good restaurants. It's where trendy locals head for a seafood dinner. Bars and restaurants line up one after the other on either side of the street. In spring and summer, they set tables out front, making the place seem even more crowded, fun, and noisy. Restaurants take pride in their *mezes* and compete to serve the widest variety. Try the casual pubs if all you want is a glass of beer and simple seafood *meze* (e.g., a platter of calamari or deep-fried mussels). Restaurants here are also casual, but they'll serve you a full meal with all the frills. The prices and variety of food are similar to those in the Flower Passage, listed earlier.

$$$ Pano Şarap Evi, in a beautiful Art Nouveau building near the fish market, dates from the late 1800s and is the oldest wine house in Istanbul. Their menu is rich with pastas and grilled dishes. The colorful, over-the-top interior is picturesque to some, but overkill to others. Reservations recommended (daily 16:00–1:00, Hüseyin Ağa Mahallesi, Hamalbaşı Caddesi 12, Beyoğlu, +90 212 292 6664, www.panosarapevi.com).

$$$ Habeşa Café Restaurant, a few blocks north of the Armenian Orthodox Church, is a low-key place dishing out traditional Ethiopian cuisine served on flatbread. Upstairs is an Ethiopian-style bar featuring traditional music, dance, and a coffee ceremony—coffee beans are roasted, ground, and brewed on the spot (daily 12:00-24:00, Hüsetin Ağa, Ekrem Tur Sokak 5, Beyoğlu, mobile +90 532 226 7066).

West of Galatasaray High School

$$ Ara Café, between the old post office and İstiklal Street, is owned by Ara Güler, the renowned Turkish-Armenian photojournalist. A popular place to see and be seen, the café attracts intellectuals, yuppies, and models. Grab a table outdoors in nice weather, or opt for a spot in the cozy split-level interior (daily 9:00-23:30, Tosbağa Sokak 2, +90 212 245 4105).

$$$$ Litera is a terrace restaurant and lounge club with sprawling views over the city and the Bosphorus. Come during happy hour (16:00-18:00) for a *meze* and a main course to share between two, plus a glass of wine or beer each, at discount prices. Check out their good, diverse wine list. Reservations recommended (daily 16:00–02:00, RS%—show this book for discount, light jazz and blues music on some weekends; near Galatasaray High School at Tomtom Mahallesi Yeni Çarşı Caddesi 32/6, +90 212 292 8947 or +90 212 292 8950, www.literarestaurant.com).

$$$ Reyhun Restaurant, near Litera, is a dedicated Persian establishment (don't be put off by the tacky neon sign). Its roomy interior offers seating in a modern, white-washed section or in a more traditional section with brick walls and tiled tables. Or, enjoy the large terrace in back that's shaded by the massive walls of St. Anthony's Church (daily 12:00-22:30, reservations suggested for dinner, no alcohol, Yeni Çarşı Caddesi 26/1, Beyoğlu; +90 212 245 1500, www.iranyemekleri.com).

$$$$ 360 is a hip restaurant with a 360-degree view of the city from a terrace atop an Art Nouveau building not far from Galatasaray High School. After hours, the restaurant becomes a club with a diverse clientele (cover charge). Reserve ahead to dine among the jet set, consulate employees, and businesspeople who enjoy the pricey international cuisine (Tue-Sun lunch starts at 12:00, dinner served in two seatings: 20:00-22:00 & 22:00-24:00, closed Mon; nightclub open from 24:00 Thu-Sat in summer, Fri-Sat in winter; İstiklal Caddesi, Mısırlı Apartmanı 163, 8th floor, Beyoğlu, +90 212 251 1042, www.360istanbul.com).

$-$$ Fıccın, across İstiklal Caddesi from St. Anthony's Church, serves tasty cuisine of the Caucasus (they're best known for their dumplings) and is a popular lunch spot with both blue- and white-collar workers. It morphs into a *meyhane* for dinner, with live *oud*, *saz*, and zither music (Mon-Sat 07:00-23:00, Sun 12:00-23:00, Kallavi Sokak, Beyoğlu, +90 212 293 3786).

$$$ ÇokÇok Thai Restaurant, a block off İstiklal, is a good choice if you want a break from Turkish food—they even import organic ingredients from Thailand. You'll choose from a menu created by a chef who has cooked for the Thai royal family, and dine in an interior designed by an award-winning architect. Owner Mr. Bekir values Rick Steves travelers, and if he's around you may receive a small gift as a gesture of his appreciation (daily 12:00-

23:00, Meşrutiyet Caddesi 51, Tepebaşı, Beyoğlu, +90 212 292 6496, www.cokcok.com.tr).

Near the Pera Palace Hotel

In addition to these places, consider **Meze by Lemon Tree,** described in "The New Istanbul Style" sidebar, earlier.

$$$ Canım Ciğerim, spread across three floors with some outdoor tables in the front, is a typical Turkish restaurant. Their specialty is lamb liver, the Turkish counterpart of foie gras. Main courses come with grilled onions, peppers, fresh arugula, and a tomato-based *meze*. It's fun to watch the action in their open kitchen (daily 11:00-02:00, no alcohol, staff speaks no English, just point and use body language, Asmalı Mescit Minare Sokak 1, Beyoğlu, +90 212 252 6060).

$$ Sisore Pide ve Kebap is a simple restaurant that serves mainly *pides* from the Black Sea, along with a variety of dishes and soups prepared fresh each day. Try *kavurmalı* (roasted meat) or *pastırmalı* (pastrami) on *pide* (daily 7:00-24:00, near the Pera Palace Hotel at Oteller Sokak 6, Asmalı Mescit Mahallesi, Beyoğlu, +90 212 245 4900).

$$ Pera Thai, a small, modest restaurant close to the Şişhane metro stop, serves up delicious Thai food, including vegetarian options. The food does not contain MSG, and spice levels can be customized. Head waiter İsmail Saydır is eager to please. Reserve ahead on weekends, especially in fall and winter (Mon-Sat 12:00-23:00, closed Sun; Meşrutiyet Caddesi 94/A, Tünel, +90 212 245 5725, www.perathai.com.tr).

$$$ Sahrap Restaurant, owned by popular Turkish food writer Sahrap Soysal, is frequented by smartly dressed locals and expats. Though it's brightly lit and spotlessly clean, it still feels warm and welcoming, with its old-style floor tiles, turquoise wall decorations resembling traditional Seljuk ceramics, and wooden furniture. Well-trained waiters literally wait on you, keeping a comfortable distance (off of the Meşrutiyet Caddesi and close to İstiklal Street at General Yazgan Sokak 13, Asmalı Mescit, +90 212 243 1616, www.sahraprestaurant.com).

Near the Tünel End of İstiklal Caddesi

In addition to these places, consider **Yeni Lokanta,** described in "The New Istanbul Style" sidebar, earlier.

$$$$ Leb-i Derya is an elegant, white tablecloth kind of place with a beautiful view. Offerings include grilled octopus, stuffed kalamari, and delicacies of Antakya, formerly Antioch of biblical fame. It's a popular spot, especially during dinner—reservations are a must (daily 16:00-01:00—order dinner before 22:30,

Şahkulu Mahallesi, Kumbaracı Yokuşu 57, Tünel, Beyoğlu, mobile +90 541 366 8480, www.lebiderya.com).

$$$ House Café, part of a trendy, gay-friendly chain, makes up for its slow service with good ambience and a wide variety of eclectic food. In addition to the İstiklal Street location (in the Mısırlı Apartmanı building at #163, Mon-Thu 9:00-2:00 in the morning, Fri-Sat until 4:00 in the morning, Sun until 24:00, +90 212 251 7991), you'll find branches at Tünel (Asmalımescit Sokak 9), and literally right on the Bosphorus in the Ortaköy district (on Salhane Sokak 1).

IN CİHANGİR

This neighborhood between İstiklal Caddesi and the Karaköy district is known for its bohemian atmosphere, narrow lanes, and street cafés, which historically attracted artists and writers.

$$$ Bilsak 5.Kat ("Bilsak 5th Floor"), decorated with dramatic flair, is a fine restaurant with sweeping views of Istanbul. It's owned and operated by theater director/producer Yasemin Alkaya, with help from her mom. The gay-friendly Bilsak is a key player in Istanbul's evening scene, with a faithful clientele. The menu has something for every taste. Reservations are smart (daily, bar from 17:00, dinner 19:00-24:00, close to Taksim Square at Soğancı Sokak 7, 5th floor, Cihangir, +90 212 293 3774, www.5kat.com).

$$ Kahvealtı, near the Firuzağa Mosque in Cihangir, is a popular, gay-friendly restaurant and café serving tasty organic and natural food (daily 9:30-21:30, Akarsu Caddesi, Anahtar Sokak 13/A, +90 212 293 0849).

$$$ Cuma, in a small house with a side porch and outdoor seating, offers casual, retro dining set amid antique and collectible shops. Their wide-ranging menu includes international dishes, and they make their own bread using flour from native non-GMO wheat (RS% offered by manager Banu Tiryakioğlu, Mon–Sat 09:00-24:00, Sun 09:00-20:00, Çukurcuma Caddesi 53/A, Beyoğlu, +90 212 293 2062, www.cuma.cc).

$$$$ SalonCuma, on the second floor of Cuma, above, comes with chandeliers, candlesticks and hardwood floors—it feels like dining at an aristocrat's home. Reservations are recommended (RS% offered by manager Banu Tiryakioğlu, dinner only Thu-Fri 18:00-24:00 or later, Çukurcuma Caddesi 53/A, Beyoğlu, +90 212 293 2062, www.cuma.cc).

$$$ Susam Café Restaurant is a good place to go to mingle with locals. Serving Mediterranean cuisine and offering a rich wine-and-beverage menu, its casual ambience is inviting and relaxing (daily 10:00-01:00, Cihangir Mahallesi, Susam Sokak 11, Beyoğlu, +90 212 251 5995).

$$$ Kasabım Ethane, a carnivore's dream, is a longtime

butcher shop that's now a meat-and-kebab restaurant. Try their staple "İskender kebab," a *döner kebab* served with tomato dressing and butter (daily 11:00-22:30, Kılıç Ali Paşa, Şimşirci Sok 4/A, Beyoğlu, +90 212 251 2575).

$ Parsifal, an acclaimed vegan/vegetarian restaurant, is cozy and pleasant, with lots of framed pictures on the walls and vintage wooden chairs and tables. The food is healthy and cheap; their mushroom burger and oyster-mushroom wrap are particularly delicious (RS% by manager Nahit Tütüncüoğşu, daily 12:00-22:45, Havyar Sokak 34, Cihangir, +90 212 243 5025).

$$$ Hayat Meyhane is a fresh and roomy "new age" restaurant/bar serving *mezes* that are a fusion of Turkish and international cuisine, along with standard *meze* fare. Try the fish that's cooked on a charcoal grill. English-speaking owner Tarkan often takes time to introduce guests to Turkish *meyhane* jargon and culture (daily 14:00-24:00, Kılıç Ali Paşa Caddesi, Akarsu Yokuşu 25/1 Beyoğlu, +90 212 293 5374).

$$ Geyik Coffee Roastery and Cocktail Bar is a cool hangout and meeting point for locals that serves only simple finger food to have with your drink (daily 16:00-02:00, Cihangir Akarsu Yokuşu 22, Beyoğlu, mobile +90 532 727 0957).

$$ Swedish Coffee Point is a neat and tidy local hangout with a large coffee menu. The half-Swedish, half-Turkish owner—a self-appointed ambassador of Swedish desserts—bakes up tasty cinnamon rolls and cakes. The small outdoor space offers good people-watching, if you can stand the cigarette smoke (daily 8:30-22:00, Kuloğlu Mahallesi, Firuzağa Cami Sokak 2E, Cihangir, +90 212 243 9453).

IN KARAKÖY

These restaurants, along with **Neolokal** (described in "The New Istanbul Style" sidebar, earlier), are located in the up-and-coming neighborhood of Karaköy. See the map on page 334 for locations.

$$ Karaköy Lokantası, with a down-to-earth ambience and flashy blue tiles, is a well-known landmark famous for its vegetarian and seafood *mezes* and main courses, such as sea bass baked in foil. Rushed service hasn't hurt its popularity (Mon-Sat lunch served 12:00-16:00, tavern-style dinner served 18:00-23:00; Sun dinner only; Kemankeş Caddesi 37A, +90 212 292 4455).

$$$ Köşebaşı Restaurant, a typical Turkish grill, is small but feels spacious thanks to its floor-to-ceiling windows. You'll find fresh flowers on every table, and the respectful waiters speak just enough English. A favorite of locals, reservations are recommended for dinner (daily 11:30–23:00, a short walk from all my hotels in this area, at Necatibey Caddesi, Gecekuşu Sokak 6, +90 212 293 1999, www.kosebasi.com/sube/karakoy/).

EATING

Cooking Classes

Spanning three continents, the Ottoman Empire united various peoples—and cuisines. Innovative palace chefs worked hard to please a discerning sultan, bringing together the culinary traditions of European, Asian, and Middle Eastern nations to create one of the world's most diverse cuisines. For an introduction to the tricks of the Turkish kitchen, spend a few hours (or a few days) learning how to make a meal fit for a sultan.

Cooking Alaturka: This restaurant in the Sultanahmet area is run by Rocco Strazzera and his Turkish wife Leyla. The couple teach students in English how to cook a Turkish meal—soup, cold appetizer cooked in olive oil, main course, and dessert—in about two hours (€65 or equivalent in other currencies, price includes 5-course meal and beverages; several classes weekly usually 10:30-14:30 or 16:30-20:30, other times available on request, closed Sun; Akbıyık Caddesi 72A, a few blocks from the Blue Mosque, +90 212 458 5919, Rocco's mobile +90 539 982 3360, www.cookingalaturka.com).

Turkish Flavours: These cooking lessons are taught by a small group of culinary specialists in their uptown condos on the Asian side of the Bosphorus. The half-day experience includes shopping in a food market followed by a hands-on cooking experience. Recipes are geared for home-cooking, and the menu changes seasonally. The team is headed by Selin, who can also share Jewish delicacies from her Sephardic heritage ($100-125/person, mobile +90 532 218 0653, www.turkishflavours.com).

Istanbul Cooking School: This school, in Tarlabaşı near Taksim, is run by several young chefs ($70/class, cash only, sessions run daily 10:30-15:00 and 15:30-20:00; Kamer Hatun Mahallesi, Tarlabaşı Bulvarı 117/2, Beyoğlu, mobile +90 545 554 6677, www.istanbulcookingschool.com).

$$ Lokanta Mimi is a tiny place serving sustainable, seasonal, and healthy food that's mostly slow-cooked in the oven. Find their daily menu on the chalkboard, and check out the seasonal menu at each table. This is a good choice for breakfast, lunch, or an early dinner. Show this book and you may receive a thank-you gift from owner/chefs Dilruba and Ferhat (Mon-Sat 8:00–20:00, closed Sun, Hacimimi Mahallesi, Necatibey Caddesi 87, mobile +90 533 582 9255).

$$ Namlı Gurme Şarküteri is a deli with table service just a few steps from the cruise port. Popular and bustling with locals, it's renowned for its breakfast. There's no menu: Just pick and choose from the colorful displays and pay by the weight (daily 7:00-22:00, Kemankeş Caddesi, Kat Otoparkı Altı 29, +90 212 293 6880).

$$$ Ma'Na Restaurant is located right at the entrance to the French Passage, a characteristic alley passing through a historic 19th-century building. Neat and elegant with crisp white tablecloths, it offers indoor dining as well as an outdoor patio with several tables (daily 12:00-23:00, Kemankeş Mahallesi, Fransız Geçidi 53, +90 212 293 0993).

$ Dem Karaköy, a cross between a teahouse and a *pattiserie*, is a good choice for breakfast or just to take a break. Choose from a vast selection of teas to enjoy in this roomy space along with its youthful clientele (daily 10:00-21:00, near the base of the Tünel funicular, Arap Cami Mahallesi, Söğüt Sokak 1, +90 212 243 6885).

$$-$$$ Karaköy Gümrük is hip, casual and stylish, with a local clientele. Their Mediterranean menu includes some traditional Anatolian tastes as well, plus they have a good list of both local and rare Thracian wines. It's busy with office workers during lunch, and reservations are recommended for dinner (Mon-Sat 10:00-23:00, Necatibey Caddesi, Gümrük Sokak 4—a short walk from the Galata Bridge and the Tünel funicular station, +90 212 244 2252).

For Dessert: $ Baklavacı Güllüoğlu is the most recognized name in quality baklava. Their main shop is right across from the cruise port at Rıhtım Caddesi, Katlı Otopark Altı 3-4, Karaköy (+90 212 293 0910, www.karakoygulluoglu.com). You'll spot other Baklavacı Güllüoğlu shops around the city—they're owned and operated by rival brothers and cousins, vying for the right to use the popular brand name. All serve fine baklava (for more on this honey-infused treat, see the sidebar on page 472).

BEYOND THE NEW DISTRICT

Kumpir **Stands in Ortaköy:** At the entrance to a popular pedestrian area on the Bosphorus, a row of stands serve *kumpir* (kuhm-peer): baked potatoes topped with your choice of ingredients. Often, you'll find additional options, such as stuffed or deep-fried mussels. Buy your food, follow the local crowd toward the water, and look for an empty bench (or sit at a waterfront coffee-shop table and get a drink) and enjoy the view of Asian Istanbul and the Old Town's silhouette. Weekends are crowded, especially in nice weather (daily 10:00-1:00 in the morning, Mecidiye Köprüsü Sokak, Ortaköy).

In Asian Istanbul

$$ Kadı Nimet Balıkçısı, at the heart of Kadıköy market area, provides seating indoors surrounded by photos of Atatürk and early national leaders, or at outdoor tables amid the hubbub. The food is great (try the hard-to-find nettle salad), but the service is not. You may see a pet goose—like the one on the restaurant's logo (daily 12:00-23:00, Serasker Caddesi 10/A, Kadıköy; for location, see the "Kadıköy" map on page 310; +90 216 348 7389). For other Kadıköy eating options, see the "Kadıköy Neighborhood Walk" (beginning on page 309).

$$$$ Lacivert, a classy seafood restaurant with magnificent views and tables right on the water, has a boat that will pick you up anywhere along the Bosphorus. It's best when it's warm enough for outdoor seating. Reservations are essential (daily 12:00-17:00 & 18:00-24:00, Körfez Caddesi 57/A, Anadolu Hisari, Beykoz, on the Asian bank of Bosphorus, just under the Fatih Sultan Mehmet Bridge, +90 216 413 4224, www.lacivertrestaurant.com).

EATING

SHOPPING IN ISTANBUL

Shopping can provide a good break from Istanbul's mosques, museums, and monuments. And diving into the city's bustling, colorful marketplaces can be a culturally enlightening experience. In this chapter, you'll find information on shopping for textiles, ceramics and tiles, gold and silver, carpets, spices, souvenirs, and bargains.

İndirim (een-dee-reem) is Turkish for "sale." July, August, January, and February are the big months for sales; in January, sales start right after the shopping frenzy for New Year's Day is over (most Turks don't celebrate Christmas, but they do buy gifts for New Year's).

Istanbul's merchants, especially at the Grand Bazaar and touristy areas in the Old Town, can be aggressive and may try to engage you in casual conversation as an entrée to offering products for sale. It's OK to say, "No, thanks"—firmly—and walk on by. (For more tips, see the sidebar on page 195.)

For information on VAT refunds and customs, see page 455.

WHERE TO SHOP

Shopping in the Grand Bazaar and at other Old Town merchants (such as the Arasta Bazaar craft market tucked behind the Blue Mosque) is lively, memorable, and fun, and prices can be low—but the quality is often questionable. Though it's also touristy, you won't want to miss the colorful, aromatic Spice Market.

Istanbul's residents prefer shopping at the

more expensive but reliably good-quality stores on and near İstiklal Street in the New District. This area is less colorful—it feels like a shopping street in any big European city—but you won't feel preyed upon or pressured by vendors.

This book includes self-guided tours of most of these areas (see the Grand Bazaar Tour, New District Walk, and Old Town Back Streets Walk chapters); you could combine your shopping with one of those tours.

WHAT TO BUY
Textiles, Silk, and Leather

Turkish textiles—known around the world—are the country's biggest industry and a source of local pride. While Turkey was once a major manufacturer for international clothing labels, competition from China has forced local clothing-makers to change tactics: Turkey now focuses on producing its own labels, in the hope of competing in the world market. These **clothing** brands, such as Mavi Jeans, are well made and affordable. To get the best merchandise, go beyond the Old Town to the New District and other uptown neighborhoods; İstiklal Street and the Taksim Square area are your best bets.

Many people associate Turkey with **pashminas**—high-quality shawls traditionally made with Himalayan goat wool. And, in fact, the Old Town is a pashmina paradise, with every color of the rainbow. But Turkey doesn't produce pashmina wool, so the ones you see here are either imports or imitations. Still, they're practical and fun, and cheaper than similar imitations sold in the US.

A *peştemal* (pehsh-teh-mahl) is a large, thin, cotton **bath towel** that Turks wrap around themselves at the baths; nowadays they're also used as curtains or tablecloths. Bathing Turks scrub away dead skin and dirt with *kese* (keh-seh)—simple rectangular **mittens** made out of raw silk or synthetic fabric.

Turkey produces wonderful **silk,** but be careful: In the Grand Bazaar and other Old Town shops, scarves and other items billed as silk are often made of polyester or, at best, low-grade silk. Most **leather** goods are a better deal in the US than in Turkey. Shoes and bags are the exception: If you're into Italian-style leather shoes, you're in the right place. For real silk scarves and shawls, and quality leather shoes, head to İstiklal Street in the New District.

In the Grand Bazaar: Cashmere House carries a wide array of shawls and scarves in materials ranging from synthetic to high-end cashmere and pashmina wool. Items have price tags, but there is still a little wiggle room for bargaining. Owner İlyas and his brother Yusuf take time to give you accurate information about their products (RS%—bargain anonymously, then show this book for an added discount of up to 5 percent). To locate the shop, enter the Grand Bazaar at the Nuruosmaniye Gate, walk straight and turn right at the fourth street, keep walking down the hill until you see the fountain, then find Cashmere House on the right corner at Keseciler Caddesi 49.

Look for authentically Turkish bath towels and mittens at the **Eğin Tekstil** and other shops on Yağlıkçılar Caddesi in the Grand Bazaar (see page 201).

The **Sivaslı Yazmacı** shop carries a wide collection of hand-made textiles, including the traditional gauzy cotton *yazma*, the head covering worn by rural Turkish women (on the same street as Eğin Tekstil, Yağlıkçılar Caddesi 57, Grand Bazaar).

Nurem carries fabrics from the heart of the Silk Road (specialties: Uzbek and Uighur needlework known as *suzani* and dyed ikat fabrics). They sell items such as pillowcases and handbags, as well as fabric priced by the meter (prices fixed, RS%—10 percent discount with this book, Yağlıkçılar Caddesi, Çukur Han 63/4, Grand Bazaar, +90 212 519 5926, mobile +90 533 313 2379).

In the Spice Market: Tuğra carries quality leather goods and bags. Prices are negotiable (RS%—bargain anonymously, then show this book to owner Mehmet Gülçek or senior staffer Mehmet Akif for an added discount of up to 10 percent; Spice Market 70, +90 212 527 6701).

At Arasta Bazaar, Near the Blue Mosque: Run by a Canadian expat, **Jennifer's Hamam** sells bath towels, bathrobes, *keses*, and tablecloths at set prices. They're made by a small group of fine weavers from throughout Turkey, using organic fibers on old-style shuttle looms (Arasta Bazaar 135 & 43, +90 212 518 0548).

Ahmet owns two eclectic stores in the Arasta Bazaar. **Sufi,** at #27, offers fine felt works, a wide spectrum of pashminas from cheap synthetics to expensive originals, handmade olive oil soaps, and dresses. All items carry price tags, but there's room to bargain. **Art East,** at #46, sells collectibles, semiprecious jewelry, art, and handicrafts (RS%—bargain anonymously, show this book for an added discount of up to 10 percent).

In the New District: Near St. Anthony's Church on İstiklal Street, **İpek Silk Shop** has knowledgeable employees and reliable, quality silk. Isaac and his helpful staff speak English and are happy to demonstrate the latest in scarf fashion (İstiklal Caddesi 120, +90 212 249 8207).

Carpets and Kilims

If you're considering buying a Turkish carpet, it's worth knowing a bit about what you're looking for—if only to avoid advertising your inexperience. For example, folding a carpet to check the knots not only will give you away as a novice but can actually ruin a silk carpet. Rubbing a carpet with a piece of wet tissue to test its colorfastness is akin to licking a shirt before you buy it. And beware of shopkeepers who stress "authenticity" over quality. Authenticity is an important consideration when shopping for traditional wool-on-wool carpets. But for wool-on-cotton or silk-on-silk, it can actually be better to get a piece made with newer techniques, which produce tighter weaves, brighter and more durable colors, and more intricate patterns.

Carpets range in price from several hundred dollars to several thousand or more, depending on the age, size, quality, and uniqueness. Merchants will ship them home for you, though many tourists find it cheaper and more foolproof to carry them back (the carpets can be folded and tied tightly into a squarish bundle).

Wool-on-wool carpets, which are made of wool pile on a wool skeleton (formed by vertical warp and horizontal weft threads), are the most traditional kind of Turkish carpet. These are still being woven in countryside villages, though that is becoming less common. Each region has its own distinctive, centuries-old design-and-color combination. In general, wool-on-wool carpets cost less than other Turkish rugs. The best way to gauge the authenticity of a wool-on-wool carpet is to look for natural, less-vibrant colors that come from vegetable dyes made from local plants. Density—the number of knots per inch—is less important to the quality of a wool-on-wool carpet. Fewer knots don't signify a lower-quality wool rug, but they do mean that the rug is more likely to stretch over time.

Newer carpet styles, such as **wool-on-cotton** (wool pile on a cotton skeleton) and **silk-on-silk,** first appeared in the 19th century. The new materials allowed weavers to create more intricate floral and geometric patterns than those found in traditional designs. (A weaver can fit more knots onto a cotton skeleton than onto a wool one.) Professional designers make these patterns with the exact thickness of the yarn in mind—so irregular hand-spun wool won't work. Wool-on-cotton and silk-on-silk carpets are colored with chemical dyes, which can be as good as natural dyes or even better. If someone tries to sell you a wool-on-cotton carpet

How to Get the Best Bargain

Many visitors to Istanbul are surprised to find that bargaining for a lower price is no longer common in much of the city. At modern stores or shopping malls, posted prices are final. But in the tourist zones—such as the Grand Bazaar, Spice Market, and other shops around the Old Town—merchants know you're expecting to haggle...and they're happy to play along. (Local shoppers have less patience for this game. Notice that even in the Grand Bazaar, locals don't often haggle—if they think  something is overpriced, they either ask for a discount or simply walk away.)

In the Old Town market areas where bargaining is common, you'll constantly be bombarded by sales pitches. If you aren't interested in what they're selling, try not to establish eye contact. Although this may feel rude, it's the best way to avoid unnecessary conversations and save your time and energy for the items you do want.

If you are interested in an item, don't make it obvious. Take your time, browse around, and pretend you might just wander off at any moment—feigned disinterest is part of the game. You're better off keeping a low profile—this isn't the time to show off your nicest clothes, jewelry, and wads of cash.

Merchandise often doesn't have price tags, because shop owners want you to ask—giving them an opening to launch into a sales pitch. Don't suggest a number; let them be the first to mention a price. When they do, assume it's elevated. Even if you counter with only half their original offer, you may find your price easily accepted—meaning you've already offered too much.

More likely, a spirited haggling war will ensue. If you don't like to bargain, you'll pay more than you should. Play along to get a lower price and a fun cultural interaction. These haggling sessions can drag on for some time, as you sip tea (usually apple flavored) offered by shopkeepers who want to keep you around. When you start to walk away, that last price they call out is often the best price you'll get.

There's room for bargaining even on fixed-price commodities, such as gold and silver, where you're being charged not only for the precious metal but also for the workmanship.

If you're haggling over something unique, be prepared to pay a premium. Shopkeepers already know that you won't be able to find it elsewhere.

by advertising that it's "made with hand-spun wool" or "dyed with vegetable colors," or that it "features a traditional design, passed from mother to daughter," walk away. Unlike wool-on-wool carpets, density is important in assessing quality for wool-on-cotton and silk-on-silk carpets.

The towns of Hereke and Kayseri are famous for their carpets. **Hereke** (heh-reh-keh) carpets are denser, require much more workmanship, and are more expensive. Authentic Hereke carpets are becoming rare, and cheap imported knockoffs are in the market nowadays, so watch out. **Kayseri** (kigh-seh-rih) wool-on-cotton and silk-on-silk carpets generally have floral designs. Their wool-on-wool carpets are favored for their unique patterns and lively colors.

Kilims (kee-leem) feature a flat weave without the pile, similar to a Navajo rug. These also have traditional designs and natural colors. Used in the past as blankets and bedspreads, they're mainly popular now as decorative items (and can be used as wall hangings). Kilims are generally inexpensive, but old and rare pieces can cost several thousand dollars. For a wearable, affordable kilim, consider a vest made from the material; you'll see these at the Grand Bazaar and elsewhere.

Ultimately, locals explain, it's a toss-up whether you pay less for a carpet in Turkey or at a good importer back home. But for many travelers, buying a Turkish carpet in Turkey is worth the premium. If that's your preference, be a smart consumer and equip yourself with good information.

Shopping Suggestions: At both of the following places, shop anonymously as you haggle, then, before you pay, show this book for an additional discount.

Punto of Istanbul, a couple of blocks away from the Grand Bazaar's Nuruosmaniye Gate, carries a wide variety of carpets—from simple kilims to fancy silk carpets—and has down-to-earth prices compared to most (RS%—show book to manager Metin, Nuruosmaniye Caddesi, Gazi Sinan Paşa Sokak, Vezirhan 17, +90 212 511 0854).

Nearby **Vezirhan Handmade Carpets,** owned and operated by the Abi family from eastern Turkey, has a good collection (at decent prices) of tribal carpets and kilims, as well as vintage carpets and the usual varieties found elsewhere. The owners are easy to communicate with and eager to come to a mutually satisfactory agreement (RS%—show book to any of the Abi family members, Nuruosmaniye Caddesi, Gazi Sinan Paşa Sokak, Vezirhan 1, +90 212 519 5510).

Tiles and Ceramics

A Turkish ceramic specialty is çini (chee-nee), which is usually translated in English as "**tile**" (or "quartz tile"). The word *çini* can describe flat tiles used for architectural decoration or functional items such as bowls, vases, and cups. The clay in *çini* products has a high quartz content and is difficult to work with. High-quality glazed *çini* tiles were at their peak in the 16th and 17th centuries, and the style is considered very traditional in Turkey. Other ceramics (*seramik;* seh-rah-meek) don't have much of a history here—though you will find them sold in markets. You'll also see **pottery** (*çömlek;* chuhrm-lehk): simple, fired earthenware objects shaped on a wheel, usually without any design or glaze.

Many stores sell copies of old, authentic tiles as well as new designs. When comparing tiles for quality, keep these tips in mind: Recycled clay has a creamy, darker look and costs much less than higher-quality white clay. To check the clay and glaze for cracks, balance the item on your fingertips (or your hand, if it's heavy) and flick the edge with your finger. If the sound is

clear and the piece rings like a bell, it's free of cracks. The value is determined by the quality of the workmanship, combined with the chemical formula of the glaze, clay, and dyes. Superior-quality tile or ceramic has quartz (or kaolin) in the clay, little or no lead in the glaze, and metal oxide dyes. Also check whether colors have smeared over one another. Intricate, multicolored, and hand-drawn designs are the most prized.

Shopping Suggestions: High-quality items are often too costly for regular stores to carry. If you are seriously interested in the best ceramics and tile, try the **İznik Foundation,** which carries on Turkey's long-established tile tradition. Their main store is in the Kuruçeşme neighborhood, north of the New District, by the Bosphorus Bridge at Öksüz Çocuk Sokak.

If you're looking for something simple, you'll find plenty of inexpensive, pretty pieces at souvenir stores all around the Old Town and Grand Bazaar.

Traditional Arts: *Hat, Tezhip, Ebru,* and *Minyatür*

Hat (pronounced "hot") is artful Arabic calligraphy. To make written words appear more beautiful, the calligrapher (*hattat;* hot-taht) bends grammatical rules and often takes liberties with the forms of letters. Over the centuries, this decorative art has reached a very sophisticated level of expression, almost like a painting. Turks are proud of *hat,* saying, "The Quran was revealed in Mecca and Medina, recited in Egypt, and written in Istanbul."

Tezhip (tehz-heep) is the illumination and embellishment of manuscripts, scrolls, and books with geometric or floral patterns. The Arabic word *tezhip* literally means "gilding," and designs often incorporate gold. Gold is crushed into powder and then mixed with a solution of gelatin before being used as a paint.

Hat and *tezhip* artists work closely together. When a *hattat* finishes a piece of work, it's passed on to the *tezhip* artist for further decoration. Artists generally work with a magnifying glass and use a very fine brush, traditionally made with a few hairs from the neck of a kitten.

Ebru (ehb-roo) is the art of transferring colored designs from water to paper and is better known as "marbling" for the designs it sometimes produces. Paper colored in this way was traditionally used for *hat* and *tezhip,* as well as for official documentation and contracts (as a fraud deterrent; if someone tried to change a document's wording, the designed paper would be damaged). Today it is considered an independent art, much like abstract painting.

Minyatür (miniature) was the dominant form of painting in Turkey from the 13th through 19th century. Traditionally called *nakış* (nah-kush), *minyatür* artists drew or painted illustrations related to a text. Unlike Western paintings of this time, artists of Turkish miniatures ignored lighting, perspective, and realistic colors, instead turning scenes into abstract or decorative motifs.

In Asian Istanbul: For the highest-quality *ebru*, visit **Ebristan,** on the Asian side of the city (near the Üsküdar pier). This is the studio and home of the colorful, world-famous *ebru* artist Hikmet Barutçugil and his hospitable wife, Füsun, a *tezhip* artist. If you happen to visit while Hikmet is teaching, you're welcome to watch him or his students at work. The gallery shows *ebru* pieces, along with multidisciplinary works that combine calligraphy, illumination, paper marbling, and miniature painting (Mon-Sat 9:30-18:00, closed Sun, Salacak, Hafız Mehmet Bey Sokak 8, Üsküdar, +90 216 334 5934, www.ebristan.com).

Near Ebristan, the **Klasik Türk Sanatları Vakfı** (Foundation of Classical Turkish Art) is dedicated to continuing Turkey's classical arts. Here Turkey's most respected artists pass their skills on to students of their crafts (crash a class when you visit). Art by resident teachers is shown in the center's gallery (daily 9:30-18:00, a short walk from the Üsküdar pier, Doğancılar Caddesi 82, Üsküdar, +90 216 391 1122).

In the Old Town: Owned and operated by helpful İsmail Akşahin, **İznik Works** carries one of the best collections in the overcommercialized Grand Bazaar. They have beautiful *tezhips, hats,* and other traditional crafts, all created by teachers from leading art schools (Mon-Sat 9:30-19:00, closed Sun, Takkeciler Sokak 43-45).

If you're just curious, the **Turkish Handicrafts Center** near Hagia Sophia is a good place to visit. The center offers courses in traditional arts ranging from bookbinding to lacemaking, and a small gallery displays works for sale. You're welcome to watch amateur artists learning the techniques of *ebru*, *tezhip*, and *hat*, and musicians practicing classical music on the *ney* (reed flute), *kanun* (zither), and *ud* (lute). The center is in the historic and lovely Caferağa Medresesi, built in 1599 by the imperial architect Sinan. Each room around the madrassa's peaceful courtyard is assigned to a particular art form (Tue-Sun 8:30-19:00, closed Mon; kitchen serves basic meals, snacks, tea, and coffee; Caferiye Sokak, Soğukkuyu Çıkmazı 1, next door to Yeşil Ev Hotel on a dead end along Hagia Sophia's outer wall, +90 212 513 3601).

For traditional dolls, visit the **doll shop** in the handicrafts center by the Blue Mosque at Kabasakal Caddesi 5. The folk dolls made by Lütfiye Bakutan and Selma Yurtlu are masterpieces you can't find anywhere else. Look for Selma's unique wall hangings featuring dolls playing flutes, praying, and more (daily April-Oct 9:00-18:00, until 17:00 in winter, Sultanahmet).

Gold Jewelry

Gold is a good buy in Turkey. Prices change with the daily rate of gold; when you ask the price of a piece, the shopkeeper will weigh it for you. The Grand Bazaar's many displays of 22-carat gold bracelets reflect Turkey's distrust of banks—many people literally wear their life's savings on their sleeves in the form of these bracelets. These simple bangles often cost little more than the gold itself.

Most mass-produced jewelry is made from molds with 14-carat gold, as it is harder and cheaper. Handmade items are the most expensive; in some pieces, the fine workmanship is more valuable than the gold itself. While the cheaper items (14-18 carat) cost around $25-40 per gram, the price can go as high as $50-75 per gram for finely crafted pieces. Semiprecious stones are generally paired with 14-carat gold, and precious stones with 18-carat.

Shopping Suggestions: Like several other jewelry masters in the Grand Bazaar, **Sevan Bıçakcı** (a.k.a. Lord of the Rings) is Turkish Armenian. His unique style of ringmaking gained him his nickname. He carves intricate forms in precious stones, colors them with special techniques, turns them upside down, and mounts them on gold rings in unusual shapes: a gladiator helmet, the dome of Hagia Sophia, a whirling dervish. Difficult to make and very expensive, they are somewhat like a snow globe on a ring—but without the snow. If you want to see more than what's on display, Herman (Sevan's cousin), Natali, or İda will gladly comply (Nu-

SHOPPING

ruosmaniye Caddesi, Gazi Sinanpaşa Sokak 16, Cağaloğlu, www.
sevanbicakci.com).

Viktor Öcal, another Armenian master, produces similarly
inspiring jewelry at more reasonable prices (a short walk from the
Hippodrome, at Klodfarer Caddesi, Servet Han 29, Sultanahmet,
+90 212 520 5281).

Silver Jewelry and Collectibles

Silver jewelry, with or without semiprecious stones, is a good and
affordable alternative to fancy gold pieces. As with gold, silver
items usually are sold by weight and won't have a price tag. Look
around a bit in the Grand Bazaar to get an idea of what's available
and the range of prices.

You can also find beads to make your own jewelry. A few shops
in the Grand Bazaar (in and near Cevahir Bedesten, see page 201)
carry silver jewelry and semiprecious stone beads.

Shopping Suggestions: In the Grand Bazaar, **Kalcılar Han**
is a production center for silver items, with shops on its lower and
upper levels (see map on page 197). Most of the silver you see in the
Grand Bazaar shops is handcrafted on site. In Kalcılar Han, silver
master **Aruş Taş** and his son **Dikran,** an inlayer, make and sell
decorative and functional silver objects (Barocco Silver, Kalcılar
Han, main floor 37, upper floor 31).

In the Arasta Bazaar, at **Art East** whose owner Ahmet also
runs Sufi (listed under "Textiles, Silk, and Leather," earlier),
you'll find collectibles, semiprecious jewelry, art, and handicrafts
(RS%—prices are marked, but feel free to haggle—then show this
book to get an added discount, Arasta Bazaar 46).

In the New District, designer **Emel Toktaş** makes interesting, basic jewelry and ceramic items at reasonable prices. She
sells her crafts in a small shop managed by friendly Nur Atınç (off
İstiklal Street at Şehir Muhtar Caddesi 33A, Taksim, mobile +90
535 896 4779).

Spices, Coffee, and Tea

A short walk through the Spice Market can be a great learning and
shopping experience. But too often travelers leave this wonderful
market with a pack of powdered "apple tea" and a strip of mysterious little spice bags. Armed with a little knowledge, you can bring
home authentic Turkish items.

For Turks, real apple tea is made by boiling dried apple skin
or adding some dried apple skin to regular black tea, or simmering
dried apple skin with cinnamon. (Meanwhile, the apple tea sold to
tourists is a mix of sugar, citric acid, ascorbic acid, tricalcium phos-
phate, apple flavoring, and caramel coloring.) Go for the real deal;
several shops in the Spice Market carry dried apple skin. Make it

tastier by adding honey or cinnamon. Dried fruits and vegetables, nuts, and spices are irreplaceable ingredients in Turkish cuisine. But contrary to what many believe, Turkish cuisine is not really all that spicy. Turkish cooks use just enough spices to enhance the taste (the exception being cuisine from the southeastern part of the country, largely because of the ethnic backgrounds of the people who live in that region).

If you would like to cook a true Turkish meal at home, here are the top 10 spices and food items to look for in the Spice Market (or elsewhere in Istanbul):

Sumak (sumac) looks like pepper with a dark red/burgundy color, but in fact it is a berry, dried and crushed. It has a sour lime taste. *Sumak* is mainly used with kebabs and salads, especially those containing onions, as it suppresses the strong flavor and scent.

Çam fıstığı (pine nuts) is a luxury item that is grown in the mountains of the Aegean coastline. It adds a matchless taste to rice pilaf, dolma, and desserts.

Nar ekşisi (pomegranate molasses) is a thick syrup that can be used anywhere in place of lemon. It is mostly used in salads.

Çörek otu (nigella seeds, a.k.a. black cumin) is known for its healing properties and is traditionally believed to help with the digestive system. Turks generously sprinkle it over savory pastries and salads.

Kimyon (cumin) is used in meatballs, meat dishes, and the local spicy sausage, *sucuk*.

Wild *safran* (saffron) is said to be the best, but local varieties of this spice are comparable in quality—and relatively inexpensive. For good saffron, look for a bright red color and fine strands. It may cost as much as 25 TL for a gram (shopkeepers treat *safran* like diamonds and handle it using fine tweezers), which sounds expensive, but it's still a good deal compared with what this spice costs in the States.

Kekik (oregano) is the most common spice used in grilled and barbecued meat dishes. It is a natural antiseptic as well. *Kekik* oil is effective in treating upper-respiratory-system diseases.

İsot (Urfa pepper) is a sun-dried red pepper with a dark red/ purple color and a smoky taste. It is used extensively in southeastern cuisine, especially in regional kebabs.

Pul biber (flaked red pepper) is a staple in Turkey and takes its place alongside salt and pepper in most restaurants and kitchens. It's the go-to spice for just about any food.

Nane (dried mint) is mostly used in soups and salads and is also added to lamb and mutton dishes. *Nane*, when boiled with lemon, is often used for treating nausea.

Shopping Suggestions: While you're at the Spice Market, be sure to visit **Hayfene**, a 200-year-old spice business. Bilge

Kadıoğlu, who studied in the US, is the fifth-generation owner of the shop. She and her brother Ahmet conduct spice-tasting sessions for interested visitors and teach about spices and how they're used. Bilge also willingly shares recipes she's tried and tested herself. In addition to spices, they carry essential oils and rose oil (RS%— show this book for a discount of up to 5 percent, Spice Market 51, +90 212 528 2895, www.hayfene.com).

Another Spice Market standby is **Topkapı,** where you can sample and buy Turkish Delights, spices, and a house-made pomegranate infusion. Managers Murat Onur and Metin Çiftçi are eager to serve Rick Steves readers (RS%—show this book for up to a 5 percent discount, Spice Market 13, +90 212 514 3500).

Also near the Spice Market entrance is **Kurukahveci Mehmet Efendi Mahdumları,** a locally famous spot to buy high-quality ground coffee.

Souvenirs and Trinkets

The Grand Bazaar is filled with stalls hawking endless mountains of junk, most of it imported. Those hats with tiny circular mirrors

are common not because they're crafted by local artisans (they're made outside of Turkey) but because the merchants know tourists will buy them. Fortunately, the bazaar is also filled with plenty of affordable, authentically Turkish trinkets that make wonderful gifts.

You can't miss the **"evil eyes"** (*nazarlık;* nah-zahr-luhk)—blue-and-white glass beads that look like eyes. Traditionally thought to ward off negative energy from jealous eyes, these are a kind of good-luck charm popular among Turks. You'll see them on doorways, hanging down from rearview mirrors, or anywhere else people want protection. Babies wear them, adults wear them, and teenage girls braid them in their hair. *Nazarlık*s are authentically and uniquely Turkish, which makes them good gifts. They come in various sizes—some with a metal frame, others on a hooked pin, still others embedded in tiles.

Small Turkish **tea glasses,** made of clear glass and shaped like a tulip blossom, are easy to find. Buy them toward the end of your trip to minimize the risk of breaking them as you carry them around.

Machine-made textiles with traditional designs make good tablecloths, pillowcases, bedspreads, and sofa throws. Some are velvet, with silky-looking, colorful embroideries.

Coffee and pepper grinders don't break easily, since they're made of brass or wood.

The same goes for **backgammon sets** and **inlaid wooden boxes.** The best are inlaid with mother-of-pearl, while the cheapest are inlaid with plastic.

If you decide to buy a glass **water pipe** (*nargile;* nahr-gee-leh), get the kind that separates into parts and is easily reassembled. For more on water pipes, see page 75.

Mined in central Turkey, **onyx** is plentiful, affordable, and popular in decorative objects such as vases and bowls, as well as chess sets (but not so common in jewelry).

Gifts for children are more limited. Consider Halloween **costumes.** You'll find tiny, colorful Turkish princess outfits, with coins adorning the sleeves and trousers. Cheap knockoffs of **soccer jerseys** also abound.

ENTERTAINMENT IN ISTANBUL

Lively Istanbul is a happening place, with thousands of nightclubs and bars, regular stage performances, and several annual world-class festivals. But if you're expecting nightlife full of shimmying belly dancers, you may be disappointed. Belly dancing in Istanbul is as popular as square dancing is in New York City. Until very recently, belly dancing was looked down upon by modern Turks, though its presence on TV and in competitions is growing.

So rather than seeking out cultural clichés, spend your Istanbul evenings enjoying modern, international activities...with a Turkish flair, of course.

Concerts and Performances

WHIRLING DERVISHES

Touristy, fake "Whirling Dervish" performances spin through many of Istanbul's theaters and restaurants. But to see the authentic two-hour religious ritual (called Sema) performed by the Mevlevi, followers of the Muslim mystic Rumi, visit the Galata Dervish Monastery or the Foundation of Universal Lovers of Mevlana, both described next (for more on Rumi and the whirling dervishes, see the sidebar).

Galata Dervish Monastery (Galata Mevlevihanesi)

This *mevlevihane* (mehv-leh-vee-hah-neh) or monastery is easy to reach (at the southern end of İstiklal Street at Galip Dede Caddesi 15). This is a rare opportunity to witness a dervish ritual enacted by real worshippers, rather than performers. The lackluster museum is skippable (see page 64).

Seeing a Service: Services are generally Sundays at 17:00; extra services may be held on Saturdays as well (about 120 TL,

Rumi and the Whirling Dervishes

In the 13th century, a Muslim mystic named Rumi (better known to Turks as Mevlana, meaning "master" in Persian) began to incorporate whirling meditation into his teachings. He believed that a dervish, spinning in a circle, becomes part of the universal harmony. A *mevlevihane* is a gathering place or residence for dervishes.

If you get a chance to watch dervishes whirl, consider the theology behind this unusual ceremony (called Sema). Rumi believed that the purpose of life was to purify oneself, to become free of the material desires of the flesh that entrap the soul, such as greed, rage, and jealousy. When rid of negative influences, a person's soul can attain eternal happiness. To accomplish this, one must "die before death"—so the dervish ritual symbolizes finding enlightenment through the death of one's self (unchaining the soul from worldly desires). Even the costume worn by dervishes evokes death: a tall camel-felt hat, resembling a tombstone, and a black cloak that represents earthly attachments. As the ritual begins, the black cloak is removed, revealing a long, white dress—similar to the shroud that deceased Muslims are wrapped in when they are buried.

Everything in the universe whirls, from the smallest to the largest particle. By whirling, the dervish becomes one with the created and the Creator.

confirm schedule by dropping by the monastery or calling +90 212 245 4141). Tickets are available at the monastery on Saturday and the day of the performance; show up no later than 16:00 to be sure you get a ticket. For advance tickets, try contacting event organizer Tebit Çakmut (mobile +90 530 584 3430).

Once inside, it's open seating, so try to get a seat as close as you can to the center of the hall. As this is a prayer service rather than a show, it's pensive and very slow-paced (about two hours total)—not ideal for impatient camcorder-toting tourists who wish those guys would just start spinning already. To slow down your pulse, ponder what a dervish told me: "As I spin around, my hand above receives the love from our Creator, and my hand below showers it onto all of his creation."

Foundation of Universal Lovers of Mevlana

Whirling dervishes can also be seen at the service held by this nonprofit organization (EMAV), which was established to spread Rumi's philosophy. On certain evenings they hold a Sema ceremony, which begins with a sermon at 19:30, followed by the whirling ceremony around 21:00 (lasts about an hour). This is one of the rare events in which you can see both male and female *semazen* whirl together. If you visit, dress modestly and remove your shoes before entering (and keep them with you). There's a 70-TL charge to attend, and donations may be requested for the maintenance of the facility (Yeni Tavanlı Çeşme Sokak 6, Mevlanakapı Mahallesi, Silivrikapı, near the outer city walls, about 10 minutes and 30 TL by taxi from Sultanahmet; +90 212 588 5780 or mobile +90 552 524 3494, www.emav.org). If you can't get your questions answered at one of the official numbers, call helpful Sevtap Demirtaş (mobile +90 505 498 9923, fluent in English).

Hodjapasha Cultural Center

Dervishes also whirl in the Old Town in this converted 15th-century Turkish bath, with hour-long performances taking place most nights at 19:00. Reserve seats in person or online (from $26, children from $16; Ankara Caddesi Hocapaşa Hamamı Sokak 3B, Sirkeci, +90 212 511 4626, www.hodjapasha.com).

Zorlu Performance Art Center (Zorlu PSM)

This state-of-the-art performance center comprising seven venues is a great place to catch high-profile entertainment, including touring Broadway shows, pop concerts, dance performances, and a jazz festival. Tickets for most events cost around $15, and Broadway musicals go for a fraction of what they would back home ($30-40). Located in the Levazım neighborhood well north of the New District, it's part of the Zorlu shopping, entertainment, and residential complex that also offers an assortment of dining and drinking options (for show details, check www.zorlupsm.com; Zorlu Center, Levazım Mahallesi, Koru Sokak No:2/PSM/70, Beşiktaş, +90 850 222 6776).

OPERA, BALLET, AND SYMPHONY

The Atatürk Cultural Center (AKM) at Taksim Square, the venue for top-notch performances by the Istanbul State Opera, State Ballet, and State Symphony Orchestra, is closed for renovation through 2022.

In the meantime, performances have shifted to alternative venues such as Hagia Irene in the Topkapı Palace grounds, the Fulya Show Center, or the Süreyya Opera House in Kadıköy. The state-subsidized tickets are dirt cheap; front-row tickets can cost

ENTERTAINMENT

Buying Tickets

To avoid an unnecessary trek to a venue's box office, consider buying tickets online. Biletix (www.biletix.com) sells tickets for most events, including movies and soccer games. Buy your ticket online, and then pick it up at the ticket office on the day of the performance—just show the credit card you used for the online purchase. The deadline to pick up your ticket is usually an hour before the start of the event.

Two other sites, Biletiva (www.biletiva.com) and Biletinial (www.biletinial.com), concentrate on theater tickets, but also provide tickets to alternative events not available through Biletix.

For popular events, tickets can sell out fast. Even if a performance is sold out online, try going to the ticket office the day of the show to see if there have been any returns—your chances of scoring a ticket are fairly decent.

as little as 20-30 TL. Symphony tickets are available a week in advance; see www.idso.gov.tr for performance details. For opera and ballet, see next.

Süreyya Opera House

The Süreyya Opera House in Kadıköy is the temporary home for opera and ballet in Istanbul, with a performance season running from September through June. Tickets are released online 30 days before a performance and usually sell out within a day. Reserve (and print) a ticket online before your trip (www.operabale.gov.tr; choose Istanbul from the menu). The opera house also hosts occasional chamber orchestra concerts on Saturdays and Sundays (likely at 15:00 or 16:00, same online ticketing system).

If you can't snag a ticket online, you can try showing up the day of a show. Locals sometimes sell or give away their tickets outside the main entrance. Or, head to the box office (Bahariye Caddesi, Caferağa Mahallesi 29, Kadıköy). If there are no-shows, theater staff may let you take an empty seat. The dress code for these performances is casual.

For more on the opera house, see the Asian Istanbul Walks chapter.

FESTIVALS

The Istanbul Foundation of Culture and Arts organizes several city-wide festivals every year, including the International Music Festival (June), the International Jazz Festival (early to mid-July), and the International Film Week (mid-Oct). Every other year in the fall, Istanbul also hosts Turkey's largest contemporary art show, the International Istanbul Biennial. Schedules for these festivals vary from year to year, and tickets can go fast, so it's worth checking the foundation's site at www.iksv.org.

The music and jazz festivals are worthwhile, partly for their venues. The jazz concerts take place in lively music clubs and on outdoor stages, while music events are often held at historic monuments. Past festival performers have included members of Milan's La Scala Opera House and the New York Philharmonic.

Nightlife

LOW-KEY EVENINGS ON THE GOLDEN HORN AND THE BOSPHORUS

Warm, clear evenings in Istanbul are perhaps best enjoyed with a short walk across the **Galata Bridge** to watch the sun go down. Take in the Old Town's magnificent skyline, dominated by floodlit domes and minarets. After sunset, head to the lower level of the Galata Bridge, where you'll find several moderately priced tavern-style eateries (*meyhane;* mehy-hah-neh) and seafood restaurants.

Restaurants, bars, and clubs along the Bosphorus tend to be expensive, but some areas are more affordable than others. For instance, the **Ortaköy neighborhood,** by the European side of the Bosphorus Bridge, is a pedestrian area with many bars, teahouses, and restaurants. In nice weather, especially on weekends, the area is packed with hundreds of people strolling its streets and alleys. Even on the warmest evenings, you'll want to bring along a sweater or shawl, as a cool breeze blows along the Bosphorus at night (in bad weather, the area is often empty). If you're on a tight budget, get a baked potato or a sandwich from one of the numerous summertime food stalls. Grab a drink from a grocery store and enjoy your evening picnic on a bench by the Bosphorus, watching the boats pass by, with the bridge lit up like a pearl necklace and the Ortaköy Mosque as its backdrop. A couple of teahouses with good views of the Bosphorus are usually packed with Turks playing backgammon or a tile game called OK. To get to Ortaköy from Taksim Square in the New District, catch bus #40 or #40T (from the transit tunnels below Taksim Square).

ENTERTAINMENT

PARTYING ON İSTIKLAL STREET

In the evenings, the neighborhood surrounding İstiklal Street, in the New District, is transformed into a vast enter-
tainment center. The street
itself has several bars, jazz
clubs, and *meyhanes* (taverns), all popular among
the locals.

Fasıl Music

Many visitors enjoy *fasıl*
(fah-suhl) music, often
performed in the inviting ambience of a *meyhane*. *Fasıl* is a performance of live, old-time Istanbul songs or classical Turkish tunes,
played by a trio of musicians. Locals sing along as they drink *rakı*
(firewater) and nibble on *mezes* (appetizers). You won't pay a cover
charge for the music, but it's customary to tip the musicians—
watch locals and imitate.

One good venue is **Şahika** (shah-hee-kah), in a narrow town-
house on Nevizade Sokak (enter the fish market by the corner of
Flower Passage/Çiçek Pasajı, then take the first right). A different
style of music, including *fasıl* and contemporary, is played on each
of its five floors. If you're a solo male, they may not let you in, so
find a fellow traveler to bring along.

Note that some of the restaurants in the Flower Passage and
others on İstiklal Street feature "Gypsy music," which is louder,
faster, and more danceable than *fasıl*.

Clubs and Nightspots

If you're serious about nightlife, dip into one of the many night-
spots on or near İstiklal Street. These generally get rolling late in
the evening, around 23:00 or later, and hit their peak around 1:00
to 2:00 in the morning. Quite a few clubs stay open until 4:00. To
get tickets in advance for big-name shows, see the "Buying Tickets"
sidebar, earlier. Here are some clubs to consider near İstiklal Street
and beyond Taksim Square:

Nardis Jazz Club, hosting both local and international performers, has been called Istanbul's best live-music club. There's live
jazz daily except Sunday, with programs starting at 21:30 on weekdays and 22:30 at weekends (50-TL drinks, 50-70-TL cover charge
based on who's performing, Kuledibi Sokak 8, Galata, +90 212 244
6327 or mobile +90 532 244 5778, www.nardisjazz.com).

The prestigious **IKSV Salon** hosts quality jazz and classical
music performances. Schedules are irregular, so check their website
for the latest (50-90-TL seats, 25-50-TL standing tickets, 25-50

ENTERTAINMENT

percent student discount on standing tickets, Sadi Konuralp Caddesi 5, Şişhane, +90 212 334 0752, www.saloniksv.com).

Love Dance Point is a classy, predominantly gay dance club with popular DJs, special events, and occasional theme parties. Doors open on weekends at 23:30, and they party until 4:00 or 5:00 in the morning (50-75-TL cover charge, open Fri-Sat only but check website for additional days, north of Taksim Square and across from the Military Museum at Cumhuriyet Caddesi 349/1, Harbiye, +90 212 296 3358, www.lovedp.net).

Babylon, in the former Bomontiada brewery two miles north of Taksim Square, is a popular club featuring international bands and performers. It usually has jazz and ethnic music, but it's not unusual to see reggae or percussion bands. Its box office opens at noon, although for more popular performances, you might want to buy tickets in advance (Tarihi Bomonti Bira Fabrikası, Birahane Sokak 1, Şişli, +90 212 334 0190, www.babylon.com.tr).

ENTERTAINMENT

ISTANBUL CONNECTIONS

This chapter covers Istanbul's main airports, train stations, bus station, and cruise port. Plan ahead and reserve any major transportation connections well in advance. For specifics on using the tram system and other public transportation in Istanbul, see the Orientation chapter.

The following website has good information about transportation within and from Istanbul: www.turkeytravelplanner.com.

By Plane

ISTANBUL AIRPORT (İSTANBUL HAVILIMANİ)

Located northwest of the city center, on the European side of the Bosphorus, Istanbul's huge, modern airport is the city's hub for Turkish Airlines and international flights (code: IST, airport info +90 444 1 442, www.istairport.com). Domestic carriers such as Anadolujet (www.anadolujet.com—the budget wing of Turkish Airlines), Pegasus Airlines (www.flypgs.com), SunExpress (www.sunexpress.com), and Onur Air (www.onurair.com) also provide service from this airport to Turkish cities including Ankara, İzmir, and Trabzon.

The airport has five concourses, dubbed "piers," that extend from the central terminal to the gates. Concourses A, B, D, and F handle international flights; concourse G is domestic. Shops, eateries, duty-free stores, and exchange desks are located in the central terminal. There are no trains or trams between the concourses, but the lofty ceilings and glimmering lights may distract you from all the walking—use the moving sidewalks when possible.

Arrivals: To exit the concourses, take an escalator down to baggage claim. From there, continue through customs and exit onto the arrivals floor. As you leave customs, there's a TI kiosk to the right (open daily until 23:00), and ATMs flank each end of the hall. Car rental desks, city transportation options, and other services are also located on this floor. Shuttle buses (Havaist and IETT) are near door 13.

Getting Between Istanbul Airport and Downtown

You can reach the Old Town or the New District by taxi, private transfer, or shuttle bus. A Metro line connecting the airport and the city center is under construction and may be operational in 2021.

By Taxi or Private Transfer: The airport is a one-hour taxi ride from either the Old Town or the New District. Taxis wait outside door 9 of the arrivals floor (available 24/7, about 200-250 TL to the Old Town; 170-190 TL to the New District).

Private car transportation can be booked directly through your hotel for about €50, with a customary 10 percent tip. Ask when you reserve your room. Note that many Old Town travel agencies arrange less expensive airport shuttles—but to return to the airport, you'll likely depart from the travel agency, not your hotel.

By Shuttle Bus: Depending on traffic, shuttle buses take 1.5 hours (much longer during rush hour) to reach the city center. They depart from near door 13 of the arrivals level. Buy tickets at the bus stop (cash or credit card) or on the bus (credit card only).

Havaist runs luxury buses between the airport and city center, with onboard Wi-Fi and USB outlets. The IST-1 line runs into the Old Town; IST-19 serves the New District (departures every 30-50 minutes, 18 TL, www.hava.ist).

For those staying in the New District, the cheapest option is run by Istanbul's public transit agency, **IETT**. Its H2 shuttle line connects to the New District at roughly 15-minute intervals (18 TL, www.iett.istanbul).

SABİHA GÖKÇEN AIRPORT

This smaller airport on the Asian side of town offers a range of domestic and international flights. It's served mainly by smaller airlines such as Pegasus, EasyJet, Onur Air, and AnadoluJet. Bus connections and transfer services into town are available, or figure 250 TL for a taxi to the city center; it takes at least 90 minutes—depending on traffic (code: SAW, +90 216 588 8888, www.sabihagokcen.aero).

By Train

Istanbul is in the middle of a long-term project to overhaul and rehabilitate its national rail service. In the end, trains will travel seamlessly between Asia and Europe, with more connections from

Istanbul to the rest of Europe. In the meantime, some stations are closed and others are being used only temporarily. Be sure you confirm any rail logistics in advance. See a travel agent or the Turkish Railways website (www.tcdd.gov.tr) for more information.

On Istanbul's European side, west of the Old Town, **Halkalı Station** connects Istanbul with Sofia and Bucharest (and points west in Europe) with one daily night train (the station is on the Marmaray commuter rail line). **Sirkeci Station,** once the Old Town terminus of the Orient Express, now handles just the Marmaray commuter line.

Istanbul's main Asian-side train station—Haydarpaşa—is closed for renovation with no trains arriving or departing. The **Söğütlüçeşme Station** in Kadıköy is—for now—the main station on the Asian side. Many trains that connect Istanbul to other Turkish cities terminate there, including the new high-speed service that runs between Istanbul and Ankara in about five hours—about half the time it takes on regular trains (85 TL each way, 9-10/day).

The Marmaray commuter rail line links Söğütlüçeşme Station with the Old Town (via Sirkeci Station). Or, you can travel to the Asian side by ferry (from Eminönu or Karaköy) to Kadıköy, and then pick up the Marmaray line to Söğütlüçeşme.

There are no trains between Turkey and Greece.

By Bus

Buses arrive at the city's **main bus terminal** (*otogar;* oh-toh-gar), located in the Esenler district on the European side. Some bus lines stop at other points in the city, which may be closer to your hotel—ask when you buy your ticket. Some bus companies offer a free transfer to other locations in the city.

From the main *otogar,* it's about a 30-minute taxi ride to either the Old Town or New District. Or catch the light rail train from the *otogar* to the Aksaray stop, where you can take the tram to your destination in the Old Town (Sultanahmet stop) or in the southern part of the New District (Karaköy stop for Galata district hotels). If your hotel is near Taskim Square, take the light rail to Yenikapı and transfer to the Metro for Taksim.

Traveling by Bus Within Turkey
Turkey has a good network of highways, and the bus system is easy to figure out. Every major city or town in Turkey has a bus terminal, usually located close to the city center and lined with small ticket offices run by competing companies. Additional, centrally located offices are linked to the *otogar* by shuttle. Service and prices are similar—just take whichever bus leaves soonest for your destination.

Bus rides cost about 50-70 TL for every 60 miles. Turkish buses are quite comfortable, and usually have WCs and tea/coffee/snack service aboard. Buses stop every two hours or so for breaks. Most bus lines make local stops. A few companies have nonstop express services to major destinations.

Bus companies that stand out for their good service include Ulusoy (www.ulusoy.com.tr) and Kamil Koç (www.kamilkoc.com.tr). While you'll pay more to travel with these companies, they typically have more centrally located bus terminals than competitors.

By Cruise Ship

Istanbul's cruise port on the Bosphorus, bordering the Karaköy and Tophane areas of the New District, has been rebuilt from scratch.

Part of an urban development project called Galataport, the cruise terminal itself is underground, freeing up the waterfront for restaurants, shops, and a pedestrian promenade.

The nearest tram stops are Karaköy, near the Galata Bridge, and Tophane. To reach the Sultanahmet stop in the Old Town, take the southbound tram in the direction of Bağcılar. For Taksim Square and İstiklal Street, walk to the Tünel station and take the historic funicular (see page 35). For transit ticket details, see "Getting Around" in the Orientation chapter.

If your trip includes cruising beyond Istanbul, consider my guidebook, *Rick Steves Mediterranean Cruise Ports*.

CONNECTIONS

BEYOND ISTANBUL

Ephesus & Cappadocia

Istanbul is the natural first stop for any visitor exploring Turkey and merits a stay of several days. But if you're intrigued to venture deeper into Turkey, this section will point you in the right direction. I've selected the two most rewarding Turkish destinations beyond Istanbul: the remarkable ancient ruined city of Ephesus, near the port of Kuşadası; and the rural region of Cappadocia—the heartland of historic Asia Minor—which puts you in touch with "village Turkey" and offers a dramatic landscape and welcoming people. Taken together, Istanbul, Ephesus, and Cappadocia form the "Golden Triangle" of Turkey for travelers.

GETTING THERE

These two destinations are far from Istanbul: Ephesus is about 330 miles to the south, along the Aegean coast; and Cappadocia is 500 miles southeast, deep in Turkey's interior. To reach either one, the best option is to fly.

By Plane: Various airlines connect Istanbul to both areas frequently and affordably—cheaper than a bus or train. Options include Turkish Airlines (www.turkishairlines.com), AnadoluJet (www.anadolujet.com), and Pegasus Airlines (www.flypgs.com), as well as some smaller, no-frills carriers. You can search for options at www.skyscanner.com.

To reach **Ephesus**, use Adnan Menderes Airport (code: ADB) in **İzmir**, which is 40 miles north of the archaeological site (about an hour drive, www.adnanmenderesairport.com).

Cappadocia has two airports: **Erkilet Airport** (code: ASR, https://kayseri.dhmi.gov.tr), in Kayseri, is about 45 miles from central Cappadocia (about an hour drive); **Cappadocia Airport** (code: NAV, https://kapadokya.dhmi.gov.tr), in Nevşehir, is about 25 miles from the center (a 30-45-minute drive). Between the vari-

ous airports in Istanbul and Cappadocia, there are more than 20 direct flights from Istanbul daily; the flight takes 1.5 hours or less.

In addition, Pegasus and SunExpress offer two direct flights between Cappadocia's Kayseri Erkilet Airport and İzmir (almost daily, about 1.5 hours).

All of these airports offer the expected services including car rental desks.

To visit all three major destinations in Turkey, connect them in this order: Istanbul, then Cappadocia, then Ephesus. From İzmir Airport (near Ephesus), you can catch a direct flight to a major European hub to connect to your journey home.

By Tour: Various tour companies offer multi-day packages that include Istanbul, Ephesus, and Cappadocia. Most subsidize their programs with lots of shopping, optional tours, and expected tips—do your research before going this route.

By Cruise: Coastal Ephesus is a popular destination for cruises (using the port of Kuşadası, or sometimes İzmir). For details on getting from Kuşadası to Ephesus, see the Ephesus chapter.

EPHESUS

Efes

Some 300 miles south of Istanbul lie the ruins of the grand, ancient metropolis of Ephesus (eff-eh-suhs)—one of the most important cities of the Roman Empire—and among the top archaeological sites anywhere. Whether you're strolling the broad boulevards, appreciating the pillared facade of the famous Library of Celsus, peeling back the layers of dust to understand the everyday lifestyles of the rich and Roman at the Terrace Houses, or testing the acoustics in the theater where the Apostle Paul famously spoke, Ephesus is a perfect place to time-travel back to the grandeur of Rome.

Near Ephesus is the Aegean port city of Kuşadası (koo-shah-dah-suh), Turkey's second-busiest cruise destination (after Istanbul). With extra time, you can visit the House of the Virgin Mary, where it's believed Mary spent the last years of her life; the town of Selçuk (sell-chuck), with its Ephesus Museum, displaying some of the best artifacts from the site, plus the ruined Basilica of St. John, where the apostle is said to be entombed; and the stony mountain village of Şirince (shih-rihn-jeh), overlooking it all.

GETTING THERE

From İzmir's Adnan Menderes Airport: A taxi to the Ephesus area costs around $50-70. Prearranged private transfers can be booked through SRM Travel and run $70-90 (+90 216 266 5839, www.srmtravel.com). More affordable is to take a shared shuttle (around 30 TL, or about $5, per person): Choose between Havaş (no need to book ahead—buses wait outside the terminal, pay driver, www.havas.net) and Kuşadası Havalimanı (prebooking required, look for driver in bag claim holding sign with your name,

Ephesus & Kuşadası Area

pay a little extra for hotel drop-off, call or text +90 256 614 5555, www.kusadasihavalimaniservis.com). Both shuttles stop in Selçuk (near Ephesus), then at the bus terminal in Kuşadası.

From Kuşadası to Ephesus by Taxi: It's a 30-minute trip straight to the site—ask to be dropped off at the upper gate. Figure about $35 one-way, $80 round-trip with waiting time. If you're quoted a much higher price, negotiate or ask the next driver.

From Kuşadası to Ephesus by Public Transit: This option is slower and more complicated than a taxi but much cheaper. You'll take a short ride within Kuşadası on one *dolmuş* minibus, then switch to a different *dolmuş* for the longer ride to Ephesus (figure about 30-40 minutes total one-way), followed by a 15-minute walk to the site's lower entrance gate.

Just past the Kuşadası TI, bear left at the taxi stand and wait at the sign with the boxed "D". Take any minibus marked *Kadınlar Denizi* ("Ladies' Beach") and tell the driver you're going to Selçuk; after just a few minutes, he'll tell you where to change to the next *dolmuş*. (Your stop is after the yellow "taxi office" sign.) Cross the street to the stand at the corner, and look for the Kuşadası-Selçuk *dolmuş*. A minibus leaves from here about every 20 minutes and takes about 30 minutes—tell the driver you want to go to Efes (ehfehs; the stop is also called *Efes Yolu*, "the road to Ephesus"). From here it's a slightly uphill, half-mile walk to the entrance; when the road forks to the right, keep going straight (even though the right fork is signed for Ephesus—that's for drivers).

PLANNING YOUR TIME

Ephesus deserves a half-day to see the sprawling ancient site. Ideally, visit early in the morning or late in the day—when it's cool, the organized tour crowds are gone, and the stone is bathed in rich warm light. Round out your day by visiting the other sights in the area.

With round-trip flights, Ephesus can be seen as a one-day side trip from Istanbul, but it's a stretch. A better plan is two overnights, either in little Şirince or big Kuşadası. **Şirince**, in the hills above Selçuk, is a historic, touristy village with some hotels and restaurants (about 10 minutes from Selçuk, 15 minutes from Ephesus). **Kuşadası**, a midsize port city with the benefits of a larger town, is more practical for most travelers (about 30 minutes south of Ephesus). It has a pleasant waterfront promenade with cafés and restaurants crowded with locals at sundown.

The big city of **İzmir**—with the nearest major airport—is about an hour north of Ephesus (or 75 minutes from Kuşadası). İzmir is primarily a transit hub and not worth squeezing into a short visit.

Ephesus Archaeological Site

At its peak in the first and second centuries AD, Ephesus was one of the grandest cities of the ancient world, ranking among the four leading centers of the Roman Empire (along with Alexandria, Antioch, and Rome itself). With a staggering quarter-million residents, Ephesus was the second-biggest city in the empire, after Rome. The Ephesus we see today reflects the many civilizations—Greek, Persian, Roman, and Christian—that passed through Asia Minor (today's Turkey) in the days before the Ottomans. Julius Caesar, Anthony and Cleopatra, St. Paul, St. John—and maybe even the Virgin Mary—all walked these same marble roads.

The area was first settled around 1000 BC. The city grew as a seaport and the worship center of the goddess Artemis. By 500 BC,

it was a bustling cultural capital on the Mediterranean. It sported the enormous Temple of Artemis, famous in its day and now a delicate, much-photographed ruin.

Ephesus was in Ionia, an important and sophisticated

EPHESUS

Ephesus

Old Harbor (dry)

Bus Stop from Kuşadası
B Bus Stop to Kuşadası
B
515

CHURCH OF THE VIRGIN MARY
HARBOR BATHS
HARBOR GYMNASIUM
GYMNASIUM
STADIUM
KORESSOS GATE
To Selçuk
HARBOR ROAD
P
WC **LOWER GATE & TICKETS**
MARBLE ROAD
Mt. Pion
CAVE OF THE SEVEN SLEEPERS
COMMERCIAL (LOWER) AGORA
17
SERAPIS TEMPLE
15
M & M GATE
16
GREAT THEATER
LIBRARY OF CELSUS
14
12
HELLENISTIC WALL
TERRACE HOUSES
13
11 TEMPLE OF HADRIAN
10 BATHS
HELLENISTIC WALL
8
9
6
7 HERCULES GATE
DOMITIAN TEMPLE
STATE AGORA
1
3
4
TOUR BEGINS
5
2
Mt. Koressus
EAST GYMNASIUM
WC
DOMITIAN SQUARE
MAGNESIA GATE
To Selçuk
UPPER GATE & TICKETS

N
100 Meters
100 Yards

To House of the Virgin Mary

1 State Agora
2 Stoa Basilica
3 Odeon
4 Prytaneion
5 Sacred Way
6 Domitian Square
7 Hercules Gate
8 Curetes Road
9 Trajan's Fountain
10 Baths
11 Temple of Hadrian
12 Public Toilets
13 Terrace Houses
14 Library of Celsus
15 Commercial Agora
16 Great Theater
17 Harbor Road

center of the Greek world. The Ephesians spoke Greek, produced "Greek" philosophers such as Heraclitus (who said the only constant is change), and popularized the Ionic style of Greek columns (topped with scroll-like capitals). Over the centuries, more war-like people—Lydians, Persians, Athenians, Alexander the Great, and Romans—overran Ephesus, but everyday life carried on in this cosmopolitan city.

Oddly, the physical location of ancient Ephesus moved over time. The Meander River (whose meandering course gave us the word) tended to shift its path, and the valley's sandy soil constantly moved. Ephesians had to adjust accordingly. When the river's access to the sea silted up in the fourth century BC, the Ephesians relocated their city farther up the valley, where the ruins now sit.

It was under Roman rule that Ephesus reached its peak. In AD 27, Emperor Augustus made the city the capital of the Roman province of Asia (roughly corresponding to today's Turkish west coast). The harbor at Ephesus bustled with goods and slaves traded from throughout the vast Roman Empire. By AD 100, Ephesus had become a city of marble buildings and grand monuments, with an infrastructure that could support hundreds of thousands of toga-clad citizens. The ruins you'll see today date largely from the city's Roman heyday in those first two centuries after Christ.

Ephesus' prominence attracted some of the earliest followers of Christ, and some of the oldest texts of the New Testament were likely written here. St. Paul came to Ephesus (about AD 50), where he conducted missionary work and wrote his First Epistle to the Corinthians ("Love is patient, love is kind. It does not envy, it does not boast, it is not proud"). St. John also may have come to Ephesus (about AD 90), having been charged with spreading Christianity in the Roman province of Asia. And the Virgin Mary supposedly retired to Ephesus (brought by John, who cared for her after the Crucifixion).

As the Roman Empire fell, so fell Ephesus. In AD 263, invading barbarians looted the city, and it never really recovered. Ephesus limped along under the wing of the Byzantine Empire—the Christian empire ruled from Constantinople (today's Istanbul). By the seventh century AD, that same old problem—the silting up of the harbor inlet—finally closed Ephesus' port for good. The marshy ground bred mosquito-borne malaria that plagued the population. The impressive buildings were scavenged for their conveniently precut stones. Earthquakes further leveled the monuments. Forgotten and buried, ancient Ephesus was ignored until the 1860s, when a series of British, German, and Austrian archaeologists excavated the site. Many of its treasures are now on display in Vienna's Ephesus Museum, and others are in the British Museum in London. While the site seems vast, 85 percent of the sprawling ancient city remains unexcavated.

ORIENTATION

Cost and Hours: 100 TL, sold on-site and online. The site is open daily 8:00-19:00, off-season 8:30-17:00.

Information: +90 232 892 6010, www.muze.gov.tr.

Getting In: The site has two entrance gates, about 1.5 miles apart. I've oriented this tour the way most visitors see Ephesus, beginning at the upper gate and working down to the lower gate. (Cruise-line excursions and taxis drop you at the upper gate.) If you instead arrive on a *dolmuş* minibus, you'll begin at the lower gate. In that case, hike or take a taxi to the upper gate, or simply see the site uphill (holding this book upside down).

EPHESUS

Tours: 🎧 To sightsee on your own, download my free **audio tour** of Ancient Ephesus (see sidebar on page 22). At the site, you can rent an audioguide.

Local Guides: Hiring a private guide is a great way to have an informative, well-organized visit. For the best experience, book a guide in advance. Arrange to meet at your hotel or at Ephesus (figure about $250/half-day). Guides who can sometimes be booked independently include **Mert Taner** (mobile +90 532 263 6430, merttaner@hotmail.com), **Can Yiğit** (mobile +90 532 426 6335, guidecan68@yahoo.com), **Levent Üzüm** (mobile +90 532 265 9753, leventuzum@yahoo.com), and **Kerem Özbaş** (mobile +90 532 251 1316, keremozbas@yahoo.com). For bureaucratic reasons, these guides may ask you to book them through a separate company; this is a common and fair practice. Another option is to contact **SRM Travel** for either a customized package or a private guide (+90 216 266 5839, www.srmtravel.com).

If you didn't arrange a guide in advance, you can generally hire one at the site. Guides hang out at each entrance—talk to a few to decide which one's personality and language skills you prefer.

Be Prepared: Bring a hat, sunglasses, and sunscreen, and wear sturdy shoes to traverse the uneven, sometimes steep terrain.

Eating: The on-site eateries are basic; consider bringing some snacks (but a full-blown picnic is not allowed). Those with rental cars might want to wait and eat in Selçuk or Şirince, not far from the site (see those sections, later).

➲ SELF-GUIDED TOUR

To trace the route of this tour, see the "Ephesus" map, earlier in this section.

The excavated area of Ephesus basically represents the city center—the "downtown" of the ancient metropolis. Beginning at the **upper gate** and working downhill, our tour passes through the government center, a residential neighborhood, a shopping area, and a theater and nightlife district. Along the way, you'll walk parts of three different roads: the Curetes (Priests') Road, connecting the upper gate to the Library of Celsus; the Marble Road, between the library and the Great Theater; and the Harbor Road, connecting the theater to the harbor (and, along the way, today's modern lower gate).

• *Just inside the upper gate is a large, rectangular space ringed with the ruins of various buildings. Stand here, at the top of the site with your back to the modern upper gate, and survey what's been excavated of the ancient city. Residential zones sprawled up the ridges high above you on the right and the left. Between these neighborhoods was this vast upper square, which was the Forum, a.k.a. the State Agora.*

❶ State Agora (Forum)

The State Agora (or Upper Agora) was an open-air courtyard surrounded by covered arcades. Here citizens could get out of the sun and rain, catch up with their neighbors, talk politics, make business deals, and ponder philosophy. This agora—about 500 feet long and 240 feet wide—originally had a temple to the goddess Isis in the center.

While there's little left of the buildings, you can see evidence of extensive plumbing in the dirt near the stack of terracotta pipes.

Ephesus had one of the ancient world's most sophisticated public waterworks systems. Runoff from the surrounding hills streamed into a network of four major aqueducts before being funneled into the city. Logically, the main reservoir was here, at

the high end of the city. From here, with the help of clay pipes (like those piled here) and gravity, water flowed to the city's fountains and the homes of the wealthy.

• *Walking beyond the pipes, you'll find what was a ceremonial road lined with columns and the remains of the...*

❷ Stoa Basilica

The northern side of the agora was a colonnaded, covered walkway (called a stoa), which was eventually remodeled into a basilica-like structure. The double row of pillars in the middle of the field marks the footprint of a typical basilica floor plan: a large central hall flanked by two narrower side aisles. The columns are Ionic—slender, fluted, and topped with (mostly missing) scroll-like capitals. While today the word "basilica" signifies a church, back then—centuries before the first basilica-style church—it meant a business center, like this, where disputes between merchants were resolved.

• *Beyond the Stoa Basilica, cut into the hillside, the largest structure you see (with semicircular rows of seats) is the...*

❸ Odeon (Bouleterion)

Dating from around AD 150, this indoor theater—once topped with a wooden roof—seated 1,500. Compared with the huge open-air theater we'll see later, this was an intimate venue. It functioned primarily as the meeting place *(bouleuterion)* for the city council, but also hosted plays and concerts. According to records, every Thursday morning, 450 aristocrats would assemble here to hash out the civic business of Ephesus. While some of the lower marble seats are original, with elegant lion-feet armrests surviving, the upper seats were

restored on the cheap in the 1950s. (By the way, to get a sense of how deeply this site was excavated, note that the theater was once buried up to its top seats.)

• *At the end of the colonnaded stoa, on the right, the two big Doric columns mark the...*

❹ Prytaneion

The Prytaneion was a kind of town hall and the seat of the Roman governor, the proconsul of Asia Minor. It was from here that a committee of six officer-type priests (or *curetes*) made decisions about city administration. This important site was where the "eternal flame" was kept (in the rectangular pit). Just as Rome had its eternal flame tended by Vestal Virgins, honored citizens of Ephesus made sure this fire always flickered, to guarantee

the city's continued prosperity. The eternal flame of Ephesus was finally snuffed out when paganism was outlawed in AD 395.

• *Just next to the Prytaneion, enjoy the viewpoint at the top of the...*

❺ Sacred Way

From here, looking far beyond the city stretching below, you might catch a glimpse of the Aegean Sea. While the sea once lapped at the gates of the city, 1,500 years of silt and big-city drainage left Ephesus high and dry. Beyond the State Agora, to your left, is the site of the Domitian Temple (currently being excavated). Ahead of you is the path called the Sacred Way (a procession honoring Artemis proceeded here annually). This short road leads downhill from the State Agora to Domitian Square.

Notice hints of Roman engineering: Drainage pipes under the road kept sewage flowing. (However, the runoff from the water used by Ephesians contributed to the silting up of the harbor, which eventually spelled the end of the city.) Metal rings in the road were probably a later addition by early archaeologists to move the wagons carrying silt outside the ancient city. Crosshatching on the street stones gave ancient sandals a better grip when wet.

You'll come to two stone pillars with carved reliefs. These were directional aids: One, facing the market, is a marble block with a relief of Hermes (god of merchants); the other, facing a pharmacy, is a carving of Asklepios (symbolizing medicine). Cosmopolitan Ephesus was filled with traders and merchants who spoke a Babel of languages, so these pictograms helped arriving sailors find their way.

• *Just past these carved stones, enter Domitian Square and turn left.*

❻ Domitian Square

The square was ringed by important buildings and monuments. The highest surviving arch (on the left) marks what was a public water fountain. The cen-

terpiece of this quarter (straight ahead) was the **Temple of Domitian,** dedicated to the notorious first-century AD Roman emperor. Though little remains today, the temple was large—two stories tall (as the ruin suggests) and covered the area of a football field. A bit of the temple facade still stands, with statues capping a couple of columns. Domitian was the cruel, lunatic emperor who, it is believed, sent John the Prophet into exile to the nearby island of Patmos, where he worked in a rock quarry and wrote the Book of Revelation.

According to oral tradition, only two men received direct revelations from God (without Gabriel as the messenger): Moses and John. As John later penned in his Gospel, God commanded him with the task of teaching true faith to seven communities, including Ephesus (and communities within two days' walk of Ephesus). These places—also including Smyrna and Pergamon—are known as the "Seven Churches" or the "Churches of Revelation."

Opposite the Temple of Domitian stood a monument with carved reliefs describing the great deeds of the Roman tribune Gaius Memmius, which was probably the Roman equivalent of the "unknown soldier" monument.

Resting on the ground across from the temple site, look for an impressively carved piece of stone—the **Nike frieze,** which once topped a gate. This depicts the Greek goddess Nike giving the wreath of victory to the Romans.

• *Walk 30 yards farther down to the...*

❼ Hercules Gate

This gate—intentionally too narrow to let chariots pass—marks the transition from pedestrian-only upper Ephesus to the commercial Curetes Road. Just before the gate, notice the remains of a road branching off to the left: It provided the ancient equivalent of a "truck bypass route" detour leading around to the harbor. Also, look around to see pieces of the original arch that once welcomed pedestrians. There's a little perch a couple of steps up, just to the right of the gate, that provides a great photo op. Pass through the gate and look back at its pillars to see its namesake draped with lion skins.

• *Now begin your stroll down...*

❽ Curetes Road

This lane gives you a small glimpse of the epic scale of Ephesus at its peak. Mentally replace the tourists with toga-clad ancients to imagine the Roman metropolis in its heyday. Statues, bubbling fountains, arches, and shops lined the street. Columns supported a covered sidewalk for pedestrians, while chariots, wagons, and men on horseback traveled the road. In the shade of the arcades, people could hang out and play games such as backgammon. The buildings on either side of the street had shops below and homes above.

• *About 50 yards down from the Hercules Gate, on your right is...*

❾ Trajan's Fountain

This public fountain, a huge reservoir basin (66 by 33 feet), is topped by a pediment on stilts. Beneath the pediment once stood a statue of the powerful emperor Trajan proudly gazing over the pond. While the wealthy had indoor plumbing, fountains like this were the sole source of water for everyone else. The carving of Trajan with his foot on an orb and the phrase "Trajan ruled the world with his right foot" provide clear evidence that ancient Romans assumed the world was round. Little holes on the lower left of the fountain

are a reminder that to let loose a stream of water to cool and clean their town, Ephesians would just uncork the fountain.

Cross the street and step up to the bannister to survey the fine mosaic sidewalk of a colonnade once lined with shops that likely catered to the fancier aristocracy.

• *About 30 yards below Trajan's Fountain, take a little detour through...*

❿ The Baths

Like all Roman baths, the bath complex at Ephesus was divided into rooms with special purposes: a changing room, a cooling-off room *(frigidarium)*, a warm room *(tepidarium)*, a hot steam room *(caldarium)*, and so on. The tradition of large public baths in Mediterranean lands has continued through the centuries—from Romans to Byzantines to Ottomans to today's Turks. Back in Kuşadası, contemporary locals are enjoying the steamy descendants of bath complexes just like this.

• *Pop back out onto the main street and notice the next building down, one of the most photographed in all of Ephesus. The Corinthian columns and lone surviving curved arch mark the ruined vestibule of the...*

⓫ Temple of Hadrian

Symbolism abounds on this structure. The central relief over the arch is Tyche, the goddess of fortune and good luck. The figure in the lunette over the entrance to the temple proper likely represents the snake-haired **Medusa—or possibly** Hadrian's lover, a man named **Antinous** (considered the most ravishing beauty in all the realm), whom the heartbroken Hadrian had deified after his early death.

The eggs on the portal frame and the little flowers carved into the stone are symbols of fertility. The swastika-like repeating geometric pattern could suggest the Meander River (which brought life and prosperity to the people) or the rising sun (a promise of good fortune). One of the friezes shows the legend of Ephesus' founding by Greek prince **Androklos** (stalking a wild boar; originals are in the Ephesus Museum in Selçuk).

• *A few steps farther down Curetes Road, go in the little doorway by audioguide marker #143 to find...*

⓬ Public Toilets

The U-shaped latrine room features marble seating surrounding an

EPHESUS

open-air courtyard with a fountain. Few Ephesians could afford private bathrooms, so most people took care of business at a public latrine like this one. Visiting the loo evolved into a social event, and this room had seats for a rollicking party of 40. A wooden roof once topped the seating area. A constantly flushing stream of water ran beneath

the seats, whisking waste immediately to a sewer. Along the floor was a second stream with clean water for washing.

• *Across the street is a separate sight, which requires its own ticket. It's well worth the extra fee to visit the...*

⓭ Terrace Houses

This modern complex protects seven three-story homes, each with its own courtyard and elaborate decorations. They present a vivid

picture of the lifestyle of upper-class Ephesians. Excavated in 1999, the Terrace Houses offer an unparalleled opportunity to see how the ancients lived and to watch ongoing excavations. Visitors follow a one-way route through the complex, appreciating carefully restored mosaic floors and frescoed walls. I've

mentioned several things to watch for, but because excavations are ongoing, your route may differ. To get oriented, consult the handy floor plans and room descriptions displayed throughout the complex.

The buildings and decor you'll see date from the early Roman Imperial period—from roughly the first two centuries after Christ. The basic architectural unit was an open courtyard, lined by columns, with main rooms and utility rooms arranged around it.

Dwelling Unit 6 shows features typical of all upper-class **Roman homes:** living and dining rooms on the ground floor, bedrooms upstairs, and an open-air courtyard in the center. This allowed air to circulate, while the lack of windows on the outer walls kept out dust, noise, and sun—a system still used in homes of both the wealthy and the poor in hot climates around the world. Beneath the courtyard floor is a cistern that collected rainwater to supply the house. Although most of the walls today are rough brick (stripped of their original decoration), they once were covered with marble or frescoes, generally depicting mythological scenes.

Keep an eye out for surviving **water pipes** in the passages. While ordinary Roman citizens used shared bathing and latrine facilities (like the complex you saw across the street), the wealthy enjoyed private plumbing. There were two systems of pipes in these homes: one for water, and one (under floors and between walls) to carry hot air for heating.

The **Marble Hall** was the dining room, where homeowners entertained casual guests. This one had all marble floors and walls; archaeologists have identified some 120,000 fragments, which they are trying to piece back together (you may see workers sorting the marble like a huge jigsaw puzzle). In the middle of the room, a gurgling pool provided both decoration and a soothing soundtrack.

The huge vaulted hall of the **Basilica,** with its restored ceiling, was used as a formal reception room. It housed a decorative pool. Remnants of frescoes can still be seen along the walls.

Continuing upstairs to the bedrooms, you'll have a good view down into the courtyard of Dwelling Unit 7. But keep heading up toward Units 5 and 3. You may see a small **storage room** that held amphorae (pointy-bottomed clay jugs) containing household supplies such as wine or olive oil. The amphorae were partially buried in soil or sand to keep their contents cool. On the walls, overlapping layers of several frescoes are faintly visible (successive waves of earthquakes and fires over the generations forced homeowners to periodically redecorate).

You'll see **frescoes, drawings,** and **mosaics** of gladiators and animals, graffiti poems, and scenes promoting themes such as education and social values. Keep an eye out for the following: a lion, Dionysus (god of wine), Medusa (though evil, she protected this house), the philosopher Socrates, Eros (a.k.a. Cupid), Apollo (god of art) and the nine Muses (guardians of artistic inspiration), a fish and a duck (in the kitchen), and so on.

In Dwelling Unit 2, look for the small **bathroom.** Like the large latrine across the street, this one was communal, with two side-by-side seats (even in a wealthy household, pooping was a social event) and a constantly flowing channel of clean water at one's feet for washing.

From the very top of the complex, look down through the glass walkway to a particularly well-preserved **mosaic floor,** with the sea

EPHESUS

god Triton on the right, and a Nereid (protector of sailors), riding a seahorse, on the left.

• *Leaving the Terrace Houses, a lane leads back to the main road. From there, turn left to face the commanding facade of the Library of Celsus. Before approaching the library, look to your right, down the Marble Road. Little survives along this road (which is generally open to visitors only on weekends). It ran along the side of the commercial agora (which you'll walk through momentarily) to the theater and the road leading to the harbor.*

Now set your sights on one of the most iconic Roman-ruin images in the world, the...

⓮ Library of Celsus

This breathtaking structure epitomizes Ephesus at its peak. With some 12,000 volumes, it was the third-largest library of the ancient world (behind the collections in Alexandria, Egypt, and Pergamon—110 miles north). Its namesake was a well-read governor of this province, whose son built the library as a mausoleum in his honor in AD 123. The ruined library was restored to its current appearance in the 1970s.

The library's facade—two monumental stories tall—features a distinctive grid of columns and recessed niches. Those **Corinthian columns** (topped with leafy capitals) on the ground floor are 40 feet tall. There were three grand doorways, each matched by windows above. The four statues in the niches represent the traits of Celsus: wisdom, knowledge, intelligence, and valor. An optical illusion causes this grand facade to seem even bigger—the outer columns are actually shorter than the central ones, making the facade appear to bulge in the middle.

Begin climbing the steps to the library. On the second step from the top, on the right side, look for the metal box that protects an image of a **menorah** lightly carved into the step. Ephesus had a large Jewish population that was on relatively good terms with the Romans (since, unlike Christians, the Jews never attempted to convert pagans to their own faith).

Step into the small interior, and picture it in its prime. The walls and floors were once gleaming **marble** (which covered the restored brick understructure we see today). Light poured in through the big east-facing windows, which caught the morning sun. The niches that you see once held scrolls. A three-foot-wide gap between the inner and outer walls helped to circulate air to preserve the delicate documents.

The library's collection included two types of scrolls. The earliest **scrolls** were made of Egyptian papyrus. As the collection at the Pergamon library grew, rivaling that of Alexandria in Egypt, the Egyptians jealously refused to export any papyrus. So the Pergamonians invented a different material: parchment, made of dried-out animal skin. (Eventually the sheets of parchment, rather than being rolled, were stacked and bound at one end—creating the book format that you're holding right now.)

Back outside, notice the triple-arched **gate** next to the library. This was one of three monumental entrances to the commercial agora. The gate is inscribed in bronze letters with two names: Mazaeus and Mithridates. These were slaves who, freed by their master Emperor Augustus, became wealthy enough to build this gate in appreciation of their liberty.

• *Step through the gate into a huge empty square that was once the...*

⓯ Commercial Agora

This large marketplace was the main supermarket and shopping mall of Ephesus. Like standard agoras throughout the ancient Mediterranean, this was an open courtyard (360 feet square) surrounded by columns that supported a portico to shade businesses. From the array of shops stocked with goods brought in from the nearby harbor, Ephesians could buy anything they wanted. Engraved marble slabs out front pictured what each shop sold: a cleaver for the butcher, an olive branch for the oil vendor, a fish for the fishmonger, and so on. The raised island of pine trees in the center of this area—nearly seven feet overhead—illustrates how much dirt archaeologists removed when they excavated this part of Ephesus.

• *Walk across the agora (keep parallel to the Marble Road, above you to the right), and follow the crowds up a ramp to the top end of Harbor Road. Fanning out across the hill to your right is the...*

⓰ Great Theater

Before climbing the steps and entering the theater, notice the stones lined up, identified, and awaiting reconstruction. And swing by the

lovely Greek **fountain** (just to the right of the steps leading into the theater), with two graceful, fluted Ionic columns, once an elegant place for theatergoers to stop for water. Dating from Hellenistic Greece, at least a century before Christ, this is one of the oldest structures you'll see at Ephesus. (Its elegant design was obscured when Romans expanded it centuries later.)

Now, climb halfway up the stairs and follow a tunnel-like gallery (perhaps the actors' entry) to your right, which deposits you right on the stage floor.

It's huge. The theater held about 25,000 spectators (possibly the largest anywhere). Since a Roman theater was typically designed to accommodate 10 percent of its city's population, experts guess that ancient Ephesus had 250,000 residents.

Although the theater is partly ruined, the **acoustics** are still so good that performers don't need microphones to be heard (as tour guides and would-be divas love to demonstrate).

Check out the 66 rows, divided into the classes of Roman society. The lower level was reserved for VIPs and the emperor's box. Many seats here were covered in marble, with comfy seatbacks. The middle level held Roman citizens (most middle-class Ephesians). The upper level was bleacher seating for the lower classes—free men and women, and foreigners.

The ancient Greeks built the theater in the third century BC. When the Romans came, they enlarged and modified it for their particular brand of entertainment, raising the stage and adding a backdrop. They enlarged the stage wall (to 60 feet high) to improve acoustics and framed the stage area with pillars, creating a proscenium. Notice the wall around the orchestra (in front of the stage). When the theater hosted gladiator fights, this wall protected spectators from the action.

In modern times, the theater became a popular venue, presenting concerts by everyone from Sting to Pavarotti (who sang with no microphone in a performance that people still talk about) to Diana Ross.

This theater played a role in the dramatic story of the **Apostle Paul,** who lived in Ephesus about AD 50-54. While Christianity's message that all are created equal in God's eyes resonated with "the 99 percent," it threatened and offended that society's elites. Paul also ruffled feathers by strongly denouncing the worship of idols. Remember that the cult of the goddess Artemis was big business in Ephesus. Artemis idol carvers and silversmiths didn't like Paul's interference one bit. According to the Bible (Acts 19), they stirred up an angry mob and snatched some of Paul's Christian companions. Shouting "Artemis is great," the rabble-rousers dragged the captured Christians to this theater. Paul wanted to save them, but cooler-headed colleagues held him back. Fortunately, the enraged crowd inside calmed down and spared the Christians from harm.

• *Step back outside the theater. Standing at the top of the steps, look down the big road that once led to the sea (now over three miles away).*

⑰ Harbor Road

In ancient times, most visitors entered Ephesus on this road, which links the city and the harbor. It made a powerful first impression: marble paved, 35 feet wide, lined with covered sidewalks, and lit with 50 street lamps (a luxury rare in the ancient world). Like the Strip in today's Las Vegas, this was the city's glitzy main drag. The shops along the way sold a dazzling array of goods from around the known world. While the functional Marble Road is rutted with tracks from cart wheels, this showcase boulevard (also known as the Arcadian Way) is in great condition. Ceremonial processions traveled this route, and it was also *the* place in town to promenade—just as families around the Mediterranean still enjoy an evening stroll.

The original **harbor** sat at the far end of this road, a third of a mile away, on an inlet of the distant sea. This was the west end of the Royal Road—the chief thoroughfare of the Roman East—making Ephesus an important port in its day. The harbor gradually silted up over the centuries—first becoming marshland, and then solid ground—leaving today's waterfront miles away. Trade dried up with the harbor, and the city declined. Eventually Ephesus was literally buried and forgotten. Fortunately for us, archaeologists reopened this cultural time capsule and brought the treasures of Ephesus back to life.

• *Your visit to ancient Ephesus is over. To exit, walk down the Harbor Road a short distance, and look for the row of trees on your right. This marks the path (with great photo ops through the trees to the theater) leading to the lower gate, where* **taxis** *await to take you back to* **Kuşadası,** *to the* **House of the Virgin Mary,** *or to the nearby town of* **Selçuk.** *Note that there is no public transportation from Ephesus to the House of the Virgin Mary—only taxis.*

Sights Near Ephesus

HOUSE OF THE VIRGIN MARY (MERYEM ANA EVI)

Many Christians believe that the hillside of Mount Koressos above the ancient city of Ephesus is where the Virgin Mary, mother of Jesus Christ, spent the last 11 years of her life. (For the whole story, see the sidebar on page 402.) While the House of the Virgin Mary is a major Catholic and Orthodox pilgrimage site, Muslims also consider this a special place and appreciate Mary as the mother of a great prophet, referring to her as "Mother Mary."

Cost and Hours: 45 TL, daily 8:00-18:00, Nov-March until 17:00, about four miles outside Selçuk, www.hzmeryemanaevi. com.

Visiting the House: The experience of visiting the house is powerful to some, underwhelming to others. After twisting up a high road above Ephesus, walk through the beautiful **garden,** on a path lined with olive trees. You'll pass a large hole in the ground, which may have been a cistern (see the water pipes buried in the ground) or a baptistery. Then you reach an outdoor amphitheater, where priests celebrate outdoor Mass.

The stone **house** itself—a rebuilt shrine on the original foundations—is small and humble. The earlier structure was likely a typical Roman house: two stories, made of stone, and with four or five rooms. The red line on the outside wall marks the house's first foundation. Inside, devoted visitors shuffle through and say a prayer. The house has two rooms open to sightseers: the large living room and the small bedroom.

Down the hill in front is a wall of spouting **fountains.** The natural spring water is blessed as holy water, which the faithful believe has healing powers. The wishing wall nearby is full of and notes with requests for the Virgin Mary.

SELÇUK

The sleepy town of Selçuk is the modern-day descendant of Ephesus. It's an unexceptional but pleasant small Turkish town with a pair of important sights: the Ephesus Museum (with artifacts from the ancient site), in the center of town; and the foundations of the Basilica of St. John, on a hilltop a five-minute walk beyond the museum.

Selçuk's **TI** is in front of the museum (+90 232 892 6328). **Taxis** wait nearby. The bus station (where *dolmuş* minibuses arrive and depart constantly, and with plenty of cheap eateries nearby) is a couple of blocks from the museum.

Eating in Selçuk: **$$ Agora Restaurant,** across from the Ephesus Museum, has pleasant shaded outdoor seating and specializes in *çöp şiş*—cubes of lamb on a tiny wooden skewer (Agora Çarşısı 2, +90 232 892 3053). **$$ Selçuk Köftecisi,** across from the Selçuk bus terminal (and owned by a retired wrestler named Ertan), is the nondescript haunt of tour guides and locals, who appreciate its good daily dishes (Şahabettin Dede Bulvarı 10, +90 232 892 6696).

Shopping in Selçuk: If you're seeking a Turkish carpet, **Oba Rugs and Kilims is** on the right-hand side of the road as you turn from the main road leading to the Upper Gate of Ephesus (you can stop off here if you're going to the site by taxi). They carry a wide variety of carpets—from simple kilims to fancy silk carpets—and has comparatively down-to-earth prices (RS%—bargain anonymously, then show this book for an additional discount; Meryem Ana Kavşağı, Efes Üst Küme Evler 3, Selçuk, +90 232 892 9494). For more about the carpet-buying experience, see the Kuşadası section, later.

▲Ephesus Museum (Efes Müzesi)

There's no actual museum at the ancient site of Ephesus, so if you want to see some of the artifacts found there, this is your best opportunity. A visit here can round out your understanding of Ephesus.

Cost and Hours: 25 TL, daily 10:00-19:00, Oct-April 8:30-17:00, last entry one hour before closing, Atatürk Mahallesi, Uğur Mumcu Sevgi Yolu 26, www.muze.gov.tr.

Visiting the Museum: The U-shaped museum has eight rooms and a courtyard. In the first hall, you'll see various **statues** that filled the niches at some of the fountains at Ephesus, including the Fountain of Trajan.

The second hall displays findings from the **Terrace Houses,** including some original frescoes and mosaics, as well as medical tools, cosmetics, and jewelry. In the middle of the room is an ivory frieze, reassembled from tiny fragments, showing war preparations under Emperor Trajan (second century AD). The statue in the niche (far corner of room) depicts Artemis as a hunter. While Roman-era iconography depicts "Diana" (as they called her) this

Mary in Ephesus?

When Jesus saw his mother and the disciple whom he loved standing nearby, he said to his mother, "Woman, behold, your son!" Then he said to the disciple, "Behold, your mother!" And from that hour the disciple took her to his own home.

John 19:26-27

Christian belief is split on where Mary lived late in life: Jerusalem or Ephesus? Adherents of the Ephesus tradition think she may have come here with the Apostle John, to whom Jesus had entrusted his mother. Believers offer these details: After Jesus' death, the Apostle John was sent to convert the pagans of Rome's province of Asia. He came to its capital, Ephesus—and, because of Jesus' commission, he likely would have brought Mary. To avoid antagonizing the local population of pagan Artemis worshippers, Mary lived in a house on Mount Koressos, high above the city. After 11 years, Mary was taken up into heaven (the Assumption).

Another piece of evidence that Mary lived here, say the faithful, is the existence of the Church of the Virgin Mary in the city of Ephesus (now in ruins). During the early years of Christianity, such churches were only dedicated to people who lived or died in the immediate area.

During Byzantine times (fifth and sixth centuries), "Mary's house" was converted into a chapel but sustained damage in various earthquakes. The house—and the specifics of the story surrounding it—gradually crumbled over the centuries. And yet, a ragtag band of local Christians still venerated this place. For reasons that even they were unsure of, every 10 years they would

way, we'll see the local interpretation of her later. On the left side is a fresco that reportedly shows Socrates.

The third hall features coins, and in the fourth hall, look for the **Eros** (Cupid)—many items here are decorated with the love-sick little cherub. In this hall, named "Ephesus Through the Ages,"

you'll see pottery remains, glass items, toys, jewelry, and similar findings.

From here you pass along the end of an outdoor courtyard (the fifth hall). Look for backgammon boards carved into marble—evidence that this game, invented by the Persians and still popular among Turks today, was adopted and enjoyed by Romans. You'll also

visit the site on August 15—the feast day of the Assumption of Mary.

In the early 1800s, a nun named Anne Catherine Emmerich—who lived halfway across Europe, in Germany, and never set foot in Turkey—had a vision of Mary's house on the slopes of this distant mountain. Decades later, the remains of the house were discovered by priests familiar with Emmerich's visions and the tradition of local reverence for the site. Catholic officials eventually determined that this was the final residence of the Virgin Mary and, in the late 19th century, declared it a place of pilgrimage. The house was restored and opened to visitors in 1951; since then, three sitting popes (Paul VI, John Paul II, and Benedict XVI) have visited here.

Skeptics question this entire account. For one thing, biblical scholars believe that John the Apostle, John the Evangelist (who wrote the gospel), and John the Prophet (a.k.a. John of Patmos, who wrote the Book of Revelation) were most likely three different people, whom early church fathers mistakenly amalgamated into a single person. Based on hard historical evidence, only John the Prophet is certain to have spent time in Ephesus. And even if the various Johns were one and the same, the Bible isn't explicit about precisely who became Mary's caretaker—that person is identified only as "the disciple whom Jesus loved." And the only gospel to relate this story at all was the one attributed to—guess who?—John. Is the story possible? Yes. Probable? No.

But if you do believe that this really was Mary's final home, it's comforting to imagine that, after a tumultuous life, she was able to retire in such a tranquil setting.

see a sundial that once sat in Ephesus' marketplace and some sarcophagi from excavated cemeteries.

Follow arrows into the sixth hall, which focuses on the cult of the mother-goddess in Asia Minor through the ages. On the right wall of the room, notice the display with pre-Greek/pre-Roman depictions of the **mother-goddess** (the prototype for Artemis-Diana, and arguably even Mary).

Next, the Artemis Temple Hall has **tomb findings** from different historical periods, including material from the Temple of Artemis. Look for the dfinalliagram explaining nine different historical burial methods. This collection of tomb pottery, weapons, and glass dates from a time when you *could* take it with you—which made these graves a big target for looters and tomb raiders.

The eighth hall gives visitors a sense of the dark space of the Temple of Artemis, with light only on two statues of the mother-goddess. One is the collection's highlight: a larger-than-life, first-century AD statue of **Artemis** (from the Prytaneion, the "eternal flame" temple at Ephesus). Whether the bulbous orbs hanging from her torso are eggs, breasts, or bull testicles, they certainly represent fertility. Notice how she is surrounded by the wild animals she's thought to rule over. And notice that she has no hands—the missing originals were likely made of precious ivory or gold.

Finally, in the last room, you'll see exhibits on the **emperors,** who were venerated as gods. Upon entering, you en-

counter the head and forearm of a 23-foot-tall statue of Domitian (from his namesake temple near the upper gate). Farther into the room is the original frieze from the Temple of Hadrian, depicting the legendary founding of Ephesus by the Greek prince Androklos. You'll also see busts of various other emperors.

• *To get from the museum to the Basilica of St. John, turn left as you leave the museum, walk about a hundred yards, turn left again, and head uphill.*

Basilica of St. John (St. Jean Örenyeri)

This ruined basilica, perched on a hill over Selçuk, is a pilgrimage site for Christians. While there's little to see here, it's very historic and an easy walk from the town center, affording fine views over the valley below. From here, you also get your best look at the once famous, now underwhelming ruins of the Temple of Artemis.

Cost and Hours: 25 TL, daily 10:00-19:00, Oct-April 8:30-17:00, last entry one hour before closing, www.muze.gov.tr.

Visiting the Ruins: The Basilica of St. John—the last great monument of ancient Ephesus—was built on the supposed tomb of the Apostle John. Although skeptical historians dispute accounts of John's life in Ephesus, here's the story: John, one of Jesus' disciples, is said to have come to Ephesus in about AD 90 to preach the gospel. When John died in about AD 100, he was buried at this hilltop location. (For more on the biblical John—or Johns—see the "Mary in Ephesus?" sidebar, earlier.)

The Ephesian Artemis

Throughout its history, the area around Ephesus has had a deep connection to various incarnations of a life-giving female deity: first a Hittite mother-goddess called Kubaba, then an Anatolian one named Cybele. During the Greek period, the cult of the goddess Artemis (daughter of Zeus, twin sister of Apollo) caught on here. This Greek virgin-goddess was associated with childbirth and chastity, the moon and the wilderness, and the hunt and wild animals. The Romans later worshipped her as Diana.

The Ephesian version of Artemis took on characteristics of previous local mother-goddesses. According to tradition, Artemis was born in May, when Ephesians celebrated a festival of roses. They'd sacrifice bulls at the Temple of Artemis, cut off the testicles, and drape them over the statue of Artemis to celebrate her fertility. Many depictions of Artemis show her covered with these bulbous shapes (including two famous statues in the Ephesus Museum; illustrated here is the second century AD version known as the Beautiful Artemis). Another interpretation: These are not bulls' balls but the many breasts of a life-sustaining mother-goddess. Or perhaps they are eggs, signifying her fertility.

In the sixth century BC, locals built a spectacular Temple of Artemis, one of the Seven Wonders of the Ancient World. Only a single pillar of that temple survives today, on the other side of the hill from the archaeological site at Ephesus. Through Roman times, devotees of Artemis worshipped her using small carved statues.

Some historians suggest it's no coincidence that this ancient site so connected with the cult of a mother-goddess was later believed to be the final earthly home of the Virgin Mary.

Some 400 years later, the Byzantine (and Christian) emperor Justinian built this church to venerate St. John. The church was 360 feet long (about the size of Westminster Abbey) and had six domes. Front and center, beneath the central dome, was John's tomb.

The basilica was constructed largely from stones scavenged from Ephesus and from a pagan structure that once stood nearby—the Temple of Artemis at the foot of the hill. Because Muslims were pushing into the area at the time, the basilica's builders also erected a castle nearby, with walls extending down to encompass the basilica. Ultimately the walls failed to protect the hilltop; the Muslims took over and converted the basilica into a mosque (you can just make out the top of its minaret, without its pointy cap), before it was damaged by an earthquake and fell into disrepair.

The supposed site of St. John's tomb is marked by a marble slab and four pillars, representing the four Evangelists. You'll also see the baptistery's plunge pool and (in the little chapel in the left transept—protected in a brown wooden hut labeled "*treasury*") some frescoes of Jesus, Mary, and St. John.

From the viewpoint terrace in front of the basilica ruins, in one glimpse, you can take in the full 3,000-year sweep of this region's spiritual history: the Christian basilica ruins; the more recent Muslim **İsabey Mosque** complex at the foot of the hill ("İsabey" means Jesus, who is considered by Muslims to be a prophet); and the pagan temple ruins in the distance.

Those ruins—the **Temple of Artemis**—first put Ephesus on the tourist map. Today the site is marked by a lone rebuilt pillar, one of the 127 that once supported a huge structure completed in about 550 BC. The ancients considered the fabled temple one of the Seven Wonders of the World. Financed by the famously wealthy King Croesus, the marble temple rose five stories high and was about three times as big as Athens' Parthenon—making it the ancient Greeks' all-around largest building. A giant statue of Artemis presided over an opulent interior adorned with marble, paintings, gold, and silver, which drew pilgrims and tourists from throughout the ancient world. In 356 BC, the temple was burned by a man named Herostratus, who was desperate to become famous at any cost (a motive still called "Herostratic fame" today). The Ephesians rebuilt and enlarged it, then had to rebuild it once more after the Goths trashed it. When the first Christian missionaries (including St. John) came here in the first century AD, they met resistance from locals who were still worshipping Artemis.

But soon Christians had the upper hand in Ephesus. In AD 401, the temple was destroyed for good by order of Christian authorities intent on stamping out paganism. The structure lay buried for 17 centuries, until archaeologists came prospecting. Their goal was not so much the city of Ephesus as it was this legendary structure—the place where, for centuries, the faithful worshipped the goddess Artemis.

At the Basilica of St. John, a plaque commemorates the 1967 visit of Pope Paul VI. That was a big year for tourism for this region. With the papal acceptance of the legitimacy of the "House of the Virgin Mary," Ephesus was suddenly a major destination. The next year, Kuşadası built its first cruise-ship pier.

ŞİRİNCE

This small mountain village just inland from ancient Ephesus (and Selçuk) is popular with visitors who want to get a taste of village life. Quaint but touristy, Şirince has an almost Tuscan feel, with fruit orchards and vineyards. Small hotels in historic houses, numerous eateries, and gift- and wine-shops dot the meandering, narrow, cobblestone streets. It's a handy home base for those who prefer to avoid busy Kuşadası.

Sleeping in Şirince: $$$$ Güllü Konak is a restored historic home around a nicely manicured garden, with an elegant provincial feel and views from some rooms (Şirince Mahallesi 44, +90 232 898 3225, www.marti.com.tr/gullukonak).

Eating in Şirince: $$$ Şirince Artemis Restaurant, right at the village entrance, fills a former primary school building. Its big, beautiful garden overlooks the picturesque village (service can be slow, Şehit Yüzbaşı Özülkü Caddesi, +90 232 898 3240).

Kuşadası

With a prime Aegean Sea location, lots of shops, and scores of hotels, Kuşadası has a resort-town feel. Cruise ships arrive at a pier right in the heart of town.

A city of about 65,000, Kuşadası is about 14 miles from ancient Ephesus.

While there's not much sightseeing in Kuşadası, it's an entertaining place to buy some souvenirs. Kuşadası's **TI** (+90 256 614 1103) and taxi stand are on the waterfront, near the cruise terminal.

Bazaar

The fun (if touristy) Kuşadası bazaar is pleasant to explore even if you're not shopping. From the TI, head away from the water and toward town, then turn left and pass the old stone caravanserai (inn) on the right (now a temporary exhibition hall). The bazaar is just beyond the caravanserai on the right, along the pedestrianized Barbaros Boulevard and its intersecting alleys. Many of the same items sold in Istanbul are available here, at similar prices—carpets, leather, tiles, silver and gold jewelry, and so on. Salespeople can be extremely aggressive, especially toward single women. Avoid eye contact, and ignore attention-grabbing sales pitches; even saying "No, thanks" elicits a lengthy conversation. If buying anything, it's expected that you'll try to haggle down the price. Prices get more reasonable the farther you get from the main drag.

Carpet Shops

Because Kuşadası is flooded with cruise passengers, most shops in town aren't geared toward serious buyers; they're hoping to make a quick and very lucrative sale.  The classic Kuşadası carpet experience is to sit through a carpet-weaving demonstration. The best of these are enjoyable and truly educational cultural experiences. While you enjoy free tea and snacks, your charming host poetically describes both the art and technique of carpet weaving, stressing the painstaking work involved ("A poor village woman toiled for two years at her loom to create this masterpiece...").

After a demonstration of how silk is teased from silkworms and a look at the weaving process, you'll be taken into the showroom and educated on the various types and qualities of carpets. You'll take off your shoes and walk across a carpet to feel the pile under your toes. Shop assistants unroll carpet after carpet, dizzying you with gorgeous patterns. And then it's time for the hard sell, when the carpet you fall in love with drops 20 percent in price after the first bargaining exchange, and you think: Maybe I can get a good deal here. Don't believe it. Heavy markups are involved.

Closer to the cruise port, consider **Artizan** (RS%—bargain anonymously, then show this book for an additional discount; Mahmut Esat Bozkurt Caddesi 21, +90 256 612 3969). To find the shop, with your back to the cruise terminal, turn right and walk along the water about 300 yards, watching for a white-washed clock tower. Artizan is just past this tower, on your left.

Sleeping and Eating in Kuşadası

Sleeping: $$ İlayda Hotel (Atatürk Bulvarı 46, +90 252 614 3807, www.hotelilayda.com) and **$$ İlayda Avantgarde Hotel** (Atatürk Bulvarı 42, +90 252 614 7608, www.ilaydaavantgarde.com) are sister hotels located on Kuşadası's main boulevard, right in the city center. Both have views of the Aegean and Samos Island.

$$$ La Vista Boutique Hotel and Spa, south of the cruise port, is bright and spacious, with a resort feel and sea views from every room (Güvercinada Caddesi 26, +90 256 614 1235, www.lavistahotel.net).

Eating: $$$$ Kazım Usta Restaurant, next to the cruise port, is casual, with colorful fishing dinghies moored nearby; they specialize in veggie and seafood mezes and salt-coated fish (Mahmut Esat Bozkurt Cad. 14/A, +90 256 614 1226).

$$$$ Mezgit Restaurant, across from Migros by the marina, displays the daily catch and mezes; the indoor/outdoor space is shaded by the vines flowing down the roof in summer (Atatürk Bulvarı 104, +90 256 618 0828).

$$$ Tranche, next to the public beach at the marina, is a combination butcher/steakhouse with views of the cove (Setur Marina, Atatürk Bulvarı 101, +90 256 618 2829).

$$$ Antepli Restaurant, about a mile outside of the center on the way to Ephesus and popular with locals, is a kebab restaurant with Mesopotamian mezes (Akyar Mevkii Ege Vista Alış-Veriş Merkezi 4, +90 256 618 1008).

EPHESUS

CAPPADOCIA

Kapadokya

In an arid, otherworldly landscape shaped by erosion, Cappadocia (kah-pah-DOK-yah) is often overlooked by visitors to Istanbul. But those who venture to this region in the center of Turkey are rewarded with stunning scenery, unique experiences, a distinctive local lifestyle, a rich and layered history, and small-town warmth.

A fascinating parade of cultures has shaped the history of this ancient land, but it's the striking geology that first grabs your attention. Cappadocia is famous for its exotic-looking terrain, especially its iconic "fairy chimneys."

The vast Persian Kingdom of Cappadocia occupied all of central Turkey from 330 BC to 17 AD, when it was subsumed as a Roman province. Early Christians seeking shelter—from Roman persecution in ancient times and from seventh-century Arab invaders—turned to Cappadocia's landscape. Over thousands of years, communities were carved into the rock—allowing residents to hunker down when armies passed through. This unique way of life resulted in some thrilling troglodyte sights: the church-and-chapel-filled valley at Göreme, the workaday community at Zelve, the castle-mountains at Uçhisar and Ortahisar, and entire subterranean cities in Kaymaklı and Derinkuyu.

Today, the tourists' Cappadocia is compact—most of the highlights described in this chapter are within about a 30-minute drive of each other. Beyond its stunning landscape and cave sights, Cappadocia comes with some fine communities that offer insight into its unique way of life. The village of Mustafapaşa has a proud history and makes a handy home base with all the tourist comforts.

Cappadocia

To Kalaba

To Cappadocia Airport

PEDESTRIAN BRIDGE

Kızılırmak River

To Kayseri & Erkilet Airport

Avanos

D-300

N

To Nevşehir & Cappadocia Airport

D-300

PAŞABAĞ VALLEY

Çavuşin

ZELVE OPEN-AIR MUSEUM

D-302

C A P P A D O C I A

GÖREME OPEN-AIR MUSEUM

Göreme

Ürgüp

CASTLE **Uçhisar**

D-302

CASTLE Ortahisar

To Nevşehir, Kaymaklı, Derinkuyu, Güzelyurt & Aksaray

D-302

ÜRGÜP YOLU

İbrahimpaşa

See Mustafapaşa detail map

Mustafapaşa

3 Kilometers

3 Miles

To Şahinefendi

To Güzelyurt and Ihlara Valley via Kaymaklı & Derinkuyu

Accommodations & Eateries
1. Sacred House Hotel
2. Bizim Ev Restaurant
3. MADO Restaurant
4. Millokal Restaurant
5. Şıra Rest. Wine Cellar
6. Tık Tık Kadın Emeği

Folk Shows
7. Uranos Cave Rest. & Performance Center
8. Harmandalı Cave Rest.
9. Saruhan Caravanserai

More off the beaten path is the overlooked village of Güzelyurt—a sentimental favorite of mine.

Consider splurging on a once-in-a-lifetime hot-air balloon ride over this unique, mind-bending landscape. While pricey, for many travelers, that magical activity is an unforgettable, trip-capping highlight.

PLANNING YOUR TIME

Cappadocia is worth at least two full days; a third (or even fourth) day lets you slow down and feel less rushed. This chapter covers the best of Cappadocia's "must-see" sights and less touristy villages, and recommends home-basing in the handy, well-preserved town of Mustafapaşa.

For an ideal visit, focus on what I consider the heart of Cappadocia—a triangle defined by the town of Avanos to the north, Uçhisar to the west, and Mustafapaşa to the east, plus a side trip a bit farther south to the underground cities in Kaymaklı or Derinkuyu. The following plans assume you're renting a car and packing as much as you reasonably can into each day.

Cappadocia in One Day: Visit Paşabağ Valley (with its fairy-chimney rock formations) and the Göreme Open-Air Museum (churches carved into the rock). Have lunch and a stroll in Mustafapaşa.

Two Days: Add the underground city of Kaymaklı and Uçhisar Castle; also consider visiting the pottery workshops in Avanos and soaring over Cappadocia in a hot-air balloon.

Three Days: Add the Zelve Valley to learn more about the communal lifestyle of the not-so-distant past, and enjoy a nature walk in a scenic Cappadocia valley (such as near Mustafapaşa).

With More Time: Add the town of Güzelyurt and a sturdy hike in Ihlara Valley (an hour's drive southwest of central Cappadocia).

ARRIVAL IN CAPPADOCIA

Shuttle services connect from either **Erkilet Airport** (in Kayseri) or **Cappadocia Airport** (in Nevşehir) to area hotels for about $10-15 per person one-way, but make many stops and can be slow. Direct private transfers are faster but pricier ($80-110/up to 4 people). Some hotels offer free or discounted shuttle service—ask when you reserve. Otherwise, contact **SRM Travel** for shuttle options (cappadocia@srmtravel.com). Taxis, which wait at the airport and use their meters, run about $50-75 for the ride to the heart of Cappadocia.

GETTING AROUND CAPPADOCIA

While you can explore Cappadocia on your own, it's slow by public transit. Consider renting a car at the airport or joining an organized tour (see next).

By Public Transportation: Public transit in Cappadocia is designed for locals and doesn't serve tourist needs well. Service is infrequent outside of work and market hours, and journeys may require several changes. But if you have more time than money, plus a keen sense of adventure, this can be a memorable way to travel. Major towns in Cappadocia have central bus terminals (called *otogar*). Smaller villages have designated points with services and transport to neighboring communities.

By Rental Car: Both airports have rental car desks for big international outfits (i.e., Avis, Budget, Sixt, Enterprise); for the best prices and availability, book ahead.

By Taxi or Private Driver: You can splurge on a taxi or private driver to link destinations; arrange either in advance with your hotel. If you'll be town-hopping, rates start at about $75 by taxi for up to four passengers.

TOURS IN CAPPADOCIA

Group Day Tours: A grab-bag of companies offer interchangeable itineraries connecting Cappadocian highlights in 16- and 24-seat tour buses (figure $60-110 per person, including admissions and lunch). Most tours set out from Cappadocia-area hotels around 9:30 or 10:00 and return around 17:00. Your hotelier can help you find a tour operator that works for you.

Private Guides: The following guides can accompany you in your rental car as you tour the area.

SRM Travel, operated by this book's co-authors, offers private tours of Cappadocia and can arrange private guides; mention this book to receive free trip-planning advice when you buy any travel service (private guides from $235/half-day, $265/full-day, +90 216 266 5839, www.srmtravel.com).

Mustafa Uysun specializes in Christian history and early Christian art ($250/full-day tour focusing on Christian aspects of Cappadocia, also offers photography tours, mobile +90 532 435 9694, muysun@gmail.com). **Deniz Ozbucak Turgut** is experienced with Rick Steves travelers and enjoys teaching both history and contemporary Cappadocian life ($235/half-day, mobile +90 532 587 4724, ozbucakdeniz@hotmail.com).

HELPFUL HINTS

Sightseeing Info and Advance Tickets: Most sights in this chapter are run by Turkey's Ministry of Culture and Tourism. To buy advance tickets, which can be a great timesaver for popular sights such as the Göreme Open-Air Museum, check www.muze.gov.tr (Cappadocia sights are listed under the city of Nevşehir). It's also smart to reserve ahead for hot-air balloon rides or folk shows.

Sightseeing Passes: Busy sightseers may save some money with either the Cappadocia Museum Pass or the Turkey Museum Pass, both of which cover most of the sights mentioned in this chapter. Figure out which sights you plan to visit and do the math. You can buy a pass online (www.muze.gov.tr) or at the first major sight you visit (including Göreme, Zelve, Kaymaklı, and De-rinkuyu). Pass holders are sometimes allowed to skip ticket-buying lines at popular sights.

Cappadocia by Season: Summer is hot and dry, with long days; because most Turks head to the beach for summer vacation, landlocked Cappadocia is quieter from late June through August. Spring and fall (April-late June, Sept-mid-Nov) are pleasant but crowded with student groups and Turkish urbanites on weekend breaks. Winter is off-season, with lower prices and shorter days.

Festivals: In late summer (Aug-early Sept), the Klasik Keyifler chamber music festival enlivens Cappadocia with performances at historic caravanserais (lodging for caravans) and al fresco shows in the shadow of a fairy chimney (www.klasikkeyifler.org).

Accommodations: Rooms here fall into two broad categories: Big, modern hotels and characteristic "cave" properties that have been converted into small hotels. Modern hotels are required to be set at a distance from natural wonders (to protect the landscape)— meaning there's not much to do in their immediate vicinity. Cave hotels are often in more atmospheric settings but can vary widely in quality and modern amenities: Some are slick and boutiquey, while others feel like the Stone Age. Cave hotels truly are caves: Even high-end places can feel humid, smell musty, and occasionally sprinkle little bits of earth from the ceiling.

Eateries: I've recommended good places to eat in three strategically located areas: in the home-base village of Mustafapaşa; in the pottery-making town of Avanos, near the Göreme Valley; and in Uçhisar.

Packing Tips: Cappadocia is a high desert. In all seasons, temperatures can vary drastically from day to night. Pack layers and plan for all temperatures. Shoes with good traction are necessary for dusty terrain, especially if you're planning to do valley walks.

Sights in the Heart of Cappadocia

These places are all within about a 30-minute drive of one another, in the heart of Cappadocia (see the "Cappadocia" map near the beginning of this chapter). I've listed them roughly in order of sightseeing priority.

▲▲▲Fairy Chimneys of Paşabağ Valley

The amazing Paşabağ (puh-suh-buh) Valley is a forest of massive fairy-chimney formations. Centuries of volcanic eruptions left huge boulders atop layers of hardened volcanic ash. As the softer rock eroded, the harder rocks were left precariously balanced atop the pinnacles that have become the icons of Cappadocia. (Some

Cappadocia's Volcanic Geology 101

Over thousands of years, several volcanoes blanketed Cappadocia with a thick layer of ash. Some of this accumulation was covered in lava that cooled into layers of volcanic rock. Under the pressure of this top layer, the ash solidified into the soft rock we call tufa.

Wind, rain, and snowmelt gradually eroded the land, leaving behind parts of the hard, volcanic rock, and the tufa layer just underneath—which was partially protected from erosion by the rock on top. This is how the "fairy chimneys" were born: a column of softer tufa, capped with a "capital" or "parapet" of volcanic rock.

These stunning formations are vulnerable to the elements: Eventually, earthquakes, erosion, and frost topple the rock cap; once that's gone, the unprotected soft tufa body cannot survive for long, and eventually erodes away. Erosion is also what keeps the cycle going. Older chimneys are continuously being wiped away, while new ones come into existence in massive accumulations of tufa. This process will go on as long as the wind blows and the rain falls.

international travelers, noticing the phallic shape of the pillars, have nicknamed this "Love Valley.")
Most chimneys are multibodied and multipeaked, and many have chapels or residences carved inside.

Cost and Hours: 18 TL, daily 8:00-19:00, Nov-March until 17:00, +90 384 271 3535.

Visiting the Valley: Allow about 45 minutes to wander around. Park your car in the lot just outside the valley and walk to the turnstiles to buy your ticket (WCs at entrance but not in valley). For the best views, climb the hill west of the fairy chimneys and then slowly descend into the valley.

The Göreme (goh-reh-meh) Valley was home to a continuous Christian monastic tradition for almost 900 years, into the 13th century. The monks carved churches and chapels deep into the rock, along with spaces to support their lifestyle: refectories, kitchens, and dormitories. Today the valley is an open-air museum, giving visitors full access to the caves. You'll also see church decorations, wall paintings, and frescoes that date back to the late Byzantine period.

Cost and Hours: 75 TL, 25 TL extra for Dark Church, to avoid ticket-buying lines buy in advance online at www.muze.gov.tr, open daily 8:00-19:00, Oct-March until 17:00, +90 384 271 2167.

Background: At its peak, the Göreme Valley was home to over 300 rock-carved churches and monasteries. Today, the open-air museum incorporates just a slice of this huge medieval complex. Unlike the "underground cities" you'll see elsewhere in Cappadocia, this complex dates from a time when it was no longer necessary to hide from invading armies: Churches here are out in the open, carved in large tufa blocks or hillsides, some with inviting sculpted facades. (Some of the rock-cut spaces here predate the valley's Christian heritage—originally carved for a different purpose, they were later converted to places of religious significance.)

As you explore, you'll see that interior decorations vary. Wealthier churches boast wall paintings and frescoes designed to fit a particular space; others have simple, monochrome, geometric patterns. Most of the decoration is intended to give the impression that you're in a freestanding church, with fine domes, columns, and vaults rather than hand-hewn walls.

The writings of the Cappadocian Fathers (see sidebar) and scenes depicted in wall paintings of the churches illustrate the unique monastic lifestyle at Göreme. Death loomed large, and the focus of religious life was salvation. The torture of Jesus Christ on the Cross, the suffering of early Christians, and persecution by Iconoclasts were all mourned communally in the valley's tiny churches.

○ Self-Guided Tour: Allow 2-3 hours for your visit. Park in the smaller lot just across from the museum entrance. After entering, hang on to your ticket—you'll need it to visit sights inside. Head into the park and get your bearings.

We'll tour the site counterclockwise, stopping at the churches listed below.

• *Past the turnstiles, take the visitors route. Start with the Chapel of St. Basil (first on the right).*

Chapel of St. Basil: Through the doorway, you enter a burial chamber. The holes in the ground were graves. The larger ones were

Three Cappadocian Fathers (and One Mother)

Four Cappadocians from the fourth century—who grew up together, worked together, and knew each other intimately—left a lasting mark on Christianity.

The "greatest" was Basil the Great. He was born around the year 330 to a prominent Christian family, at a time when early eastern Christianity and paganism still coexisted. Basil was homeschooled by his sister, Macrina, alongside his kid brother Gregory ("of Nyssa"). When Basil went off to college, he met a fellow student named Gregory of Nazianus, and they soon became fast friends. Though these four people would go their separate ways over the years, they were united in their strong Christian faith and opposition to what they saw as heretical ideas that were dividing their homeland.

Basil continued his studies in Constantinople and Athens, soaking up both the Greek classics and early Biblical teachings. But what called to him was the solitary life of the monk. He founded a commune near Uluköy, in northern Turkey, and established a regimen of work and prayer that set the tone for monastic life. His erudite writings helped solidify Christian doctrine, and his eloquent prayers have become part of the everyday liturgy. (A great place to commune with this holy man is in the rustic Chapel of St. Basil in Göreme.)

Basil's unassuming brother, Gregory, stayed home and became bishop of Nyssa in Cappadocia. He wrote a popular ode to his pious sister, Macrina, who chose a humble life studying scripture.

Meanwhile, Gregory of Nazanius traveled the Christian world, studying philosophy in Athens and Alexandria, and becoming bishop of Constantinople. Eventually, he retired back home in Güzelyurt (where you can visit the Church of St. Gregory—see page 429).

Together, the Cappadocian Fathers helped confirm the Christian doctrine of the Holy Trinity (one God in three persons: God, Jesus, and the Holy Spirit). Followers of a teacher named Arius asserted that, because Jesus was physically born of God, the Trinity must be three separate entities. All of Christianity was divided. But in fiery sermons and scholarly treatises, the Cappadocian Fathers successfully championed the three-in-one concept, known today as the Nicaean Creed (for the Turkish city of Nicaea—now İznik) which some Christians still recite today: "I believe in one God..."

The Fathers were eventually granted sainthood in the Eastern Orthodox and Eastern Catholic churches. Macrina was canonized for inspiring them, and for her legendary asceticism: She lived a life of chastity and died lying on the hard ground because a bed would be too hedonistic.

for the church's benefactors, and the smaller ones were probably for orphans admitted to monastic life before puberty.

In the connecting chapel, the small main apse has a painting of Jesus. As you face the apse, on the left wall, notice the Cappadocian St. Basil (next to St. Theodore on a red horse). The chapel is dedicated to St. Basil, who stressed the importance of communal monastic life over the seclusion and asceticism that were popular among early Christians at that time. His belief in the equal importance of work and prayer paved the way for monasteries that followed. (Today, the Benedictine Order—named for Europe's patron saint—still follows the motto *Ora et labora*—pray and work.)

On the opposite wall is a painting of St. George mounted on his white horse. George and Theodore—the martyred equestrian saints—were natives of Anatolia and soldiers in the Roman army. Their stories were popularized in Europe by Crusaders, who passed through here on their way to the Holy Land. That's how St. George—who was from Cappadocia—became the patron saint of England, Catalunya, and many places in Western Europe.

• *Back outside on the visitors route, walk up the hill. Past the Apple Church on the right, in about 50 yards, is the...*

Chapel of St. Barbara: This space was designed with a cross plan, domes, and the main apse flanked by two niches. The two large holes in the ground (to the left as you enter) were probably used for baptisms. Just beyond, on the left wall, you'll find a painting of St. Barbara. This patron saint of architects, stonemasons, and gravediggers was a martyr from Nicomedia (today's İzmit, near Istanbul). Notice how both the main apse and the niches have altars for the bread and wine during the Eucharist—a common feature in Cappadocian churches.

More distinctive are the unique red geometric designs—Christian iconography. For example, find the large cross at the center of the main dome. It represents Jesus, and the four pairs of arrows around it depict Archangels. Together they represent the Ascension of Christ. These geometrical patterns are also thought to be magical—symbols to protect priests against Satan's temptation.

• *Back outside, a few steps up the path puts you in front of the...*

Chapel of St. Onuphrius (a.k.a. the Snake Church): This narrow, rectangular church was dedicated to St. Onuphrius, portrayed as a nude hermit on the barrel vault (Onuphrius spent 70 years in seclusion in the Egyptian desert). Look for the two horseback martyrs—St. Theodore and St. George—killing a huge snake (giving this chapel its name). Next to St. Theodore (red horse), St. Helen and her son Constantine hold a cross between them, symbolizing that they are the protectors of the true Christian faith. Helen was made a saint for her quest to find the "true cross" upon which Jesus was crucified.

• *As you walk up the hill, peek into the chamber marked as the* **refectory**. *Inside, everything is hewn out of rock: the stairs, the tables, and the benches around them. These halls were used by the monks for communal meals, meetings, special events, and funerals. At one time more than a dozen refectories operated in the valley, each one associated with a different monastery.*

At the top of the hill, you'll see a stairway leading up to the...

Dark Church: Stairs lead to a courtyard in front of the church entrance. This courtyard was once a huge inner hall, but the rock facade eroded and eventually collapsed. A second set of stairs takes you to inside the Dark Church (covered by a separate ticket).

The church interior barely sees any daylight—giving it its name. However, this darkness has helped preserve the impressive frescoes decorating the interior, which were probably painted by visiting artists from Constantinople (roughly between 1000 and 1050). Vividly colorful frescoes cover every surface of the church. From the top down, they tell stories about God and celestial beings, the life of Christ and his followers, and early saints. There are themes from the Old and New Testaments, as well as the so-called apocryphal bibles (written around the same time, but not accepted as canonical).

Tune into the symbolism of the colors. Purple represents celestial rulers, including Mary. Blue represents the Kingdom of God—heaven. The clothing is indicative of daily medieval life here. Notice that most women are covered head to toe, as if clad in a burka—this local tradition predates not only Islam, but even Christianity, going all the way back to pagan times.

• *As you exit the open-air museum, keep walking down the hill along the road. After a short walk, on the right, you'll see the entrance to the...*

Tokalı Church: Tokalı is the largest and most impressive of all the churches in Göreme. With its design, size, and elevated ceiling, it almost feels like a freestanding structure, carved in stages.

Entering the Old Church, scenes on the vaulted ceiling portray the life of Christ—starting with the Annunciation and continuing to the Resurrection, as Jesus saves Adam and Eve by breaking the gates of hell and trampling Satan under his feet.

Farther into the cave, the New Church (c. late 10th or early 11th century) has a distinctly different style. It was funded by influential donors who could afford to import artists from Constantinople—so the style reflects that of the capital city. As if to further show off their wealth, large amounts of precious lapis lazuli were crushed to create the dominant blue color, and the halos of Jesus and Mary were painted with real gold.

▲▲Avanos Pottery Workshops

Avanos (ah-vah-nohs)—about 10 minutes north of Göreme—is one of Cappadocia's larger towns, built on the banks of the Kızılırmak River (Turkey's longest). For millennia (at least 4,000 years, dating back to the Hittites), locals have taken advantage of the soft, moldable riverbank clay to make pottery. You can browse a variety of pottery workshops in town, most of which are handed down from father to son. Potters eagerly invite you in, offer you tea, show off their kick-wheel skills, and even let you try throwing your own pot. While free, these presentations come with an expectation that you'll buy something.

Eating in Avanos: $$ Bizim Ev Restaurant, close to the main bridge on the Kızılırmak River, is a traditional eatery with seating inside under a vaulted ceiling and out on the terrace (Orta Mahalle, Baklacı Sokak 1, +90 384 511 5525). **$$ MADO,** part of a well-known Turkish ice-cream chain, is also a full-service restaurant. It's on the bank of the river overlooking an isle with a small duck colony (Asmaaltı Köprü Yani, Kızılırmak kenarı, +90 384 511 5023).

▲▲▲Underground Cities of Kaymakli and Derinkuyu

Located at the heart of Anatolia, Cappadocia was a crossroads for invading armies—and warfare was a fact of life. As early as the second millennium BC, locals took advantage of the soft tufa rock to carve hidden underground shelters. Over time, these shelters were gradually enlarged and connected—becoming entire underground cities where thousands could live safely for months at a time, without ever emerging into the light of day. They were designed to include communal spaces, as well as churches, stables, kitchens, storage units, cellars, grape presses, and even toilets.

Cappadocia has an estimated 150 such underground shelters—mostly near or below homes, or under cemeteries, to provide an easy escape in case of attack. Hidden tunnels lead to communal parts of the complex. And most of these tunnels (and parts of the underground complexes) are still in use today, as cellars, storage units, and stables.

About two dozen underground cities are known, and two in particular are well set up for visitors and only a 10-minute drive apart: **Kaymaklı** (which could have held 5,000 people) and **Derinkuyu** (20,000 people).

Choose just one to visit, as the experience is similar, and allow about 1.5 hours to explore. Kaymaklı has tighter spaces, including a couple of long, narrow tunnels—you'll only be able to stand up straight in a few of the chambers. For some, this is the most atmospheric and authentic "cave dwelling" experience. But if you're tall or wary of tight spaces, go instead to Derinkuyu, which has larger halls and higher ceilings.

Cost and Hours: 50 TL each, daily 8:00-19:00, Oct-March until 17:00. To avoid lines in peak season, buy tickets online in advance at www.muze.gov.tr.

Visiting the Underground Cities: This experience is not for everyone: The narrow tunnels, low ceilings, and lack of daylight will make some feel claustrophobic. You can usually walk down to the first level to get a feel for it and decide whether to proceed. Once you head farther in, know that you'll be on a one-way route through a veritable labyrinth with no backtracking.

Once inside the underground city, you'll follow a marked path to explore the networks of streets and plazas. You'll find kitchens, cramped living spaces, massive roll-away-the-stone doors, and ingenious ventilation shafts to bring fresh air to the many underground levels. The tunnels are tight—you'll have to hunch down to move around. But that was all part of the plan to make any would-be invader vulnerable. It must have been a long, dark wait down here while armies and oppressors raged above. But it's inspiring to think of the persecuted Christians who decided to go—literally—underground. The underground cities are a remarkable example of their determination to live free and true to their faith.

▲▲Uçhisar Castle

Standing at 200 feet, Uçhisar (ooch-hee-sahr) Castle is a huge natural rock formation pocked with numerous man-made caves. This castle-mountain's high vantage point was ideal for exerting control over the area. It was used as a stronghold for centuries and could house upwards of 1,000 people. Hardy hikers who tackle the steep and often irregular steps are rewarded with a 360-degree view of central Cappadocia.

Cost and Hours: 20 TL, daily 7:30-20:00, Oct-March until 18:30, +90 384 219 2005.

Eating in Uçhisar: $$$$ Millokal Restaurant is upscale and offers a view (Tekelli Mahallesi, Karlık Sokak 30, +90 535 1000 1925 or +90 384 219 2288, www.millocalrestaurant.com). **$$$$ Şıra Restaurant Wine Cellar** has a good wine collection—both local and national—and has a wine-pairing menu for Cappadocian dishes (Tekelli Mahallesi, Göreme Caddesi 87, +90 384 219 3037).

CAPPADOCIA

▲Zelve Archaeological Park

One of scores of similar cave communities here in Cappadocia, Zelve (zehl-veh) was continuously inhabited from the 10th century until the 1960s. Eventually abandoned due to landslide risk, today it's an open-air museum similar to Göreme. While Göreme is all about churches and chapels—and their art— Zelve gives a better sense of everyday life in a troglodyte community, with a wider variety of dwellings...including a mosque mixed in among the churches.

Cost and Hours: 20 TL, daily 8:00-19:00, Nov-March until 17:00, at the end of the road past Paşabağ Valley.

Visiting the Park: Zelve consists of three separate valleys that converge at what was the "central square." Exploring this pink landscape, you'll see hundreds of cave dwellings connected by stairs and tunnels. Imagine this place centuries ago: It was a thriving community, with thousands of inhabitants. Caves served as ancient condominiums, with holes dug out as cooking pits. They were also equipped with natural pantries—cubby holes carved for storage of food and wine. Big, animal-powered stone wheels ground grain. The residents ingeniously used whatever nature offered them. For example, watch for the many holes burrowed into the rock face. This allowed easy collection of pigeon droppings, which were valuable fertilizer to assure a good harvest in the valley below (especially for vineyards).

▲Ortahisar Castle

Like Uçhisar, the castle-mountain of Ortahisar (ohr-tah-hee-sahr) served as an fortress to control the area. Its main appeal is that it's far less touristy and easier to climb. The coffee shop overlooking the castle is busy with locals and welcomes visitors.

Cost and Hours: 20 TL, daily 7:30-20:00, Oct-March until 18:30.

Experiences in Cappadocia

▲▲▲Hot-Air Ballooning

A wonderful way to appreciate Cappadocia's bizarre landscape is from above. For me, the most exciting balloon ride anywhere is here in Cappadocia. It's pricey (usually around $250 per person, more in peak season) but memorable.

Tours start before sunrise: A shuttle bus whisks you to the departure point—which can change depending on conditions.

Cappadocian Wines

Cappadocia's winemaking tradition dates back more than 4,000 years. Archaeologists have dug up golden wine cups, clay jugs, and Assyrian cuneiform script describing the wine trade and harvest season. In pagan times, wine was offered to the gods, and early Christians used it for Eucharist through Byzantine rule. Even under the Muslim Turks, production continued (although in lesser volume) by the Orthodox population. One branch of Islam that permits the drinking of wine—Bektashi—has its roots in Cappadocia. Coincidence?

The taste of Cappadocian wine is shaped by climate and terrain: the drastic temperature difference between day and night, and the contrast between freezing cold winters and sun-baked summers. The local grape varietal, Emir, produces award-winning whites. Red wines feature adopted Öküzgözü and Boğazkere grapes from the Euphrates basin. Grapes grow just above the dirt, and are not elevated. After harvest, the plant is trimmed down to its roots and buried in the soil so it can survive the winter frost. In addition to wine, local grapes are used to make juice and molasses.

Groups gather in a desolate field that suddenly becomes a hive of activity. Noisy burners are fired up and balloons filled. You'll climb into the basket, meet your captain who fills up the balloon with a sound like a fire-breathing dragon, and—skimming the grass—you slowly lift off. While scary for some, the feeling I get is one of graceful stability...with majestic views. Soon, scores of tourist-filled balloons share the sky in silent wonder. Pilots skillfully maximize the drama of this unforgettable landscape—a forest of pinnacles honeycombed with ancient dwellings.

Due to limited air space and the number of balloons, baskets fill up quickly. Booking in advance for peak season is a must. To avoid scams, book direct with the balloon company or via a reputable third party such as your hotelier or tour guide. **Butterfly Balloons** (www.butterflyballoons.com) is a well-established company with experienced crew; if they're full, **SRM**  **Travel** (cappadocia@srmtravel.com) can help you find another good option.

▲Folk Shows

Touristy but fun folk shows abound in Cappadocia. These are typically held in caves, which are often large and impressive in their own right. The standard routine is for one group of dancers to perform samples from a half-dozen different parts of Turkey, with costume changes and live-music accompaniment. The $30-50 price tag includes snacks and a drink; booking ahead is a must. Reputable options include **Uranos Cave Restaurant and Performance Center** in Avanos (Gülşehir Caddesi, Akbel Mevki, İkinci Taş Köprü Karşısı, +90 384 511 3560), and the smaller **Harmandalı Cave Restaurant** in Uçhisar (includes belly dancing, Aşağı Kavak Köyü Yolu, +90 384 219 2364).

Another option is to attend a whirling dervish ritual at the 13th-century **Saruhan Caravanserai** in Avanos (€25, reservation required, daily at 18:00 and 21:00, New Kayseri Road, Km 6, +90 384 511 3795, www.saruhan1249.com).

Villages in Cappadocia

MUSTAFAPAŞA

The village of Mustafapaşa (moos-tah-fah-puh-shah), worth ▲▲, is a good home base for exploring the area. Mustafapaşa was once

a predominantly Greek settlement called Sinasos—home to the wealthiest community in all of Cappadocia. Remarkably well preserved, the village provides a "Cappadocia in miniature" look at the way local settlements evolved through the centuries, from the earliest cave dwellings to the stately mansions of the 1800s. A walk through Mustafapaşa peels back layers of history, geology, and culture. I also like Mustafapaşa because it's one of the few villages in the region not overrun by mass tourism: The government has carefully protected both its charm and architectural authenticity.

Until about a century ago, the people living here were predominantly Greek Christians and the local economy was limited to humble agriculture. Beginning in the 1700s, villagers began to head to Constantinople for better prospects. Once there, the Sinasites (as they were called) carved out a niche as oil millers and fishmongers. Their guild came to monopolize the trade of dried fish, fish roe, and caviar—exporting it as far as Paris. The Sinasites eventually became the sole supplier for ships passing through the Bosphorus.

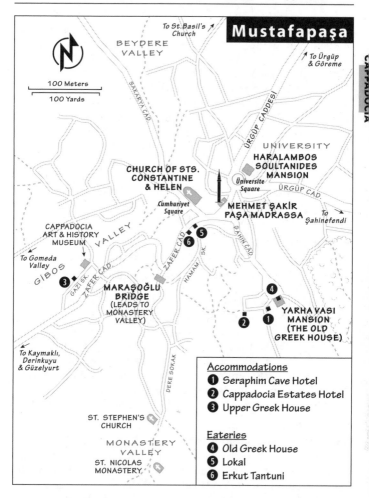

Map: Mustafapaşa

BEYDERE VALLEY
To St. Basil's Church
To Ürgüp & Göreme

100 Meters
100 Yards

SAKARYA CAD.

ÜRGÜP CADDESİ

UNIVERSITY

CHURCH OF STS. CONSTANTINE & HELEN

HARALAMBOS SOULTANIDES MANSION

Üniversite Square

ÜRGÜP CAD

Cumhuriyet Square

MEHMET ŞAKİR PAŞA MADRASSA

To Şahinefendi

CAPPADOCIA ART & HISTORY MUSEUM

To Gomeda Valley

GİBOS

ZAFER CAD.

GAZİ SK.

VALLEY

ZAFER CAD.

HAMAM SK.

ŞAHİN CAD.

3

MARAŞOĞLU BRIDGE
(LEADS TO MONASTERY VALLEY)

6 **5**

4

2 **1**

YARHA VASİ MANSION (THE OLD GREEK HOUSE)

To Kaymaklı, Derinkuyu & Güzelyurt

DEKE SOKAK

ST. STEPHEN'S CHURCH

MONASTERY VALLEY

ST. NICOLAS MONASTERY

Accommodations
1 Seraphim Cave Hotel
2 Cappadocia Estates Hotel
3 Upper Greek House

Eateries
4 Old Greek House
5 Lokal
6 Erkut Tantuni

With their success, once-rural Sinasos became urban. The Sinasites generously invested in their hometown, building stately mansions, public buildings, baths, caravanserais, churches, and schools. During the village's heyday, it was home to 4,500 Christian Greeks and 1,500 Muslim Turks.

After World War I, the Treaty of Lausanne mandated a massive population exchange between the Turkish Republic and newly independent Greece: Christians in Turkey were to move to Greece, and Muslims from Greece were to replace them in Turkey. Though wealthy, the Sinasites feared they would be looked down on as refugees when they returned to Greece. They hired a photographer to document their town and carefully chronicle every detail of their lives. These records were preserved, capturing a priceless snapshot of life in Sinasos, just before it became Mustafapaşa.

Sights in Mustafapaşa
Church of Sts. Constantine and Helen
The largest freestanding church in Cappadocia was built in record time. Under Ottoman rule, non-Muslim communities (like Sinasos) were rarely granted permission to build a new church—just to renovate an old one, under strict time limits. The clever Sinasites came up with a plan, stashing all of the needed supplies next to their soon-to-be-demolished church. As soon as the permit was granted, they tore down the old church and rebuilt a new one in just 80 days. All able-bodied villagers worked in the 1850 "restoration," and this sparkling new church was the result.

Mehmet Şakir Paşa Madrassa
A fine example of Turkish stone carving and architecture, this impressive building (1898-1900) greets you at the entrance of the village. Mehmet Şakir Paşa was a statesman and a general in the Ottoman army. Attracted by tales of the beauty of Sinasos, he paid a visit and was saddened at how much wealthier local Christians were than Muslims. To level the playing field, he commissioned the construction of this school. Today it's home to Kapadokya University, with over 5,000 students. While not a museum, the school welcomes discreet visitors who are careful not to disturb students. The facility is particularly busy during the annual Klasik Keyifler chamber music festival, when international musicians gather here for rehearsals.

Haralambos Soultanides Mansion
Haralambos Soultanides was the richest man in Sinasos; fittingly, his beautifully preserved mansion (from 1892)—today housing the university administration—dominates the entrance to the village. A double staircase and the gracefully carved stone facade give way to the main hall, decorated with frescoes depicting social life. Ask permission at the main gate to take a quick look at the lobby.

Maraşoğlu Bridge
This bridge—built by a wealthy local in 1865 to connect densely populated neighborhoods of old Sinasos—is one of the most popular "selfie spots" in town. The inscription reads: "Like a link connecting two separate pieces, I am connecting the two parts of the village, and also immortalizing the virtues of my citizens like a triumphal arch."

Cappadocia Art and History Museum (a.k.a. Doll Museum)
A traditional Turkish doll is made by kneading paper or cotton with a natural gum (tragacanth) to create a dough that's hand-

shaped into a doll. Once formed, the dolls are dressed in handsewn traditional costumes. This museum—humbler than its ambitious name, yet still endearing—collects the life's work of a local doll-maker in themes that tell the story of Turkish life: dervishes, street vendors, women in a harem, and so on.

Yarha Vasi Mansion ("The Old Greek House")

Dating from 1876, this mansion is arguably the best-preserved example of civil architecture in all of Cappadocia. You'll see the original frescoes and detailed stone and wood-work. If it is crowded with Turks, that's because the mansion was recently a filming location for a popular soap opera, adding to its fame.

Hiking in and Around Mustafapaşa

Four river valleys nearby are ideal for nature hikes. Hoteliers are happy to give you details.

Gibos Valley, known as the "hidden valley," is southwest of the village. The walk here is manageable, mostly flat, and the natural extension of a stroll through town. Along the way you'll see the Theodarakis Church.

In **Monastery Valley,** just beyond the arches of Maraşoğlu Bridge, a wealthy monastery once hosted visitors at no cost. These efforts were funded by a sericulture center (raising worms and producing silk). Of the several churches here, the recently restored ninth-century St. Nicholas Monastery—named for the patron saint of Sinasos—is worth a visit. This was also an important site for the Muslims of Sinasos, who in times of trouble would come here to pray and tie a piece of fabric on the tree in the courtyard.

Gomeda Valley works for a longer nature hike (allow 2 hours). Along the way, you'll see impressive natural formations, pigeon lofts, and multistory rock dwellings, once home to thousands of locals. The valley also has several churches. You may need to repeatedly cross a small creek that meanders through the valley (the water level is higher in early spring). In the summer, the trail can be very dusty—good shoes are essential.

Beydere Valley stretches about a kilometer to the north of the village. Adventurers can descend into the valley through a narrow subterranean tunnel from St. Basil Church (Hagios Vasilios).

Sleeping in Mustafapaşa

This village is an ideal home base for exploring Cappadocia. As a bonus, its dense rock structure makes its cave hotels less humid and more appealing than those elsewhere in Cappadocia. The first two places are a short walk from the village center.

$$$ Seraphim Cave Hotel is a plush cave hotel with 22 rooms, a relaxing garden, and an indoor pool/spa (for best rate book direct on their website, +90 384 353 5323, www.seraphimcavehotel.com, contact@seraphimcavehotel.com).

$$ Cappadocia Estates Hotel, with a variety of historic cave mansions around beautiful courtyards and gardens, makes you feel like the houseguest of an well-off local friend (RS%, +90 384 353 5020, www.cappadociaestates.com, info@cappadociaestates.com).

$ Upper Greek House, in the upper part of the village, is a cozy, friendly, and well-maintained historic home with cave and masonry rooms (Yukarı Mahalle, Gazi Sokak 60, +90 384 353 5413, www.uppergreekhouse.com, info@uppergreekhouse.com).

Near Mustafapaşa, in Ürgüp: $$$$ Sacred House Hotel, with over-the-top medieval décor, is tucked away on a side street at the center of the larger town of Ürgüp—a 10-minute drive north of Mustafapaşa (Dutlucami Mahallesi, Barbaros Hayrettin Sokak 25, +90 384 341 7402, www.sacredhouse.com.tr, info@sacredhouse.com.tr; for location, see the "Cappadocia" map near the beginning of this chapter).

Eating in Mustafapaşa

$$ Old Greek House offers homemade dishes prepared by village women, served in a courtyard under arches and vines or inside the historic mansion (Şahin Caddesi, 16, +90 384 353 5306, www.oldgreekhouse.com).

$$ Lokal, owned and operated by Kapadokya University, is central and affordable (Mehmet Şakir Paşa Caddesi, +90 353 5540).

$ Erkut Tantuni is a favorite of university students for a quick, inexpensive lunch of tasty grilled beef wraps (unpredictable hours—sometimes also open for dinner, Mehmet Şakir Paşa Caddesi).

Near Mustafapaşa, in Ürgüp: $ Tık Tık Kadın Emeği, owned and operated by women, serves modest but delicious local dishes at good prices. Watch the cooks roll their dough on their large round tables (better for lunch, Yeni Cami Mahallesi, İstiklal

Caddesi 13, +90 382 341 3373; for location, see the "Cappadocia" map near the beginning of this chapter).

GÜZELYURT AND NEARBY

This area—a bit farther from the core of the tourists' Cappadocia (about an hour's drive southwest of Mustafapaşa)—is skippable on a very short visit. But with more time, this is one of my favorite parts of Turkey, precisely because it's removed from the mass tourism of central Cappadocia.

▲▲Güzelyurt

Tucked away from the tourist crowds, the town of Güzelyurt (gew-zahl-yurt) lacks the attention it deserves. But that's exactly why I love it: It's off the beaten path, preserving the rural character and charm of the past. Here in Güzelyurt, time stands still.

Güzelyurt means "beautiful land." It's best known in Turkey as the place where historic enemies—Greeks and Turks — lived together in peace. The town is a harmony of cultures, history, architecture, and religions.

Known as Gelveri in Greek, the village was once a thriving Christian community—the Ottomans even granted them the right to mint coins. But today things are much humbler, preserving the town's delicate history. The ancient town seems one with the rock out of which it was carved. Sixteen centuries ago, monks built monasteries into the cliffside. Erosion has driven most of the residents here to more stable dwellings, but some remain. Residents somehow eke out a living from these crumbling terraces and neglected gardens.

Park at the central square in the village and explore. Near the tin dome of the modern mosque, the **market square** is the heart of Güzelyurt. It's busy with people enjoying petite glasses of sweet çay and the happy clatter of backgammon dice.

To see more, head down the hill through the so-called **"Antique Valley"** (or, to avoid the uphill walk back, drive down). You'll pass a ticket office and pay a modest fee to enter the valley and visit the historic church-turned-mosque.

While Güzelyurt is Muslim today, Christians worshipped here for centuries. But the huge Greek-Turkish population swap in the 1920s drastically changed the demographics. Today Güzelyurt's historic, Byzantine-style Christian **Church of St. Gregory** is a mosque with a single minaret and honors St. Gregory of Nazianzus (c. 329-390). Born nearby, he traveled to Athens to study and rose through the ranks of the church hierarchy, serving briefly as the Archbishop of Constantinople. In his later years, Gregory lived a modest life in his native Cappadocia and built this church later named for him. The structure you see today dates largely from the late 1800s, but you can still see the remnants of the original fourth-century church behind the main apse in the garden (essentially the substructure—irregularly lined stone blocks). This mosque doesn't have a large congregation, because the community prefers the heated mosque in the village center instead of this cold, stone building. Plans are afoot to restore it as a church/museum.

For a sweeping view, walk to a **viewpoint** at the far side of town, toward the snowy slopes of the Fuji-like Mount Hasan volcano that rules the horizon. From this perch, the vista extends out over a lush and living gorge. The cliff rising from the gorge is stacked with building styles: Upon a 1,600-year-old church sit troglodyte caves, Selçuk arches, and Ottoman facades. And on the horizon gleams the tin dome of a 20th-century mosque, with its twin minarets giving a constant visual call to prayer. The honey that holds this architectural baklava together is the people.

Eating in Güzelyurt: The village has just two eateries, both in the village center: Next to the coffee shop is a basic **$** *pide* **house** and across from the entrance to the underground city is **$ Güzelyurt Gelveri Restaurant,** which serves local stew and a savory "immigrant's pastry" (named for the Turks who made it after moving here during the population exchange with Greece a century ago).

▲Ihlara Valley

The surprising green Ihlara (uh-lah-rah) Valley, just south of Güzelyurt, is famous for its seven-mile hike amid poplar groves, eagles, vultures, and early Christian churches cut into the rocks. More a canyon than a "valley," it slices through a plateau dominated by majestic Mount Hasan (Hasan Dağı). Today an archaeological site, Ihlara was a monastic complex for centuries, but only a few of the 50 churches still carry the legacy of the past. This is a great spot for an ambitious hike following the river along the valley floor—be ready to climb more than 600 steps (45 TL to enter, good trail map posted at valley entrance, plan on 3-4 hours for the 7-mile loop, shorter routes possible).

Ağzıkarahan Caravanserai

For a trip back in time—to the 13th-centry Silk Road—add a visit to this historic site in the village of **Ağzıkarahan,** about 20 miles northwest of Güzelyurt (50 miles west of Mustafapaşa). To encourage caravans and merchants to travel through and spend more time (and money) in Anatolia, the Selçuk sultans built several caravanserais on trade routes. While these began as isolated military outposts protecting trade caravans, communities soon sprung up nearby. This prime example is on the intercity road between Nevşehir and Aksaray, 10 miles before Aksaray (confirm opening times locally).

TURKISH HISTORY

Istanbul—Turkey's biggest and most venerable city—is a microcosm of the country. Because it straddles two continents, the city reflects Turkey's vibrant mix of East and West.

Istanbul is a city of churches, mosques, palaces, and ancient ruins. In its infancy, it was home to nomads on horseback and traders in sailing ships. Then it basked in years of imperial glory—from Greek emperors to Roman emperors to Byzantine emperors. Its citizens included Orthodox priests, Catholic crusaders, and Muslim scholars. It has seen sultans in turbans, concubines in harems, old viziers, and Young Turks. In modern times, Istanbul became the heart of a proud Muslim democracy. And all these eclectic elements have come together to make that rich cultural baklava we call Istanbul.

Istanbul and Turkish History

The Early Years (6,000 BC-AD 500)

The place we now call Istanbul began life as a small Neolithic settlement around 6,000 BC. Turkey itself goes back much farther—in fact, the world's oldest megalithic ritual structure, Göbekli Tepe in southeast Turkey, was built some 12,000 years ago, when people were still living as nomads. And one of the world's oldest "cities" (7500 BC) is Çatalhöyük, 300 miles southeast of Istanbul. But for millennia, the peninsula that now constitutes Asian Turkey (also called Anatolia or Asia Minor) was little more than small cultural groups in scattered villages.

Then around 2000 BC, Anatolia was settled by the **Hittites.** These Indo-European people developed an advanced legal system and a civilization that rivaled Egypt. By uniting all of Anatolia,

Turkey Almanac

Official Name: Türkiye Cumhuriyeti (Republic of Turkey)—or simply Turkey.

Population: About 82 million. Turkish people are a mixture of more than 30 ethnic groups, but most consider themselves Turks, who make up about 75 percent of the population. Kurds are the largest minority at 19 percent. There are also about 4 million Syrian refugees. Over 98 percent of the population identify as Muslim (Sunni), with the rest mostly Christians and Jews.

Istanbul Latitude and Longitude: 39°N and 35°E; similar latitude to Washington D.C, San Francisco, Madrid, and Lisbon.

Area: 302,535,000 square miles, slightly larger than Texas.

Geography: The part of Turkey to the west of the Bosporus Strait is geographically part of Europe, but most of the country lies in Asia. Turkey occupies a unique and strategic location at the crossroads of Europe and Asia and controls the entrance to the Black Sea. It borders Bulgaria, the Black Sea, and the Republic of Georgia to the north; Armenia, Azerbaijan, and Iran to the east; Iraq, Syria, and the Mediterranean Sea to the south; and the Aegean Sea and Greece to the west. Most of the country sits on a high central plateau (Anatolia), which is surrounded by mountains and bound by narrow coastal plains to the north, south and west. It has a temperate climate, with hot, dry summers and wet, mild winters (harsher in the interior). The highest point is Mt. Ararat (16,945 feet) in the eastern part of the country.

Biggest Cities: Istanbul (more than 15 million), Ankara (the capital, about 5.5 million) and Izmir (almost 4.3 million).

Economy: The GDP is $771 billion, with a per capita GDP of over $27,000. Clothing, agricultural products, textiles, manufactured metals, and transport equipment are among the major exports. Germany is Turkey's largest trading partner.

Government: A presidential republic, ruled by a president who is both the chief of state and head of the government, and is elected by majority vote for up to two five-year terms. Current president Recep Tayyip Erdoğan is a member of the central-right, conservative Justice and Development Party (AKP). Executive power rests with the Council of Ministers, which is appointed and headed by the president. Legislative power is vested in the Grand National Assembly (600 seats), elected by a proportional vote to serve five-year terms.

Language: Turkish

Flag: A white crescent moon and star on a red background.

The Average Turk: The average Turk is 32 years old, will live to age 79, and has two children. They own their own home, work 48 hours per week, and drink four cups of tea per day.

the Hittites created the first glimmers of what we would come to know as Turkey.

Around 1200 BC, the Hittite empire, following territory losses to the Assyrians and a mysterious group known as the Sea Peoples, splintered into dozens of kingdoms: The Lycians fringed the southern coast. The Lydians (yes, they were different from the Lycians) took the west and invented the harp and coinage. And the Phrygians in the middle of Anatolia were known for their bravery, artistic tombs, and legendary King "Touch-of-gold" Midas. (Artifacts from these early peoples can be seen in the Istanbul Archaeological Museums).

While Anatolia floundered, larger empires swept in from the east and west. Assyrians from Mesopotamia (present-day Iraq) annexed eastern Anatolia, while the Greeks colonized the western coast (they called it Ionia). Among the Greeks' city-states, one soon rose to prominence: Byzantium.

Byzantium—The Greek Years
(mid-7th century BC-AD 1)

Byzantium was founded about 660 BC by a Greek named Byzas. He built a hilltop city surrounded by walls located at the tip of a peninsula—basically, today's Old Town. The city quickly prospered, thanks to its strategic location along the east-west highway between the Mediterranean and the Black Sea, with a sheltered harbor perfect for sea trade.

As a crossroads, Byzantium drew from both Greek culture to the west and Assyrian (followed by Persian) culture to the east. In 490 BC, when Persian emperor Darius the Great threatened Greece, he built a bridge of boats across the narrow Bosphorus Strait near Byzantium, allowing thousands of troops to cross. In 334 BC, Alexander the Great came through in the other direction, pushing the Persians out and settling Anatolia with Hellenistic ("Greek-style") cities and introducing the Greek language and culture. (Impressive remnants from that era include the Hippodrome and Alexander's sarcophagus in the Istanbul Archaeological Museums.)

After Alexander's death in 323 BC, Anatolia was divided among his successors. Now vulnerable to marauders, Turkey looked for security to the new rising empire: Rome.

The Roman Empire—"Byzantium" becomes "Constantinople" (AD 1-500)

As the Roman Empire took over Anatolia (making it the Province of Asia), the land prospered. Under Emperor Vespasian (AD 73), Byzantium became an important Roman center. Under Septimius Severus (AD 200), this strategically located city was fortified with even stronger walls. By 300, Byzantium was facing raids from barbarian Goths, an early warning sign of the Empire's decline. But fortune would again smile on Byzantium, when a new, visionary emperor took over the reins of Rome: Constantine the Great.

To shore up the declining empire, Constantine moved the capital from the decaying city of Rome to a more strategic position in the east. After considering Troy, he chose Byzantium, roughly midway between the European and Asian halves of the empire. Constantine officially renamed the city Nova Roma ("New Rome"), though everybody just called it "The City of Constantine"—Constantinople.

Constantine and his successors began making Constantinople the greatest city on earth. They beefed up the walls, constructed a massive royal palace (where Sultanahmet Park is today), and built huge churches (as Rome became increasingly Christian). They raised the triumphal arch called the Milion, which served as the zero-mile marker, and laid out the main street called the Mese Odos. Soon, Constantinople had a population of 500,000 and ruled over a Roman Empire that stretched from Spain to Syria.

But Rome continued its decline. Theodosius I (r. 379-395) was the last Roman emperor to rule a united Roman Empire from Constantinople. By 400, the empire had split in two, and by 500, the western half fell to barbarians and the Dark Ages. But Constantinople remained strong. This surviving eastern half of the Roman Empire would live on under a new name: the Byzantine Empire.

The Byzantine Empire at its Peak (500-1000)

For the next 500 years—while Western Europe floundered in darkness—the Byzantine Empire remained prosperous, peaceful, and highly cultured. Constantinople was the capital of an empire that encompassed Turkey, Greece, Palestine, and Egypt. It was Greek-speaking and Orthodox Christian.

One Byzantine emperor stands out: Justinian (r. 527-565). Under Justinian, the empire expanded, even temporarily reconquering its lost Roman territories. Justinian established a code of law (the Codex Justinianus) that provided a foundation for many other legal codes in Europe. He built the mammoth Basilica Cistern to bring water to his people. And greatest of all, Justinian constructed the magnificent church of Hagia Sophia—the St. Peter's Basilica of the East.

Though the Byzantine Empire declined after Justinian, it remained the most powerful force in medieval Europe. The Byzantines refined the art of glimmering mosaics and golden icons. Emperors were crowned at the "navel" of the world, on the Omphalion inside the Hagia Sophia. The Orthodox patriarch in Constantinople rivaled the Catholic pope in Rome (eventually leading

A City of Many Names

Istanbul has had several names through its history, including Byzantium, Nova Roma, Constantinople, Konstantiniye, and finally, Istanbul.

Byzantium, which means "the city of Byzas," was named for its legendary Greek founder. When Constantine proclaimed Byzantium as the new capital of the Roman Empire, the official name was changed to Nova Roma ("New Rome"). However, the people of the city called it Constantinople, or "the city of Constantine." That name survived during the period of the Ottoman Empire as Konstantiniye, the Arabic rendering of Constantinople.

So, when did the city's name become Istanbul? It was officially renamed in 1930, but actually, Constantinople was always Istanbul. The word "Istanbul" comes from the Greek phrase "(i)stin poli(n)," which means "to the city." When people used this phrase, it meant that they were going into *the* city...that is, to Constantinople. The Turks kept using the adopted version of this phrase and called the city Istanbul.

to the Great Schism between the two in 1054). For 500 years, the Byzantine Empire was a beacon of light.

But Byzantium was slowly crumbling from within, even as it was facing threats from both the east and the west.

Decline of the Byzantine Empire (1000-1453)

Over the next four centuries, Byzantium entered its long decline. The bureaucracy became unwieldy (inspiring our use of the word "byzantine" for something overly complex), farms were abandoned, taxes went uncollected, and marauders threatened. The once-vast empire gradually shrank to (basically) parts of Anatolia and Greece.

Then, from the east, they were threatened by an upstart religion: Islam. A group of nomads out of Iran called the Selçuk Turks rode a rising tide of Islam, conquered most of Turkey (1037-1243), and established it as a Muslim region. Only Christian Constantinople held out, along with their possessions in Greece. The Selçuks were highly cultured. Their great poet and mystic, Rumi (who inspired Turkey's whirling dervishes) wrote: "Love lies beyond dogma. In all mosques, temples, and churches, there is only one altar, because there is no religion but the one God." (You can enjoy the Selçuks' beautiful architecture and ornate tiles in the Istanbul Archaeological Museums and Museum of Turkish and Islamic Arts.)

In 1204, Constantinople was threatened from the west by fellow Christians, no less. During the Fourth Crusade, greedy Italian mercenaries sacked the rich city and carried off its treasures. They stuck around for 50 years as the "Latin Empire" before the Byzantines regained control. (With friends like these, the Byzantines hardly needed enemies, but look out...)

In 1243, the Mongol hordes (from the far east) trampled through Anatolia and scattered the Selçuks. Along with the Islamic Mongols came other Turkic tribes, settling Anatolia as they crept ever closer to Constantinople. One of these peoples would soon become the predominant power in Anatolia: the Ottomans.

In 1453, the Ottomans laid siege to Constantinople. The Byzantines pleaded for help from Christian allies in the West. But when their appeals went unanswered, the Byzantine clergy decided: "We would rather be ruled by the Ottoman turban than by the Catholic miter."

For two months, Constantinople held out. Its walls were the strongest in the world, and a large chain stretched across the entrance of the Golden Horn stopped enemy fleets. But the Ottomans simply pulled their ships out of the water, slid them over the hills, and went around the chain. Soon the Ottomans' state-of-the-art cannons were bombarding the walls. And on May 29, 1453, Constantinople—and a thousand years of Byzantine greatness—fell.

The Ottoman Empire at Its Peak (1453-1750)

The new ruler, Mehmet II "the Conqueror" (r. 1451-1481), made Constantinople the capital of his Islamic empire. Byzantine lands became Ottoman. The church of Hagia Sophia became a mosque. The city name was Turk-ified to "Konstantiniye." Mehmet II made the grand city even grander. He was an enlightened sultan who spoke six languages and fostered art and science. Both Christians and Muslims were welcome in his court, beginning a long practice of religious tolerance in the Ottoman Empire.

A few decades later, under Süleyman the Magnificent (r. 1520-1566), the Ottoman empire reached its peak, stretching from Austria to the Middle East, and as far south as North Africa. One-third of Europe's population lived within its borders, and Istanbul was the largest and most prosperous city in the world.

Süleyman (along with his favorite wife Roxelana and personal architect Sinan) beautified the city with huge buildings. The sprawling Topkapı Palace was a world in itself. Lavish rooms were decorated with colorful İznik tiles, fountains, elaborate thrones, and lush carpets. Süleyman built a huge mosque for himself, which set the tone for the even more over-the-top Blue Mosque built by

Ahmet I at the beginning of the 17th century. Istanbul was the de facto capital of global Islam, and all its treasures poured in—from elegant silk fabrics to jeweled swords to Muhammad's sacred sandals. (For more on the era of Süleyman, see page 206.)

For two centuries more, the Ottoman Empire was peaceful, prosperous, and enlightened, with Istanbul as its opulent capital. Forward-thinking sultans preserved what was best from the Muslim world while also exchanging goods, ideas, and new technologies with the Christian West. (For more on the enlightened "Tulip Era" see page 48.) But while the West continued racing into the modern world, too many sultans seemed content to smoke their hookahs and rest their pointy-toed shoes on their ottomans.

Decline of the Ottomans (1750-1918)

By the mid-1700s, the Ottoman Empire was in serious decay. The titles of the later sultans—Selim the Sot, İbrahim the Mad—tell the story. Incompetent rulers, palace intrigue, lavish spending, over-taxation, clumsy bureaucracy, and rampant corruption were taking their toll. Istanbul became a tired city, though occasionally brightened with new sultan-financed fountains and bazaars.

Some progressives tried to reform the obsolete empire and learn from the West. A Reformation Decree (1839) brought a small measure of democracy. In 1876, a (reluctant) sultan allowed a (weak) parliament. A handful of Istanbul-based intellectuals dubbed the Young Turks printed progressive newspapers calling for reform. But despite these efforts, the decaying Ottoman Empire was becoming known as the "Sick Man of Europe"...and then a war took it off life support.

When World War I broke out in 1914, the Ottomans sided with Germany, hoping to regain possessions in the Balkans and Middle East. The Ottomans fought valiantly, especially at the bloody battle of Gallipoli (150 miles southwest of Istanbul).

During the war, the Ottoman government forcibly relocated its Armenian population—during which hundreds of thousands of Armenians died. Were those deaths the regrettable collateral damage of war, or intentional ethnic cleansing? That controversial issue is still hotly debated today.

At the end of the war, the Ottomans found themselves on the losing side. Allied troops marched through the streets of Istanbul. The eager winners—France, Britain, and Italy—could hardly wait to carve up Turkey and share in the feast.

Former Ottoman lands were partitioned, eventually becoming independent nations like Iraq, Syria, Israel, Armenia, and Egypt. The rump that was left over (essentially, Turkey) remained in the hands of the Ottomans...for now.

Top 10 Figures in Istanbul History

Byzas (seventh century BC): Greek colonist who founded a namesake city on the Bosphorus: Byzantium.

Constantine the Great (r. 306-337): Roman emperor who legalized Christianity and moved the capital of his vast empire from Rome to Byzantium (renamed Constantinople).

Justinian (r. 527-565): Byzantine emperor who expanded the empire to its greatest extent, codified law, and built Hagia Sophia.

Rumi, a.k.a. **Mevlana** (1207-1273): Great Selçuk philosopher and mystic who inspired the order of whirling dervishes.

Osman I (1258-1326): Founder of a small Anatolian principality that eventually grew into a 600-year-long empire, which bore a modified version of his name—"Ottoman."

Sultan Mehmet II, **the Conqueror** (r. 1451-1481): Successfully laid siege to Constantinople, putting the Ottoman Empire on the map as a world power.

Sultan Süleyman the Magnificent (r. 1520-1566): With his wife, Roxelana, vastly expanded Ottoman territory and financed many fine buildings. See page 206.

Mimar Sinan (1489-1588): Süleyman's magnificent architect, whose grand but tastefully restrained buildings and monuments still rank among Istanbul's best. See page 209.

Kösem (1590-1651): Favored wife of Sultan Ahmet I who essentially ran the Ottoman Empire through her underage sultan son. See page 93.

Mustafa Kemal Atatürk (1881-1938): The "father of the Turks" who liberated his people from western invasion at the end of World War I, founded the modern Turkish Republic, and enacted sweeping reforms that made Turkey more European than Asian. See page 262.

The once-mighty Ottoman Empire had gone down in flames. But from the ashes rose the great hero of modern Turkey: Atatürk.

Atatürk and the 20th Century

The final sultan was allowed to keep his ornate throne as long as he gave the rest of Europe whatever they wanted.

But proud Turkish patriots, led by field marshal Mustafa Kemal (1881-1938), seized the moment to take control of their country. A former officer who'd fought bravely in

Libya and at Gallipoli, Kemal led a campaign to kick out the occupying armies and topple the sultan. In 1923, he established the Turkish Republic, the modern nation of Turkey we know today. For his leadership, he was given the honorary last name "Atatürk"—which literal means "father of the Turks," but also carries a connotation of greatness.

Atatürk enacted sweeping reforms to propel Turkey into the 20th century and orient it West rather than East. Every aspect of Turkish life was affected. He banned veils and encouraged more Western dress. The Latin alphabet replaced Arabic script. The new government was structured to mirror Western democracies. From lifestyle to education to language, it was a total transformation. The nation's capital was even moved to a small town in the center of Turkey, Ankara. And the city of "Konstantiniye" was officially renamed "Istanbul." (For more on the visionary and much-revered Atatürk, see page 262.)

After Atatürk's death, the country floundered as it searched for leadership and wrestled with its fledgling democracy. Though Turkey remained neutral during World War II, financial losses from the war years continued to hold the country back. Heated political clashes occasionally prompted the military to intervene and restore order (most recently in 1980), but they always returned control back to the people.

Over time, Turkey's political minds—believing that factionalism and military interventions have hampered the country's progress—have steered the country toward allowing a stronger, more centralized executive branch. The senate was abolished, leaving only a single national assembly, and the position of prime minister was eliminated, giving the president more power. That trend culminated in 2014 with the election of a strong (some would say authoritarian) president, Recep Tayyip Erdoğan.

Istanbul and Turkey Today

Today, Istanbul is the biggest city in a modern and prosperous nation. Home to one in every five Turks, Istanbul is the country's financial and cultural center.

As prime minister (2003-2014) and now president, Erdoğan, though popular, has raised eyebrows with his conservative social policies and authoritarian style. In May 2013, pro-secular Turks took to the streets to protest—perhaps the largest anti-government uprising in the history of the republic. Erdoğan labeled it a "coup" and clamped down on dissent (see the "I Was in Taksim" sidebar on page 258).

Visitors to today's Turkey will encounter a number of hot-button issues. There's the constant tension between liberal secular Turks and more conservative Islamic parties.

There's also that issue of the hundreds of thousands of Armenians who died in Turkey during World War I. Armenians and others insist that the Turkish nation take responsibility for those deaths. Most Turks would prefer if this question were debated by historians, rather than politicians. One sign of progress: In 2009, Turkey reestablished diplomatic relations with its neighbor Armenia.

Another challenge Turkey faces is how to deal with its ethnic minorities, particularly the 10 million Kurds in the southeast. Some of Turkey's Kurds (along with their fellow Kurds in Syria, Iraq, and Iran) are demanding their own independent nation, but Turkey is reluctant to share a border with that potential state.

Exacerbating the ethnic-minority problem is the civil war in Syria, which has sent refugees pouring toward Turkey. In 2019, Turkey sent troops into Syria to create a buffer zone to secure its border.

Turkey applied long ago to join the European Union. But both sides know it's not an easy fit. Europe (mostly white and Christian) already struggles to welcome its own Muslim minorities, much less Turkey's vast Muslim population. The (relatively liberal) EU is wary of Turkey's (conservative) ruling party, and over time Turkey has become less eager to join the club.

Despite these challenges, Turkey is enjoying a period of unprecedented wealth, and its grand traditions and history continue to bridge Europe and Asia.

HISTORY

UNDERSTANDING ISLAM

Turkey offers Western visitors a excellent opportunity to explore a land that's fully Muslim, moderate, and welcoming. This chapter, written by the Turkish Muslim authors of this book, explains the practice of Islam in Turkey to help travelers from the Christian West understand and respect a very rich but often misunderstood faith.

"Islam" is an Arabic word meaning "to surrender"—to submit to God's will. The word "Muslim" refers to a person who surrenders to God in all things.

Over 98 percent of Turks identify themselves as Muslims, mostly of the Sunni sect. But the decision to practice Islam, and to what degree, is an individual choice—a freedom protected by the secular state. Turks don't talk much when it comes to religion, considering it a private matter. An old saying goes, "You never know who's got the faith, or who's got the money." Islam, with many different sects, is practiced in diverse ways among Turkish people. Turks, who have a tradition of tolerance, accept the various sects, as long as none tries to impose its individual interpretation on others.

THE ROOTS OF ISLAM
The Prophet Muhammad (AD 570-632) was born in Mecca (in today's Saudi Arabia), in a community he believed was in the throes of moral decadence. Most of the Arab people at the time worshipped idols.

Muhammad sought a new way. He retired to a cave for a whole month every year to meditate and seek truth. When Muhammad was 40 years old, the Archangel Gabriel appeared to him in the cave and said that God had chosen Muhammad to be God's prophet.

The first revelation Muhammad received was "Read in the name of Allah who created you." (*Allah* is Arabic for "God.") Revelations kept coming over the next 21 years. Muhammad's followers memorized and wrote down the revelations, and compiled them in a book called the Quran, which Muslims believe is a faithful recounting of God's word.

Muhammad didn't introduce a new religion. Rather, he invited people to return to the religion of Abraham: submitting to one god. That alone was enough to cause trouble, as Muhammad's words clashed with the personal interests of local community leaders and even Muhammad's own tribe. Early converts to Islam had a difficult time in Mecca, where they were persecuted. Seeking freedom to practice their beliefs, a group of Muhammad's followers migrated to the city of Medina in 622. This event and date mark the beginning of the Muslim calendar.

THE FIVE PILLARS OF ISLAM

Most Muslims largely accept these five essential practices, or "pillars," of Islam as the basis of their faith:

1. Say and believe, "There is no other god but God, and Muhammad is his prophet." This is called *şehadet* (sheh-hah-deht) in Turkish, which means "testimony" or "witness." A Muslim bears witness by accepting and declaring the fundamentals of the faith.

2. Pray five times a day. *Namaz* (nah-mahz) is the word for daily ritual prayers. It means to pray, to recite God's name— "Allah,"—and to prostrate oneself before God.

3. Give to the poor. Charity, or *zekat* (zeh-kaht), is required of Muslims who can afford a decent living for their family. They should give away one-fortieth (about 2.5 percent) of their annual income to help the needy. Their giving should be discreet—undertaken without boasting and with care not to hurt the feelings of the receiver.

4. Fast during Ramadan. Devout Muslims in good health are required to fast (*oruç*; oh-rooch) from sunrise to sunset during the month of Ramadan. If for some reason a believer cannot fast, he or she must instead feed the poor. Fasting is not just about staying away from food and drink all day; it is about self-discipline and becoming closer to God. (See the sidebar on page 72.)

5. Make a pilgrimage to Mecca. Muslims who can afford it, and who are physically able, are required to go on a pilgrimage, called a hajj (hahdge), to the sacred sites in Mecca and Medina at least once in their lifetime. The highlight of this journey to Islam's holiest places is a visit to the Kaaba, the iconic cube-like building in Mecca. Muslims believe the Kaaba was built by the prophet Abraham and is dedicated to the worship of the one God (in Arabic, *Allah*).

God requires more than just these five elements from those who truly "submit." To Muslim Turks, God's will is recorded in

An Essential Part of Prayer

Fatiha (fah-tee-hah) means "the opening"—specifically, the opening chapter of the Quran. *Fatiha* is an important part of Muslim worship: No spiritual contact, or prayer, is complete unless it is recited. On Turkish tombstones, you'll often see the phrase *"Ruhuna El Fatiha"* ("fatiha for the soul"). People praying with open hands at shrines recite the words of the *fatiha*:

In the name of God, the Beneficent, the Merciful.

Praise be to God, Lord of the Worlds, the Beneficent, the Merciful.

Owner of the Day of Judgment,

You alone we worship; you alone we ask for help.

Show us the straight path,

The path of those whom you have favored; not the path of those who earn your anger, nor of those who go astray.

the Quran—giving believers a more extensive code of ethics governing daily conduct. Muslims also follow the Prophet Muhammad's works and life, known as the *sünnet* (sew-neht; "the path"), which appear in the hadith, the recorded works and words of the Prophet.

COMPONENTS OF ISLAM
Prayer

Mainstream Islam asks believers to perform *namaz* (ritual prayer) five times each day: morning, noon, afternoon, evening, and night. The exact times of prayers change each day according to the position of the sun and are announced by the call to prayer, or *ezan* (eh-zahn). This very Eastern-sounding chant warbles across Istanbul's rooftops five times daily. However, you won't see Turks in shops, restaurants, and on the streets suddenly prostrate themselves in prayer; people pray mainly in mosques.

No matter where they are in the world, Muslims face Islam's holy city of Mecca when they pray. Muslims are not required to go to a mosque to pray, except for the Friday noon prayer, which the Quran tells believers to perform with their congregation. But Friday is not a day of rest like the Christian or Jewish Sabbath—the Quran says Muslims should go back to work when the service is over.

The Mosque

The English word "mosque" comes from the Arabic *masjid* (mahs-jeed), meaning "place for prostration." The Turkish word for mosque is *cami* (jah-mee), meaning "place for congregation." Turks also use the word *mescit* (mehs-jeet; from the Arabic *masjid*) for a small mosque, or a simple chamber to perform *namaz*.

The mosque grew from the need to provide a safe place for Islamic congregations to practice their religion, protected from the world and the blazing desert sun. Mosques are not described in the Quran, so there is no prescribed architectural form. A building's function is what makes it a mosque.

Even within the predominantly Muslim world, religious architecture varies according to place and time. Istanbul's older mosques, to a great extent, were built in the Ottoman style. The classical Ottoman architecture in the Old Town gives way in the New District to a more eclectic style with Western influences.

The most common form of mosque (exemplified by the Blue Mosque and the Mosque of Süleyman the Magnificent) has a central dome, with cascading semi- and quarter-domes. The concept of a massive central dome supported by pillars was first used at Hagia Sophia, built originally as an Eastern Orthodox Christian church. In the centuries since, Turkish architects have refined this traditional design, which is still reflected in many contemporary mosques.

Because early Muslims were turning away from the pagan worship and idolatry of their time, Islamic tradition prohibits portrayals of humans in places of worship. It was believed that icons could distract followers from worshipping God as the only god, and mainstream Islam continues this tradition today. Mosques are instead decorated with fine calligraphy and floral and geometric patterns, often displayed on colored tiles.

Minarets—the tall, skinny towers near a mosque—were originally functional: From here, the call went out five times a day to let people know it was time for prayer. Even though the call to prayer is now usually broadcast electronically, minarets remain a symbolic fixture of mosque architecture, like bell towers on Christian churches in Europe.

Prayer services in a mosque are generally segregated, with women and men in different parts of the mosque or separated by a screen. This is for practical reasons: Islamic prayer involves different body positions, such as kneeling with one's forehead on the floor, and early believers thought it could be distracting to have members of the opposite sex doing this in close proximity.

For details on the proper protocol for visiting a mosque, see page 71.

Ablution

Ablution (*abdest;* ahb-dehst) is the physical—and spiritual—cleansing prescribed for a Muslim before prayer. It involves ritual washing of the body: hands and arms to the elbows, feet and lower legs, mouth, nose, face, and ears. The fountains and water taps you'll see outside every mosque are for ablution.

The Imam

In Turkey, the imam is the Muslim counterpart of a Christian priest or Jewish rabbi. His primary role is to lead the service in a mosque, five times a day. In the past, the imam was more active in Turkish society, in both religious and social matters. Though the imam's influence has waned in urban areas, villagers in rural Turkey usually go to their imam when they need advice.

The imam is usually responsible for calling the congregation to prayer. At large mosques, this duty is delegated to the muezzin, a person chosen for his talent in correctly voicing the call to prayer.

Although Turkey is a secular country, both imams and muezzins are civil servants, appointed and paid by the state's Religious Affairs Directorate (Diyanet). To become an imam, you must complete a four-year university degree in theology (studying Islam as well as other religions) and pass a rigorous final exam. The government regulates the rotation of imams, but there is no hierarchy among them (as for example with the bishops and cardinals in the Catholic Church).

ISLAM, CHRISTIANITY, AND JUDAISM

The Quran refers to Muslims, Christians, and Jews as "People of the Book" and to people in general as either "believers" or "nonbelievers." Just as the word "catholic" can mean "universal," the words "Islam" and "Muslim" can have a wider meaning in the verses: "Muslim" can be taken to mean all those who have faith in the one God and "Islam" as all those who submit to God's will. For instance, in a verse related to "People of the Book," the Quran says, "There are good Muslims among them."

The Quran recognizes 28 prophets by their names, including Abraham, Noah, Moses, Jesus, and Muhammad. According to the Quran, God sent hundreds of prophets to take his message to humankind.

The Quran speaks of an afterlife (heaven and hell) but no eternal punishment and no original sin. There is no confession in Islam—faith and repentance are strictly between God and the believer.

MUSLIM WOMEN: SCARF OR NO?

Islam advises modesty for both men and women in attire and attitude. Some Muslims interpret this as an order for women to cover their bodies from head to toe. Veils or black coverings are not traditionally a part of Turkish culture, but in Turkey you'll sometimes see these trends borrowed from Arab Muslim cultures farther east.

The majority of Turkish Muslims prefer a more liberal interpretation of modesty. The way a woman dresses is left to individual choice, and less than half of Turkish women cover their hair. On the streets of Istanbul, you'll mostly see women dressed in contemporary styles, ranging from conservative dresses to miniskirts. But you'll also see many women wearing headscarves. The most popular headscarf style in cities is a turban—not like those once worn by Ottoman dignitaries, but an elegant scarf that covers the head and the neck.

Although rare in Turkey, you may see a few devout women wearing the black, robelike çarşaf (similar to a burka). For the most part, the women you see in çarşaf in Istanbul's Old Town and Grand Bazaar are tourists from other Muslim countries.

How does a Turkish woman decide how to dress? Her particular community, personal beliefs, family, status, age, education, and profession all play a role. Wearing a head covering or scarf does not always have religious significance but is more of a cultural act.

In poorer and more rural areas, women tend to dress more conservatively. The young women generally dress however they like, as long as they are modest, but elderly women typically wear a scarf in public, often accompanied by a cloak that looks like a long raincoat. In the countryside, it's traditional for women to wear a simple white or colorful scarf—not only as part of their religion but also as practical protection from the sun and dust.

PRACTICALITIES

This chapter covers the practical skills of European travel: how to get tourist information, pay for things, sightsee efficiently, find good-value accommodations, eat affordably but well, use technology wisely, and get between destinations smoothly. For more information on these topics, see RickSteves.com/travel-tips.

Tourist Information

Turkey's national tourist website provides a good introduction to the country's major destinations, attractions, history, culture, and food (www.goturkey.com). The Turkish Ministry of Culture and Tourism website at www.ktb.gov.tr is also helpful and has short video clips on some of the country's main sights—useful for pretrip viewing.

In **Istanbul,** the city's tourist information office (abbreviated TI in this book) often misses the mark, but it's worth stopping in to pick up a free map. For branch locations, see the Orientation to Istanbul chapter.

Travel Tips

Travel Advisories: For updated health and safety conditions, including any restrictions for your destination, consult the US State Department's international travel website (www.travel.state.gov).

Visa Requirement: You're required to obtain a three-month tourist visa prior to entering the country. You can get a visa at a Turkish consulate or embassy, but it is easier to apply for it online at www.evisa.gov.tr at least 48 hours before your departure ($50; Canadians pay $60—only US currency accepted). The visa will be emailed to you directly. You must print the visa and be prepared to show it to airport officials and customs officers when you arrive, and to carry it with you at all times during your stay in Turkey.

Emergency and Medical Help: For any emergency service—ambulance, police, or fire—call **112** (operators may not speak English; ask a willing local for assistance in making the call). If you get sick, do as the locals do and go to a pharmacist for advice. Or ask at your hotel for help—they'll know the nearest medical and emergency services.

Any ambulance summoned by 112 will quickly deliver a patient to the nearest public hospital, whose emergency rooms are fast and free. Once stabilized, patients can choose to be transferred to a newer, private hospital, where most staff speak English. (It's possible to call a private hospital directly for an ambulance, but response and travel times will be longer than dialing 112.)

Private hospitals in the city include the American Hospital (in the New District at Valikonağı Caddesi, Güzelbahçe Sokak 20, Nişantaşı, +90 444 3777—dial ext. 9 for English, then 1 for ambulance services, www.amerikanhastanesi.org); the International Hospital (west of the city center at Istanbul Caddesi 82, Yeşilköy, +90 212 468 4444; for an ambulance call +90 444 9724, www.acibadem.com.tr); and Liv Hospital Ulus (north of the New District at Ulus Ahmet Adnan Saygun Caddesi, Canan Sokak, Beşiktaş, +90 444 4548 for information or ambulance, www.livhospital.com).

Theft or Loss: To replace a passport, you'll need to go in person to a consulate (see next). If your credit and debit cards disappear, cancel and replace them (see "Damage Control for Lost Cards" on page 454). File a police report, either on the spot or within a day or two; you'll need it to submit an insurance claim for lost or stolen rail passes or electronics, and it can help with replacing your passport or credit and debit cards. For more information, see RickSteves.com/help.

US Consulate: For 24-hour emergency assistance dial +90 212 335 9000, Üç Şehitler Sokak 2, İstinye Mahallesi, http://tr.usembassy.gov.

PRACTICALITIES

Canadian Consulate: Buyukdere Caddesi 209, Tekfen Tower, Levent 4; general info +90 212 385 9700, after-hours emergency tel. in Ottawa—call collect +1 613 996 8885; www.turkey.gc.ca.

Time Zones: All of Turkey is in the same time zone. Istanbul, which is one hour ahead of most of continental Europe, is generally seven/ten hours ahead of the East/West Coasts of the US—but note that Turkey does not observe daylight savings time. For a handy time converter, use the world clock app on your phone or download one (see www.timeanddate.com).

Business Hours: Most shops are open daily 9:00-19:00; on Sundays, they open a little later in the morning. On holidays, most museums and shops in tourist areas are open (and shops may stay open a little later than usual).

Most government offices and banks are open Monday-Friday 9:00-17:00; some are also open Saturday 9:00-12:00. On the day before a national or religious holiday, many government offices and banks close in the afternoon.

Watt's Up? Europe's electrical system is 220 volts, instead of North America's 110 volts. Most electronics (laptops, phones, cameras) and appliances (hair dryers, CPAP machines) convert automatically, so you won't need a converter, but you will need an adapter plug with two round prongs, sold inexpensively at travel stores in the US. Avoid bringing older appliances that don't automatically convert voltage; instead, buy a cheap replacement in Europe.

Discounts: Discounts for sights are generally not listed in this book. Children under 8 (with a passport for proof) can get in free to museums and sites run by the Turkish Ministry of Culture and Tourism, including Topkapı Palace, Chora Church, Turkish and Islamic Arts Museum, and Istanbul Archaeological Museums. Some discounts are available only for Turkish citizens.

Online Translation Tips: Google's Chrome browser instantly translates websites; Translate.google.com and DeepL.com are also handy. The Google Translate app converts spoken or typed English into most European languages (and vice versa) and can also translate text it "reads" with your phone's camera.

Going Green: There's plenty you can do to reduce your environmental footprint when traveling. When practical, take a train instead of a flight within Europe, and use public transportation within cities. In hotels, use the "Do Not Disturb" sign to avoid daily linen and towel changes (or hang up your towels to signal you'll reuse them). Bring a reusable shopping tote. To find out how Rick Steves' Europe is offsetting carbon emissions with an innovative self-imposed carbon tax, go to RickSteves.com/about-us/climate-smart.

Money

Here's my basic strategy for using money in Europe:
- Upon arrival, head for an ATM at the airport and withdraw some local currency, using a debit card with low international transaction fees.
- In general, pay for bigger expenses with a credit card and use cash for smaller purchases. Use a debit card for cash withdrawals.
- Keep your cards and cash safe in a money belt.

PLASTIC VERSUS CASH

Although credit cards are widely accepted in Europe, cash is sometimes the only way to pay for street food, taxis, tips, and local guides. Some businesses (especially smaller ones, such as B&Bs and mom-and-pop cafés and shops) may charge you extra for using a credit card—or might not accept credit cards at all. Having cash on hand helps you out of a jam if your card randomly doesn't work.

I use my credit card to book and pay for hotel reservations, to buy advance tickets for events or sights, and to cover most other expenses.

WHAT TO BRING

I pack the following and keep it all safe in my money belt.

Debit Card: Use this at ATMs to withdraw local cash.

Credit Card: Handy for bigger transactions (at hotels, shops, restaurants, travel agencies, car-rental agencies, and so on), payment machines, and online purchases.

Backup Card: Some travelers carry a third card (debit or credit; ideally from a different bank), in case one gets lost or simply doesn't work.

A Stash of Cash: I carry $100-200 in US dollars as a cash backup, which comes in handy in an emergency (for example, if your ATM card gets eaten by the machine).

What NOT to Bring: Resist the urge to buy **Turkish lira** before your trip or you'll pay the price in bad stateside exchange rates. Wait until you arrive to withdraw money. European airports have plenty of ATMs.

BEFORE YOU GO

Use this pre-trip checklist.

Know your cards. US debit cards with a Visa or MasterCard logo will work in any European ATM. As for credit cards, Visa and MasterCard are universal, American Express is less common, and Discover is unknown in Europe.

Know your PIN. Make sure you know the numeric, four-digit

Lira, Euros, and Dollars

In this book, we list most prices in Turkish liras (*Türk lirası*, or TL, also indicated as TRY). But many Turkish businesses in tourist areas price their services and accept payment in either euros or dollars. This is partly for convenience but primarily to protect vendors from a declining lira. Hotels almost always list prices in euros, and we've followed suit in the Sleeping in Istanbul chapter.

At the time of publication, 1 Turkish lira equaled about US $0.15 or €0.13. Like the dollar, one Turkish lira (TL) is broken down into 100 cents, or *kuruş* (koo-roosh abbreviated Kr). Coins range from 1 *kuru* to 1 TL, and bills from 5 TL to 200 TL. So that 25-TL coffee-and-baklava break is about $4, that 90-TL shawl is about $15, and that 200-TL taxi ride is...uh-oh.

Check www.oanda.com for the latest exchange rates for either lira or euros.

PIN for all of your cards, both debit and credit. Request it if you don't have one, as it may be required for some purchases in Europe (see "Using Credit Cards," later). Allow time to receive the information by mail—it's not always possible to obtain your PIN online.

Report your travel dates. Let your bank know that you'll be using your debit and credit cards in Europe, and when and where you're headed.

Adjust your ATM withdrawal limit. Find out how much you can take out daily and ask for a higher daily withdrawal limit if you want to get more cash at once. Note that European ATMs will withdraw funds only from checking accounts, not savings accounts.

Ask about fees. For any purchase or withdrawal made with a card, you may be charged a currency conversion fee (1-3 percent) and/or a Visa or MasterCard international transaction fee (less than 1 percent). If you're getting a bad deal, consider getting a new debit or credit card. Reputable no-fee cards include those from Capital One as well as Charles Schwab debit cards. Most credit unions and some airline loyalty cards have low or no international transaction fees.

Using Cash Machines

Cash machines have English-language instructions and work just like they do at home—except they spit out local currency instead of dollars, calculated at the day's standard bank-to-bank rate.

In most places, ATMs are easy to locate—in Turkey ask for a *Bankamatik* (bahn-kah-mah-teek), though some banks use different names—"24," "self-service," or *paramatik*—literally "money-matic." When possible, withdraw cash from a bank-run ATM located just outside that bank.

If your debit card doesn't work, try a lower amount—your request may have exceeded your withdrawal limit or the ATM's limit. If you still have a problem, try a different ATM or come back later.

Avoid "independent" ATMs, such as Travelex, Euronet, Moneybox, Your Cash, Cardpoint, and Cashzone. These have high fees, can be less secure, and may try to trick users with "dynamic currency conversion" (see next).

Dynamic Currency Conversion

When paying with a credit card, you'll often be asked whether you want to pay in dollars or in the local currency. Always refuse the conversion and choose the local currency. While DCC seems convenient, it comes with a poor exchange rate, and you'll wind up losing money. Many ATMs also offer DCC—again, always select "continue without conversion."

Exchanging Cash

Minimize exchanging money in Europe; it's expensive (you'll generally lose 5 to 10 percent). In a pinch you can find exchange desks at major train stations or airports. Banks generally do not exchange money unless you have an account with them.

Using Credit Cards

US credit cards generally work fine in Europe—with a few exceptions.

European cards use chip-and-PIN technology; most chip cards issued in the US instead require a signature. When presented with a US card, European card readers may generate a receipt for you to sign—or prompt you to enter your PIN. At self-service payment machines (such as transit-ticket kiosks), US cards may not work. In this case, look for a cashier who can process your card manually—or pay in cash.

"Tap to pay" cards and smartphone payment apps work in Europe just as they do in the US, and sidestep chip-and-PIN compatibility issues.

Drivers Beware: Drivers may encounter automated pay points (tollbooths, parking meters, gas pumps, etc.) where US cards are not accepted. Carry cash as a back-up and be prepared to move on to the next gas station if necessary (some gas stations sell prepaid gas cards, which you should be able to purchase with any US card).

Security Tips

Pickpockets target tourists. Keep your cash, credit cards, and passport secure in your money belt, and carry only a day's spending money in your front pocket or wallet.

Before inserting your card into an ATM, inspect the front. If anything looks crooked, loose, or damaged, it could be a sign of a card-skimming device. When entering your PIN, carefully block other people's view of the keypad.

Don't use a debit card for purchases. Because a debit card pulls funds directly from your bank account, potential charges incurred by a thief will stay on your account while the fraudulent use is investigated by your bank.

While traveling, to access your accounts online, be sure to use a secure connection (see the "Tips on Internet Security" sidebar on page 475).

Damage Control for Lost Cards

If you lose your credit or debit card, report the loss immediately to the respective global customer-assistance centers. With a mobile phone, call these 24-hour US numbers: Visa (+1 303 967 1096), MasterCard (+1 636 722 7111), or American Express (+1 336 393 1111). From a landline, you can call these US numbers collect by going through a local operator.

You'll need to provide the primary cardholder's identification verification details (such as birth date, mother's maiden name, or Social Security number). You can generally receive a temporary card within two or three business days in Europe (see RickSteves.com/help for more).

If you report your loss within two days, you typically won't be responsible for any unauthorized transactions on your account, although many banks charge a liability fee.

TIPPING

Tipping in Turkey is similar to the US—for special service, tips are appreciated, if not expected. As in the US, the proper amount depends on your resources, tipping philosophy, and the circumstances, but some general guidelines apply. A 10 percent tip is average.

Restaurants: In restaurants with table service, tip 10 percent for good service, even if your bill includes a service charge. See the "Eating" section, later, for details.

Taxis: For a typical ride, round up your fare to the next lira (for instance, if the fare is 24 TL, pay 25 TL); for a long ride, round to the nearest 5 TL (for a 47-TL fare, pay 50 TL). If the cabbie hauls your bags and zips you to the airport to help you catch your flight, you might want to add a little more.

Services: In general, if someone in the service industry does a super job for you, a small tip of a few liras is appropriate...but not required. If you're not sure whether (or how much) to tip for a service, ask a local for advice.

GETTING A VAT REFUND

Wrapped into the purchase price of your Turkish souvenirs is a Value-Added Tax (VAT) of 18 percent. You're entitled to get most of that tax back if you purchase more than 118 TL (about $17) worth of goods at a store that participates in the VAT-refund scheme. Typically, you must ring up the minimum at a single retailer—you can't add up your purchases from various shops to reach the required amount. (If the store ships the goods to your US home, VAT is not assessed on your purchase.)

Getting your refund is straightforward...and worthwhile if you spend a significant amount.

At the Merchant: Have the merchant completely fill out the refund document (they'll ask for your passport; a photo of your passport usually works). Keep track of the paperwork and your original sales receipt. Note that you're not supposed to use your purchased goods before you leave Europe.

At the Border or Airport: Process your VAT document at your last stop in Turkey (such as the airport) with the customs agent who deals with VAT refunds. At some airports, you'll have to go to a customs office to get your documents stamped and then to a separate VAT refund service (such as Global Blue or Planet) to process the refund. At other airports, a single VAT desk handles the whole thing. Note that refund services typically extract a 4 percent fee and can refund your money in cash immediately or credit your card. Otherwise, you'll need to mail the stamped refund documents to the address given by the merchant. Allow plenty of extra time at the airport to deal with the VAT refund process.

CUSTOMS FOR AMERICAN SHOPPERS

You can take home $800 worth of items per person duty-free, once every 31 days. Many processed and packaged foods are allowed, including cheeses, dried herbs, jams, baked goods, candy, chocolate, oil, vinegar, condiments, and honey. Fresh fruits and vegetables and most meats are not allowed, with exceptions for some canned items. As for alcohol, you can bring in one liter of alcohol duty-free (it can be packed securely in your checked luggage, along with any other liquid-containing items).

To bring alcohol or liquid-packed foods in your carry-on bag on your flight home, buy it at a duty-free shop at the airport. You'll increase your odds of getting it onto a connecting flight if it's packaged in a "STEB"—a secure, tamper-evident bag. But stay away from liquids in opaque, ceramic, or metallic containers, which usually cannot be successfully screened (STEB or no STEB).

For details on allowable goods, customs rules, and duty rates, visit http://help.cbp.gov.

Sightseeing

Sightseeing can be hard work. Use these tips to make your visits to Istanbul's finest sights meaningful, fun, efficient, and painless.

MAPS AND NAVIGATION TOOLS

A good map is essential for efficient navigation while sightseeing. The maps in this book are concise and simple, designed to help you locate recommended destinations, sights, hotels, and restaurants. Simple maps are generally free at TIs and hotels.

You can also use a mapping app on your mobile device, which provides turn-by-turn directions for walking, driving, and taking public transit. Google Maps, Apple Maps, and CityMaps2Go allow you to download maps for offline use; ideally, download the areas you'll need before your trip. For certain features, you'll need to be online—either using Wi-Fi or an international data plan.

PLAN AHEAD

Set up an itinerary that allows you to fit in all your must-see sights. For a one-stop look at opening hours, see "Istanbul at a Glance" (page 42); also see "Daily Reminder" on page 29. Most sights keep stable hours, but you can easily confirm the latest by checking with the TI or visiting museum websites.

Don't put off visiting a must-see sight—you never know when a place will close unexpectedly for a holiday, strike, or restoration. Many museums are closed or have reduced hours at least a few days a year, especially on religious holidays, New Year's Day, and Republic Day (Oct 29). A list of holidays is in the appendix; check for possible closures during your trip. In summer, some sights may stay open late. Off-season hours may be shorter.

Going at the right time helps avoid crowds. This book offers tips on the best times to see specific sights. Try visiting popular sights very early or very late. Evening visits (when possible) are usually peaceful, with fewer crowds. Late morning is usually the worst time to visit a popular sight.

Study up. To get the most out of the self-guided tours and sight descriptions in this book, read them before you visit. Hagia Sophia is much more fascinating if you've been busy learning about Byzantine architecture.

RESERVATIONS AND ADVANCE TICKETS

Given how precious your vacation time is, I recommend getting reservations for any must-see sight that offers them.

To deal with lines, many popular sights sell advance tickets that guarantee admission at a certain time of day, or that allow you to skip entry lines. It's worth giving up some spontaneity to book in advance. While hundreds of tourists sweat in long ticket-buying lines—or arrive to find the sight sold out—those who've booked ahead are assured of getting in. In some cases, getting a ticket in advance simply means buying your ticket earlier on the same day. But for other sights, you may need to book far in advance. As soon as you're ready to commit to a certain date, book it.

See "Sightseeing Strategies" in the Sights chapter for specifics.

AT SIGHTS

Here's what you can typically expect:

Entering: You may not be allowed to enter if you arrive too close to closing time. And guards start ushering people out well before the actual closing time, so don't save the best for last.

Many sights have a security check. Allow extra time for these lines. Some sights require you to check daypacks and coats.

At mosques, respect the dress code (covered knees and shoulders for all, and headscarves for women). For more information, see "Visiting a Mosque" on page 71.

Photography: If the museum's photo policy isn't clearly posted, ask a guard. Generally, taking photos without a flash or tripod is allowed. Some sights ban selfie sticks; others ban photos altogether.

🎧 **Audioguides and Apps:** I've produced a free, downloadable audio tour for my Ephesus Tour. For more on my audio tours, see page 22.

Many sights rent audioguides with recorded descriptions in English. If you bring your own earbuds, you can often enjoy better sound. And if you don't mind being tethered to your travel partner, you'll save money by bringing a Y-jack and sharing one audioguide. Museums and sights often offer free apps that you can download to your mobile device (check their websites).

Temporary Exhibits: Museums may show special exhibits in addition to their permanent collection. Some exhibits are included in the entry price, while others come at an extra cost (which you may have to pay even if you don't want to see the exhibit).

Expect Changes: Items can be on tour, on loan, out sick, or shifted at the whim of the curator. Pick up a floor plan as you enter and ask museum staff if you can't find a particular item. Point to the photograph in this book and ask, *"Nerede?"* (neh-reh-deh; "Where is?").

Services: Important sights usually have a reasonably priced on-site café or cafeteria (handy and air-conditioned places to rejuvenate during a long visit). The WCs at sights are free and generally clean.

Before Leaving: At the gift shop, scan the postcard rack or thumb through a guidebook to be sure you haven't overlooked something that you'd like to see. Every sight or museum offers more than what is covered in this book. Use the information I provide as an introduction—not the final word.

Sleeping

Extensive and opinionated listing of good-value rooms are a major feature of the Sleeping chapter in this book. Rather than list hotels scattered throughout a city, I choose hotels in my favorite neighborhoods that are convenient to your sightseeing.

My recommendations run the gamut, from dorm beds to luxurious rooms with all the comforts. I like places that are clean, central, relatively quiet at night, reasonably priced, friendly, small enough to have a hands-on owner or manager, and run with a respect for Turkish traditions. I'm more impressed by a convenient location and a fun-loving philosophy than flat-screen TVs and a fancy gym. Most of my recommendations fall short of perfection. But if I can find a place with most of these features, it's a keeper.

Book your accommodations as soon as your itinerary is set, especially if you want to stay at one of our top listings or if you'll be traveling during busy times. Popular places are even busier on weekends...and can be inundated on three-day weekends. Hotels are crowded in May, June, September, and October.

Major Christian holidays (Easter and Christmas, including the weeks before and after) can cause prices and demand to spike in Muslim Turkey, because Europeans flock here when they have time off. Conversely, Muslim holidays do not generally affect Istanbul hotel prices, as many Turks travel away from the city during those times. Most hotel rates go down from mid-November through mid-March (except around New Year's, when they charge peak rates). Some places also offer small discounts in July and August, when the city is hotter and quieter.

See the appendix for a list of major holidays and festivals in Istanbul.

RATES AND DEALS

I've categorized my recommended accommodations based on price, indicated with a dollar-sign rating (see sidebar). Most hoteliers give

Sleep Code

Hotels in this book are categorized according to the average price of a standard double room with breakfast in high season. Turkish hotels generally quote prices in euros.

$$$$	**Splurge:** Most rooms over €180
$$$	**Pricier**: €140-180
$$	**Moderate**: €100-140
$	**Budget**: €60-100
¢	**Backpacker:** Under €60
RS%	**Rick Steves discount**

Unless otherwise noted, credit cards are accepted, hotel staff speak basic English, and free Wi-Fi is available. Comparison-shop by checking prices at several hotels (on each hotel's own website, on a booking site, or by email). For the best deal, *book directly with the hotel*. Ask for a discount if paying in cash; if the listing includes **RS%**, request a Rick Steves discount.

prices in euros to protect themselves from the changeable value of the Turkish lira. Room prices can fluctuate significantly with demand and amenities (size, views, room class, and so on), but relative price categories remain constant. Taxes, which can vary from place to place, are generally insignificant (a dollar or two per person, per night).

Room rates are especially volatile at hotels that use "dynamic pricing" to set rates. Prices can skyrocket during festivals and conventions, while business hotels can have deep discounts on weekends when demand plummets. Of the many hotels I recommend, it's difficult to say which will be the best value on a given day—until you do your homework.

Booking Direct: Once your dates are set, compare prices at several hotels. You can do this by checking hotel websites and booking sites such as Hotels.com or Booking.com. After you've zeroed in on your choice, book directly with the hotel itself. This increases the chances that the hotelier will be able to accommodate special needs or requests (such as shifting your reservation). And when you book by phone or email, the owner avoids the commission paid to booking sites, giving them wiggle room to offer you a discount, a nicer room, or a free breakfast (if it's not already included).

Getting a Discount: Some hotels extend a discount to those who pay cash or stay longer than three nights. And some accommodations offer a special discount for Rick Steves readers, indicated in this guidebook by the abbreviation "**RS%**." Discounts vary: Ask for details when you reserve. Generally, to qualify for this discount, you must book direct (not through a booking site), mention this book when you reserve, show this book upon arrival,

Making Hotel Reservations

Reserve your rooms as soon as you've pinned down your travel dates. For busy holidays, it's wise to reserve far in advance (see the appendix).

Requesting a Reservation: For family-run hotels, it's generally best to book your room directly via email or phone. For business-class and chain hotels, or if you'd rather book online, reserve directly through the hotel's official website (not a booking website). Almost all of my recommended hotels take reservations in English.

Here's what the hotelier wants to know:
- Type(s) of room(s) you want and number of guests
- Number of nights you'll stay
- Arrival and departure dates, written European-style as day/month/year (18/06/22 or 18 June 2022)
- Special requests (en suite bathroom, cheapest room, twin beds vs. double bed, quiet room)
- Applicable discounts (such as a Rick Steves reader discount, cash discount, or promotional rate)

Confirming a Reservation: Most places will request a credit-card number to hold your room. If the hotel's website doesn't have a secure form where you can enter the number directly, share this info via a phone call.

Canceling a Reservation: If you must cancel, it's courteous—and smart—to do so with as much notice as possible, especially for smaller family-run places. Cancellation policies can be strict; read

and sometimes pay cash or stay a certain number of nights. In some cases, you may need to enter a discount code (which I've provided in the listing) in the booking form on the hotel's website. Rick Steves discounts apply to readers with either print or digital books. Understandably, discounts do not apply to promotional rates.

TYPES OF ACCOMMODATIONS
Hotels

In this book, the price for a double room ranges from $60 (very simple—toilet and shower down the hall) to more than $300 (grand lobbies, maximum plumbing, the works), with most clustering around $140-170.

Most hotels have lots of doubles—sometimes called "French beds" in Turkey—and a few singles and triples. Rooms that sleep four are rare, though some hotels may have family-friendly connecting rooms.

Arrival and Check-In: Hotel elevators are common, though small, and some older buildings still lack them. You may have to

From: rick@ricksteves.com
Sent: Today
To: info@hotelcentral.com
Subject: Reservation request for 19-22 July

Dear Hotel Central,

I would like to stay at your hotel. Please let me know if you have a room available and the price for:
• 2 people
• Double bed and en suite bathroom in a quiet room
• Arriving 19 July, departing 22 July (3 nights)

Thank you!
Rick Steves

the fine print before you book. Many discount deals require pre-payment and can be expensive to change or cancel.

Reconfirming a Reservation: Always call or email to reconfirm your room reservation a few days in advance. For B&Bs or very small hotels, I call again on my arrival day to tell my host what time to expect me (especially important if arriving late—after 17:00).

Phoning: For tips on calling hotels overseas, see page 476.

climb a flight of stairs to reach the elevator (if so, you can ask the front desk for help carrying your bags up).

Hotels are required to collect your name, nationality, and ID number. When you check in, the receptionist will normally ask for your passport and may keep it for up to a couple of hours. If you're not comfortable leaving your passport at the desk for a long time, bring a photocopy to give them instead.

If you're arriving early in the morning, your room probably won't be ready. You should be able to safely check your bag at the hotel and dive right into sightseeing.

In Your Room: Most hotel rooms have a TV, telephone, and free Wi-Fi (although in old buildings with thick walls, the Wi-Fi signal might be available only in the lobby). Simpler places rarely have a room phone.

There's a reason many bathrooms in Old Town hotels have a small wastebasket next to the toilet: sensitive plumbing. Many places prefer that you don't flush toilet paper; use the wastebasket instead.

Breakfast and Meals: Turkish hotels see a good breakfast as

Using Online Services to Your Advantage

From booking services to user reviews, online businesses play a greater role in travelers' planning than ever before. Take advantage of their pluses—and be wise to their downsides.

Booking Sites

Booking websites such as Booking.com and Hotels.com offer one-stop shopping for hotels. While convenient for travelers, they're both a blessing and a curse for independent, family-run hotels. Without a presence on these sites, small hotels become almost invisible. But to be listed, a hotel must pay a sizable commission...and promise that its own website won't undercut the price on the booking-service site.

Here's the work-around: Use the big sites to research what's out there, then book direct with the hotel by email or phone, in which case hotel owners are free to give you whatever price they like. Ask for a room without the commission mark-up (or ask for a free breakfast if not included, or a free upgrade). If you do book online, be sure to use the hotel's own website. The price will likely be the same as via a booking site, but your money goes to the hotel, not agency commissions.

As a savvy consumer, remember: When you book with an online booking service, you're adding a middleman who takes roughly 20 percent. To support small, family-run hotels whose world is more difficult than ever, book direct.

Short-Term Rental Sites

Rental juggernaut Airbnb (along with other short-term rental sites) allows travelers to rent rooms and apartments, often providing more value, space, and amenities than a cookie-cutter hotel. Airbnb fans appreciate feeling part of a real neighborhood and getting into a daily routine as "temporary Europeans." Depending on the host, Airbnb can provide an opportunity to get to know a local person, while keeping the money spent on your accommodations in the community.

---

a badge of honor, and they are quite competitive—so unless you're sleeping at a dive, you can expect a decent breakfast. (Breakfast is almost always included in the room rate.) A Turkish hotel breakfast often consists of cheese, olives, bread, jam or honey, butter, tomatoes, cucumbers, eggs (usually hard-boiled), Turkish tea, and instant coffee. Don't expect thick "Turkish coffee" for breakfast—Turks drink this as a digestive after meals. Fresh-squeezed fruit juice may be available for an additional charge.

Checking Out: While it's customary to pay for your room upon departure, it can be a good idea to settle your bill the day before, when you're not in a hurry and while the manager's in.

Hotelier Help: Hoteliers can be a good source of advice. Most

Critics of Airbnb see it as a threat to "traditional Europe." Landlords can make more money renting to short-stay travelers, driving rents up—and local residents out to more affordable but less charming districts. When those long-term renters go, traditional businesses are replaced by ones that cater to tourists. And the character that made those neighborhoods desirable to the tourists in the first place goes too. Some cities have cracked down, requiring owners to obtain a license and to occupy rental properties part of the year (and staging disruptive "inspections" that inconvenience guests).

As a lover of Europe, I share the worry of those who see residents nudged aside by tourists. But as an advocate for travelers, I appreciate the value and cultural intimacy Airbnb provides.

User Reviews

User-generated review sites and apps such as Yelp and TripAdvisor can give you a consensus of opinions about everything from hotels and restaurants to sights and nightlife. If you scan reviews of a restaurant or hotel and see several complaints about noise or a rotten location, you've gained insight that can help in your decision-making.

But as a guidebook writer, my sense is that there is a big difference between the uncurated information on a review site and the vetted listings in a guidebook. A user-generated review is based on the limited experience of one person, who stayed at just one hotel in a given city and ate at a few restaurants there. A guidebook is the work of a trained researcher who forms a well-developed basis for comparison by visiting many restaurants and hotels year after year.

Both types of information have their place, and in many ways, they're complementary. If something is well reviewed in a guidebook and it also gets good online reviews, it's likely a winner.

know their city well, and can assist you with everything from public transit and airport connections to finding a good restaurant or a late-night pharmacy.

Hotel Hassles: Even at the best places, mechanical breakdowns occur: Sinks leak, hot water turns cold, toilets may gurgle and smell, the Wi-Fi goes out, or the air-conditioning dies when you need it most. Report your concerns clearly and calmly at the front desk.

If you find that night noise is a problem (if, for instance, your room is over a nightclub or facing a busy street), ask for a quiet room in the back or on an upper floor. To guard against theft in your room, keep valuables out of sight. Some rooms come with a safe, and other hotels have safes at the front desk. I've never bothered using one and in a lifetime of travel, I've never had anything stolen from my room.

If you need to do laundry, it's best to have your hotel do it or send it out—self-service launderettes are rare.

For more complicated problems, don't expect instant results. Above all, keep a positive attitude. Remember, you're on vacation. If your hotel is a disappointment, spend more time out enjoying the city you came to see.

Short-Term Rentals

A short-term rental—whether an apartment or house—is an increasingly popular alternative, especially if you plan to settle in one location for several nights. For stays longer than a few days, you can usually find a rental that's comparable to—and cheaper than—a hotel room with similar amenities. Plus, you'll get a behind-the-scenes peek into how locals live.

Many places require a minimum stay and have strict cancellation policies. And you're generally on your own: There's no reception desk, breakfast, or daily cleaning service.

Finding Accommodations: Websites such as Airbnb, FlipKey, Booking.com, and the HomeAway family of sites (HomeAway, VRBO, and VacationRentals) let you browse a wide range of properties. Alternatively, rental agencies such as InterhomeUSA.com and RentaVilla.com provide a more personalized service (their curated listings are also more expensive).

Before you commit, be clear on the location. I like to virtually "explore" the neighborhood using Google Street View. Also consider the proximity to public transportation and how well-connected the property is with the rest of the city. Ask about amenities (elevator, air-conditioning, laundry, Wi-Fi, parking, etc.). Reviews from previous guests can help identify trouble spots.

Think about the kind of experience you want: Just a key and an affordable bed...or a chance to get to know a local? Some hosts offer self check-in and minimal interaction; others enjoy interacting with you. Read the description and reviews to help shape your decision.

Confirming and Paying: Many places require you to pay the entire balance before your trip, usually through the listing site. Be wary of owners who want to take your transaction offline; this gives you no recourse if things go awry. Never agree to wire money (a key indicator of a fraudulent transaction).

Apartments or Houses: If you're staying in one place for several nights, it's worth considering an apartment or rental house (shorter stays aren't worth the hassle of arranging key pickup, buying groceries, etc.). Apartment or house rentals can be especially

---

Keep Cool

If you're visiting Istanbul in the summer, you'll want an air-conditioned room. Most hotel air-conditioners come with a remote control that generally has similar symbols and features: fan icon (click to toggle through wind power, from light to gale); temperature (20 degrees Celsius is comfortable); louver icon (choose steady airflow or waves); snowflake and sunshine icons (cold air or heat, depending on season); and clock ("O" setting: run X hours before turning off; "I" setting: wait X hours to start). When you leave your room for the day, do as the environmentally conscious Europeans do, and turn off the air-conditioning.

---

cost-effective for groups and families. European apartments, like hotel rooms, tend to be small by US standards. But they often come with laundry facilities and small, equipped kitchens, making it easier and cheaper to dine in.

Other Options: Swapping homes with a local works for people with an appealing place to offer (don't assume where you live is not interesting to Europeans). Good places to start are HomeExchange.com and LoveHomeSwap.com. To sleep for free, Couchsurfing.com is a vagabond's alternative to Airbnb. It lists millions of outgoing members, who host fellow "surfers" in their homes.

Hostels

A hostel provides cheap beds in dorms where you sleep alongside strangers for about €14-18 per night. Travelers of any age are welcome if they don't mind dorm-style accommodations and meeting other travelers. Most hostels offer kitchen facilities, guest computers, Wi-Fi, and a self-service laundry. Hostels almost always provide bedding, but the towel's up to you (though you can usually rent one). Family and private rooms may be available on request.

Independent hostels tend to be easygoing, colorful, and informal (no membership required; www.hostelworld.com). You may pay slightly less by booking direct with the hostel. **Official hostels** are part of Hostelling International (HI) and share an online booking site (www.hihostels.com). HI hostels typically require that you be a member or else pay a bit more per night.

Eating

For listings in this guidebook, I look for restaurants that are convenient to your hotel and sightseeing. When restaurant-hunting, choose a spot filled with locals, not the place with the big neon signs boasting, "We Speak English and Accept Credit Cards."

Restaurant Code

Eateries in this book are categorized according to the average cost of a typical main course. Drinks, desserts, and splurge items can raise the price considerably.

$$$$	**Splurge:** Most main courses over 90 TL
$$$	**Pricier:** 60-90 TL
$$	**Moderate:** 30-60 TL
$	**Budget:** Under 30 TL

In Turkey, kebabs, sandwiches, and other takeaway food are **$**; a basic café or sit-down restaurant is **$$**; a casual but more upscale restaurant is **$$$**; and a swanky splurge is **$$$$**.

Venturing even a block or two off the main drag leads to higher-quality food for a better price.

RESTAURANT PRICING

I've categorized my recommended eateries based on the average price of a typical main course, indicated with a dollar-sign rating (see sidebar). Obviously, expensive specialties, fine wine, appetizers, and dessert can significantly increase your final bill.

The categories also indicate the personality of a place: **Budget** eateries include street food, takeaway, order-at-the-counter shops, basic cafeterias, and bakeries selling sandwiches. **Moderate** eateries are nice (but not fancy) sit-down restaurants, ideal for a straightforward, fill-the-tank meal. Most of my listings fall in this category—great for a taste of the local cuisine at a reasonable price.

Pricier eateries are a notch up, with more attention paid to the setting, presentation, and (often inventive) cuisine. **Splurge** eateries are dress-up-for-a-special-occasion swanky—typically with an elegant setting, polished service, and pricey and intricate cuisine.

RESTAURANTS

Traditionally, the evening dinner is the big meal of the day in Turkey. As in other Mediterranean countries, dinner is eaten late (generally between 20:00 and 21:00), and it can last for hours. But most restaurants are ready to serve dinner much earlier, and you can make your meal as long or as short as you like. Except for high-end, international places, restaurants in Turkey generally have a single menu and price list for both lunch and dinner. For the most part, once a restaurant is open, it serves meals nonstop until closing time.

Some restaurants don't serve alcohol, as noted in the listings in the Eating chapter. Alcohol permits are expensive, and some restaurants are located too close to a place of worship or a school to qualify.

Restaurants (indoor spaces) are nonsmoking. Water pipes (a.k.a. hookahs) are available at many restaurants in the Old Town; see page 75 for more information on this pastime.

During the religious festival of Ramadan, Muslims fast during the day, then gorge themselves at sunset. This means that restaurants are likely to be empty during the day, and a few may close altogether. But as the sun sets, you might see long lines. For more on Ramadan, see page 72.

Tipping: If you order your food at a counter, don't tip, though it's nice to leave a lira or two on the table for the busser. At cafés and restaurants that have a waitstaff, tip 10 percent for good service. Be ready to tip in cash even if paying with a credit card (you can't add a tip to the payment slip). Some upscale restaurants may include a service charge in the bill; this fee goes to the restaurant, not the servers, so it's still appropriate to round up your bill about 10 percent. If you're not sure whether your bill includes the tip, just ask.

PRACTICALITIES

Types of Restaurants

A **kebab lokantası** or **kebabçı** (keh-bahb-chuh) serves the traditional Turkish kebab. Places run the gamut from upscale to hole in the wall. Kebab restaurants usually start serving around 11:00 and stay open until about 23:00.

People usually go to a tavern-style **meyhane** (mehy-hah-neh) to enjoy *rakı* (anise-flavored liqueur) and *mezes* (appetizers). A mey-

hane is judged not by its main courses, but by the quality and the variety of its *mezes*. Such restaurants may be open during the day, but they do most of their business at dinner and later, when live music is usually offered.

A **balık lokantası** or **balıkçı** (bah-luhk-chuh) serves fish and seafood as well as *mezes* and salads made with calamari, octopus, shrimp, or mussels. Waiters usually bring out a tray of cold *mezes* to choose from. *Rakı*, the classic Turkish alcohol, is commonly served with seafood, but almost all seafood restaurants also sell wine and soft drinks. When selecting a fish dish, ask how big the

May It Please the Sultan

Cooks in royal kitchens concocted quite a few creative dishes to please the sultan. Who else would have thought of cooking stuffed melon, mixing rice with almonds and apricots, or stewing eggplant jam? At restaurants that serve traditional cuisine, you may come across dishes listed as *hünkar beğendi* ("the sultan liked it"), *imam bayıldı* ("the imam loved it"), or *dilber dudağı* ("belle's lips"). These names show the close link between food, people, and the palace.

portions are: One portion may be enough for two or three eaters to share. Often fish is priced daily and sold by weight. To avoid tourist-gouging, ask your server to explain the pricing if it's not outlined in the menu.

"Self-servis" restaurants are cafeterias but with restaurant-quality food. These are some of the best-value and most atmospheric places to eat in town. Don't be put off by the absence of menus—simply survey the scene, and point to what looks good. For tips on navigating self-service restaurants, see the sidebar on page 470.

An *esnaf lokantası* ("workers' restaurant") offers a real "Back Door" eating experience. These simple eateries, usually hiding out on back streets in low-rent areas and business districts, serve up inexpensive, wholesome food for local workers. They're usually only open for lunch (standard hours are 11:00-16:00) and don't accept credit cards. Most *esnaf lokantası* (ehs-nahf loh-kahn-tah-suh) don't have menus—customers choose from the cooked food that's on display. You'll usually find at least one type of stew, a few vegetable and meat dishes, and side dishes such as rice, bulgur pilaf, pasta, or potatoes. Go early—the best dishes go fast.

TURKISH CUISINE

Understanding the basics of typical Turkish food will help you better enjoy the cuisine.

Meze (meh-zeh) is the general term for any appetizer, served hot or cold in small portions, usually eaten before the main course. Typical **cold *mezes*** (*soğuk mezes;* soh-ook meh-zeh) include cheese, stuffed grape leaves, eggplant salad, and *cacık* (jah-juhk), a thick mix of yogurt, cucumbers, and garlic with olive oil, similar to Greek *tzatziki*. **Hot *mezes*** (*sıcak mezes;* suh-jahk meh-zeh) are traditionally served after the cold *mezes* and can include tiny meatballs, grilled or deep-fried calamari or shrimp, or *börek* (boh-rehk; see below). *Mezes* can be a meal in themselves, so save room if you're ordering a main course.

When ordering, keep in mind that waiters are not used to the

American custom of sharing appetizers. If you ask for a *meze* you plan to share, your waiter will likely think you want portions for every person at your table. You can avoid confusion by having each person at the table order one appetizer, then share after the *mezes* arrive.

Soup (*çorba;* chor-bah) is often served at the beginning of the meal. *Mercimek* (mehr-jee-mehk) *çorba* is made with mashed lentils, and *yoğurt çorbası* is made with yogurt and served hot.

Zeytinyağlı (zey-teen-yah-luh; "in olive oil") is a common term for vegetables cooked in olive oil. Vegetables can be a main course or—if they're deep-fried, chilled, and served with yogurt—an appetizer.

Seafood is an essential part of Istanbul cuisine. For details on the local varieties of fish, see the sidebar on page 296.

Turks eat a lot of **yogurt,** usually made from cow's milk. The thick, savory yogurt called *cacık* (jah-juhk) is popular.

Kebabs—generally marinated, skewered, and grilled—are the primary means of preparing and serving meats. Kebabs have different names based on how they're prepared. A *şiş* (skewer) *kebab* means is any meat cut into small pieces and grilled on a skewer. For a *döner* (doh-nehr; "to spin") *kebab,* the chef cuts thin slices from a big chunk of meat grilled on a vertical rotisserie, then wraps it in pita or sandwich bread. Traditional  *döner kebabs* are veal or a mix of lamb and veal, but more recently chicken (*tavuk;* tah-vook) and fish have become popular.

Dolma (dohl-mah; stuffed) refers to stuffed vegetables such as bell peppers, tomatoes, eggplant, zucchini, or grape leaves. When stuffed with rice, raisins, or onions—and cooked in olive oil—dolma is a vegetarian dish served as a cold *meze.* When stuffed with rice and meat, dolma is a main course, often accompanied by yogurt (not to be confused with *dolmuş*—a minibus stuffed with people).

Savory ***börek*** (boh-rehk) is made of phyllo dough with cheese, herbs, and/or minced meat nestled between the pastry layers. *Su böreği* (soo boh-reh-ee) is prepared with thick sheets of dough that are briefly dipped in boiling water before they're layered over the stuffing. *Sigara böreği* (see-gah-rah boh-reh-ee), a deep-fried cheese roll, is a popular *meze.*

Pide (pee-deh) is Turkish-style pita bread (sans pocket) usually topped with vegetables and cheese. Take a thin, flat *pide,* top

Self-Service Survival Guide

Self-service, cafeteria-style restaurants are common in the city, especially along the street with the tram tracks (Divan Yolu) in the center of the Old Town, and on İstiklal Street in the New District. Serving freshly cooked, typical Turkish food at good prices, they are perfect for travelers who are short on time—simply choose your food, pay for it, eat it, and leave.

Before you get in line, survey the counter to see what's available. Most eateries don't label the dishes in English, so if you need advice, ask a cook or the person next to you. Keep an eye out for what others are ordering; locals know what's good. Make up your mind quickly—busy lunchtime eaters aren't too tolerant of dilly-dallying.

Point to what you'd like, and the staff will hand it to you. Prices are set and for a full portion. Even if you ask for smaller portions to construct a sampler plate, you'll still pay the full price per item. If you're with a companion and want to sample several items, it's easiest if you both order full portions and then split them at your table.

Keep things moving by being ready to pay (cash or credit card). When you've finished eating, don't bus your dishes, but do leave a lira or two for the staff.

Here are some of the dishes you'll likely find in a self-service restaurant:

Soup *(Çorba):* Most places will have at least one kind of soup. *Yayla çorbası* (yay-lah chohr-bah-suh) is a light, delicious yogurt soup with rice, flour, and egg. You'll also see lentil soup (*mercimek;* mehr-jee-mehk); the slightly spicy *ezogelin* (eh-zoh-geh-leen) with rice or bulgur, lentils, tomato-and-pepper paste, garlic, and a few spices; and tomato soup (*domates;* doh-mah-tehs).

it with meat, onions, and parsley, and you have *lahmacun.* Or try *lavaş* (lah-vahsh), a flat bread that, when baked fresh, arrives on your table looking like an inflated pillow. **Gözleme** (gohz-leh-meh) is flat bread cooked on a convex steel sheet.

One of Turkey's most popular **desserts** is **rice pudding** (sütlaç; sewt-lahch); variations include *fırın* (fuh-ruhn), rice pudding with a burned top, and *keşkül* (kash-kuhl), milk pudding with coconut, vanilla, and eggs. You'll also want to sample Turkish **baklava,** served with cream or crushed nuts; **shredded wheat** is combined with crushed nuts and sweet syrup (*kadayıf;* kah-dah-yuhf) or with unsalted cheese (*künefe;* koo-nef-ay). **Bread pudding** (*ekmak*

Side Dishes: Try rice pilaf (*pirinç pilavı;* pee-reench pee-lah-vuh), *hıngal* (huhn-gahl; potato-filled steamed dumplings), *patates* (pah-tah-tehs; potatoes served mashed, steamed, or deep-fried), and *bulgur pilavı* (bool-goor pee-lah-vuh; pilaf made with cracked wheat and fresh tomatoes and/or tomato paste).

Pasta *(Makarna):* While not that common, you might see spaghetti or macaroni and cheese (*fırında makarna,* fuh-ruhn-dah mah-kahr-nah).

Vegetarian Dishes: Most common are green beans (*yeşil fasulye,* yeh-sheel fah-sool-yeh) and different types of dolma (stuffed vegetables) cooked in olive oil.

Meat Dishes: Many main courses combine meat with vegetables. For example, *karnıyarık* (kahr-nuh yah-ruhk; "split tummy") is made by cutting an eggplant open and stuffing it with minced veal, onions, and tomatoes. When cooked in olive oil and made without meat, it's called *imam bayıldı* (ee-mum bah-yuhl-duh, "the imam loved it"). For *musakka* (moo-sahk-kah), the eggplant is chopped into slices or rings.

Veal *(dana;* dah-nah) is common (usually cooked with tomatoes, onions, green pepper, and/or potatoes), but you'll generally also find **chicken** (*tavuk;* tah-vook)—steamed, cooked with vegetables, or grilled. **Lamb** *(kuzu),* particularly the shank (*kuzu haşlama;* koo-zoo hush-lah-mah), is a local favorite. Lamb is often cooked and served with carrots, potatoes, and onions. **Meatballs** (*köfte;* kohf-teh), usually made of minced veal or lamb, are grilled or cooked with vegetables and often accompanied by french fries, fresh tomatoes and peppers, or rice. *İçli köfte* (eech-lee ko-hf-teh) is a bulgur pouch filled with meat, onions, and spices.

Salad: You can count on at least two kinds of salads being available at most restaurants: *Çoban salatası* (choh-bahn sah-lah-tah-suh; "shepherds' salad"), made with chopped tomatoes, cucumbers, onions, and peppers; and green salad (*yeşil salata;* yeh-sheel sah-lah-tah), which usually has tomatoes, onions, and/or shredded carrots.

PRACTICALITIES

kadayıfı; ehk-mehk kah-dah-yuh-fuh) is served with thick cream of water buffalo milk (*kaymak;* kahy-mahk). The **quince dessert** (*ayva tatlısı;* ahy-vah that-luh-suh) is topped with *kaymak* and/or crushed nuts; semolina **cookies in honey syrup** (*şekerpare;* sheh-kehr-pah-reh) are moist bites of sweetness.

DRINKS

Ayran (eye-rahn) is a popular, everyday beverage made of yogurt diluted with water and seasoned with a pinch of salt. This refreshing drink pairs well with many local dishes. You'll even see it on the menu at McDonald's and Burger King. Most eateries serve bottled

Turkish Baklava

For centuries, baklava has reigned as the queen of desserts. At its most basic, it consists of very thin layers of phyllo dough, baked and soaked in syrup. Of the countless variations, Turks tend to favor baklava with pistachios.

When you visit a *baklavacı* (bahk-lah-vah-cuh) specialty shop, use all five senses to tell good baklava from bad. First, it must be crisp—neither hard nor spongy—with no excess syrup visible, and should smell deliciously of butter and nuts. Poke it with a fork; if it has been baked just right, you'll hear a crunch. And as you take that first heavenly bite, the fine layers of dough should melt in your mouth. In Istanbul, **Baklavacı Güllüoğlu** is the go-to place for the best baklava (see page 355).

ayran made from pasteurized milk and safe drinking water. If yours isn't served from a bottle (or in a sealed plastic cup), ask whether it was made with bottled water or request bottled *ayran*.

Turkish coffee (*kahve;* kah-veh) is unfiltered coffee, with the grounds mixed right in. It's typically drunk as a digestive after dinner, and sometimes after lunch—but never at breakfast (for more details, see page 73).

Tea (*çay;* chai)—both black and herbal—is a more common drink among Turks than coffee. Turkish tea, grown locally along the Black Sea coastline, is similar in taste to English breakfast or Earl Grey. Turks never put milk in their tea. *Adaçayı* (ah-dah-chah-yuh; sage), *ıhlamur* (uh-lah-moor; linden), and *kuşburnu*

(koosh-boor-noo; rosehip) are popular herbal flavors. When you ask for herbal tea, unless you're in a specialty café, you'll be given a teabag and a cup of hot water. In the Old Town, you'll likely be offered apple tea made with granulated apple and sugar. The real thing is made from dried and boiled apple skin (available at the Spice Market; see the Shopping chapter).

Rakı (rah-kuh) is the quintessentially Turkish firewater you'll see anywhere alcohol is allowed. Distilled from grapes and flavored with anise seed, it has a strong licorice taste. Turks dilute it with water or ice, which turns the drink a cloudy white color. *Rakı*—like Greek ouzo—is an acquired taste. It's particularly good with a light meal, meat, fish, or some *mezes*. If you drink a lot of *rakı*, watch out—too much will give you a mega-headache the next morning.

Şerbet (shehr-beht) is boiled fruit juice with sugar added; the flavors change with the season). During meals, sultans didn't drink water, but *şerbet*.

Fresh-squeezed juice (*suyu*, soo-yoo) is widely available at cafés, restaurants, and street stands, and usually quite cheap. The most popular squeezable fruits are orange (*portakal*, por-tah-kahl) and pomegranate (*nar*, which is very tart—try it mixed with OJ.

Remember, don't drink the **tap water** in Istanbul. Bottled or canned drinks are, of course, perfectly fine. Most restaurants serve safe-to-drink water in plastic cups with peel-off tops.

STREET-VENDOR FARE

Common street-vendor fare includes *döner kebabs,* sandwiches, bagel-like *simit*, mussels, and sheep intestines...which taste better than you might expect.

Döner kebabs, described earlier, are the most popular type of Turkish fast food.

For **sandwiches,** locals usually use white bread. Ordering *yarım ekmek* (yah-ruhm ehk-mehk; "half bread") will get you half a sandwich. For a smaller snack, request a quarter-sandwich: *çeyrek ekmek* (chehy-rehk ehk-mehk).

Simit (see-meet) is made by dipping a ring of dough in grape molasses *(pekmez)* and sesame seeds before baking. You can buy one from a street vendor (for as little as 2 TL) or from one of the growing number of *simit* chains, such as Simit Sarayı, where you'll find a range of choices similar to a bagel shop. For a cheap picnic, buy a crunchy, freshly baked *simit,* and top it with tomatoes, cucumbers, and some *beyaz peynir* (beh-yahz pehy-neer; white cheese made from cow's or sheep's milk) from a grocery.

Midye tava (meed-yeh tah-vah), deep-fried mussels, are served either in a sandwich or on a plate, and usually come with *tarator* (tah-rah-tohr), a dip made of breadcrumbs, yogurt, garlic, vinegar, and sometimes walnuts. A local delicacy is *midye dolma*—mussel shells stuffed with olive-oil-soaked rice, raisins, and herbs.

Standing by the Galata Bridge on the Golden Horn, even from a distance, you'll smell the *balık ekmek* (bah-luhk ehk-me-

Hurdling the Language Barrier

The language barrier in Istanbul is no bigger than in Western Europe. In fact, visitors often find that it's easier to communicate in Istanbul than in Madrid. Most people in the tourist industry, and quite a few young people, speak English.

The Turkish people are among the friendliest in the world. The locals you meet will often invite you to have tea with them. You'll likely be able to communicate with them in English, but it's fun to know some key Turkish pleasantries (see "Turkish Survival Phrases" on page 489). In this hospitable country, you'll find that doors will open to you regardless, but you'll get more smiles when you can speak a few words of the language.

hk)—grilled mackerel, onions, and lettuce sandwiched in bread—being prepared on small boats tied by the ferry docks in Eminönü. A few stands, pubs, and restaurants along the bridge (lower level, pedestrian area) also serve *balık ekmek*.

A big favorite among Turks is ***kokoreç*** (koh-koh-retch)—sheep intestines that are chopped up, grilled, seasoned, and served with tomatoes and peppers. (If this sounds inedible, remember that sausages are traditionally packed in sheep intestines.) To give this a try, ask for a small *çeyrek ekmek* (chey-rehk ehk-mehk; "quarter-portion"). A popular place for this local treat is **Şampiyon Kokoreç** (described on page 269).

Staying Connected

One of the most common questions I hear from travelers is, "How can I stay connected in Europe?" The short answer: more easily and affordably than you might think.

The simplest solution is to bring your own device—phone, tablet, or laptop—and use it just as you would at home (following the money-saving tips below, such as getting an international plan or connecting to free Wi-Fi whenever possible). Another option is to buy a European SIM card for your US mobile phone. Or you can use European landlines and computers to connect. More details are at RickSteves.com/phoning. For a very practical one-hour talk covering tech issues for travelers, see RickSteves.com/mobile-travel-skills.

USING YOUR PHONE IN EUROPE

Here are some budget tips and options.

Sign up for an international plan. To stay connected at a lower cost, sign up for an international service plan through your carrier. Most providers offer a simple bundle that includes calling,

Tips on Internet Security

Make sure that your device is running the latest versions of its operating system, security software, and apps. Next, ensure that your device and key programs (like email) are password-protected. On the road, use only secure, password-protected Wi-Fi. Ask the hotel or café staff for the specific name of their network, and make sure you log on to that exact one.

If you must access your financial info online, use a banking app rather than accessing your account via a browser, and use a cellular connection, not Wi-Fi. Never log on to personal finance sites on a public computer. If you're very concerned, consider subscribing to a VPN (virtual private network).

messaging, and data. Your normal plan may already include international coverage (T-Mobile's does).
airport).

Before your trip, research your provider's international rates. Activate the plan a day or two before you leave, then remember to cancel it when your trip's over.

Use free Wi-Fi whenever possible. Unless you have an unlimited-data plan, save most of your online tasks for Wi-Fi. Most accommodations in Europe offer free Wi-Fi. Many cafés (including Starbucks and McDonald's) offer hotspots for customers; ask for the password when you buy something. You may also find Wi-Fi at TIs, city squares, major museums, public-transit hubs, airports, and aboard trains and buses.

Minimize the use of your cellular network. The best way to make sure you're not accidentally burning through data is to put your device in "airplane" mode (which also disables phone calls and texts) and connect to Wi-Fi networks as needed. When you need to get online but can't find Wi-Fi, simply turn on your cellular network (or turn off airplane mode) just long enough for the task at hand.

Even with an international data plan, wait until you're on Wi-Fi to Skype, download apps, stream videos, or do other megabyte-greedy tasks. Using a navigation app such as Google Maps can require lots of data, so download maps when you're on Wi-Fi, then use the app offline.

Limit automatic updates. By default, your device constantly checks for a data connection and updates app content. Check your device's menu for ways to turn this off, and change your email settings from "auto-retrieve" to "manual" (or from "push" to "fetch").

Use Wi-Fi calling and messaging apps. Skype, WhatsApp, FaceTime, and Google Hangouts are great for making free or low-cost calls or sending texts over Wi-Fi worldwide. Just log on to a

PRACTICALITIES

How to Dial

Here's how to dial from anywhere in the US or Europe, using the phone number of one of my recommended Istanbul hotels as an example (0212 517 7173). If dialing internationally, drop the initial 0 from the number.

From a US Mobile Phone

Phone numbers in this book are presented exactly as you would dial them from a US mobile phone. For international access, press and hold the 0 key until you get a + sign, then dial the country code (90 for Turkey) and phone number.

▶ To call the Istanbul hotel from any location, dial +90 212 517 7173.

From a US Landline

Replace + with 011 (US/Canada international access code), then dial the country code (90 for Turkey) and phone number.

▶ To call the Istanbul hotel from your home landline, dial 011 90 212 517 7173.

From a European Landline

Replace + with 00 (Europe international access code), then dial the country code (90 for Turkey, 1 for the US) and phone number.

▶ To call the Istanbul hotel from a Greek landline, dial 00 90 212 517 7173.

▶ To call my US office from a Turkish landline, dial 00 1 425 771 8303.

Wi-Fi network, then connect with friends or family members who use the same service. If you buy credit in advance, with some services you can call or text anywhere for just pennies.

Buy a European SIM card. If you anticipate making a lot of local calls, need a local phone number, or your provider's international data rates are expensive, consider buying a SIM card in Europe to replace the one in your (unlocked) US phone or tablet. In Turkey, buy a SIM card from a mobile-phone shop such as Vodaphone, Turkcell, or Avea (easily found at the Istanbul airport).

WITHOUT A MOBILE PHONE

It's less convenient but possible to travel in Europe without a mobile device. You can make calls from your hotel and check email or get online using public computers.

Most **hotels** charge a fee for placing calls—ask for rates before you dial. Some hotels have **public computers** in their lobby for guests to use. On European keyboards, use the "Alt Gr" key to the right of the space bar to insert the extra symbol that appears on some keys. If you can't locate a special character (such as @), simply copy and paste it from a web page.

From One Turkish Phone to Another

To place a domestic call (from a Turkish landline or mobile), drop +90 and dial the phone number (including an initial 0). Within the same area code, just dial the seven-digit number.

▶ To call the Istanbul hotel from Kuşadası, dial 0212 517 7173.

▶ To call the Istanbul hotel from the 212 area code, just dial 517 7173.

More Dialing Tips

Local Numbers: European phone numbers and area codes can vary in length and spacing, even within the same country. Mobile phones use separate prefixes (for instance, in Turkey, mobile numbers begin with 5). When a European phone number begins with 0, drop it when dialing internationally (except when calling Italy). Special numbers in Istanbul that start with 444 (such as 444 3777, the American Hospital) do not have an area code. From a US cell phone, though, you would need to dial +90 before the number.

Toll and Toll-Free Calls: It's generally not possible to dial European toll or toll-free numbers from a US mobile or landline (although you can sometimes get through using Skype). Look for a direct-dial number instead.

Calling the US from a US Mobile Phone, While Abroad: Dial +1, area code, and number.

More Phoning Help: See HowToCallAbroad.com.

MAIL

You can mail one package per day to yourself worth up to $200 duty-free from Europe to the US (mark it "personal purchases"). If you're sending a gift to someone, mark it "unsolicited gift." For details, visit www.cbp.gov, select "Travel," and search for "Know Before You Go." The Turkish postal service works fine, but for quick transatlantic delivery (in either direction), consider services such as DHL (www.dhl.com).

Resources from Rick Steves

Begin Your Trip at RickSteves.com

My mobile-friendly **website** is *the* place to explore Europe in preparation for your trip. You'll find thousands of fun articles, videos, and radio interviews; a wealth of money-saving tips for planning your dream trip; travel news dispatches; a video library of travel talks; my travel blog; our latest guidebook updates (RickSteves.com/update); and the free Rick Steves Audio Europe app. You can also follow me on Facebook, Instagram, and Twitter.

Our **Travel Forum** is a well-groomed collection of message boards, where our travel-savvy community answers questions and shares their personal travel experiences—and our well-traveled staff chimes in when they can be helpful (RickSteves.com/forums).

Our **online Travel Store** offers bags and accessories that I've designed to help you travel smarter and lighter. These include my popular carry-on bags (which I live out of four months a year), money belts, totes, toiletries kits, adapters, guidebooks, and planning maps (RickSteves.com/shop).

Our website can also help you find the perfect **rail pass** for your itinerary and your budget, with easy, one-stop shopping for rail passes, seat reservations, and point-to-point tickets (RickSteves.com/rail).

Rick Steves' Tours, Guidebooks, TV Shows, and More

Small Group Tours: Want to travel with greater efficiency and less stress? We offer more than 40 itineraries reaching the best destinations in this book...and beyond. Each year about 30,000 travelers join us on about 1,000 Rick Steves bus tours. You'll enjoy great guides and a fun bunch of travel partners (with small groups of 24 to 28 travelers). You'll find European adventures to fit every vacation length. For all the details, and to get our tour catalog, visit www.ricksteves.com/tours or call us at +1 425 608 4217.

Books: This book is just one of many books in my series on European travel, which includes country and city guidebooks, Snapshots (excerpted chapters from bigger guides), Pocket Guides (full-color little books on big cities), "Best Of" guidebooks (condensed, full-color country guides), and my budget-travel skills handbook, *Rick Steves Europe Through the Back Door*. A complete list of my titles—including phrase books, cruising guides, and travelogues on European art, history, and culture—appears near the end of this book.

TV Shows and Travel Talks: My public television series, *Rick Steves' Europe,* covers Europe from top to bottom with over 100 half-hour episodes—and we're working on new shows every year (watch full episodes at my website for free). My free online video library, Rick Steves Classroom Europe, offers a searchable database of short video clips on European history, culture, and geography (Classroom.RickSteves.com). And, to raise your travel I.Q., check out the video versions of our popular classes (covering most European countries as well as travel skills, packing smart, cruising, tech for travelers, European art, and travel as a political act—RickSteves.com/travel-talks).

Audio Tours on My Free App: I've produced dozens of free, self-guided audio tours of the top sights in Europe. For those tours and other audio content, get my free **Rick Steves Audio Europe app,** an extensive online library organized by destination. For more on my app, see page 22.

Radio: My weekly public radio show, *Travel with Rick Steves,* features interviews with travel experts from around the world. It airs on 400 public radio stations across the US. An archive of programs is available at RickSteves.com/radio.

Podcasts: You can enjoy my travel content via several free podcasts. The podcast version of my radio show brings you a weekly, hour-long travel conversation. My other podcasts include a weekly selection of video clips from my public television show, my audio tours of Europe's top sights, and live recordings of my travel classes (RickSteves.com/watch-read-listen/audio/podcasts).

PRACTICALITIES

APPENDIX

Holidays and Festivals

This list includes selected festivals in Istanbul, plus national holidays observed throughout Turkey. Many sights and banks close on national holidays—keep this in mind when planning your itinerary. Dates for Muslim holidays are set according to a lunar calendar, so the specific dates vary from year to year. Even though Christian holidays (such as Easter, Ascension, and Christmas) are not celebrated in Istanbul, the city can be especially crowded with visiting Europeans during these times.

Before planning a trip around a festival, verify the dates with the festival website, Turkey's tourist office (www.goturkey.com), or my "Upcoming Holidays and Festivals in Turkey" web page (www. ricksteves.com/europe/turkey/festivals).

Jan 1	New Year's Day (national holiday)
March/April	Istanbul Film Festival (http://film.iksv.org)
March/April/May (adjusts with lunar calendar)	Ramadan: April 13-May 12, 2021; April 2-May 1, 2022; March 22-April 20, 2023 (followed by Eid-al-Fitr feast days)

April	Easter (Western): April 4, 2021; April 17, 2022; April 9, 2023
April/May	Easter (Orthodox): May 2, 2021; April 24, 2022; April 16, 2023
April 23	National Sovereignty and Children's Day (national holiday)
May	Ascension Day (Western): May 13, 2021; May 25, 2022; May 18, 2023
May 1	Labor and Solidarity Day (national holiday)
May 19	Atatürk Commemoration and Youth Day (national holiday)
May/June	Ascension Day (Orthodox): June 10, 2021; June 2, 2022; May 25, 2023
June	Istanbul Music Festival (muzik.iksv.org)
June/July	Kurban Bayramı (Muslim festival): July 19, 2021; July 9, 2022; June 28, 2023
Early July	Istanbul Jazz Festival (caz.iksv.org)
July 15	Democracy and National Unity Day (national holiday)
Aug 30	Victory Day (national holiday)
Sept	International Istanbul Biennial (four weeks, held in odd years, bienal.iksv.org)
Mid-Oct	October Film Festival (filmekimi.iksv.org)
Oct 29	Republic Day (national holiday)
Dec 24-Jan 1	Christmas Week

Books and Films

To learn more about Istanbul and Turkey past and present, check out a few of these books or films.

Nonfiction

Atatürk: The Biography of the Founder of Modern Turkey (Andrew Mango, 1999). A comprehensive biography of Turkey's legendary statesman.

Crescent & Star (Stephen Kinzer, 2001). A look at Turkey as a bridge between East and West, both politically and geographically.

The Drop That Became the Sea (Yunus Emre, 1999). A compilation of 13th- and 14th-century Sufi poetry, tinged with Islamic mysticism.

Eat Smart in Turkey (Joan Peterson, 2004). A culinary guidebook to Turkish cuisine.

An Istanbul Anthology: Travel Writing Through the Centuries (Kaya Genç, 2015). Impressions and perspectives on Istanbul by writers as diverse as Arthur Conan Doyle, Gustave Flaubert, and Ernest Hemingway.

Istanbul: Memories and the City (Orhan Pamuk, 2005). An intimate portrait of Istanbul by Turkey's leading contemporary writer.

Istanbul: The Imperial City (John Freely, 1996). A brief history and gazetteer of the city's sights.

Osman's Dream: The History of the Ottoman Empire (Caroline Finkel, 2005). An epic history of the empire from its ascendency in medieval times to its downfall in the 20th century.

The Pleasantries of the Incredible Mulla Nasrudin (Idries Shah, 1968). A collection of Sufi wisdom as told by mystics and masters.

Sailing from Byzantium: How a Lost Empire Shaped the World (Colin Wells, 2006). The fascinating story of how Byzantium preserved and contributed to Western civilization.

A Short History of Byzantium (John Julius Norwich, 1997). An authoritative chronicle of Byzantium's rise and fall.

Suleiman the Magnificent (André Clot, 1992). A history of the most celebrated of Ottoman sultans.

Tales from the Expat Harem (Anastasia M. Ashman and Jennifer Eaton Gökmen, 2006). The personal adventures of foreign women living in Turkey.

Turkish Odyssey: A Cultural Guide to Turkey (Serif Yenen, 2003). A comprehensive guide to Turkish society and culture.

Turkish Reflections: A Biography of a Place (Mary Lee Settle, 1991). Settle recounts two visits to Turkey, 15 years apart.

Fiction

The Bastard of Istanbul (Elif Shafak, 2006). A young Armenian girl living in Arizona travels to Istanbul to uncover her identity and cultural heritage.

Birds Without Wings (Louis de Bernières, 2004). Bernières depicts a village tragedy amid the fall of the Ottoman Empire.

The Black Book (Orhan Pamuk, 1990). After an Istanbul lawyer's wife disappears, he begins assuming the identity of her ex-husband.

Bliss (O. Z. Livaneli, 2002). After intense trauma, a young Turkish girl begins a journey of transformation in Istanbul.

Human Landscapes from My Country (Nazim Hikmet, 1966). Verse vignettes tell the story of Turkey's emergence as a modern, secular country.

Memed, My Hawk (Yashar Kemal, 1955). A bandit-hero seeks justice in the Turkish countryside.

My Name Is Red (Orhan Pamuk, 1998). Part mystery, part love story, set in 16th-century Istanbul.

One for Sorrow (Mary Reed and Eric Mayer, 1999). The first in a series of six mysteries set in Byzantine Constantinople.

Portrait of a Turkish Family (Irfan Orga, 1950). A wealthy Ottoman family disintegrates at the end of the Ottoman Empire.

Snow (Orhan Pamuk, 2002). An exiled poet returns to Turkey and faces suspicion after making a controversial report.

Film

Crossing the Bridge: The Sound of Istanbul (2005). A fascinating musical portrait of modern Istanbul.

Distant (2002). A photographer and his unemployed cousin try to connect in snow-covered Istanbul in this award-winning film.

Gallipoli (1981). Two Australian soldiers (including a very young Mel Gibson) fight in the Gallipoli campaign during World War I.

Hamam (Steam: The Turkish Bath) (1997). An Italian inherits a traditional public bath in Istanbul.

Midnight Express (1978). The hair-raising tale of an American imprisoned in Istanbul on drug charges.

Tinker Tailor Soldier Spy (2011). Parts of this Cold War drama take place in the heart of Istanbul.

Topkapi (1964). Peter Ustinov won an Oscar for his role in this crime caper, worth seeing for its grand tour of 1960s Istanbul.

A Touch of Spice (2003). A Greek boy growing up in Istanbul learns about both food and life from his grandfather.

Uzak (Distant, 2002). An unemployed young man from the countryside tries to adjust to life in Istanbul.

Yol (1982). Five political prisoners in Turkey struggle to readjust to the outside world.

Books for Kids

Delilah Dirk and the Turkish Lieutenant (Tony Cliff, 2011). The Indiana Jones-esque heroine of this graphic novel causes trouble in Constantinople.

Istanbul for Kids (Burçak Gürün Muraben, 2014). Stories and histories presented in an easy-to-read format.

The Road from Home: The Story of an Armenian Girl (David Kherdian, 1979). A non-fiction account of the life of Kheridian's mother, who survived the Armenian genocide as a girl.

The Stone of Destiny: Tales from Turkey (Elspeth Tavaci, 2012). A poor stonecutter journeys to Istanbul.

Turkish Delight: A Kid's Guide to Istanbul, Turkey (Penelope Dyan, 2011). Using poetry and photographs, this guide focuses on what children might find interesting in the city.

Conversions and Climate

Numbers and Stumblers

- Europeans write a few of their numbers differently than we do. 1 = 1, 4 = 4, 7 = 7.
- In Europe, dates appear as day/month/year, so Christmas 2022 is 25/12/22.
- Commas are decimal points and decimals are commas. A dollar and a half is $1,50, one thousand is 1.000, and there are 5.280 feet in a mile.
- When counting with fingers, start with your thumb. If you hold up your first finger to request one item, you'll probably get two.
- What Americans call the second floor of a building is the first floor in Europe.
- On escalators and moving sidewalks, Europeans keep the left "lane" open for passing. Keep to the right.

Metric Conversions

A **kilogram** equals 1,000 grams (about 2.2 pounds). One hundred **grams** (a common unit at markets) is about a quarter-pound. One **liter** is about a quart, or almost four to a gallon.

A **kilometer** is six-tenths of a mile. To convert kilometers to miles, cut the kilometers in half and add back 10 percent of the original (120 km: 60 + 12 = 72 miles). One **meter** is 39 inches—just over a yard.

1 foot = 0.3 meter	1 square yard = 0.8 square meter
1 yard = 0.9 meter	1 square mile = 2.6 square kilometers
1 mile = 1.6 kilometers	1 ounce = 28 grams
1 centimeter = 0.4 inch	1 quart = 0.95 liter
1 meter = 39.4 inches	1 kilogram = 2.2 pounds
1 kilometer = 0.62 mile	32°F = 0°C

Clothing Sizes

When shopping for clothing, use these US-to-European comparisons as general guidelines (but note that no conversion is perfect).

Women: For pants and dresses, add 30 in Turkey (US 10 = Turkish 40). For blouses and sweaters, add 8 for most of Europe (US 32 = European 40). For shoes, add 30-31 (US 7 = European 37/38).

Men: For shirts, multiply by 2 and add about 8 (US 15 = European 38). For jackets and suits, add 10. For shoes, add 32-34.

Children: Clothing is sized by height—in centimeters (2.5 cm = 1 inch), so a US size 8 roughly equates to 132-140. For shoes up to size 13, add 16-18, and for sizes 1 and up, add 30-32.

Turkey's Climate

First line, average daily high; second line, average daily low; third line, average days without rain. For more detailed weather statistics for destinations in this book (as well as the rest of the world), check Wunderground.com.

J	F	M	A	M	J	J	A	S	O	N	D
48°	49°	53°	63°	70°	79°	82°	82°	77°	68°	60°	52°
35°	36°	39°	45°	53°	60°	65°	66°	60°	53°	45°	39°
13	14	17	21	23	24	27	27	23	20	16	13

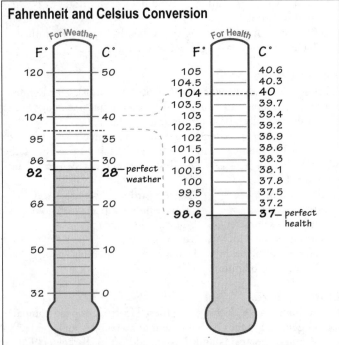

Fahrenheit and Celsius Conversion

Europe takes its temperature using the Celsius scale, while we opt for Fahrenheit. For a rough conversion from Celsius to Fahrenheit, double the number and add 30. For weather, remember that 28°C is 82°F—perfect. For health, 37°C is just right. At a launderette, 30°C is cold, 40°C is warm (usually the default setting), 60°C is hot, and 95°C is boiling. Your air-conditioner should be set at about 20°C.

APPENDIX

Turkish Language and Survival Phrases

The Turkish language is unfamiliar to most American ears. Yet Turkish is spoken by more than 200 million people worldwide and is the native language of some areas of Asia and the Balkans.

For a millennium, the people of today's Turkey spoke a mix of Turkish, Persian, and Arabic—depending on the subject and the speaker. Turkish was written in the Arabic alphabet. But in 1928, when modern-day Turkey was founded, the reforms that swept the country included an overhaul of the language. The Arabic script was abandoned in favor of the Latin alphabet. Not only did this nudge the country further toward Europe, but it was also more effective for conveying Turkish sounds than Arabic had been. As a result, more Turks became comfortable with their written language; today, the nation's illiteracy rate is less than 3 percent.

Most urban Turks speak at least a little English—and even if they don't, they will do their best to communicate with you. Still, it helps to know a few Turkish words and phrases. The Turkish people love visitors, and a friendly greeting in their language is an easy icebreaker.

To hurdle the language barrier, bring a phrase book (see the Turkish Survival Phrases on the next page), or use a translator app. A good supply of patience helps too. To make transactions clearer, have vendors write down prices.

If you master only four phrases, learn and use these: To say hello, say *merhaba* (mehr-hah-bah). Please is *lütfen* (lewt-fehn). Thank you is *teşekkür* (teh-shehk-kewr). For good-bye, say *hoşçakal* (hohsh-chah-kahl).

You may hear these common phrases: *inşallah* (een-shah-lah; God willing), *maşallah* (mah-shah-lah; may God keep it so), *kolay gelsin* (koh-lay gehl-seen; may it be easy), and *rastgele* (rust-geh-leh; may you receive some).

Since Turkish is pronounced exactly as it's spelled, it's easy to sound things out—once you learn a few new characters. And Turkish includes a few diacritics below and above letters that change their sound (see the next page).

Vowels

a sounds like "ah" as in "call"
e sounds like "eh" as in "egg"
ı (with no dot, capitalized I) sounds like "uh" as in "the"
i (with a dot, capitalized İ) sounds like "ee" as in "bee"
o sounds like "oh" as in "old"
ö sounds like "uhr" as in "urn" (the same as the German Ö/ö)
u sounds like "oo" as in "ooze"
ü sounds like "ew" as in "dew" (the same as the German Ü/ü)

Consonants

The consonants q, x, and w don't exist in the Turkish alphabet. Most consonants are pronounced just as they are in English. Here are the exceptions:

c sounds like "j" as in "jet"
ç sounds like "ch" as in "church"
g sounds like a hard "g" as in "good"
ğ is almost silent, and makes the preceding vowel longer (so the word *Ağa* is pronounced "aah-ah")
j sounds like "zh" as in "leisure"
ş sounds like "sh" as in "shoe"
v usually sounds like "v" as in "viper," but sometimes like "w" as in "wiper"

Turkish Tips

Turkish is usually pronounced rather flatly, without much emphasis on certain syllables—unless you're asking a question. If you want to invite someone to coffee *(kahve)*, you'd say, "kahh-VEH?" (accent on the second syllable).

Also note that the word order in Turkish can be different from English. For instance, to ask for a beer, you'd say, *"Bira lütfen"* (bee-rah lewt-fehn; "Beer, please"). But to ask where the toilet is, you'd say, *"Tuvalet nerede?"* (too-vah-leht neh-reh-deh; literally "Toilet where is?").

Adding *-lar* or *-ler* to the end of a word makes it plural (which one you add depends on which vowel comes last). Words in Turkish don't have a gender, and the language doesn't use articles.

Turkish Survival Phrases

In the phonetics, pronounce "ī" as the long "i" sound in "light"; "ew" as "oo" (with your lips pursed); and "g" as the hard "g" in "go."

English	Turkish	Pronunciation
Hello.	Merhaba.	mehr-hah-bah
Good day.	İyi günler.	ee-yee gewn-lehr
Good morning.	Günaydın.	gew-nī-duhn
Good evening.	İyi akşamlar.	ee-yee ahk-shahm-lahr
How are you?*	Nasılsınız?	nah-suhl-suh-nuhz
Do you speak English?	İngilizce biliyormusunuz?	een-gee-leez-jeh bee-lee-yohr-moo-soo-nooz
Yes. / No.	Evet. / Hayır.	eh-veht / hah-yur
I understand.	Anlıyorum.	ahn-luh-yoh-room
I don't understand.	Anlamıyorum.	ahn-lah-muh-yoh-room
Please.	Lütfen.	lewt-fehn
Thank you (very much).	Teşekkür (ederim).	teh-shehk-kewr (eh-deh-reem)
I'm sorry.	Üzgünüm.	ewz-gew-newm
Excuse me. (to pass)	Afedersiniz. / Pardon.	ah-feh-dehr-see-neez / pahr-dohn
No problem.	Sorun yok.	soh-roon yohk
There is a problem.	Sorun var.	soh-roon vahr
Good.	İyi.	ee-yee
Goodbye. (said by person leaving)	Hoşçakal.	hohsh-chah-kahl
Goodbye. (said by person staying)	Güle güle.	gew-leh gew-leh
one / two	bir / iki	beer / ee-kee
three / four	üç / dört	ewch / dirt
five / six	beş / altı	behsh / ahl-tuh
seven / eight	yedi / sekiz	yeh-dee / seh-keez
nine / ten	dokuz / on	doh-kooz / ohn
How much is it?	Ne kadar?	neh kah-dahr
Write it?	Yazar mısınız?	yah-zahr muh-suh-nuhz
Is it free?	Ücretsiz mi?	ewj-reht-seez mee
Is it included?	Dahil mi?	dah-heel mee
Where can I find...?	...nerede bulurum?	neh-reh-deh boo-loo-room
Where can I buy...?	...nereden alabilirim?	neh-reh-dehn ah-lah-bee-lee-reem
I'd like / We'd like...	...istiyorum / istiyoruz.	ees-tee-yoh-room / ees-tee-yoh-rooz
...a room.	Oda...	oh-dah
...a ticket to ___.	___'ya bilet...	___ yah bee-leht
Is it possible?	Olası mı?	oh-lah-suh muh
Where is...?	...nerede?	neh-reh-deh
...the train station	Tren istasyonu...	trehn ees-tahs-yoh-noo
...the bus station	Otobüs durağı...	oh-toh-bews doo-rah-uh
...the tourist information office	Turizm enformasyon bürosu...	too-reezm ehn-fohr-mahs-yohn bew-roh-soo
...the toilet	Tuvalet...	too-vah-leht
men / women	bay / bayan	bī / bah-yahn
left / right	sol / sağ	sohl / saah
straight	doğru	doh-roo
What time does this open / close?	Ne zaman açılıyor / kapanıyor?	neh zah-mahn ah-chuh-luh-yohr / kah-pah-nuh-yohr
At what time?	Ne zaman?	neh zah-mahn
Just a moment.	Bir saniye.	beer sah-nee-yeh
now / soon / later	şimdi / birazdan / sonra	sheem-dee / bee-rahz-dahn / sohn-rah
today / tomorrow	bugün / yarın	boo-gewn / yah-ruhn

*People will answer you by saying, *"Teşekkür ederim"* (Thank you very much).

In a Turkish Restaurant

English	Turkish	Pronunciation
restaurant	*lokanta / restaurant*	loh-kahn-tah / rehs-toh-rahnt
I'd like / We'd like to make a reservation.	*Rezervasyon yapmak istiyorum / istiyoruz.*	reh-zehr-vahs-yohn yahp-mahk ees-tee-yoh-room / ees-tee-yoh-rooz
One / Two persons.	*Bir / İki kişilik.*	beer / ee-kee kee-shee-leek
Non-smoking.	*Sigarasız.*	see-gah-rah-suhz
Is this table free?	*Bu masa boşmu?*	boo mah-sah bohsh-moo
The menu (in English), please.	*(İngilizce) menü lütfen.*	een-ghee-leez-jeh meh-new lewt-fehn
tax included	*KDV dahil*	kah-deh-veh dah-heel
tax not included	*KDV hariç*	kah-deh-veh hah-reech
service included	*servis dahil*	sehr-vees dah-heel
service not included	*servis hariç*	sehr-vees hah-reech
"to go"	*paket*	pah-keht
and / or	*ve / veya*	veh / veh-yah
menu	*menü*	meh-new
meal of the day	*günün yemeği*	gew-newn yeh-meh-ee
portion / half-portion	*porsiyon / yarım porsiyon*	pohr-see-yohn / yah-ruhm pohr-see-yohn
daily menu / special	*günün menüsü*	gew-newn meh-new-sew
appetizers	*meze*	meh-zeh
bread	*ekmek*	ehk-mehk
cheese	*peynir*	pay-neer
sandwich	*sandöviç*	sahn-doh-veech
soup	*çorba*	chohr-bah
salad	*salata*	sah-lah-tah
meat	*et*	eht
poultry	*tavuk*	tah-vook
fish	*balık*	bah-luhk
seafood	*deniz ürünleri*	deh-neez ew-rewn-leh-ree
fruit	*meyve*	mey-veh
vegetables	*sebze*	sehb-zeh
dessert	*tatlı*	taht-luh
water	*su*	soo
milk	*süt*	sewt
orange juice	*portakal suyu*	pohr-tah-kahl soo-yoo
coffee	*kahve*	kahh-veh
tea	*çay*	chī
wine	*şarap*	shah-rahp
red / white	*kırmızı / beyaz*	kuhr-muh-zuh / beh-yahz
beer	*bira*	bee-rah
glass / bottle	*bardak / şişe*	bahr-dahk / shee-sheh
big / small	*büyük / küçük*	bew-yewk / kew-chewk
Cheers!	*Şerefe!*	sheh-reh-feh
more / another	*biraz daha / bir tane daha*	bee-rahz dah-hah / beer tah-neh dah-hah
The same.	*Aynısından.*	ī-nuh-suhn-dahn
Bill, please.	*Hesap, lütfen.*	heh-sahp lewt-fehn
tip	*bahşiş*	bah-sheesh
Delicious!	*Nefis!*	neh-fees

Packing Checklist

Whether you're traveling for five days or five weeks, you won't need more than this. Pack light to enjoy the sweet freedom of true mobility.

Clothing

- ☐ 5 shirts: long- & short-sleeve
- ☐ 2 pairs pants (or skirts/capris)
- ☐ 1 pair shorts
- ☐ 5 pairs underwear & socks
- ☐ 1 pair walking shoes
- ☐ Sweater or warm layer
- ☐ Rainproof jacket with hood
- ☐ Tie, scarf, belt, and/or hat
- ☐ Swimsuit
- ☐ Sleepwear/loungewear

Money

- ☐ Debit card(s)
- ☐ Credit card(s)
- ☐ Hard cash (US $100-200)
- ☐ Money belt

Documents

- ☐ Passport
- ☐ Tickets & confirmations: flights, hotels, trains, rail pass, car rental, sight entries
- ☐ Driver's license
- ☐ Student ID, hostel card, etc.
- ☐ Photocopies of important documents
- ☐ Insurance details
- ☐ Guidebooks & maps

Toiletries Kit

- ☐ Basics: soap, shampoo, toothbrush, toothpaste, floss, deodorant, sunscreen, brush/comb, etc.
- ☐ Medicines & vitamins
- ☐ First-aid kit
- ☐ Glasses/contacts/sunglasses
- ☐ Sewing kit
- ☐ Packet of tissues (for WC)
- ☐ Earplugs

Electronics

- ☐ Mobile phone
- ☐ Camera & related gear
- ☐ Tablet/ebook reader/laptop
- ☐ Headphones/earbuds
- ☐ Chargers & batteries
- ☐ Phone car charger & mount (or GPS device)
- ☐ Plug adapters

Miscellaneous

- ☐ Daypack
- ☐ Sealable plastic baggies
- ☐ Laundry supplies: soap, laundry bag, clothesline, spot remover
- ☐ Small umbrella
- ☐ Travel alarm/watch
- ☐ Notepad & pen
- ☐ Journal

Optional Extras

- ☐ Second pair of shoes (flip-flops, sandals, tennis shoes, boots)
- ☐ Travel hairdryer
- ☐ Picnic supplies
- ☐ Water bottle
- ☐ Fold-up tote bag
- ☐ Small flashlight
- ☐ Mini binoculars
- ☐ Small towel or washcloth
- ☐ Inflatable pillow/neck rest
- ☐ Tiny lock
- ☐ Address list (to mail postcards)
- ☐ Extra passport photos

INDEX

INDEX

MAP INDEX

Explore Europe

At ricksteves.com you can browse through thousands of articles, videos, photos and radio interviews, plus find a wealth of money-saving travel tips for planning your dream trip. And with our mobile-friendly website, you can easily access all this great travel information anywhere you go.

TV Shows

Preview the places you'll visit by watching entire half-hour episodes of *Rick Steves' Europe* (choose from all 100 shows) on-demand, for free.

ricksteves.com

your travel dreams into affordable reality

Radio Interviews

Enjoy ready access to Rick's vast library of radio interviews covering travel tips and cultural insights that relate specifically to your Europe travel plans.

Travel Forums

Learn, ask, share! Our online community of savvy travelers is a great resource for first-time travelers to Europe, as well as seasoned pros.

Travel News

Subscribe to our free Travel News e-newsletter, and get monthly updates from Rick on what's happening in Europe.

Classroom Europe

Check out our free resource for educators with 400+ short video clips from the *Rick Steves' Europe* TV show.

Audio Europe™

Rick's Free Travel App

Get your FREE **Rick Steves Audio Europe**™ app to enjoy…

- Dozens of self-guided tours of Europe's top museums, sights and historic walks

- Hundreds of tracks filled with cultural insights and sightseeing tips from Rick's radio interviews

- All organized into handy geographic playlists

- For Apple and Android

With Rick whispering in your ear, Europe gets even better.

Find out more at rickssteves.com

Gear up for your next adventure at ricksteves.com

Light Luggage

Pack light and right with Rick Steves' affordable, custom-designed rolling carry-on bags, backpacks, day packs and shoulder bags.

Accessories

From packing cubes to moneybelts and beyond, Rick has personally selected the travel goodies that will help your trip go smoother.

Shop at ricksteves.com

Save time and energy

This guidebook is your independent-travel toolkit. But for all it delivers, it's still up to you to devote the time and energy it takes to manage the preparation and logistics that are essential for a happy trip. If that's a hassle, there's a solution.

Rick Steves Tours

A Rick Steves tour takes you to Europe's most interesting places with great guides and small groups. We follow Rick's favorite itineraries, ride in comfy buses, stay in family-run hotels, and bring you intimately close to the Europe you've traveled so far to see. Most importantly, we take away the logistical headaches so you can focus on the fun.

Join the fun

This year we'll take thousands of free-spirited travelers—nearly half of them repeat customers— along with us on 50 different itineraries, from Athens to Istanbul. Is a Rick Steves tour the right fit for your travel dreams?

Find out at ricksteves.com, where you can also check seat availability and sign up. Europe is best experienced with happy travel partners. We hope you can join us.

See our itineraries at ricksteves.com

BEST OF GUIDES

Full-color guides in an easy-to-scan format. Focused on top sights and experiences in the most popular European destinations

Best of England
Best of Europe
Best of France
Best of Germany
Best of Ireland
Best of Italy
Best of Scotland
Best of Spain

COMPREHENSIVE GUIDES

City, country, and regional guide printed on Bible-thin paper. Pac with detailed coverage for a mu week trip exploring iconic sight and venturing off the beaten pa

Amsterdam & the Netherlands
Barcelona
Belgium: Bruges, Brussels,
 Antwerp & Ghent
Berlin
Budapest
Croatia & Slovenia
Eastern Europe
England
Florence & Tuscany
France
Germany
Great Britain
Greece: Athens & the Peloponn
Iceland
Ireland
Istanbul
Italy
London
Paris
Portugal
Prague & the Czech Republic
Provence & the French Riviera
Rome
Scandinavia
Scotland
Sicily
Spain
Switzerland
Venice
Vienna, Salzburg & Tirol

E BEST OF ROME

Italy's capital, is studded with
 remnants and floodlit-fountain
s. From the Vatican to the Colos-
with crazy traffic in between, Rome
erful, huge, and exhausting. The
 the heat, and the weighty history

of the Eternal City where Caesars walked
can make tourists wilt. Recharge by taking siestas, gelato breaks, and after-dark
walks, strolling from one atmospheric
square to another in the refreshing evening air.

*Pantheon—which
dome until the
2,000 years old
ver 1,500).*

*thens in the Vat-
s the humanistic*

*diators fought
ther, entertaining*

Complete your library with...

Credits

CONTRIBUTOR
Gene Openshaw

Gene has co-authored more than a dozen Rick Steves books, specializing in writing walks and tours of Europe's cities, museums, and cultural sights. He also writes for Rick's public television series, produces audio tours on Europe, and is a regular guest on Rick's public radio show. Outside of the travel world, Gene has co-authored *The Seattle Joke Book.* As a composer, he has written an opera called *Matter,* a violin sonata, and dozens of songs. He lives near Seattle, where he enjoys giving presentations on art and history, and roots for the Mariners in good times and bad.

ACKNOWLEDGMENTS

Thank you to Cameron Hewitt, for his help in shaping the Beyond Istanbul section, and to Robyn Stencil, for some vital on-the-ground assistance. Thank you also to Risa Laib, for her 25-plus years of dedication to the Rick Steves guidebook series.

PHOTO CREDITS

Front Cover: Lamp shop, Istanbul © Abdul Hafiz Ab Hamid, EyeEm, Getty Images

Back Cover: (from left) Hagia Sophia © Anton Aleksenko, Dreamstime.com; Istanbul street market © Derketta776, Dreamstime.com; Bosphorus cruise © Anton Aleksenko, Dreamstime.com

Dreamstime: 12 (bottom) © Iuliia Kuzenkova; 258 © Ihsan Gercelman

Public Domain via Wikimedia Commons: 206 (left)

Additional Photography: Lale Surmen Aran, Tankut Aran, Dominic Arizona Bonuccelli, Cameron Hewitt, Rosie Leutzinger, Rhonda Pelikan, Carol Ries, Rick Steves, Gretchen Strauch, Laura Van Deventer. Photos are used by permission and are the property of the original copyright owners.

Avalon Travel
Hachette Book Group
1700 Fourth Street
Berkeley, CA 94710

Text © 2021 by Rick Steves' Europe, Inc. All rights reserved.
Maps © 2021 by Rick Steves' Europe, Inc. All rights reserved.

Printed in Canada by Friesens.
Eighth edition. First printing January 2021.
ISBN 978-1-64171-367-2

For the latest on Rick's talks, guidebooks, tours, public television series, and public radio
show, contact Rick Steves' Europe, 130 Fourth Avenue North, Edmonds, WA 98020,
+1 425 771 8303, RickSteves.com, rick@ricksteves.com.

Rick Steves' Europe
Managing Editor: Jennifer Madison Davis
Assistant Managing Editor: Cathy Lu
Editors: Glenn Eriksen, Suzanne Kotz, Rosie Leutzinger, Teresa Nemeth, Jessica Shaw,
    Carrie Shepherd, Meg Sneeringer
Editorial & Production Assistant: Megan Simms
Editorial Intern: Maxwell Eberle
Graphic Content Director: Sandra Hundacker
Maps & Graphics: David C. Hoerlein, Lauren Mills, Mary Rostad
Digital Asset Coordinator: Orin Dubrow

Avalon Travel
Senior Editor and Series Manager: Madhu Prasher
Associate Managing Editors: Jamie Andrade, Sierra Machado
Indexer: Stephen Callahan
Production & Typesetting: Lisi Baldwin, Scott Kimball, Jane Musser, Ravina Schneider
Cover Design: Kimberly Glyder Design
Maps & Graphics: Kat Bennett, Mike Morgenfeld

COLOR MAPS

*Istanbul's Old Town • Istanbul's New District
• Istanbul Transit*

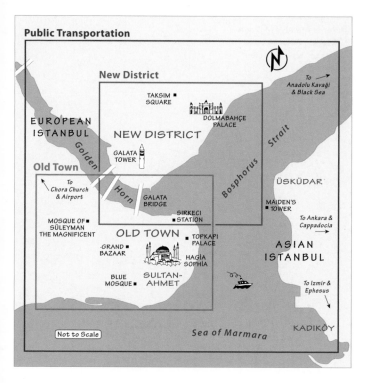

Public Transportation

New District

To
Anadolu Kavağı
& Black Sea

TAKSIM ■
SQUARE

NEW DISTRICT

DOLMABAHÇE
PALACE

EUROPEAN
ISTANBUL

Golden

GALATA
TOWER

Old Town

To
Chora Church
& Airport

Horn

GALATA
BRIDGE

SIRKECI
■ STATION

MOSQUE OF ■
SÜLEYMAN
THE MAGNIFICENT

OLD TOWN

TOPKAPI
PALACE

GRAND ■
BAZAAR

HAGIA
SOPHIA

BLUE
MOSQUE ■

SULTAN-
AHMET

Bosphorus Strait

ÜSKÜDAR

MAIDEN'S
■ TOWER

To Ankara &
Cappadocia

**ASIAN
ISTANBUL**

To Izmir &
Ephesus

Not to Scale

Sea of Marmara

KADIKÖY

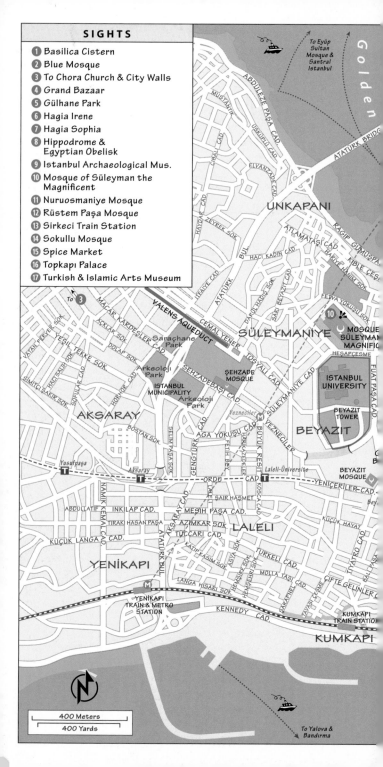

SIGHTS

1. Basilica Cistern
2. Blue Mosque
3. To Chora Church & City Walls
4. Grand Bazaar
5. Gülhane Park
6. Hagia Irene
7. Hagia Sophia
8. Hippodrome & Egyptian Obelisk
9. Istanbul Archaeological Mus.
10. Mosque of Süleyman the Magnificent
11. Nuruosmaniye Mosque
12. Rüstem Paşa Mosque
13. Sirkeci Train Station
14. Sokullu Mosque
15. Spice Market
16. Topkapı Palace
17. Turkish & Islamic Arts Museum

400 Meters
400 Yards

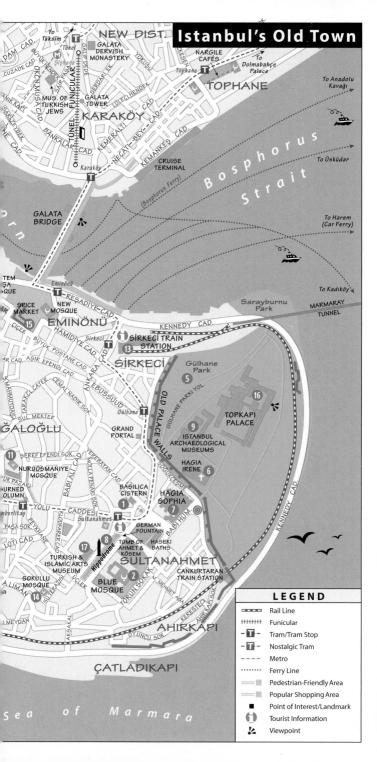

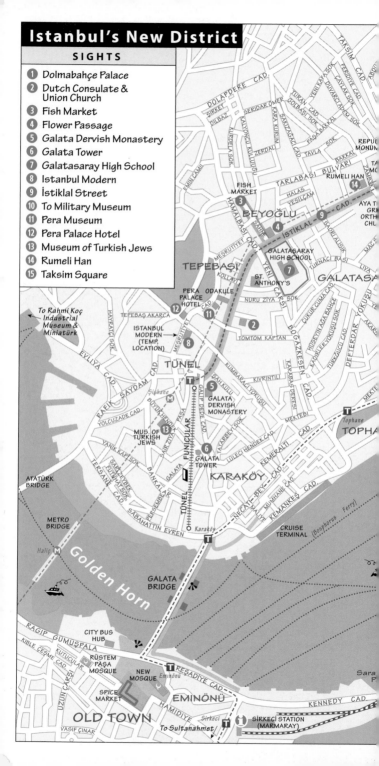

Istanbul's New District

SIGHTS

1. Dolmabahçe Palace
2. Dutch Consulate & Union Church
3. Fish Market
4. Flower Passage
5. Galata Dervish Monastery
6. Galata Tower
7. Galatasaray High School
8. Istanbul Modern
9. İstiklal Street
10. To Military Museum
11. Pera Museum
12. Pera Palace Hotel
13. Museum of Turkish Jews
14. Rumeli Han
15. Taksim Square

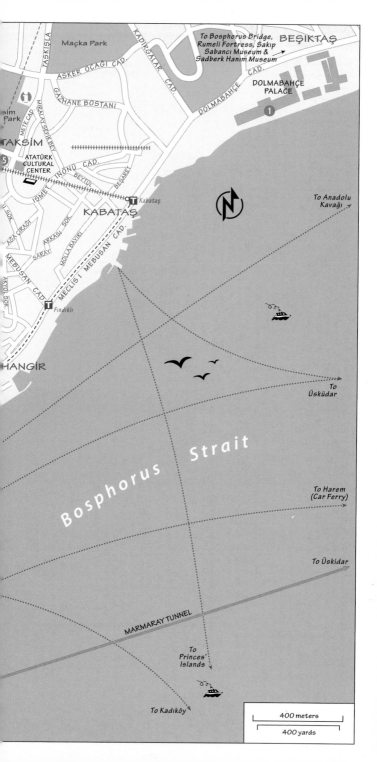

TAŞKIŞLA

Maçka Park

BEŞİKTAŞ

KADIRGALAR CAD.

ASKER OCAĞI CAD.

To Bosphorus Bridge,
Rumeli Fortress, Sakıp
Sabancı Museum &
Sadberk Hanım Museum

GAZHANE BOSTANI

DOLMABAHÇE PALACE

DOLMABAHÇE CAD.

MİRALAY ŞEFİK BEY

METE CAD.

sim
Park

1

TAKSİM

İNÖNÜ CAD.

5 ATATÜRK CULTURAL CENTER

İSMET

BEYTÜL

To Anadolu
Kavağı

BEŞARET

Kabataş

KABATAŞ

İL SOK.

AĞA ÇIKAĞI

ARKASI SOK.

SARAY

MOLLA BAYIRI

MECLİS İ MEBUSAN CAD.

MEBUSAN CAD.

AKYOL SOK.

Fındıklı

HANGİR

To Üsküdar

Bosphorus Strait

To Harem
(Car Ferry)

To Üsküdar

MARMARAY TUNNEL

To Princes'
Islands

To Kadıköy

400 meters

400 yards

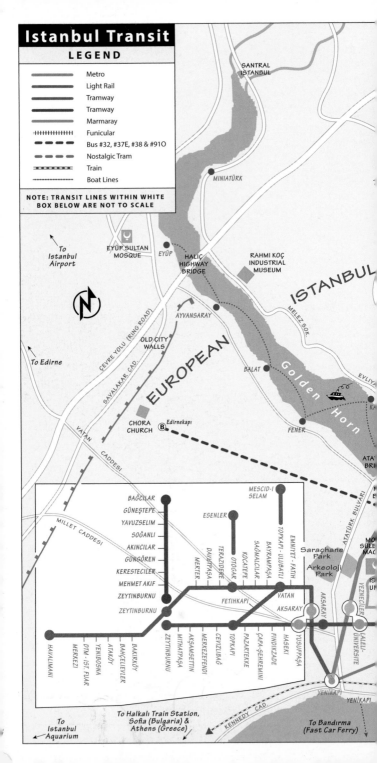

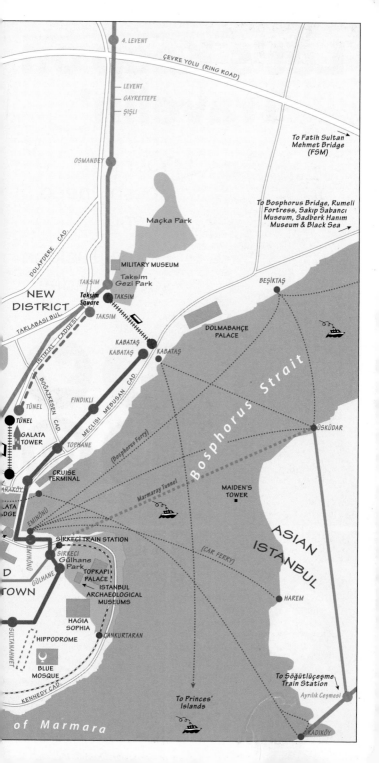

Let's Keep on Travelin'

Your trip doesn't need to end.

Follow Rick on social media!